BOMB GROUP

The Eighth Air Force's 381st and the Allied Air Offensive over Europe

PAUL BINGLEY AND MIKE PETERS

Published in the United States of America and Great Britain in 2022 by
CASEMATE PUBLISHERS
1950 Lawrence Road, Havertown, PA 19083, USA
and
The Old Music Hall, 106–108 Cowley Road, Oxford OX4 1JE, UK

Hardback Edition: ISBN 978-1-61200-960-5
Digital Edition: ISBN 978-1-61200-961-2

A CIP record for this book is available from the British Library

Printed and bound in the United Kingdom by TJ Books

Typeset in India by Lapiz Digital Services, Chennai.

For a complete list of Casemate titles, please contact:

CASEMATE PUBLISHERS (US)
Telephone (610) 853-9131
Fax (610) 853-9146
Email: casemate@casematepublishers.com
www.casematepublishers.com

CASEMATE PUBLISHERS (UK)
Telephone (01865) 241249
Email: casemate-uk@casematepublishers.co.uk
www.casematepublishers.co.uk

Front cover: B-17G-70-BO 43-37675 VE-N *Flak Magnet* pictured in formation with B-17G-35-DL 42-107112 VE-O *Sleepy Time Gal.* Both aircraft belonged to the 532nd Bomb Squadron and would survive their time in combat over Europe. (U.S. Air Force photo)

Contents

Foreword

Wandering the old airfield of Ridgewell today, the ghosts of the past do not seem very far away. Parts of the old runway and perimeter track still cross a wheat field and skirt a hedgeline—cracked concrete sprouting grass and weeds. Once, this concrete bore the weight of numerous B-17 Flying Fortress heavy bombers; now only tractors and farm vehicles use it. During the war, Ridgewell airfield was home to an entire bomb group of Americans—thousands of young men and women—and this quiet rural backwater morphed into a small, makeshift town. Not so very long ago an old baseball bat was discovered on the airfield, a reminder of the transformation this place underwent during the war.

Some buildings still remain. In one corner of the old site, mounting swathes of brambles, alder, and nettles bar much of the way to what appears at first to be an old barn, but which was, in fact, once the station cinema. Half close your eyes and it's not too hard to imagine the place filled with young airmen, safe for that night's screening at any rate. Cigarette smoke clouding the room, the cellulose projected onto a far wall. Men sitting in rows, cheering when there needed to be a cheer, laughing when there was a funny moment. Off the back of the cinema was another room, almost like an annexe. This belonged to the chaplain of the 381st Bomb Group, Captain James Good Brown. It was his task to serve the spiritual needs of the young men who were expected to take to the skies in their B-17 Flying Fortresses until they had completed their twenty-five mission tour, but who—for much of the time the 381st was stationed in this corner of Essex—statistically had little chance of reaching that golden number. Brown struggled to make sense of the terrible struggle these men faced flying bomber missions over the Reich, but certainly did his best to offer what solace he could. Another of his unenviable tasks was to write letters to bereaved families; it was an almost daily duty.

The 381st certainly suffered, as did most of the heavy bomb groups of the US Eighth Air Force stationed in England. The summer and autumn of 1943 were particularly brutal and Brown had to watch the morale of the men plummet after the lofty optimism they arrived with in June that year was punctured over Schweinfurt, Regensburg and other distant targets deep in the Reich. "As for comradeship," he wrote in October 1943, "this was no more, for our comrades were gone." The despair was palpable.

It's easy to talk in terms of broad-brush strokes when considering the strategic air war against Germany. On a certain date, a certain number of bombers bombed a certain target. A certain number failed to return. Figures, numbers, statistics. What this book on the 381st reminds us that the bomber war was fought by individuals and groups of young men. By homing in on one particular location and one bomb group, we are able to see the immense human drama of the bomber war through the experiences of these airmen. Of course, every man is different, and squadrons and bomber groups also had their own identities and cultures. Nonetheless, the story of the 381st was certainly indicative of the wider experience of American heavy bomber crews operating out of England during the war and so it is brilliant that Paul Bingley and Mike Peters have focussed on this one place, one bomb group and one set of crews.

The story of the 381st at Ridgewell is certainly a remarkable one, in which they played a vital part in the Eighth's overall impressive wartime contribution, picking up two Distinguished Unit Citations during the two years they were based there, and sending out bomber crews on almost every major operation undertaken from England.

This is a book born of deep knowledge and, perhaps even more importantly, passion. It is a means of honouring those who lived and fought from this corner of the Essex countryside, long since abandoned as an airfield, but whose traces are still felt. The survivors are a generation slipping away all too fast, but as this book shows, their legacy remains.

James Holland
June 2022

Acknowledgements

The authors wish to thank the following for their assistance, support, advice and encouragement during the writing of this book:

Alan and Monica Steel, Sarah and Darren Allen, Jim, Jenny and Chris Tennet, Derek Wyndham Mayes, Robert and Vanda Root, Tony and Ann Goodchild, Anthony Wallbridge, Becky Benfield-Humberstone, Michael Land, Jane Bevan, Stuart Day, Andrew Cox, Graham Thrussell, Richard Flagg, James and Claudia Grey, Ross and Lynne Greene, Don and Jana Madar (and the late Charles Denosky), Jared Cummings and Amy Beechler, Ron Mackay, John Howland Jr., James Holland, Peter Caddick-Adams, Geert Van Den Bogaert, Sean Claxton, Colleen Brennan, Roland J. Ramirez, Elizabeth Yee (and the late Leonard L. Spivey), Andrea Lerum (and the late George R. DeVoe), Norman Wells, Mark S. Copeland, Michael Faley, Dave Sutton, Nathan Howland, Paul Woodadge, Michael Hutchins, Ivor Ramsden, Paul Bellamy, Jeff Hawley, Peter Worby, Merryn Walters, Kevin Wilson at the 381st Bomb Group Memorial Association; Scott W. Loehr and all at the National Museum of the Mighty Eighth Air Force, Savannah, Georgia, including Al Pela Jr., John J. O'Neil III, Heather Thies and Dr. Vivian Rogers-Price; all those at the Imperial War Museum (London and Duxford), RAF Museum (London), and Essex Records Office; Camille Noel, Scott Liggett, Bill Cullen, John Silvernale, Bob Korkuc, Ron Pegg, Bill Yancy, Pär Henningsson, Pat Tarashuk, Brian Piazza, Veli-Pekka Pelttari, Stephan Creutzburg, Tim Hollenkamp, Steve Snyder, Joost de Raaf, Bart Robberechts, Frances Bekafigo, Andy Laing, Matthew Walsh, Linda Beckum, Steve Hale, Darryl Parker, Tony Brown, Iryna Danko, Lara Fiegel, Ruth Sheppard and all at Casemate Publishers, Max and Toby Curwen-Bingley, Alan and Mary Bingley, Sheila, Brian and Laura Tallant, Aki Bingley and Karen Peters.

Finally, to the late, great David R. Osborne, who "taught Paul Bingley all he knows"; Bob Gilbert, who never failed to answer a torrent of questions; Edward Carr, who delved deep into his memory to fill in the gaps; Ray Ater, one of the unsung heroes; and Casey Bukowski, who finally came back and brought it all to life.

Thank you all.

Prologue

Casey Bukowski wears a feather in his cap. He found it among some pinecones and a pile of leaves next to a tall, granite memorial. Gray and angular, the monument stands beneath several swaying conifer trees. To its right sit two black, corrugated buildings, their dormer windows protruding from semi-cylindrical roofs. Hospital wards 75 years before, Bukowski had tried avoiding them back then. He's doing the same now as he carefully studies the gold-leaf inscription.

> DEDICATED TO THE HONOR OF THOSE MEMBERS WHO VALIANTLY SERVED AND GALLANTLY DIED IN DEFENSE OF BRITAIN AND THE FREE WORLD AGAINST TYRANNY AND OPPRESSION SO THAT WE ALL MAY LIVE IN PEACE AND FREEDOM WITH DIGNITY.

Casimer "Casey" Bukowski is one of those members. When this memorial was first erected in 1982, however, he hadn't been among the one hundred or so of his compatriots who had stood before it. Bukowski had last seen this place slip below his feet on February 22, 1944. Over 27,000 days had passed since then, during which time he had married, fathered three children, studied mechanical engineering, then retired as a purchasing agent with the United States Department of Veterans Affairs. Now, he had returned.

"I'm finally back home," he said, the feather shaking in his cap.

This is Ridgewell, a rural corner of Essex, England, where this once fresh-faced boy from Buffalo, New York, had first arrived on November 16, 1943. Back then, Bukowski had been a replacement B-17 Flying Fortress waist gunner assigned to the 381st Bomb Group, the so-called "hottest outfit to reach the ETO."[1]

Within days of his arrival, he was routinely being woken from his sleep by the glare of a torch in the face. He would stumble out of bed ("with a few unsavory words"), get dressed, then stagger to breakfast. He would sometimes eat fresh eggs ("never a good sign"), before being told where he was going. Mostly it was Germany, and he'd hadn't liked it at all.

In truth, he hadn't cared much for any of the European cities he'd seen after arriving in England. Brunswick, Bremen and Kiel—they were all as bad as each other. Oschersleben? That was the worst. However, as a waist gunner in the ten-man crew of a Flying Fortress called *Friday the 13th*, his job wasn't to admire the sights of Europe. It was to tell the difference between a German Focke-Wulf Fw 190 and an American P-47 Thunderbolt. Get it wrong and there was hell to pay.

There was no mistaking the Fw 190 fighters over Oschersleben on January 11, 1944. There were hundreds of them. For three hours, Bukowski had slid on empty shells in the paper-thin waist of *Friday the 13th*, shooting at enemy fighters for all his worth. When his B-17 landed back at Ridgewell, it skidded off the runway with a flat tire, burst hydraulics and two bloodied officers. Bukowski's reward was to sew a neat, blue Distinguished Unit Citation ribbon onto the breast of his tunic—another feather in his cap. But then he was ordered to go back to Oschersleben.

February 22, 1944. Seven hours after taking off from Ridgewell, Bukowski came to. He was lying on his back, squinting at the sun through an open escape hatch. His 16th mission was unravelling spectacularly.

Things had started to go awry shortly before take-off when his navigator had spilt his parachute on the ground at Ridgewell. By the time a replacement was brought to their B-17, the rest of the 381st was already in the air. When his pilot finally caught up with the formation, he clung onto its tail-end. "Purple Heart corner," as Bukowski referred to it.

Thirty minutes from the target, "head-on" fighter attacks then left *Friday the 13th* fatally damaged. His fellow waist gunner was struck by cannon fire and fell dead beside him. Bukowski was also wounded by the blast. Drifting in and out of consciousness, he dragged himself towards the hatch before tumbling out, pulling the parachute ripcord as he went. Amid machine gun fire ("I thought those fighters were shooting at me"), he dropped unconscious.

"I hit the ground next to an autobahn, but knew little of it," Bukowski recalled. Although he knew his first duty was to evade capture, he was not in the best place. "My legs hurt, my back hurt, my head hurt, and I couldn't stand." He was soon discovered by two German civilians, who dragged him to a nearby farmhouse. There, he was shoved onto a stool in the middle of a room where they began rifling through his pockets. An elderly woman screamed at them to stop and tried pulling them away, but their frisking only intensified. Finally, she grabbed a broom and began striking them.

"I can only think she had a son who was away fighting like me," Bukowski remembered. "I guess she didn't want him treated in the same way as me. If it wasn't for the 'frau' of that house, I might not be here now."

It is astonishing that he is here at all. Shortly after being handed over to German soldiers, he was taken to a military hospital where he was treated for his wounds. His right eye was so badly damaged it had to be removed by doctors. He was then taken to *Stalag Luft IV*, close to the Baltic Sea, where he remained for almost a year. Then, in February 1945, with the Soviet Army advancing west, he and his fellow campmates were force-marched across Germany at gunpoint. It was a debilitating three-month journey that saw many of them disappear. Those who were unable to keep up were sent to a truck at the rear. "You didn't want to end up in that truck. Some that did, were never seen again."

Bukowski is finally seeing his old base again. After surviving the war, which culminated in the loss of some of his closest friends and his job (his former defense employer wouldn't re-hire him as a machinist because of his damaged eyesight), he left his wartime experiences behind and married his sweetheart, Rita. Sadly, two years before his return to Ridgewell, she passed away.

"The feather's an Indian sign," he said, adjusting it in his cap. "Rita passed away twenty minutes into the New Year. Finding this means she's here with me now. I know it sounds stupid, but I believe that stuff."

A chance meeting in a hot-dog queue brought him back to Ridgewell. His cap—adorned with rows of ribbons and the words "US Army Air Corps"—prompted someone to ask about his story. His reply saw a new friendship flourish, culminating in his trans-Atlantic crossing and a long and winding bus ride through the English countryside.

> WANTED: CASIMER BUKOWSKI FOR DEFECTING FROM HERE WITHOUT PAYING HIS BAR BILL: EIGHT SHILLINGS AND TUPPENCE.

The sign in Ridgewell's *White Horse* pub is intended as a joke. It's a place Bukowski had last visited before his fateful flight in 1944. Standing there, he chuckles, but takes it in his stride, pointing out parts of the building to the present-day owner. It's barely recognizable now.

It's the same at his former airfield—RAF Ridgewell. Little remains of what had previously been "Essex's only long-term heavy bomber base." Where B-17s once taxied towards Nazi Germany, more peaceful aircraft now fly. It is the home of the Essex Gliding Club.

Bukowski climbs into one of its gliders painted in the markings of his former bomb group. As the pilot adjusts the straps on his parachute, he instructs him on what to do in the event of an emergency. "I've used one of these before," Bukowski jokes. Moments later, he's back in the air over Ridgewell. Down below, faded patches of soil mark where some of its hardstands once stood. Nearby, a sliver of the main runway still exists. It is next to this that his glider eventually floats in for a safe landing, something he wasn't able to do 75 years before.

Casey Bukowski is one of over a thousand American airmen who were unable to land back at Ridgewell during World War II. More than half never returned home to their families. It is to them, and those like them, that this book is dedicated.

CHAPTER 1

Baptism by Fire

Early on Sunday morning, December 7, 1941, a formation of 12 United States Army Air Forces (USAAF) B-17 Flying Fortresses approached the islands of Hawaii. The crews were nearing the end of a 2,400-mile flight from California. The radio operator on each aircraft was tuned into *KGMB*, a commercial radio station located in Honolulu. It was playing pleasant Hawaiian music. More importantly for the B-17 navigators, though, it allowed them to take a bearing on its transmitter signal and follow the beam until they made landfall. *KGMB* was then due to give a detailed weather report intended for the incoming formation.

The B-17s had taken off at 15-minute intervals the night before from Hamilton Field, California. By 0700 on Sunday morning, they were 175 miles northeast of the Hawaiian coast. Unaware of the imminent Japanese attack on the US Pacific Fleet at Pearl Harbor, the crews were looking forward to landing at Hickam Field and the end of what had been an uneventful, but tiring, flight.

The B-17s were part of an American plan to reinforce the USAAF's presence in the Philippines. The flight was one of a series to augment the 19th Bombardment Group (19th BG) with an additional squadron. Hawaii was a welcome staging post at the end of the first leg of an important transfer of heavy bombers to the Pacific.

The original USAAF orders for the reinforcement operation had detailed a total of 16 B-17s to move to Clark Field in the Philippines. Eight aircraft were provided by the 38th Reconnaissance Squadron based at Albuquerque, New Mexico. The other half of the force was drawn from the 88th Reconnaissance Squadron (88th RS) from Fort Douglas, Utah. Planning for the mission soon identified the distances involved were challenging, even for an unladen B-17. In order to conserve fuel and extend the range of the aircraft, a decision was made to fly with reduced crews.

With no bombload and no threats expected, the bombardier and four other gunners usually making up part of the B-17's ten-man crew, were surplus to requirement. Each bomber would fly with two pilots, a navigator, one flight engineer and a radio operator. The redundant crew members were to follow on in transport aircraft to meet up with their respective crews at Hickam Field. There were, however, several passengers—mainly mechanics—essential to maintaining the B-17s on their arrival.

In an effort to further reduce weight, no ammunition was allowed. Each aircraft carried its own guns, but they were stowed, along with the bombsight. This decision had caused concern. International tensions were high in the Pacific region and the risks of flying with unarmed aircraft needed to be considered. Immediately prior to departure, the mission commander, Major Truman H. Landon, had raised the question of defensive armament face-to-face with General Henry H. Arnold, commander of the USAAF. Arnold had visited the crews and stayed to watch their B-17s depart Hamilton Field. He was firmly of the view there was no requirement or weight capacity for guns during the flight to Hawaii. Nevertheless, he did assure Landon the B-17s would be fully armed and crewed when they left Hickam for their onward flight to Clark Field.[1]

Even after the reduction of crew numbers, concern remained about fuel capacity and aircraft endurance. A further modification was made to extend the reach of the B-17s. Each aircraft was modified to carry a tank in its empty bomb bay. Nevertheless, even with the extra fuel, the margin for error was tight. As a precaution, the launching of the mission was delayed until 1800 on December 6, due to head winds. When authorization for take-off was finally given, three aircraft aborted with minor engine problems. A fourth turned back shortly after take-off. The remaining 12 pressed on, with four B-17Cs and eight B-17Es split into two flights of six, with 10 minutes' interval between each one.

Ironically, Landon's B-17s—the most heavily-armed aircraft of World War II at the time—were about to fly into combat for the first time with no weapons and no bombs.

* * *

The famed Flying Fortress was about to inadvertently play a part in masking the approach of the Imperial Japanese Navy's attempt at dealing a devastating blow to American naval power in the Pacific. At 0702, the US Army radar station at Opana Point identified a large blip that the duty operator, Private George Elliott, interpreted as a formation of 50 aircraft approaching Hawaii at 137 miles range. Elliott informed the switchboard operator at the Fort Shafter Information Center at 0720, critically omitting the number of aircraft from his report.[2] The majority of duty staff were at breakfast, but First Lieutenant Kermit Tyler was still on duty and took Elliott's call. During the conversation, Tyler remembered the inbound B-17s expected at about the same time and from the same direction. The incoming B-17s offered a logical explanation for the radar contact.

The Japanese attack force flew on undetected—the strike leader, commander Mitsuo Fuchida also tuning into *KGMB*. Following the same beam intended for the approaching B-17s, Fuchida received the confirmation he needed: "partly cloudy skies mostly over the mountains, ceiling 3,500 feet, visibility good."[3] He then fired flares signaling the attack option his commanders were to take.

Ten minutes after listening to the *KGMB* weather update, Captain Richard H. Carmichael, leading "A Flight" in B-17E *Why Don't We Do This More Often*, reported Oahu in sight. At 0745, he attempted to contact the control tower at Hickam. The transmission was broken and intermittent. Hickam tower did not respond. Carmichael put this down to atmospherics and saw no reason to change course. Minutes later, the leading B-17s crossed the coastline and were at last flying over land. At this point, they sighted approaching fighters. Unaware of an impending attack, Landon and his crews wrongly identified what were actually Japanese Mitsubishi A6M "Zero" fighters as P-36 Hawks. Given the distance from Japan, and the fact the two nations were not at war, the logical deduction was these aircraft were a USAAF escort dispatched from Hickam. Any doubt about the identity, or intent of the approaching fighters was swiftly dispelled when the fighters began to attack the formation.

In spite of their fatigue, the B-17 crews reacted quickly and in an unconventional way. Their bombers epitomized the contemporary US doctrine of daylight, precision bombing. This was especially true of the USAAF concept of defense. The B-17E, in particular, was designed to fly through any fighters it encountered en route or over any target. Bristling with heavy caliber machine guns, the B-17 deserved its fortress name. American thinking on defense was based on collective defense and mutual support. The massing of B-17s in tight "box" formations would, it was thought, create an impenetrable cloud of firepower generated by dozens of gunners with interlocking arcs of fire. The B-17 would, therefore, be able to beat off any attack and punch its way through to the target.[4]

The obvious problem that Landon and his crews faced that morning over Oahu—other than almost dry fuel tanks—was that their guns were stowed. They also had no ammunition and no gunners to operate them. The order was given to break formation and scatter; every aircraft for itself. The pilots had few options, however. They were low on fuel and, as yet, unaware of the ferocity of the attack on Hickam Field. As the lead B-17s came within visual range of Hickam, the crews could make out large, billowing pillars of smoke. First Lieutenant Bruce G. Allen was flying B-17C 40-2063[5] in the second wave, "B Flight," on the approach:

> ...the thick, rolling clouds of smoke were hard to miss—and some wondered if a drill or exercise was underway. Sergeant Albert Brawley was certain that the rows of burning aircraft were the result of a pilot crashing on the flight line; 1st Lt. Bruce Allen didn't even realize that the fires were actually at Hickam—he was sure that the smoke came from nearby sugar cane fields being burned off. It wasn't until the pilots began asking for flight traffic control at Hickam for landing instructions that the truth was confirmed for them.[6]

The eventual response from the Hickam tower was unflustered and professional. Captain Gordon Blake, the base operations officer, calmly gave the B-17 crews the airfield wind speed and direction, before periodically reminding them that "the field was under attack by unidentified aircraft."[7]

Ahead of Bruce Allen, the leading B-17Es of "A Fight" began making their approaches to the Hickam runway, landing east to west, as instructed by Blake. Captain Richard Carmichael, the commanding officer of the 88th RS, approached Hickam while the Japanese attack was at its peak. He quickly decided to abort the approach and try to land elsewhere, eventually managing to get *Why Don't We Do This More Often* into Haleiwa Auxiliary Field. His aircraft was subsequently damaged by strafing "Zeroes," but not destroyed. His B-17 was successfully followed by another "A Flight" aircraft, *Naughty But Nice*, flown by First Lieutenant Harold N. Caffin.

The third B-17E, *The Last Straw*, flown by First Lieutenant Robert E. Thacker managed to avoid interception and landed his aircraft at Hickam, although with a burst tire. First Lieutenant Frank Bostrom had less luck, however. He also attempted to land a fourth "A Flight" B-17E, *San Antonio Rose*, but was driven off by repeated Japanese attacks. He managed to evade the "Zeroes," making a forced landing on the nearby golf course at Kahuku.

The last two B-17Es also managed to avoid interception and slipped into Hickam during a lull between the Japanese attacks. First in, avoiding Japanese fire and US anti-aircraft fire, was the B-17E (41-2433) flown by First Lieutenant Harry Brandon. Brandon made a good landing assisted by his co-pilot Robert Ramsey.

The last of the "A Flight" aircraft to land was B-17E 41-2434 with First Lieutenant David G. Rawls at the controls. Having attempted to land at Hickam, Rawls had then flown off to try his luck at Wheeler Field. Finding Wheeler under attack, he returned to attempt another landing at Hickam. On route, the B-17 drew fire from US Navy guns. On landing, the taxiing B-17 was then strafed. The crew survived, but only after abandoning their aircraft and running for cover.

Amid the chaos, "B Flight" had crossed the coast and its pilots were desperately looking for somewhere to land. Its commander, Truman Landon, was lucky. His aptly named *Lucky 13* was able to make a safe landing at Hickam. The Japanese attack then abated, as the second B-17E, flown by First Lieutenant Karl Barthelmess landed, untroubled. He was followed by First Lieutenant Bruce G. Allen's B-17C, 40-2063, which also landed unopposed. As Allen taxied looking for somewhere safe to park, Captain Raymond T. Swenson then brought his B-17C in. Swenson's co-pilot Ernest (Roy) L. Reid remembered the sight:

> What I saw shocked me. At least six planes were burning fiercely on the ground. Gone was any doubt in my mind as to what had happened. Unbelievable as it seemed, I knew we were now in a war. As if to dispel any lingering doubts, two Japanese fighters came from our rear and opened fire. A tremendous stream of tracer bullets poured by our wings and began to ricochet inside the ship. It began to look as though I would probably have the dubious distinction of being aboard the first Army ship shot down.
>
> Without waiting for an order from Captain Swenson, I pushed the throttles full on, gave it full RPM, and flicked the "up" switch on the landing gear. It seemed only logical to get

> quickly into some nearby clouds and try to escape almost certain destruction, since we had no way of fighting back.
>
> I had no sooner taken these steps than smoke began to pour into the cockpit. The smoke was caused by some of their tracer bullets hitting our pyrotechnics, which were stored amidships. Captain Swenson and I both realized there was now no choice but to try to land. The captain yanked the throttles off, and I popped the landing gear switch to the down position again. The wheels had only come up about halfway, and they came down and locked before we hit the ground.[8]

Swenson's crew had just gained the unwanted distinction of being the crew of the first American aircraft shot down in World War II. A combination of a hard landing, internal fire, and further strafing runs by two Japanese "Zeroes" saw the burning B-17's fuselage split in half. The crew then came under fire as they ran for cover—among them, First Lieutenant William R. Shick, a flight surgeon. He was wounded during the attack and later died in hospital of his wounds, having refused medical attention.[9]

The next B-17C that attempted to land at Hickam was *Skipper*, flown by First Lieutenant Robert H. Richards. With the airfield still under attack, he aborted his approach and turned towards Bellows Field. He then landed downwind, overshooting the runway—*Skipper* finally coming to a halt nose down in a ditch. In spite of the rough landing and repeated strafing by Japanese fighters, there were no casualties. Finally, the last B-17C, 40-2054, approached Hickam with First Lieutenant Earl J. Cooper landing the last of the "B Flight" bombers. Cooper's crew had also been relentlessly attacked by "Zeroes," as well as being engaged by US anti-aircraft fire, but they had arrived on the ground at Hickam, and with no casualties.

All 12 B-17s had made it across the Pacific, demonstrating the reliability of Boeing's four-engine bomber. The flight had also said much for the quality of the USAAF's crews and their training. The survivability of the B-17's rugged design was clearly evident. The amount of punishment some had absorbed was impressive. This survivability soon became legendary. The number of combat crews that survived crashes or forced landings, to walk away from a damaged aircraft, added to the B-17's reputation as an aircraft that would "get its crew home" no matter what.

In the wake of Pearl Harbor, the B-17 did sterling service in the Pacific theater, flying bombing missions against Japanese forces, while acting as a transport aircraft and hunting submarines and surface vessels. The 7th, 11th, and 19th Bomb Groups made good use of the B-17s that were committed to the Pacific. They flew numerous bombing raids in the battles that followed, before being withdrawn and replaced by Consolidated B-24 Liberators. Yet, the characteristics of the now battle-proven B-17 were needed elsewhere. This aircraft was to spearhead a new daylight bombing offensive in Europe—the role for which it was arguably designed and built.

CHAPTER 2

The Hottest Outfit

January 1–June 2, 1943

Deep in Texas' "Big Bend" country, close to the western edge of a ramshackle town called Pyote, a new airfield was taking shape. A single road led towards the site, which extended for some 2,700 acres. Construction workers had taken less than four months to scrape the sagebrush, lay two 8,400-foot-long concrete strips, and erect several large buildings and scores of wooden huts. Officially known as the United States Army Air Forces' (USAAF) new Pyote Army Air Field, its setting would give rise to a more apt nickname—"Rattlesnake."

When excavators first began scraping their way across the hardpan surface, countless diamondback rattlesnake dens were uncovered. As the reptilian bodies piled up, signs were hurriedly erected warning workers to "wear boots or high-top shoes and leggings," and to watch where they stepped or reached. When work was completed, the signs remained in place, while a more striking one was designed. Block capital letters mounted on either side of the entrance welcomed visitors to the "Rattlesnake Bomber Base."

The first tenants to arrive at the new field had endured a long and fraught journey to reach it. In the wake of its heroic deeds in the Pacific, the 19th Bomb Group had returned home as the US Army's most highly decorated fighting unit. When a cadre of its airmen began filing through Pyote's main gates on New Year's Day 1943, the group had already been awarded four Distinguished Unit Citations (DUC) and two Medals of Honor.[1]

The 19th's men were followed by their battle-weary B-17s, which were ferried from Pocatello, Idaho. "Rattlesnake"—the group's new Texan base—had been chosen as the ideal location to demonstrate its expertise to the USAAF's growing number of new airmen, one of whom was Second Lieutenant William R. Dendy.

Dendy found it easier than most to reach Pyote's new training base. Arriving the same day as the 19th, the 15-mile journey from his hometown of Wink ensured he was the first member of his new unit to arrive. Finding none of his fellow recruits there, however, he promptly turned around and drove home.

Dendy's new commanding officer, on the other hand, faced a 500-mile trek from Tucson, Arizona. Leaving by train on New Year's Day 1943, Lieutenant Colonel

Joseph "Joe" J. Nazzaro arrived at Pyote 24 hours later. His first task was to begin selecting buildings for his men, most of whom had been drafted in from the 39th and 302nd Bomb Groups. Nazzaro's ultimate directive, however, was to establish the Eighth Air Force's newest heavy bombardment group—the 381st.

* * *

Raised in Brooklyn, New York, 29-year-old Joe Nazzaro was a graduate of West Point and a rising football star. Having first served in the infantry, he'd transferred to what had previously been known as the United States Army Air Corps (USAAC). A two-year stint flying in the Philippines then followed, before he was shipped back to the US, where he'd taken command of the 302nd Bomb Group. With chiseled good looks and an uncompromising manner, Nazzaro was every inch the type of leader the Eighth was looking for. On arrival at Pyote, however, he was soon searching for his wayward new chaplain, James Good Brown.

Brown's journey to Pyote had been an arduous one. Travelling from Massachusetts via Spokane, Washington, he'd found himself faced with a 23-hour train delay in El Paso, Texas. On a whim, he'd decided to go sightseeing. A brief stroll across the Rio Grande and he was soon in Mexico. A short while later, having been swiftly robbed of his camera by bandits, he was staring at the walls of a Juárez courthouse. Still dressed in his US Army "pinks and greens," he was eventually released by a judge who told him to "get out of here" as soon as possible. Brown needed no invitation. Fleeing back across the border, he then found himself stood to attention before Nazzaro—his "trial" all set to continue.

> Behind the desk sat a man with a stern look on his face. His eyes looked directly into mine. They looked right through me. They never wavered. He had no semblance of a smile on his face. He offered no congenial words of friendliness, no pleasant "hello." Instead, he just looked at me, through and through. His first words were: "Where have you been? You're a day late."[2]

As soon as Brown explained the story of his brush with Mexican law, Nazzaro shouted in disbelief. It was a startling moment for Brown. For as long as he could remember, he had never been admonished. His parents had raised him to be a "model child"—one "who never lied, cheated or stole." Hoping he would follow in his father's ministerial footsteps, his parents had set the bar high.

"[They] had given me the middle name of Good," he later recalled, "so, I felt an obligation to live up to that name and be exactly that."

Stood before Nazzaro, Brown felt like an errant schoolboy. Yet, he had also harbored the same ambitions as his parents. After enrolling at college in Pennsylvania, he'd earned a theology degree. Graduating from Yale, he'd then been awarded a divinity degree. A doctorate followed a short while later. He'd then become the minister of a small church in Lee, Massachusetts, and was eventually married with three young daughters. Yet, as his male congregation fast disappeared from the pews following the outbreak of war, Brown soon "grew tired of waving goodbye." At the age of 41, he'd enlisted as an army chaplain.[3]

* * *

Shortly after Brown's arrival at Pyote, the ranks of the 381st began to swell. Hundreds of men were assigned to its four numbered squadrons—the 532nd, 533rd, 534th and 535th—each of which was equipped with a single B-17. The new bombers quickly became the responsibility of four "model crews," a total of 16 officers and 24 enlisted men handpicked by Nazzaro to lead the rest of his 381st Bomb Group to war.

The group's new operations officer, 24-year-old Major Conway S. Hall, arrived at the base a few days later. Hall was accompanied by Spot, a mongrel dalmatian he'd picked up by the roadside in Arizona. Hailing from Little Rock, Arkansas, Hall had already flown four combat missions with the Twelfth Air Force in North Africa. Sandy-haired and diminutive in stature, he stood tall when it came to making tough decisions. Within days of his arrival, he was soon sending the model crews into the air regardless of weather conditions. When Nazzaro questioned his new officer's judgement, Hall replied testily: "If they can't fly instruments in the US, they won't survive long in England."[4]

On the ground, conditions were equally challenging. Desert winds whipped the dust into such a pall that the men had to be equipped with respirators. Wooden huts also had to be tethered to the ground—many of them still not fully constructed.

"Between the dust storms, we had no engine stands, for example, for our B-17s," recalled Conway Hall. "But there was a theater being built and they had a lot of lumber laying around. So, we made ourselves some stands and the cost of the theater 'overran'."[5]

James Good Brown, who had been warned about Pyote ("that Godforsaken place") by a sympathetic Texan railroad conductor, was unimpressed with his surroundings. "I walked through the sand to the mess hall and there wiped the sand off the table before I began to eat."[6]

The young girls working in the canteen asked Brown not to blame them for it, but he had already made up his mind. Pyote was "the laughing stock of the air force."

With limited facilities on the base, the airmen were given 24-hour passes to visit the nearby towns. Most headed for the roadhouses of Odessa, some 80 miles away, while others chose the closer Monahans. Few, though, visited Pyote.

"[There was] nothing but rattlesnakes, jack rabbits and sand," recalled the 535th's First Sergeant Charles D. Butts. "Wasn't anything of the town to speak of. Very few houses … businesses, or anything."[7]

Once an "oil boom" town with 18,000 people and 150 companies, Pyote had become a "ghost city." A mere 75 residents lived along a single street that housed two general stores and a post office. Nevertheless, the new bomber base brought opportunities. One of three cafés in Pyote—the Aztec—became a focal point for many airmen—its beer bottle-stacked walls making for an illuminating spectacle on sunny afternoons. The town's trailer colony with its spoil of "attractive women" also appealed to the men. However, after spotting several 381st jeeps in the area, a displeased Nazzaro ordered his men to give precise details of "where they will be" each time they left the base.

* * *

A month after arriving at Pyote, Nazzaro's 381st began its first phase of training. By now, four additional B-17s had been allocated to each squadron. On January 31, they took off on a "sea-search mission" over Muroc Lake, California, a ten-hour round-trip from Pyote.

The base's growing fleet of bombers soon began to cause equipment problems, however. There was a distinct shortage of practice bombs. Nevertheless, an astute William Dendy sourced a constant supply. Hiding from the neighboring 98th Bomb Group's crews as they loaded their bombs onto trolleys, Dendy routinely hitched them onto his own jeep before speeding away. Coupled with the systematic theft of building materials to bolster its shelters, the 381st soon earned a reputation for "thievery."

To avoid the frequent dust storms that threw up a 2,000-foot veil, the first phase of flight training for the B-17 crews took place between midday and 1600. It consisted of practice take-offs and landings, as well as simulated attacks on a bombing and gunnery range at Alamogordo, New Mexico, over 200 miles away. Yet, each day would start the same—the 381st's ground crews herding cattle, prairie dogs and rabbits away from the runways, before spraying the surfaces with water to remove dust and scrub.

Tougher elements of flying came with the 381st's second training phase, which began on March 3. Nazzaro's intensive program shifted to high-altitude formation and long-range flying—most of which was operated under "simulated combat conditions." His regime had become so rigorous that the crews were under considerable strain to keep the aircraft flying.

"Many came to me in the chaplain's office and said 'we can take it no longer. Colonel Nazzaro is too hard on us'," wrote James Good Brown. The chaplain's reply was terse. "He is getting you ready for war."[8]

Brown was unaware the group had completed its second training phase, when Nazzaro informed him they would be leaving Pyote. The 381st was to finish its third and final phase at Pueblo Army Air Field in Colorado—a more established flying training school with better facilities. The chaplain was only too pleased to dust off his bags and begin packing.

Three days later, the 381st began moving the 475 miles north to Pueblo. While the ground crews travelled by train, the combat crews followed in their B-17s. One of the first to lift off from Pyote was the newly named *Strato Sam*, piloted by First Lieutenant Marvin D. Lord. His B-17F was loaded with five crew members, as well as six ground crewmen who'd missed the train; a mistake that almost cost them dearly.

As *Strato Sam* took off into a warm and cloudless sky, there was a sudden vibration followed by a loud "thud." Glancing out of his window to check, Lord's radio operator saw a wheel bounce past, closely followed by a sizeable chunk of the axle. Leaving the undercarriage extended, Lord circled Pyote where controllers confirmed that much of his port landing gear was missing. He was then ordered to head for Tinker Army Air Field, 400 miles away in Oklahoma, where repairs could more easily be carried out.

Lord instructed his passengers and crew to prepare for a "wheels up" landing. As they checked their parachutes, he asked if anyone wanted to bail out "while they had the chance." No one volunteered. Even so, unable to jettison the ball turret[9] without the necessary tools, they faced the prospect of the bomber breaking its back on landing. It could rupture the bomb bay fuel tank and ignite any fuel. Lord and his crew elected to drop the fuel tank instead. As *Strato Sam* approached Tinker, the bomb bay doors were opened and the tank was successfully jettisoned into a marsh. Lord then made an "extremely smooth, flaps down, wheels-up" landing with no injuries to passengers or crew. With *Strato Sam* also largely repairable, the 381st's first flying accident had ended surprisingly well.[10]

* * *

Two days after leaving Pyote, the 381st's ground crews found their arrival at Pueblo much more welcoming. Led by a marching band, they arrived at a larger base next to a sizeable town. It was a far cry from the "primitive" and snake infested Pyote.

The 381st's other B-17s all arrived safely, led by Captain Landon C. Hendricks, commanding officer of the 533rd Bomb Squadron. Hendricks, of Pike County, Kentucky, had joined the 381st not long after Nazzaro and shared his commander's strict attention to detail. As soon as he landed at Pueblo, Hendricks set about ensuring his men were prepared for what lay ahead. Dental appointments, medical lectures and immunization checks were quickly organized. Powers of attorney and wills were also drawn up.

"It isn't the individual, not the [squadron] as a whole," Hendricks wrote in his diary, "but the everlasting plugging of every living soul."[11]

Two days later, the first of 41 brand-new B-17Fs began landing at Pueblo. With production shared between Boeing, Douglas and Vega, Flying Fortresses were starting to pour off the assembly lines. The 381st's four squadrons were allocated an additional 10 B-17s each. Almost immediately, the crews decorated them with names and artwork to add some character. The likes of *Sweet Eloise*, *Caroline* and *Georgia Rebel* lined Pueblo's taxiways. Others, like *Whaletail* and *Tinker Toy* were already famous in their own right, both having been filmed being built at Vega's Burbank plant, which served as the backdrop for a Hollywood movie called *Hers to Hold*, starring Deanna Durbin.

The 381st and its squadrons also began taking on their own identities. New emblems were designed; the 381st's being a silver shield and two falling bombs (one blue, depicting the group's training; the other, red, indicating "bravery and tenacity") beneath the group's motto, "Triumphant We Fly."

The 535th Bomb Squadron's insignia was designed by a member of the ground crew of *Tinker Toy*, who decided his unit was going to "give 'em HELL until it's over, over there" by drawing a "heavy-set, grinning red Devil" carrying a large blue bomb; the blue denoted that, since its activation, the 535th had been "out to do more than its share for 'Uncle Sam'." With designs accepted and "tentatively approved," the badges were eventually being sewn onto every airman's A-2 jacket.[12]

As each new bomber arrived, it was quickly calibrated and prepared for mock bombing and leaflet drop missions. The 381st's pilots were also being lectured by returning crews on combat conditions in both the European and Pacific Theaters. The pace of training, both in the air and on the ground, was relentless.

At 0400 on April 21, Pueblo sprang to life. The B-17s were each loaded with a mix of pyrotechnics, practice bombs and one live 500lb bomb. The crews were then briefed for their next training mission—a test of the US West Coast's defenses. Two hours later, 40 B-17s took off from Pueblo bound for Hammer Field, California—a five-hour flight away.

For the next five days, the 381st's bombers joined 160 others in what was publicly declared to be the "most ambitious air-sea maneuver yet attempted."[13] Flying with all four squadrons in formation on the first day, the 381st extended its reach 300 miles into the Pacific. Returning across Los Angeles in the dark, the formation was then bracketed by searchlights. To add realism to the "unpleasant" experience, Bell P-39 Airacobras were also scrambled to intercept.

The next day, the crews flew over San Francisco, past the Golden Gate Bridge and out into the Pacific once more, this time for a 700-mile round trip. It was followed a day later by a simulated bombing attack on the city, which included two other B-17 groups, 25 medium bombers and numerous defending P-39s. The "attack" was declared a success.

Returning to Pueblo, Nazzaro was then greeted with new orders. The group was to prepare for its overseas movement. Within a week, an advance party of officers left for New York to begin the process of transferring the 381st's men and equipment. On May 4, Nazzaro took off from Pueblo bound for Smoky Hill Army Air Field, Kansas. His B-17F had been nicknamed *Nobody's Baby* after several pilots had refused to fly it. Its cockpit had been stenciled with the words *Peedie*—the nickname of the 532nd Bombardment Squadron's (BS) commanding officer Captain Robert F. Post—and *Peewee*—Conway Hall's nickname. The B-17's passenger list also included Hall's dog, Spot, who was known to have left his mark on the female canine populations of Texas and Colorado.

For the 381st's B-17 crews, it was apparent the group was bound for the European Theater of Operations (ETO). Their instructors had "dropped" Japanese fighter recognition lectures from their briefings. For the ground crews, however, their destination remained unknown.

At Smoky Hill, the airmen were given their individual equipment and personal weapons. Officers were issued with service pistols, while enlisted men received M1 carbines. Flight engineers also wielded sub-machine guns. Modifications were then made to the group's new B-17Fs—bomb bay fuel tanks being installed. Finally, lectures were held on the Atlantic crossing, chemical warfare and security discipline. A six-day furlough was also granted. Smoky Hill's use as a staging point for newly trained bomb groups heading to Europe was clearly evident.

"The barracks showed the anxiety of foregoing crews who had been processed here," noted Landon Hendricks. "The walls were covered with large ragged holes and small round holes made by fists and .45 slugs."[14]

The 381st's ground crews left Pueblo two days after the B-17s, bypassing Smoky Hill. Instead, hauling duffle bags, knapsacks, helmets and mess kits, they trudged to Pueblo's station where four trains were waiting for them.

"We were not good soldiers," remembered James Good Brown. "We didn't know how to march. We just kept our own pace as fitted the length of our legs, and suited our taste."[15]

Hot, crowded and stuffy, the trains took diverging routes across the United States, before delivering the men to Camp Kilmer, New Jersey—the US Army's overseas processing center. Although not immediately clear to many of the men, some, like Chaplain Brown, had already guessed where they were heading.

* * *

While the ground crews of the 381st crossed the country towards New York, Winston Churchill had already arrived after sailing the Atlantic on board RMS *Queen Elizabeth*. The luxury liner, which had been converted into a troopship, had delivered him to the US for a second conference with President Franklin D. Roosevelt. During an address to both Houses of Congress, Churchill acknowledged the part being played by the Allied air forces:

> Progress [in the air war] is swift and sure. But it must be remembered that the preparation and development of airfields, and the movement of the great masses of ground personnel on whom the efficiency of modern air squadrons depends, however earnestly pressed forward, is bound to take time.[16]

Landon Hendricks wasted no time in squeezing himself into the cramped cockpit of *Tinker Toy*. After two weeks at Smoky Hill, he was keen to get going. The date was May 16. It was high time he put the things he had been scribbling in his diary to good use. He checked them once again:

> At approximately 10 degrees west, notify Prestwick you are shifting from 6500 to 4420 KC voice[17] to work "Dogwatch."[18] If message is not acknowledged immediately, shift to 4420 using trailing antenna and call "DW."[19]

Among the other B-17s lined up at Smoky Hill, Joe Nazzaro and Conway Hall busied themselves in *Nobody's Baby*. The repaired *Strato Sam*, under the command of the 532nd's senior officer, Captain Robert Post, sat close by, its three crew members and five passengers onboard. Captain David E. Kunkel, commanding officer of the 534th Bomb Squadron, was running through his checklist in *Whaletail*, while First Lieutenant Frank G. Chapman was waiting to lead the 535th in his eponymous *"Chap's" Flying Circus*. Almost 350 men of the 381st would soon be off the ground and heading for Europe.

The crews were instructed to make their own way, taking one of several North Atlantic ferry routes. Landon Hendricks planned to avoid poor weather over Canada by taking a more southerly course. He expected to make refueling stops in both Bangor, Maine, and Gander, Newfoundland. If the weather allowed, he would then take *Tinker Toy* out across the ocean for a 12-hour, direct flight to Prestwick, Scotland.

Lifting off from Smoky Hill at 0800, Hendricks steered his B-17 northeast. Flying at 5,000 feet, he then reached Des Moines, Iowa, before banking right towards Illinois. Heavy rain and poor visibility forced him down to 3,000 feet, but he eventually picked out the dark ribbon of the Mississippi River in the distance. Descending lower still, he banked towards the small town of Morrison. On approach, he finally pushed the control column forward, forcing *Tinker Toy* down to tree-top height. Hendricks's co-pilot, Captain John H. Hamilton Jr., knew what was coming. It was his hometown. *Tinker Toy* tore straight along Morrison's Main Street, allowing Hamilton one last wave.

Eleven hours after leaving Smoky Hill, *Tinker Toy* landed at Dow Army Airfield, Bangor. Two days later, Hendricks and his crew were back in the air again, this time bound for Gander, Newfoundland. Thirty minutes into the flight, they crossed the American coastline for the last time, Hendricks "not realizing then how dear to us it was."[20]

On landing at Gander a few hours later, Hendricks and his crew discovered the Royal Canadian Air Force base "very cold … and conveniences, few."[21] With weather over the Atlantic also forecast to be poor, they were ordered to wait for five days. It left one unfortunate enlisted man having to sleep in *Tinker Toy* for the sake of security. Nevertheless, just as the sun slipped below the horizon on May 27, Hendricks and his crew took off again, climbing to 10,000 feet, where they would remain for the next 10 hours.

Not far behind, First Lieutenant Leo Jarvis of the 532nd was snoozing at the controls of his unnamed B-17. Several hours after taking off from Gander, he'd fallen asleep, leaving his co-pilot, Second Lieutenant Eugene E. Mancinelli, flying the bomber. Of the 10 men on board, only Mancinelli and the navigator, First Lieutenant Richard P. Riley, were awake. Suddenly, halfway across the Atlantic, one of the bomber's engines failed. Mancinelli quickly feathered[22] its windmilling propeller, but the commotion startled Jarvis, who, half-asleep, involuntarily feathered a second. The bomber rapidly lost airspeed and dropped several thousand feet before Jarvis restarted it. He and his crew remained wide awake for the rest of the flight. On landing at Prestwick, their bomber was promptly named *Feather Merchant.*

* * *

By May 29, most of the 381st's B-17s had arrived at Bovingdon airfield in Hertfordshire—the Eighth Air Force's primary training base for new groups arriving in England. Over the next 10 days, it served as the 381st's indoctrination school, with the crews receiving instruction from veteran airmen.

The 381st's ground crews, however, were only just leaving the US. Laden with equipment and weighed down by the tearful hugs of wives and sweethearts who'd made their way to New Jersey, 2,000 of them had trudged out of Camp Kilmer on May 26, led by a marching band. The men then climbed aboard several trains and numerous ferry boats for the one-hour journey to Manhattan's West 44th Street Pier.

Berthed alongside the vast Cunard White Star terminal building was the liner, RMS *Queen Elizabeth*, which had delivered Winston Churchill to the US a week earlier. Painted slate gray and glistening under heavy rain, it was about to begin ploughing across the Atlantic as part of Operation *Bolero*—the American troop build-up in the United Kingdom.

* * *

For 48 hours, some 14,000 troops clambered up the gangplank, lugging 75-pounds of equipment each. Among them was James Good Brown.

"I have never before seen such tired, weary, depleted and sweaty men as these young troops," he observed. "No gleam in the eye. No accomplishment in the end. Perhaps death."[23]

Their destination was unknown, but Chaplain Brown had already made an educated guess after being issued with woolen underwear at Camp Kilmer. When his summer khaki uniform was taken away from him, he'd become quite sure. He was finally convinced when he climbed aboard a "British ship" to be greeted by "British sailors." His hunch proved to be correct when *Queen Elizabeth* sailed out of New York and began surging east. Yet, conditions aboard the liner were far from luxurious.

"We were crowded into every corner and cranny of the ship," Brown noted. "As many as five hundred men were lying in rope beds hung from the ceiling in a room designed for a few people in peacetime. I was in a room with eighteen officers; a state room designed for two passengers."[24]

To avoid German U-boats, the unescorted[25] vessel regularly changed course, on one occasion lurching so violently it left many of the passengers ill. Their predicament wasn't helped by a full-blown gale, which erupted halfway through the voyage. The chaplain, who quickly found his sea legs, noted how "vomit was everywhere," with some men even "sleeping in their own."[26]

After seven days at sea, during which time one 381st airman was found to have smuggled his pet dog aboard ("Nick the collie" avoided being thrown overboard and was allowed to continue his voyage), RMS *Queen Elizabeth* slipped quietly into Gourock, Scotland. The Americans eagerly scanned a scene that was teeming with naval activity. Countless warships were moored everywhere.

"Now we knew we were in the war zone," wrote Brown.[27]

The process of disembarking 14,000 troops from a ship at anchor was a lengthy one. It wasn't until the next day that all 2,000 men of the 381st could leave the confines of *Queen Elizabeth* on a fleet of tugboats.

"We knew for certain that we were in Britain when we heard the Scottish bagpipes," wrote Brown. "We heard, too, the quaint Scottish accent of the lassies who served us a cup of tea on the dock."[28]

It was Brown's "first real proof" that the 381st was to be stationed on British soil. His self-proclaimed "hottest outfit" had reached the ETO.[29]

When the 381st's ground crews crossed the English border on three trains on June 3, they were on course to join an estimated 100,000 American servicemen already in the country, a country that was fast becoming the greatest operating military base of all time.

At 0600 on June 3, 1943, the first of three London and North Eastern Railway trains rolled into Great Yeldham Station, Essex. Some 600 Americans immediately swamped its platforms, which were quickly strewn with kitbags and equipment. They had come from all over—Louisville, Kentucky; Chelsea, Massachusetts; Brantley, Alabama. After months of training in Texas and Colorado, they were now squeezed together on two narrow platforms in a small corner of the world that many of them couldn't pronounce. They were also on "Hitler's doorstep." Yet, as James Good Brown noted, "We were home, for it was to be our home … until the end of the war in Europe."[30]

Intermission: The Airfields

Within weeks of Pearl Harbor, the decision had been taken in Washington, D.C., to deploy US forces to Europe. On January 8, 1942, the US War Department then authorized the activation of a US military presence in the British Isles. From the outset, this included a fledgling bomber command. A small team of USAAF officers, under the command of 46-year-old Brigadier General Ira C. Eaker, arrived in the UK on February 20. Eaker's six-man team joined the US Army Special Observer Group in London. The observer group, under the command of Major General James E. Chaney, had been in England since May 1941.

The newly arrived team had numerous tasks. However, priority was given to identifying the sites for the headquarters, airfields and logistic infrastructure required to support the newly formed Eighth Air Force, the initial plan for which was ambitious.

The projected order of battle had envisaged four commands: Bomber, Fighter, Ground Air Support, and Composite. Eaker needed to identify home airfields for 60 combat groups; 33 of these new formations were bombardment groups, 17 of which were designated as heavy bomber units. Airfields were also required for 12 fighter groups, eight transport groups, and seven observation groups. All these units were to be established in the UK by May 1943. Breaking this down to the operational level, the new air force would field 3,500 aircraft organized in 220 squadrons.

Fortuitously for Eaker, the airfield construction program was a national priority for the British. At the program's height, over a third of Britain's hard-pressed wartime construction industry was dedicated solely to airfield work. By the end of the war, more than 400 new airfields had been constructed on British soil. The years 1941–42 were the peak period; at one point, contractors handing over a new airfield to the government every three days.

Although there was disagreement between the newly arrived Americans and their Royal Air Force (RAF) hosts on the best way to prosecute a bombing offensive against Germany, Eaker and his team received enthusiastic support from the British. By May 1942, they had reached the conclusion that East Anglia would best suit the needs of the Eighth's VIII Bomber Command. The obvious advantage of basing in East Anglia was its geographic proximity to potential targets in Germany and occupied Europe. Eaker was also keen to keep his aircraft away from the congested airspace around the multitude of RAF bomber stations further north along the east coast of England in Lincolnshire and Yorkshire.

The final decision to center on East Anglia was made late in May. The small number of Eighth Air Force bomb groups that were already in place in Cambridgeshire and Northamptonshire would stay where they were. The massive expansion of the Eighth would be centered on the rural counties of Suffolk, Norfolk, and Essex. It would operate from 92 British airfields, occupying 75 of them for the duration of the war.

East Anglia would host the lion's share, accepting 53 airfields. In August 1942, each of the airfields allocated to the incoming USAAF was given its own unique identification number. Heavy bomber stations were numbered in the 100 range, while fighter stations were allotted a 300 number. So began the deep association between the people of the rural counties of East Anglia and the men and women who made up the Eighth Air Force.

CHAPTER 3

Big Leagues

June 3–July 14, 1943

Just as the Eighth was being formed in Savannah, Georgia, to carry out the USAAF's strategic bombing campaign in Europe, so a new airfield was carved from the English soil. In September 1941, 600 acres of farmland straddling a broad plateau on the Essex–Suffolk border had been requisitioned by the Air Ministry. Its Directorate General of Works then oversaw construction of the site by civil contractor, Constable Hart & Co. Ltd. It took the company's laborers less than 15 months to complete.

Built to the RAF's "Class A" design—the highest standard for operational airfields—enough concrete had been laid for three intersecting runways, 36 hardstands and five miles of service roads.[1] Two transportable hangars, a 30-acre bomb storage facility and a 68-building technical site supported the airfield, which had originally been slated for RAF Bomber Command use. Following America's entry into the war, however, the site was reallocated to the Eighth's VIII Bomber Command (VIII BC). To accommodate its envisaged 50 bombers per group, a further nine pans and five loops were added after June 1942.

Sprawled across some 200 acres south of the airfield were two communal areas, a 17-bed hospital and nine "domestic" sites. A mass of brick buildings, Nissen huts and Seco demountables were scattered beneath trees and in the dips of undulating fields. In total, more than 400 structures had been erected to accommodate almost 3,000 people.

RAF Ridgewell turned operational just as the Rattlesnake Bomber Base opened its main gates. With the 381st in training, its intended British home was loaned to a homeless RAF unit—No. 90 Squadron—which had arrived in Essex on December 29, 1942. Eighteen months earlier, the former Royal Flying Corps fighter squadron had held the distinction of being the RAF's only B-17 Flying Fortress unit. However, 90 Squadron's 20 B-17Cs—the first of the type to engage the *Luftwaffe* over Europe—failed to impress. The unit was disbanded after just 20 operations, having lost three of its bombers in combat.[2]

Reformed in November 1942, 90 Squadron was then equipped with Short Stirling heavy bombers. In the six months that followed, its aircrews carried out

51 bombing and minelaying operations from Ridgewell. By the time they left for Cambridgeshire's RAF West Wickham at the end of May 1943, they had lost 28 Stirlings in raids and non-operational accidents, while 132 airmen had been killed in action. When the 381st arrived at the newly numbered "Army Air Forces Station 167," a handful of RAF officers and one unserviceable Stirling remained.

* * *

Named after a nearby village, Ridgewell airfield lay two miles beyond Great Yeldham's station. With no trucks waiting to greet them, James Good Brown and some of his men began hiking along a road once used by Roman legionnaires.

"We did not march, we just walked," Brown wrote in his diary. "How fortunate we were, to be set in East Anglia, where the villages looked exactly like the picture calendars we hang in our American homes. There were no numbers on the houses ... each house had a name ... like names in story books."[3]

On arrival at his new home, Brown found few comforts except for a canteen filled with civilians who had been repairing Ridgewell's runways following 90 Squadron's departure. The chaplain acquainted himself with the English waitresses and soon developed a taste for tea and crumpets. Within days of his arrival, however, the workers and waitresses were gone and the canteen torn down.

As a way of welcoming the Americans to Ridgewell, its local vicar had converted an upstairs storeroom at the village's congregational church into another canteen. Despite complaints from some of his parishioners, its doors were opened for "the foreigners" to play board games, darts and music. Local woman Olive Foulds was drafted in to serve tea, food and cigarettes. She was startled by the difference in manners.

"The treats were boiled eggs," she recalled. "The Americans gave me a strange look when I first served them ... they'd never seen an egg cup." She was equally bemused when one American began tucking into his boiled egg "with a fork."[4]

As the ground crews continued to pour into Ridgewell, the first official task of the 381st headquarters' personnel was to lower the RAF ensign and replace it with a large American flag. It proved to be a symbolic moment for many, including "Axis Sally," later known as the American-born propagandist Muriel Gillars. In a broadcast made over the airwaves from Berlin, she "welcomed" the men of the 381st to England, even greeting some of its officers by name. A briefing on "base security" was hastily arranged for the next day.

Notable by their absence were the B-17s and combat crews, all of whom had found their way across the Atlantic without incident. After arriving at Bovingdon, the crews had been given a morale-boosting talk by Brigadier General Ira C. Eaker, commander of the Eighth Air Force. The officers were told that, after successfully completing 25 missions, one in four would be kept in England as instructors while the rest would be sent back to the US to oversee operational training units. Those enlisted men "who do good work" could also expect to be given commissions and transferred to these units as instructors.[5]

It wasn't lost on the men that in order to "successfully" complete 25 missions, they'd first have to survive. The gravity of their task was driven home by the 533rd's commanding officer, Landon Hendricks, who delivered a speech to his men before they departed for Ridgewell.

"Your life depends on … your capabilities as a crew," he stated. "No matter how good your guns work or airplane flies, if your crew doesn't work together, you're going to lose … you're in the big leagues … you can't slip up."[6]

The 381st had become the 19th American bomb unit to arrive in England. When Joe Nazzaro coaxed *Nobody's Baby* in for landing at Ridgewell on June 6, "Station 167" became VIII BC's newest operational base. Over the next few days, the rest of the 381st's B-17s flew the short distance from Bovingdon. It was a novel sight for the residents of Ridgewell, who turned out to watch the sleek bombers descend over their homes. It was also a joyful occasion for the ground crews, who'd last seen their Fortresses depart from Pueblo a month earlier.

First Lieutenant Jack B. Painter of the 532nd BS had piloted *Sweet Eloise* the 4,800 miles from Colorado. As his B-17 touched down at Ridgewell, a lapse in concentration saw the wrong switch flicked. Instead of seeing the bomber's flaps slide under the wings, Painter felt its undercarriage retract instead. He could only watch as Ridgewell's runway rose inexorably towards him. *Sweet Eloise* slumped to the ground and a grinding halt.

In something of a design flaw, Boeing had positioned the B-17's flap and undercarriage switches "side-by-side." The 381st's operations officer, Major Conway Hall, was quick to remedy the situation. He immediately ordered the group's engineers to move the flap switches "a foot away, before another airplane takes off." It was too late for *Sweet Eloise*, however. The wrecked bomber was dragged to the outside of a hangar where it remained until almost every part was stripped away. Crowned the 381st's inaugural "hangar queen," *Sweet Eloise* also became its first "loss."

* * *

On the day of *Sweet Eloise*'s demise, the Combined Bomber Offensive (CBO) officially began. The Allied policy, which had been hatched at the Allies' Casablanca Conference in January, signaled the start of "round-the-clock" Anglo-American bombing operations from Great Britain. While the 381st and other VIII BC bomb groups would carry out the precision bombing of enemy targets by day, RAF Bomber Command would continue to attack strategic city areas by night. It was hoped the coordinated efforts would bring about the "progressive destruction and dislocation of the German military, industrial and economic systems and the undermining of the morale of German people …"[7]

The 381st's arrival in England saw its attachment to the 101st Provisional Combat Bombardment Wing (101st PCBW) of VIII BC's 1st Bombardment Wing (1st BW). Under the command of Colonel William M. Gross, the 101st PCBW comprised the Bassingbourn-based 91st Bomb Group (BG), which had arrived in England the previous October, and the 351st Bomb Group, which had made Northamptonshire's Polebrook airfield its home in April. Following the arrival of the 381st, the three 101st PCBW groups could contribute a total of 131 Flying Fortresses to the CBO.[8]

The 381st was joining illustrious company. The 91st BG had previously been assigned the distinguished B-17F *Memphis Belle*, one of the first heavy bombers to complete 25 missions over Europe. Its 10 crewmen, under the command of Captain Robert K. Morgan, had flown most of their missions in the aircraft. They had then starred as the subjects of a US War Department film shot by director and producer, William Wyler. *Memphis Belle* left England for the US to carry out a publicity tour, just as the 381st's B-17s landed at Ridgewell.

The 351st BG was also hosting a celebrity of its own in the guise of movie star-turned-observer-gunner, Clark Gable, who had been assigned to the group to help make a recruitment film for the USAAF. Gable had flown his first mission several weeks before the 381st established itself at Ridgewell.

* * *

It was some time before the 381st had the opportunity to fly its first mission. Almost as soon as its combat crews arrived at Ridgewell, their gunners were packed off to Snettisham, Norfolk, for gunnery training over The Wash. Days later, Landon Hendricks and the 381st's three other squadron commanders travelled to Bassingbourn to join the 91st on a raid, which was subsequently cancelled. It wasn't until June 21 that the 381st's teletype machine whirred into action, spewing out "Field Order 152B."

The 381st was tasked with joining another new arrival, the 384th BG, for an attack on an industrial area in the Belgian port city of Antwerp. However, in the early hours of the morning, after a flurry of nervous activity across the base, the 381st's introduction to combat was cancelled before it could get off the ground. With bombs loaded and crews briefed, the "scrubbed" mission did little for morale.

Nevertheless, just after midnight on June 22, Field Order 153B was received at the 381st operations office. The raid on Antwerp was back on. The ground crews were ordered to re-load five 1,000lb general-purpose bombs on each of the 22 B-17s. The adjutants then scoured the domestic sites, waking the crews who were tasked with flying. James Good Brown, who had "confiscated" a small room next to the chapel, was sleeping fitfully when there was a knock on his door. He needed no invitation to get up.

The 381st's inaugural mission would involve the first large-scale daylight raid on Germany's Ruhr Valley. While 235 of VIII BC's B-17s were attacking Hüls's synthetic rubber plants, the 381st would be targeting Ford's and General Motors' plants in Antwerp. The group's ultimate aim was to draw the *Luftwaffe* away from the Hüls force, effectively acting as "bait." It would join the equally untested 384th BG, embarking on a series of feints over the southeast of England, flying as far west as Oxford, before heading back along the south coast and crossing the English Channel at North Foreland, Kent. There, the crews could expect to meet 136 Republic P-47 Thunderbolts of VIII Fighter Command (VIII FC). To observe his escort fighters, Brigadier General Frank O'Driscoll Hunter, commanding officer of VIII FC, would be flying with the 381st. At the briefing, Joe Nazzaro asked the chaplain, James Good Brown, to say a few words.

"The hour had arrived," Brown noted. "The time for which these men had been preparing."

He avoided issuing a sermon, instead instructing the crews to keep their "strength and courage of mind and of heart." Brown then recited a short prayer before they were dismissed.

"No exuberance was there," he recalled. "All the fun had gone out of flying. This was war. This was death. And they knew it."[9]

As the crews filed out of the briefing room, they were handed sweets by the medical staff. Once at their bombers, ambulances then toured the hardstands delivering coffee and cookies. Just before 0700, a single flare fired from the control tower told the pilots to start their engines. Moments later, a second flare signaled the start of taxiing. Leading his group on its first combat mission, Lieutenant Colonel Joe Nazzaro's B-17 was the first to start moving. Chaplain Brown could only stand and wave goodbye, "one of the loneliest men in the world."[10]

* * *

Nazzaro was airborne at 0709, by which time the 384th's B-17s—led by its commanding officer, Colonel Budd J. Peaslee—were already circling overhead. One of the 381st's bombers aborted with mechanical problems, but the others eventually got airborne, albeit 43 minutes behind schedule. Both groups then set off for the one-hour detour around England. Several minutes were shaved by "cutting Oxford short," but by the time the formation reached the Kent coast it was still half an hour late. With no escort fighters in sight, Peaslee elected to press on towards Antwerp, climbing to the 384th's assigned bombing altitude of 24,000 feet, with the 381st trailing 1,000 feet higher.

Some two hours after take-off, the novice groups finally reached enemy territory for the first time. Then, just six minutes after crossing the Belgian coastal town of Knokke, the *Luftwaffe* appeared. At first, Jack Painter's navigator, Second Lieutenant Lloyd L. Duke, was perplexed by the "morse code" signals blinking in the haze up ahead. He watched closely as the flashes appeared to move before picking up speed and hurtling past. He quickly realized it was tracer ammunition and he was the target.

At a closing speed of 500 miles per hour, an estimated 60 Focke-Wulf Fw 190s of *Jagdgeschwader* 26 (JG 26) screamed in head-on, turning upside-down and swooping beneath the formation before peeling away. Although the B-17 gunners were initially caught by surprise, they soon began firing in concert. The first wave of German pilots then climbed to attack from the rear, making sure they kept the sun behind them.

Approaching the Initial Point (IP)[11] at the Dutch border town of Sas van Gent, the formation was spared any further fighter attacks by the onset of flak.[12] *Little Chuck*, a B-17F of the 533rd BS, under the command of First Lieutenant Inman G. Jobe, was almost immediately hit, fragments knocking out an engine, tearing a hole in one wing, and damaging the electrical system. *Little Chuck* slid from the formation as it neared the target.

Another 533rd aircraft, *Devil's Angel*, was also suffering problems, having been struck by cannon fire during the initial fighter attack. Pilot First Lieutenant Martin L. Shenk was left clinging on to the formation. Yet, it was his element leader First Lieutenant John J. Martin who appeared to be in most trouble.

With its number two engine smoking,[13] Martin's B-17 was seen to drop from the formation chased by a German fighter. Although he rang the bail-out bell, only two crewmen managed to jump before the aircraft entered a spin. The bombardier, Second Lieutenant Wallace W. Hoag, and the navigator, Second Lieutenant Harry R. Long, both escaped through the nose hatch, although the latter broke his leg as he tumbled past the open bomb bay doors. Parachuting 25,000 feet, both men glided to the ground only to find their B-17 already embedded in the mud of the Scheldt estuary. Promptly captured by German soldiers, they then watched as the bodies of their eight crewmates were recovered from the crashed bomber.

The battle was still raging overhead when Brigadier General Hunter's P-47s finally arrived to engage the *Luftwaffe*. Nevertheless, flak continued to pound the formation as it left the target. First Lieutenant Earl B. Horr's *Iron Gut Gert* had already sustained several strikes and soon began falling. Pursued by a German fighter, Horr had no option but to ring his bail-out bell. At 15,000 feet, he and his crew jumped, one of them having been seriously wounded.

Ball turret gunner, Staff Sergeant Charles P. Henry had been struck by cannon fire as he prepared to jump. Two other crew members—navigator Second Lieutenant George P. Griffith and tail gunner Staff Sergeant Arthur A. Jones—managed to "throw" the incapacitated Henry out of the aircraft, before following. Unfortunately, Henry landed in the Scheldt estuary and was too weak to disentangle himself from his parachute. His body was later washed ashore close to the Dutch city of Terneuzen.

Most of the Horr crew was quickly rounded up by German soldiers, although George Griffith was apparently shot by a patrol as he tried to escape from the water. His body was never found. Only the bombardier, Second Lieutenant Chester L. Hoover avoided immediate capture. Despite being badly injured during his fall,

Hoover evaded the Germans for three days. When he was finally found, he was partially paralyzed. Hoover would spend the rest of the war in a "full body cast" and *Stalag Luft III*.[14]

As the formation left the target area, *Little Chuck*—flying alone on three engines—also came under persistent attack. Its pilot, Inman Jobe, put the bomber through a series of violent evasive maneuvers, but was unable to prevent a second engine being damaged by more fire. With many of its control cables also severed, Jobe could only fly the bomber using its Automatic Flight Control Equipment.[15] It was only a matter of time before *Little Chuck* became the 381st's third casualty. Fortunately, though, a group of P-47s tore into the German fighters, scattering them in all directions. Several American fighters then pulled alongside *Little Chuck* as Jobe struggled to maintain airspeed and altitude crossing the English Channel.

Despite jettisoning the bombs and machine guns, Jobe's battle to keep the B-17 airborne wasn't helped by the loss of a third engine, which seized and burst into flames. Luckily, he was nearing the Kent coast, where he quickly spotted a potato field. Ordering his crew to assume "crash positions" in the radio room, he brought the bomber in for a "graceful" belly-landing. Only a concrete pole prevented the aircraft from stopping in one piece, its port wing sliced cleanly in two. Even so, Jobe and his crew—who'd christened their bomber after a name they routinely called each other—could celebrate the luckiest of escapes.

* * *

Twenty-one B-17s had taken off from Ridgewell earlier that day. Only 17 made it back.

"I shall never forget the look on Colonel Nazzaro's face as he came along the walk towards the interrogation building on his return from Antwerp," wrote James Good Brown. "He looked haggard and worn."[16]

Devil's Angel, which had been struck by flak and relentlessly attacked by the *Luftwaffe*, eventually crash-landed at Framlingham airfield with six wounded crewmen. One of them—radio operator, Technical Sergeant John D. Sinclair—had given first aid to his seriously wounded tail gunner before taking over the tail guns, despite being wounded himself. Sinclair would later be awarded the 381st's first medal for gallantry, a Silver Star. His crewmate, tail gunner Staff Sergeant Charles W. Brinton, wouldn't be so lucky, however. He died from his wounds three days later.

Another 381st crewman also lost his life during the group's first mission. Tail gunner Staff Sergeant Arnold B. Lorick was the first of its combat crew members to be brought back to Ridgewell having been killed in action (KIA). Another tail gunner had to be hospitalized after returning in "a state of acute emotional shock."

"The aircrews had no idea what they were getting into," remembered Conway Hall, the 381st's operations officer. "I had been in combat in Africa and I knew the horrors of aerial warfare. But this was never discussed with our aircrews and [after Antwerp] they all woke up and grew up to what aerial combat was. It's a deadly business."[17]

Chaplain James Good Brown was of the same opinion after attending the interrogation.

> I listened for two solid hours. I did not have to ask the fellows to speak: they were talking to one another. They could not keep quiet. Each was telling the other what he saw. I heard more in two hours than one man wants to hear in a lifetime. It was a lifetime for them. And it was a death-time for others. What of their faces? They had aged ten years.[18]

* * *

The 533rd BS had suffered appallingly during the Antwerp mission. One aircraft lost, two destroyed in crash-landings, and a dead tail gunner: all proof of its rough introduction to combat. Nevertheless, the squadron's ground crews were ordered to load six of its bombers with almost 30,000lb of bombs and 36,000 rounds of ammunition for a second consecutive mission the following day.

Among the 533rd's aircraft inventory was *Caroline*, the B-17F that had carried Brigadier General Frank Hunter to Antwerp. While *Caroline*'s four officers were briefed for their second mission over Europe, the bomber's gunners were preparing their guns. Also working on and around *Caroline* were its ground crew, as well as several electrical specialists and numerous ordnance personnel, one of whom was Staff Sergeant Joe H. Willis.

"My job was to go to each plane and make sure they had everything they needed and everything was working alright," he later recalled. "The last plane I came to [*Caroline*], I walked around and everything seemed to be alright … and then I started to walk away and one of the armament men up in the plane hollered out, 'We need a box of .50-caliber ammunition for this plane'."[19]

Willis took a nearby truck to collect the ammunition from the storage area, approximately 180 yards away. On his way back to *Caroline*, he heard a massive explosion. Thinking the Germans were attacking his base, he instinctively jumped out of his moving vehicle and scrambled into a ditch.

"You've been out in a wind storm when the sand stings your face? That's what it felt. I looked in the direction where the explosion came and the first thing I saw was one of those big wheels off of a B-17, looked to me like a hundred foot in the air."[20]

The blast wasn't the result of German bombs, but American. *Caroline* had accidentally exploded on the ground. Francis "Bud" E. Owens, a gunner who'd been cleaning his guns on an adjacent B-17 named *Connie*, was sprinting to safety when he spotted an injured man crawling beneath the bomber. Grabbing him by the shoulders and dragging him clear, Owens quickly found some cover. Seconds later, there was another explosion.

With debris raining down and ammunition "popping," several others, including the 533rd's ordnance officer Captain Julius L. Eichenbaum, raced to help Owens evacuate the injured airman. Private First Class Glenn W. Burkland had suffered a compound leg fracture. Lifting him into a nearby vehicle, they then checked inside *Connie*. Slumped dead in its nose was the bombardier, Second Lieutenant Paul E. Tull. After removing his body, they then began fighting fires and defusing bombs before towing the badly damaged bomber away from what was left of *Caroline*.

"Where a Flying Fortress had been standing, there was none," wrote James Good Brown. "There was only flat earth … the largest single piece I saw was the small part of an engine far away."[21]

Caroline had practically vaporized. So, too, had those who had been preparing the bomber for its second mission. As soon as the area was declared safe, the grim task of retrieving their remains began.

"This required many hours," noted the 381st's Flight Surgeon Major Ernest Gaillard. Jr. "Ten soldiers … unaccounted for. Thirteen bodies, or portions of bodies … positively identified; but the mutilation and charring of the remains made the task extremely difficult."[22]

One officer, 22 enlisted men—both combat and ground personnel—and one British civilian worker, who'd been cycling past *Caroline*, were killed. Three other servicemen and several civilians had also been injured.

As well as the complete destruction of *Caroline*, four B-17s had been damaged by the explosions, one seriously. *Connie*, which had sustained severe fire and shrapnel damage, was declared scrap three days later. The others were largely repairable. Even so, the 533rd BS was unable to muster a single aircraft for the Bernay-Saint-Martin mission, which still went ahead after the perimeter track had been cleared of wreckage.

Taking off later that afternoon, the 381st's B-17s failed to rendezvous with the 384th BG. All were then recalled due to bad weather, with the crews forced to "salvo" their bombs in the English Channel before returning to Ridgewell.

At the end of a long and painful day, those convalescing in the base hospital following the explosion of *Caroline* were joined by several others who returned from their futile mission nursing "first-degree frostbite."

* * *

In just two days, the 381st had lost 45 of its airmen, either missing in action (MIA) or killed. Yet, it was the loss of those in the *Caroline* incident that troubled James Good Brown the most.

"To lose men in battle was one thing," he wrote. "To have 23 men killed from a bomb explosion was another … an unexpected tragedy."[23]

He quickly set about arranging the burial of the bodies at Brookwood Military Cemetery in Surrey, a task made all the more difficult by the number. "There were too many caskets to be placed inside the little chapel," he wrote. "The funeral, therefore, was held at the graves." Brown also lamented the fact that few from the group could attend the ceremony. "The men had to stay with their tasks on the base."[24]

A subsequent report into the explosion of *Caroline* found that the first blast was caused by "eight or nine bombs" exploding "high up in the bomb bay," while the second was "probably of one or two 300lb bombs which were finned and fuzed [sic] and were in cradles ready to be moved." All had been set to "instantaneous." There were also eyewitness statements to suggest that *Caroline* had caught fire, "since there was a cloud of black smoke and fire observed … before the blast."[25]

* * *

Two days after the explosion of *Caroline*, on June 25, Field Order No. 155 tasked the 381st with providing 24 B-17s for an attack on the Klöckner aircraft engine factory in Hamburg. As soon as the group took off into heavy rain at 0545, however, the mission ran into problems.

Having been briefed to bomb from 18,000 feet, the crews were forced to climb 7,000 feet higher in order to break out of the clouds. Once clear, they found themselves scattered. Persistent contrails (exhaust condensation trails) then hampered close formation flying.

Over the coast of northwestern Germany, a combination of flak and an estimated 125 German fighters conspired to bring down another 533rd BS aircraft. First Lieutenant Robert K. Schrader's unnamed B-17F dropped from the formation and disappeared into the clouds. Nothing was seen of it again; although later reports indicated that it crashed into the German Bight. The bodies of bombardier 2nd Lt. Edward G. Samara, top turret gunner TSgt. William K. Cutting, and tail gunner SSgt. Lewis E. Frisbee were all found washed ashore on the Frisian Island of Wangerooge. The bomber's left waist gunner, Sgt. Stephen Kurnafil, was found alive, but in a serious condition. He later died in a German naval hospital. No mention was made of the rest of the crew, which included the 533rd's operations officer, Capt. John Hamilton—Landon Hendricks's co-pilot across the Atlantic, and the 381st's highest-ranked loss so far.

Another 381st crewman was also lost on the mission. Staff Sergeant Ivan J. Tieman of the 534th BS—1st Lt. Dexter Lishon's left waist gunner—was struck by cannon fire and killed. His body was returned to England, but only thanks to the skill of Lishon, who was able to crash-land *Whaletail* at RAF Foulsham, Norfolk, despite losing two engines and the use of his control cables.

The Hamburg mission had been another setback. Poor weather conditions had seen both the 1st and 4th BWs search fruitlessly for breaks in the clouds, with most of their bombs dropping on targets of "opportunity" and "last resort."[26]

The following day, the 533rd was relieved of combat duty while the 381st took part in an equally ineffective raid. Nineteen B-17s were dispatched from Ridgewell to bomb an "air depot" at Vélizy-Villacoublay in the suburbs of Paris. Again, heavy cloud cover and poor visibility prevented them bombing. Despite the failed attack, however, an encounter with the *Luftwaffe* saw the mission credited. More troublingly, though, seven of the group's B-17s, including the lead aircraft flown by the 381st's deputy commander, Lt. Col. Leland F. Fiegel, had to return early with mechanical failure.

* * *

Despite the horrors of combat, the deaths of the 23 airmen in the explosion of *Caroline* were still weighing heavily on the minds of the men. James Good Brown had received numerous requests to organize a memorial service.

"This I had not expected," he noted, "but it indicates the tremendous feeling of loss which permeated the whole atmosphere of the base."

Brown, who preached with "no reference to any particular church or creed," had recently been joined by a Roman Catholic chaplain, Capt. Martin J. Collett. Both men discussed how such a service should proceed, with Collett suggesting that he conduct one for the Roman Catholics, while Brown plan another for the Protestants on the base. Brown argued the men "should not be separated" and suggested a common service.

"If we cannot come as one group—the 381st—to meet together in commemoration of our own buddies whom we lost, there is something wrong with our religion."

Three days after the tragedy, a "non-denominational" service took place at the base chapel. Some 400 men crammed inside the building, with most of the 533rd Bomb Squadron filling the seats. Hundreds of others stood outside to pay their respects. Just as Brown had expected, the service was listened to "intently and reverently and in deep sorrow."[27]

* * *

In the wake of the *Caroline* incident, bomb loading procedures were changed. Only four ordnance and armaments personnel were allowed near the aircraft when bombs were being loaded. Once they were hooked onto the racks, the armaments men would then vacate the area while the ordnance crew "fused" them.

"That was just a safety precaution to keep some men from getting killed at one time," recalled 533rd ordnance worker, Joe Willis.[28]

Willis and his fellow ordnance crews had a particularly weighty bomb-loading task on June 28, when VIII BC scheduled its 69th mission for an attack on the German submarine pens in the French port of Saint-Nazaire. To penetrate the four-foot-thick, reinforced concrete locks, each of VIII BC's B-17s were loaded with two 2,000lb general-purpose bombs. Twenty-two of the 381st's bombers were tasked for the raid, which was led by Joe Nazzaro, flying his fifth consecutive mission.

Taking off at 1410 into clear skies, Nazzaro and the 381st formed up with the rest of the 101st PCBW. He then led the entire formation toward the target. Encountering little opposition, 54 B-17s "squarely hit" Saint-Nazaire's port and locks, leaving columns of smoke "10,000ft high." On their return to England, however, the B-17s were intercepted by the *Luftwaffe* whose Me 109s and Fw 190s attacked the formation as it began making its way across the English Channel.

"An FW [190] made a head-on attack at us from 10 above," wrote the 533rd's commander, Landon Hendricks, who was co-piloting *King Malfunction II*. "A 20mm explosive shell entered the nose under the astrodome, came through the instrument panel in a direct line with me. It veered off … came through my flying suit … hit the engineer in the leg and stopped in the rear of the ship."[29]

Both Hendricks and the engineer, TSgt. John P. Kapustka, who was flying his first mission, would later receive Purple Hearts.

Another struggle was also taking place on *Georgia Rebel*, which had been fending off the fighter attacks. During one pass, the B-17's life raft suddenly broke loose from its external compartment, wrapping itself around the tail. The pilot, 1st Lt. Osce V. Jones was unable to control the shuddering bomber, which soon began spiraling down. Only the quick thinking of his co-pilot, 1st Lt. Melvin R. Hecker, prevented the crew's demise. Fighting his way back through the diving aircraft, he was able to wrench the life raft free by tying its lines around one of the waist guns and using the gun as "leverage." In the commotion, *Georgia Rebel*'s gunners managed to shoot down two of the chasing German fighters.

After landing back at Ridgewell, several other gunners claimed five enemy aircraft "destroyed." The combat crews also declared the mission to be the 381st's "most successful," the target being "completely demolished." Consequently, it proved to be VIII BC's last planned attack on Saint-Nazaire.

The final raid of the 381st's first month in England came the following day when it returned to France to attack another *Luftwaffe* airfield at Triqueville, near Le Havre. Despite reaching the target, none of the 101st PCBW's 40 B-17s were able to drop their bombs due to solid cloud-cover. Still, the 381st's 14 crews were "credited" with the mission, which was described by the group's public relations officer, Capt. Saul B. Schwartz, as a "no-runs, no-hits, no-errors trip."[30]

Unfortunately, that same day, an error in judgement cost the life of one of the group's ground crew members. During a "friendly discussion" in their barracks about whether his Thompson sub-machine gun was clean, Sgt. Martin L. Miller accidentally shot his friend, Sgt. Robert H. Anderson, in the chest. After being rushed to the base hospital, Anderson was pronounced dead a short while later. His death brought the group's growing casualty list—those recorded as MIA, KIA, or killed in service—to 57. The 381st's baptism had proven to be an unholy one.

* * *

The beginning of July marked the first anniversary of the arrival of the first B-17E on British soil. *Jarrin' Jenny* of the 97th BG had landed at Prestwick exactly a year earlier. Although the aircraft wasn't used for VIII BC's first heavy bomber raid, which occurred on August 17, 1942, one B-17E that did take part in that first mission was 41-9043 *Peggy D*, which was assigned to the 97th's 342nd BS. Deemed surplus to requirements by July 1943, the B-17E was transferred to Ridgewell to serve as the 381st's "group hack."[31] It was given fresh markings—"GD-A1"—and a new name, *Little Rock-ette*.

Several weeks earlier, the 1st BW had issued a notice to all of its bomb groups about the "indiscriminate" naming of aircraft.

"The Commanding General of the Eighth Air Force is concerned … and desires that each Group observe some definite system with regard to such names," the notice read. "In this connection the following possibilities are suggested: names of states, cities, famous flyers, airfields, and so forth."[32]

Little Rock-ette largely adhered to this instruction, having been named by Conway Hall after his hometown in Arkansas. *T.S.*, on the other hand, required some clarification. Not until its co-pilot, 2nd Lt. Robert L. Weniger from Houston, was challenged to explain its meaning did it become clear. *T.S.* had been named in honor of his beloved "Texas State." Weniger's nine crewmates knew otherwise, however. *T.S.* was actually an abbreviation for "Tough Shit"—a term it would live up to in the weeks that followed.

Aside from some dubious nicknames, the 381st's B-17s had carried few markings since their arrival in England. All of its bombers sported the USAAF's insignia; a serial number; two-letter squadron code and aircraft letter. By July, in an effort to aid the assembly of its bomber formations, VIII BC introduced a new system of identification. Based on the "brand marks" used by cattle ranchers, its proposed "tail markings" consisted of a geometric shape and capital letter. The 381st ground crews were duly instructed to paint an 80-inch-wide white triangle on either side of the B-17s' tails, overlaid by a letter "L." The new symbol identified the bombers as being part of the 1st BW and 381st BG respectively.

* * *

After a "scrubbed" raid intended for the French city of Le Mans on July 2, VIII BC's 71st mission finally took place two days later on American Independence Day. The 1st BW was ordered to attack aviation plants in both Le Mans and Nantes. The 381st's 21 B-17s were aiming for Le Mans and what was believed to be a Focke-Wulf engine factory. The group was led by the 91st BG, with the 351st trailing behind.

Everett F. Malone, a co-pilot with the 535th, was flying in *Man o' War*—the B-17F he and his crew had flown all the way from Pyote. As the formation neared France, Malone's aircraft was at its assigned bombing altitude of 21,000 feet.

"So far we had met no opposition, flak or fighters, and everyone was flying very good and tight formation," he recalled. "Only a few minutes away was our IP. Suddenly, I saw fighters—Fw 190s and Me 109s—about 12 of them diving at our formation."

Up ahead, several Me 109s "raked" the 533rd's unnamed 42-29928, which was being flown by 1st Lt. Olof M. Ballinger. His co-pilot, 2nd Lt. John M. Carah, was unaware that their B-17F had been hit until one of the gunners exclaimed that the oxygen system had been cut. Cannon fire had also struck the right waist gunner and ball turret gunner, killing them both. It was imperative that the aircraft descend below 10,000 feet for the other gunners to breathe.

"The Luftwaffe pilots sensed a kill and three of them attacked us continually down to about 6,000 feet," remembered Carah.

His B-17 then suffered a direct flak hit, which jammed the controls and pushed the aircraft into a steep climb. Carah immediately rang the bail-out bell and scrambled to the escape hatch, where he met the bombardier, 2nd Lt. George C. Williams.

"[Williams had] his parachute unfurled in his arms. I told him to jump anyway, but he just shook his head."

As Carah tumbled out of the aircraft, the right waist gunner Bud Owens was desperately trying to help the wounded radio operator TSgt. John K. Lane. Owens, who'd recently been commended for saving the life of Glenn Burkland following the explosion of *Caroline*, found himself saving the life of another airman. Clipping a parachute onto the semi-conscious Lane, Owens dragged him to the rear escape hatch, pushed him out and pulled the parachute cord as he went. Owens then followed.

John Carah landed safely in an orchard at La Coulanche, having been "rocked" in his parachute by a passing Me 109, and the subsequent explosion of his B-17 as it crashed nearby. Rescued by the French Resistance, he eventually made his way to Switzerland—becoming one of the first American airmen to successfully do so.[33]

Pilot Olof Ballinger, who was the last to bail out of the stricken B-17, also landed in the same orchard, as did Bud Owens. Both managed to make their escape, which subsequently took them through France and on towards Spain. John Lane, the wounded radio operator, was quickly captured by German troops. He survived his wounds as well as 22 months in captivity. Three others, including the bombardier George Williams, were killed in the crash.

"I will never know why Lt. Williams chose his fate as he did," wrote John Carah. "We had been briefed that in case of accidentally pulling the rip cord, to bundle up the spilled chute and jump anyway."[34]

After watching the group return from the Le Mans mission and realizing there was one B-17 missing, James Good Brown was close to tears.

"Not until you have 'sweated out a mission' will you ever know what 'sweating it out' means," he wrote. "I saw a buddy of Ballinger 'sweat out' this raid. Long after the planes were in and the waiting group had disappeared, he stood there looking into the skies. He stood there alone. I felt like crying, but I did not dare."[35]

* * *

The 381st's B-17s remained grounded for the next five days, as did the rest of VIII BC's. It gave the men time to ponder their situation, with some even devising new ways of fighting the war. James Good Brown was "all ears" when one airman began describing his strategy.

"We will only fly in cloudy weather so that we cannot see the enemy," he explained. "When we do encounter the enemy, we will turn around and come back. If we keep this up long enough, we will finally wear the enemy planes out …" Brown could only admire the man's "stamina of spirit."[36]

The strength of some men's stomachs was tested when several arrived at the base hospital on July 6 complaining of nausea, vomiting, and diarrhea. The number steadily rose until there were some 30 cases. The illness made a change for the medical staff, who'd been treating a spate of injuries resulting from bicycle accidents (the frequency of which was "almost beyond reason," according to the station's surgeon, Maj. Ernest Gaillard). While investigations were carried out into the cause of the mystery illness, Gaillard's superior, Maj. Garfield P. Schnabel, the group surgeon, sampled his first taste of combat while accompanying the 381st as an observer on its eighth mission on July 10.

The group took off during the afternoon leading the 101st PCBW, which included the 351st and its own observer, Capt. Clark Gable. They were revisiting the *Luftwaffe* air depot at Vélizy-Villacoublay, a target they'd failed to attack two weeks earlier. Much like the previous attempt, however, the mission was thwarted by solid cloud-cover. All 22 of the group's B-17s returned to Ridgewell still carrying their bombs.

Four days later—Bastille Day—the group found itself France-bound yet again. An attack on Amiens–Glisy's *Luftwaffe* airfield was ordered as part of a combined effort by 264 B-17s on several French bases. The raid on Amiens–Glisy would be carried out solely by the 101st PCBW, which was to be led by the 351st.

Twenty-four 381st crews were scheduled to be woken for the mission, but they were jolted awake just after midnight by an air raid alarm warning of approaching German bombers. Although the base escaped detection, several bombs landed on the nearby village of Helions Bumpstead. Fortunately, there were no casualties.

The 381st's B-17s took off just after 0600 to make up the 101st PCBW's low group. All 64 bombers assembled together between Cambridge and Ely, before proceeding south towards Beachy Head. The 533rd's *Red Hot Riding Hood* was climbing to 15,000 feet when its pilot, 1st Lt. Charles E. Hedin, noticed a problem with his number four engine. He asked the radio operator, TSgt. Robert L. Potts, to check from his window. Potts spotted a flame from the rear of the engine and told

Hedin to "feather" it. Almost as soon as Hedin had done so, Potts found himself "standing in mid-air."

Red Hot Riding Hood's number four engine had wrenched itself away from the wing, smashing the tail off and snapping the aircraft in two. Briefly suspended, Potts's quick thinking saw him yank his parachute rip cord. He then watched as his B-17 fell away and disintegrated.

Only four crew members survived the break-up of *Red Hot Riding Hood.* Navigator 2nd Lt. Donald F. Hamm, bombardier Frank E. Cappel, and top turret gunner TSgt. Richard H. Hanna were thrown clear and parachuted to safety. The others were killed when the bomber crashed near Rattlesden airfield, Suffolk. Among the dead was Hedin's co-pilot, 2nd Lt. William D. Burroughs, who had been assigned to the group just six days earlier and was flying his first mission. The surviving members of the Hedin crew, who had already mourned the death of their original tail gunner Arnold Lorick, were all hospitalized. Only one of them—Richard Hanna—would ever fly again.

Despite the loss of *Red Hot Riding Hood*, the formation flew on, reaching Beachy Head at 0715. By the time it crossed the French coast at Le Tréport, nine squadrons of P-47s were on-hand to escort the bombers to and from their target. Turning left at Poix, the formation then headed towards Amiens–Glisy, before dropping over 230 tons of general-purpose and incendiary bombs on the airfield.

As the formation made a sharp, left-hand turn away from the target, Robert Weniger, the co-pilot of *T.S.*, spotted two Fw 190s climbing at speed. He alerted his pilot, Capt. Edwin R. Manchester Jr., at which point the fighters began a "balls-to-the-wall" forward pass.

"Prior to coming into range, you could see their wing guns belching fire," Weniger recalled. "All gunners aboard our ship were firing … but they kept right on coming. At this point, I knew we were in for a real problem."

The first fighter flew in head-on before rolling beneath *T.S.*, almost taking its ball turret guns with him. The other fighter followed.

"The wingman in the second Fw 190 … was either dead when he rolled … or damned mad at us for bombing his airfield," remembered Weniger. "His aircraft was perpendicular to our wing when he crashed into us between the number three engine and the fuselage."

The Fw 190 instantly broke apart, its nose and propeller gouging the B-17's number four engine, which "poured forth a big black stream of oil resembling a Texas oil gusher." The rest of the fighter careened down the B-17's fuselage, striking its horizontal stabilizer and tail before "cartwheeling" away.

"That's the hard way to knock down one of Jerry's fighters and is not recommended for [the] longevity of bomber crews," noted Weniger.

The collision had left *T.S.* on the verge of stalling, but Weniger and Manchester kept the B-17 airborne by forcing it into a dive while pushing the throttles forward.

Despite heavy vibrations, damaged electricals and only two functioning engines, the bomber flew on. However, it was soon left behind by the fast-disappearing formation.[37]

During the attacks, few had seen another of the 381st's B-17s, *Widget*, leave the formation. Either struck by flak or damaged by a fighter, the bomber was thought to have crashed off the French coast near Berck-sur-Mer with the loss of 1st Lt. Robert J. Holdom and his entire crew. *Widget* became the 535th's first loss of the war.

T.S.—another 535th B-17—floundered on. Approaching the English Channel, it flew over a flak battery, which succeeded in peppering over a thousand holes in its fuselage. Moments later, another fighter attack from the rear saw a 20mm shell explode in the cockpit beneath Manchester's seat. Fortunately, he remained unscathed. His crew's luck was further boosted by the sudden appearance of P-47s, which began attacking the *Luftwaffe* fighters.

"After the Germans were driven off, a P-47 piloted by Capt. [Charles "Chuck"] London appeared just off our right wing," recalled Robert Weniger. "This was one of the most beautiful sights I believe every member of the crew had ever seen."[38]

London would later be awarded the Distinguished Service Cross (DSC)—partly for this mission—after he "fearlessly and without regard for his personal safety led his flight to attack greatly superior numbers of enemy fighter aircraft which were attacking a damaged bomber."[39]

During an exchange of hand signals to explain that their radio was out, Weniger received London's acknowledgement that he would provide continuous escort back to England. The *T.S.* crew then began jettisoning heavy equipment to lighten their load.

"Could we get across the Channel or would we have to ditch? We were going to England come hell and hopefully, no water," said Weniger.

Despite a brief moment of anxiety when it seemed that *T.S.* might be brought down by barrage balloons off the English coast, the crew soon spotted a landing strip. Lining up with what turned out to be RAF Manston, Manchester and Weniger then worked together to land the heavily damaged bomber.

"No flaps, no landing gear, RPM at the peg … over the end of the runway at 120 miles per hour and then a full reduction of power."

After sliding to a halt, the 10-man crew promptly evacuated the smoldering B-17 without a moment's hesitation.

"The English airdrome officer came out after a short while to advise us we should not have landed on that runway," wrote Weniger, "because it had been mined in the event the Germans tried to land. Eddie [Manchester] dryly remarked to him, 'we just did.'"

As the Manchester crew inspected *T.S.*, they found one of the Fw 190's machine guns firmly embedded in the wall of the radio room. Their bomber, which would eventually be declared salvage, had lived up to its name.[40]

* * *

The 381st's ninth mission had seen the loss of two more bombers, bringing the total number to eight in just three weeks of combat. After learning that Manchester and his crew were safe, James Good Brown was "torn between elation and sadness." There was still no news of *Widget*, but he had to turn his attention to the task of burying those killed in the *Red Hot Riding Hood* crash.

"I think the tearing of the personality is as hard as anything in the war," he later wrote in his diary. "One lives a strained life. It is not a life of ease and peace ... this war business is ugly. It literally breaks the heart. But we must not let it break the mind."[41]

CHAPTER 4

Forward Together

July 15–30, 1943

Three days after the loss of *Red Hot Riding Hood*, James Good Brown once more travelled the 100 miles to Brookwood Cemetery. The 381st was still only three weeks and nine missions into its war, yet here he was again, this time, stood over the flag-draped coffins of 1st Lt. Charles Hedin and five of his crew. It was yet another tragedy that Brown had forlornly hoped he would never experience.

He remembered the young British Women's Auxiliary Air Force member he'd seen walking along the road while making his way to Brookwood several weeks earlier. He and several other officers had instructed their driver to stop and give her a ride. Although she hadn't said much on their journey, Brown was struck by something she did say. "You men have been here in England only a short time." Brown asked her how she knew. "Because you are all so happy."

He was taken aback. The British had certainly suffered—far longer than the Americans—but the men of the 381st were also suffering. They'd been in England only a few weeks, but, as far as Brown was concerned, they were "growing older by the day and by the hour."[1]

To compensate for its recent losses, the 381st began to receive additional B-17Fs rendered expendable by other groups. Several had arrived from the 96th BG based at nearby Andrews Field. They included *TARFU* (a tacit abbreviation for "things are really fucked up"), which was immediately rechristened *TS Too* by the 535th BS, in recognition of its mischievously named, *T.S.* The group also found its combat crew complements increased from nine per squadron to 12. It allowed the 381st to put up its largest number of B-17s for its 10th mission two days later.

In accordance with the CBO's *Pointblank* directive,[2] VIII BC planned to target the German rail and aviation industry for its 74th raid. The 4th BW was tasked with attacking the latter at Hamburg, while the 1st BW would aim for the former at Hanover. VIII BC's new-found capability to launch a "maximum effort" raid was illustrated by the 101st PCBW, which scheduled 83 of its bombers—more than the entire VIII BC had at its disposal the previous winter. The 381st alone would be supplying 30.

Loaded with 500lb general-purpose bombs, the 381st's B-17s, again led by Joe Nazzaro, began taking off into low cloud at 0715. Among them was a B-17F flown by the 532nd's first "replacement" crew, led by its pilot Flight Officer (FO) Jack S. Pry and navigated by 2nd Lt. Roger W. Burwell.

Burwell had graduated top of his navigation class in Texas and had immediately been offered an instructor's role at a stateside navigation school. Instead, he'd chosen to go into combat and was assigned to Pry's crew shortly before leaving the US. Within weeks, he found himself with the 532nd at Ridgewell and about to take part in his first combat mission.

The weather over England on July 17 made Burwell's task a difficult one. Several 381st crews had to abort the mission early, having failed to take over from the formation leader when he, too, had aborted. Further difficulties were encountered during assembly with the 101st PCBW and the rest of the 1st BW at the English coast. Nevertheless, most of the 381st's B-17s continued on their way to Hanover, but then came a recall message.

As the unescorted 1st BW neared Hanover, the reason for the recall became clear. The 381st and several other groups were immediately set upon by some 70 German fighters. Roger Burwell had no time to fear the attacks.

"Between trying to navigate on a miniscule desk to keep track of our location, and at the same time man a machine gun on each side of the nose of the plane," he wrote, "was like a one-armed paperhanger trying to eat his sandwich while at the same time trying to paper a wall."[3]

The target was heavily obscured by cloud, causing the lead group to bypass the primary and split off in search of targets of opportunity. Nazzaro followed, eventually dropping his bombs near a German village. He was followed by another 13 381st B-17s, which had managed to fend off the *Luftwaffe* fighters, destroying at least five in the process. They had also avoided the worst of Hanover's flak.

Returning across the North Sea, the 381st was met by a squadron of Spitfires. It was then that Roger Burwell's pent-up anxiety finally eased.

"I had time to feel totally exhausted, shaking and scared."[4] It was a pattern that would repeat itself for him and many others, who frequently found themselves faced with the same gnawing fear.

* * *

Replacement engineer and top turret gunner TSgt. John S. Comer felt anxious as his truck approached a rain sodden Ridgewell two days later. Glancing around his crewmates, each pondering their own fates, Comer wondered if they were destined to replace others who'd been lost from the 100th Bomb Group, an infamous unit whose casualties were well-known. "Please!" thought Comer. "Not that unlucky snake-bit command."[5]

At 33 years of age, John Comer was considerably older than most of his crewmates. But he was beginning to question his wisdom. A depth-perception weakness had ended his hopes of becoming a pilot 10 years earlier. The events of Pearl Harbor and the insatiable need for bomber crews had then seen him race from his aircraft mechanic's school to enlist. The medical examiner, noting Comer's poor eyesight and mechanical skills, offered to waive the defect if Comer was certain he wanted to become a flight engineer. "It will probably mean combat," said the examiner. "Is that what you want?" Comer's response was unequivocal. "Sounds great to me!"[6]

When Comer arrived at Ridgewell, he was relieved to hear that he and his crew had been assigned to the 381st BG. They were also being sent to the 533rd BS, which was low on crews. One of Comer's crewmates asked the officer about the group's losses. Comer was stunned to hear that the 381st had only been at Ridgewell for 60 days and had already lost "a hundred and one percent" of its combat personnel. Comer was sure it was a joke, but a smile never appeared on the officer's face.

"Our strength is down and we are happy to have you with us," the officer said meekly.

Comer's anxiety was not helped by several "veteran" gunners who burst into his hut as he unpacked a short while later.

"Hey kid, you're about my height," shouted one. "What size blouse you wear?"

The question was met with a testy response from one of Comer's crewmates, but the veteran continued his morbid examination.

"At the 381st they don't issue any replacement clothes," he said. "If you tear your pants, or ruin a blouse, you sweat it out until a gunner your size don't make it back."

Comer insisted he would "make it,"[7] but the odds were stacked against him four to one.[8]

* * *

A few days later, Comer found himself marveling at the standard of the base's food supply. Although the British were strictly rationed, Ridgewell seemed to have a plentiful supply of meat. Even so, the ongoing spread of the mystery illness, which had affected scores of men from two squadrons, only increased the number of inspections. "Embalmed beef"—frozen 40-pound cuts of meat, which required several hours to thaw—were thought to be the culprits. Still, over the next few days, checks of the mess halls, kitchens and sewerage found the base's water supply to be "contaminated." A new well, pump house and purifier were soon installed.

As quickly as Ridgewell's infrastructure was being bolstered, so Germany's was being dismantled. A report issued by the British Joint Intelligence Committee estimated that the *Luftwaffe* was employing more than half its fighter strength to protect the German transportation system and synthetic rubber industry, as well as fuel, iron and coal factories in the Ruhr Valley. On July 24, Operation *Gomorrah* was put into effect, the main target being Hamburg and its array of shipyards, U-boat pens and oil refineries. Concentrated "round-the-clock" bombing by the Allies was planned to last for a week. It was the first time VIII BC was invited to participate in an RAF Bomber Command "battle."[9]

The 381st's target on July 24 lay 400 miles north of Hamburg, on the Norwegian peninsula of Herøya. It was to be a 1,900-mile round trip from Ridgewell and easily the 381st's (and VIII BC's) longest raid so far. The primary target for the 381st and the 1st BW was Norsk Hydro's aluminum and magnesium plants, which had been constructed over the previous two years by the *Luftwaffe*-operated *Nordische Aluminium Aktiengesellschaft*. While the 1st BW was selected to destroy the plants, the 4th BW was tasked with attacking the port areas of Trondheim and Bergen. Over 300 American heavy bombers were loaded and ready for their first attacks on Norwegian soil.

At 0330 on July 24, 1st Lt. Osce Jones was sleeping soundly when a loud voice startled him. It announced that he and his crew were flying a mission. Despite rumors the evening before, there had been nothing to suggest where they were going. It was only at the briefing, when Joe Nazzaro turned to the map and traced a long ribbon from Ridgewell to Norway, that the crews finally knew.

Jones and his crew were one of the most respected in the 535th BS. Yet, for the Herøya mission, they would see several enforced changes. First, they would have to do without their usual navigator, Leonard L. Spivey. He'd been tasked with filling in for the group's lead navigator, who had been called away from his desk at the 381st's headquarters. Secondly, Jones's regular co-pilot Melvin R. Hecker had been replaced by the 535th's operations officer, 1st Lt. George B. McIntosh. Jones's was a makeshift crew cobbled together for a challenging mission.

Georgia Rebel had been repaired since its "life raft incident," and was loaded with nine 500lb bombs when Jones and his crew arrived an hour before take-off. After a green flare was fired from the control tower at 0800, Jones began taxiing the bomber out from its hardstand as the lead B-17 of the 535th.

Just after take-off, Jones turned south before entering thick cloud, which extended for several thousand feet. *Georgia Rebel* then homed in on a new navigational aid, a "Splasher" radio beacon, which had been installed 12 miles south of Ridgewell. On reaching it, Jones orbited until all 22 of the 381st's B-17s were in formation. They then headed north to link up with the rest of the 1st BW, using several more beacons along the way. It was the first time the beacons were used to aid assembly in overcast weather.

Flying a course of 353 degrees true at an altitude of 10,000 feet, the 1st BW's 180 B-17s headed for the Skagerrak strait—a wide body of water between Norway, Sweden and Denmark. Approaching Herøya, the formation then climbed to its bombing altitude of 17,000 feet, before skirting around the peninsula and turning southeast for the bomb run. It had been almost five hours since take-off.

The low-altitude approach seemed to work. There was no fighter opposition. Even so, the new aluminum and magnesium plants had been equipped with a collection of 88mm flak guns, which soon homed in on the formation. Explosions rocked *Georgia Rebel*, but Osce Jones had already switched control to 2nd Lt. Charles W. Nevius's Norden bombsight,[10] which continued guiding the B-17 straight and level. Very quickly, the German gunners began finding their range. Just after bombs away, *Georgia Rebel* was slammed by an explosion which put its number two engine out of action. Jones quickly regained control and feathered the damaged propeller, but one blade was badly twisted. He then steered southwest and began the arduous task of nursing the bomber back to Ridgewell.

Approximately 150 miles from Herøya, *Georgia Rebel*'s number three engine began malfunctioning. Although Jones was unaware, another pilot flying alongside also spotted fuel leaking from *Georgia Rebel*'s port wing. Jones's B-17 slowly slipped behind the rest of the formation, which was still four hours' flying time from England.

Jones conferred with McIntosh and the rest of the crew. It was clear that *Georgia Rebel* wasn't going to make it. The thought of crash-landing in either Nazi-occupied Norway or Denmark didn't appeal to the crew. The safest option was to head for neutral Sweden, an hour's flight away. It was also something that had never been achieved by an American crew before.

Jones turned *Georgia Rebel* back over the Skagerrak and headed northeast, before crossing Oslofjord. The crew dumped classified documents and equipment into the water, including the Norden bombsight. Jones then banked the bomber east towards the Norwegian coastline and across the towns of Fredrikstad and Sarpsborg. The crew prepared for flak and German fighters to appear, but the bomber remained undetected and staggered on towards the Swedish border.

Jones's stand-in navigator, 2nd Lt. Arthur L. Guertin, had no accurate maps of the area and could only estimate the location of the Swedish border. However, a lack of fuel soon forced Osce Jones's hand. Flying over seemingly endless forests and hilly terrain, he eventually spotted a railroad track and descended to 600 feet in order to follow its course. Then, travelling another 20 miles north, he spotted a long field next to the tracks. Flying alongside for a brief survey, the crew confirmed it looked suitable. Jones then made a sweeping 360-degree turn to approach from the south.

Several local inhabitants watched the bomber bank at low level, before descending towards the field, one even managing to capture a photograph. Deciding against using the undercarriage, Jones chose to "belly land" the bomber instead. With the crew braced in the radio room, *Georgia Rebel* touched down and slid along, snapping pine saplings as it went. Then, slowed by the boggy ground, it came to an abrupt halt just short of a telegraph pole. When the uninjured crew emerged from the bomber, a young man from a nearby farm was first on the scene. In perfect English, he confirmed they had landed in Sweden.

Swedish border troops and curious civilians soon arrived at the bomber, which was proudly shown off by its crew. The Americans were then whisked away by car to a nearby courthouse where they were served coffee and sandwiches. A day later, Osce Jones and his men were taken to the nearby town of Falun, where their Swedish internment began in the comfort of a large, rented house. Osce Jones and the *Georgia Rebel* crew had become the first Americans to be interned in Sweden during World War II.[11]

* * *

"Gentlemen, the target for today is Hamburg." There was silence, before the low groans rose to a steady din. Most crews had flown the Herøya mission the day before and were still bleary-eyed from their 11-hour flight. They were now wide awake again.

Second Lieutenant Philip P. Dreiseszun, a navigator with the 532nd, was in a "state of numb awe, of mixed feelings of fear and wonder"[12] as he sat listening to the briefing officer. Dreiseszun was nudged by his fellow crewmate and bombardier James H. Houck, who shook his head. Hamburg wasn't going to be like Herøya. The *Luftwaffe* would see to that. The bomber crews would also have to wave goodbye to the escorting P-47s somewhere over the North Sea. Dreiseszun's only hope was that he would get the chance to meet his English date in the village of Clare later that evening.

The crews' briefed route would take them 200 miles over the North Sea on a northeasterly heading, before swinging southeast for another 200-mile leg in towards the bomb run. At 1300, in fair weather and good visibility, 24 B-17s began lifting off from Ridgewell to head for their assembly area with the 101st PCBW. By the time the 91st and 351st BGs arrived, however, the 381st was way ahead of them. It was forced to circle back, which then left it too far behind. As the formation crossed the East Anglian coast at Cromer, the 381st was still fighting to catch up.

In the nose of *Lethal Lady*, Dreiseszun and Houck donned their oxygen masks and test-fired their guns. Their pilot, 1st Lt. William R. Moore and others in the group were flying as hard as they could to reach the 101st PCBW, but the formation was slipping further away. Several 381st B-17s then aborted, including that of the leader, Maj. George G. Shackley. His place was taken by the deputy leader, David Kunkel, who attempted to catch up by cutting across the approach path to the target. Dreiseszun knew they were now facing a dangerous situation.

"In a tight formation, our wing was a formidable target," he later wrote, "as stragglers, [we] were an easy mark for destruction."[13]

Just after 1630, the 381st entered a heavy flak barrage that shook the crew of *Lethal Lady*. Down below, Hamburg was covered by a thick pall of smoke left by a heavy RAF bombing raid the night before. The 1st BW's target area was hidden yet again. Amid heavy explosions, the formation turned north to find a target of opportunity. But then the *Luftwaffe* appeared.

Swarming in from all directions, countless Me 109s pounced on the 381st. Dreiseszun and Houck braced themselves against each other as they frantically swung their machine guns. Cannon fire then struck *Lethal Lady*, spinning Houck around and knocking Dreiseszun into his worktable. Although he hadn't been hit, he could see that Houck was. The bombardier had collapsed to the floor with a gaping chest wound. Despite Dreiseszun's attempts to stem the flow of blood, Houck lay dead.

William Moore was struggling to hold *Lethal Lady*, which had had part of its horizontal stabilizer shot away. Smoke was also billowing from an engine. With several guns still rattling away in the back of the aircraft, Moore gave the bail-out order. Philip Dreiseszun left Houck and crawled back to the nose hatch. He paused for a few seconds while he considered whether to extricate his dead crewmate from the nose so he could be parachuted for burial. It was an agonizing decision, but Dreiseszun decided to leave him. He kicked open the hatch and rolled out headfirst.

Dreiseszun counted as he dropped, pulling his ripcord after 2,000 feet. He was jerked violently and glanced up to check on the parachute's condition. To his horror, he saw it was riddled with rips and tears—presumably, he thought, from being hit during the fighter attack. Buffeted by strong winds and swinging wildly from side to side, Dreiseszun "curled up" and let the parachute carry him down some 25,000 feet. He thought back to the intelligence briefings at Ridgewell and quickly threw away his high school ring and Hebrew-identifying dog tags. He then began falling faster and straighter.

"There was not enough buoyancy to easily float down," Dreiseszun recalled, "just enough to prevent a free drop. The rate of closure between myself and the ground increased frighteningly."

Seeing a group of people rushing to the spot where he was going to land, Dreiseszun thought back to his training lectures. Then everything went black.

"My eyes opened to see a German soldier sitting on me. I put my hand to [his] chest... and pushed him off me."

Dreiseszun then raised himself up and reached for a pocket where he kept his cigarettes. Several other soldiers instantly raised their rifles. "Cigarettes..." Dreiseszun gingerly explained. But there were none left. They'd fallen out on his way down.[14]

* * *

As Philip Dreiseszun was being dragged to his feet in front of a hostile German crowd, another 381st B-17 was in trouble overhead. First Lieutenant Jack H. Owen was fighting with the controls of *Sad Sack*, which had been flying alongside *Lethal Lady*. Owen's B-17 had been hit by flak over Hamburg and, with fire spreading along the starboard wing and large holes in the fuselage, the crew began bailing out. *Sad Sack*'s radio operator TSgt. Roy L. Slater exited the rear hatch, but he struck the B-17's tail assembly, which dislocated his hip. Slater fared better than his co-pilot 2nd Lt. William E. Bohan, however. He was shot in the chest by German civilians on landing. Fortunately, Bohan was "rescued" by German troops and went on to recover in a prisoner of war (POW) camp.

For several of *Lethal Lady*'s crew, though, their luck had deserted them. The body of tail gunner Sgt. John M. Watkins Jr., who was thought to have been killed during the fighter attack, was recovered from the bomber's wreckage at Rethwischhof, Bad Oldesloe. So, too, that of James Houck. But it was the fates of co-pilot 2nd Lt. Dale G. Wendte and waist gunner SSgt. Joseph G. Kralick that were most disturbing.

Just after *Lethal Lady*'s radio operator TSgt. Edward W. Usher had crashed through the branches of a tree and landed on a haystack, he was picked up by German troops. Loaded onto a wagon, he was shocked to see Kralick lying there dead, a clean bullet wound to his forehead. Usher was convinced Kralick had been shot after landing. The same fate befell Wendte, who had bailed out "uninjured" ahead of pilot William Moore. He, too, was found to be shot. When Moore was processed through the *Luftwaffe*'s *Dulag Luft* (transit camp) the next day, several downed RAF airmen told him they had seen "17 Americans" hanging on telegraph poles in Hamburg. Philip Dreiseszun learnt why on his way to the same camp.

"Enroute to [*Dulag Luft*] we were taken in groups escorted by armed guards," he recalled. "As we passed through Hamburg train station, we encountered an enraged citizenry who were prepared to lynch us. Our guards cleared the way for us, shoving Germans aside and fending off those more belligerent trying to reach us."[15]

In addition to the losses of the Moore and Owens crews, a third—that of Capt. Joseph E. Alexander—was also missing. His B-17 has also been damaged by flak over Hamburg and was making its long flight back to Ridgewell. A short way over the North Sea, however, the aircraft was seen to vibrate violently before turning back towards Europe. It was the last time Alexander's B-17 was seen, although it later transpired that he'd managed to belly land in a meadow where his bombardier promptly destroyed the Norden bombsight before German soldiers arrived. For Alexander—who'd once remarked that "war would be a hell of a great time if no one got hurt"—the war was over.

The 381st's 12th mission had proved to be its costliest so far. Only 14 B-17s had managed to bomb. Seven of them had been damaged, while 30 men were missing in action. One crewman also returned to Ridgewell in a critical condition, suffering from anoxia. Operation *Gomorrah* was taking its toll.

* * *

James Good Brown's insistence on "sweating out" the group's missions had not diminished. But he'd noticed that too few of the ground crews were on hand to watch the bombers return from their raids. He approached Joe Nazzaro with a suggestion.

"I thought it was imperative that as many as possible get up to the flying field and watch the fellows return," Brown wrote.[16]

A day after the first Hamburg raid, he was delighted to see more ground crews than usual assemble for the bomber's return from another mission. Yet, they were all in for a shock.

Earlier that morning, 22 of the group's B-17s had followed the same route to Hamburg as the day before. This time, they also led the 1st BW's 100 other B-17s along the Nordelbe and over the Blohm & Voss U-boat yards. However, a combination of smoke from previous bombing raids, and an artificial smokescreen created by the Germans conspired to cover the primary target. Instead, the formation dropped on the nearby Howaldtswerke U-boat yard, flattening it.

Tinker Toy, piloted by 1st Lt. Frank Chapman, had just dropped its 500lb bombs and turned south when it was rocked by an explosion. Flak fragments pierced the nose of the aircraft and struck Chapman's replacement navigator, 1st Lt. Sidney Novell, who was flying his first mission. Novell was floored by the blast, which left his left thigh bleeding heavily.

Elsewhere in the formation, explosions and shattered plexiglass had incapacitated one of the 534th's navigators; while the 532nd's lead bombardier was suffering from frostbite after removing his gloves to manipulate the bomb sight over Hamburg.

Unlike the previous day, the 381st headed back to England largely intact. Only one of its B-17s was forced to divert after crossing the English coast. Short of fuel, its pilot made an emergency landing at an airfield still under construction, which sent workers scattering in all directions. The rest of the B-17s returned to Ridgewell.

One of the first to land was *Tinker Toy*, with a red flare being fired from the radio room on its approach. Three of Frank Chapman's crew had suffered anoxia during the flight, each claiming the other two were "dead." All three were revived, but it caused much confusion. The same couldn't be said for their navigator, Sidney Novell, however. As soon as *Tinker Toy* arrived on its hardstand, it was quickly surrounded by a large group of men.

"When the engines were turned off, they saw something which is not pleasant," James Good Brown wrote in his diary, "but I think it was the best thing that could have happened."

Frank Chapman stepped out of the aircraft weighed down by his parachute and equipment. Handing it to Brown, he announced that the navigator had "got it." In the nose, Sidney Novell lay dead, his femoral artery cut. Brown went to assist the medics as they removed the navigator's body from the aircraft. Lowering him down, blood began seeping over Brown, staining his clothes and covering his hands. Amid gasps of horror, Brown thought it was the "best lesson" the group had learned since arriving in England.

"Unless these men see the price we are paying," he later told Frank Chapman, "They will never know what corrective measures to take ..."[17]

* * *

On July 27, the 1st BW was temporarily stood down from Operation *Gomorrah*, while Brig. Gen. Frederick L. Anderson Jr., newly appointed commanding general of VIII BC, joined the RAF for its continuing assault on Hamburg. Flying as an observer in an Avro Lancaster, he watched as almost 800 bombers pounded the city for a second night. A combination of high temperatures, tinder-dry conditions, and concentrated targeting caused a massive firestorm, which raged for several hours. It claimed the lives of some 40,000 people, many of whom were asphyxiated. An estimated 16,000 buildings were also destroyed.[18]

At 0745 the next morning, 20 B-17s took off from Ridgewell for the group's 14th mission. Hamburg was spared this time. Instead, the 1st BW's 182 bombers were aiming for the Gerhard Fieseler works in Kassel, a plant churning out Bf 109 and Fw 190 fighters. Over 100 P-47s of the 4th, 56th and 78th Fighter Groups (FG) escorted the bombers, which included a further 120 B-17s from the 4th BW. Their primary target was another aircraft factory in Oschersleben. It was planned to be VIII BC's first long-range, fighter-escorted mission.

Frustratingly, the weather intervened again. Approaching the target, the 1st BW's commander aborted the attack due to solid cloud cover. Several groups searched for targets of opportunity, but the 381st circled Kassel and headed back for England with its 20 bombloads intact. Still, the 4th FG achieved a notable first when its P-47s, equipped with jettisonable fuel tanks, penetrated German airspace while engaging the *Luftwaffe* over the Netherlands.

After several days of training, John Comer and his crew were still waiting for their first encounter with the Germans. That looked set to change at 0230 on July 29 when the lights of their hut snapped on and a voice announced they were flying a mission. When Comer arrived at the mess hall, he was too nervous to eat his "fresh eggs."

"I watched the men come and go in anxious fascination," he later wrote. "I envied the confident air of the vets, who appeared totally unperturbed. I wondered if I would survive long enough to develop such a carefree attitude."[19]

Comer's anxiety rose when he realized he'd left his heated flying suit in the hut. While the rest of his crew were taken by truck to the operations building, Comer ran through the darkness and across muddy fields to retrieve his equipment. When he arrived at the briefing, it was already over. The 381st would be attacking Kiel's U-boat yards using 22 B-17s. Comer and his crew would be flying *Nip and Tuck*, a B-17F that had been transferred in from the 96th BG a month earlier. When the crew arrived at their bomber, however, its 12 machine guns were nowhere to be seen. Another frantic dash across the airfield to locate the missing guns saw *Nip and Tuck* almost miss its take-off time.

Once in the air, Comer's pilot, 2nd Lt. Paul W. Gleichauf, informed the crew that they could expect a "hot reception" from several hundred fighters. He also told them to prepare for attacks halfway across the North Sea. Ten minutes from the German coastline, however, *Nip and Tuck*'s number four engine began to vibrate before slowing down. Gleichauf had no option but to feather the propeller and bank round for the long flight back to Ridgewell.

The rules for a "mission credit" were clear. If a crew flew all the way to the target and dropped bombs, it was credited. If the crew dropped on another target, the mission still counted. Finally, if the crew failed to drop, but engaged the enemy in combat or encountered flak, it, too, would count. With the Kiel mission aborted before the enemy coast, Comer and his crew could count on another 25 missions. "It was a long, tiresome and frustrating day and all for nothing," remembered Comer.[20]

Of the 24 B-17s dispatched from Ridgewell, 18 of them managed to hit the target just after 0900. Turning for home, *Martha the II* of the 533rd BS began to slip behind the formation. The bomber then attracted the attention of several German fighters, one of which disabled its number two engine with cannon fire. Despite further withering attacks, *Martha the II* somehow caught up with the formation. Its navigator, 2nd Lt. John C. Donovan, also destroyed one of the fighters with a burst from his machine gun. The other fighters peeled away and the bomber was finally left alone.

Whaletail, under the control of 1st Lt. William C. Wroblicka and carrying the 534th's operations officer Capt. Arthur F. Briggs, had suffered a series of engine problems and lost power and altitude over the North Sea. By the time it reached the English coast, there was only one functioning engine left. Descending over Norfolk, Wroblicka was forced to crash land near Thetford, the bomber bouncing across a wheat field before slewing to a halt. As Wroblicka stepped out, an irate farmer approached him complaining about the damage to his crops. Wroblicka calmly explained the aircraft was there for good reason—their "mutual survival."

* * *

Later that evening, as the 381st's officers were being entertained by a singer at Ridgewell, James Good Brown saw a young officer sitting alone in a corner. The chaplain went over and sat with him. First Lieutenant Guerdon W. Humason, a co-pilot with the 532nd BS, hailed from Orange Cove, California. Brown noted he was a "nice looking chap … with clear eyes and a straightforward look." The two chatted before Humason rose to his feet to return to his barracks. He was expecting to fly a mission the next day. "I can fly better if I get my rest," he explained.

Brown accompanied Humason to his hut while the two talked about the *Luftwaffe*'s fighter pilots and Nazi philosophy.

"We were fighting a German youth dedicated to [Hitler's] cause," Brown told him. "Now it is showing itself. It is evident in the air. We are meeting it in a well-trained German air force."

Humason could only reply that he "wished it were over."[21]

In the early hours of July 30, Guerdon Humason was awoken for the 381st's sixth raid in a week. He was to fly as "deputy lead" pilot, with the 532nd's commanding officer Maj. Robert Post sat beside him in the co-pilot's seat. Together, they would lead the 1st BW.

At the briefing, Joe Nazzaro announced that 18 of the group's aircraft would be returning to Kassel to bomb the Bettenhausen Fieseler works. James Good Brown noted how Nazzaro's voice "didn't shake" as he explained how dangerous the mission would be. Brown glanced around the room at the grim faces, including Humason's.[22]

By 0900, the 381st was at 31,000 feet leading another 100 B-17s over Kassel. Humason's bombardier had already dropped their bombs when flak exploded below the aircraft, bucking it violently. Three of its engines were knocked out, the oxygen system cut, and an elevator jammed. The B-17 immediately dropped from the formation, chased by German fighters.

Several of the gunners had been wounded by the flak explosion and scrambled for the waist door to bail out. Unable to prise it open, SSgt. Walter J. Anderson elected to jump through a waist window instead. The other gunners and radio operator followed, all landing safely. It later emerged, however, that Walter Anderson had struck the horizontal stabilizer as he exited. He was later found dead with an unopened parachute.

As Humason's B-17 reached 10,000 feet, cannon fire from an Me 109 struck the cockpit, hitting Post in the leg and taking out one of his eyes. Humason was also slightly wounded, but he pushed the B-17 into another dive before levelling out at 3,000 feet. Remarkably, the aircraft was flying well on one engine, but with the loss of fuel from punctured wing tanks and all ammunition expended, Humason knew time was almost up.

As the B-17 dropped lower, it was "pasted" by the fighters and hit the ground near Apeldoorn, the Netherlands, before skidding into a small forest. Humason and three others managed to escape the wreckage just as the fighters began strafing it. Shortly afterwards, he was captured by German troops.

Robert Post had become the most senior ranked officer lost by the 381st. However, his fate, and those of Guerdon Humason and crew, were unknown. It was a bitter blow. Operation *Gomorrah* had cost the group dearly. Five B-17s and fifty men were missing. As James Good Brown noted in his diary, "we have been in the war only five weeks, but already the reaper of death has cut a deep swathe into the 381st."[23]

Intermission: The Bomb Group

If the B-17 and the B-24 bombers were the individual building blocks that the Eighth Air Force was constructed of, then its bomb groups were the operational currency by which it traded every day. This was the foundation on which the Americans' European strategic heavy bombing campaign was built.

Flying daylight, precision bombing missions with VIII BC was an entirely different proposition to that experienced by the crews of RAF Bomber Command. British and Commonwealth bomber crews lived as a squadron. They flew their operations at night, operating as solitary aircraft in a bomber stream. In almost complete contrast, the American crews that made up VIII BC lived, trained, and fought together, flying into battle, in formation, frequently as an entire group.

In 1942, an Eighth Air Force bomb group usually operated 35 aircraft, three of which belonged to the group headquarters. Within most bomb groups, four frontline squadrons each maintained eight aircraft. As the number of available aircraft increased, most squadrons were issued a ninth aircraft that was employed as a "staff ship." By the autumn of 1943, there was a planned increase in bomb group strengths. Each squadron was supplied with enough additional aircraft, personnel, tools, and spares to operate 14 bombers.

Second Lieutenant Theodore "Ted" Homdrom, a navigator, gives some insight into the organization of the 381st BG while describing the management of its navigators:

> Our 381st Bomb Group had four squadrons. The 381st Group Navigator chose the four squadron navigators, as well as handling a lot of administration and paperwork. When someone who had been a squadron navigator finished his tour of combat, he could be promoted to Group Navigator if there was a vacancy. We squadron navigators also had a hand in the training of replacement crew navigators and in aids that came into cope with the European weather, like *Gee*-box [a radio navigation system used to fix an aircraft's position]. Squadron Navigators usually flew when their squadron led the 'combat wing' of 54 bombers. So that is how the navigation worked.
>
> On a mission, though the number varied later, in 1942 a squadron put up six aircraft and a group put up three of its four squadrons, resting one. Therefore, at three groups to a wing, a "combat wing" had 54 aircraft, while a "division" could consist of two or more wings. That is a lot of aircraft and a lot of guns—over 500 big .50 [caliber machine guns] per wing alone. As you can see, a "wing" could provide a lot of firepower against enemy fighters.[1]

The squadrons were supported in every aspect by the ground crews of the group's "sub depot" (and subsequent "air service group"). They were located together on a shared airfield, under one commander who, in turn, was supported by the headquarters staff. A heavy bomb group airfield could accommodate anywhere between 2,000 and 3,000 personnel.

CHAPTER 5

A Matter of Time

July 31–August 17, 1943

At the end of Operation *Gomorrah*, which had been dubbed "Blitz Week" by the Americans, VIII BC announced a stand down from combat. Its hard-pressed bomb groups could finally take a break after six exhaustive missions in seven frenetic days. The respite hadn't come soon enough for the 381st, however. Over the course of 39 days, its strength had been whittled by a third. A total of 15 B-17s and 134 airmen had been lost in raids and accidents. By July 31, just nine of its 45 assigned bombers remained operational.[1] The 381st's surgeon, Ernest Gaillard, was mindful of the effects "the heaviest operational schedule ever maintained" was having on the crews.

"I feel the men have withstood the strain well, and while very tired, are definitely not jittery," he noted. "They need a rest and change now."

Gaillard also pondered the consequences for his group having lost its first squadron commander, the 532nd's Robert Post, who had been promoted to the rank of major just three days earlier.

"I believe they [the crews] will be adjusted to the loss in a short time," he wrote. "However, as they must have realized … some squadron CO would be shot down sooner or later if they continued to participate in raids."[2]

On August 2, Ridgewell airfield was officially handed over to Joe Nazzaro by the RAF. A British officer and a handful of civilians had remained on site to provide care and maintenance, but the formal ceremony at the 381st headquarters' site marked the start of a new beginning. The cleanliness of the base's facilities and the wellbeing of its thousands of inhabitants were still giving cause for concern, however.

After a lengthy inspection by several 1st BW officers, Ridgewell's "unsatisfactory conditions" persisted. So much so that, within days, some 75 officers and men had contracted diarrhea after drinking water that was "unusually cloudy." It led to an Eighth Air Force medical inspector and a major from the chief surgeon's office being sent to Ridgewell. A list of nine recommendations were subsequently drawn up, including "ample, clean clothing for mess personnel" and "feces exams for all food handlers." Nevertheless, "odoriferous" latrines, "sloppy" kitchens and the "dirty fingernails" of cooks were still being found several days later.[3]

While the Eighth's medical department was busy scrutinizing Station 167's sanitary conditions, the 381st's senior officers made their way across London for a briefing at *Pinetree*, VIII BC's ornate headquarters at High Wycombe in Buckinghamshire. Led by commanding officer Joe Nazzaro, the party consisted of the squadron commanders—including Robert Post's replacement, Arthur Briggs—as well as the group's stand-in lead navigator Leonard Spivey.

Spivey, a farmer's son from Artesia, New Mexico, had graduated from navigator's school in November 1942. Shortly afterwards, he'd been assigned to the embryonic 381st at Pyote, where he was soon made "first navigator" of the 535th's "model crew." By the time he reached Ridgewell, Spivey had become the 535th's "squadron navigator." At Pinetree, his status was elevated once more, in what turned out to be his "most fascinating experience of the war."

"Here was a young first lieutenant, 22 years of age, and everybody else were field grade officers or generals," he recalled. "I walked into the anteroom and a long table was lined with hats, gold braid ..."

After being introduced to "the whole command staff," including the Eighth's commanding officer Ira Eaker, as well as the head of the US Army in Europe, Lt. Gen. Jacob L. Devers, Spivey was led out into the expansive grounds of the mansion, which had previously been Wycombe Abbey School. Entering a small "kiosk," he was then ushered into an elevator, which descended underground. Emerging into a "huge room lined with charts," Spivey learned the reason for his being there.

> An intelligence officer got up and said: "We're planning a mission into Germany and the target will be ball-bearing plants where a large percentage of the ball-bearings manufactured in Germany are. It's right there in Schweinfurt; a small town."
>
> They had a mock-up of Schweinfurt, to scale ... and from the intelligence, reconnaissance of the flak guns, and the plants and locations ... there was something like ... 80 emplacements, which made me shiver, because I hated flak.[4]

As Spivey was counting the model's anti-aircraft guns, an RAF officer, who was also a flak expert, turned to him and explained the plan was to go in "at 16,000 feet." The 381st had never bombed that low before. When Spivey was asked what he thought, he meekly replied, "we'll be a much easier target."

On Spivey's return to Ridgewell, his *Pinetree* visit and the Schweinfurt mission remained "highly-classified."

"We were told, before that mission comes up, you cannot fly over occupied Europe, for obvious reasons," he recalled. "Be that as it may, I got orders after that to fly missions—and I flew them."[5]

* * *

While VIII BC's stand down continued, the 381st ground crews worked tirelessly to patch up and mend battle-damaged B-17s. In addition to carrying out the necessary test flights after repairs, the group's combat crews also attended ground schools, or took 48-hour passes to enjoy some much-needed rest. Nevertheless, three "scrubbed" missions, including one to Schweinfurt, punctuated the downtime.

"We were to hit the target [Schweinfurt] in the afternoon [of August 10] and the RAF was to hit it that night with 1,000 planes," noted Landon Hendricks in his diary. "The mission was delayed because of weather."[6]

Thirteen days after the group's last mission, enough B-17s were fixed to embark on VIII BC's 81st raid—another assault on Germany—in particular its synthetic oil facilities in the Ruhr Valley. The 381st scheduled 20 of its B-17s, although the 535th was supplied with a spare from the 91st at Bassingbourn. *Yankee Eagle*, flying in the group's lead position, was co-piloted by the 535th's commanding officer, Maj. William W. Ingenhutt, and navigated by the supposedly "mission-banned" Leonard Spivey.

Sat in the tail gun position of Spivey's B-17 was its usual co-pilot Everett Malone, who was there to monitor the rest of the 381st as it assembled.

"Reached our bombing altitude—28,000ft," he noted in his log. "Temp -44 [degrees centigrade]. Very cold."[7]

The temperature indicated at the briefing was expected to be -38, but the drop caused numerous cases of frostbite, including to Malone, whose feet became "terribly cold." Worse still, the recent diarrhea outbreak had left others in "serious difficulty."

After crossing the Dutch coast at 0828, the formation, led by the 351st, turned on the IP at 0853. Two minutes later, heavy flak pounded the B-17s as they overflew Essen.

William Wroblicka, piloting *Devil's Angel*, had originally taken off from Ridgewell as a "spare," but he'd been forced to slot into a vacant position left by another 381st B-17, which aborted over Norfolk. Already showered with flak over the Dutch city of Nijmegen, *Devil's Angel* was hit again as it headed along the bomb run, its number one engine catching fire.

"We dropped our bombs as we began to lose altitude fast and fell away from the group," recalled Wroblicka's bombardier, 2nd Lt. Lester W. Schneider. "As soon as this happened we were immediately attacked by two Me 109 fighters and raked by cannon fire."[8]

The attack put another engine out of action, set the port wing on fire, and damaged the rear of the bomber. Wroblicka ordered his crew to bail out but, as they did so, *Devil's Angel* was struck by more bullets. Only the radio operator SSgt. Fred M. Smith managed to avoid being hit as he bailed out. The other four gunners were reportedly killed before they could jump. All four officers and the top turret gunner managed to escape through the nose hatch before the B-17 crashed northwest of Bonn. William Wroblicka, who'd crash-landed *Whaletail* in Norfolk just two weeks earlier, was the last to bail out. After landing, he set off in a westerly direction, evading capture for several days. He was then taken prisoner, as were the rest of his crew, including Lester Schneider.

"I was interrogated by a [*Luftwaffe* captain] who asked many questions," he recalled. "I was completely surprised when he told me all about myself, my army life and my family."

Schneider was taken to *Stalag Luft III*, where he would spend the next year and a half. He and his crew had become the 534th's first loss.[9]

The 381st's remaining B-17s followed the rest of the 101st PCBW towards the target, which was found to be covered by "the smoke of a million chimneys." The leading 351st sought a target of opportunity and dropped its bombs on a steel factory at Bochum. It then turned northwest for the return to England.

As the formation crossed the Dutch border, *Margie Mae* of the 532nd BS was badly damaged by flak over the city of Maastricht. Its pilot, 2nd Lt. Theodore L. Moon, had no option but to order his crew to bail out. All ten succeeded in jumping, although they were quickly rounded up by the German military.

Another 381st B-17 was also lost on the return to Ridgewell. The formation was due to be met by P-47s at the Belgian–German border but *Forget Me Not* was being harried by a German fighter, which succeeded in bringing it down. The pilot, FO Fred G. Evans, was killed before he had a chance to bail out of the bomber, as were four other members of his crew. The remaining five were taken prisoner.

James Good Brown was on hand to meet the crews as they returned from yet another torturous mission.

"You look for faces, and they are not here," he wrote in his diary. "... of Evans and his crew; of Wroblicka and his crew; and of Moon and his crew ... But I see some of the men's faces when they walk off alone. I walk over and stand by a man's side ... I do not say a word."

Thursday, August 12 had ended with the loss of three more B-17s and 30 men. Brown closed his diary with the words, "I don't feel like eating supper."[10]

* * *

After a two-day break in which Ridgewell's water supply was thoroughly analyzed and chlorinated, the 381st's crews were back in the air for the group's 18th mission. Engineer and top turret gunner John Comer, whose first two missions hadn't been credited, was hopeful this one would count after his B-17, *Nip and Tuck*, took off to bomb an aircraft plant near Brussels.

"How long was it going to take to get in 25 missions?" he wrote. "But ... clouds began to form heavily underneath the formation and halfway over the North Sea it became a solid blanket."[11]

Arriving over Belgium, the 381st then searched fruitlessly for its target, before turning back for England. "Three attempts and all that work for nothing!" wrote Comer.

Despite this, a report of flak from the lead B-17 confirmed the mission as being credited. While Comer's crewmates argued whether any flak had actually been seen, he was confident he'd got his first combat mission officially recognized. The lack of any visible flak was also something to be thankful for.

"We were lucky to ease into combat with sorties [like this], because each time we had learned some valuable lessons, gained confidence, and increased the odds for surviving ..."[12]

The next day, Comer and his crew were back in *Nip and Tuck* for another short-haul mission to a *Luftwaffe* airfield at Le Bourget, near Paris. Yet, this time, he was to get his first taste of both flak and fighters.

With four groups of P-47s providing area cover, the 381st, under the command of Joe Nazzaro, led the 101st PCBW towards the target. However, it wasn't long before elements of the *Luftwaffe* side-stepped the American fighters and intercepted the bombers.

"I was tracking four suspicious fighters at nine o'clock and wheeled around just in time to get my sights on the fighter attacking us," recalled John Comer. "It was headed straight for our nose spitting deadly 20mm cannon shells and 30-caliber machine gun bullets. I was so fascinated by the sight that I froze ..."[13]

Comer failed to fire his guns in anger, immediately drawing the ire of his co-pilot, 1st Lt. Herbert Carqueville. Even so, *Nip and Tuck* survived its first encounter with the *Luftwaffe*, although flak then began bursting around the aircraft.

"As the bursts crept ever closer I could feel the hair on my head trying to push up against my helmet," recalled Comer. "All the German gunners needed to do was make one final correction, and they would have had us bracketed, dead center."[14]

Fortunately, *Nip and Tuck* and 170 of the 1st BW's other B-17s made it through to the target, where almost 795,000lb of bombs were dropped during an eight-minute period. The main concentration of bombs photographed by the trailing 351st showed craters spread over "the main field for 4,401 feet," while smoke covered hangars, workshops and dispersal areas. The *Luftwaffe*'s field repair depot was largely destroyed.

At the interrogation back at Ridgewell, the jubilant crews were served with coffee, hot chocolate and Spam sandwiches. Lieutenant Colonel Nazzaro wandered the room offering words of comfort and congratulations. Having led the 101st PCBW on one of its most effective raids so far, Nazzaro was later awarded the Silver Star for his "conspicuous gallantry and intrepidity." For John Comer, though, the intensity of the Le Bourget mission had left him drained. After cleaning and stowing his guns, he trudged wearily back to his Nissen hut.

"I literally fell into bed, with part of my clothes on, and in two minutes was oblivious to everything ..."[15]

* * *

"It is now the wee hours of the morning," wrote James Good Brown in his diary on Tuesday, August 17. "The time does not matter. What is time these days! Nothing. It all flows together one day into another. No one is interested in time alone."[16]

It was just after 0200 and Brown was preparing to attend the combat crews' briefing for the group's 20th mission. Unknown to many, including John Comer, they'd unwittingly paved the way for VIII BC's 84th raid by "softening up" the *Luftwaffe*'s defenses in Belgium and France. At the briefing, the curtain was drawn back to show the map of Europe. A long, red line stretched far into Germany towards Schweinfurt. Although Leonard Spivey and the squadron commanders were familiar with the route, many were horrified by their intended flight path.

"Our crew had been lucky so far," recalled 2nd Lt. Robert E. Hyatt, a navigator with the 534th. "Nine missions without any trouble, no one injured, no serious damage. But I had the distinct premonition that we were going to get it ... how could you penetrate that deep and get in and out safely?"[17]

By coincidence, August 17 marked the first anniversary of American heavy bomber operations from England. While the 381st and eight other groups of the 1st BW were attacking Schweinfurt's ball-bearing plants, the 4th BW would be targeting a Messerschmitt factory in Regensburg. The 4th BW, under the command of Col. Curtis E. LeMay, was expected to "fight its way in" before swinging south to land in North Africa, while the 1st BW, commanded by Brig. Gen. Robert B. Williams, would battle its way back to England. The ambitious plan was designed to disperse the *Luftwaffe* and dilute its fighting ability.

At 0630, with clear, high-pressure weather extending across much of Europe, the 381st was scheduled to depart. However, Ridgewell, like many VIII BC bases, was shrouded in fog. A red flare fired from the control tower at 0600 signaled the start of an ominous wait for the crews. Hourly postponements then followed as they remained by their aircraft.

"A truck came out with Spam sandwiches," remembered nervous ball turret gunner Ken Stone, who was flying in the lead B-17, *Big Time Operator*. "I managed to eat two of them."[18]

The 4th BW had trained extensively on instrument take-offs and assembly. With a shrinking daylight window in which to land in North Africa following the raid, its B-17s were launched after a 90-minute delay. The 1st BW, meanwhile, remained firmly grounded. The nub of the "double strike" plan had been lost.

* * *

The 381st's B-17s began moving out from their hardstands almost four hours after the Regensburg force had taken off. *Uncle Sammy*, a B-17F of the 533rd BS faced a three-mile journey around the perimeter track before reaching the runway. One of its waist gunners, SSgt. Hubert A. Goss, glanced at the control tower where men were waving, a sight he'd not seen before.

The 1st BW was to be divided into two "task forces." The 381st's 26 B-17s were allotted a forward position in the leading 2nd Air Task Force (2nd ATF), under the command of Col. William M. Gross. The Third Air Task Force (3rd ATF), led by

Col. Howard M. Turner of the 40th Combat Bombardment Wing, would follow 12 minutes behind. Unhindered during assembly, the 1st BW reached the Dutch coast where it was met by an escort of RAF Spitfires. However, just as they were being replaced by two American fighter groups near the Belgian city of Antwerp, the weather closed in.

After noticing a build-up of heavy cloud, William Gross ordered his 2nd ATF to descend to 17,000 feet. The trailing 3rd ATF, however, remained at its assigned altitude of 21,000 feet. It proved to be an ill-timed decision. The 4th FG, which had been sent to escort the 2nd ATF, searched vainly for the B-17s. By the time the P-47s reached them, they were at the extent of their range. Their pilots could do no more than wave and turn back to England. Robert Hyatt watched them leave.

"They wiggled their wings and went back to their barracks and beer. We all knew we were going to be meeting the Germans soon. It was an awful empty feeling watching our fighters go."[19]

Minutes later, elements of JG 26 attacked the 381st head-on. First Lieutenant Weldon L. Simpson's *Lucky Lady* was immediately struck by cannon fire from an Fw 190, which damaged the leading edge of one wing. Simpson dropped the B-17 out of formation and turned back for England. *Lucky Lady* was then attacked "from all sides" until it rolled over and entered a spin, which Simpson fought to control as his crew bailed out. The aircraft then broke apart and crashed near Turnhout, Belgium, killing the doomed pilot. It was to Simpson's great credit that his crew survived. Eight were taken prisoner, while another—bombardier 1st Lt. Douglas C. Roraback—would eventually evade capture.

The 381st was soon attracting relentless enemy attention and Robert Hyatt's unnamed B-17 was also raked by cannon fire.

"They came in from eleven o'clock high—two FWs with yellow cowlings," remembered his crewmate, top turret gunner SSgt. Paul F. Shipe. "Coming in dead on the nose like that was a dirty trick. You hadn't a chance."[20]

Shipe subsequently went back through the bomb bay to find all the hatches open. Everyone in the rear of the aircraft had already bailed out. His pilot, 1st Lt. Hamden L. Forkner, had feathered one damaged propeller but could do nothing about a second which burst into flames. He waved to the pilot flying alongside him and was the last to bail out behind Shipe. Their crewless B-17 then flew a further 25 miles before crashing near Teuven, Belgium. Forkner and three of his crew were taken prisoner. Shipe, Hyatt and four others managed to escape.

German fighter controllers had been monitoring the Schweinfurt force since its assembly over England. After establishing that the Regensburg bombers would not be returning to their English bases, the controllers swiftly vectored 13 groups of fighters towards the 1st BW formation—by now, entering Germany. Flying from his base at Wiesbaden-Erbenheim, *Leutnant* Alfred Grislawski had already attacked the

4th BW. With a closing speed of 500mph, he aimed his Bf 109 at the right-hand side of the 1st BW.

Flying in the rear of the 2nd ATF was *Sweet Le Lani* of the 534th BS. Grislawski carried out a frontal attack, setting the B-17's number three engine on fire. Quickly realizing the situation was hopeless, its pilot, 2nd Lt. Neil H. Wright, switched on the bomber's Automatic Flight Control Equipment (AFCE) and issued the bail-out order. All 10 men jumped but were promptly captured. *Sweet Le Lani* went into a long, shallow dive before crashing near Simmern, Germany. It was the third 381st B-17 to be shot down in just 13 minutes.

As the formation continued on, *Hauptmann* Hermann Staiger of JG 26 focused his attention on the 533rd, which was flying in the 2nd ATF's high group. A leading *Viermot* [21] killer, he already had 63 heavy bomber claims to his name. Sixty seconds after *Sweet Le Lani* had been shot down, *Strato Sam* came into his sights. Staiger's cannons sent a hail of bullets into the B-17. Its pilot, FO James C. Hudson, immediately rang the bail-out bell, but bombardier 2nd Lt. Kenneth E. Robinson's parachute had spilled inside the aircraft. Tangled lines then left him unable to jump. He was killed when the aircraft crashed near Pesch. His nine crewmates were captured.

The 381st's operations officer, Maj. Conway Hall, was leading the group in *Big Time Operator*. Fifteen minutes earlier, he'd watched his deputy, Weldon Simpson, lost from his starboard wing. Shortly afterwards, *King Malfunction II*, flown by 1st Lt. Jack Painter, had moved into the vacant position. At 1423, a Bf 110 tore through the formation, cannon fire striking Painter's wing, which forced him to drop away. Moments later, the B-17 slid into a steep dive before breaking in two. Several parachutes were seen to leave the aircraft before it crashed, with Painter still at its controls.

Two of those who managed to bail out of *King Malfunction II* were its co-pilot 1st Lt. Robert E. Nelson and waist gunner SSgt. Raymond A. Genz. Descending over the German countryside, both were shot at by a German farmer. Avoiding his gunfire, they then took cover in a nearby wood. It was to be the starting point of a remarkable journey.

By now, the formation was overflying Bonn, whose flak gunners had found their range. A hole was blown in the number one engine of *Uncle Sammy*, which began leaking fuel before erupting in flames. Its pilot, 1st Lt. Challen P. Atkinson, decided he could go no further.

"He put her down in a turn towards home," remembered waist gunner SSgt. Peter A. Katsarelis. "So steeply that I was pinned to the floor by the centrifugal force. I couldn't move an inch."[22]

Pursued by fighters, Atkinson weaved a zigzag course allowing his gunners a "close-up shot." By then, however, most of them were out of ammunition. When *Uncle Sammy* was struck by more cannon fire, Atkinson rang the bail-out bell. In the pandemonium that followed, Hubert Goss spilled his parachute and was forced to frantically search for another. Luckily, he found one and was the last to bail out before the aircraft crashed close to Kesseling. Landing in a tree, he then managed to summon the strength to evade capture for 72 hours. Two of Goss's crewmates were less fortunate, however. Both Atkinson and ball turret gunner SSgt. James C. McGoldrick were allegedly shot and killed by Germans after landing on the ground.

Overhead, four B-17s of the 384th, 351st and 379th Bomb Groups were shot down in quick succession. Another aircraft went spinning out of control and plunged through the 381st's formation. The 534th's 1st Lt. Reinhardt M. King, flying *Hell's Angel*, was forced to make a violent maneuver to avoid being hit by another B-17, which was also attempting to dodge the falling aircraft. Moments later, however, there was nothing he could do to elude a Bf 109, whose cannon fire ripped through one of his B-17's engines and set its starboard wing on fire.

Hell's Angel, which had been assigned to the group at Pueblo four months earlier, eventually crashed near the town of Wiesbaden. All 10 men managed to bail out, including King's navigator, 2nd Lt. Edward C. McGlynn, who avoided being tracked by a pack of wolves overnight ("probably the worst night of my life"), before being captured by civilians several days later.[23]

* * *

During the planning of the Schweinfurt mission, the 1st BW was expected to fly south of the town before turning 180 degrees to bomb from the east. The sun would have been positioned behind the bombers, providing a natural hindrance to fighter attacks. After the delayed take-off, however, the plan had been hurriedly changed. Of the 230 B-17s which began the mission, 198 reached the IP at Gemünden. They then headed directly to Schweinfurt from the west. William Gross's earlier decision to reduce the altitude of his force then caused difficulties once more.

Approaching Schweinfurt, the trailing 3rd ATF soon gained ground on the 2nd ATF, which was still climbing to reach its bombing altitude. The 3rd ATF was forced to fly a meandering course to create an interval for its groups to fall into line. Second Lieutenant Harry M. Smith of the 535th BS was unaware of the problems behind as he wrestled with the controls of *Damfino*. His aircraft had been badly damaged in an earlier fighter attack. As he approached the Kugelfischer ball-bearing plant, he managed to hold his B-17 long enough for the bombardier to release their payload. Turning for home, *Damfino* was then set upon by a German fighter, which succeeded in damaging one of Smith's engines. For a short while the B-17 flew straight and level, but it then developed a spin from which Smith was unable to recover. Ten more men of the 381st bailed out to become POWs.

The "bunching up" of the task forces and the twisting route taken by the 3rd ATF led to a largely unsuccessful attack on Schweinfurt. The 1st BW released its bombs in almost a dozen places, approximately four miles in length. A few bombers struck small sections of Schweinfurt's three main ball-bearing plants, but many bombs landed in open fields nearly two miles beyond. Leonard Spivey's fears about the German flak batteries around the town were also being realized. Manned by those who worked in the factories, their 88mm guns pounded the formation as it passed overhead. One shell exploded directly in front of the 532nd's *Ole' Swayback*, badly wounding its bombardier, 2nd Lt. William D. Lockhart.

"It was like being hit in the face by a brick," he later recalled. "Like someone hitting you with a baseball bat. The physical impact of being hit and stopping it with your body was considerable. A piece of shell had hit me in the chin, passed through the cheek and lodged behind my left eye."[24]

Ole' Swayback, piloted by 1st Lt. Leo Jarvis, flew on before being attacked by a Bf 110. Ken Stone was watching from the ball turret of *Big Time Operator* as Jarvis's right waist gunner "waved goodbye." *Ole' Swayback* then dropped from the formation while its 10 crewmen bailed out.

"Chutes were all over the sky," Stone remembered. "White ones [of the Americans] and the brown chutes of enemy pilots. It looked like a parachute invasion."[25]

Ole' Swayback finally crashed near Ebrach, Germany, where its crew was quickly captured. William Lockhart, now a prisoner of war, eventually lost an eye as a result of his wounds. The German civilian medical staff even wrapped the piece of flak in some gauze and placed it in his pocket. "Some souvenir," he noted.[26]

Shortly after bombing Schweinfurt, the 1st BW turned north and then west before beginning the long trek back to England. By now, nine of the 381st's B-17s had been lost in action. There followed an hour's respite before the *Luftwaffe* attacked again.

Chug-A-Lug Lulu, piloted by 1st Lt. Loren C. Disbrow, had so far escaped the worst of the attacks. But at 1620, a German fighter pilot caught sight of it. A sustained assault left three of the B-17's engines badly damaged. The fourth then seized before the aircraft went into a spin. Disbrow issued the bail-out order and all 10 men jumped. Six were taken prisoner, while four managed to evade capture, including ball turret gunner SSgt. Joseph J. Walters, who was quickly spirited away by the Belgian Resistance. *Chug-A-Lug Lulu* had become the 32nd B-17 lost by the 1st BW.

Leonard Spivey, flying in *"Chap's" Flying Circus*, the 535th's lead B-17, had expended close to 4,000 rounds of ammunition in the nose of his aircraft. "Ankle-deep" in shell casings, he began navigating his squadron back to England.

"I could see plumes of smoke from where planes had crashed on the ground," he recalled. "We could almost fly those lines of smoke as landmarks to get home by."[27]

The persistent fighter attacks had left *Rum Boogie* with two disabled engines. Its pilot, FO George R. Darrow, was forced to reduce the power on the other two in order to conserve fuel. Finally reaching the English Channel, his fuel warning lights then came on and the aircraft began losing altitude. Moments later, the two remaining engines suddenly gave out and his heavy bomber became "a huge glider."

"Without the engines running, it was very quiet," Darrow remembered. "We could holler from the cockpit to the radio room and give status reports to the crew in the rear of the plane."[28]

Twenty miles from the English coast, the Fortress ditched—its nose and cockpit plunging beneath the waves before the aircraft bobbed back up. Darrow and his crew managed to escape before it sank in less than a minute.

"Here we were, ten very tired, hungry, wet and scared crewmen sitting in two little yellow rafts in the middle of the English Channel," recalled Darrow.[29]

He and his crew were eventually picked up by an RAF air-sea rescue boat after floating in their dinghies for an hour and 15 minutes. *Rum Boogie* had become the eleventh and final B-17 to be lost by the 381st on August 17. The group's remaining aircraft limped back across the English countryside to Ridgewell. Chaplain Brown, who'd been "sweating out" the crews after their take-off earlier that morning, had decided to help out on a local farm to take his mind off things. As he rode his bicycle back towards the airfield, he spotted some aircraft on the horizon.

"We had sent out all we had," he wrote in his diary. "As they came nearer, I began to count them. I counted all of them. 'I made a mistake,' I said to myself … They must be another group just flying over our field … They would go on to a field more distant, perhaps the 91st Bomb Group. We had sent out many more."[30]

Brown was shocked to discover that the bombers bore the letter "L" on their tails. As they began circling over Ridgewell, the terrible truth dawned. Only 15 had made it back, 14 of them severely damaged.

"When those wheels touched the ground, I was the happiest person on earth," remembered Ken Stone. "We had made the deepest penetration yet flown by B-17s … we were told that it would shorten the war by six months."[31]

His fellow crew members were also informed that the Germans "had all the women and kids in the city picking up ball bearings."

Some of the Eighth Air Force "brass" were waiting in Ridgewell's interrogation room to hear the exhausted crews describe their missions.

"There were several generals in there and one of them asked me … about it," recalled Conway Hall. "I said, 'the SOB that planned this one should have been on it.'"[32]

The 1st BW had dispatched 230 B-17s to Schweinfurt. Thirty-six had failed to return. The 4th BW had attacked Regensburg with 146 aircraft, losing 24. A total of 60 VIII BC bombers had been lost, taking with them 601 men. One hundred and ten were lost from Ridgewell alone. Five had been killed in action, 83 were prisoners of war, and 12 were evading capture. George Darrow and the crew of *Rum Boogie* would eventually return to Ridgewell the following day.

In just 203 minutes, the 381st's losses had almost doubled. It had also suffered the heaviest loss of any group on the Schweinfurt–Regensburg raid.

Later that evening, the crews took to the pubs to drink away the day's events. In the officers' club, 1st Lt. Arthur M. Sample was sitting at the bar with a dejected Joe Nazzaro, who was agonizing about having to "rebuild" the group. Sample became agitated and had to be pulled away by his friend, Roger Burwell. According to Sample, Nazzaro was more concerned about his "workload" than Schweinfurt.[33]

Nazzaro, however, had already been instructed to prepare the group for VIII BC's next mission, despite declaring it "non-operational." It would prevent the Germans from realizing how hard the group had been hit, he was told.[34]

Ridgewell's domestic sites were a stark reminder, as James Good Brown found when he accompanied some of the men back to the huts they shared with missing crews.

"As they stood there looking at the empty beds, they knew they would have to continue to fly the next day and the next day and the next day until their 'turn' came up. There did not seem to be one shred of hope that they would survive. As for the flying ability of the 381st—it is crippled."

CHAPTER 6

Deception

August 18–September 9, 1943

> Men eat in silence. They arise and leave the table in silence. If they ask for anything at the table, it is in a low murmur. Or they may go without butter in order not to talk. If any man were to walk boisterously into the dining room, throwing his conversation around loosely, he would be scorned … Ridgewell Aerodrome is like this. It is like a city morgue.[1]
>
> JAMES GOOD BROWN, AUGUST 18, 1943

Ridgewell's mess halls were a pitiful sight. Usually bustling with men, they were largely empty. Over 100 men—many of whom James Good Brown had seen and spoken to the morning before—had vanished. But his thoughts were also with those who'd survived the Schweinfurt mission. "What of the atmosphere which encompassed [them]?" he asked. "Grasp the feeling which gripped their minds when they entered their Nissen huts and saw the empty beds of one hundred of their buddies."[2]

For John Comer, things had also changed. The anxieties he'd once harbored had disappeared. Paying bills or "meeting a sales quota" seemed trivial in the extreme. Not knowing what to expect each day was now the new norm.

"It boiled down to revising my mental priorities to accept a new way of looking at things," he wrote. "A new mental attitude that would have been alien and totally unacceptable six months ago."[3]

Unknown to those at Ridgewell, many of the missing crews had survived the Schweinfurt raid, although most had been taken prisoner by the Germans. A number were still evading capture, including *King Malfunction II*'s co-pilot Robert Nelson and waist gunner Raymond Genz.

Just after midnight on August 18, they'd left their hiding place to help the wounded ball turret gunner SSgt. Allen P. Kellogg and waist gunner SSgt. Norman G. Whitman reach a nearby road. Unable to walk, both had chosen to surrender to the Germans in order to seek medical attention. Nelson and Genz, armed with their escape kits and compasses, then made off in a southwesterly direction, hoping it would take them to Switzerland.

Back at Ridgewell, there was some fleeting good news. Flight Officer George Darrow's former B-17 *Big Time Operator* was dispatched to RAF Manston to collect him and his crew after their ditching in the English Channel. Still dressed in the RAF uniforms given to them by their rescuers, they were interrogated on their arrival at Ridgewell. Darrow was then awarded a Distinguished Flying Cross (DFC) on what was his 22nd birthday.

With much of the 4th BW still on the ground in North Africa, and a large part of the 1st BW disabled because of battle damage, VIII BC chose to restrict its operations to close-range targets. A *Luftwaffe* airfield at Gilze en Rijen was selected as the primary for the 1st BW on August 19, with a total of 125 B-17s scheduled for the mission.

Having suffered more than any other group on the Schweinfurt raid, the 381st could only muster seven. The 532nd and 535th Bomb Squadrons were both stood down, but several of their B-17s were allocated to the other two squadrons. The 533rd BS would supply five, which surprised John Comer—even more so when he learnt that he and his crew would be flying one. Still, after being told the details of the mission (there would be fighter escort and they'd only be over enemy territory for a short while), Comer was relieved. He was also pleased to learn his B-17 would be carrying one of the group's medical officers, 1st Lt. Bernard E. Cohler.

Another of the 533rd's other B-17s, *Man o' War*, was to be flown by a composite crew made up of four men from the 533rd and six from the 535th. The latter comprised several who had been part of the 535th's "model crew" at Pyote, including navigator Leonard Spivey. His engineer and top turret gunner SSgt. Leo I. Perkins and radio operator SSgt. Arthur L. Everett were also with him. *Man o' War* would lead the 381st, flown by another "original" 535th pilot, 1st Lt. Orlando H. Koenig.

At the briefing, Spivey was still looking "glassy-eyed" after the Schweinfurt raid when he was told by Joe Nazzaro that "the war must go on." Sat in the nose of *Man o' War* as the group's lead navigator, he then began guiding it on a series of feints over England, before heading out across the North Sea. Shortly before reaching the Dutch coast, the formation was then met by P-47s, which proceeded with them towards the target.

Spivey could clearly see the IP and the target through broken clouds, but an order came through to abort the mission due to "visibility." Amid the confusion, the lead bomb group continued on over the airfield, but failed to drop its bombs. It then turned immediately across the target, rather than continuing on for another minute. Spivey looked on in disbelief. "God, are we going around again?" he thought. "We'll be sitting ducks."[4]

German flak guns tracked the formation as it began a long, 360-degree turn. The flak intensified as the lead group lined up for a second attempt. *Man o' War* was then struck by flak which damaged its starboard wing, causing a fuel leak. It flew on, but Fw 190s swiftly began attacking. Spivey and the bombardier Edward T. O'Loughlin had no time to react, but Spivey managed one burst. A dark, acrid smoke then began filling the nose.

Spivey called Koenig on the intercom to tell him about the smoke, but Koenig had other problems. Fire had taken hold of the wing and was spreading rapidly. He ordered his crew to bail out. Within seconds, Spivey was at the hatch. He nodded to Koenig, who was coming down from the cockpit. Kicking open the door and diving out, Spivey then blacked out before coming to, having unwittingly pulled the ring on his parachute chest-pack.

Spivey's fall from 19,000 feet was a lengthy one. It was cold and he was swinging 40 degrees from side-to-side beneath a 24-foot parachute that was threatening to fold. Looking down, he was hopeful that he could land somewhere quiet so he could find some cover. The flash of several flak guns and the noise of shells whistling past told him otherwise. He then saw two Me 109s approaching him. Thinking they might shoot him, he prepared to "spill" his parachute to drop faster. Just as they got closer, Spivey even seeing the pilots' faces, they quickly banked away, wiggling their wingtips. Spivey was so relieved he saluted them.

After drifting some 13 miles, Spivey came down over a city crammed with buildings and towers. He pulled the parachute to guide himself clear of power lines, before descending towards an open area. Faces looked up as he landed on a stretch of grass next to a busy railroad station. He'd arrived in the Dutch city of Schiedam, close to Rotterdam. He was immediately greeted by a sizeable crowd and a group of German soldiers, one of whom waved a hand grenade shouting "hands up." Spivey answered in German, "I have no pistol," but he was apprehended and taken away to muted cheers and several "Victory" signs.

Spivey had survived the downing of *Man o' War*, which had killed four gunners. But he, Koenig and four others were now POWs. Like Philip Dreiseszun just a few weeks earlier, Spivey found himself processed through Frankfurt's *Dulag Luft*, before being taken to *Stalag Luft III*—his "home" for the next 17 months.

* * *

Back at Ridgewell, news of the Koenig crew's loss was met with more dejection. Ernest Gaillard, the 381st's flight surgeon, whose subordinate Bernard Cohler had safely returned with John Comer, quickly noticed the effect the "easy" mission had had on the combat crews.

"If losses can be sustained on the simple ones," he wrote, "what chance does anyone have?"[5]

The following morning, the base loudspeaker crackled into life. At 15-minute intervals, a voice repeatedly ordered the combat personnel to assemble at operations. John Comer and his crewmates were unimpressed. So, too, were many of those who trudged alongside them. "Another one of those aircraft recognition classes!" yelled one. "I know what a 190 and 109 look like!"[6]

Lieutenant Colonel Joe Nazzaro, mindful of the mood gripping his men, had called them all together. A planned mission to a *Luftwaffe* airfield in Villacoublay, France, had been "scrubbed" earlier that morning, but it gave him the opportunity to drive home the group's aims and the broader objectives of the Eighth Air Force. He then gave an outline on the Germans' situation and the need for the Allies to keep up the pressure. Finally, he pointed out that their fellow crews—those who'd recently been taken prisoner—wouldn't appreciate any inactivity. "Each effort," he stressed, "no matter how small, shortens their restriction."[7]

Surprisingly, he then ordered that each combat crewman be given an immediate four-day pass, an advance in pay, and transport to London. When the cheering had died down, there was a scramble to get ready. Before dark, John Comer and most of his friends were already reveling in London.

* * *

Over the next four days, the 381st's ground crews set about feverishly repairing the group's battle-damaged bombers. There was also a flurry of aircraft transfers between the 381st and 305th Bomb Group, based at Chelveston, Northamptonshire—five B-17Fs heading in opposite directions. It left the 381st with 26 on hand; of which only 15 were fully operational.

While VIII BC stood down its heavy bomb groups, the 482nd Bombardment Group arrived at Alconbury in Huntingdonshire. It was formed with just three squadrons, two equipped with B-17s and one with Consolidated B-24 Liberators. The bombers were fitted with a variety of navigation aids, including two that had been developed by the RAF—*H2S* and *Oboe*. The 482nd's overriding function was to supply a "pathfinder" force of radar-equipped aircraft to VIII BC's three bombardment wings. Its crews would also be selected from a range of heavy bomb groups, including the 381st. Its ultimate aim, however, was simply to bomb through clouds.

* * *

John Comer's trip to London had certainly been a hazy one. His last night ("a real bash!") was followed by a "super bender" the next day. It culminated in him being physically held up by his crew mates as they staggered through Waterloo Station trying to avoid the Military Police. Somehow, they'd all made it back to Ridgewell unnoticed.

It took extra effort for Comer to get out of bed when he was roused for his next mission on August 24. His pilot, Paul Gleichauf, had already attended the briefing at 0145 when Comer and the other gunners met him outside operations. As soon as Gleichauf told them their altitude would be "25,000 and the temperature, forty below," Comer could only quip, "It's gonna be a balmy day in th' waist!"[8]

Again, the 381st was only able to supply seven B-17s for the mission, which had previously been scrubbed the day the crews had been given their four-day London pass. VIII BC's 86th raid was to strike at an air depot near Paris. The 381st's B-17s were scheduled to take-off just before 0500, but the weather soon intervened. After the formation had departed Ridgewell, it was forced to turn back.

Later that day, the same crews were briefed for the same destination. At 1430 they were back in the air and bound for the *Luftwaffe* air depot at Villacoublay. Comer's crew in *Nip and Tuck* were flying as the "spare," in case another of the 381st's B-17s should abort. Sure enough, 10 minutes from the French coast, *"Chap's" Flying Circus* pulled out of the formation and headed back to England. *Nip and Tuck* took up its position.

Shortly after crossing the European coastline, P-47s arrived. They were just in time to engage a group of Fw 190s attempting to reach the bombers. John Comer was transfixed.

"I wonder if there has ever been a sight … as watching a series of dog fights between good pilots," he later recalled, "I sometimes forgot briefly that I was a part of the drama. At times I almost felt like it was a highly realistic war movie in which I was a bit player."[9]

As the formation reached Paris's Eiffel Tower—the IP—it began its turn towards Villacoublay. Heavy flak then buffeted *Nip and Tuck*, but it flew on before dropping all but one of its bombs. A single 500-pounder remained firmly shackled, "hung up."

Comer offered to release it, but he was told to hold his position. A new regulation prohibited bomber crews from jettisoning anything over occupied Europe. Despite a precarious journey along *Nip and Tuck*'s "catwalk" sometime later, he managed to release the bomb, with a flick of his screwdriver, into the English Channel.

* * *

The 381st attempted to cross the Channel twice more over the next few days. On August 26, having been woken up at 0400, the combat crews were recalled just as their B-17s were forming up over Essex, heavy weather once again being responsible. The next day they got their chance to strike at a new kind of target—one that was considered too close for comfort.

Ten days earlier, on the day the 381st attacked Schweinfurt, the RAF had bombed a German rocket facility at Peenemünde on the Baltic coast. It was believed to be developing and testing ballistic missiles. Unknown to the Allies, engineers from Peenemünde had also travelled to France to plan the construction of a launch facility near Saint-Omer in the Pas-de-Calais region. When the new buildings were discovered by an RAF reconnaissance aircraft in May, their purpose wasn't immediately clear. Lord Cherwell, Winston Churchill's scientific advisor, was equally mystified, although he did suggest that "if it is worth the enemy's while to take all the trouble of putting them up, it would seem well worth our while—or rather the Americans—to knock them down ..."[10]

After consulting with Sir Malcolm McAlpine, head of the British construction firm Sir Robert McAlpine Ltd (who recommended striking the site while the concrete was still wet), the Allies pressed ahead with an attack. Loaded with two 2,000lb general-purpose bombs each—the largest bombs capable of being carried internally by the Flying Fortress—10 B-17s were dispatched by the 381st.

Taking off at 1700, they joined a formation of 224 bombers from both the 1st and 4th Bomb Wings. Flying "line-astern" and escorted by a combination of RAF and VIII FC fighters, they climbed to an altitude of 16,000 feet for the attack, which lasted for almost an hour. When they had done their work, most of the site was beyond saving, especially when the concrete had set. The 381st crews were triumphant on their return to Ridgewell. Ten B-17s and a hundred men had successfully achieved their objective without a scratch.

"As time goes on and tension eases through comparatively easy missions," wrote the 381st's surgeon, Ernest Gaillard, "the situation is getting better." Yet, the specter of Schweinfurt still cast a long shadow. "I believe the morale is increasing gradually now," he continued, "...[but] a half empty dining room is a rather sinister reminder."[11]

Among those absent from its breakfast tables were the 532nd's Robert Nelson and Raymond Genz, who were still evading capture in Germany. As they continued following their southwesterly course, sleeping in forests and barns, they still had no idea of their whereabouts. Only when they came upon roads could they check signposts.

"This almost got us into serious trouble," recalled Nelson. "When we rounded a curve ... [we] saw an armed German soldier with two prisoners approaching us. We just managed to get into a field where we crawled around a haystack while the German passed."[12]

Still dressed in their flying gear, and with hunger making them increasingly desperate, the airmen eventually approached two men working in a field.

> We went up to the younger of the men and motioned we were hungry. He gave us a cigarette. While we were having a sign-language conversation, the older man came over to see what was happening. As soon as he learned we were American aviators, he shook hands with us. Our morale went up when this happened, but we were still hungry. The old man could give us nothing but apples, cigarettes and directions.

Although they weren't in Switzerland, Nelson and Genz learned they were in Luxembourg. More importantly, they were no longer in Germany. They had hiked almost one hundred miles in under two weeks. "We left them feeling happier than at any other time since parachuting," recalled Nelson.

The next day, both men found themselves under the guidance of the Resistance. But the hardest part of their escape from Germany was yet to come. It would take them via Paris, across the Pyrenees, through Spain and on into Gibraltar. Just before they left for England, they sent a telegram to Joe Nazzaro. It read:

> CREW OF A.C.—140—O.K. Two slightly injured. Two of us in safe hands, and on way. Will see you. Left Waist Gunner and "Nellie"[13]

* * *

By the end of August, the 381st had recovered sufficiently to increase its contribution to VIII BC's missions. Nineteen B-17s were scheduled on August 31 for an assault on a *Luftwaffe* airfield at Romilly-sur-Seine, 50 miles east of Paris. Joe Nazzaro was set to lead the mission, accompanied by Col. William Gross, commanding officer of the 101st PCBW.

One hundred and seventy B-17s began taking off from nine East Anglian airfields in the afternoon. By the time they arrived over their target, they found it obscured by solid cloud-cover. However, William Gross was able to demonstrate why he was an advocate for using radio communication to aid assembly and "control" formations.

When the 306th and 384th Bomb Groups turned off of the target after being unable to see it, Gross immediately warned the trailing groups to cancel their approach. Instead, he announced a new IP and directed the formation back to the cloudless Amiens–Glisy airfield, which he'd spotted along the way. At 1807, the formation arrived over its new target, 70 miles north of Paris.

Not only was Gross's move a stroke of genius, it was also a huge stroke of luck. Amiens–Glisy had previously been attacked on July 14 when VIII BC had hit one side of the airfield. During the intervening period, the Germans had repaired and camouflaged the area. However, they had "shifted the center of visual interest" to the opposite side. Just over 100 B-17s dropped 735 500-pounders in 17 minutes, flattening that, too.

All 19 of the 381st's B-17s had bombed "effectively." As the combat crews congratulated each other on the ground back at Ridgewell, a satisfied William Gross looked on. He'd "commanded" rather than led the mission. Even though VIII BC had been following the RAF's rule of "radio silence," Gross proved it could be used to positive effect. It was the first time VHF was used to improvise an attack on an unbriefed target.[14]

The following day, Joe Nazzaro entertained another senior officer at Ridgewell, when Brig. Gen. Robert B. Williams, commander of the 1st BW, arrived to watch the group's B-17s head off on a mission to bomb another *Luftwaffe* airfield at Conches-en-Ouche. Once again, the weather intervened, forcing a recall at the French coast. Much to the crews' frustrations, the mission wasn't credited. Despite this, the 381st's surgeon, Ernest Gaillard, was noticing that the men seemed to be benefiting from the shorter-range missions.

"There is a considerable improvement in morale during the past week," he wrote. "Operational flights have been comparatively easy and no casualties or losses resulted. This has increased the feeling of confidence a great deal."[15]

John Comer and his fellow gunners were feeling extremely confident. So much so, that when one of them found some paint, they instinctively painted *Nip and Tuck*'s engine cowlings bright red. "Didn't a hot crew need a hot airplane?" joked Comer.[16]

As an enlisted man, Comer was not privy to the officers' briefings. However, he and his crew had devised a way of learning how "tough" a mission was likely to be. The next day he was stood outside the briefing room waiting to hear the reactions. Listening to the groans, he judged the mission to be "medium tough." Despite it being against regulations to load more than the standard 7,000 rounds of ammunition, he asked *Nip and Tuck*'s armorer to load an extra thousand.

The 381st's target for September 3 was Romilly-sur-Seine—the same airfield the 1st BW had been unable to hit several days earlier. Twenty-two B-17s started taking off at 0600. Among them was *Big Time Operator*, which was being flown by a composite crew made up of several veterans, along with some "replacements" flying their first mission.

One of the veterans onboard, waist gunner Charles F. Bang, was cursing his luck. Usually part of Frank Chapman's crew, Bang was embarking on his 11th mission. While training in the US, he'd broken his leg and had been told by doctors to remain there while his crew travelled overseas. Against doctors' orders, he'd made the trans-Atlantic crossing with the ground echelon onboard the *Queen Elizabeth* in order to re-join his crew.

As an armorer–gunner, Bang had been busy preparing *Big Time Operator*'s machine guns when it took off. The early morning light had been so dim that he'd been unable to see his fellow crew members' faces. By the time it was light, they'd donned their oxygen masks.

"Instead of being a member of a crew whose every move I could anticipate," he later wrote, "I found myself amid a group of absolute strangers of whose ability I knew nothing."[17]

On the way to the target, one of the other veterans onboard, radio operator Edwin R. Myers, noticed *Big Time Operator*'s pilot, 2nd Lt. Benjamin J. Zum, was having great difficulty in holding formation. As a 10-mission veteran, Myers knew that a "throttle-jockeying" pilot was a "red flag" to the *Luftwaffe*.

The formation was being led by Landon Hendricks, who skirted around several flak areas along the French coast, before heading inland. A number of B-17s aborted and turned back for England, while another of the 381st's lost an engine and was forced to maintain maximum power on the remaining three to keep up.

Ten minutes over the coast, P-47s appeared in the distance. Comer's ball turret gunner then spotted an "oddly-marked" B-17 trailing the formation. It was being escorted by what appeared to be Spitfires. Bizarrely, the B-17 then started firing at the other bombers. It quickly became apparent that the Fortress was a captured aircraft and the "Spitfires" were Me 109s.

Almost immediately, the sky turned into a melee. It was also uncomfortably close to the 381st, but the group escaped any major damage and continued on to its bomb run. Light flak then exploded below the formation, but it was able to drop its bombs successfully. After turning away from the target, it was then attacked by a swarm of Me 109s.

Unknown to the American crews, the commander of the *Luftwaffe*'s fighter force, Adolf Galland, had issued a recent directive to his pilots. They were to engage only one wave of enemy attack "continuously" and with "the mass of all fighter units."

Big Time Operator was trailing the formation and had just turned west of the target when it was "attacked most viciously" by German fighters.[18] Suffering heavy damage, Benjamin Zum immediately gave the order to bail out. Other crews reported seeing 10 parachutes leave the B-17 before it exploded. However, the body of the bombardier, Luther C. Clark, was later found with an unopened parachute. The other nine crewmen landed safely, although several were quickly captured, including Charles Bang. Edwin Myers and two others made off in search of cover. It was the start of another fraught journey for more 381st men.

John Comer and the gunners of *Nip and Tuck* had managed to fend off the "pecking" fighter attacks with some "dandy shots," when a squadron of Spitfires appeared. They fought off the Me 109s just as the English Channel came into view. Once *Nip and Tuck* was safely over the water, an angry Paul Gleichauf soon came on the intercom to remonstrate about the "red paint," which had "drawn in" the fighters. John Comer knew it had been a "foolish notion" that they were a "hot crew." That evening, the red paint was painted olive drab.

* * *

Three days later, Comer was woken up at 0230. It was an early one, which could only mean one thing—an extra-long mission. Later, as he stood outside the briefing room, a prolonged groan was followed by silence. "We had a super mean one coming up."[19]

The target was an industrial area in the German city of Stuttgart, a round-trip of 1,350 miles. It was to be VIII BC's first deep penetration raid since Schweinfurt. The 381st scheduled 21 B-17s for the 1st BW formation, which would number 181.

Comer was expecting to fly in *Nip and Tuck*, but as he was preparing its ammunition he was told to drop everything and move to another B-17. It would have more fuel capacity for the long trip. However, when Comer saw the replacement B-17, he was stunned.

"Of all the planes, we got *Tinker Toy*," he recalled. "No one wanted to fly that plane. It was the jinx ship of the 381st. No crew had ever flown her on a routine mission."[20]

The 381st's B-17s were each loaded with 42 incendiary bombs and began taking off from 0600. Some four hours later, despite encountering heavy cloud near Strasbourg, the 1st BW arrived over Stuttgart. The primary target was hidden, so the formation circled looking for suitable targets of opportunity. The 381st eventually bombed a large marshaling yard at Offenburg and turned for home. However, the circling and unpredicted winds had consumed a lot of fuel, with yellow warning lights striking up on some B-17s just after they'd bombed.

Despite suffering oxygen supply problems and several hung up bombs, *Tinker Toy* banked away. Comer then calculated the chances of making it to England. "We have about five hundred gallons—three hours using our altitude," he told his crew. It was another three-and-a-half hours to Ridgewell.

By the time the French coast came into view, *Tinker Toy*'s gauges were reading empty. Once over the water, it dropped out of the formation and slowed down, almost idling. The crew then began jettisoning everything heavy, including the three bombs.

Eventually, Paul Gleichauf spotted an RAF airfield just after crossing the English coast. A flare was fired to indicate he was landing without normal procedures. *Tinker Toy* then touched down safely, closely followed by several other distressed B-17s. Twelve more from other groups were forced to ditch in the sea, while another of the 381st's bombers crash-landed at Ashford in Kent, its crew escaping uninjured. Six more diverted to different airfields across the southeast England.

The "Stuttgart" mission was considered a disaster—45 bombers lost, a haphazard bombing pattern, and tons of fuel wasted. Yet, despite *Tinker Toy*'s jinxed reputation, Comer and his crew had made it.

"She had a malevolent disposition," he recalled, "as if she were determined to punish the men who forced her to endure the tortures of combat … she was not like other airplanes."[21]

Still, the tortures of combat continued unabated. The next day, September 7, 17 B-17s lifted off from Ridgewell at 0545. They were tasked with striking at Brussels's Evere airfield. Just before 0900, they arrived over the target, dropping 40 tons of bombs in the space of only three minutes. For once, however, they remained unmolested.

Since Schweinfurt, every raid had been leading up to VIII BC's 93rd mission—a joint operation with the RAF. It began with a night attack on a German long-range gun battery in the Boulogne area. On the evening of September 8, five B-17s from Chelveston's 305th BG were temporarily attached to the RAF for the raid, which proved unsuccessful.[22] Nevertheless, the 381st was ordered to supply 18 B-17s for an attack on Lille-Nord's airfield the following day.

Comer was preparing the guns on *Nip and Tuck* when Paul Gleichauf arrived at the aircraft. He was excited. "The long-awaited invasion may be on this morning," he said. "All crews are warned to make no comments on the intercom about anything they may see crossing the Channel."[23]

Half an hour later, they were taxiing around Ridgewell's perimeter track under the cover of darkness, before taking off for France. Comer was expecting to take part in a "diversionary" raid to disperse the *Luftwaffe*. Yet, crossing the English Channel, his attention was suddenly drawn to the sea below.

"Ships were strung out in a long line from the British coast halfway across the Channel. It looked like the invasion was on."

Over 300 vessels were steaming towards France, while 19 heavy bomb groups were heading for nine separate French targets. "It was an exhilarating view," recalled Comer.[24]

As *Nip and Tuck* crossed the French coastline, flak opened up. Comer could hear fragments strike the aircraft and in an instant the ball turret gunner called out that he'd been hit. Fortunately, he wasn't badly wounded. After checking he was okay and could still man the guns, Gleichauf flew on, *Nip and Tuck* dropping its bombs at 0830. The gunner was then removed from the turret and treated by the bombardier, who wrapped him in blankets.

Once back at Ridgewell, he was lifted onto a stretcher and into a waiting ambulance. Comer, however, was depressed by both the ball turret gunner's wounds and the mission as a whole. At the interrogation, he learned nothing more about the ships in the Channel. He was also ordered to leave *Nip and Tuck*'s guns mounted in the aircraft for another mission, which never came.

Operation *Starkey* was the invasion "that never was." It was designed to deceive the Germans into thinking an assault on Boulogne-sur-Mer was under way. The ships—mostly cross-channel steamers—were largely empty. Thirty minutes after the 381st had dropped its bombs, the "armada" turned through 180 degrees back towards England. The feint attracted little response from the Germans, but the bombing claimed the lives of 376 French citizens in the village of Le Portel.

"I was bothered by my part," John Comer later recalled of *Starkey*. "I think most of the men who manned the bomber crews were uneasy whether they admitted it or not … war is not glorious—or noble … [it] is incredible brutality and inhumanity beyond description."[25]

Intermission: Evolution of the B-17

While its primary role was to deliver bombs in order to destroy, the Boeing B-17 Flying Fortress's sleek and elegant profile has become iconic. It is synonymous with the hard fought, and costly, US daylight bombing offensive in Europe. Yet, what most people think they know about the B-17 is almost entirely overshadowed by dramatic accounts of the intense and bloody air battles that took place from 1943 through to the late spring and early summer of 1945. In fact, the story of the Boeing Airplane Company's iconic four-engine bomber goes back 10 years before the great missions of that period, right back to the production of the first design blueprints for Project 299 in 1934.

In what was considered to be a huge commercial gamble, Boeing invested $432,000 in its radical new design—the huge, all-metal Y1B-17. At the time, the prototype Pratt & Whitney-engine-powered bomber was considered to be cutting-edge. On completion of the first prototype, it was the largest land-based aircraft ever built in the US. The Y1B-17's modern, sleek lines reinforced the impression that it was something different to the outdated aircraft then in American military service.

Standing 19 feet tall, with a 74-foot-long fuselage, and wings spanning 104 feet, the new metal bomber, with its enclosed cockpits, and multiple defensive machine gun positions, captured the imagination of everyone who saw it.

The prototype first flew on July 28, 1935, from Boeing Field, Seattle, with Leslie Tower at the controls. On seeing the huge bomber, a reporter from the *Seattle Daily News* supposedly enthused: "Why, it's a 15 ton Flying Fortress!"[1]

It is difficult to comprehend the huge leap in capability that the Y1B-17 represented. It could fly higher, faster, further, and carry a heavier bomb load than any other bomber in US service. Considering the many technological advances, and the significantly enhanced capabilities that the Boeing design incorporated, it is obvious why the US Army ordered 13 of the new type. After further test flights, the Y1B-17 was accepted into service and re-designated the B-17. It was subsequently named the Flying Fortress.

There is, however, some speculation about the origin of the name. The obvious, and popularly accepted narrative is that the point of origin, for what is one of the most apt names for an aircraft type, was the Seattle reporter's exclamation. On seeing the prototype's five prominent gun positions, more than twice that on any conventional bomber at the time, he saw a huge, imposing leviathan bristling with weapons—a "flying fortress."

There is also an alternative theory, linked to the inter-service politics of American defense strategy during the 1930s. It has been argued an agreement between the US Navy and the USAAC—equipped with its new high-flying B-17s and their secret, super accurate Norden bombsights—meant the latter could defend the US coastlines from any naval threat, releasing their surface fleets to range further afield. This coastal defense role made the B-17 the equivalent of a fortress defending the American shoreline.

Prior to the attack on the US naval fleet at Pearl Harbor, the new B-17 Flying Fortress attracted the attention of the British, whose air force was supplied with a batch of 20 B-17C variants. The type was designated "Fortress I" by the RAF.

The use of the Fortress I on combat operations eventually accelerated the technical advancement of the B-17. However, at the outset, the USAAC advised that the aircraft was not ready for combat operations. In the spring of 1941, ignoring American advice, the RAF allocated the Fortress I to 90 Squadron, the unit that would eventually make RAF Ridgewell its temporary home in early 1943.

What occurred in the summer of 1941 was a series of experimental raids. Flying Fortresses were sent out by 90 Squadron in very small numbers to attack a series of German targets. Operating at high altitude, it took the unproven B-17C and the inexperienced crews to the limits of performance capabilities. The use of penny packet formations against heavily defended targets proved disastrous, however. The loss of eight aircraft to accidents and enemy action during just 20 operations only reinforced the arguments for the RAF's night bombing policy.

Nevertheless, while the Fortress I may not have been a success operationally, a huge number of modifications were made to the B-17's design. Not least, the significant increase in the size of the tail that would be incorporated into the B-17E, which subsequently improved stability at altitude.

The myriad of modifications made to almost every system on the early B-17s would eventually result in the B-17G, the ultimate Flying Fortress—one that was fully equipped to spearhead the Eighth Air Force's daylight bombing campaign over Europe.

CHAPTER 7

Jinxed Ships

September 10–October 8, 1943

By early September, the 381st was carrying out an average of one mission every three days. Although individual airmen weren't called upon to fly each one, many were flying for extended periods of time. The demanding schedule was soon noticed by the 1st BW's medical officers, who declared the 381st "bottom of the statistical list" in granting leave.[1] They recommended that any crews "completing 15 or more missions should automatically get a week of leave … at a rest home."

Ridgewell was home to 237 officers and 1,984 enlisted men, including 220 combat crew members. It also had 26 B-17Fs on hand, three fewer than the minimum required. *The Lucky Strike*, *Flat Foot Foogie* and *Smilin' Thru* were all ferried in from Chelveston on September 11.

Two days later, the 381st found itself under a new chain of command. VIII BC was reorganized into three divisions formed from the complements of its bombardment wings. The 1st and 3rd Bombardment Divisions (BD) replaced both the 1st and 4th Bomb Wings (BW) respectively, while the 2nd BW became the 2nd BD. In addition to the renaming of its wings, VIII BC's "provisional" combat bombardment wings were also replaced by properly constituted units. On September 13, the 101st PCBW became the 1st Combat Bombardment Wing (Heavy), with the 381st now part of the 1st Combat Bombardment Wing (CBW) of the 1st BD.

* * *

Several weeks earlier, the 381st had received new equipment for the installation of external bomb racks on its B-17s. On September 15, 10 of its Fortresses were fitted with a rack beneath each wing. Two 1,000lb bombs were then hoisted and hooked, while a further 6,000lb of general-purpose bombs were loaded in their bomb bays. The 381st's next mission would see its heaviest individual loads carried yet.

The group's destination was the *Luftwaffe* "air depot" at Romilly-sur-Seine, an airfield it had bombed two weeks earlier. Described by the 1st CBW intelligence section as a "juicy target," the 381st would once again carry wing commander Col. William Gross.

Following his successful improvisation after being prevented from bombing Romilly on August 31, Gross hoped to fine-tune his method with the 381st. Arriving at Ridgewell, he was furnished with a "four-leaf glassine folder" detailing the entire course of the raid. It served as his prompt to check the weather conditions over potential targets along the way. Gross's procedure would go on to become the "norm" for all combat bombardment wings in the 1st BD.

Gross climbed aboard Joe Nazzaro's B-17 to lead the 1st CBW to France. Arriving over the target at 1850, the formation's heavily-laden B-17s then released their bombs, each "concentrated in the immediate target area." The hefty loads had taken their toll, however. Increased fuel consumption saw several of the 381st's B-17s land elsewhere in southern England, while other 1st CBW bombers, also fitted with racks, followed suit. One of the 351st's B-17s crash-landed short of Polebrook after running out of fuel, its uninjured pilot confirming the racks were "not feasible for trips any farther inland than Paris."[2]

The B-17s that made it back to Ridgewell landed in darkness after 2100—a "canopy of searchlights" leading the crews to their base for the first time. Despite the heavy challenge, the mission had been successful—no aircraft lost and Romilly's airfield "polished off."

* * *

Another French destination was the group's 30th target the next day, when 20 of its B-17s took off just after midday bound for Nantes. The city's harbor installations and a nearby airfield were to be attacked by 147 B-17s flying from eight British bases. John Comer and his crew were in their usual aircraft, *Nip and Tuck*, while Comer's former co-pilot Herbert Carqueville was piloting a new B-17F, *Big Bust* (whose name had eluded the censors). It was Carqueville's first mission as "first pilot."

Flying a sweeping route around London and Oxford, the formation left the south coast at Selsey Bill before reaching its bombing altitude halfway across the English Channel. Overflying Rennes, German fighters then appeared, most quickly homing in on the 381st.

"We could never be certain what they looked for," wrote John Comer. "We knew they looked for the weakest formations and suspected that they tried to spot green crews … [but] when they recognized the opposition by the insignias, they may have changed their tactics."[3]

Seven Me 109s simultaneously attacked in single file, during which time a combination of Comer's top turret guns and the tail guns of Harold Harkness converged to damage one. Comer and his navigator Carl Shutting then switched their attentions towards another fighter, which was circling "about twelve hundred yards" away. Both 381st men began "lobbing" shells at the German fighter, which immediately dived straight on them.

"We picked the wrong man to mess with," recalled Comer. A series of attacks were fended off, only for Comer's pilot, Paul Gleichauf, to lecture both of his crew members for making the German pilot "mad."

During one attack, Herbert Carqueville's B-17 had been "riddled" with cannon fire. Comer and the crew of *Nip and Tuck* looked on anxiously at their friend's bomber, which, although damaged, appeared to be under control. The formation continued on over the target, only to find it obscured by cloud. Amid light and inaccurate flak, the lead B-17 sought out another objective before dropping its bombs. The 381st followed, before swinging west out over the Bay of Biscay for the long journey back to England—their lengthy route eventually shaking off any chasing fighters.

As the B-17s arrived back over Ridgewell, Carqueville's *Big Bust* was one of the first to land, flares having been fired by its gunners to indicate it had wounded aboard. After stopping, the bomber was immediately surrounded by ground crews. Carqueville hadn't been wounded, but several of his crew were. However, the medics struggled to reach them.

"The difficulties in ... evacuation were overcrowding ... and lack of sufficient number of medical department soldiers to handle litters and give necessary aid," noted the 381st's flight surgeon, Ernest Gaillard.

As a result of the congestion, he recommended that four medics with "Red Cross brassards" be assigned to each ambulance. Only they could approach bombers landing in emergency.[4]

John Comer and his crew had avoided any flak, but their attempt to hit an enemy fighter that wasn't attacking hadn't gone down well. "When we landed, Major Hendricks ... sent for Shutting and me," remembered Comer. "The major was usually a mild-mannered man, but when we reported, he was steaming."

Hendricks reprimanded both men for "drawing" the fighters, which, he said, took the "prize for stupidity." Luckily for them, the 381st was short of crews, meaning he was unable to mete out anything other than a warning about "severe disciplinary measures." Comer and Shutting considered themselves told.[5]

* * *

Of three new crews to arrive at Ridgewell later that evening, 1st Lt. Robert J. Miller and his officers also found themselves in trouble. They'd arrived late from Bovingdon having visited "three or four villages" along the way to "sample the wares of their pubs." They were ordered to present themselves at the 381st headquarters building the next morning.

As the four waited, they were laughing nervously when the door "flew open." Joe Nazzaro then strode purposefully to the middle of the room where he turned and glared.

"The first thing I noticed were his eyes," recalled navigator 2nd Lt. David A. McCarthy. "Dark and so piercing they could destroy an army tank at five hundred yards with just a glance." Nazzaro began listing their responsibilities and obligations. "His tone was soft; he did not raise his voice, but boy, did we listen," noted McCarthy. Each officer was then issued with a set of restrictions and confined to the base until further notice.[6]

After being assigned to the 534th BS, McCarthy and his crewmates were then introduced to its commanding officer, Maj. David Kunkel, whose face was "filled with the thunderclouds of anger." After outlining the behavior expected of them, McCarthy and the others were left in no doubt. "In something under three minutes we had been 'chewed out', humbled, and dismissed."

Nazzaro's anger was not unfounded. Earlier that morning, he'd assembled his crews for a mission to Frankfurt. Just before the briefing, the 532nd's new commanding officer, Capt. Arthur Briggs, had approached one of the medical officers to tell him that he "did not wish to go on the mission" and that he had "ideas of homicide and suicide." He also insisted the "odds" were stacked against him.

"It is rather hard to decide whether it was the feeling for [his] personal safety or the weight of responsibility of leading the group into combat that was responsible for his attitude," wrote surgeon Ernest Gaillard. "It was pointed out to him that he was one of the leaders in the group and that personnel looked to him for direction and guidance."[7]

Nazzaro had subsequently taken Briggs to one side, explaining that the decision to go on the mission was "squarely" up to him. After agreeing to attend the briefing, Briggs finally learned the mission had been scrubbed.

"Since the Schweinfurt raid … Captain Briggs states he has not slept well … he was quite introspective and downcast … and stated that he had no desire whatsoever to get near a B-17," noted Gaillard. "Another mission is [needed] to restore confidence … following the mission, a period of rest is needed … in the meantime, we are going to do our utmost to ensure adequate sleep."[8]

* * *

That day, the first B-17G landed at Ridgewell. Built by the Douglas Aircraft Company, it was assigned to the 535th BS. The bomber had originally been designated a B-17F, but the installation of an electrically driven Bendix chin turret had seen it reclassified as a B-17G. Nicknamed *Lucifer Jr III*, the new bomber would enable its bombardiers to aim defensive fire directly at enemy fighters attacking head-on, thus protecting the most vulnerable part of the aircraft.

The arrival of *Lucifer Jr III* heralded a flurry of aircraft transfers, the majority being older B-17Fs. Over the next few days, several were ferried in from the newly activated 482nd "Pathfinder" group at Alconbury, while others arrived from the US.

Another new B-17, *Whodat – The Dingbat!*, was also assigned to the 534th BS. It brought the group's total inventory of operational bombers to 42—five short of its assigned number.

Despite the increase in B-17s and replacement crews, the 381st remained grounded. Even so, four missions were briefed and scrubbed, including one that saw the group's aircraft take-off and climb to 14,000 feet before being recalled. Once again, the cancellation did nothing for morale. For John Comer and crew, though, their optimism was set to improve, albeit temporarily.

Granted leave after completing nine missions, the crew had been signed off for a week's "respite" by the 533rd's medical officer, Capt. Louis G. Ralston. They were each given a $14 allowance and packed off to one of the Eighth's "rest homes" at Moulsford Manor in Berkshire. After being handed his bed sheets on arrival ("sheets? I had forgotten about such things."), Comer donned civilian clothes, played tennis and took boating trips along the river Thames. "[Moulsford] was one of the most pleasant weeks I have ever experienced," he wrote. "It was a week's interlude of tranquility in the midst of war."[9]

* * *

The war was a "constant background" for 15-year-old John Davis, who lived close to Comer's base at Ridgewell. "By day we would see the B-17s ... forming up," he remembered. "In the evening it would be British aircraft filling the sky, all at various heights and all flying east. The air was just alive ..."[10]

On September 22, the 381st was stood down, while the 305th Bomb Group's 422nd BS was in action, taking off from Chelveston in the evening to accompany RAF Bomber Command on VIII BC's first night raid into Germany. Five B-17s joined more than 700 British bombers for a heavy attack on the city of Hanover.[11]

Among the RAF bombers were 137 Stirlings, 19 of which had taken off from Cambridgeshire's RAF Wratting Common (formerly known as West Wickham). The Stirlings belonged to 90 Squadron, past tenants of Ridgewell. James Good Brown was sitting in Ridgewell's officers' club when he was alerted to the sight of the Stirlings climbing in the distance. He also spotted something odd coming from one of them.

"As it moved along in the sky, it left a long trail of smoke behind it," recalled Brown, who also saw "blinking lights," which turned out to be flames. The Stirling then began "diving straight down."

"When the plane was halfway down there occurred what no flier wants to see," wrote Brown. "A burst of fire as big as a house. In an instant the plane exploded in mid-air."[12]

Schoolboy John Davis was in the kitchen of his house at Brockley Green when he "felt the ground shake" and saw the sky light up. Both he and his sister raced outside to investigate. They were met by a shocking sight.

"The sky was full of smoke and falling pieces of aircraft," he recalled. "Some dropping like stones, some twisting and turning slowly down. Some of it was burning. On the ground there were huge flames from several sites of wreckage."[13]

Within minutes, three ambulances were scrambled from Ridgewell for a six-mile journey to the crash site.

"The plane and its occupants were spread over an area of 500 yards and parts of the burning plane hit a nearby farmhouse, causing a severe fire …" noted Ernest Gaillard. "In the midst of the burning incendiary bombs and unexploded 1,000-pound bombs, the members of this station proceeded to evacuate the bodies of the RAF personnel …"[14]

Six of the crew were dead, although, miraculously, one of the gunners was found alive. Severely injured, Flight Sergeant George L. Duffy survived the incident. After witnessing the event, James Good Brown scanned the faces of those around him.

"They did not like it," he wrote. "Lieutenant [Charles W.] Dowell, one of the oldest and steadiest pilots in the outfit and now one of our long-time original men, spoke up and said, 'I've always said these things aren't practical.'"[15]

* * *

After a week's pause, VIII BC went back to war for the 100th time. The practicalities of bombing Nantes the week before hadn't lived up to the plan. On September 23, the 1st BD was sent back to the French port—although this time its primary target was the Dutch-built, German-seized, submarine supply ship SS *Kertosono*, which had been missed the first time.

Twenty-two B-17s began taking off from Ridgewell at 0430 and steered the same course as before, leaving the English coast at Selsey Bill. However, bad weather during assembly quickly left the 533rd BS lost and alone. Unable to locate the rest of the group, its B-17s aborted the mission and returned to Ridgewell.

The weather also forced the formation to descend by 6,000 feet in order to avoid dense clouds over France. The B-17s then encountered some 50 German fighters near Rennes.

The 532nd's 1st Lt. Melvin R. Hecker, who was flying in the tail position of the group's lead B-17—the newly-assigned *Big Time Operator II*—quickly secured his first "kill" and eventual DFC after downing one of the fighters. Even so, shortly after the formation turned on the IP, accurate flak struck his B-17. Fortunately, Hecker wasn't wounded, but his navigator, 1st Lt. Frank J. Shimek, was hit in the leg.

The formation succeeded in dropping almost 100,000lb of bombs—a "string" of which burst across the area where the *Kertosono* was berthed. The B-17s then turned out over the Bay of Biscay before heading north. The 1st BD had escaped without losing a single bomber. However, 41 had been damaged, including *Big Time Operator II.*

It was some time before reconnaissance photos showed the results of VIII BC's 100th raid. "The *Kertosono* was still upright and unsunk," noted the 1st CBW's diarist, "but 68,000 tons of other shipping had been sunk or destroyed in addition to very heavy damage inflicted to port installations." Nevertheless, it was eventually discovered that the *Kertosono* was sitting "securely on the river bottom."[16]

Melvin Hecker had sustained some damage of his own. Although he'd returned unhurt, his shirt was shredded and the toe of one boot had been torn off. Luckily, he wasn't "in them" at the time; they'd been hanging behind his tail position in a bag. "It was close enough tho," he said.[17]

* * *

For many, the standard of personal equipment was a constant source of irritation. Ill-fitting oxygen masks ("the Gestapo must have designed it"), insufficiently heated electric gloves ("why in the hell did they put the heat in the palm of the hand?") and electric boots that always seemed to be in short supply, were just some of the "gripes." As an engineer, John Comer had taken to modifying, fixing and designing his own equipment, including "electric overshoes," which he made "out of scraps and with crude tools."[18]

It was with some irony, then, that the 381st rolled out the red carpet for the chairman of the US War Production Board, Donald M. Nelson, on September 25. Nelson—who'd asked American citizens to "answer honestly" if they were "doing everything within [their] power … to put more weapons into the hands of our fighting men"—was visiting Ridgewell after meeting with British production officials in London. Escorted by the Eighth's commander, Maj. Gen. Ira Eaker, Nelson was the first civilian dignitary to officially visit Ridgewell.

By the time he departed, the 381st was gearing up for its 32nd mission—an attack on a fighter assembly plant at Les Mureaux, northwest of Paris. Soon after taking off at 1445 on September 26, however, the formation—led by Nazzaro and the 381st—flew into clouds that extended for some 25,000 feet. After blindly venturing 20 miles inside France, Nazzaro took the decision to abandon the raid. Light but accurate flak over Dieppe on the return trip duly confirmed the mission as being credited.

"And that is what is known as getting a mission the easy way," quipped one of the 381st's returning crewmen.[19] Nevertheless, five others had sustained varying degrees of frostbite, mainly due to ill-fitting oxygen masks and failed electric gloves.

* * *

The weather was not expected to be an issue the following day, when VIII BC's 1st BD and 3rd BD took off to bomb the industrial areas of Emden in northwestern

Germany. Leading the formation of 308 B-17s was the 482nd Bomb Group—the "Pathfinder Force" (PFF)—whose four radar-equipped B-17s had been dispatched from Alconbury to lead the divisions.

The Emden mission signaled a number of firsts. The PFF B-17s had been fitted with the British-designed *H2S* radar, which scanned the ground while feeding images to an indicator unit inside the aircraft. The images produced a "maplike picture" of the ground, showing dark, light and bright areas for water, ground and conurbations respectively.[20] At 25,000 feet it could cover a radius of 50 miles, although it also had an average "circular error" of two miles. Still, it allowed PFF navigators to recognize cloud covered towns and cities by their sprawl, the shape of any rivers, or even the span of a bridge. Flying in the lead position, PFF bombardiers would then release smoke bombs to mark the release point for the B-17s that followed.

Another first for the mission was the "pursuit coverage" of P-47s, which had been fitted with 108-gallon reinforced paper tanks under their wings,[21] taking their "radius of action" to 325 miles. It meant the 1st and 3rd BD formations would be escorted over a much greater distance than before.

"Off they went again into the dawn, winging their way through the clouds, headed for Emden," wrote James Good Brown, of the 381st's departure from Ridgewell. "It is a beautiful sight to see them take off one after the other. I am getting more and more eager to fly with them in combat, but Colonel Nazzaro's answer is a flat 'No'."[22]

Nazzaro was not leading the mission this time—that task had been assumed by the 1st CBW's commander, William Gross, who was flying in a PFF B-17 from Bassingbourn. It led the wing, while the 381st's 18 bombers followed in the low position at 23,000 feet. The entire formation eventually reached Germany some three hours after take-off.

"Just over the enemy coast, which was covered with clouds, fighters attacked," noted Everett Malone, who was co-piloting *"Chap's" Flying Circus*. "Our escort was ahead of us and above and couldn't do us any good whatsoever."[23]

Flying in the low element of the low squadron was FO Daniel D. Hagarty. Just after take-off, his co-pilot, Capt. Howard N. Kesley, had noticed a barrage balloon that had broken from its moorings "being shot down by a Spitfire." He thought it was "some kind of omen." As the formation headed along the bomb run, Kesley then saw his first B-17 shot down in a similar vein. "It seemed as though someone tried to pull it from this dive when it broke in half," Kesley recalled. "The ball turret went spinning off, like a baseball ..."[24]

After making one pass, the German fighters returned, this time firing from behind. Kesley's B-17 suddenly became the prime target and "all hell broke loose."

"We felt the tremor when we were hit," remembered Kesley. "Our #3 engine took a shot right through the propeller hub ... I was almost hypnotized by the sight of oil gushing from the propeller and freezing instantly ... piling up on the engine nacelle like big globs of rubber."[25]

Unknown to Kesley and his pilot, five of their crew had been wounded during the attack, one seriously.

"We never saw this one fighter," remembered waist gunner SSgt. John R. Crawbuck. "He was directly below us and looped two 20mm shells into the waist between [SSgt. James W.] Dunn and me."[26]

Crawbuck was wounded in the hip, but he then saw Dunn lying on the floor of the aircraft ("one leg was gone"). Crawbuck quickly applied a tourniquet and administered a shot of morphine before returning to his gun to fire at the fighters.

The loss of one engine had forced Hagarty to drop from the formation. A second engine then gave out, which also had to be feathered. Luckily, despite becoming a "sitting duck," the B-17 was left alone to make its way back across the North Sea.

"As we limped on towards the English coast, losing altitude all the time, we wondered if we could get high enough to clear the coastal cliffs," recalled Kesley. "We began to throw overboard everything that was loose, including ammunition."[27]

Despite being wounded himself, the bombardier, 2nd Lt. Richard E. Rylands, was sent back to give first aid to both waist gunners. Hagarty was finally able to land the bomber at Great Ashfield, Suffolk, where several ambulances transported the wounded crewmen to an evacuation hospital near Diss, Norfolk. It would be another six weeks before John Crawbuck flew again, but he was eventually awarded the Silver Star for his bravery. James Dunn would ultimately survive his wounds.

The 381st's remaining B-17s landed back at Ridgewell just after noon, 10 of them damaged. The first PFF-led mission was deemed to be effective, although it had been impossible to observe the results due to clouds. It was eventually established that "some bombs" had found their target, but most had fallen in and around Emden's city center.

* * *

David Kunkel, commander of the 534th BS, had led four of the 381st's missions during September. The West Point graduate had also seen his squadron through 16 consecutive raids without loss. On September 30, he learned that he was to be awarded the group's third Silver Star. Two days later, he found himself leading the group once more, this time to the same target it had bombed five days earlier—Emden.

John Comer and his crew had just returned from their week of rest and were scheduled to fly the group's 34th mission. It was to be Comer's 11th raid, but he'd noticed a change at Ridgewell.

"The combat mess hall was getting crowded again with the influx of new men," he wrote. "It was easy to pick out the recent arrivals. I could see the anxiety written on their faces and in their gestures."[28]

Yet, the angst was also affecting "veterans." SSgt. Clarence M. Jones, a ball turret gunner with the 532nd, was due to fly his seventh mission. Jones—a member of

George Darrow's crew, which had ditched *Rum Boogie* in the North Sea on the return from Schweinfurt—suddenly "became hysterical" and refused to take part. He was promptly stood down but would later return to combat duty.

Still grumbling about the paucity of their equipment, the combat crews were given some life-saving gear for the Emden mission. Over 160 men were provided with "flak suits"—heavy canvas vests containing steel plates. Most chose to wear them, but some used them as "pads" to protect the bottom of the aircraft and their own "nether regions."

The second Emden mission saw external bomb racks re-fitted to the group's 20 B-17s. Once again, the 482nd's PFF aircraft led the formation of some 350 heavy bombers, while P-47s escorted them all the way to the target. Just after 1600, almost a thousand tons of bombs were unleashed on Emden's port.

Only the 533rd's newly assigned B-17G, *Gremlin's Delite*, failed to drop all of its bombs successfully. Those in the bomb bay stubbornly refused to fall. Only when the radio operator kicked them, did one side fall out. The other side remained firmly lodged, until the bombardier, 2nd Lt. John C. Leverette, Jr., "defused" them before "throwing" them into the North Sea. *Gremlin's Delite*, which had been christened by the crew just before take-off, was well-named.

* * *

A renaming ceremony took place the following day, when the 381st's inaugural, chin-turret equipped B-17, *Lucifer Jr III*, was retitled *Bacta-Th'-Sac*. Luckily, most of the group's combat crews were allowed to stay in their beds on a day that brought no mission. However, three crews, including that of John Comer, were woken to perform air–sea rescue duties.

The next day, October 4, the crews were roused for the group's 35th raid—an attack on Frankfurt's industrial areas. Among them was navigator Roger Burwell, who was flying his 16th mission.

"Our squadron [532nd] was to lead the group and the group was to lead the [1st BD]," he recalled, "so our squadron was to lead the whole Eighth Air Force."[29]

Just before the group's 21 B-17s began taking off from Ridgewell, a head-on collision on the perimeter track between a weapons carrier and a staff car injured six ground crewmen, two of them seriously. Fortunately, both survived. Roger Burwell, however, soon began questioning his chances of survival over Europe.

> We were on the route in and had just passed Aachen, Germany, when we lost oil pressure on one engine … the first thing that I knew, Jack [Pry, the pilot] had put the plane into an almost vertical dive after feathering the engine. He was headed down for a low cloud layer with some fighters trying to get on our tail. He called on the intercom for a heading back to our base but I was pinned against the bulkhead and couldn't move. My immediate thought was, "I guess we are going to buy the farm this time."[30]

Burwell's was one of nine 381st B-17s to abort the mission early, leaving just 12 to reach the target. However, heavy clouds, a thick smoke screen, and a frozen bombsight in the lead aircraft forced the commander, David Kunkel, to select another target. Unfortunately, the 1st CBW's bombs and incendiaries landed "in a cemetery."

Roger Burwell's B-17 landed back at Ridgewell, having avoided any flak by skirting "every town in Belgium." It made it home without so much as a scratch.

"Having survived so many missions with near misses, I then decided that we had just about run out our string of luck."[31]

* * *

New navigator David McCarthy was yet to experience his first taste of combat. Having spent three weeks flying orientation missions and attending gunnery training over The Wash, he returned to Ridgewell where he immediately sensed "an air of foreboding." On October 7, he was woken for his first mission.

"I was so frightened I had trouble getting into my clothes," he wrote. "In the mess hall, while the others were apparently relishing their fresh eggs, I sat there having trouble swallowing my coffee."[32]

After attending the briefing for the mission to Germany, McCarthy's confidence slowly returned. However, not long after assembling over the Norfolk coast, the raid was scrubbed and the B-17s returned to Ridgewell. "That aborted mission did serve me well, though," remembered McCarthy. "I never again experienced mind-altering fear."[33]

Just after the crews landed at Ridgewell, some were photographed with their B-17s. One of them was 24-mission veteran Dexter Lishon, who posed with his crew in front of their newly assigned B-17F *Bobby T.*

Lishon was one of 16 officers sharing David McCarthy's barracks. McCarthy looked upon him as a "big brother"—a "compassionate young man" who patiently explained the "mechanics" of formation flying; *Luftwaffe* tactics; and the "personalities" of the 381st's senior officers.[34] Only a week earlier, Lishon had been promoted to captain. He had also been made the 534th's operations officer.

* * *

In the early hours of October 8, Lishon moved around the hut with a flashlight, quietly calling out the names of McCarthy's crew. They were scheduled to fly the day's mission.

"This morning, however, unlike the previous morning, I enjoyed my bacon and eggs … and looked forward to the day with confidence," noted McCarthy.[35]

John Comer was also woken up for the group's next mission. However, when his name and the last three digits of his bomber's serial number were read out, he was upset to learn he wouldn't be flying in *Nip and Tuck*. Due to a clerical error, his usual "765" had been given to another crew. He and his crew would now be flying "755." It was named *Last Straw*.

Another of those who'd been woken for the mission was navigator Roger Burwell. He'd just returned from a 48-hour pass, "well hungover." Burwell's friend, co-pilot Arthur Sample, had taken up an offer to become the pilot of a new crew and was set to fly his first mission with them. Burwell was assigned to fly with his usual pilot, Jack Pry, who was "more nervous, uptight than usual." Pry's uneasiness only intensified during the briefing.

"The moans and groans arising out of the throats of the pilots and co-pilots seemed louder than usual when the curtain was pulled back," Pry remembered. "Colonel Nazzaro [then] said, 'our target for today is Bremen, Germany.' We knew Bremen would be heavily defended, and the briefing confirmed this belief."[36]

The group's targets were the city's submarine pens and ship-building yards, which were thought to have produced 10 percent of German U-boats a year earlier.[37] Encircled by "250 flak guns" and defended by some 200 *Luftwaffe* fighters, the pilots were told it could be "rougher than expected." Nevertheless, the formation would be escorted to and from the IP by six groups of P-47s. The 381st would be led by the 535th's commanding officer, Maj. William Ingenhutt, who would trail the 1st CBW in its low position.

David McCarthy and his crew, led by pilot Robert Miller, were slated to fly in the rear of the 381st's formation. "We … being the newest crew and therefore the most expendable," he recalled. "*Tail End Charlie*."

McCarthy's crew was assigned a new B-17F—*Our Mom*—which had recently been transferred in from Chelveston. Bremen would be its first raid. McCarthy's co-pilot, Joseph Doerfler, was the only one with any combat experience. He'd flown one mission.

Taking off just before midday, the group's 21 B-17s assembled into the 1st CBW before forming up with the rest of the 1st BD over Cromer.

"As we crossed the coast the sun was shining brightly," recalled David McCarthy. "I was elated and excited … nothing could possibly happen … the day was far too beautiful and peaceful …"[38]

After crossing the Dutch island of Texel, the formation encountered a few bursts of anti-aircraft fire, but continued on, turning southeast towards the IP. On reaching it, the escorting P-47s then turned back for England. As soon as they'd gone, *Luftwaffe* fighters appeared. John Comer was alerted to them by his tail gunner.

"When I spun around I could hardly believe what I saw," wrote Comer. "Four fighters were flying so close together they looked like one enormous four-engine aircraft." It was the cue for the B-17s to demonstrate their massed fire power.

"Almost all top turrets, some balls and all tails poured a heavy barrage at those four unfortunate fighters," remembered Comer. "The enormous mass of fifty caliber slugs was so devastating that there were four puffs of black smoke and a sky filled with debris that erased four poorly-trained German pilots."[39]

Roger Burwell was firing from his nose position in *Feather Merchant.* "There were German planes coming at us from all directions," he recalled. "There were the usual Fw 190s and Me 109s, but, unbelievably, there were twin-engine Ju 88 dive-bombers and twin-engine Me 210s equipped with wing racks hanging off just out of our machine gun range."[40]

The fighters were hanging back for good reason. *Feather Merchant* was entering the "flak zone." It was immediately struck by a direct hit, which disabled its number two engine. Burwell was wounded in the hand by shrapnel, although not seriously. However, the blast had severed the nose compartment's intercom, meaning he and the bombardier, Theodore Snyder, were unable to know what was going on in the rest of the aircraft. All they could hear was the rattling propeller, which suddenly "froze up." It then tore off the wing and flew away.

By this time, *Feather Merchant* had released its bombs and was joined by Arthur Sample's *Ole Flak Sack*—both now dropping from the formation with flak damage. Almost immediately, however, Sample's B-17 was hit by a German fighter.

"One moment the plane and crew were flying along with us, a little behind us and to the side," recalled Jack Pry. "The next instant, a huge fireball, angry red, orange and black smoke. Then nothing."[41]

Miraculously, two crewmen were blown free from *Ole Flak Sack.* Both the co-pilot Edward A. Cytarzynski and the left waist gunner James R. Forbes parachuted down into the hands of the Germans. Arthur Sample and seven others were killed in the explosion.

Jack Pry continued to fight with the controls of *Feather Merchant,* which was then hit by "something" that ripped off the left wingtip.

"Things were happening all over now," Pry remembered. "Hardly a moment passed that the plane did not shudder with the impact of more hits."[42]

Further explosions in the waist section led to the complete loss of another engine. Half of the right horizontal stabilizer was also blown away. The worsening damage soon rendered the B-17 uncontrollable. Pry screamed for his crew to bail out. He then attempted to ram an Fw 190 after becoming "angry" with its pilot for his persistent attacks. Roger Burwell was also incensed by another Fw 190, whose pilot slowed down to study the B-17, just as Burwell was trying to destroy its radar equipment.

> He was so very close to our wing that I could see his face as he looked out of the plane. It made me so mad that ... I grabbed my machine gun and emptied the last rounds in the belt. The fighter was so close that I couldn't miss. I saw him crumple over in the cockpit and the engine blew up in fire as he fell off on a wing. I thought, "At least I got that bastard for me and Art Sample..."[43]

Amid more exploding shells, Burwell quickly bailed out behind Jack Pry and their bombardier, Theodore Snyder. Several others jumped from the rear, including their severely wounded left waist gunner Carl A. Baird. "How he managed the strength and fortitude to get to the door to jump when he was so badly wounded … I'll never know," said Jack Pry.[44]

The other waist gunner, SSgt. Alfred A. Johnson, had a "horrible misfortune," however. His parachute had popped and spilled open in the fuselage. Although both Baird and the top turret gunner SSgt. Edward R. LaPointe had gathered it up and handed it to him, Johnson was not seen to have jumped. He was later found dead close to the wreckage of *Feather Merchant*, which also contained the body of ball turret gunner Irvin W. Smith. He was thought to have been killed by a 20mm cannon shell.

Overhead, Dexter Lishon's *Bobby T* was also under attack. Although he'd taken off as a "spare," Lishon had elected to join another group over the North Sea. Despite this, as he attempted to slot into the formation next to another B-17, its pilot tried to force him out.

"We fought this phenomenon all the way to the target," remembered Lishon's navigator Robert Gluck. "Every attempt by us to join the formation was met with resistance."[45]

Approaching the IP, Lishon was again forced out of the formation, although this time it left him five miles behind. *Bobby T* was alone and at the mercy of six Fw 190s. In quick succession, three of its engines were disabled before the aircraft caught fire. After issuing the bail-out order, Lishon and his crew jumped. Landing safely, all were taken prisoner.

Much later, at the POW processing center, the *Dulag Luft* in Frankfurt, Robert Gluck met the pilot of the B-17 that had forced them out of the formation on the way to Bremen. He, too, had been shot down. Gluck learned that the pilot, a member of the 100th Bomb Group who'd been flying his first mission, thought *Bobby T* had been captured and was being flown by a *Luftwaffe* crew, "because of the Triangle L on the tail."[46]

* * *

Just before the 381st released its bombs, the group's unnamed lead B-17, flown by William Ingenhutt, had its number two engine struck by flak. Turning off the target, another engine was put out of action—Ingenhutt was forced to feather it. With shrapnel "rattling against the fuselage" and flames consuming his number two engine, Ingenhutt pushed the B-17 into a steep dive. He succeeded only in blowing the cowling panels off the blazing engine. Unable to extinguish the flames, Ingenhutt then issued the bail-out order.

As the navigator Edwin D. Frost put on his parachute pack, he gestured to his friend, bombardier Robert C. Black, to do the same. "I believe he shook his head," remembered Frost, "… he seemed dazed."[47]

Frost knew there was "no alternative but to jump" and did so from 11,000 feet. He was followed by Ingenhutt, who checked the aircraft was empty before bailing out. Robert Weniger, the former co-pilot of *T.S.*, who'd been flying in the tail gunner's position, also jumped. On landing, he was gathering his parachute when a German woman yelled at him. "American airmen must get drunk to fly over Germany," she shouted. Weniger made his escape, only to be captured within an hour, as was the rest of the crew. One was missing, though—the bombardier, Robert Black.

"The only explanation that I can offer," wrote Edwin Frost, "is that [Black] did bail out, but hit the bomb bay doors after leaving …"

The others could only surmise, some even suggesting Black may have evaded capture only to be "caught by the SS or Gestapo" before "dying in prison." Whatever the outcome, Black's body was never found.[48]

* * *

TS Too, the B-17F that had been named in honor of Robert Weniger's *T.S.*, almost collided with Weniger's B-17 as it went down, although Capt. Edwin Manchester managed to avoid it. He then took over the lead, but soon lost an engine to flak before being further damaged by a fighter. With only two engines functioning, *TS Too* peeled out of the formation chased by German fighters.

Fifteen miles west of Bremen, and with parts of its oxygen system shot away and several crew members wounded, Manchester's co-pilot, Capt. Elton D. Jukes, "garbled" the words, "bail out."

"Then something hit the nose," remembered bombardier Keith D. Moore. "Whatever hit us did a good job of it. The bombsight was canted to the side, about 30 degrees, and almost the whole nose glass was gone."[49]

Moore and the navigator, Marvin L. Smith, were "thrown back to the catwalk area" of the B-17, where they scrambled out through the nose hatch. With the aircraft on fire from the cockpit back, other crew members went to bail out, but the aircraft broke in two from the ball turret back.

Tail gunner Wade McCook had been treating the wounded left waist gunner Matthew Berk in the rear section of the bomber when it disintegrated. Both men were pinned inside the tail, which "floated" down 20,000 feet "like a leaf." Astonishingly, McCook and Berk survived, as did Keith Moore and Marvin Smith. Edwin Manchester and the others perished.

* * *

John Comer's *Last Straw* had so far evaded the worst of the fighter onslaught and Bremen's flak belt, but it had sustained numerous strikes—one of which disabled its number three engine. However, it was Comer's "faithful old aerial warhorse," *Nip and Tuck* that seemed in more difficulty.

Under the command of 2nd Lt. James W. Hartje, *Nip and Tuck* ("last squadron, last element, last plane") had two engines burning and was seen turning away from the formation.

"I watched '765' fall back with mounting apprehension," remembered John Comer. "As she rolled back within my sight far below, I felt stabs of anguish. It was like losing an old friend with whom I had shared both escapades and harrowing experiences."[50]

The crew of *Nip and Tuck* began bailing out, although the ball turret gunner, Clayton M. Boykin, hadn't been heard from since his guns were put out of action by a fighter. Edward Czyz was also "sitting on the floor" of the aircraft, fearful of jumping.

The aircraft crashed some 25 miles from Bremen, the two men still inside. The body of the top turret gunner, Eugen W. Kaseman, was found lying some distance away from the wreckage, his parachute unopened. The rest of the crew were taken POW.

The loss of *Nip and Tuck* had left *Tinker Toy* at the back of the formation. The B-17—"riddled from the ball to the tail"—was quickly set upon by two fighters. "They … hit her dead center of the cockpit," said John Comer. "I saw a small explosion."[51]

Unknown to Comer and his crew, the pilot of *Tinker Toy*, 1st Lt. William J. Minerich, had been decapitated. His co-pilot, 2nd Lt. Thomas D. Sellers, had also been wounded, while both the bombardier and navigator were left dazed in the nose, its plexiglass having been blown off.

With blood covering the cockpit and the top turret gun's plinth, Sellers and his engineer, TSgt. Henry L. Miller, set about trying to fly the damaged bomber back to England.

"One wing was badly torn and an engine cowling knocked off," noted John Comer. "But she flew on."[52]

While *Tinker Toy* of the 535th BS limped home, another 535th bomber, *Ron Chee*, went down. Unseen by any of the other crews, the fate of its men remained unknown. Led by 1st Lt. Leslie A. Kemp, all 10 were subsequently found to have been killed when the bomber crashed 45 miles southwest of Bremen. It was the third 535th bomber to be lost and the 381st's seventh overall.

* * *

"That which happened to us can never be described in words," wrote chaplain James Good Brown of the Bremen raid. "Only those who lived on the base … can comprehend the impact on the entire Group."[53]

Brown followed one of the 381st's returning B-17s as it taxied to its hardstand after landing. He rode alongside an ambulance, whose driver explained that "a man on the plane had been killed." The plane was *Our Mom* and its navigator was David McCarthy. Once it stopped, he and several others climbed out to check on its condition.

"The crew counted 375 flak holes, twenty-two 20mm cannon projectile holes, a shattered and smashed plexiglass nose and a tail assembly that was almost blown off," McCarthy recalled.[54] Yet, worse was inside.

After the formation had left the island of Texel on its return to England, McCarthy had slumped to the floor of *Our Mom*, exhausted. The bombardier, Edward A. Klein, had also been "grasping the handles of his machine with his head resting on his arms," when their pilot, Robert Miller, had called the crew to check for injuries and damage. All but the tail gunner, Stephen J. Klinger, had answered. McCarthy had gone back to check on him.

"One look and my heart [leapt] into my throat," McCarthy recalled. "Steve was dead. He was still seated upon the bicycle seat with his legs folded under him … I knelt there looking at him in horror."[55]

Back at Ridgewell, McCarthy watched some men crowding around the ambulance and aircraft. He climbed back inside to retrieve the tail gunner's body, quietly aided by James Good Brown. As they lifted Klinger's body into the ambulance, McCarthy could no longer hold back.

"Watching all those people stare at Steve, I became very angry and lashed out verbally," he recalled. "I thought of them as the same morbid curiosity-seekers that appear at the scene of all tragedies." McCarthy then turned to Brown weeping. Klinger was "only twenty years old."[56]

"The experience in beholding such a ghastly sight shattered him," wrote James Good Brown. However, another, more horrific sight was to greet the chaplain as he moved on to "the jinxed ship," *Tinker Toy*. There, he helped place the body of its pilot, William Minerich, on a stretcher, with his severed head beside him.

"Too many words cannot be said of [Minerich's co-pilot] Lieutenant Sellers," Brown later wrote. "There he sat, having seen his pilot's head shot off … He could 'go to pieces' or be a man and fly back home, bringing his crew to safety. This is what he did."[57]

The Bremen mission had resulted in the 381st's second highest loss of the war so far. Seven aircraft had been shot down, while 11 of its remaining B-17s had been heavily damaged. Seventy-two men had been killed or were missing in action, while three had returned wounded. Collectively, they'd accounted for 28 enemy fighters—either destroyed, probably destroyed or damaged.[58] The feat would earn the group its first DUC for "gallantry, determination and esprit de corps."

Nevertheless, a "high percentage" of veterans had been taken, including the 535th's commander, William Ingenhutt. Now a prisoner of war, he would eventually be awarded a Silver Star. Despite his squadron having suffered its heaviest loss "since Schweinfurt," it had also earned the group its highest individual award.

"For extraordinary heroism in connection with military operations against an armed enemy while serving as Co-Pilot of a B-17 Heavy Bomber," Thomas Sellers of the 535th was duly awarded the DSC.

> Despite severe wounds, and cold from the open cockpit, Lieutenant Sellers, with superb skill, courage, and determination to save the airplane and its crew, brought the heavily damaged plane into formation, guided it through two hours of ceaseless fighter attacks, and returned the plane and its crew safely to their home base. His courage, calmness, and heroism were an inspiration to his comrades and reflect great credit upon himself, the 8th Air Force, and the United States Army Air Forces.[59]

"I sat with the pilots at the very last meeting," wrote James Good Brown in his diary. "There was Ingenhutt … Minerich, Manchester, Kemp … Hartje … Pry … Sample … Lishon, and all their co-pilots. These men we lost today are typical of the men I knew and loved … My heart is torn within me. I am lonesome and will miss them."[60]

CHAPTER 8

Beating the Odds

October 9–22, 1943

James Good Brown awoke to the sound of engines just after 0700. The incessant drone could only mean one thing. After the "blood, hell and terror" of the day before, the group was going out on another raid. Brown, though, couldn't understand why he'd not been woken. He'd gone to sleep just after midnight. His last diary entry had read, "one of the worst days of my life."[1] It seemed October 9 hadn't started so well, either.

Unknown to Brown, his usual helper, Captain Julius L. Eichenbaum, had left on a pass and no one else had thought to wake him. He didn't know where the group was going, or who had gone. "I feel guilty," he wrote. "I was not there in the briefing to wish them 'good luck.'"[2]

John Comer had been one those who'd taken off that morning. He'd also had trouble waking up, still feeling groggy from the Bremen raid the day before. Many of those who'd flown the mission to Bremen had been given sodium amytal to sedate them. Surgeon Ernest Gaillard noted that those who'd received the dose "were in much better shape" than those who hadn't.[3]

When Comer had arrived at operations earlier that morning his mood had quickly been lifted. His pilot, Paul Gleichauf, explained they were being given a new B-17G that had arrived two days earlier. Just before he left operations, however, Comer was quickly brought back down to earth. An "ominous groan" from the briefing room told him all he needed to know. Hurrying to his new B-17, daubed with the name *Hellcat,* he immediately asked the armorer for extra ammunition.

The 381st had been ordered to attack the Arado aircraft plant in the town of Anklam—over 550 miles away in the northwestern corner of Germany. For the first time, each of the 381st's B-17s had been loaded with 2,700 gallons of fuel for the eight-hour round trip.

VIII BC tasked the 1st BD and elements of its 3rd BD with flying at an unusually low altitude of 13,000 feet, crossing over Denmark, before banking right into northern Germany. It was hoped they would draw the *Luftwaffe* into battle, while other 3rd BD groups, and the 2nd BD with its B-24s, flew unopposed to the Polish ports of Danzig and Gdynia, 200 miles further on.

With the route being so close to German fighter bases, Comer told Gleichauf they had "better put on all the ammunition we can carry." Gleichauf didn't want to carry the extra weight, but Comer concluded he hadn't disagreed. With that, he loaded 13,500 rounds, almost double the regulated amount.

When it came for *Hellcat*'s turn to take-off, the B-17 failed to respond to Gleichauf's attempts to lift. At 123mph, with the end of the runway rapidly approaching, the B-17 began a groping climb. Its wheels were retracted, which narrowly missed several trees, before it started sinking.

"For the only time in my life I gave up all hope of survival," wrote Comer. "I knew that no one survived a crash on a take-off with an overloaded airplane."

The B-17 fell towards an open field as Gleichauf frantically ordered the wheels to be lowered. They snapped into position just as the B-17 hit the ground. It then bounced back into the air where its wheels were retracted again. The aircraft descended a few feet and then slowly began inching its way up, narrowly avoiding more trees.

As soon as it was flying straight and level, a relieved Comer went back to investigate. To his shock, he found the gunners had moved much of the ammunition towards the rear. The tail gunner had also been sat in his position. Comer was furious.

"We were 1,300lb too heavy at the tail. That must have been the worst successful take-off since Orville Wright made the first one."[4]

By 1140, the 381st formation had successfully circumvented one *Luftwaffe* interception before arriving over Anklam. All 16 B-17s then swiftly dropped a combination of 1,000lb general-purpose and 100lb incendiary bombs. After a four-minute bomb run, they turned northwest before beginning the long flight back across Denmark and the North Sea.

By now, the *Luftwaffe* was on high alert. As the 381st approached the Danish coast, German fighters attacked. One of the 532nd's aircraft, piloted by 2nd Lt. Douglas L. Winter, was hit, a 20mm shell exploding in the cockpit. Winter was briefly knocked unconscious. By the time he came to, all four crewmen in the front of his B-17 were bailing out, one of them giving him a farewell salute before jumping. With a fire taking hold and the aircraft banking steeply, Winter corrected the turn, engaged the AFCE and fought the flames. When they were finally extinguished, he continued flying with his five remaining crewmen.

Battlin' Bombsprayer, piloted by 2nd Lt. James "Jim" L. Loftin, was badly damaged by a Bf 110 near the Danish coast.

"Jim's crew became actively mobile," remembered David McCarthy, who was flying alongside in *Our Mom*. "They were removing their oxygen masks and snapping their parachutes to their harnesses. Lt. Beckerman, the navigator, leaned over his desk, gave us the 'V' for victory sign, and with a quick wave of his hand he departed the ship through the nose hatch."

At least eight of the crew, including Loftin, bailed out and were later captured. Two of its crew members, however—radio operator Charles G. Silverburg and tail gunner Allen T. Alford—were later found to have been killed. For David McCarthy, watching the parachutes "blossom" was a poignant sight.

"The four officers of that crew were the last of our barracks mates," he said. "Now our crew was to be alone …"[5]

John Comer had spotted some Me 210s holding off at a distance. Suddenly, what appeared to be flak began bursting around the formation. It soon became apparent that the "flak" bursts were rockets being launched from the German fighters. One exploded close to Comer's aircraft. However, the gunners were unable to reach the fighters with effective fire because of the distances involved.

Unknown to Comer, *Forget Me Not II*, flown by his former pilot Herbert Carqueville, had also come under attack. Unseen by the rest of the formation, his B-17 disappeared from view and was later found to have ditched in the North Sea with the loss of all 10 men.

Major Landon Hendricks, commanding officer of the 533rd, was leading his squadron in one of the group's original B-17Fs. His crew included the squadron's lead navigator, Capt. William T. Turner; its lead bombardier, Capt. Leo K. English; Capt. Robert L. Withers, original pilot of the doomed B-17F, *Caroline*; and pilot 2nd Lt. William L. Duggan, who was flying in Hendricks's tail gunner's position to direct the squadron formation.

Halfway across Denmark, their unnamed B-17 was hit by a rocket, which struck the number one engine. The loss of power to Hendricks's aircraft forced the trailing bombers to slow down. Gleichauf was flying on Hendricks's left wing, and his crew were trying all they could to disable the Me 210s, but the German pilots had judged their distance perfectly. *Hellcat*'s machine guns just couldn't reach.

Scanning the scene from his top turret, Comer watched Landon Hendricks leave his cockpit, before returning a few moments later. His aircraft then dropped out of formation with its undercarriage extended to signal it was surrendering the lead.

"Take a good look at Hendricks," Comer thought to himself. "I doubt if we will ever see him again."[6]

Intermittent fighter attacks continued out into the North Sea, before a Bf 109 struck Hendricks's number two and three engines, fatally damaging it. Several crews reported seeing up to six parachutes sprout from the B-17, before it dropped and exploded on contact with the water. It would later transpire, however, that Hendricks and his crew were all killed.

When the remaining B-17s landed back at Ridgewell, four were missing (Douglas Winter was forced to land elsewhere). At the interrogation, Comer discovered his good friend Carqueville was among them. He hadn't been aware that Carqueville was flying the mission because he'd been temporarily attached to the 535th. Comer went numb. He also didn't know the fate of Hendricks and his crew.

When James Good Brown sat down with Comer and the rest of the Gleichauf crew after their interrogation, he asked them what happened to Hendricks. To a man, they expressed their belief that he had "deliberately sacrificed himself so as not to let the squadron fall back too far behind the rest of the group and to draw the concentrated fire of the rocket fighters."

Later that evening, Brown took to his diary to pay tribute to Landon Hendricks. "You were a gentleman," he wrote. "This war. This is hell. These are great men."[7]

* * *

The loss of two squadron commanders within 48 hours of each other was a bitter blow. Worse still, the group had lost 27 of its original crews—three-quarters of whom had formed the 381st at Pyote. Landon Hendricks and Robert Withers were the latest to be shot down. "Here was our only chance to bring through the few remaining veterans," lamented James Good Brown. "We did not succeed. They are gone."[8]

After surviving his first two missions, replacement navigator David McCarthy was stood down, but he struggled with the sudden change.

"In only two days, we had adjusted our lives to flying combat missions," he wrote. "Now we were expected to relax, write letters and take it easy. It was a very difficult adjustment."[9]

The attrition in bombers was also wearing heavily on the 381st. In two days, 10 of its B-17s had been lost and 22 were heavily damaged. A day later, the group was only able to ready eight serviceable bombers for a third consecutive field order—one that saw VIII BC turn its attention towards the railroads and waterways of Münster.

Taking off into thick cloud at 1130, the 381st formed a composite group with the 91st BG, which was leading the 1st BD. The 3rd BD was out in front, while the 2nd BD sent 39 B-24s on a "diversion." Within hours, one of the most concentrated air battles of the war had claimed 30 bombers and over 300 men.

The 381st was one of the more fortunate groups, largely avoiding the slaughter. However, all of its B-17s were damaged, including one that had two large holes blown out of the side of its radio room. Nevertheless, the group had lost none of its airmen. Only one was wounded, while another had survived a period without oxygen after the supply to his ball turret had failed. Yet, other groups had sustained terrible casualties.

Of the 30 bombers lost on VIII BC's 114th mission, 25 were from the 13th CBW—its 100th BG faring the worst, losing 12 of its B-17s. In just three raids, the so-called "Bloody Hundredth" had lost almost half its strength. The cost of VIII BC's war was mounting with each passing day.

Mindful of the losses, British Prime Minister Winston Churchill wrote to the commander of the US Army in Europe Gen. Jacob Devers the following day. In his letter, Churchill expressed his admiration for the crews and how they'd "ranged over the length and breadth of Germany, striking with deadly accuracy." He continued, "I am confident that with the ever-growing power of the 8th Air Force, striking alternate blows with the Royal Air Force Bomber Command, we shall together inexorably beat the life out of industrial Germany and thus hasten the day of final victory."[10]

The Münster raid had also proved to be a costly one for the *Luftwaffe*. Over 250 claims (enemy aircraft destroyed, probably destroyed or damaged) were made by VIII BC gunners. However, such numbers were often the result of multiple gunners on different aircraft claiming the same fighter. The 390th BG alone had claimed 60 fighters—an all-time record for enemy aircraft destroyed by a single group on one mission.[11] Yet, the raid had also cost the lives of some 700 German civilians, killed by an attack whose aiming point was the city center itself.

David McCarthy had gone to Ridgewell's flight line to watch the B-17s return from Münster. He was standing with a group of airmen when they appeared on the horizon.

"The grounded fliers around the control tower then reverted from grim, anxious men, to the teenagers they had been only a few months ago," he noted. "Laughing, grinning kids, punching each other on the shoulder, slapping their neighbors on the back and a couple of them performing impromptu jigs. A stranger might have concluded that the war had ended."[12]

* * *

Two days after Münster, a reshuffle of senior officers took place at Ridgewell. Frank Chapman assumed command of the 535th from George Shackley, who'd initially replaced the missing William Ingenhutt four days earlier. Shackley was given command of Hendricks's 533rd BS. However, another valued officer was giving cause for concern.

Captain Arthur Briggs, the 535th's operations officer, who'd been co-pilot to Conway Hall on the Schweinfurt raid and who'd crash-landed *Whaletail* in a Norfolk field alongside Dexter Lishon, had finally seen enough. Three days after Münster, he informed Joe Nazzaro that he was refusing to fly the group's 39th mission, an attack on Emden's port area. Nazzaro gave Briggs a warning: he was one of the 381st's senior officers and any such a refusal would have a disastrous effect on group morale, something that was already at its lowest. The choice was his—stay and risk the consequences of disgrace and court-martial or fly the mission. Briggs reluctantly agreed. Shortly after take-off, however, the 381st's B-17s were recalled after encountering heavy weather. The mission was duly scrubbed, which only exacerbated Briggs's mounting anxiety.

His troubles had begun on the evening of August 17, when he'd returned from the group's disastrous mission to Schweinfurt. That evening, he'd got into a fight with a ground crew officer who'd said the wrong thing. Briggs immediately took off for London, where he'd spent several days drinking. By the time he returned to Ridgewell, he'd become withdrawn and suicidal. He'd also had thoughts about shooting his friends and kept reliving missions in his sleep. Finally, on September 17, he'd refused to fly another mission—one that was also scrubbed.

After being heavily sedated at the base hospital for several days, then spending a week at an officers' rest home in Hampshire, Briggs's decline had worsened. The day after his refusal to fly the Emden mission, the 381st's surgeon, Ernest Gaillard—under the direction of Nazzaro—drafted a letter to the US Army's medical board. In it, he acknowledged that the 381st had flown missions "on three consecutive days, lost two squadron commanders, a number of old crews, and a total of ten aircraft"—but, for refusing to fly, Briggs had "voluntarily accepted the punishment and disgrace that might be facing him." Gaillard signed off with the words, "lack of moral fibre."[13]

* * *

When the curtain was pulled back to reveal a long, red ribbon stretching all the way to Schweinfurt on October 14, there were loud groans. Men winced as they heard the "swearword" Schweinfurt. Most could be forgiven for following Arthur Briggs when it was announced the 381st would be flying in the 1st CBW's low position. All John Comer could do was curse his own "stupid" luck.

A day earlier, Comer's crew had been stood down from combat status after Paul Gleichauf had developed a bad case of flu. It gave Comer the chance to fix a problem with *Hellcat*'s chin turret guns, which had jammed on the last raid. Comer's bombardier, John J. Purus, had been none too happy, so he and Comer had fitted mechanisms to prevent the problem from happening again. They also fitted the same to another of the 533rd's B-17Gs, *Gremlin's Delite*. When Comer explained to the armaments officer that the guns could only be adjusted "during combat," the officer insisted Comer fly the next mission in the navigator's position (to assist the bombardier with firing the guns). "We don't want some navigator foulin' up this test and that is what we're going to get…" the officer said. "I never saw a navigator who knew anything about guns except which end the bullets come out."[14]

Comer accompanied the officer to operations, where the officer-in-charge was asked to assign Comer as navigator on *Gremlin's Delite* for the group's next mission. He was also asked for any hint about the next mission. The officer refused to say, but the armaments officer already knew the planned bomb load. "We're going to be loading block busters," he whispered. The last time the 2,000lb "block buster" bombs had been used were on submarine pens. Comer deduced that the mission would be on the coast—an easy target on the coast—a "milk run."[15]

He couldn't have been further from the truth. Comer and the *Gremlin's Delite* crew weren't outside the briefing room when the target was announced. They hadn't heard the loud groans and profanities that followed. As soon as the co-pilot Stanley G. Parsons arrived and told the gunners they were going to Schweinfurt, all of them thought he was a joking. "We're going over the middle of Germany to Schweinfurt an' back," he retorted. "If we get back."[16]

Comer was in shock; the joke was on him, especially as 500lb demolition bombs had been loaded instead of "block busters." He was joined in the nose of the aircraft by John Leverette, the crew's bombardier, who'd recently been checked out as a navigator. With the usual navigator grounded because of illness, Leverette was assigned to fly the mission as navigator–bombardier, with Comer alongside to reload the guns. He was immediately told by Leverette they would be in the low position and facing "1,200" enemy aircraft along the way.

Gremlin's Delite was one of 17 B-17s to begin taking off from Ridgewell at 1035. The forecast 4,000 feet of fog turned out to be 6,000 feet higher than expected, meaning each aircraft had to feel its way for much longer than expected. By the time the bombers broke free of the clouds, they were scattered across the sky. Much time and fuel was then spent assembling into formation before the group headed off towards the Suffolk coast.

The 381st was joining three divisions, two of which were targeting Schweinfurt, while the third—the 2nd BD—was flying a diversionary route into northwestern Germany. The 1st BD and 3rd BD comprised 291 B-17s loaded with a combination of 500lb and 1,000lb bombs, plus 100lb incendiaries. Their route would take them across the North Sea, over Belgium, the Netherlands and Germany, before sweeping round to overfly northern France and the English Channel. A group of P-47s would escort each division into the continent, while another would provide withdrawal support, backed up by two squadrons of RAF Spitfires. VIII BC's 115th mission was already unravelling, though.

The 381st's delay in forming up had seen it miss the 1st CBW's assembly. Another delayed group—the 305th—had also lost sight of its wing, but it caught up with the 1st CBW and slotted into its vacant low position. When George Shackley, leading the 381st, found the 1st CBW, he was surprised to find the 305th in his position. He quickly chose to pull up to the high group, led by the 91st. It would turn out to be a fortuitous move.

The fighter escort was also adding to the confusion. Two fighter groups had been hampered by the weather back in England, while another was unable to find the bomber formation and turned back on reaching the European coastline. The fighters that did reach the 1st BD arrived too early, leaving them short of fuel. Once over the coast, they turned back for England.

At this point, one of the 381st's B-17s aborted the mission. Robert Miller, pilot of *Our Mom,* was convinced there was a problem with his two port engines. His co-pilot, Joe Doerfler, disagreed, claiming there was nothing wrong.

"A heated argument ensued between the two pilots about whether or not they should abort," remembered navigator David McCarthy. "Of course, the entire crew could hear the argument, and all of us were concerned about the discord that existed in the flight deck."[17]

As commander of the aircraft, Miller won the argument by pulling *Our Mom* out of the formation. Its position was taken over by the "spare" B-17F, *Flat Foot Foogie*.

John Comer, in the nose of *Gremlin's Delite*, could clearly see a mass of German fighters gathering in the distance. He would soon have to fire his modified chin turret guns.

Alongside, another 381st B-17, *This Is It!*, was facing its own trouble. Due to the heavy bomb and fuel load, its pilot, David D. Hutchens, had held the brakes on take-off at Ridgewell. He'd then throttled to maximum power. As soon as he let go, the aircraft lurched forward, snapping both waist guns from their mounts. The crew had debated aborting the mission, but the waist gunners managed to fix one of them to the aircraft so it could be fired.

Scores of German fighters tore through the 1st BD in groups of three and six, dividing the B-17s' defensive fire. John Comer also noticed that some Ju 88s were keeping their distance, but continually hurled rockets into the formation, as had been the case at Münster. However, it was the low group—the 305th—that was being attacked mercilessly. Turning towards the target at Würzburg, the attacks intensified, the Germans' discovering the formation's destination.

"The battle was as furious as any I saw over Europe," recalled John Comer. "Flak [then] began to burst all around the formation and I could hear heavy shrapnel striking the ship."[18]

Nevertheless, the fighters kept on coming as the formation approached Schweinfurt's ball-bearing plants. *Flat Foot Foogie*, which had been transferred in from the 305th a few weeks earlier and had taken up the position of *Our Mom* after it had aborted, was struck by flak just after bombs away. With one of its engines disabled, it then suffered a withering attack by a Bf 109 before exploding. Only four of its crew survived the explosion.

As the fighter attacks continued, David Hutchens's *This Is It!* suffered an oil pressure loss from its number one engine. He shut it down and attempted to feather the propeller, but the mechanism failed to work. The sudden drag immediately slowed the bomber, which began to drop from the formation. It was then chased by several German fighters.

At 20,000 feet, Hutchens saw thick cloud cover down below. Cutting the B-17's power, he pushed it into a dive, which almost threatened to rip the port wing off and push its airspeed indicator past the red line. He then pulled up, almost into a stall, causing the chasing fighters to overshoot. Hutchens then dived again, into the relative safety of the clouds.

With the wind-milling propeller causing severe vibrations, Hutchens ordered the crew to prepare to bail out. The vibrations then stopped. He discussed a possible landing in Switzerland, but the decision was made to go home using cloud cover, wherever possible.

Back in England, the weather had worsened. It meant that the fighter groups tasked with the bombers' withdrawal had remained grounded. However, the skies over France were almost clear. Just as the 1st BD skirted Paris, still under fighter attack, the city's flak guns opened up. *This Is It!* avoided the worst of it as it continued escaping the clutches of the *Luftwaffe*, although fuel was running extremely low.

Luftwaffe fighters continued to attack elements of the formation as it flew out across the English Channel, but *This Is It!* remained unopposed. With its fuel lights blinking, David Hutchens steered the B-17 on a northerly heading towards what he hoped was England. It wasn't until he landed on a coastal runway and saw "a beautiful British Spitfire" that he was sure he and his crew were safe.

At 1730, the 381st began landing back at Ridgewell. Most of the other 1st BD stations were closed due to the weather and the ground crews had been warned to expect the entire division. In the end, only a handful of others landed, including two that ground-looped.[19]

Of the 17 B-17s dispatched by the 381st that morning, only five returned undamaged. The group was also missing three B-17s, including two that landed elsewhere in England. Overall, VIII BC lost 60 bombers—its highest loss on a single raid. Shockingly, the 305th BG, which had taken the 381st's position in the formation, lost 13 of its 16 B-17s. The battle had raged for over three hours across some 800 miles of airspace.[20]

"For me ... that high bank of fog hovering over our assembly space that morning was an incredible stroke of good fortune," remembered John Comer. "Although we bitterly cursed the fate that put us in that ten thousand foot layer of murk, it turned out to be the difference between acceptable losses and disaster ..."[21]

What could have been a disaster for the Miller crew had also turned out be a stroke of luck. However, both Robert Miller and his co-pilot, Joe Doerfler, were "chewed out" by the 534th's commander, David Kunkel. They had aborted the mission without good reason.

"Bob Miller was never a coward," remembered David McCarthy. "He may possibly have been overly cautious, but he was a courageous man. No man ever completed 25 missions without courage to spare."[22]

For Joe Nazzaro, however, the strain was starting to show. "[He was] more visibly affected by this mission than by any that I have yet observed," noted the 381st's surgeon, Ernest Gaillard. "He stated last night that he was more tired than when he, himself, had flown missions." Gaillard also saw how Nazzaro felt the anguish of his men, but knew the missions needed to be carried out. "He truly is a good man," wrote Gaillard.[23]

The public reaction to the second Schweinfurt raid and the significant losses it had incurred was one of shock. Although the ball-bearing plants had suffered significant damage (some estimates suggest 67 percent was knocked out), there had been over 600 casualties. Nevertheless, at a press conference three days later, commander of the USAAF Gen. Henry Arnold, encouraged by post-mission assessments of the damage, boldly stated, "now we have got Schweinfurt!" However, for those who survived their visit that day, it would forever be known as "Black Thursday."

* * *

The shock of the last few raids resonated deeply at Ridgewell. James Good Brown had noticed that many of the combat crews were resigned to their fate.

"The possibility of reaching 25 missions seemed gone," he wrote. "It was the one hope of the new crews—the replacements … the truth is there was little hope."[24]

David Kunkel, the 381st's only remaining original squadron commander, called a meeting the day after the second Schweinfurt raid.

"Every man in this room is a volunteer," he said. "You chose to fly in these B-17s. No one forced you to fly. If you are shot down after your bombs are released on your 25th mission, you can go down with the satisfaction of knowing you completed your obligation to your country." It was a harsh address but, as Kunkel pointed out, "this is war. Some die and some survive."[25]

Comer and his crewmates continued debating their chances of survival. Some thought the odds "stretched thinner" the closer a man got to the end of his tour. Comer thought otherwise. James Good Brown, on the other hand, was troubled by the repeated losses.

"Replacements now come in almost every day," he wrote. "Before we learn to know them, they have gone down in combat." Nevertheless, he reasoned that "men will come and men will go … the 381st will go on."[26]

The group was stood down for the next five days, allowing its combat crews some respite. The ground crews also had time to fix the damaged bombers. Unknown to the crews, a mission to Düren was scrubbed prior to briefing on October 17. The next day, eight B-17s were sent to Thurleigh, home of the 306th BG. They were due to make up a composite group for an attack on Düren—again, though, the mission was scrubbed, this time after take-off.

Düren finally came into VIII BC's sights on October 20. The German city served as a major rail center between Cologne and Aachen, although its industrial areas were selected as the primary target for three divisions. The 1st BD comprised nine groups with 103 B-17s. Again, the 381st sent eight of its aircraft to Thurleigh at 0615, where the crews were briefed to join the 306th's high squadron.

For the first time, the 1st BD used two Pathfinder B-17s equipped with the RAF's *Oboe* blind-bombing device. Shortly after take-off, however, one of them aborted, while the other struggled to pick up radio signals from England. The formation also found itself leap-frogging high-altitude clouds, which hampered bombing. Only the 3rd BD was able to attack, while just 17 of the 1st BD's force hit a *Luftwaffe* airfield at Woensdrecht in the Netherlands. All others, including the 381st, returned to England with their bomb loads intact. Despite the "recall," the mission was credited for the 381st's crews.

* * *

Technical Sergeant Edwin Myers had recently returned to Ridgewell. The 535th radio operator's journey had started on September 3, when his B-17, *Big Time Operator*, was shot down over France. Myers's escape had taken him through French towns and villages before he stumbled into the hands of the Resistance. A protracted journey through Paris saw him eventually reach the port of Brest. Despite its German naval activity, the port was being used as the assembly point for Allied evaders. Myers found himself crammed into a French fishing vessel with 17 other airmen. After being stuck in port for six days, he arrived in southwest England after a two-day voyage. On his arrival at Ridgewell, he became the first 381st combat crew member to successfully return after being shot down over Europe.

Two other downed crew members, Robert Nelson and Raymond Genz, who'd both been shot down on the first Schweinfurt mission, were also making their way through Spain; while another missing 381st airman, waist gunner Bud Owens, was about to reach the country after being shot down on July 4.

On October 22, Owens began an ascent of the Pyrenees with a small group of Allied airmen led by a French mountain guide. Their route would take them into Spain via Andorra and on towards Barcelona. A short way into the climb, Owens's former pilot Olof Ballinger began struggling. He told the guide he was unable to move because of severe cramping. The guide told Ballinger to hide and wait for his return, which was expected to be a week later.[27]

The rest of the group continued to climb, but one of them became ill after taking too many Benzedrine tablets (to generate energy). Owens volunteered to carry the sick man, which he did for the next 30 hours. However, the lack of food, combined with "ersatz" footwear, left Owens and several others unable to walk. Slumping to the snow on the Andorran side of the mountains, they could go no further. The guide, in a fit of rage, pulled out his pistol and fired into the snow next to one of the airmen's heads. It had no effect. The guide and the others reluctantly moved on, leaving Owens and two others behind. Sometime later, they succumbed to freezing temperatures and died.

Bud Owens had been hailed a hero after dragging an injured ground crewman to safety after the explosion of *Caroline* on June 23. Eleven days later, he'd saved the life of his incapacitated radio operator after hooking a parachute to him and pushing him out of their doomed B-17. Finally, while attempting to help a fellow evader cross the Pyrenees, Owens had lost his life.

Glen Burkland, the ground crewman, and John Lane, the radio operator, both survived the war and returned home. Bud Owens's body was recovered in 1950 and his remains were later interred at the Ardennes Military Cemetery in Belgium—another 381st combat crewman unable to beat the odds.

Intermission: Making a Home Run

The original crews that made up the first bomb groups that landed in England in 1942 had no idea how long they would be staying in Europe, nor how many missions they would be expected to fly. Once the first raids had been mounted, and the first aircraft had been shot down, these questions quickly became important.

The open-ended nature of the combat tour and the rate of attrition among the bomber crews began to have a negative impact on morale. Concerned about this, the Eighth's chief surgeon, Col. Malcolm C. Grow, suggested a tour length of fifteen combat missions be introduced for bomber crews. Another contributing factor to fatigue, and low morale, was the low number of available crews—those that were fit to fly had to fly more often. The morale problems were compounded by the lack of respite for increasingly worn-out crews.

Despite combat losses, the number of crews available increased through the spring of 1943, at this point Ira Eaker extended the tour length from 15 to 25. Very few crews could realistically expect to reach that milestone and make a home run. The fighter groups were also given a tour length of 200 combat flying hours.

October 1943 was a particularly dramatic month for the Eighth. Four full strength, maximum effort raids had been mounted at considerable cost. The summary of aircraft losses for the month showed that 214 aircraft had been lost. Analysis also showed that 10 percent of those launched had not returned. An even greater number were damaged, but limped home carrying wounded crew members. The overall total of losses amounted to more than half the strength of VIII BC. The onward projection of these stark figures at Eighth Air Force headquarters, produced the grim conclusion that the entire bomber force would be lost and have to be replaced within just three months.

On February 11, 1944, Henry Arnold informed James "Jimmy" Doolittle (eventual commander of the Eighth Air Force), that, given the current attrition rate among his bomber crews, and the anticipated increase in the intensity of bombing operations leading up to D-Day, 25 combat missions was no longer sustainable as a tour length. The cold mathematics of the air war indicated that if the rate of flying and the number of aircraft available for missions was to be maintained at an effective level, then crews would simply have to complete more missions. Tour length was extended again to 30 missions in April.

The brutal reality of this decision for the Eighth's crews was that any extension of tour length resulted in a corresponding reduction in their chances of survival. For most of 1943, the chances of completing a tour were calculated at 40 percent. Surviving unwounded, just 35 percent. Later in 1944, with the *Luftwaffe*'s threat waning, the mission total was increased to 35 for the bomb groups, while the fighter groups' tours were extended to 300 hours. Every airman who served with the Eighth has their own story to tell. Each, however, follows the same chronology—the mission count, making the final mission, and their home run.

CHAPTER 9

Scrub the Sky

October 23–December 1, 1943

Heavy fog and bad weather crept across Europe during the second half of October, hindering VIII BC's efforts to launch any major bombing raids. Only occasional night leaflet drops could be made over northern France. "There was a persistent rumor that Bomber Command weather officers came over from the States in good health and went home a month or so later in straitjackets," joked the 1st CBW's intelligence section.[1]

For the men of the 381st, the poor weather brought ground schools, test flights and practice missions. The group's strength was also reinforced by the arrival of yet more replacement crews. Although morale remained "a problem," John Comer and his crewmates found time to lighten their mood by "initiating" the new airmen in Ridgewell's mess halls.

> The temptation was too much to resist ... immediately we launched into a morbid discussion of combat raids in drastic detail: explosions, aircraft fires, dead crewmen, amputations, planes falling in spins out of control. We made it a point to act as if we did not realize they were listening. When the conversation was particularly gory, there was no sound of knife or fork from the next table. I noted with satisfaction when we left that the newly arrived officers were no longer hungry. It was our warm and friendly welcome to the 381st [Bomb] Group and Ridgewell Airdrome.[2]

The higher echelons had recognized that October's losses could no longer be sustained. The 1st BD alone had lost a total of 106 bombers, 91 of which were missing. News filtered through to the combat crews that things were set to change.

"For the next several weeks our missions were to be flown at altitudes of 25,000 feet or higher in an effort to reduce the effectiveness of the enemy's anti-aircraft guns," noted navigator David McCarthy. "Command would [also] plan the missions to keep the bombers' targets within the range of our fighter escort."

McCarthy was pleased to hear the news, even if it was just hearsay. "We were not looking for guarantees, only for a ray of hope."[3]

* * *

The arrival of the novice 401st BG at Deenethorpe in Northamptonshire saw a further reshuffle in the ranks of VIII BC. A fourth wing was added to its 1st BD to accommodate the 401st BG and several others that were set to arrive in England. The 92nd CBW was duly activated on November 1.

The move would ultimately affect the 381st. Its fellow 1st CBW group, the 351st, was set to be transferred to the new wing to supplement the 401st. Consequently, the 1st CBW's 381st and the 91st would have to pool a composite group between them until another new unit could be assigned.

Further changes took place on November 3, when VIII BC issued field orders for its first bombing raid in 14 days. It would call upon more than 500 bombers, 11 of which would be equipped with blind-bombing devices. Two would carry the existing *H2S* sets, while nine would be fitted with the new, American-developed *H2X* version.

While *H2X* would enable a broader area of land to be scanned, it relied on distinguishing between water and land in order to work effectively. Consequently, its use was mainly limited to coastal towns and cities. On November 3, VIII BC planned to use it for an attack on the German North Sea naval town of Wilhelmshaven.

Another new addition to VIII BC's arsenal would be the use of Lockheed P-38 Lightnings for support. With a marginally greater range than the P-47, the twin-engine P-38s were expected to give the bombers better protection. When John Comer's crew heard about their presence, they were delighted.

"There were whoops of joy," he recalled. "We were completely unaware that P-38s had arrived in England … [their] main feature was long range and strong construction … there was no doubt that they could easily handle the rocket-carrying fighters."[4]

Comer's *Hellcat* and 26 others began taking off from Ridgewell at 0920 bound for Wilhelmshaven. After assembling into the 1st CBW, the 381st then joined with the rest of VIII BC's divisions before leaving the English coast near Grimsby. According to one of the airmen, the sky was "solid with B-17s as far as 50 miles ahead and behind."[5]

After reaching the IP at Papenburg, the formation then turned northeast towards the aiming point—Wilhelmshaven's port. The 1st CBW's lead B-17's PFF equipment then malfunctioned, causing the 381st to drop on parachute flares left by the lead combat bombardment wing. The group then fled back to England.

The 381st's only casualties were 2nd Lt. George Darrow and SSgt. Shirley E. Goucher. The latter, an engineer and top turret gunner on 1st Lt. Martin L. Shenk's *Linda Mary*, which had aborted the mission early, fell from his top turret, fracturing his upper arm. The former, who'd landed *Big Time Operator II* at Ridgewell, was almost shot in the leg by a ball turret gun, which was accidentally fired while being cleared. Fortunately, Darrow was only slightly injured by flying debris.

Although the bombing results had been unobserved due to solid cloud cover, the Wilhelmshaven mission was hailed a success. It was thought that the aiming point had been "completely destroyed." The new *H2X* and P-38-escorted bombing raid had seemingly improved the crews' chances of survival. John Comer was pleased.

"No airman at the 381st had succeeded in completing 25 raids," he noted. "It was past time that some of the earliest arrivals should have been through. For the first time I began to feel a cautious optimism that before long the 381st was going to turn out some graduates."[6]

* * *

Forty-eight hours later, 21 of the group's B-17s were back in the air and bound for Gelsenkirchen's marshaling yards. Lieutenant Colonel Nazzaro, using callsign "Bo-Peep," had been given the task of air commander—leading the entire 1st BD in one of the 482nd's new PFF B-17s, *Spirit of Franklin County, Missouri*—a "bond-bought Fort."[7]

For the second consecutive mission, more than 500 heavy bombers were being sent to Germany, escorted by almost 400 fighters. Flying the 381st's forty-second raid was 2nd Lt. Cornelius J. Donovan, a navigator with the 532nd, who was on his 15th.

"To the dreaded Ruhr Valley—for the second time," he noted. "The target was the same one I went to on August 11th … [today] I had my iron hat on, and for the first time, I wore a flak suit."[8]

Climbing to a bombing altitude of 28,000 feet, the formation reached the IP near the Dutch town of Hoogeveen. It then turned southeast for a 20-minute bomb run in towards Gelsenkirchen.

Despite the presence of numerous P-47s, several enemy fighters "filtered through," one striking the 534th's lead B-17, flown by Capt. Charles P. Ohl. Shot in the stomach by a 20mm cannon shell, the wounded pilot was dragged from his seat and carried to the radio compartment where he was given medical attention by the bombardier, George P. Heinz. Ohl's co-pilot, 1st Lt. Martin H. Downey—himself wounded and falling in and out of consciousness—was joined in the cockpit by the navigator, 1st Lt. Harold L. Stralser, who helped fly the bomber towards the target.

Arriving over an "open" Gelsenkirchen, some 100,000lb of high explosives and incendiaries were released by all 21 of the 381st's B-17s. Then, two minutes later, heavy and accurate flak knocked out two of Joe Nazzaro's engines, slowing his bomber down to 130mph. Several other 381st B-17s were also damaged by cannon fire, three seriously.

Blowin' Bessie, piloted by 1st Lt. Donald K. Hopp, lost part of its number two engine just after its bombs had been dropped. It then slowed down before falling from the formation, where its crew began firing flares. Although Hopp issued the bail-out order, only he and two others managed to escape before the bomber plunged into the Netherlands Diep estuary. Hopp; his navigator Marshall E. Tyler; and top turret gunner, Alexander M. Girvan, were all taken prisoner. Only one other crew member's body was found.[9]

Last Straw, piloted by 1st Lt. William D. Butler, had also been struck by flak just west of the target. Flying at 28,000 feet, Butler issued the bail out order to his crew, six of whom duly jumped. His bombardier, 2nd Lt. Hayden T. Brown, however, was quickly overcome by anoxia after removing his oxygen mask. Brown collapsed near the nose hatch, accidentally deploying his parachute, which billowed outside before wrapping itself around the ball turret. Brown was trapped with one leg hanging outside the aircraft. He remained in the same position for 90 minutes while Butler struggled to fly the damaged bomber back to England, finally making an emergency landing at West Malling in Kent.

Remarkably, Hayden Brown survived his blackout, exposure and injuries. He, William Butler and two others returned to duty. The six who bailed out were all taken as POWs, including the left waist gunner, TSgt. Francis R. McGinty, a friend of John Comer's, whose *Hellcat* had also been damaged by anti-aircraft fire.

"A hunk of flak … tore through the empty bomb bay with a fearsome noise," remembered Comer. "As soon as we got to a lower altitude, and the threat of fighters had eased, I got out of the turret and looked for any damage I could see."

He found the hydraulic fluid had been lost, meaning the braking system wouldn't work on landing. A subsequent discussion took place as to how Paul Gleichauf might try to "ease off into the sticky mud" on landing at Ridgewell.[10]

Elsewhere, navigator Harold Stralser was also wondering how he and the semi-conscious Martin Downey might be able to land their B-17. Overflying the Netherlands, they'd been unable to keep up with the formation—at one point, dropping from their squadron and extending the undercarriage to signal they should be left alone. The other B-17s followed. Stralser, under Downey's instruction, pulled back into the formation and continued on to Ridgewell.

Joe Nazzaro's *Spirit of Franklin County, Missouri* had been trailing smoke for two hours by the time it crossed the English coast at Orford Ness. The 381st's B-17s then began arriving back over Ridgewell almost six hours after they'd taken off. Among them was the hydraulic-less *Hellcat*, which now faced another problem. Both sides of the runway were lined with people as it approached. The possibility of swinging into the mud was lost.

"Gleichauf was infuriated," recalled Comer. "The high speed of the aircraft meant nothing to them … then it was too late."

Hellcat careered off the end of the runway, crossing "rough ground, roads and ditches" before coasting across a country lane where an English soldier was riding his bicycle. John Comer felt a "slight impact," then cringed as the bomber headed for a barnyard where two women were sitting on a fence.

"There was a sizeable ditch and the wheels dropped into it," recalled Comer. "The aircraft came to a lurching halt, with the nose of the plane resting about where I saw the two ladies sitting a few seconds earlier."[11]

Fortunately, both were unhurt, as was the English soldier who'd miraculously avoided being hit by the B-17's number four propeller. The only casualty was Comer's ball turret gunner, Harold Harkness, who'd been wounded by plexiglass which had shattered in his face when *Hellcat* had been struck by flak.

More remarkable was the safe return of Charles Ohl and his crew. Not only had they successfully completed the mission and landed without their pilot, but they'd also safely delivered the 381st's first combat crewman to survive his 25-mission tour-of-duty. The crew's bombardier, George "Pappy" Heinz, who'd nursed his wounded pilot all the way back from Gelsenkirchen, had beaten seemingly insurmountable odds.

Charles Ohl would also win his battle. Despite being critically wounded, he underwent an operation that saved his life.

"There I saw one of the greatest examples of courage that I had ever witnessed," noted James Good Brown, after the surgery. "Captain Ohl looked up from his bed and said, 'I will conquer this. I still have my head.'"[12]

* * *

After a day's break, the 381st was called back into action, this time as part of a streamlined 1st BD. Acting as the entire division, the 1st CBW was tasked with bombing the German city of Wesel, 20 miles east of the Dutch border. Fifty-nine B-17s were loaded with 125 tons of high explosives and incendiaries, which were to be delivered on the town's marshaling yards.

Navigator David McCarthy had missed the group's two previous missions, while his crewmates hadn't. They were now stood down for the Wesel mission, while he wasn't. McCarthy would have to fly as part of another crew.

"Our crew was a team," he noted. "We worked, played, flew and fought together; without them, I felt naked and abandoned."[13]

Taking off at 0820, the 381st met the rest of the 1st CBW over Ely. The formation then crossed the North Sea above a "swelling, turbulent" cloud base, which rose to 24,000 feet. Fortunately, it kept the *Luftwaffe* at bay, but also adversely affected the mission. The *Oboe* blind-bombing device fitted to the lead PFF B-17 failed and the ordnance was left widely scattered. Nevertheless, no flak and fighters meant a milk run. When the group returned to Ridgewell just after 1300, it was in much more orderly shape than 48 hours earlier.

"The sense of relief that everyone feels when the ships come back, flying a good formation, and with none of them peeling off or shooting flares, is notable," wrote flight surgeon Ernest Gaillard. "It is a release to the anxious tension that we all feel when the ships are out on another mission."[14]

* * *

Bad weather persisted for the next few days, which further frustrated the crews. "The ground where there was no pavement became a sea of mud," wrote David McCarthy. "The footpath between our barracks and the flying crews' mess hall was a quagmire that loaded our boots with pounds of mud. We truly earned our rations …"[15]

The conditions stymied any VIII BC operations until November 11, when the crews finally awoke to a "beautiful morning." Briefed at 0620 and airborne by 0920, 17 of them headed for the same target they'd visited four days earlier, Wesel. Yet, as their B-17s neared the Dutch coast, towering clouds up to 29,000 feet meant they would have to climb another 2,000 feet to bomb. A recall was ordered, and the crews returned to Ridgewell with two cases of anoxia, one of frostbite, no mission credited, and "plenty of disappointment."

Two days later, the crews were briefed for yet another raid on Bremen and its port areas. The 1st CBW was due to meet over Ridgewell at 9,000 feet. Members of the medical detachment, including Ernest Gaillard, were invited to join the group's operations officer, Maj. Conway Hall, in a spare B-17 to observe the wing's assembly.

"Cloud cover was up to 20,000 feet. Went up without oxygen," noted Gaillard. "There were three masks for the five of us, and at 17,500 feet, [one passenger] decided to pass out."

From then on, the occupants were forced to exchange oxygen masks, including Major Hall, who was piloting the bomber. When Hall's ears "got good and blue," Gaillard would pass the mask back to him. When they were "pink," Gaillard would take it back.

"The whole trip was a monument to our own stupidity," noted Gaillard. "We were dressed for 9,000 feet, or zero weather, and it was -22 [degrees] Centigrade at 20,000 feet."[16]

The Bremen mission was finally abandoned and the 381st's B-17s began groping their way back down to Ridgewell.

"These recalls are harder on the crewmen than a stiff mission," wrote the 535th's diarist. "Officers and men alike are never more bitter than after flying several hours at altitude and sub-zero temperatures."[17]

* * *

A numbing journey was in store for the crews on November 16, when 21 of them were briefed for a 1,050-mile round trip to attack a molybdenum processing plant at Knaben in Norway.

Responsible for supplying its entire output to Germany, the mine's steel-strengthening mineral was being quarried under the watchful eyes of occupying forces, who'd fortified its surroundings with numerous flak guns. Knaben was deemed the "most important economic industrial target in Norway."[18]

As part of a formation of 189 bombers, the 381st flew in the high position of the 1st CBW, which climbed to 19,000 feet to clear the overcast. Just before reaching the Norwegian coastline, the formation then descended to 15,000 feet for its attack. This was expected to clear the barrage balloons strung across the approach.

"[The mine was] very hard to find," wrote navigator Cornelius Donovan, who was flying his 17th mission. "We circled all over Norway, searching for the target before finding it."[19]

"The target area was possibly one of the best nature-camouflaged targets yet encountered," noted the 1st CBW's lead bombardier, Capt. Harvey H. Wallace. "Snow covered the rocky mountains and the fjords were so numerous that landmarks for pilotage points were few."[20]

On approach to the target, the 532nd's lead B-17, *The Joker* almost dropped more than its payload. Pilot William J. Baltrusaitis's ball turret gunner SSgt. Wallace B. McGaughey spun his turret to the rear of the B-17, but as he did so its door flew open and blew off. The gunner was left suspended. Struggling against the wind and without a safety belt, the fortunate McGaughey clambered back inside. He was flying his 25th mission.

Two bomb runs were carried out—the second being made after a very steep 360-degree turn to avoid losing the target. All 22 of the 381st's B-17s then dropped their bombs, although it wasn't easy to determine if they'd found their target. Another hapless gunner, Sergeant Clarence T. Williams, flying in the 535th's *The Hellion* attempted to take a look out of his waist window, only to instantly freeze his face. Fortunately, his frostbite wasn't serious.

The group's B-17s landed at Ridgewell after a seven-and-a-half-hour flight. For the second consecutive mission, they'd returned without any major casualties. No fewer than 12 men had also finished their tours of duty, including Wallace McGaughey.

"The crews at the interrogation were all in good spirits," noted Ernest Gaillard. So, too, was Charles Ohl, who was recovering in hospital after the Gelsenkirchen raid. One mission short of his tour, he'd learned that he would be "allowed his 25th" after records revealed he'd taken part in an aborted raid that was now credited.[21]

* * *

Chaplain James Good Brown was surprised at how quickly the 381st had become a "seasoned group." No longer did the same tensions hang over the briefing room as they had done in June. The replacements had more confidence and could see more chance of survival. Yet, he was also aware they were a "strange crowd … strangers to each other."

> Only a few of our original fliers remain, those whom we call "veterans." It is hard to grasp the fact that in just five months the original 381st Group of our flying personnel are almost gone. It is a lonely feeling. Something is missing. We came to Ridgewell Aerodrome as a "family," both the flying personnel and the ground echelon. We knew each other. Now I look around in the briefing room and in the airmen's mess and see only a few of the original men.[22]

It was also true of the group's aircraft. Very few of the original B-17s remained. On November 21, several new B-17Gs were transferred in from Deenethorpe, home of the new 401st BG. Among them was one of four assigned to the 532nd BS.

Serial number 42-37786 hadn't been given a name. Its new ground crew chief was highly superstitious and believed it was better off without one. He'd inscribed his first B-17 with a name, number of fighters destroyed, and bombing missions, but it was shot down on its eleventh raid. Strangely, the same fate had then befallen his next B-17.

"Enter the *Hit Paraders*, my crew," remembered replacement engineer and top turret gunner Sgt. Alfred F. Suchy, whose crew was assigned the new B-17. "He refused to add our name … the number of planes destroyed, or number of missions as we flew them … he said it was bad luck …"[23]

One replacement crewman with renewed confidence was navigator David McCarthy, who'd returned from a 48-hour pass in London. He'd purchased some "calf-high, cowhide boots." On his return to Ridgewell, he was showing them off in the officers' club when the 533rd's commanding officer George Shackley walked past. Shackley informed McCarthy his boots were not regulation.

"He studied the boots for a few seconds and then commanded, 'Don't wear them on missions'," recalled McCarthy. "I asked, 'Why not?' and his answer was, 'Because when you get shot down, they are mine'."

With his "trademark grin" and a slap on the shoulder, Shackley walked away. The boots now represented new optimism for McCarthy's survival.

"Without that hope and confidence, I would have drunk the five pounds away, and not invested it in a pair of boots for Major Shackley to inherit."[24]

* * *

After a nine-day stand down, during which time several missions to Bremen were planned and scrubbed, the men of the 381st were given their first taste of home. Thanksgiving was celebrated in Ridgewell's mess halls on November 25, complete with evenly spaced candles, linen tablecloths and waiters. New replacement Robert L. Singleton was quick to report back to his wife, Norma.

"Our dinner was really swell … a real Thanksgiving feed … we had turkey, mashed potatoes, filling, peas and corn, cranberry sauce, celery, pickles, parker house rolls, coffee, cake, fruit and candy … it really was super, no kiddin'!"[25]

For more established airmen, however, the meal was met with melancholy. "It was with a lonely heart that each of us greeted this holiday," wrote David McCarthy. "We were alone in a foreign land and we pictured, in our minds, past holidays spent surrounded by our families."

The next morning, McCarthy and 300 others were scheduled to take part in the group's 45th mission. He was "excited" as he tucked into his eggs and bacon at breakfast. "The last several days had been a real source of irritation for us," he wrote. "Being grounded was nerve-racking and disastrous to our morale."[26]

Nevertheless, as the map was unveiled at the briefing, he saw a long line stretching towards Bremen—the "City of Hell"—over which his tail gunner, Steve Klinger, had been killed six weeks earlier. McCarthy's only thought was one of "impending doom."

Captain Robert O. Fricks was also questioning his own mortality. One of the group's few remaining original pilots, Fricks was embarking on his 25th and final mission. Chaplain James Good Brown was alone with him in the briefing room as he changed into flying gear.

> A few minutes before, he [Fricks] was fooling around with the men in fun and jest. He was saying to them that he knew he would go down and that all the fellows were hoping he would go down so that they could divide up his personal belongings ... but when we were in this room alone he said: "'I'm more nervous now over this 25th trip than I was over any other since the first. I feel terrible."[27]

Fricks was one of 29 pilots taking part in the mission, which would see the group join in with the "biggest show put on by the Eighth Air Force to date."[28] However, a protracted climb up through 19,000 feet of solid cloud cover saw VIII BC's three divisions emerge widely scattered over Lincolnshire. The 381st's *Hellcat* had burnt too much fuel reaching the altitude, so its pilot, Paul Gleichauf, elected to abort the mission for fear of not having enough for his return. Four more 381st B-17s followed.

Our Mom successfully assembled into formation and flew on across the North Sea. However, as it neared the IP, the ball turret gunner, SSgt. John A. West, informed the crew that his turret was "locked." One of the waist gunners said he would help him out, but several minutes later West called again. Silence from the waist led the bombardier, Edward Klein, to investigate. He found both waist gunners and the radio operator unconscious—their oxygen hoses having been accidentally unhooked.

Fortunately, Klein was able to revive one, who helped revive the others, but with no functioning ball turret and several incapacitated and frostbitten gunners, the pilot, Robert Miller, turned back for England. As he dropped from the formation, he was spotted by two German fighter pilots who gave chase. Luckily, Miller was able to dive into the undercast before making good his escape.

"We were home; but were we?" wrote navigator David McCarthy. "As we attempted to cross the [English] coastline, the anti-aircraft guns protecting the coast fired four rounds at us and we turned back to sea."

After making a 360-degree turn, *Our Mom* tried again but was fired at a second time. Eventually, a P-47 appeared and escorted the B-17 to RAF Waterbeach in Cambridgeshire, where the gunners were evacuated for medical treatment. Miller subsequently discovered that his Identification Friend or Foe (IFF) antenna had broken off after the bombs had been salvoed.

The 381st's remaining 23 B-17s dropped their bombs through clouds using the flares of a PFF aircraft. Largely unscathed, they then returned to Ridgewell—Robert Fricks's *Four Aces, Pat Hand* among them.

"His plane touched down safely and a great sigh of relief came from us," noted James Good Brown. "In the interrogation room, men crowded around Fricks. What a glorious moment!"[29]

Robert Fricks had become the fourth officer to complete 25 missions, and the fourteenth 381st man overall. Yet, as Chaplain Brown noted after six months in combat, "there is not one whole crew that came through intact."[30]

One crew thought to be missing over Germany was Robert Miller's. After his gunners had been treated at Waterbeach, Miller flew *Our Mom* back to Ridgewell, landing long after the others had returned from Bremen. There was a shock in store when his crew arrived at their barracks.

"Our belongings, including my brand-new boots, were gone," recalled David McCarthy. "When we pulled out of formation and dove into the clouds with two German fighters on our tail, the crews that witnessed our dive assumed we had been shot down and reported our loss during their briefing … Fortunately, Major Shackley did not get my boots."[31]

* * *

The bad weather continued to plague the 381st, so much so that, by the middle of November, its B-17s had taken off eight times only to return to Ridgewell without having bombed. By the end of the month, airborne cancellations reached double figures.

On November 29, the group took off bound for Bremen once more. This time, though, the clouds topped 29,000 feet forcing the B-17s to return to Ridgewell. It was a similar story the next day, when 22 B-17s took off to attack an aircraft engine factory in the German city of Solingen. Halfway across the North Sea, cloud cover intervened yet again.

Solingen came back into VIII BC's sights on December 1, when it tasked several of its combat bombardment wings with attacking the city's industrial areas. At the same time, the 381st BG and 1st CBW (minus the 351st, which had now been reassigned to the 92nd CBW) would target Leverkusen, 10 miles further south.

Replacement waist gunner Sergeant Carlton A. Josephson from New Britain, Connecticut, was woken at 0430 to fly the mission. The evening before, he and his fellow gunners had taken themselves off to *The Fox* pub in nearby Tilbury Juxta

Clare—their favorite hangout and one that was managed by "Big Bill," a "big Limey with a handlebar moustache." During the course of the evening, the pub's black cat had jumped onto the shoulders of the crew's tail gunner, Sgt. John F. Healy, sparking some nervousness.

"Known as a bad luck omen, we mentioned this to Big Bill," remembered Josephson. "In England this was just the opposite. It was a sign of good luck. We all felt better after he said this."[32]

Carlton Josephson quickly dressed for his seventh mission and headed to the mess hall, where, to his consternation, he was served powdered eggs. "Usually, it was a breakfast of fresh eggs whenever we had a mission," he said. "We were robbed."[33]

Arriving at his bomber—a newly assigned B-17G, *Mission Belle*—Josephson set about preparing his guns in darkness. Only when his pilot, Flight Officer Harland V. Sunde, arrived at the aircraft was he made aware of their destination. "It was in the Ruhr Valley," noted Josephson. "Better known as 'Happy Valley'."[34]

The group's 25 bombers began taking off just after 0800 led by Major Kunkel, whose own B-17 soon developed mechanical problems. While the 381st was still forming up over Ridgewell, Kunkel landed and swiftly transferred to a spare. He then took off again to lead the formation to the target.

Carlton Josephson's *Mission Belle* had also developed a technical problem when its flaps failed to retract after take-off. Crossing the coast at Cromer, the pilot Harland Sunde considered aborting, but Josephson managed to manually crank the flaps into position. *Mission Belle* and the rest of the 381st continued southeast carried by a 90-knot tailwind. Bypassing Leverkusen, they then approached the target from the opposite direction.

Just as the formation neared the IP, flak struck *Mission Belle*'s number three engine, which Sunde was unable to feather. The aircraft began falling back. He then told his crew to prepare to bail out.

While doing so, several of them unhooked their oxygen masks, but Sunde told them to hold their positions. Carlton Josephson almost passed out, but was saved by his waist gunner, Charles Culver, who also revived the ball turret gunner, Doyle McCutchen.

Having salvoed the bombs, bombardier 2nd Lt. O. D. Tully was still awaiting the bail-out command. "After getting out of the flak, German fighters swarmed us," he recalled. "We knew we were in for a long day."

Mission Belle came under attack, which wounded both Josephson and McCutchen. Sunde then immediately dropped some 6,000 feet in order to find cloud cover—just about making it before two Fw 190s whistled in.

"The look inside the ship—it looked as though a cyclone had hit," remembered engineer and top turret gunner Claudio "Steve" Carano. "Parachute bags were strewn about everywhere, ammunition boxes and belts were all over the ship, the odor of burnt powder and flesh prevailed in every corner …"

After hiding in clouds for 40 minutes, *Mission Belle* then broke out into clear skies just above Aachen, close to the border with Belgium and the Netherlands. Almost immediately, the city's flak guns erupted, bombarding the aircraft with fragments until it resembled a sieve.

"It sounded like a kid running a stick along a corrugated tin building," remembered Carano. "Holes appeared in all parts of the ship … everyone in the waist had been hit by flak."

Down to almost tree-top height, the B-17 was again picked up by German fighters, which proceeded to attack—even flying as close as 25 feet when the pilots realized the radio operator's gun was the only one still functioning. Wounded in the cockpit, Harland Sunde continued to fly towards the Dutch coast, still "five minutes" away.

The crew's nominated first aid officer, O. D. Tully had moved through the aircraft to treat those who'd been wounded. As he was pulling John Healy from his tail gun position, an Fw 190 attacked, striking Healy with 20mm shells. Although Tully was left with a "bloody, gory sight" in his lap, he wasn't hit.

As *Mission Belle* flew low over the Rhine, Sunde came on the intercom to give his crew three choices—they could either bail-out, crash-land or ditch. Although the crew favored bailing out, the B-17 was unable to climb. Sunde's only choice was to ditch the ailing bomber.

"There was no warning, no expecting it, no nothing," remembered Steve Carano. "Just an impact that pinned me to the bulkhead, a terribly loud noise, two lurches then silence. The water was knee-high before I realized that we had crashed."

The surviving crew members began trying to make their escape from the sinking bomber but were only able to inflate one life raft. With five in the dinghy, O. D. Tully; his pilot, Harland Sunde; and waist gunners, Doyle McCutchen and Charles Culver found themselves in the water. *Mission Belle* then sank nose-first, its tail snapping off and slamming back down on the water. Unfortunately, McCutchen was beneath it and was killed. The others were swept away by the fast-flowing current.

Only Tully and Culver would survive, both being rescued by Dutch civilians. Sunde drowned, while Healy, who'd questioned the luck of a black cat in *The Fox* the evening before, had "died at his guns."[35]

* * *

At the time *Mission Belle* was struck by flak, another 535th B-17 had also been hit. *Bacta-Th'-Sac*, the group's first B-17 with a chin turret, had its number three engine disabled. It, too, then slipped from the formation before being pounced on by fighters, which succeeded in damaging another engine.

Fighting the bomber's tendency to "nose up," while also vying with a frozen windshield and exploding oxygen bottles, pilot 2nd Lt. Warren C. Hess headed for the clouds. However, the reprieve was only temporary. After emerging a short while later, two Me 109s intercepted *Bacta-Th'-Sac*, pouring cannon fire into it and wounding several crew members, including tail gunner SSgt. Edgar G. Delp. Somehow, all 10 men bailed out before the bomber crashed near the Belgian city of Huy.

Warren Hess and seven of his crew were rounded up by the Germans, while two others—the bombardier, 2nd Lt. Robert F. Wernersbach, and co-pilot, 2nd Lt. Charles L. Smith—began their escapes. Wernersbach would subsequently make it back to England the following May, while Smith was captured by the Germans in Belgium (although he would later be freed by British troops). Of those taken POW, tail gunner Edgar Delp died as a result of his wounds, the only member of Hess's crew to lose their life.

Another 535th B-17 fell from the formation, when *Four Aces, Pat Hand*, flown by 2nd Lt. Donald E. Noxon, was struck by flak. Having dropped his bombs over the target, Noxon's aircraft was seen to turn "slightly away" from the lead position with its bomb bay doors still open. *Four Aces, Pat Hand*, which had been so named because of the last four digits of its serial number (42-31111), then disappeared into the clouds, seemingly under control.

Nothing was heard from Donald Noxon and his crew, which included 2nd Lt. George E. Giovannini—Harland Sunde's usual co-pilot. *Four Aces, Pat Hand* was later thought to have crashed in the North Sea with the loss of all 10 men, most of whom had just returned from a rest home.

Another 381st B-17 disappeared from the formation, but only as it neared the French coast. *Full Boost!*, a B-17F with the 532nd BS, had been flying "rather erratically" on the way to the target according to other crews. Pilot 2nd Lt. Jason H. Duncan appeared to be banking and "not in formation" before the bombs were dropped. The aircraft was then hit by flak, causing a momentary fire which was soon extinguished. Dropping from the formation, it stayed on course but gradually lost altitude. It was then seen to "turn about" and head back towards Germany.

Full Boost! was attacked by an Me 109, which succeeded in killing six of its crew. Four others managed to bail out, including Duncan, before the B-17 exploded in mid-air over the French commune of Steenvoorde. It was less than 30 miles from the English Channel.

Struggling back across the Channel was an unnamed B-17G (42-39808) belonging to the 534th BS. It had been damaged by flak and was short of fuel when its pilot, 1st Lt. Harold H. Hytinen, spotted an airfield at Allhallows, Kent. Crash-landing, Hytinen sustained a fractured skull, while his co-pilot, 2nd Lt. William R. Cronin, suffered a broken nose and their navigator, 2nd Lt. Richard I. Maustead, fractured ribs. The four-mission bomber was salvaged, but never flew again.

The 534th's David McCarthy, who'd been stood down for the mission, was apprehensive, having learnt where his fellow crews had been sent. During the afternoon, he walked to the flight line to wait for the group's return.

"That period of time, that waiting, was interminable," he recalled. "Finally, 15 minutes after the ETA [Estimated Time of Arrival], the planes were approaching the base. Aloud, we started counting them as they came into sight." McCarthy was saddened to learn five were missing, three from the 535th alone.[36]

"We live in a fool's paradise," wrote James Good Brown in his diary. "We build up the false notion that our losses in combat will diminish … why can we not accept the hard reality that we are in a war? I guess it is as simple as this: We do not like war."[37]

CHAPTER 10

Snow and Skis

December 2–31, 1943

Except for a single foray over Knaben's snow-covered molybdenum plant during November, the 381st had been targeting Germany for two months. Since October, the group had also lost almost 100 men—40 on the Leverkusen mission alone. Yet, some of them were still evading capture, while several others had returned to Ridgewell.

Captain Robert Nelson and SSgt. Raymond Genz had arrived back at their old base at the beginning of November. Members of Jack Painter's *King Malfunction II* crew, both had successfully escaped and evaded capture after being shot down on the first Schweinfurt raid. It was an astonishing achievement by two men who were thought to be the first Americans to successfully return to England after bailing out over Germany.[1]

On December 2, Nelson and Genz, alongside several other 381st evaders, lectured the group's combat crews on escape and evasion techniques. While some details were kept secret, the resourceful airmen spoke candidly about the psychological and physical traumas involved.

"I am interested to see the reaction of the fliers," noted James Good Brown. "They cling to the accounts like men to a life raft ... when they see in person one of their buddies who bailed out, then made his way to safety and home, it gives them hope."[2]

Several days earlier, SSgt. Joseph Walters had also returned to Ridgewell. A member of Loren Disbrow's crew, whose *Chug-A-Lug Lulu* had also been shot down on the first Schweinfurt raid, Walters had made his escape from Belgium. Moving by foot, bicycle and train, he'd ended up walking across the Pyrenees into Spain. Along the way, he'd picked up several souvenirs, including "a fez and a bunch of bananas."

A few days after Walters's arrival, his fellow 535th crew member and the group's first evadee Edwin Myers departed for the US. Like George Heinz's 25-mission achievement a month earlier, it was a celebratory moment for the 381st.

Among other lectures, the replacement crews also received one from the group's surgeon, Ernest Gaillard, who'd noticed their deficient levels of equipment. "It seems rather futile to lecture these groups about what they should have and then not be able to supply it," he noted. Still, it gave him an opportunity to discuss the "mental mechanisms, the development of fear reaction [and] operational exhaustion."[3]

Gaillard's lecture was also followed by another on the source of "Piccadilly flak,"[4] which he noted was delivered by "three rather decrepit, ancient meatballs." The interrogation of the group's "wayward personnel" by elderly nursing staff was a source of amusement for Gaillard. "What an odd way for three nice, old ladies to make a living," he wrote.[5]

Unfortunately, the nurses' lecture was a timely one. The previous evening, a 533rd BS ground crewman who'd contracted gonorrhea and was being treated at the US Army's 121st Station Hospital in nearby Braintree, died from the disease. His body was among the first to be buried at the newly opened American cemetery at Madingley, near Cambridge.

* * *

John Comer was upset when he found himself assigned to a new crew for the group's 47th mission on December 5. Climbing into the truck to go to the aircraft, he was even less happy with the gunners' "conversational drivel."

"We got us a new boy flyin' navigator today," exclaimed one. "Our navigator's got the clap—on that last pass to London."[6]

When the truck arrived at *Hellcat*, the crew chief informed Comer that the aircraft had a technical problem and wouldn't be flying. After being forced to wait for another truck, the airmen were eventually delivered to a spare B-17. The delay saw them take off 20 minutes behind the rest of the group.

As John Comer's despondency increased, his officers were rather pleased. Unknown to the gunners, the pilots had been briefed to attack the *Luftwaffe* airfield at Paris–Ivry. Although any target in France was never easy, it wasn't German. The most important factor, however, was that the bombers would be escorted by newly arrived North American Aviation P-51 Mustangs. It would be their first opportunity to provide support. As Comer's pilot briefed the crew on the intercom, the gunners cheered the good news.

"The secret had been well kept from the bomber crews," recalled Comer. "With those beauties, my prospects looked far brighter."[7]

Unfortunately, the weather wasn't so bright over Paris. All 216 B-17s of the 1st BD found their targets solidly cloud-covered. Prohibited from dropping any bombs on obscured areas in occupied Europe, the 381st headed back to Ridgewell. Despite the lack of flak and fighter attacks, the mission was still credited.

"There were light hearts in all the fliers when they stepped out of their planes and touched the solid earth of England," wrote James Good Brown. "It was a special day for one … and he didn't hesitate to relate this fact to the men."[8]

A day before his 20th birthday, the 381st's youngest-ever pilot, 1st Lt. Donald J. Rutan had flown his 25th and final mission. Instead of peeling off to land, Rutan made straight for the center of the field at near-ground level, before screaming over the control tower. Rutan's was one of Ridgewell's first "buzz" jobs.

* * *

A brief period of calm descended on Ridgewell following the Paris–Ivry raid. Weather conditions thwarted missions, allowing the combat crews a break. James Good Brown began planning a Christmas program, complete with a "Festival of Music." It saw him scour the local villages looking for suitable female voices to join his chorus. The ploy worked, as a steady flow of local women arrived at the base for rehearsals. The chaplain soon shelved the idea, however, when different groups of men joined each night.

The poor weather kept the 381st grounded for almost a week, but it didn't prevent the *Luftwaffe* from making an appearance in the skies over Essex on December 10. At 1915, the base Tannoy wailed into life warning of an approaching air raid. A number of the airmen were watching a Red Cross show when several explosions interrupted the entertainment. They spilled out into the darkness to see parachute flares descending in the distance. Anti-aircraft guns were also firing close by. Ridgewell's lights were quickly turned off, but it was clear the raiders were searching for it.

"This was one time that bombing in this vicinity was a little too close for comfort," wrote 381st surgeon Ernest Gaillard.[9]

The German raid had missed Ridgewell but found another military target seven miles away. A new USAAF airfield being constructed by the US Army's 833rd Engineer Aviation Battalion at Gosfield was bombed and strafed by several German aircraft, leaving four servicemen dead and 15 others wounded. Explosives were also dropped around the vicinity, many falling on farms and in fields. Fortunately, the civilian population was unharmed. It was a taste of what the 381st and other Allied bomber units were meting out on a round-the-clock basis.

The following morning, 300 men were woken for the group's 48th mission—a raid on Emden's industrial areas, 300 miles across the North Sea. The crews were met by thick clouds and wet snow as they made their way to the bombers. It gave many of them an uneasy feeling, especially John Comer, who squinted through the murk as *Hellcat* began its long climb. "I know how many green pilots are taking off this morning all over England," remarked one of Comer's crewmates. "That's what bothers me the most in this stuff."[10]

Despite a near miss with a "dark blob," which turned out to be a black cloud, *Hellcat* emerged into bright sunshine at 9,000 feet. Again, though, the long climb up had delayed assembly, with squadrons once again scattered across the sky. A strong headwind then slowed the formation down.

By the time it arrived over the target, an estimated 400 fighters were waiting. The 3rd BD's seven groups were hardest hit, with 14 B-17s lost, while the 1st BD largely avoided the flak and fighters to deliver almost 600 tons of bombs.

One B-17 that couldn't drop its load was *Hellcat*. Three of its bombs were still hanging from the racks, including a thousand-pounder, which was lodged beneath two swaying 500lb bombs. As the flight engineer, it was usually John Comer's task to free any errant bombs, yet they were in such awkward positions that he couldn't gain access without the help of another crew member. Balanced on the narrow catwalk 15,000 feet above the North Sea, Comer and his bombardier, John Purus, managed to release the bombs. However, the B-17, pushed by a strong tail wind, was almost at the English coastline when the first of the smaller bombs dropped, splashing perilously close to a British seaplane base.

When the 381st arrived back at Ridgewell, Daniel Hagarty of the 534th BS was biding his time. Ignoring the group's usual landing circuit, he let *The Green Hornet* swoop in towards the center of the field. He then buzzed the tower, half-rolled and returned for a second attempt, quickly followed by another. His navigator, David McCarthy, watched the tower fill the plexiglass nose for a third time before it fast-disappeared underneath. He also saw an angry Conway Hall waving a flare gun at the passing B-17. For McCarthy, the end of Hagarty's 25th "was the most exciting event of the entire mission."[11]

* * *

Although the frequency of men finishing their tours increased, none of the 533rd's combat crew members had reached their 25th missions. "A psychic wall was slowly developing in the minds of those who were getting close to the magic number," wrote John Comer.[12] He was one of them—just six short himself—when he was woken to fly to Germany on the morning of December 13.

Led by four PFF B-17s from the 482nd, the 381st and four other 1st BD groups began taking off at 0900 destined for Bremen's port areas. Another 14 groups were attacking Kiel's submarine yards, while fighter support was being provided by eight groups of P-38s, P-47s and P-51s. Despite delays in assembly and heavy, but inaccurate, flak over the cloud-covered target, 171 of the 1st BD's 182 bombers dropped successfully. All 30 of the 381st's B-17s returned to Ridgewell intact, although 11 had been damaged.

On landing, six of the 533rd's crew members had finally "broken the jinx." "It could be done!" thought Comer. Later that evening, the local pubs were filled with the squadron's crews celebrating the news that some of their number had survived. "There was now little doubt in my mind," wrote Comer, "that I would soon join the selected band."[13]

The next day, Comer and his crew were assigned for an air–sea rescue mission over the North Sea. Their eight-hour task proved fruitless, leaving most of the crew "half-sick." Unlike their fellow combat crews, however, they'd not been stunned by the mission briefing at 0230 that morning.

"When the men enter the room, they immediately look up to see … who is flying and in what position," wrote James Good Brown. "Then the screen is rolled up … with the red cord leading from Ridgewell, Essex, England, to the place of the mission. This day it was Berlin. BERLIN!"

It was the first time the combat crews had seen the name pinpointed on the map. Brown was sitting next to a 533rd pilot who was flying his 25th mission. "He was grave, said hardly a word, and had no smile," recalled Brown.[14]

Images of the target were then projected, showing the Mean Point of Impact (MPI) as Berlin's Air Ministry building—a headquarters that housed some 4,000 people. When the 381st's intelligence officer outlined the route's main flak areas, he announced there were reported to be some 200 guns in Berlin. This drew another groan from the crews. His briefing was followed by that of the weatherman, radio officer, and, finally, Joe Nazzaro. When the briefing was over and the men began filing out, one of them turned to James Good Brown. "Keep on your knees all the time today," he said.[15]

A short while later, just as the crews were waiting in their B-17s for the "engines start" flare, the mission was scrubbed. John Comer heard cheering echo across the field.

* * *

Yet again, the British weather was blamed for another cancellation. As the combat crews trudged back from their bombers, the 381st's ground and medical officers added insult to injury by carrying out an inspection of their Nissen huts. With winter taking hold, the thin, corrugated walls would soon provide little defense against the plummeting temperatures. Many of the huts were found to be in a "deplorable" condition. "They were dirty, crowded, inadequately blacked out, damp [and] inadequately heated," wrote Ernest Gaillard.[16]

Each hut was equipped with a Tortoise stove[17] and its occupants rationed with a daily supply of coal—usually on a first-come, first-served basis. Compared to civilians in the surrounding villages, who had to make do with four hundredweight (200 kg) of coal each month, the airmen were better off. Still, many had resorted to chopping down trees, including Comer and his crewmates, who'd stumbled across an abandoned crosscut saw and immediately put it to good use. The green wood often failed to burn though, leaving the airmen damp and cold.

"Many of them spend a great deal of their time as scavengers looking for fuel," noted Gaillard. "Just the other night … [two pilots] were seen running at full speed across a [ploughed] field with a sack of coal (dubbed 'midnight requisitioning'), and an Englishman close behind them."[18]

Gaillard also noted how some of the officers had been "sleeping in their flying clothing in order to keep warm," while other "ingenious members" had discovered that shoe polish was a "good substitute for kindling wood." "Praise the Lord and pass the shoe polish!" joked Gaillard. Yet, he was keenly aware that it was "mandatory for the physical efficiency and morale that [the combat crews'] lot be bettered."[19]

Two days after the scrubbed Berlin mission, the 381st marked a milestone by celebrating its 50th with a second consecutive raid on Bremen. Thirty-one B-17s took off at 0845, led by a PFF B-17 flown by one of the 533rd's crews. The aircraft's navigator Cornelius Donovan found himself "cramped in the nose" surrounded by "secret navigational equipment" and a "radio man."[20] Nevertheless, his B-17 was able to release "brilliant flares" over the primary target, while the rest of the 381st followed to drop approximately 113,000lb of bombs and incendiaries.

The only difficulty during the mission was encountered on the return to Ridgewell, which saw the group's B-17s individually descend through a solid undercast to land beneath an extremely low ceiling. "It was interesting, but dangerous," remarked one crew member.[21]

On December 18, 2nd Lt. Thomas Sellers travelled to the Eighth Air Force's *Widewing* headquarters at Bushy Park in southwest London. He was there to receive the DSC for his actions on October 8, when he'd flown the badly damaged *Tinker Toy* back to Ridgewell after his pilot, William Minerich, had been killed during a fighter attack.

Sellers received the award from Ira Eaker; as did Brig. Gen. Robert Williams, commander of the 1st BD, who was awarded his DSC for leading the first Schweinfurt raid. Lieutenant John C. Morgan of the 92nd BG was also there to receive the Medal of Honor. His pilot had also suffered a head wound on a mission in July, which had caused him to grapple with Morgan for control of the aircraft. Morgan had managed to keep formation, bomb and return to England. At the ceremony, Eaker instructed Morgan to "fly no more combat." Morgan refused. Within months, he'd been shot down and was a POW.

Thomas Sellers's former B-17, *Tinker Toy*, continued to belie its jinx reputation. On December 20, it was assigned for the group's 51st mission—a revisit to Bremen and its heavily-targeted shipyards. *Tinker Toy* was one of 28 B-17s scheduled to fly with the 381st, which would form five percent of the total force of VIII BC bombers. Nine combat wings were taking part, with the 1st CBW expected to be third in line on the bomb run.

At 0815, the 381st's bombers began lifting off from Ridgewell into a beautiful sunrise. John Comer's unnamed B-17G reached 120mph and began a shallow climb, flying straight ahead for two minutes before banking left to begin a slow orbit of the base. The bombing altitude was 29,000 feet and the temperature was expected to be 60 degrees below. "It turned out to be the coldest temperature I have ever had to endure," recalled Comer.[22]

An hour after take-off, Comer and his crewmates donned their oxygen masks. Another hour later and the 1st CBW had assembled into the 1st BD and was heading out across the North Sea. Comer's bombardier suggested a more regular check of the oxygen supply, which turned out to be fortunate.

Fifteen minutes into Germany, a check failed to raise a response from the tail gunner, SSgt. Walter A. Wisneski. Armed with a portable oxygen bottle, the waist gunner, SSgt. James D. Counce, went to investigate. He found Wisneski unconscious and began reviving him. Counce's own oxygen then failed and he slumped over the tail gunner. The other waist gunner, SSgt. Mitchell J. LaBuda, was ordered to investigate, when he, too, passed out. With three unconscious men in the tail, Comer was ordered to the back of the aircraft.

As soon as began making his way, his oxygen bottle instantly failed. He quickly realized it was the demand regulator freezing. A simple tap with a screwdriver cleared it. Comer grabbed several more bottles and moved towards the tail. "I kept telling myself, 'You must not make any mistakes—if you do some people are going to die.'"

When Comer arrived, he quickly revived LaBuda, who then assisted him with the other two. "Both of their faces were as black as coal," Comer recalled. Successfully reviving Counce, he and LaBuda then dragged Wisneski out of the tail position where they could work on him. "There was no doubt in my mind that the tail gunner was dead."

Comer made every effort to revive him, even increasing the oxygen flow rate, running the risk of serious injury. Then, with a sudden twitch of his leg, Wisneski began to revive. Comer was mentally congratulating himself, when Wisneski—a wild look on his face—drew back his arm and punched Comer squarely in the face, knocking his head against the fuselage and momentarily incapacitating him. Fortunately, Counce came to Comer's aid, before they helped a fully revived Wisneski back to his guns.[23]

As the formation approached Bremen, the crews could see that, despite being briefed to bomb through solid cloud cover, the city was entirely clear. It was also patently obvious that it wasn't clear of flak. Comer's aircraft bounced around as he began moving back to his top turret. Just as he was traversing the ball turret, the gunner rotated it. Comer lost his footing, plus the two oxygen bottles he was carrying. As he hit the floor, the bottles struck him on the head. "Two knockout blows in ten minutes," recalled Comer.[24]

A few minutes into the bomb run, the 381st's lead B-17, *Big Time Operator*, was set to drop its bombs. Bombardier Thomas J. Hester was adjusting the Norden bombsight when he was struck in the forehead by a piece of flak. Hester was immediately slammed back into the navigator, but somehow had the strength to make his way back to the bombsight and drop his bombs. Fortunately, the plexiglass had slowed the fragment just enough to save Hester's life.

After dropping its bombs, *Tinker Toy* was attacked by several German fighters, one of which rammed the B-17's tail. Locked together, the two aircraft immediately fell from the formation and spun end-over-end before exploding a few seconds later. Comer hadn't seen it, but he was told by his navigator that *Tinker Toy* had "got it."

"Some of the men heard Lord Haw Haw predict that they would shoot down *Tinker Toy*," remembered Comer, who often wondered if the German pilots had "some special vendetta" against it.[25]

Another 381st B-17, *The Rebel*, was also being targeted by several fighters. Three minutes after *Tinker Toy* exploded, *The Rebel* dropped from the formation and was attacked before eventually catching fire. Its pilot, 1st Lt. Waldo B. Crosson, gave the bail out order, but in the process of jumping, his co-pilot, James R. Opitz, was struck in the neck by cannon fire. A 14-year-old German schoolboy near Finna, 12 miles northwest of Bremen, had seen *The Rebel* approach at low altitude chased by the fighters. He saw a man drop from the B-17, who then crashed through some trees before striking the ground headfirst. His parachute remained unopened. It was James Opitz, who had only been flying the mission as a replacement for Crosson's usual co-pilot.

At about the same time, one of the 381st's newly assigned B-17s was also hit by fighters from behind. It was the first mission for *Great Profile*, which had also been the first B-17G to be manufactured.[26] Piloted by 1st Lt. Bernard F. Hollenkamp, the aircraft was on fire, its tail framework clearly visible to other crews. As the officers began bailing out, Hollenkamp wrestled with the controls. Everyone from the radio room back had been killed in the attack. Just ten minutes after the bomb run had begun, *Great Profile* crashed into a marsh at Stapeler Moor, 45 miles northwest of Bremen. Bernard Hollenkamp was later found dead in the wreckage.

As the 381st's remaining 25 bombers flew northwest, 15 of them had been damaged by a combination of flak and fighter attacks. *Whale Tail II* had had its port elevator almost completely shot away, while much its tail had been badly damaged by flak. Still, it flew on under the control of 2nd Lt. Leo Canelake, making a dog leg at 1245 to turn southwest towards England. Fifty minutes later, other crews watched as Canelake dropped from the formation. "Due to his normally erratic formation flying, I paid no attention," said Richard J. Niederriter, who was flying alongside.[27] *Whale Tail II* was last seen making a 180-degree turn close to the water. It was not seen again.

The group's third consecutive Bremen mission had been one of its worst. In addition to the 40 men who were now classified as missing in action, one returning crewman had died as a result of anoxia. Several others had also been wounded by flak.

Whodat – The Dingbat! had suffered the loss of one engine and its undercarriage had been damaged. As it approached Ridgewell, its crew found the right landing gear wouldn't lower. Circling for the next 30 minutes trying to lower it proved unsuccessful. Eventually, the B-17 made a belly-landing, severely damaging its fuselage. Its crew, however, remained uninjured.

"Our ship, 'Tinker Toy' was lost over the target area," wrote base surgeon, Ernest Gaillard after the Bremen mission. "We all feel the loss a bit more keenly than would have been anticipated … [we] looked on it with mixed horror and affection."[28]

John Comer was equally struck by *Tinker Toy*'s loss. "Her end was as weird and spectacular as her reputation," he wrote. "A ship with such a bloody and storied record could not have had an ordinary ending like other airplanes."[29]

* * *

On December 22, Ira Eaker received new orders to command the Allied air forces in the Mediterranean Theater of Operations. He was soon replaced by Maj. Gen. (later Lt. Gen.) James "Jimmy" Doolittle, Medal of Honor recipient and aviation pioneer. At Ridgewell, Joe Nazzaro had also received new orders. After guiding the group through its activation and first six months of combat, he was destined for the United States Strategic Air Forces in Europe (USSTAF), which now fell under the command of Lt. Gen. Carl A. Spaatz.

That same day, VIII BC tasked its three divisions with attacking Osnabrück's marshaling yards. The 381st supplied 22 B-17s for the mission, which was designed to cripple the central railroad link between Germany and the Netherlands. At 0845, the aircraft began taking off into clear skies.

Once again, temperatures were extremely low, down to minus 46 degrees. It led to several system failures. John Comer's B-17, for example, lost its airspeed indicator due to a frozen pitot tube.[30] Others found their Bendix chin turrets inoperable, including one bombardier whose turret guns hadn't worked on four of his last five missions. Even Conway Hall, who was leading the group, suffered a heart-stopping moment when two of his engines suddenly died over the target. As soon as he mouthed the words "this is no time for playing games," both engines restarted.

Despite occasional probing by German fighters, the 381st reached the bomb run largely unopposed. Nineteen of the group's B-17s then delivered their 500lb bombs, although *Miss Abortion*'s bombardier, 2nd Lt. Jack. S. Glazier, found his aircraft's bomb bay doors were stuck and the bombs still hung up. As flak exploded around the formation, Glazier's engineer hand-cranked the doors open before the pilot flicked the salvo switch. Most bombs fell, but some were still stuck. For the second mission in a row, Glazier gingerly edged along the catwalk to release them. As he did so, one struck another on the way out, sending a jolt throughout the B-17. Fortunately, Glazier's "run of bad luck" was at an end, especially when *Miss Abortion* landed back at Ridgewell. Glazier had been on board *Whodat – The Dingbat!* when it crash-landed at the base two days earlier.

* * *

In early December, Temporary Air Marshal Sir Trafford Leigh-Mallory, commander-in-chief of the Allied Expeditionary Air Force had been authorized to begin attacking "ski sites," areas in the Pas-de-Calais region and on the Cherbourg peninsula that were thought to be concealing missile launch sites. Under the codename *Crossbow*, attacks had begun on the sites, using the codeword "Noball."

On Christmas Eve, VIII BC selected several "Noball" sites in the Pas-de-Calais region for its 164th mission. Over 700 heavy bombers—the largest number of aircraft for a single mission to date—were to make the first major strike against the "ski sites."

When the map was uncovered in the briefing room there were loud cheers. Images were then projected showing a small target area shrouded by trees, which included several buildings shaped like skis. The 381st was heading for Cocove on what was being dubbed the "rocket gun coast."

Two hours later, 26 B-17s began lifting off into a clear sky. Ernest Gaillard had chosen to observe the raid on his first combat mission.

"I was surprised at my experiencing no fear or apprehension at any time," he wrote. "The only reaction that I had was at the time we were receiving flak hits and I wondered just what in the hell I was doing up there instead of back down on the ground where I belonged."

Gaillard instinctively went to look out of the waist window at the flak but was "unceremoniously grabbed by the tail" and shoved down by the waist gunner.[31]

The concealment of the targets and the individual aiming points saw the group make several runs over the site. John Comer, flying his 23rd mission, was wincing at the flak barrage.

"Burst after burst exploded in the middle of the squadron," he recalled. "It was incredible that with so much accuracy and so many shells thrown at us, no direct hits were made."[32]

Fragments showered the B-17s as they passed high overhead. When the 381st's bombers had finally delivered their loads, they escaped back across the English Channel to Ridgewell. Once on the ground, Comer counted 55 flak holes in his B-17. Another had over 200. Fortunately, all 281 airmen, including Ernest Gaillard, were safe.

Chaplain James Good Brown was relieved that the mission had gone well. That evening, a Christmas Eve carol service was held, with the 381st's quartet providing the musical entertainment. As navigator David McCarthy observed, "the latent talent exhibited ... was another indication of the injustice of war. In another time and place, these men would have been stars of the musical stage."[33]

The fifth Christmas of World War II was the 381st's first. There was no mission planned because of poor weather conditions. At 0800, a short service was held at the base chapel and, for the rest of the day, the base loudspeaker system played Christmas carols. The airmen had been ordered not to use public transport so British soldiers could get home. Despite numerous invitations from local people to attend Christmas lunch at their homes, most of the men chose to attend the base feast.

On Boxing Day, the locals then got their chance to sample the delights of American ice cream. James Good Brown had planned a children's party for some time. "Here we are in their midst, yet they are not allowed on the base," he noted.[34]

Instead of the anticipated 250 children arriving at his chapel, though, almost 400 appeared. Squeezed into the building, the children were shown a movie before being given gifts, most of which had been donated by the airmen.

* * *

Bad weather persisted over Europe. On December 28, a mission to the "rocket gun coast" was scrubbed. For several days, VIII BC remained grounded, although its groups continued with their work. The 381st welcomed new crews, who were soon carrying out practice flights over England. The next day, 1st Lt. Bill B. Ridley took off in John Comer's former B-17F, *Nip and Tuck*, which had had its name changed to *Chug-a-lug*. Ridley's training flight was going well until, in poor visibility, he hit some trees in Wiltshire. The B-17 remained in the air, but severe vibrations caused him to force-land in a field at Maiden Bradley. Ridley and his crew were unhurt, but the aircraft was written off.

A day later, the crews awoke to clear skies. John Comer was keen to get back in the air with just two of his 25 missions remaining. Comer's pilot, Paul Gleichauf, was flying his 25th. Theirs was one of 28 crews scheduled to attack Ludwigshafen's port areas and oil refineries.

Taking off at 0800, the 381st was assembled into its formation 80 minutes later. Although many of the crews weren't aware, Joe Nazzaro was flying his final mission before taking up his new role as deputy director of USSTAF operations—one that would see him oversee the operations of both the Eighth and Fifteenth Air Forces. The mission was also being flown by a new member, Lt. Col. Harry P. Leber, Jr., who'd been transferred in as air executive. He was set to take over from Nazzaro after the mission.

Despite head-on fighter attacks near the target, all 28 of the 381st's B-17s dropped as planned. Turning back for England, no fewer than 13 men were praying their aircraft would make it. Paul Gleichauf was one. As he guided the B-17 across Le Havre and out over the English Channel, he became a happy man.

"[He] began to whoop and sing snatches of songs," recalled John Comer. "That was the only time I saw Paul Gleichauf act up in the cockpit of a B-17."[35]

On arrival back at Ridgewell, Gleichauf planned a ceremonial buzz. However, his wing man was sticking tightly to him. Unperturbed, Gleichauf dived to low level before screaming past the control tower, the other B-17 still alongside. "I imagine there were explosions of unprintable words in the control tower," noted John Comer.[36]

Amid the joy of Paul Gleichauf and several others who'd finished their tours, one of the 381st's B-17s arrived back with a dead crewman. Somewhere over the Channel, radio operator Curtis W. Hickman's oxygen supply had failed. By the time the crew noticed him slumped in his chair, it was too late. Despite attempts to revive him for almost an hour, Hickman was pronounced dead on arrival.

* * *

Twenty-six 381st crews were hoping their journey on New Year's Eve 1943 would end safely—and with a party at Ridgewell. First, they would have to negotiate a one-thousand-mile round-trip, avoid flak and fighters along the way, and successfully bomb Bordeaux's Merignac airfield.

At 0900, the B-17s left Ridgewell bound for their assembly area over Weymouth, Dorset. Once there, the 381st formed up with another three groups of the 1st BD. In total, VIII BC had dispatched almost 600 heavy bombers for an assault on several *Luftwaffe* airfields in southwestern France. The 381st's route to its primary target would take it south of Bordeaux, before swinging north for its attack. It was expected to be a long mission, taking over eight hours to complete.

At around 1230, the formation neared the IP when the *Luftwaffe* appeared—Fw 190s vectoring in towards the 381st's high squadron. One of the group's newest B-17Gs, which had been assigned just 11 days earlier, was struck by a hail of machine gun bullets. In the shattered nose, the bombardier, 2nd Lt. Harry M. Grimball, Jr., was hit in the legs and severely wounded. The navigator, 2nd Lt. Cornelius A. Heintz, Jr., had also been hit. Their B-17 fell behind the rest of the formation and its bombs were jettisoned. The pilot, 2nd Lt. Earl B. Duarte, then caught up with the formation, but with one engine windmilling and another smoking, he elected to turn right and head towards Spain.

With severe damage and wounded crew members, Duarte was soon left with no choice but to order his crew to bail-out. All 10 men jumped and the aircraft crashed on farmland close to the outskirts of Toulouse. Seven of the crew were quickly captured, but Duarte and his co-pilot, 2nd Lt. Glen A. McCabe, along with their engineer, Sgt. Russell N. Jevons, made their escape. The latter would subsequently be captured two months later, while both Duarte and McCabe made it back to England.

James Good Brown was concerned when the B-17s hadn't arrived back as scheduled. He called the tower to be told that the field was closed because of poor weather. One of the 381st's B-17s had landed on the south coast having run short of fuel over the Channel. The others were scattered all over the southeast of England. The eagerly awaited New Year's Eve party at the officers' club would have to wait.

Seven B-17s did manage to make it back, including one flown by the 535th's commanding officer, Capt. Frank Chapman. He'd just completed his 24th mission and wanted desperately to land at his own field. When James Good Brown caught up with him, he was struck by Chapman's demeanor.

"I saw that he did not smile with his usual ease," noted Brown. "The tension is there which comes to all men when they face the last one."

Chapman was certainly sweating out his last one, but he'd also asked to be relieved of the position of squadron commander. Brown was stunned. "The position was laid on his shoulders at 21 years of age because he was one of the few … who had not gone down in combat. But he knew he was not the type for the job."[37]

Intermission: Manning the Forts

One of the most impressive, and fascinating, aspects of the USAAF's experience in the ETO is, without doubt, the speed with which the Eighth Air Force grew from an inexperienced, fledgling force into what was arguably the most powerful air force of World War II.

The development of the "Mighty Eighth" is all the more remarkable when the demographics of the manpower that filled its ranks are considered. Unlike most of the other combatant nations, the US did not enter the war with a large, well-trained air force. Although the senior hierarchy that was to lead what would become the USAAF was made up of an experienced cadre of serious career airmen, the majority of those they would send into battle were civilians in uniform.

It is this initial huge gulf in experience and knowledge that makes the ultimate achievements of those that flew in the Eighth's 43 bomb groups even more remarkable.

The B-17 needed a crew of 10 men to take it into combat, and each crew had its own complex human chemistry. Every B-17 was, in itself, a "miniature America"—a diverse microcosm of the massive citizen army that the US was generating. Although voluntary enlistment had been scrapped in December 1942, the USAAF allowed draftees to apply for voluntary induction. This allowed the USAAF to cream off the most promising draftees to serve in its rapidly expanding force

The wartime memoirs of those who flew are consistent in their description of their crew composition. The men that manned the Forts were drawn from every level, and all corners, of American society. Factory workers, Hollywood actors, ranch hands, teachers, and musicians from every state in the union flew alongside each other—every man the product of an industrial scale training program that, over the 18 months between Pearl Harbor and the beginning of *Pointblank*, grew the USAAF from a strength of 345,000 men, to more than 2.1 million. A staggering increase of 520 percent.[1]

Forging a disparate group of 10 individuals into a cohesive and effective bomber crew was not a simple process—it took many weeks and months. Initially, each airman made their own way as an individual through enlistment, into basic military training, and onward to a successful application to fly. The flying training was structured around progression through a primary syllabus to an advanced one, and then conversion to a specific bomber type. Interestingly, all crew members other than the pilots underwent gunnery training. Having successfully completed this training, and having received their "silver wings," it was time to report for the first phase of B-17 training—time to join a combat crew.

The officers in the aircrew—the would-be pilots, co-pilots, navigators, and bombardiers—were products of the Aviation Cadet Recruiting Program. The entry age for this program was lowered from 20 to 18 in January 1942. The remainder of a crew—the flight engineer, radio operator, and gunners were sergeants or enlisted men—many in their late teens. The average age of a typical bomber crew was 21.

CHAPTER 11

The 25

January 1–11, 1944

In late 1943, a report into the 381st's combat failures by flight surgeon Ernest Gaillard found that 95 percent fell into one of four categories: fear reaction; loss of "functional systems" due to combat stress; psychoneuroses; and operational exhaustion. Gaillard concluded that those in the first two were invariably "lost to combat" ("when stress returns, the symptoms return"), while others could be treated with "narcosis" ("75% returned to combat"). A wide-ranging VIII BC report in January 1944 also found that between July 1, 1942, and December 31, 1943, a total of 13,868 casualties had been reported. It equated to just over four percent of the 335,450 airmen who'd been sent out on missions. The report also suggested that crews were more likely to become casualties in their first five missions, while only one in four of them would complete their allotted 25.[1]

One of the 381st's remaining original pilots, Frank Chapman, had seen too many others fail during the six months he'd been at Ridgewell. He was now sweating out his 25th and final raid. Chapman had been with the group since its days at Pyote, but, as the 535th's commander, the 21-year-old from Old Orchard, Maine, had been held back from combat missions to focus on the needs of his crews. By the early hours of January 4, his wait was almost over.

Another pilot eager to finish his tour was 1st Lt. Cecil M. Clore of Bargersville, Indiana. Having been assigned to the 532nd BS in August, Clore had taken two months less than Chapman to clock up his tally of 24. When Clore's men were woken for the 381st's 56th mission, each member had at least 20 to his name.

Briefed for an attack on Kiel's submarine yards, their next would see them climb to a bombing altitude of 26,000 feet while facing temperatures of -52 degrees centigrade. Cecil Clore was assigned a new B-17G, which had arrived at Ridgewell two weeks earlier, while Frank Chapman would be flying his eponymous *"Chap's" Flying Circus*—the ageing B-17F he'd flown across the North Atlantic in May 1943.

Clore's navigator, 1st Lt. Ralph J. Waldman, was also flying his final mission. He'd become firm friends with fellow navigator and New Yorker, David McCarthy.

Both men had spent the previous evening together in the officers' club. Full of excitement, Waldman had talked about the "stuffed, toy donkey" he'd carried as a talisman. It had been given to him by his wife just before he'd left the US. She'd also issued strict instructions that he should carry it with him on every mission. However, he was confident he no longer needed it—McCarthy needed it more than him. As Waldman readied himself for the raid on Kiel, he grabbed the toy from his equipment bag and turned to McCarthy.

> With a big grin on his face, Ralph handed the donkey to me. I looked the animal over and then handed it back to Ralph, with a bit of advice: "You keep him until we get back. Don't break the team up now. I'll use his charm for my last fifteen missions ..." My buddy insisted that I keep the donkey, and suddenly we both became embarrassed. Here we were, two grown men, arguing over the ownership of a toy donkey that belonged in a very young child's nursery.[2]

McCarthy accepted the toy, although he harbored superstitions of his own. "I had to be the first to enter the plane through the nose hatch," he wrote. "Before we took off, I always entered the cockpit, stood between the pilot and co-pilot until we were safely airborne, and then I put an arm around their necks and hugged them." Just before 0800, his *Our Mom* began lifting off from Ridgewell. This time, however, he was unable to perform his ritual.

A "mighty explosion" ahead of another B-17 taking off in front of McCarthy's caused his pilot, Robert Miller, to bank sharply to avoid "flaming, scorched earth." With no sign of wreckage as they passed overhead, the crew quickly deduced that a preceding B-17 must have suffered a "malfunction in the bomb bay." One of McCarthy's waist gunners then spotted a low-flying B-17 heading back towards Ridgewell with one engine on fire. Before he could say any more, the aircraft struck some trees, spun into the ground and exploded. McCarthy's stunned crew could do no more than continue on to Kiel.[3]

* * *

It was Cecil Clore's B-17 that had crashed. By the time Ridgewell's ambulances reached the scene, they were too late. Only the tail of the bomber was recognizable, stood tall among the trees, surrounded by wreckage and flames. Strewn around were five bodies. The medical crews recovered them and took them to the base hospital, less than a mile away.

"When the accident occurred, I was called immediately to go to the hospital," wrote James Good Brown. "It was not known then if the men would be brought back to the hospital alive. I went there and saw the bodies of five of my men, torn and broken and cut and slashed."

Brown then went to the crash site with the medics to help retrieve the other bodies still trapped among the wreckage.

"Everything was massed together—a black mess," he wrote. "We saw what looked like a body … a leg was gotten hold of—the rest of the body must be there. We pulled. We tugged … with our hands, we had to pull aside the burned material."

Eventually, the remains of all five were recovered, but they'd been burnt beyond recognition. Despite the awfulness of the group's first major flying accident, Brown tried to remain calm as he took to his diary.

> How do I feel about all of this? I hardly know what to say. I did not get sick as did one of the officers who went back in the ambulance. Neither did I get angry. My men who go through this hellish war do not get angry. I had no feeling of glory, as a soldier of war, thinking that these men died in great glory. How could I think that when war is inglorious? These men were burned alive—burned alive! This can hardly be glorious.[4]

* * *

The group's 25 B-17s continued on to Kiel, led by Conway Hall in *Pistol Packin' Mama*. They joined over 500 other bombers, while being escorted by 70 P-38s and 40 P-51s. Just after turning on the IP, the 381st's B-17s were met by flak and a "few German fighters," which, according to David McCarthy in *Our Mom*, began firing "early and recklessly," but were too far away to cause any serious damage.[5]

Although John Comer had been stood down from the mission, his usual B-17, *Hellcat*, was being flown by another crew. Approaching the target, its navigator's parachute suddenly burst open and "blossomed" in the nose of the aircraft. After gathering it up, the bombardier, 2nd Lt. Adam A. Mackow, returned to his bomb sight to drop the bombs. He then turned his attention to repacking his friend's parachute—a hand-numbing task that took two hours to complete.

After the 381st turned off the bomb run, *The Lucky Strike* was also left with a problem. An early B-17F manufactured by Boeing, it hadn't been fitted with factory-mounted Tokyo tanks.[6] Instead, *The Lucky Strike* was carrying a bomb bay fuel tank for the mission. At bombs-away, one of the bombs was left hung up. In an attempt to dislodge it, the fuel tank was accidentally released, taking with it some 400 gallons of precious fuel. *The Lucky Strike* still had three-and-a-half hours of flying time ahead of it.

Although enemy fighters were kept at bay by a handful of P-38s and P-51s, flak damaged several of the 381st's B-17s, including *Our Mom*.

"An 88mm shell exploded directly in front of us," wrote David McCarthy. "The nose of our Fort had become opaque, and an 18-inch hole … provided the only visibility." For the next few hours, McCarthy and his bombardier, Edward Klein faced a "bitterly cold … 150mph wind."[7]

Faced with a struggle of his own was the 535th's 2nd Lt. Rowland H. Evans, pilot of *The Lucky Strike*, who ordered his crew to jettison anything they could find in order to conserve fuel. Descending over the North Sea, ice had formed on his windshield, completely cloaking it and the cockpit instruments. By the time the B-17 reached the Norfolk coast, its fuel was almost gone, although the ice wasn't. Evans had to crane his neck in order to see where he could land.

Approaching the village of Cawston, 12 miles inland, two attempts were made to line up with a field. Evans then bellied the bomber in, the B-17 stopping after smashing into a ditch and spinning round. When the dust had settled, the bombardier, 2nd Lt. Irving Kraut, and the ball turret gunner, Sgt. Julius E. Rivera, lay dead. Both had suffered fractured skulls. Two others were injured.

The 381st's remaining bombers landed back at Ridgewell—among them, Frank Chapman's *"Chap's" Flying Circus* and David McCarthy's *Our Mom*.

"That was when I discovered that my friend, Ralph Waldman, had died," McCarthy recalled. "Why did it happen to him? Why didn't Ralph keep his damned donkey today?" McCarthy vowed it would be his companion until he finished his tour. "Superstition, born of fear, should never be denied."[8]

Chaplain Brown cycled to the airfield to look for Frank Chapman—"the one man who finished his 25th mission." Brown found "*"Chap's" Flying Circus* standing silently in its place." He then saw one of the crewmen who told him that Chapman had missed the interrogation and gone straight to his barracks. Brown found Chapman "lying flat on his back on his bed looking up at the ceiling."

> As soon as I got inside the room, I stretched out flat on the bed on the opposite side of the room and lay there staring at the ceiling ... Then I looked over at Chapman and smiled, without a word. He smiled back, without a word. That look from him was worth more than any word he could have spoken. He was happy; it showed in his face.[9]

* * *

John Comer had been stuck on number 24 since the Ludwigshafen raid, during which time he'd developed a neck ache. A visit to the flight surgeon had seen him prescribed with pills that went into the "first trash can" he passed. "My problem was nerves," he later recalled. "The only pill that would help me was one more mission."[10]

Comer had lain awake most of the night on January 5, when his hut door finally swung open and someone shouted, "Alright, we gotcha a good one." With the day dawning clear and cold at 0500, his final mission was finally on.

Together with its 1st CBW companion, the 91st, the 381st was set to attack a *Luftwaffe* airfield near the French city of Tours. The 91st, which had given the Eighth Air Force one of the first bombers to complete 25 missions (*Memphis Belle*), was about to become the first bomb group to reach a century of missions.[11]

John Comer had flown 31 missions, including several that had been scrubbed, as well as air–sea rescue duties. He would now fly his "official" 25th in *Doll Baby*, with pilot 2nd Lt. Leven B. Ferrin, who was also flying his last mission. When Ferrin told his gunners their destination was "80 miles southwest of Paris" with "fighter escort in and out," they all whooped and cheered.[12]

The formation of 79 B-17s, which included those from the 351st and 401st BGs, took off at 0845 and overflew London before leaving the south coast at Selsey Bill.

"The run going in was without incident," remembered John Comer. "Believe me, no other crew on that mission was so alert and ready for trouble …"[13]

None materialized, and by the time the bombers arrived over Parçay-Meslay at 20,000 feet, their target was clear. Almost 200 tons of high explosives then burst across the airfield, with some 381st crews claiming that "less than two buildings were left standing."

Shortly after the formation turned north, 10 German fighters appeared, one of which fired a rocket at 2nd Lt. Jack R. Zeman's B-17F, *Baby Dumpling*. It struck one of the engines, which immediately began smoking. The aircraft, having also been raked by cannon fire, then left the formation, seemingly under control. Zeman, however, had been left "semi-conscious" by the "terrific explosion." His co-pilot, 2nd Lt. Otis A. Montgomery, managed to drag him from his seat and gave him a parachute. The dazed pilot then "crawled past the turret into the bomb bay" and "just fell out."[14]

Zeman's bombardier, 2nd Lt. William C. Walker, was scrambling to find his own parachute. The navigator, 2nd Lt. Frank R. Bisagna, quickly found a spare and handed it to Walker before going back to open the forward escape hatch.

"Then I passed out from lack of oxygen," Bisagna noted. "My chute had had the cords cut by the shells fired at us and it opened by itself. I woke up floating down."[15]

Bisagna was quickly taken prisoner, along with five of his crewmates. Three others managed to make their escape; including a badly injured Jack Zeman, who'd hit the ground unconscious. All three would eventually return to Ridgewell. However, navigator William Walker—who'd seemingly been unable to open his parachute in time—was killed.

John Comer was angry at the Germans after they twice attempted to slip in undetected. With smoke hanging over the bombed airfield still visible from 60 miles away, Spitfires then arrived to "criss-cross" below the B-17s as they escorted them back to England.

"A little later the sunlight reflecting on the Channel began to sparkle in the distance," wrote Comer. "I watched the coast slide by below with mixed feelings. When it faded into the haze I knew for sure it was all over."

After *Doll Baby* landed, Comer went to the interrogation before returning to the bomber to clean and stow his turret guns. He wouldn't be flying the next mission, but someone else might.

> On the perimeter track to the personnel site, I suddenly realized that I felt different. What was it? Then it dawned on me that the [neck] pains were gone. Just like that. It took an hour

> and a half after the mission for my ragged nerves to return to normal ... The celebration that night lasted until two a.m., and when the pubs closed it resumed at the hut. I was through![16]

* * *

Not only had the Tours mission signaled the end for John Comer, but it also marked the start of a new beginning for the Eighth Air Force. The following day, Lt. Gen. Ira Eaker was transferred to the Mediterranean to take command of Allied air operations there; while Lt. Gen. Carl Spaatz returned to England to take up his post as Joe Nazzaro's new commander. The reshuffle was complete with the arrival of "Tokyo Raider," Jimmy Doolittle, who, soon to sport a third star on his epaulettes, took over the reins of VIII BC—which was now redesignated "Eighth Air Force."

The command changes were far from the minds of the men of the 532nd BS as they assembled at Ridgewell's chapel in the afternoon of January 6. They were there to catch a truck to the new military cemetery at Madingley, near Cambridge. Their destination was its "first row" of graves, which had been freshly dug in preparation for the burials of Cecil Clore and his crew.

"The tragedy was more acute because I had picked up the bodies with my own hands," wrote James Good Brown. "And now I saw them, each one in his own casket. They were lying there before me, and I knew it."

Brown was presiding over a ceremony that also included another 14 men from other bases who'd been killed in action.

"Those 24 caskets did not make a pleasant sight ... there were more to be buried ... they were not buried today because there was not enough manpower to dig graves."

The 42-man entourage from Ridgewell observed Brown's 30-minute service, which was followed by a three-volley salute and a rendition of *Taps*. Before long, they were on their way back to Ridgewell, with most of them, including James Good Brown, deep in thought.

> Coming home in the truck, I watched those fliers. They were doing some thinking. There was no jesting in the 30-mile drive between Cambridge and Ridgewell. One of the men was doing a lot of talking. All the way home he talked of these men. I sat and listened as the truck bounced along the English roads. I had said all I wanted to say at the 24 flag-draped caskets stretched out before me.[17]

Brown had been feeling increasingly guilty that he was "not flying" with his men. "Here I sit on the base telling them that they, the fliers, must go into combat," he wrote. "By what right should they be fighting my war?" Several times he'd "begged" for Nazzaro's permission and each time he'd been answered with a "flat no." But Nazzaro was gone. Brown would have to turn his powers of persuasion on the 381st's new commander, Harry Leber.[18]

* * *

Having flown his first mission on Christmas Eve, replacement 535th BS navigator 2nd Lt. Theodore "Ted" Homdrom was woken at 0400 on January 7 for his second. The Minnesota native had first trained as a tank commander with the 5th Armored Division, but while on maneuvers in the Californian desert he'd seen Douglas A-20 Havocs flying at low level in support of the tanks. "I thought at least they [the crews] were out of all of this dust," he wrote. "Consequently, I obtained a [USAAC] form and applied."[19]

After his first mission, Homdrom had quickly deduced that being served "two fresh eggs" for breakfast meant "danger." It was with some trepidation, then, that he was given the same, before being briefed for the 381st's 58th mission.

The group's target was the German chemical conglomerate, IG Farben and its sprawling Ludwigshafen plant. Thirty B-17s, including one PFF bomber would make up a main group, plus a composite one with the 91st BG. Taking off at 0745, they began climbing to an altitude of 28,000 feet, before joining 190 others from the 1st BD.

For the second time, Ted Homdrom found himself flying with an experienced crew, including veteran pilot, Inman Jobe. Their brand-new B-17G had also just been assigned to the group, having been given to the 535th BS two days earlier. It would eventually be painted with bright-white letters spelling the name, *ASSEND*.

As he had done on his first mission, Homdrom quietly breathed "Lord, I am in your hands" as his B-17 took off. It would be a saying he used on every mission. He would also routinely carry the New Testament in his pocket.[20]

Several others were flying their final missions, including Capt. Marvin Lord, one of the originals, who was leading the composite group. Two of his crew—ball turret gunner SSgt. Kenneth Stone and right waist gunner Charles E. H. Fry—were also finishing their tours. Both were happy to know that a combination of P-38s, P-47s, P-51s and RAF Spitfires would be escorting them to Germany.

Onboard veteran B-17F *Winsome Winn – Hilda* (so-named after the wife of pilot 1st Lt. Arden D. Wilson) was replacement radio operator SSgt. Peter Kucher. He'd taken the position of Wilson's usual crew member, Richard H. Nisbet, who'd been wounded on the Tours mission.

Just after dropping its bombs, Wilson's aircraft was seen to be smoking from its number one engine. It flew on with the formation for five minutes before slowly dropping back. *Winsome Winn – Hilda* was then last seen heading for cloud cover 10,000 feet below, chased by several German fighters.

Before reaching the clouds, the B-17 was "riddled by shellfire," during which time Peter Kucher was killed. The tail gunner, SSgt. Anthony E. Greco, continued to shout evasive instructions to Arden Wilson, while egging the German fighters to "come on in and get it." They continued to damage the bomber, leaving Wilson no option but to order his crew to bail out. All did, bar Peter Kucher. The bomber then exploded 500 feet from the ground.

Landing between Ludwigshafen and Saarbrücken, the surviving crew members were quickly rounded up by German troops. When Arden Wilson was shoved into a truck, he found a body inside with "USAAF coveralls, boots and blue heating suit." The face was covered so he was unable to identify the man. Whoever it was had been shot.

It later transpired the body was Anthony Greco's. The Germans informed some of the crew that his parachute had failed to open. Bombardier Harry H. Ullom was convinced Greco's chute opened and that he was "killed by German soldiers or civilians … while attempting evasion."[21]

The rest of the 381st's bombers arrived back over Ridgewell, including Marvin Lord's *Big Time Operator II*. Lord—who'd never aborted any of his 25 missions—approached the airfield before buzzing it three times. He'd finished his tour—as had his two gunners, Kenneth Stone and Charles Fry. Both received 48-hour passes to London.

"I feel wonderful now and thank God for his careful guidance throughout my 25 combat missions in the European Theater of Operations," wrote Ken Stone.[22]

* * *

On January 8, Maj. Charles L. Halsey became the 535th Bomb Squadron's commanding officer following the departure of Frank Chapman. A day later, Harry Leber was officially sworn in as the group's commander. His predecessor, Joe Nazzaro, had one more duty to attend to before leaving the 381st for good. He pinned a DFC on the chest of John Comer, who studied the decoration carefully. It was awarded to those who'd completed 25 missions.

"I pondered why my luck had held up and tried to recall the faces of those I knew well who failed," he wrote.[23]

The next day, as Comer prepared to leave Ridgewell, several familiar faces returned. As the result of an agreement between the American and Swedish governments, all US servicemen who'd been interned in Sweden were being released for repatriation. Having spent 170 days in a house in the Swedish town of Falun, the crew of *Georgia Rebel*, including pilot Osce Jones and co-pilot George McIntosh, were reassigned to the 535th BS at Ridgewell. They found a host of new faces, among them 2nd Lt. John W. Howland who'd been assigned to their squadron two weeks earlier.

Howland had been raised in Port Chester, New York, after his family moved from Casper, Wyoming, in 1927. Like a great many young Americans, he'd enlisted in the USAAF after the Japanese attack on Pearl Harbor. His ambition to become a pilot, however, was thwarted early on when it was found he was too short. Instead, he'd trained as a navigator.

Arriving at Ridgewell in late-December with his pilot, 2nd Lt. James L. Tyson, and crew, Howland was allocated the same Nissen hut as another 535th navigator, Ted Homdrom. Both men were woken at 0400 on January 11—Homdrom for his third mission and Howland for his first.

"Briefing started at 0500 hours and a large groan went up when the curtain covering the chart was removed," wrote Howland. "We were able to see how far into Germany we were headed … the small town of Oschersleben, about [100] miles southwest of Berlin."[24]

James Good Brown was present for the briefing but noticed a difference in the group. "I believe that all of the men who [were flying] to Oschersleben this day were new men in the group," he remarked. "Thus, it is not easy for a chaplain to become acquainted overnight with these replacements. It takes time."[25]

The crews' target was a fighter assembly plant in Oschersleben. Thirty-three B-17s began taking off from Ridgewell at 0800. They were being led by another familiar face, Capt. Arthur Briggs, who'd been reinstated for duty by the 381st's medical officers.

"He [Briggs] expressed the opinion that the battle on the ground between missions was much more hazardous to the mental processes than during the mission," Ernest Gaillard noted. "That would seem to be borne out by our observations."[26]

Two of John Comer's former crewmates were also flying the mission. Radio operator George M. Balmore and waist gunner James Counce were both placed with different crews. Comer said his goodbyes at their bombers before leaving Ridgewell to return to the US.

"I had to hurry to get my bags ready for the truck that was to take us to the nearby station," he wrote. "Just before the train arrived, I looked up as I heard a formation overhead."[27] It was the 381st heading to Germany.

* * *

After forming up with the 91st into the 1st CBW, the group departed the Suffolk coast at Lowestoft.

"I was very tense and couldn't concentrate on navigation as I normally would," remembered John Howland. "My mind just wouldn't do what I wanted it to do."

Encountering a mechanical problem, Howland's pilot, Inman Jobe then called for a "heading home." Surprised by the call, Howland gave Jobe the wrong heading.

"I went back to navigating and discovered that my 245-degree course was going to take us right over Amsterdam."[28]

Fortunately, Howland corrected his error. Jobe then feathered one of his propellers before quickly diving away into cloud cover.

Meteorologists had predicted clear weather over Germany for the mission. However, conditions across Europe were deteriorating and the escorting P-47s and P-51s were unable to locate the bombers. Weather was also worsening over England, meaning many of the groups would struggle to land on their return. The decision was taken to recall the mission. However, only the 2nd BD and 3rd BD received it. The 1st BD continued on to both Oschersleben and its other target, Halberstadt, completely unescorted and oblivious.

As the formation crossed the Dutch coast, flak opened up, immediately striking John Comer's former B-17G, *Hellcat.* With its number three engine on fire, the pilot, 2nd Lt. Donald E. Nasen, gave the bail-out order. Several of the crew managed to jump before the aircraft plunged into the Zuiderzee. Only one man—waist gunner Sgt. John R. Lantz—survived his time in the water. Lantz was eventually rescued by Dutch fishermen. His nine crewmates, however, were all declared dead or KIA.[29]

As the formation proceeded across the Netherlands, the *Luftwaffe* appeared. An estimated 175 fighters began attacking with increasing ferocity—mainly focusing on the 533rd BS, which was flying as the high squadron.

Yankee Eagle, under the command of 2nd Lt. Wilfred R. Perot, soon collided with an Fw 190, which sheared off the B-17's port wing, causing it to explode. The right waist gunner, SSgt. Edwin B. Bosley, was blown out but managed to parachute to safety. He was the crew's only survivor and was soon captured by the Germans.

Yankee Eagle was quickly followed by another 533rd B-17F, *Fertile Myrtle,* which was hit by cannon fire and eventually crashed near Osnabruck. Its pilot, 2nd Lt. Matthew J. McEvoy, and his crew survived, only to be captured.

Big Time Operator II, which had brought Marvin Lord's crew safely back to Ridgewell four days earlier, was also struck by cannon fire, disabling several engines. It then broke apart—its navigator, Louis H. Gill, suddenly finding himself "alone in mid-air." Seven others also managed to escape the disintegrating bomber. Two, however, had already been killed. Ball turret gunner Stanley A. Wright and John Comer's close friend James Counce were both killed before the aircraft crashed close to the town of Minden.

Almost at the same time as *Big Time Operator II* was lost, two more of the 533rd's B-17Gs also went down. Struck by flak, which caused it to drop from the formation, the unnamed B-17G of 1st Lt. Gordon W. Crozier was then attacked by fighters. Slumped dead inside its radio room was John Comer's other friend, George Balmore. He'd been killed by cannon fire. His nine crewmates managed to bail out before the B-17 crashed near Paderborn.

Doll Baby, under the command of 1st Lt. Billy F. Chason, was also struck by fighters, which ignited a fire in its number one engine. Chason managed to extinguish it, but his number three was also hit, forcing it out of the formation. All 10 men bailed out to become POWs.

Originally flying as a spare, *Betty Lou* was also being targeted by fighters when one of them exploded close by. The fighter's flaming engine smashed through the B-17's fuselage, breaking it in two—the ball turret spinning off with its gunner, TSgt. Harold F. Prestwood, still inside. Only two of its crew—waist gunners Bernard M. Keene and L. T. Patterson—managed to parachute to safety. Eight others were killed when *Betty Lou* crashed in a forest six miles from Oschersleben. Keene and Patterson later learned through a Lord Haw Haw propaganda broadcast that Prestwood's ball turret had been found "buried six feet in the ground" with him still inside.[30]

Just as the formation turned on the bomb run, a combination of flak and fighters conspired to bring down the 534th's *Green Hornet*. All but the right waist gunner, SSgt. Ross N. Defenbaugh, survived and were captured. Defenbaugh was killed when the aircraft crashed southwest of Oschersleben. Those captured included SSgt. John Crawbuck, who'd been awarded a Silver Star and Purple Heart for his actions on the group's 42nd mission in November 1943.

Bombardier 2nd Lt. William R. Farrell, flying in the 532nd Bomb Squadron's *Friday the 13th*, had been hit in the leg by fragments of a 20mm shell and was blown out of his stool on the bomb run, but he still had the strength to return to his bombsight before dropping the aircraft's load. He then "knocked down" a fighter using the B-17's turret guns, treated his wounded navigator, Flight Officer Benjamin N. Saporta, and returned to fire the nose guns until they were out of ammunition. Both Farrell and Saporta would subsequently be awarded Silver Stars and Purple Hearts for their gallantry.

After being led "off-course" across the "heavy flak installations" of the Ruhr Valley by the 91st, the 381st arrived back over England to find heavy cloud had closed in. Most of the group's bombers were forced to divert to Hardwick airfield in Norfolk. Of the 33 that had taken off from Ridgewell in the morning, only a handful returned. Eight of the group's B-17s had been lost, six from the 533rd BS alone. The only positives were the "destruction" of 28 enemy fighters—the group's biggest claim so far. Along with other groups in the 1st BD, the 381st would receive its second DUC, having flown to Oschersleben without fighter protection.

Back at Ridgewell, David McCarthy learned that his friend, Gordon Crozier, had been lost on the Oschersleben mission. He also learnt about the missed recall and the carnage that followed as a result—the crews looking on the disaster with incredulity.

"They simply could not believe that Command would abandon them to such brutal punishment so callously," he wrote. "Morale and faith in the High Command was lost."[31]

"This was the day the Eighth Air Force fouled up," wrote James Good Brown. "It was a blunder. But when our men saw the next day the reports in the papers which wrote up the Oschersleben raid as a great accomplishment, our men could but shake their heads in disgust … this was the second highest loss …"[32]

It wasn't until three days later that John Comer learnt about the 381st's Oschersleben disaster. He was met at Lancashire's Chorley replacement control depot by one of his former pilots, Leven Ferrin, who told him about the mission and the 533rd's catastrophic part in it. Comer then discovered his two best friends, George Balmore and James Counce, were both listed MIA.

> I turned away from Ferrin and stumbled blindly from the crowded bar. He followed and told me the meager details that were known. But I had quit listening. My mind was in shock. Right then I could not talk to anyone. The night was bitterly cold and it was raining. I walked blindly in the rain without cap or raincoat for a long time, because a man does not cry in front of other men.

CHAPTER 12

Ridgewell's Revenge

January 12–February 15, 1944

The 381st crews that landed at Hardwick after the Oschersleben raid were collected by truck and driven to Ridgewell later that evening. Among them was Ted Homdrom and crew. Not knowing that his hutmates had made it back to England, John Howland went to sleep feeling worried. When he awoke the next morning, he was glad to see them in their beds. Later in the day, he then heard the horrific details of their mission.

"There's no way we can win this air war or survive our missions if the Brass is going to screw up like that very often," he wrote.[1]

Heavy battle-damage and poor weather conditions kept the 381st grounded for the next nine days. Several missions were planned and scrubbed, while a number of new B-17s flew in to replace those recently lost. There were also changes in the group's ranks when the 534th's commander, Maj. David Kunkel was promoted to lieutenant colonel and transferred to the 381st headquarters as operations officer. His role was filled by the fully rejuvenated Arthur Briggs.

There was also some cheer in the air on January 17, when a bachelor party was held for the 381st's surgeon, Ernest Gaillard. The medical officer from Louisville, Kentucky, was to be married to local girl, Dorothy Nash. The next day, their party took off to the Savoy Hotel in London—the wedding ceremony itself taking place in the nearby chapel. The marriage, according to Gaillard, "exemplified the pinnacle of Anglo-American unity."[2]

* * *

John Howland had also been in London on a 48-hour pass. After bumping into "a few Piccadilly Commandos,"[3] he travelled back to Ridgewell to embark on a "cross country hop" with new pilot 2nd Lt. William A. Pluemer. However, on approach back to the airfield, they were ordered to divert elsewhere because of bad weather. Attempting to land at another airfield 50 miles away, they were then told to go back to Ridgewell.

"We were in a squadron of nine ships," remembered Howland. "We were number nine to land … just as we broke clear of the low hanging clouds, we were ordered to go around again and use an alternate runway."

Two B-17s had taxied into each other after landing on the main runway. Although the crews were uninjured, both B-17s were badly damaged, *Squat n' Droppit* slicing the tailfin off *Return Ticket*.

Making a third attempt to land on an alternate runway, Howland's pilot finally brought their B-17 in for a downwind[4] touchdown with 1,800 gallons of fuel and 6,000lb of unfused bombs. "It was quite a mess," wrote Howland. "It's almost safer to fly missions."[5]

Mission number 60 came the next day (January 21) when 36 B-17s took off from Ridgewell to attack two "Noball" sites in northern France. John Howland was stood down for the mission, but Ted Homdrom and his original crew, under the command of 2nd Lt. James R. Liddle, were woken to take part.

"This 'milk run' was welcome after the 'massacre' we went through on the 11th," Homdrom wrote. "We tried to locate rocket gun emplacements, but from about 12,000ft high, and hazy clouds below, we at first could not locate our briefed target."[6]

While Homdrom's squadron made five runs across the area, another circled over it 10 times. For a total of one hour and five minutes, the group overflew enemy territory without any threat of opposition. Although the mission was later described by the group's new commanding officer, Harry Leber, as a "bombardier's dream," several B-17s brought their bombs back to Ridgewell due to cloud cover. David McCarthy's *Our Mom* was one, but he was glad to have finished his "feared" 13th mission unscathed.

Just as the 381st returned from its brief visit to France, the RAF dispatched more than 800 aircraft to an assortment of destinations in Europe. Magdeburg was the main objective, with almost 650 aircraft taking part in the RAF's first major raid on the city. At the same time, over 100 Avro Lancasters and Short Stirlings followed up the Eighth's attacks on "Noball" targets by carrying out their own raids on the Pas-de-Calais rocket sites. However, it was a combination of the raid on Magdeburg and the re-appearance of the *Luftwaffe* that focused the 381st airmen's minds for the next 24 hours.

During the evening of January 21, parts of southeast England came under attack by German bombers. The raid—largely in retaliation for the "round-the-clock" bombing of Germany—was mainly focused on London. John Howland could clearly see "bomb flashes and the ack-ack down to the south" from his hut at Ridgewell.[7] A number of flares and incendiary bombs were also seen in the direction of the nearby village of Sible Hedingham, but no damage or injuries were reported.

That evening, the RAF lost a total of 58 aircraft—its highest loss of the war so far.[8] The following day, and with no missions planned by the Eighth, 12 B-17s took off from Ridgewell to scan the North Sea for downed RAF airmen. Navigator John Howland struggled to maintain his concentration given the task in hand.

"Many course changes were made as we flew the search pattern," he recalled. "When one of the crew members called attention to a floating object, navigation charts were put aside and I became just another observer."[9] The B-17s returned to Ridgewell later that evening having spotted nothing.

Howland was woken at 0345 the next morning for a raid on Frankfurt. It had been rumored the B-17s were being loaded with fragmentation bombs, and Howland had assumed the Continental invasion was "ready to get started." Instead, he found his B-17 loaded with scores of 100lb incendiaries. Howland's frustration was compounded when his taxiing B-17 suffered a flat tire. Transferring to a spare bomber (which hadn't been fueled), his crew eventually took off 90 minutes behind the group. By the time they arrived over the assembly area, the rest of the 381st was 6,000 feet above. Howland's pilot James Tyson "tacked onto a 'triangle B' group" (92nd) which was on its way from Podington airfield, Bedfordshire.

Over the English Channel, Howland's bombardier, Frank Palenik, test-fired the chin turret's nose guns. The mechanism ground to a halt. Without functioning forward-firing machine guns, Tyson took the decision to turn back inside the French coast. Just a few minutes later, however, the entire formation was recalled because of worsening weather conditions. Much to Howland's mounting irritation, the mission wasn't credited.[10]

* * *

The real Frankfurt raid came five days later, when 39 B-17s took off into darkness. The crews had been woken at 0330, before being briefed at 0600. "Our men did not welcome this mission when they saw it uncovered on the map," noted James Good Brown. "I saw the look on their faces."[11] Matters were made worse by a partial collapse of the perimeter track during taxiing, which delayed most of the B-17s.

The Eighth's 198th raid saw the 381st divided into two groups as part of an overall force of six wings, comprising 863 heavy bombers. The darkness didn't aid assembly. It caused squadrons, groups and wings to intermingle. John Howland's *"Chap's" Flying Circus* lost the 381st over Ridgewell, then found itself flying alongside the 92nd once again.

As the bombers climbed to their assigned bombing altitude, several of the 381st's B-17s aborted and turned back for Ridgewell. One was *Bermondsay Battler*, whose right waist gunner, SSgt. Thomas G. Lawrence, had begun experiencing crippling stomach pains. After 10 minutes in agony, his pilot, Henry Putek, rapidly descended to help the ailing gunner. Lawrence felt immediate relief, but Putek decided to head back to Ridgewell where he could receive proper medical attention. On arrival, Ernest Gaillard, the 381st's surgeon, found the gunner "happily farting, hiccoughing and belching his way all over [the] station."[12]

The rest of the 381st continued on towards Germany until it reached the IP, where flak opened up. Shortly after, the *Luftwaffe* appeared.

"We ran into about 15 or 20 Fw 190s in flights of two or four," recalled John Howland. "Four … lined up astern of us and shot some rockets at us; but they did no damage."[13]

Just behind Howland's aircraft, one of the 534th's newly assigned B-17Gs, flying its first mission, wasn't so fortunate. Hurtling in from the right, several German fighters riddled it with cannon fire. Second Lieutenant Robert W. Mohnacky's aircraft then fell from the sky. All those in the front of the aircraft were killed when it crashed near Koblenz. Those in the rear managed to bail out but were soon captured.

Another 534th B-17G, flying its third mission, was also hit, wounding several of its crew. The pilot, 1st Lt. Lawrence H. Mickow, immediately prepared to bail out. As he rose from his seat, he instructed his co-pilot, 2nd Lt. William H. Hennessey, to do the same. Hennessey, flying his first mission, was frozen to the controls and refused to move. Mickow shook him, but it was no use. Seconds later, the aircraft exploded, blowing Mickow out. Miraculously, he survived, along with four others. Hennessey and four enlisted men were killed.

As the 381st turned off the target, Harry Leber could see the "sky was black" and the formations behind had "caught hell."[14] Frankfurt itself was also suffering. Over 800 bombers were attacking the city, delivering almost 2,000 tons of high explosives and incendiaries. It was the first Eighth Air Force mission in which more than 700 aircraft bombed "effectively."

On arrival back at Ridgewell, Sgt. Raymond M. Castellano, a gunner on board *Honey*, was marveling at his flak jacket. Attacked by fighters over Frankfurt, he'd seen part of the aircraft's vertical stabilizer shot away and a hole torn in its fuselage. He'd then felt a "burning sensation" in his side and asked for medical assistance. The radio operator found a "deep graze," before pointing to Castellano's flak jacket. "There was a hole made by a 30-caliber bullet, and at the approximate position of my abdomen," recalled Castellano. "In no fewer words can I say, '[I lived] by my flak suit.'"[15] James Good Brown, though, could only lament the taking of more of his men. "Sad is the loss," he wrote in his diary. "The bell tolls again."[16]

The alarms wailed later that evening as the *Luftwaffe* overflew Ridgewell on yet another London raid. Several explosives were dropped on nearby farmland, but no one was injured. The 381st airmen also had no time for sleep. At 0345, they were roused for a second consecutive raid on Germany. An hour later, James Good Brown attended their briefing. He found himself sat next to 535th pilot, 1st Lt. Carl O. Baer.

"He was so tall," recalled Brown, "I had to look far into the air to see him … he was a big fellow, not fat, just big."

Baer struggled to find clothes that fitted him and constantly asked the chaplain for help. "I freeze every time I go into the air," he'd told Brown.[17] Baer had missed the group's last few missions having contracted influenza. The virus had kept him hospitalized for a month. On January 30, he was fully recovered and fit to fly *"Chap's" Flying Circus*, the 535th's last original B-17. Its namesake pilot, Frank Chapman, had now finished his tour of 25 missions, but the veteran bomber had exceeded that number thanks to other crews.

The 381st's 62nd mission marked a milestone for the Eighth, which was embarking on its 200th raid. Almost 800 heavy bombers were sent to attack Brunswick's aviation plants deep in the heart of Germany. Thirty-one of them began taking off from Ridgewell at 0820, including *"Chap's" Flying Circus*, which led an element of the 535th. Eighty minutes later, all of the 381st's B-17s were assembled into formation. They then set off on a meandering course around East Anglia, before overflying Lowestoft and out across the North Sea.

Shortly after leaving the Suffolk coast, John Howland's B-17 began losing oxygen pressure. It soon became apparent the dwindling supply wouldn't be sufficient for the time needed at altitude. Acting quickly, Howland's pilot, James Tyson, dropped his undercarriage and turned back for Ridgewell. It was the second 381st B-17 to abort the mission.

The bombers were being escorted by a combination of P-38s, P-47s and P-51s but, as they neared the target, flak began exploding and the *Luftwaffe* attacked. *Martha the II* was hit by an Fw 190 and slipped from the formation just after the target. Its pilot, 1st Lt. Henry D. Steele, salvoed everything in the bomb bay to lighten the load, but his B-17 began lagging behind.

The 535th's *Wolverine* also came under attack and was badly damaged. Its pilot, 2nd Lt. Robert P. Deering, found the bomber unflyable and ordered his crew to bail out. *Wolverine* promptly entered a spin and dropped from the formation. Few saw its last moments, but the aircraft was thought to have exploded in mid-air, its wreckage crashing in a street 20 miles southwest of Brunswick. Eight of the crew were later found dead, while two others—the co-pilot, Robert P. Williams, and the bombardier, Paul O. Crabtree—were both captured alive after being blown clear.

The 381st's gunners continued to fend off sporadic attacks by Me 109s as the group withdrew from the target and began the long flight back to Ridgewell. Still, thick contrails, haze and clouds made it difficult for them to distinguish friendly fighters from the enemy.

Badly damaged, *Martha the II* peeled away from the group and dropped 2,000 feet with its landing gear lowered. Although it appeared to be under control, it was going down. The co-pilot, 2nd Lt. James R. Settle, had issued the bail out order and clambered towards the engineer, instructing him to bail out from the waist along with the gunners. Eight men jumped while two others remained "frozen" in the aircraft. They were killed when the B-17 crashed shortly after crossing the Dutch border. Two other enlisted men—radio operator Wilbert E. Eason and waist gunner Peter Hlynsky—were subsequently killed during their descent, Eason after his parachute failed to open and Hlynsky having seemingly drifted backwards and crashed into a fence, breaking his neck.

The remainder of the 381st continued across the Netherlands. Five minutes short of the Dutch coast, Carl Baer's *"Chap's" Flying Circus* began running low on fuel and slowed down. Baer called the 535th's leader, 1st Lt. Bill Ridley, by radio and informed him that he only had 108 gallons left and was "three miles behind." Five minutes later, Baer called again requesting fighter support. A further conversation between the two established that Baer was jettisoning his guns and was doubtful he would make it to England. "Have a good supper ready for me when I get back," Baer told Ridley.[18]

When the rest of the 381st landed back at Ridgewell, six B-17s were immediately readied to help in the search for *"Chap's" Flying Circus*. However, the RAF's air–sea rescue had already been alerted by the 381st's crews.

"When our men entered the interrogation room," wrote James Good Brown, "they told us what had happened. We waited throughout the evening … for good news. But no word came."[19]

Four days later, Carl Baer's body was washed ashore at Great Yarmouth. The bodies of his crew and the wreckage of *"Chap's" Flying Circus* were never found.

* * *

"Chap's" Flying Circus was the 63rd B-17 lost by the 381st. On average, one aircraft and ten men were being lost for every mission flown. Yet, the 381st had grown steadily since the start of its combat operations. In June 1943, 18 aircraft were being sent out on missions. The group's mission to Frankfurt on January 29 had seen it dispatch twice that number.

Frankfurt was again the briefed target for 30 crews on January 31. John Howland was among them, having been woken at 0400. Just as he arrived at the aircraft, the mission was scrubbed. It gave him the chance to pick up his pay ("sent 50 bucks home and kept $100 for a trip to London and for interest-free loans to the enlisted crew members when they go broke about the middle of the month.") and purchase some cigars from the post exchange (PX).[20]

Not far from the PX was the base chapel, which also served as Ridgewell's gymnasium and cinema. Howland cycled there during the afternoon to watch an air–sea rescue movie. He couldn't help but think of Carl Baer and his crew, from whom there was still no word. "I hope air–sea rescue was on the ball yesterday," he reflected.[21]

Meanwhile, James Good Brown was watching his chapel being converted into a ladies' "powder room" for a 381st dance.

"I saw five kegs of beer rolled into the gymnasium," he noted. "There seemed enough to float a battleship. I wondered and asked if all that was to be consumed at one party. I was told flatly and promptly: 'Yes.'"

Despite a plea from the group's Roman Catholic chaplain that the chapel not be used as a powder room, Brown—"the 381st chaplain"—saw no objection, claiming, "it may be the nearest they will ever get to the holy altar." When he returned to his small room at the back of the chapel the following evening, the dance was in full swing.

"The vigor and hurling and throwing were not due entirely to the conscious will on the part of the thrower," noted Brown, "but to the over-enthusiasm which comes from a wee bit too much beer."

Sure enough, the next morning, only one of the five kegs remained. Brown calculated that each man present must have consumed at least nine pints. "It seems scientifically impossible," he wrote. But he was also happy to discover that his holy altar "was as holy as before."[22]

The combat crews were woken at 0430 that same morning to attend another briefing for Frankfurt. Again, the mission was scrubbed just prior to take-off. A full 24 hours passed before they were reassembled for yet another field order—this time, a raid on Wilhelmshaven's U-boat yards.

John Howland's crew had been allocated an ageing B-17F. Even so, a 100-knot tail wind sped the bomber across the North Sea. Forced to climb to 28,500 feet to avoid clouds and heavy contrails, the 10-mile-long bomber stream then dropped on the signal of a PFF B-17. As usual, bombing through solid cloud yielded unseen results. Despite this, the German flak gunners were able to detect the bombers.

"[Flak] was popping all around us," recalled John Howland. "Those guys really [had] some good radar equipment to shoot that high, and without being able to see us."

Howland was unable to see anything at all. His old B-17 had no ventilation in the nose, which frosted up the higher it flew. He was forced to use a pocket-knife to cut a hole in the plexiglass, which achieved little. For the rest of the mission, Howland sat watching his compass, "dead-reckoning" his way back to Ridgewell.[23]

All 33 B-17s landed at Ridgewell safely. The standout performer of the day was the 534th's ironically named *Miss Abortion*, which returned from its 26th mission without aborting—a 100 percent record. Nevertheless, higher authority had deemed its nickname unsavory. *Miss Abortion* was painted over with the single word: *Stuff.*

* * *

Wilhelmshaven was the first of four consecutive raids that would eventually see the 381st launch over 120 sorties. It was also the group's 63rd accomplished mission out of 121 issued field orders. To date, almost half of the 381st's briefed raids had been scrubbed.

On February 4, John Howland was again woken at 0400. At the briefing, he was told his destination—Frankfurt. This time, the route in and out would follow the Ruhr Valley while bypassing a hotbed of flak guns. Once again, the lead aircraft would be supplied by the 482nd BG. Howland was pleased to learn a *Gee* box had been fitted to his B-17, which would enable him to track the mission's progress.

Taking off at 0845, the 1st BD's formation of 287 bombers headed out across the North Sea towards Rotterdam. As soon as they reached the coast, the sky erupted with flak. Howland then noticed the formation was 10 miles left of its course. Flying on at 26,000 feet, he also spotted a heavier concentration of flak up ahead. For the next 15 minutes, he logged light, heavy and accurate flak, which soon turned into a barrage.

Another 381st B-17, *Mickey Finn*, piloted by John Kuhl, was hit, disabling two of its engines and splattering oil across the windshield. The B-17 slowly slipped back through the formation, but John Kuhl carried on towards the target knowing he'd be protected from any enemy attacks by the ample fighter escort.

Yet again, though, the crews found the target covered by cloud. They followed the lead of the PFF B-17 by "toggling" their bombs on its release. The formation then headed back along the same route it had flown.

"That dumb lead navigator took us right back up 'Happy Valley'," noted John Howland.

Forty-five minutes later, Howland's aircraft was rocked by flak, although it kept flying. This time he realized the lead navigator was even further off course—some 40 miles south of where they'd first entered Germany. Fortunately, they avoided any further flak and escaped back across the North Sea.[24]

John Kuhl's *Mickey Finn*, however, was floundering. Kuhl's co-pilot, 2nd Lt. Ashley L. Hamory, flying his first mission, suggested making an emergency landing in Belgium. The rest of the crew encouraged Kuhl to try to reach England. They began jettisoning everything heavy, including armor plating. When they reached the Belgian coast, an RAF Mosquito unexpectedly appeared. For now, Kuhl and his crew were safe.

John Howland's B-17, meanwhile, had arrived over Essex and was circling in thick clouds. His pilots were attempting to locate the radio beacon that would direct them towards Ridgewell, but its signal wasn't working. When Howland saw that his *Gee* box had managed to fix their location, he shouted to the pilots. The co-pilot, William J. Doherty, yelled at him to keep quiet as they continued trying to locate the beacon's signal, but Howland insisted they listened and instructed them to turn 360 degrees. His assertion proved right when Ridgewell appeared through the murk.

The strain of the mission was affecting many. Just after landing, one of the 532nd's co-pilots inadvertently retracted his B-17's undercarriage instead of its flaps. The aircraft immediately collapsed on the main runway.

Captain David Hutchens, meanwhile, wasn't interested in the runway. He and seven of his crew had just survived their 25th mission. He gleefully pointed his B-17 at the control tower and tore towards it at ground level, pulling up at the last moment. Not for the first time, a flare gun was brandished in the direction of the buzzing bomber. This time, a red flare shot straight up and embedded itself in the aircraft's number two engine. A fortunate, red-faced Hutchens was able to make an emergency landing.

First Lieutenant John Kuhl and crew, though, were still nursing their troubled B-17 back to Ridgewell. They'd almost been given up for lost by the ground crews when they approached the base some three hours later. With one landing gear retracted and the other partially extended, Kuhl made a crash-landing, his second since *Whodat – The Dingbat!* six weeks earlier. Mercifully, the B-17 slid to a halt without causing any injuries.

Having survived their ordeal, Kuhl's crew were called back together for a celebratory photograph with the hapless *Mickey Finn*. Shortly afterwards, their co-pilot, Ashley Hamory, slumped to the ground in shock. He recovered, but that evening, as the rest of the men in his hut slept, Hamory was heard wandering around mumbling to himself. He was taken to the base hospital where he spent the next three days asleep. When he finally woke up, he didn't know where he was, nor recognize anyone. Hamory was diagnosed with "hysterical amnesia" and immediately grounded. He wouldn't finish his tour until much later in the war.

* * *

For the rest of the men, the pace of combat continued unabated. On February 5, the crews were briefed for the seventh time in ten days. At 0745, 28 of them took off led by Conway Hall, eventually linking up with the 91st. The two groups then headed for a *Luftwaffe* airfield at Avord, 125 miles south of Paris. Another 24 groups were targeting six other French airfields.

A combination of cloudless skies and the lead bombardier's steady aim saw Avord's hangars and buildings blown apart. Several gunners also watched the *Luftwaffe* ground crews' frantic attempts to disperse their aircraft. In the tail gunner's position of *Honey*, SSgt. John S. Szabo witnessed the lasting effects of the attack.

"I watched the smoke pile up for half an hour after we left," he recalled. "An hour later it was still visible."[25]

Although the 381st had bombed successfully and returned undamaged, one B-17—its ball turret doggedly stuck in the down position—unceremoniously touched down at Ridgewell. Parallel gouges along the main runway and two ground-down 50-caliber machine guns were the only wounds of the day.

More French airfields came under attack the next day when 33 B-17s took off to bomb Nancy–Essey. They were part of a stream of over 300 1st BD heavy bombers heading for both Nancy—which was being used to train German glider pilots and airborne troops—and Dijon's Longvic airfield.

As the formation crossed France, flak guns zeroed in. An explosion struck the 535th's *Touch the Button Nell*, blowing out both side windows, parts of the windshield, and astrodome. The blast also set off flares inside, sparking a fierce fire between the cockpit and top turret, where TSgt. Lifford E. French was standing.

"It burned the cockpit upholstery and the partition between the top turret and the bomb bay, where bombs hung," recalled French. "It scorched transfer hoses that passed through the wall, carrying 100-octane gasoline."[26]

French's pilot, 1st Lt. Henry Putek, quickly pulled out of the formation and instinctively rang the bail-out bell. The co-pilot, bombardier and navigator all jumped, but Putek was left stranded. His parachute had been destroyed in the fire, which Lifford French was fighting. By the time French had extinguished it, he'd sustained severe facial burns. He then instructed the five gunners to remain on board, while he went to the cockpit to take up the co-pilot's seat alongside Putek.

No sooner had *Touch the Button Nell* left the formation and jettisoned its bombs, than it was set upon by three Me 109s. Amid sustained and withering attacks, Putek carried out violent evasive maneuvers. "We nearly broke the plane in two," he recalled. The gunners also registered hits on the fighters, destroying all three. Sgt. Herbert J. Burgasser, the ball turret gunner, was seriously wounded during the attacks.

Touch the Button Nell "wallowed along" at 4,000 feet with its bomb bay doors jammed open. It was also full of holes, some of which were in the windshield. Both Putek and French donned their oxygen masks as protection against the icy wind blast. For the next two hours, they remained that way as they struggled to fly back to England without a navigator. The absence of him and the bombardier turned out to be a blessing, however, as, when skirting Paris, the B-17's plexiglass nose was blown off by flak.

Crossing the English Channel, *Touch the Button Nell* then faced another test. During the attacks, its radio and IFF transmitter had both been shot out. British anti-aircraft gunners on the ground radioed the crew. Receiving no answer and not knowing if the B-17 was one that had been captured by the Germans, they opened fire. Putek swung 180 degrees and flew back out over the sea. He then spotted an airfield dotted with several "white" aircraft.

"We hadn't been briefed on any white American planes," recalled Lifford French. "We weren't sure whether we were on British soil, but we were almost out of fuel so we had to land, whether we were in France, Germany or England."[27]

Henry Putek dipped his wings to alert those on the ground that his B-17 was damaged. He then coaxed it in for landing. Fortunately, the airfield was Dunkeswell, Devon, a US Navy station. Its white aircraft turned out to be anti-submarine Liberators.

Touch the Button Nell was damaged beyond repair. Its ball turret gunner, Herbert Burgasser, had suffered multiple lacerations to the face and subsequently lost his left eye. Lifford French, meanwhile, had suffered second degree burns to his face. Both were hospitalized at Dunkeswell.

A month later, Lifford French was awarded the 381st's second DSC. Part of his citation read: "The heroic actions of Sergeant French, remaining with the plane, undoubtedly saved the life of the pilot and made possible the safe return of the airplane."

Henry Putek was awarded the Silver Star for his actions, while Herbert Burgasser received a Purple Heart, as did Lifford French. The three officers who bailed out over France all managed to evade capture. Nancy–Essey airfield, however, managed to avoid destruction thanks to bad weather.

* * *

John Howland was also feeling under the weather. After returning from his last mission on February 4, he'd immediately travelled to Bedford on a 48-hour pass. He'd gone there to visit a navigation school roommate who was based with the 379th BG at Kimbolton. Despite enjoying their reunion, Howland had picked up a cold. Returning to Ridgewell, he was left feeling "like the devil all day long."

He arrived back to find a new navigator in his squadron. Canadian Charles P. Stormer had been assigned to the 535th from a Royal Canadian Air Force squadron. He'd taken up a role as the 381st's first "enlisted navigator." Stormer's brother, Lloyd, had been serving as a bomb aimer with Ridgewell's former tenants, 90 Squadron, at nearby Wratting Common. Sadly, he'd gone missing in action six months earlier. Charles Stormer now had to survive 25 daylight missions in the nose of a B-17.

John Howland, though, was suffering. He avoided a practice mission two days after returning from Bedford by turning up at the base hospital for treatment. The next day, he was given no choice but to fly after being woken for a raid at 0300. "I still don't feel like setting the world on fire," he wrote in his diary.[28] Howland's B-17 and others took off into darkness, but as soon as they had formed up, they were recalled and the mission scrubbed.

By the time the crews were re-assembled in the briefing room on February 11, they'd enjoyed a four-day break from combat. Howland and his crew hadn't been placed on combat status, so they were left alone, while their hutmates were roused at 0300 for the mission. The 381st crews learned they would be leading the rest of the 1st BD to Frankfurt's marshaling yards, with Harry Leber in command.

The formation left the English coast north of Felixstowe escorted by P-47s. As it climbed to 25,000 feet, George Darrow's *The Joker* suffered oxygen problems. The gunners' supply system failed, which left them needing to use portable bottles. A short while later, ball turret gunner SSgt. Richard G. Morrison was found to be anoxic. He was quickly dragged out of his turret and revived.

By the time the 1st BD reached the target, P-51s and P-38s had also arrived. So, too, had thick clouds of flak. *Tenabove*, flown by Robert V. Laux, was hit by fragments, which damaged two engines, forcing him to feather one. His B-17 then slipped back through the formation, which deviated away from a cloud-covered Frankfurt and flew south towards Ludwigshafen.

Darrow's *The Joker* then came under attack by German fighters, a 30mm bullet smashing through its fuselage and striking the ankle of Richard Morrison, who was still recovering from his anoxic episode. Darrow's violent evasive maneuvers then threw the radio operator, TSgt. Jack W. Kaufman, against the fuselage, knocking him out.

The 381st dropped on the signal of the PFF B-17 over the city of Ludwigshafen, before turning right and heading back across France. An hour and 20 minutes later, the straggling *Tenabove*, which had been repeatedly attacked by German fighters, could fly no more. Despite being escorted by friendly fighters, the B-17's left stabilizer had been shot away, its bomb bay was on fire, and it was riddled with holes. Robert Laux gave the order to bail out and all 10 men jumped from 10,000 feet, *Tenabove* eventually crashing and exploding near the French commune of Forges-Les-Eaux, just 30 miles short of the Channel. Laux and six of his crew managed to escape, later returning to Ridgewell, while three others were captured.

Thirty-two B-17s landed back at Ridgewell, including *The Joker*—one of the group's last original B-17Fs. It was peppered with holes. Nevertheless, for the 41st time, it had safely returned its crew back to Ridgewell. The wounded ball turret gunner, Richard Morrison, was evacuated to the base hospital, while two other crewmen were treated for minor wounds. Three gunners in other B-17s had also suffered frostbite. It brought the total number of 381st men frostbitten in three months to 86, the second highest rate in the 1st BD.

* * *

On February 13, the *Luftwaffe* resumed its attacks on Britain. During the evening, John Howland and his pilot, Jim Tyson, had just returned to their Nissen hut when they became aware of a raid.

"First came the muffled wail of distant air raid sirens," Howland recalled. "Several fingers of light [then] pierced the darkness as searchlight batteries sought to capture the German bombers."

Minutes later a bright, red flare fell to the ground close to the base. Almost immediately Ridgewell's Tannoy system crackled into life, announcing "condition red" and repeatedly warning people to take cover.

The Germans had dispatched Heinkel He 177 Greif long-range bombers, which appeared to be heading for London. Howland thought the flare was "some type of pathfinder marker." He then watched as several searchlights caught one of the bombers in their beams.

"Suddenly, there was a horrendous barrage of simultaneous flak bursts," he recalled. "Amidst the red yellow bursts, a white flame appeared which fell to earth like a meteorite. It grew brighter and brighter until there was a brilliant flash." John Howland took "no joy" from observing the demise of a German bomber crew.[29]

* * *

A crowd of bombed-out Londoners descended on Ridgewell a few days later to inspect four B-17Gs—three of them having been assigned to the 381st. They were led by the mayor of the borough of Bermondsey, who'd overseen a fundraising effort as part of "Wings for Victory Week." The Londoners' target had been £800,000, but they eventually raised a staggering £845,113. The sum enabled the purchase of the four bombers, which were collectively known as the "Bermondsey War Loan Fleet." One of their number was the focus of attention at Ridgewell on February 15.

"As Flatbush is to Brooklyn, so Rotherhithe is to Bermondsey," declared an official USAAF press statement. "Rotherhithe suffered the worst damage of the Blitz," the statement continued, "so the people of Rotherhithe and Bermondsey, to do their full share to help batter the enemy into submission, subscribed to war loan funds to purchase a Boeing B-17 which they christened *Rotherhithe's Revenge*."[30]

The brand-new B-17G was launched with the smash of a bottle of "Bermondsey-made ale" over its nose guns. Parked alongside was the Bermondsey fleet, including *Bermondsay* [sic] *Battler*, *Bermondsey Special* and *London Avenger*. All had seen combat. Only *Rotherhithe's Revenge* was the rookie.

For the 381st crews, respite from combat came courtesy of poor weather conditions over Europe. For the next week, *Rotherhithe's Revenge* and the other 381st B-17s remained firmly grounded. It allowed the crews much-needed time to attend to maintenance needs, with John Howland fitting "ventilator scoops" to the nose of his B-17F, which had frosted over on the recent Wilhelmshaven mission.

"I may never have to fly in this old tub again," he wrote, "but if I do, I want to be able to see out of the windows."[31]

Days later, John Howland would get the chance to see clear skies. Meteorological experts, having studied European weather patterns stretching back centuries, were predicting a "good looking sequence" of three to four days of high pressure. This meant the Allies could finally schedule a "maximum effort" for what would ultimately become "the biggest, most concentrated air battle yet of the war."[32]

Intermission: The Weather Gods

The Eighth Air Force's bombing campaign in Europe lasted for 983 days. During this time, tactics and equipment were constantly evolving, but the basic cycle of selecting a target, planning, and launching a bombing mission changed little after the raids mounted in the early months.

The majority of missions originated from the Eighth Air Force's (formerly VIII BC) headquarters. The targets selected were taken from the target lists formulated as part of the CBO. Occasionally, higher command directed the use of Eighth Air Force bomb groups away from the "strategic" bombing offensive, a good example being the massive intervention in the Ardennes on December 24, 1944, later known as the "Battle of the Bulge."

Weather was without doubt the key consideration when planning a bombing raid. Flying heavily laden bombers in close formation, in poor visibility, was high-risk. Losses while attempting to group and assemble in reduced visibility were often heavy. Equally vital was the requirement to be able to see the target to bomb accurately. An accurate prediction of wind speeds and bombing altitudes was critical to successfully hitting the target. The windspeed and cloud base were variables in the calculations programmed into the Norden bombsights used by the lead bombardiers. Also critical was the weather for the return leg of the mission. Having bombed their target and turned for home, crews had to be able to locate their home airfields and land safely.

Planning for most missions started a day in advance at Eighth (VIII BC) headquarters in High Wycombe. Meteorological forecasts were received at 1015, 1600 and 2200. Mission planners studied the forecasts, hoping for stable high pressure over England and occupied Europe. At this stage, the weather had a direct influence on mission planning. The most difficult, heavily defended targets could only be reached by large numbers of bombers flying in tight, well-organized defensive formations. Attempting to maintain massed formations in poor visibility, often with variable headwinds or crosswinds, was extremely dangerous.

If the weather forecast was favorable with clear skies, then a large-scale mission could be mounted, concentrating the maximum available number of bomb groups against a high priority target. If conditions were expected to be cloudy, then the available force would be split between two or three lower priority targets, the intent being to increase the odds of success in marginal conditions. Hopefully, at least one element would strike lucky and be able to bomb accurately. Often, however, only parts of occupied Europe were clear enough for daylight operations, which restricted the options open to the planners at High Wycombe. It also helped the *Luftwaffe* intelligence analysts anticipate which targets were likely to be attacked.

The final decision on whether to launch a mission on the following day rested with the deputy commander of operations at *Pinetree*. Immediately after receipt of the 2200 weather forecast, an operations meeting was held. The meeting scrutinized the latest weather predictions, updates on ongoing mission preparation and target intelligence. It was at this point that the planned mission was cancelled, postponed, or approved.

Despite steadily improving technology—particularly the increasing use of radar to identify targets through cloud cover—weather conditions consistently constrained Eighth Air Force operations throughout its bombing campaign.

CHAPTER 13

Trafalgar

February 16–25, 1944

A day before the *Rotherhithe's Revenge* ceremony, Supreme Headquarters Allied Expeditionary Force (SHAEF) was established at Bushy Park, the Eighth Air Force's former *Widewing* headquarters in southwest London. General Dwight D. Eisenhower had returned from the Mediterranean to assume command of the organization, which would now be responsible for the planning and execution of the Allies' intended invasion of occupied Europe.

To aid the invasion, air superiority was essential. In order to achieve that goal, destruction of the *Luftwaffe* was necessary. This included the dismantling of the airframe manufacturing and assembly plants replenishing it. Under the direction of Maj. Gen. Frederick L. Anderson Jr., VIII BC's former commander and Joe Nazzaro's immediate superior, Operation *Argument* was born.

Anderson's previous role was now in the hands of Jimmy Doolittle, whose influence quickly brought about a new tactic. No longer was the "first duty" of fighters to "bring back the bombers alive"—it was to "destroy German fighters" instead. Equipped with a growing number of long-range fighters, VIII FC, and the recently arrived Ninth Air Force Fighter Command were tasked with sending their aircraft ahead of the bombers to "seek out" enemy fighters before they reached them.

While the bombers' principal role would be to continue targeting areas key to the German economy, under the scope of Operation *Argument* they would largely be used as bait, effectively luring the *Luftwaffe* into the air. Over a week-long period, Allied fighters would hunt down operational German aircraft, while the bombers of the Eighth Air Force and RAF Bomber Command would destroy any new replacements being built on the ground.

Most of the Eighth's bomb groups had been prevented from flying missions for eight days due to poor weather. Long-range forecasts now indicated a high-pressure system settling over central and southern Germany. It was the cue for the launch of Operation *Argument* with 823 RAF aircraft being dispatched to Leipzig on the evening of February 19. Despite the promising weather predictions, however, the bombers arrived over the city too early due to unexpected winds. They then found it covered in cloud. By the end of the raid, 79 aircraft had been lost, representing RAF Bomber Command's heaviest loss of the war so far.[1]

* * *

Sunday, February 20, dawned "cold and dreary." John Howland had been expecting a stand down, but he was woken at 0500, as were almost 500 others, including navigator David McCarthy.

"The air chilled us to the bone as we trudged through the dark to the mess hall," he wrote. "Only a hot breakfast prepared us for the trip to the briefing room."[2]

James Good Brown was present when the mission was outlined.

"This was one of the mornings when quiet hung over the briefing room like a heavy cloak," he wrote. "One could feel it. The red line on the map led to Oschersleben … this day could bring disaster."

For the first time, the Eighth was sending over 1,000 bombers to Germany. They were to be escorted by some 800 fighters, 73 P-51s among them. As well as Oschersleben, the 381st would also strike at Leipzig—the same city bombed by RAF Bomber Command the evening before. Forty-seven B-17s would take off from Ridgewell, splitting into two groups for the attacks, which would see them bomb aircraft plants at both locations.

Lifting off into the clouds just before 1000, the 381st circled back towards Cambridge before leaving the English coast at Lowestoft. Overflying the Netherlands an hour later, the thick undercast began to break.

"As we made our way into Germany, the clouds that had obscured our view of the ground beneath us cleared and we had unlimited visibility," recalled David McCarthy.[3] The Eighth Air Force's weather forecasters had been right after all.

Largely unopposed, the formations split at Brunswick and aimed for their respective targets. First Lieutenant Kirch J. Cogswell's unnamed B-17G headed for its IP at Halle, before turning towards Leipzig. After doing so, Cogswell's navigator, 2nd Lt. William R. Meehan then noticed that none of the others had turned with them. "Separated from the herd," their lone B-17 became a target for a "pack of Me 110s."

Cannon fire quickly struck the right waist gunner, Sgt. Charles E. Duncan, who fell dead at his gun. Bursts of flak then succeeded in setting fire to the bomb bay and damaging two engines. Cogswell issued the bail-out order and his surviving crew members jumped, including the co-pilot, 2nd Lt. William Borrego, who laughed "hysterically" as he descended.[4]

"The most overpowering sensation is that feeling of being completely suspended in space," remembered William Meehan. "It is as if you were hung upon a hook at 1,000 miles above the earth … you suddenly have a feeling of great loneliness."

Meehan and the rest of the crew landed safely, although he was "roughed up a bit" by German civilians, as was William Borrego, who found himself pistol-whipped.

Both were eventually "rescued" by German troops and taken as POWs, along with the rest of the crew. "And there you are," wrote Meehan. "Germany on a one-way ticket."[5]

* * *

After successfully bombing their objectives, the 381st's remaining B-17s turned back for England protected by Allied fighters.

"Our spirits were high as we returned to base," remembered John Howland. "But the flares being shot from the ship in front of us indicated 'wounded on board'."[6]

One of the 533rd's new B-17Gs returning from its ninth mission—*Big Mike*—landed with a dead crew member. Top turret gunner TSgt. Edward J. Senk had not been killed as a result of enemy fire, but friendly. Somewhere over the North Sea, a gunner on another B-17 had accidentally shot Senk in the head while clearing his guns.

As James Good Brown watched the B-17s return to Ridgewell "strewn all over the sky," he noted how it had become more difficult to count them in given the numbers now being sent out. Nevertheless, he was also "surprised" that so many had returned when he'd initially "feared the worst." Apart from the loss of Edward Senk and Kirch Cogswell's crew, there was joy that three others had completed their 25th missions, two of whom were pilots.

Second Lieutenant William Butler—"no young fellow anymore," according to Brown—aimed his unnamed B-17 straight at the control tower.

"Down he came," remembered Brown. "Down, down, down. His plane was lower than the tower … I think that even the pilots who stood beside me were a bit apprehensive."[7]

After several wild passes, Butler's B-17 was followed by Capt. Alan F. Tucker's self-named *Ol' Man Tucker*, which buzzed the field a single time and "in a safe manner." Onboard was Tucker's engineer and top turret gunner Charles H. Raglin, who'd also completed his 25th mission. Both were subsequently photographed signing for their wallets, while a laughing James Good Brown was also pictured congratulating William Butler. Two weeks later, both photographs appeared in the weekly London newspaper, *The Sphere*.

* * *

Another veteran crew member about to finish his tour was TSgt. John Sinclair, recipient of the group's first major award (a Silver Star) and Purple Heart holder. He'd flown his 24th mission with William Butler on February 20 but was one of over 300 to be woken early again the next morning for the group's 69th raid.

While most enlisted men were already wide awake by breakfast, many of the group's officers were feeling "under the weather," having attended the monthly officers' dance the previous evening.

"It was with a shaking hand and an aching head that most of us attended the briefing," noted surgeon Ernest Gaillard.[8]

Briefed for an attack on a *Luftwaffe* bomber airfield at Gütersloh in central Germany, 33 crews took off from Ridgewell led by former Swedish internee Osce Jones, who was flying *Jaynee B*. Sat alongside him in the co-pilot's seat was Col. William Gross, commander of the 1st CBW, who was leading his wing to Germany. In all, three divisions of 861 heavy bombers headed for six *Luftwaffe* airfields. Navigator John Howland was "enthusiastic" about the mission.

"Perhaps it was because yesterday's big raid was so successful," he noted. "Perhaps it was the fact that today's mission was much shorter … perhaps we were just careless and cocky."[9]

Following a similar route to the day before, the 381st eventually reached the IP where the lead B-17 made an unexpected turn into clouds. The primary target was cloud-covered, forcing its navigator to look for a secondary. With the formation scattered, the *Luftwaffe* then attacked.

"I was manning my machine gun and gave up navigating for a while since I wasn't lead navigator," wrote John Howland. "We were under sporadic attack for about 30 minutes."

While flying across Osnabrück ("the lead navigator screwed up again"), Howland and the other crews were then met with a barrage of flak.

"A piece came through the glass window above my gun mount and missed me by a few inches."[10]

Osce Jones's fellow Swedish internee George McIntosh was flying *Our Desire*. It was also struck by flak, which set the nose compartment on fire and filled it with smoke. Both the panicked navigator, 2nd Lt. Allen E. Bergreen, and the bombardier, William F. Piekarski, bailed out to become POWs. Two other crewmen managed to extinguish the flames, while McIntosh regained control and flew on with the formation.

With the secondary also obscured by cloud, the formation headed northwest towards Achmer, where the group dropped over 80 tons of explosives on another *Luftwaffe* airfield. The 381st then returned to Ridgewell intact, with several B-17s nursing minor damage and one slightly wounded crewman. John Sinclair had survived his 25th mission, but he'd also been "nicked in the heels" by fragments of a 20mm shell that burst near his position.

William Gross landed back at Ridgewell on *Jaynee B* proclaiming, "excellent results with tight patterns over the target." He then boasted, "I think you can say another of their airdromes is missing."[11] For John Howland, however, the mission had left him with a slight graze on his neck and a growing frustration.

> I suppose the raid can be called successful. But I don't call it a success when the lead ship screws up … that 360-degree turn into a cloud bank in the target area was a STUPID decision. The guy who made it should pay the price for making a BAD DECISION. But the Brass will probably give the SOB a medal.[12]

* * *

Later that evening, some of the crews ventured off base to unwind in the surrounding pubs. *The Fox* was just a stone's throw from SSgt. Thomas "Tommy" L. LaMore's hut. He was six missions into his 25, yet he found the journey back from his "real home" somewhat riskier.

"I had the short walk virtually memorized," he wrote. "There was a long plank over a muddy ditch that was slippery and twisted. For some reason, it was more difficult to maintain course and altitude coming back to the hut."

Although LaMore enjoyed friendly relations with "Big Bill," the pub's landlord ("did you ruin Herr Hitler's day today?" LaMore would be asked), there was an effort on the part of both men to "keep up the illusion" that the war, and the 381st's part in it, was all fun and games.

"All of us airmen were slowly changing," LaMore noted. "Slowly becoming more serious, less carefree. There was a certain look that developed in the men who were flying combat missions. It was a hard look. Our mannerisms were changing, too. We were edgy, prone to sudden outbursts and long periods of quiet, even in a crowded pub."[13]

Second Lieutenant Francis J. Flaherty's crew were trying to take things in their stride. Their training had seen to that. Six months and nine days earlier, while on a night practice flight near Alexandria Army Air Field, Louisiana, their B-17 had suffered two engine fires. Flaherty had been faced with a dilemma—attempt to land the burning bomber in darkness or bail out. Flaherty chose the latter. It was a night he and his crew never forgot.

"I saw patterns on the ground," remembered left waist gunner SSgt. Casimer "Casey" L. Bukowski. "From the moonlit sky, with the shadows and the darker and lighter colors below, I was trying to figure out which were the swamps and which was *terra firma*, because I was thinking of alligators and snakes."

Finally bailing out, Bukowski had landed on "hard ground." Groping his way through the undergrowth ("hoping I didn't feel any water"), he was then found by a rancher who took him to a nearby town where he was reunited with his crew.

"This all occurred on Friday, August 13, 1943," Bukowski remembered. "We thought it would be a good name for a ship. We'd all survived the crash, so we named our ship, *Friday the 13th*."[14]

Five days after it had been assigned to the 381st, Bukowski's crew had flown their *Friday the 13th* for the first time. On the mission to Oschersleben on January 11, bombardier William Farrell and navigator Benjamin Saporta had both been wounded. Each received a Silver Star and Purple Heart. On Tuesday, February 22, the crew of *Friday the 13th* prepared themselves for a return.

* * *

"Up at 0500 again and briefed for Oschersleben," wrote navigator John Howland in his diary. "I didn't feel right about this mission and wasn't too enthused about going."[15]

Operation *Argument* was set to continue with a third consecutive assault on German airfields and aircraft plants. Over 800 heavy bombers and almost 700 fighters were being sent to numerous targets in Germany. Thirty-two began lifting off from Ridgewell just before 1000, but they immediately ran into difficulty. Forecast weather conditions at 11,000 feet began playing havoc with assembly.

"[Meteorologists] said it would be clear at that altitude," wrote Howland. "But we found it was quite hazy and we had dense, persistent contrails. We looked and looked, but couldn't find our group."[16]

Flying blindly around Clacton and with no sign of the 381st, Howland's pilot turned back for Ridgewell after jettisoning his bombs in the North Sea. By the time they arrived back at their base, they weren't alone. Another 18 of the 381st's bombers had followed, while two others landed elsewhere. Only 12 of the group's B-17s succeeded in forming up with 15 from the 91st. Casey Bukowski's *Friday the 13th* and Tommy LaMore's brand-new *Carnival Queen* were among them.

Things were further exacerbated when the reduced formation reached the point at which they were to rendezvous with escort fighters. They were nowhere to be seen. The two groups then proceeded across the Dutch coast and on in towards Germany.

Not long after Tommy LaMore's aircraft passed the coastline, its number two engine lost power. He and his crewmates were expecting their pilot, 1st Lt. Armour C. Bowen Jr., to announce the mission was being aborted, but he flew on.

"Everyone was grouchy as hell," recalled LaMore. "Nothing seemed to be going right."[17]

What should have been a strong formation of 799 heavy bombers had been whittled down by almost 80 percent. An hour inside Germany, it was met by a high-caliber opposition of some 200 enemy fighters.

Casey Bukowski's *Friday the 13th* was one of the first to be hit by cannon fire, which killed two gunners and detonated its oxygen tanks, setting the aircraft on fire. Four of the crew bailed out, including Bukowski. Badly wounded, he was soon taken prisoner and admitted to a German hospital where he lost an eye. The luckless *Friday the 13th* eventually crashed in the municipality of Senne II, close to the city of Bielefeld, where six of Bukowski's crewmates were found dead in the wreckage, including pilot Francis Flaherty.

In addition to heavy fighter opposition, 105mm anti-aircraft guns opened up over Bielefeld, firing 48 rounds in two minutes.[18] First Lieutenant Hal E. Roling's unnamed B-17G was hit, stopping its number three engine. Dropping from the formation, it was then attacked head-on by German fighters, which succeeded in blowing its nose off and destroying the cockpit. All five crew members in the front of the aircraft were killed, before it went spinning out of control. The surviving gunners bailed out over the Hillegossen district of Bielefeld and were quickly captured by German soldiers.

Bermondsay Battler, the 535th's new B-17G, had also been struck by fighters during the first attack and was seen dropping from the formation. With two of its engines on fire and flames in the nose, pilot, 1st Lt. Lee W. Smith's aircraft side-slipped[19] below the formation and dropped out of sight. *Bermondsay Battler* eventually struck the ground near Detmold, 15 miles southeast of Bielefeld, killing all 10 men on board.

Fifteen minutes from the target, another newly assigned 535th B-17G, flown by 2nd Lt. Henry Hustedt, was also badly shot up by fighters. Assigned to the squadron just two days earlier, his unnamed aircraft was hit by an explosion, which killed the waist gunner and radio operator. The eight remaining crew members bailed out just before it blew up in mid-air.

Tommy LaMore, kneeling in the tail gun position of *Carnival Queen*, had just destroyed an Me 109 when his bomber flew along the bomb run.

"The flak was an almost solid dark cloud over the target," he remembered. "Suddenly there was a loud sound like someone hitting a giant frying pan with a huge spoon, and the ship shuddered slightly."

LaMore was immediately buffeted by an icy blast of air, which blew through a large hole in the window next to him. After bombs away, *Carnival Queen* was struck again, this time tearing most of the number four engine from its mounting. The aircraft then dropped from the formation trailing "heavy black smoke."

> I tried to think clearly in the noise and blowing debris. I tried to find the triangle of the [parachute] ripcord, tried to remember the bailout procedure. As I looked back, I saw the formation heading off with swarms of German fighters tearing at them. I had never thought about leaving the protection of the formation. It was like being in a life raft and watching a ship sail away.[20]

Bad weather had forced the formation to miss Oschersleben and seek out a target of opportunity, which turned out to be an airfield at Bünde. It then swung left for the 400-mile journey back to Ridgewell. Among the formation was another unnamed 535th B-17G, flown by 2nd Lt. Charles H. Downey.

With a "perforated" vertical stabilizer, Downey was seen to drop from the formation with his bomb bay doors open and undercarriage extended. He then quickly lost altitude, pursued by several Fw 190s. Somewhere near the town of Hamelin, the B-17 crashed; coming to rest with seven dead crew members, including Charles Downey. Only the radio operator and two waist gunners survived.

Although it hadn't been witnessed by any of the other crews, another 381st B-17G, *Homing Pigeon*, had also been lost from the formation. Under the command of 1st Lt. Francis N. Fridgen, it was attacked by fighters and forced down at Opherdicke, near the city of Dortmund. Two of its crew were found dead at their positions, while two others had seemingly been killed bailing out. They were both found dead close to the wreckage of *Homing Pigeon*, which was discovered broken in two. Francis Fridgen and three others were taken prisoner, while two—waist gunner Lowell E. Slayton and tail gunner Walter H. Abernathy—managed to escape and evade capture.

Tommy LaMore's *Carnival Queen* was still trying to escape the grip of the *Luftwaffe*. It had earlier spiraled out of the formation with its undercarriage extended. Chased by fighters, the pilot, Armour Bowen, had then weaved in and out of clouds, during which time his co-pilot had managed to restart its number two engine. Tommy LaMore's tail guns had seized and burnt out, so he decided to take the spare ammunition forward to the waist guns, which had both fallen quiet. He found the gunners removing them from their mounts, before throwing them out of the bomber to lighten its load.

After helping the ball turret gunner from his ball, LaMore then proceeded to head towards the top turret, which had been hit during an earlier fighter attack. There, he found the engineer and top turret gunner, Oliver K. Stuart, laying on his back, his face "a bloody pulp." Stuart had been hit by 20mm cannon fire, but he was still alive. While *Carnival Queen* crossed the North Sea, LaMore and the others tended to their wounded crewmate. Their B-17 finally landed at Leiston on the Suffolk coast, where he was evacuated for treatment. LaMore was also treated for frostbite.

* * *

Twenty-four hours earlier, James Good Brown had cycled to the hardstand where *Bermondsay Battler* had parked after returning from Achmer. He'd wanted to welcome its crew, including pilot Lee Smith.

"I greeted each one as he stepped from the plane," he wrote. "There I see them as they crawl out of the plane; watch them rub their hands in the good solid ground; pick it up and kiss it; and shuffle their feet on the concrete where the plane rests."[21]

Bermondsay Battler didn't return from Bünde. Unknown to Brown, Lee Smith and his entire crew had been killed in action. Five other B-17s had also been lost, another 50 men gone with them. Only four had returned to Ridgewell. Two others, Tommy LaMore's *Carnival Queen* included, had landed elsewhere. The only positive was the return of top turret gunner TSgt. Fred T. Berg who'd completed his 25th mission. His severely frostbitten hands (the result of having to hand-crank his B-17's bomb bay doors without gloves) were just a minor setback. However, the horror of the mission was clear to see, as Brown observed.

> The men who returned from Bünde described what took place, but their description was nothing compared with the look on their faces. Some looked wild. Others looked weird. Others looked haggard and worn out. Others were disappointed. Others cried because of what they saw happening to our men. Others were almost hysterical and talked fast. Others were sick—physically sick.[22]

Most, like John Howland were angry. The decision to launch a mission "under adverse weather conditions" was to blame for the severe losses.

"At times, it looks like we might be making progress in this air war," he wrote. "But I honestly believe my chances of making it through are about 100 to one against me … I thank God I don't have a wife and children to leave behind. It is tough enough to walk this pathway alone."[23]

* * *

After a 24-hour period in which the Eighth gave its heavy bomber groups some much needed rest, 23 of them received field orders in the early hours of February 24. Aviation industry plants in five locations were their targets. For the 381st—it was Schweinfurt.

"Oh, dear God," wrote navigator David McCarthy. "Not again!"

After being briefed at 0530, McCarthy and the officers of the Liddle crew arrived under the wing of *Our Mom* to tell the rest of the crew.

"When we told them the name of the target, they thought we were kidding. Once they realized that we weren't … an aura of gloom emanated from our crew."[24]

Taking off at 0830, 32 B-17s quickly formed up with the 91st BG over Colchester before heading off to Germany. John Howland's *Squat n' Droppit* was flying in the second element of the high group.

"Our assembly was perfect," he wrote. "Everything seemed to click. Flight, Squadron, Group and Wing assembly were right on schedule. Everyone in the proper place at the proper time, and at the proper altitude."[25]

Crystal clear weather conditions over Europe and a vast escort of 767 fighters combined to inspire great confidence among the crews. Fourth to arrive over Schweinfurt's ball-bearing factories, the 381st found its aiming point obscured by the preceding attacks, but still managed to drop over 65 tons of high explosives and incendiaries. Nevertheless, although the *Luftwaffe* was largely absent, Schweinfurt's flak guns pounded the formation. Second Lieutenant Dale McCrory's B-17 was struck near the tail, which severely wounded its tail gunner, Sgt. William F. Seifermann. For the next few hours, the radio operator, Glenn M. Dick, fed oxygen to Seifermann until the aircraft landed back at Ridgewell.

The rest of the 381st arrived back at Ridgewell, including John Howland's *Squat n' Droppit*, which was met by the "donut truck." His crew were in "good spirits." They were subsequently photographed with their B-17 still eating their treats.

The 381st's third visit to Schweinfurt had proved to be a good one. Yet, the wounds sustained by William Seifermann were serious—so much so, that Chaplain Brown was called to give prayer. Three days later, the gunner died in hospital.

* * *

Friday, February 25 saw the culmination of Operation *Argument*. Many of the crews had flown each of its four previous raids, but they were woken again for what would be the group's longest mission so far. Their destination was the southern German city of Augsburg—just 50 miles from the Austrian border.

The 381st's 133rd field order would see the group fly its 72nd mission to strike at the Messerschmitt fighter assembly line in Augsburg. It was one of four German aviation-related targets selected by the Eighth to be attacked by all three of its divisions. More than 750 heavy bombers and almost 900 fighters were about to descend on the Third Reich.

"We were so weary, we didn't have much to say to each other," wrote navigator John Howland after his crew's briefing. He knew it would be a long flight ("1,380 statute miles") and that fighter escort would be good "as far as Mannheim," but Howland was left unimpressed with his crew's payload.

"We weren't carrying bombs in our plane. We were the 'paper boys'. Our bomb bay was full of propaganda leaflets called the 'Sternenbanner'."[26]

Several other crews were carrying the same, causing much consternation. "We are nothing more than the highest paid, best equipped paper boys in the world," remarked one. "What a waste of time," said another. "We could have mailed it to them."[27]

Most of the 381st's 32 B-17s were loaded with a cocktail of explosives and incendiaries. Among them, was the still unnamed 42-37786, which had been assigned to the group the previous November. Unofficially known as *Hit Parader*, its crew chief had refused to paint the name and number of missions, citing bad luck after two of his previous bombers had been shot down on their eleventh missions. *Hit Parader* was about to embark on its eleventh mission, this time under the command of 2nd Lt. Donald G. Henderson, who was flying his 25th and final one.

Just before take-off, John Howland's *Squat n' Droppit* immediately ran into trouble. Taxiing around the perimeter track, it suffered a blowout, which rather pleased the navigator. However, "everyone on that field who knew what a wrench looked like" rushed to the aircraft and had the tire changed within the hour. By the time Howland's B-17 arrived at the group's assembly point, it tacked onto the formation in its "Purple Heart Corner."[28]

Reaching Selsey Bill on schedule, the 1st CBW formation crossed the French coast near Dieppe for the three-hour flight in towards Augsburg. Again, the meteorologists were proved correct—the solid undercast dissipated over France, leaving clear skies all the way to the target. It was also largely devoid of any fighters, except for an abundance of P-38s, P-47s and P-51s. Bypassing Augsburg to the north, the bomber formation then swung 180 degrees to attack from the east.

Round Trip Jeannie, flying in the 1st CBW's lead position, was rocked by flak as it neared the target. Fragments tore into its bomb bay, which set off a smoke marker bomb. Pilot 1st Lt. John A. Silvernale had just seconds to react and salvoed his bombs before they had a chance to explode. However, it was the cue for many of the trailing B-17s to release their bombs, most of which fell short of the target. It wasn't too much of a problem for John Howland's bombardier. All he could do was shout "papers away" as he released numerous neat bundles of propaganda leaflets.

Donald Henderson's *Hit Parader* had also been struck by flak, momentarily knocking it from the formation. Fragments had also wounded his co-pilot, 2nd Lt. Jack H. Fournier. After dropping his bombs, Henderson's number four engine then began to malfunction, seemingly damaged by flak. With a distinct loss of speed and a feathered propeller, the B-17 fell back through the formation until it was some 4,000 feet below. Several Me 109s then closed in, although two were quickly shot down by Henderson's desperate gunners.[29]

Chased by a single, determined fighter, Henderson descended lower and turned his B-17 towards Switzerland. Overflying the city of Stuttgart, it then attracted the city's flak guns. Several bursts caused further damage, before the Me 109 re-engaged, raking it with yet more cannon fire. Donald Henderson finally gave up any hope of reaching Switzerland and issued the bail-out order. Only he and three others managed to jump before the aircraft struck the ground at Wilmandingen, less than 50 miles from the Swiss border. Despite being so near, Henderson was taken prisoner on his 25th mission. Worse still, six of his crew had been KIA.

* * *

Some nine hours after take-off, the group's remaining B-17s returned to Ridgewell in darkness. Despite the loss of one aircraft, the mission was declared a success—the 381st's lead bombardier later claiming that the group "knocked out at least three-quarters of the factory," while "looming columns of rolling black smoke" could still be seen 200 miles away.[30]

Although the "Trafalgar of [the] war"[31] had clearly dealt a significant blow to the *Luftwaffe*, Operation *Argument* hadn't wrought the "final extinction" Frederick Anderson had been hoping for.[32] Nevertheless, the Germans had lost more than 500 operational fighters. Their ability to produce replacements had also been hindered, with a 35 percent drop in production during the month of February alone.[33]

What would ultimately become known as "Big Week" had seen the loss of at least 266 American bombers, however—eight of them from the 381st. Eighty more men had been taken from its ranks. For the likes of John Howland and his crew, the struggle would continue.

"After interrogation, we went to bed, hoping tomorrow will be an easy day, for a change."[34]

CHAPTER 14

"Big B"

February 26–March 9, 1944

The 381st's two previous missions had seen a noticeable decrease in fighter opposition. Only the raid on Bünde had brought out the *Luftwaffe* in anything approaching significant numbers. As the fighter threat slowly subsided, Eighth Air Force commanders and the heads of the USAAF agreed to dispense with olive-drab camouflage paint for their aircraft in favor of a natural metal finish.

"It is estimated that removal of the familiar greenish-gray paint gives AAF planes a slight increase in top speed," a USAAF guide stated, "… and a weight reduction … in heavy bombardment types of from 70 to 80 pounds."[1]

On the day of the Augsburg mission, the 381st received its first natural metal finish B-17G. The Boeing-built model was among the first block of uncamouflaged B-17s to be delivered to the 1st BD. It was assigned to the 533rd BS, whose commander, George Shackley, immediately inspected it. While happy to receive the aircraft, Shackley was less than enthusiastic about its shiny livery. He ordered it to be painted olive-drab (to fit in with the rest of the group's B-17s), while the name *Dreambaby* was applied in honor of newly assigned pilot 2nd Lt. Ewing S. Watson, whose wife was pregnant.[2]

Dreambaby was one of 16 new B-17s assigned to the group in February, bringing its total bomber complement to 58. The wear and tear on each was so unrelenting, however, that many needed to be repaired several times during the month, some for damage sustained outside of combat.

One was B-17G 42-31448, which had suffered a belly-landing in training. The resultant damage had been so severe that the group's 448th Sub Depot engineers were forced to remove its chin turret. When the bomber emerged from the hangar, it resembled a B-17F. The crews duly named it *Half Breed.*

The change in aircraft colors also coincided with a significant change in combat crew tours. The Eighth's commander, Jimmy Doolittle, had increased the number of missions to 30, citing a "shortage of aircrews" and a loss rate that had declined appreciably.[3] After his decision was made public, many airmen baulked at the increase. Some did try to understand it, though, including veteran navigator David McCarthy.

Those of us with twenty completed missions [the week of Doolittle's announcement] would still be finished after twenty-five; all other fliers would have their tour requirements increased on a pro-rated basis.

When the new program was introduced I had completed only nineteen missions, so one additional raid was added to my tour. I'd have to fly twenty-six. Having that one extra mission added was depressing, but fair. We were still taking heavy losses, but were not losing nearly as high a percentage of our total flying complement. The extra mission did worry me, though. I felt it was tempting fate.[4]

* * *

One man eager to carry out his first combat mission was James Good Brown. His own "mission" had started as far back as 1942, when he was a minister in Massachusetts.

"The matter came to a head when, on Sunday mornings, I stood on the church steps saying 'goodbye' to the young men who were going off to war," he wrote. "I found myself advocating the defence of democracy, but expecting someone else to do my work."

Joe Nazzaro had persistently refused Brown's request to fly a mission, but with Nazzaro now gone, Brown turned his attention to the new commanding officer, Harry Leber. At first, Leber had also refused, claiming that Brown would be "shot down." Brown, however, noted that Leber had not said a definitive "no."

One officer who was on Brown's side was the group's air executive, Conway Hall. Hearing Brown's endless pleas to be allowed to fly a mission, Hall was only too happy to let him go.

"It might be a blessing to all in the 381st Bomb Group if you would be killed," he joked. "Or better than that: you might go down in Germany and convert the heathen." Brown could only agree with the last statement.[5]

At 0530 on March 2, Brown was sat with the crews in the briefing room when the curtain was pulled back on the map of Europe. The ribbon stretched to Frankfurt. Shortly after, Conway Hall approached Brown asking if he wanted to fly the mission. Despite an objection from Harry Leber, Brown jumped at the chance. He was then helped into combat clothing "fit for the Arctic regions," before joining the crew of Capt. Charles G. Wood for the truck ride out to their B-17, *Rotherhithe's Revenge*.

The group's first mission in almost a week would see 36 of its bombers attack Frankfurt's marshaling yards. As usual, the 381st would assemble with Bassingbourn's 91st Bomb Group, combining to make a single wing between them. *Rotherhithe's Revenge* would lead the composite group made up of both units' B-17s. It lifted off out in front, with James Good Brown riding in the nose.

"I watched beautiful England until I got to 10,000 feet, then I crawled up into the cockpit."

Donning his oxygen mask, Brown stood behind the 24-mission veteran Charles Wood and his co-pilot, 1st Lt. Robert R. Zadnik, who was flying his 25th. Crossing the English Channel at Beachy Head, Wood then led the formation east in towards Germany.

Brown was quickly motioned to the rear of the B-17 to allow its top turret gunner to move more freely. It involved a precarious walk across the bomb bay. Arriving in the radio room, Brown was unplugged from his portable oxygen bottle and connected to the aircraft's main supply. The radio operator then refilled Brown's portable bottle.

"This is what I call foresight," wrote Brown. He also realized, however, that he was giving the radioman "one more job to do."

At 26,000 feet with a temperature of -42 degrees centigrade, James Good Brown was beginning to experience what the crews endured day after day. For the first time, he saw flak ("it was to our rear and all too close"), then the bomb bay doors opened and he saw the ground far below.

"When I saw the bombs fall, I had no personal feelings at all," he wrote. "All of our men feel the same way. They are dropping their bombs on strategic targets … not on villages and towns."

After the bombs were released, Brown then made his way back through the aircraft towards the waist gunners. The flak was getting heavier and he was soon alerted to the sight of a German fighter. With *Rotherhithe's Revenge* leading the high group, he was spared any close attacks, but saw the lead group "getting it hot and heavy." At that moment, one of the 381st's B-17s was hit by a burst, which caused it to drop from the formation.

"It was right under our ship, quite far below," wrote Brown. "I saw chutes opening up below us. The men were bailing out."

Unknown to him at the time, the unnamed B-17G was being flown by his good friend, 1st Lt. Eugene Schulz, who hailed from Lockhaven, Pennsylvania, near to where Brown had been born. Schulz's B-17 crashed just across the Belgian border, although he and his crew survived their bailing out. The right waist gunner John T. Farr managed to evade capture, successfully returning to Ridgewell some six months later.

When a German fighter made a pass, Brown was pushed to the floor by one of the gunners. He was then alerted to the sight of Allied fighters, which arrived "flying leisurely" alongside the formation. Escorted all the way to the Belgian coastline, Brown knew that he was almost home.

"The men may crab about England, gripe about the food and the weather, but they surely like England when they are returning from a combat mission," he wrote. "We exclaimed with much feeling: 'good old England!'"

After eight hours in the air, *Rotherhithe's Revenge* and James Good Brown landed safely back at Ridgewell.

"What a reunion there was when we jumped onto the ground! I now experienced what I had seen so often—members of the same crew hugging each other as though they had not seen each other for six months."

Brown's joy was tempered by the loss of Eugene Schulz and crew, but he now considered himself a different person.

"I took a good deep breath of air and felt that I had a right to it … I was now on the inside with them."[6]

* * *

Navigator John Howland had also flown the Frankfurt mission, but he'd not been feeling good. He'd also frozen his back after his electric suit had burnt out. At 0330 the next morning, he was woken again, this time for an attack on a ball-bearing plant in the town of Erkner, on the southeastern edge of Berlin—"Big B" as it was commonly referred to.

When Howland studied the route over the Frisian Islands, skirting round Hamburg and back from Berlin, he decided it was "more like an aerial tour of western Europe than a bombing raid." The total trip was 1,400 miles in length, with five-and-a-half hours over enemy territory.

Thirty-six B-17s began taking off from Ridgewell at 0715. They quickly formed up at 5,000 feet, before joining with the 91st. The two groups then assembled with the rest of the 1st BD and left the Norfolk coast at Cromer.

As the formation climbed to 26,000 feet over the North Sea, the temperature plummeted to minus 60 degrees—the coldest recorded on any mission so far. After crossing the Danish coast, John Howland's B-17F then suffered an engine problem, forcing his pilot to abort the mission. Thirteen minutes later, the whole raid was scrubbed.

Persistent contrails and a rising undercast plagued the B-17s, leading to the recall inside Germany. In the pandemonium that followed, the 1st CBW, including the 381st, flew through a formation of the 4th CBW. Rocked by prop wash, two B-17s from each wing collided, with debris falling on the 381st's unnamed 42-37986, which also fell from the formation. Luckily, 2nd Lt. Robert H. Rogers and crew managed to bail out before their aircraft crashed 10 miles north of the Dutch city of Groningen. All ten were captured by German troops.

Having dropped its bombs on the town of Wilhelmshaven, the group returned to Ridgewell minus one of its number and with two cases of frostbite. John Howland, who'd been "coughing like a fiend" for two days, found himself grounded by the medical staff. The group's first foray towards "Big B" hadn't gone as planned.

* * *

Erkner was again the group's destination the next day, when 33 crews were woken at 0400. Some, like 535th navigator Ted Homdrom, were flying their third mission in as many days. Others, like John Howland, were stood down.

"Boy, it sure felt good to lay in the sack while the rest of the group went out," he wrote.[7]

On take-off at 0800, one aircraft suffered an engine fire, which was quickly doused. Several other B-17s were also forced to abort the mission early, including one whose tail gunner had become airsick. The 532nd's *Spare Parts* then began suffering engine problems at 20,000 feet. An oil leak had supposedly been fixed the previous day, but its number three engine quickly gave in. Soon after, another malfunctioned. Losing airspeed and altitude, its pilot, 2nd Lt. David D. Keyes, elected to salvo his bombs. Having done so, the bomb bay doors then refused to close. Keyes turned the heavily vibrating bomber back towards the French coast but was unable to reach the English Channel. With his aircraft too low for the crew to bail out, Keyes made a forced landing close to the French commune of Saint-Omer. Although his crew was uninjured, they were quickly captured. It was only their second mission.

Unlike the day before, the formation was flying a more direct route across Europe towards Erkner. As had happened 24 hours earlier, however, clouds gradually built up, forcing the bombers to climb to 26,000 feet. Some distance from the target, the raid was scrubbed, the crews learning they would have to look for a target of opportunity instead. Without fighter escort, and while facing heavy and accurate flak, the 381st made a 360-degree turn, flew south, north, and finally west, before dropping its bombs on the city of Düsseldorf. The group then headed back to Ridgewell.

Not long after the B-17s landed and the crews had been interrogated, Harry Leber called them all back together.

"Col. Leber chewed our asses for too many abortions," noted John Howland. "Claimed we were yellow, among other things, and got everyone pissed off at him."[8]

A total of nine B-17s had aborted the second Erkner mission. Leber forcefully outlined the group's policy, announcing it would be "more severe." Those aborting future missions "without adequate cause" would be the "subject of disciplinary action."[9]

* * *

The Eighth's 250th mission was planned for March 6—the target once again, "Big B." Three divisions of 730 bombers, plus 17 groups of some 800 fighters would make up the raid, which entailed a 1,100-mile round trip to a city that had 70 percent of the *Luftwaffe*'s fighters within range. Yet, as navigator, David McCarthy pointed out: "Berlin represented the evil heart of the Nazi empire, and to destroy a monster, one must pierce its heart. On the sixth of March we began the surgery."[10]

Of the task force, 262 B-17s were being supplied by the 1st BD, which would lead the mission. Spearheading the entire formation would be the 1st CBW, comprising the 381st and 91st, which would lead a bomber stream measuring some 90 miles in length. After the 381st's 30 crews had been briefed for their part in the mission, which would again focus on Erkner's ball-bearing plants, one of the 535th pilots noticed that the queues for the toilets were "three times as long."[11]

Taking off at 0800, the 381st made a wide sweep inland before leaving the coast at Cromer. Flying on a southeasterly heading, John Howland then noticed that the 91st was leading the formation 20 miles off of its planned route. The 1st CBW passed over Osnabrück, which invited the city's flak gunners to commence firing.

> We took some flak in the nose of our ship when a hunk of steel tore through the roof, hit the armor plate in front of the pilot, bounced off, hit my helmet, and bounced again. Never did find the piece, although it must have been about three inches long by the marks it made in the armor plate, and on my helmet. Threw out some chaff to throw their aim off. But we were too late, and those boys down there knew their stuff. They kept it right up there till we were out of range. I was quite put out about getting shot up needlessly, and all due to poor navigation.[12]

The unnamed 42-37983 being flown by 2nd Lt. Roderick T. Cahill was also struck by flak, which disabled its number four engine. Unable to maintain airspeed, Cahill dropped his bombs on Osnabrück and left the formation, turning back towards England. However, his aircraft was unable to reach it, Cahill being forced to ditch just off Foreness Point, Kent. Fortunately, he and his crew were quickly picked up by an RAF air–sea rescue unit, with the severed tail of 42-37983 later washing up just beneath the Kent headland.

John Howland was still smarting at the 91st's lead navigator when he noticed that the formation was due to pass over the city of Hanover. Howland asked his pilot, James Tyson, to call the lead crew to ask them to return to the briefed route in order to avoid more flak. After calling, Tyson was told to "maintain radio silence." However, the formation did make a left turn to avoid Hanover.

"I knew talking over the radio like that was a violation," wrote John Howland. "But I decided it was time to let the lead navigator know where he was."[13]

As the formation continued towards the IP, Charles Woods, flying his 25th and final mission, noticed "moving clouds of fighters" in the distance. David McCarthy in *Our Mom* also spotted them and watched as they prepared to attack.

"For the first time in my experience, the Germans lined up about 50 abreast, formed the equivalent of a skirmish line, and stormed into the First Combat [Bombardment] Wing."[14]

Ted Homdrom, flying his 14th mission as a navigator, counted "about 36 Me 109s" screaming towards his B-17.

> All of us on the crew who had a gun or guns were firing at those German fighters. I had a gun at each side window. As I followed one, simultaneously firing my right .50-caliber machine

> gun, I saw a huge explosion. It was the [Me] 109, but also a nearby bomber. My knees were shaking as I feared that I might have caused it.[15]

Homdrom "breathed a prayer" and continued firing, as did John Howland, who was cursing his luck. Unlike Homdrom's B-17, Howland's aircraft was only fitted with a single .50-caliber machine gun on the right-hand side of its nose. With fighter attacks coming from his left, Howland was left exposed and instinctively ducked behind the skin of the fuselage as the fighters' guns flashed. He soon realized it was "rather foolish." Seconds later, however, an explosion sent shards of plexiglass flying through the nose compartment.

"I then noticed that the window above my desk was completely gone and that both hands were bleeding," he wrote.[16]

Fortunately, Howland only received minor cuts. His bombardier, Frank Palenik, was also slightly wounded, but he continued firing the bomber's chin turret guns.

The 533rd Bomb Squadron's *Linda Mary*, one of the group's remaining B-17Fs, pulled out of the formation. Rocket-firing fighters had shot away most of its tail assembly, killing the tail gunner Raymond F. Legg, one of John Comer's former crewmates. With the underside of the right wing also on fire, its pilot, 2nd Lt. Richard W. Coyle, called for his crew to bail out. All except Legg were able to jump before the aircraft exploded in mid-air and crashed near the city of Magdeburg—*Linda Mary* becoming the last original B-17F to be lost by the 381st. Its nine surviving crew members were all taken prisoner.

As the formation turned on the IP for a northerly bomb run, *Myer's Flaw*, being flown by 1st Lt. Edward E. Haushalter, was attacked by a combination of fighters which succeeded in destroying its hydraulic system and oxygen tanks. With the aircraft "enveloped in flames," Haushalter ordered his crew to bail out. Only five succeeded in doing so. The others were found dead, including Haushalter, whose parachute had seemingly failed. His body was discovered in the street of a Berlin suburb.

As the 381st approached Erkner, the B-17G-cum-B-17F *Half Breed* was attacked by a fighter, which knocked out two engines and set one on fire. Pilot 2nd Lt. Milton A. Fastrup glided out of the formation in a wide right turn down towards clouds. Sometime later, he issued a bail-out order and his entire crew jumped before the aircraft crashed near Cologne. All 10 were captured, but *Half Breed* was no more.

The 381st's remaining B-17s followed the 91st BG over the target, although cloud cover forced the groups to seek out the secondary. While some crews reported "perfect hits," with many believing they were the first to leave their marks on Berlin, their bombs had actually fallen on the village of Zernsdorf.[17]

"We still had a long trip before we'd be safe," wrote David McCarthy. "Berlin is 380 miles from the coast of the Netherlands and 540 miles from Ridgewell. We were to be in German airspace for two and a half hours and would have to fly another hour and a half to get back to our base."[18]

After the 381st turned off the target, it was eventually met by an escort of Allied fighters, allowing the crews time to relax a little and assess damage.

"We found four holes in the nose; three made by 20mm shells and one by flak over Osnabrück," wrote John Howland.[19]

Nevertheless, when the group finally landed back at Ridgewell, almost all of them had suffered "considerable damage." Alongside John Howland and Frank Palenik, only one crewman had been wounded—tail gunner SSgt. Emery Y. Naha, a Native American from Arizona, who'd been hit in the shoulder by a cannon shell. Known as "Little Beaver" to his tribe, Naha was awarded a Purple Heart.

One of Naha's fellow 535th gunners, and the last of the squadron's original combat crewmen, SSgt. John J. Wardell, Jr., had also earned himself a medal after completing his 25th mission. In addition to a DFC, Wardell would soon find himself being awarded two gold bars after being elevated to the position of second lieutenant. A member of Frank Chapman's *"Chap's" Flying Circus*, Wardell would remain with the 381st as one of its gunnery officers. The mission to Berlin had proved costly, however, with four B-17s lost and 30 men MIA.

"The crew members seemed quite happy to see Ridgewell again," wrote surgeon Ernest Gaillard. "But are convinced that the back of the Luftwaffe is not broken."[20]

After a lengthy interrogation, John Howland and his pilot, James Tyson, were ordered to report to commanding officer, Harry Leber. He immediately berated them for breaking radio silence. Despite protestations from both men ("We weren't giving away any secrets"), Leber demanded they followed the rules. He then angrily dismissed them both. John Howland's frustration was clear.

"Thoroughly chastised, and too tired to eat, wash up or give a damn, I made my way back to our room and went to bed."[21]

* * *

The first large-scale daylight attack on Berlin had seen the loss of 69 heavy bombers and 11 fighters. It would subsequently become the Eighth's highest number of aircraft lost in a single day, yet over 1,600 tons of high explosives and incendiaries had rained down, becoming the first American bombs to be dropped in and around the German capital.

The 381st crews were woken the next morning at 0500 for another mission to Erkner, although, just prior to briefing, the mission was scrubbed. It gave John Howland the opportunity to recheck his navigator's instructions for radio procedures over enemy territory. They were quite explicit.

> THE NAVIGATOR IN A WING POSITION WILL HAVE PILOT BREAK RADIO SILENCE WHEN LEAD NAVIGATOR IS MAKING AN OBVIOUS NAVIGATION ERROR.

Howland and over 200 other combat crewmen were woken early again on March 8 for yet another assault on Erkner.

"We were all nervous about going back into the same stuff we hit Monday," he wrote. "But we were told that every available long-range fighter in the British Isles would be over the target area to help us."[22]

Part of the 1st BD's formation of 235 B-17s, the 381st crossed the Dutch coast just north of Amsterdam. In cloudless skies, they flew according to the briefed route, which satisfied John Howland. Then, some 50 miles from Erkner, a huge black cloud over the target could clearly be seen. The preceding 3rd BD's B-17s had left their mark.

Just before reaching the IP, 2nd Lt. Thomas A. Pirtle's unnamed B-17G, 42-38029, was seen to drop from the formation with a feathered engine. Half a mile behind the rest of the 381st, the newly assigned bomber, which was flying its first mission, then turned away and headed west, seemingly protected by four P-51s. Despite this, just over 90 minutes later, the bomber crashed near the Dutch village of Lettele after being shot down by a German fighter. Fortunately, Pirtle and his crew bailed out in time, with two of them—bombardier Harry F. Cooper and ball turret gunner William C. Kinney—going on to escape and evade capture. Both would eventually return to England some seven months later.

The wings ahead were being kept busy by the *Luftwaffe*, but the 381st encountered only one pass. The group remained unmolested as it flew through moderate flak to deliver just over 35 tons of bombs on Erkner.

"Strike photos showed that we clobbered the target and we felt that we wouldn't have to go back to that place again," wrote John Howland.[23]

The rest of the crews felt the same, including Capt. Melvin R. Hecker, who was leading in *Rotherhithe's Revenge*. Hecker, one of the group's originals, was flying his 25th mission.

Despite an interminable four-hour flight back to England, followed by a let-down through solid undercast, the remaining 20 B-17s landed safely at Ridgewell. The crews, while "mildly euphoric," were also tired after their almost nine-hour round trip.

"It has been quite a while since the medical department has had any real work to do on the return of a mission," noted surgeon Ernest Gaillard. "I hope that our good fortune continues."

Just over two hours later, however, Gaillard was made aware of an accident on the flight line. Sergeant Michael C. Babines, Jr., a mechanic with the 534th BS, was fatally injured when an engine caught fire on the B-17 he was working on. Jumping from the escape hatch, he inadvertently stumbled into its number two propeller. Immediately rushed to hospital, Babines died the following morning.[24]

* * *

At 0400 on March 9, the lights of John Howland's hut snapped on. He was flying another mission, one that would take him back to the suburbs of Berlin.

"Most of us are getting a little tired of going back to the same target; but "Big B" isn't as big in our minds as it used to be," he wrote.[25]

The target for 31 of the 381st's crews was a Heinkel bomber assembly plant and airfield at Oranienburg, some 15 miles northwest of Berlin's city center. It would be the third time in four days that they would have to endure a nine-hour round trip, two-thirds of which would be spent in German airspace.

"None of us could be happy about this trip," wrote David McCarthy. "How often could we tempt fate?" Three of his crew, including the bombardier, Edward Klein were flying their final mission. "Fate is not often kind."[26]

Taking off into clouds at 0800, the group assembled without trouble and headed for the coast of Norfolk. Despite having no navigational device fitted to his B-17, John Howland attempted to check their route by scanning his aeronautical charts. Only when he spotted a break in the clouds, could he identify their position as being southeast of Cromer.

"I didn't know it at that time, but we weren't going to see the ground again until we hit the coast of Holland on the way back."[27]

Led by a PFF B-17, with its "fishbowl" antenna in place of a ball turret, Howland continued plotting their course, but noticed they were making "late turns." Comparing his no wind navigation data with those forecast at the briefing ("experience had taught me to be skeptical of … wind data"), he concluded they were off course. Again, he asked James Tyson to call the lead aircraft at a point shown on his map where "information could be relayed." Asking for their position, James Tyson was met with a curt response—he was to maintain radio silence. Nevertheless, Howland continued tracking their route and after a right-turn in towards a "tremendous concentration of flak," he realized they were over the center of Berlin. He also deduced they'd been fighting a headwind 20 knots stronger than predicted.

The lead B-17 had been unable to locate the primary target, so the formation dropped on the secondary—Berlin's city center. Although the flak was heavy and covered an area of some 10 miles, Howland found it to be "the most inaccurate" he'd ever seen, with shells exploding either 1,000ft above or 5,000ft below the formation. Even so, discernible bangs of white bursts (instead of black) told him they were over a battery of larger guns.[28]

As *Our Mom* turned away from Berlin, its navigator David McCarthy was pleased to be heading home.

"We still had not met a German fighter," he wrote. "It was the considered opinion of our intelligence officers that the veteran fliers of the Luftwaffe were gone, and the replacement pilots were not yet trained sufficiently in 'blind' flying techniques for their commanders to risk their remaining planes and pilots in the thick clouds below us."[29]

All the crews could see were "thick layers of black smoke" rising through the undercast—a sight that was still visible half an hour later. Pushed by a powerful tailwind and protected by an abundance of P-38s, P-47s and P-51s, the formation droned back to England where the 381st landed at 1700. No bombers were lost, minimal damage sustained, and only one crew member was wounded. Several others had also completed their tours, including three of David McCarthy's crew. He would have to wait a while longer.

John Howland didn't have to wait long to be summoned by Harry Leber. Once again, he and his pilot had broken radio silence. In no uncertain terms, Leber angrily told them not to do it again. Later, after opening a bottle of whisky to celebrate surviving three Berlin missions, Howland again checked his notebook. It confirmed the procedures to be followed over enemy territory. Both he and Tyson were convinced Leber was wrong and considered going to see him. A jeep then arrived at their hut. He wanted to see them, too.

Before either of them had a chance to talk about radio procedures, Leber spoke up.

"I didn't bring you down here to talk about that," he said. "I want to know if you would like to go to Pathfinder school and learn how to be a lead team."

Both men were taken aback, Howland even "smelling a rat." Leber then outlined the reason for his proposal. He'd received a directive asking all commanders in the 1st BD to select two crews to be sent to the Pathfinder Force school at Chelveston—home of the 305th. There, they would be given a "study break away from combat duty" and to have "an opportunity to lead and not make the mistakes" they had observed in other lead crews. Leber finished his proposal with some strong incentives.

"You will fly the best ships in the Eighth Air Force, and there will be promotions."

Howland and Tyson could only nod in agreement. There would be no more wrong turns to "Big B." They were on their way to becoming "pathfinders."[30]

Intermission: Preparing for Battle

If the meteorological forecast for flying the next day was good, then the staff at *Pinetree* confirmed their choice of target and the size of the force to carry out the mission against it. This information was incorporated into a formal field order that could be transmitted to the three bomb divisions that made up the Eighth Air Force. A "warning order" would be issued before the field order was transmitted; this allowed the divisions to alert their combat wings, and they in turn could then inform their respective bomb groups of the impending mission.

Almost immediately the planners at division headquarters labored to produce the detailed plans and data required to choreograph a concentrated force over the target. The mission-planning cycle considered the nature of the target and the most effective ordnance required to assure its destruction. The range to the target, the fuel and bomb loads required, the route to the target, and the MPI for the bombardiers to aim for were also formulated. As well as the coordination of the bomb groups themselves, the provision of a fighter escort required careful planning.

Wing headquarters were normally warned of the mission early in the afternoon. This initial warning was received by teletype machine. It included the location of the target in an encoded format. Also detailed were the mission timings, the route, and altitudes to be flown to and from the target. Force composition—which combat wings would be flying, and in what order—were also designated. This allowed more detailed operational planning to get under way. Later the same afternoon, or early in the evening, wings would issue advance warning of the field order to their bomb groups.

Receipt of this information instantly changed the tempo and focus of life on a bomb group airfield. All elements of the group from the commanding officer down were notified and placed on alert. Military Police were posted on the doors of the operations block. At the same time, a red mission flag was hoisted over the domestic sites around the airfield. In some groups, a red light was switched on in all bars and mess facilities, banning the sale of alcohol to aircrew on station. Telephone calls and movement in and out of the airfield were also restricted.

As soon as the mission warning was circulated, squadron ground crews began the task of preparing serviceable aircraft for the mission. While engineers and mechanics worked on the aircraft, the potentially hazardous task of fueling and arming each bomber to the required mission loading began. The loading of bombs would often go on throughout the night.

In parallel with this frenetic activity out on the airfield, the crews were locked into what would become a well-practised briefing cycle. The squadrons' lead navigators and bombardiers formulated their own instructions for the squadron crew briefs. Weather, flak concentrations, alternate targets, and anticipated enemy fighter opposition, all featured in this process. The tempo of this frenzy of activity was set by zero hour—the time the mission was due to launch. This key timing was often not known until well after midnight.

CHAPTER 15

Death of a B-17

March 10–31, 1944

On March 10, the American public woke to the news that the air war had taken a "surprising turn." "Nazis Shun Battle" read the headline of a *New York Times* article, which underlined the lack of fighter opposition over Berlin the previous day. The 381st's crews who'd returned from Berlin had noticed the *Luftwaffe* was "visibly diminished." Tail gunner, Tommy LaMore was feeling confident "the tide had turned." With more men completing their prescribed missions and heading home, his morale was further boosted.

"Everything seemed possible now," he wrote. "I actually began to think I might survive my twenty-five missions."[1]

Some of the enlisted men lucky enough to survive their tours had been held back in England to serve as gunnery instructors. Most, however, were being swiftly returned to the US to help train new recruits there. Many were not keen on going back, however, as the 535th Bomb Squadron's diarist noted:

> A growing number of them do not want to go home, basing their decisions upon stories we hear from newly arrived crews … that gunnery schools at home are run by ground officers unacquainted with combat conditions over here, and more interested in misguided War Department directives than in the contributions experienced gun crews have to offer the training system.[2]

John Howland was awaiting his orders to begin training as a PFF navigator, but with the 381st stood down after six grueling missions in nine days, he and his fellow airmen were given the chance to relax. Following a lecture on the pitfalls of aborting (one pilot had been reduced to co-pilot after two aborts in a row) and a lengthy practice flight, Howland took himself off to *The White Hart Hotel* in Great Yeldham.

The "old inn" had become a favorite of Howland's, who'd taken to its "Windsor-backed chairs" and "homelike atmosphere."[3] Many of his fellow airmen referred to its landlady, Barbara Nankivell, as "The Governess," after she'd taken over the reins of the hotel when her husband was called up to the RAF. Nankivell enjoyed catering for "the boys" of the 381st.

"They surprised us at first by continually asking for water in between their courses and after their meals," she recalled. "They were very polite and pleasant about our coffee, which they honestly didn't like very much, and many of them ended up by acquiring our habit of drinking tea."[4]

John Howland was visiting the *White Hart* one evening when a fellow American had played a practical joke on some unsuspecting British visitors.

"I had the opportunity to watch a sergeant gunner from the base perform his classic act," wrote Howland. "The young American from the New York City area could speak with an absolutely perfect Cockney accent … and the sergeant would strike up a conversation."

After being asked why he wasn't serving in the RAF, the sergeant had claimed he'd been forced to leave because of its "bad food, scratchy uniforms and awful pay." Dressed in his Class A attire, he'd then sauntered back to his friends, who'd kept up the pretense through stifled laughter.

Two days after the 381st's last Berlin mission, Howland visited the *White Hart* where he immediately sensed an "atmosphere." He quickly learned that the playful sergeant had been listed as MIA.

"The [Governess] tearfully informed us that she was terribly tired of the war, and that it would be best for all concerned if we Yanks stayed on the base."[5]

* * *

Over the next few days, several new natural metal finish B-17s were ferried into Ridgewell from Glatton airfield in Huntingdonshire. Among them was *Dee Marie*, a Boeing-built B-17G, which had arrived from America just a week earlier. Immediately named after the wife of one of the group's pilots, it was subsequently inherited by a newly assigned crew led by pilot Charles E. Ackerman and his co-pilot Troy H. Jones.

Born in Sumner, Florida, Jones had been drafted into the US Army a month after the Japanese attack on Pearl Harbor. After applying to become an aviation cadet, he'd then trained as a B-17 pilot, joining Ackerman's crew in Dyersburg, Tennessee. In late February, the crew had been assigned to the 534th BS at Ridgewell. On March 16, after two weeks of acclimatization, they were split up to take part in the 381st's 79th raid—an attack on a Messerschmitt experimental airfield at Lechfeld, deep in southern Germany.

Troy Jones was among 330 airmen briefed for the mission, which would see the group's B-17s join 250 others for the nine-hour, 1,300-mile round trip. Each one had been loaded with over 200 20lb fragmentation bombs. Led by Harry Leber in *Rotherhithe's Revenge*, the group lifted off just after 0730 and arrived over the target by midday. Finding Lechfeld indistinguishable below solid cloud cover, the PFF B-17 then led the formation towards the secondary target in the city of Augsburg, 12 miles north. However, its radar operator mistook the town of Gessertshausen for Augsburg and the formation dropped its bombs in error. Amid heavy, but inaccurate flak, the 1st CBW then turned west for the four-hour flight back to England. Encountering German anti-aircraft fire for the first time, Troy Jones found it an enlightening experience.

"That flak is quite a sensation," he wrote. "If it is really close, you see not only the black puff, but also a red flame as the shell explodes ... [if] a burst occurs right under you, the plane lifts like a row boat going over a wave in pretty heavy surf."[6]

Fortunately, *Dee Marie* survived its first crossing of Germany, as did the rest of the group's B-17s. However, just 25 miles from the French coastline, a fire broke out in the cockpit of the unnamed 42-97454. As pilot 1st Lt. Rudolph G. Duncan pulled out of the formation, his co-pilot, Karl Franek, alerted the crew to the blaze. Mistakenly thinking it was a bail-out order, waist gunner William J. Yanzek immediately buckled his parachute and jumped from the B-17. Although listed as MIA on his first mission, Yanzek would escape and evade capture, returning to Ridgewell six months later.

Rudolph Duncan's cockpit fire was extinguished by engineer and top turret gunner TSgt. John T. Eylens Jr., who not only suffered frostbite, but also burns to his hands. For his actions, he was duly awarded the Purple Heart, as well as another Oak Leaf Cluster to his Air Medal.[7] On landing at Ridgewell, Eylens and his fellow airmen then received a generous liquor ration.

The Eighth's new pre-interrogation pick-me-up was warmly received by the crews, although the 381st's surgeon, Ernest Gaillard, wasn't so sure.

"I am not convinced that it has real value, nor am I convinced of the idea of having the medical department associated with a bottle of whiskey," he noted. "At the present time, we are doing about as much catering as we are medical work."[8]

Nevertheless, it gave the airmen an opportunity to toast several others who'd successfully completed their tours—including the 535th's 1st Lt. Thomas Sellers DSC—the co-pilot who'd returned the crippled *Tinker Toy* back to Ridgewell five months earlier. Sellers, the group's highest award winner and Purple Heart holder, could finally return home to Norfolk, Virginia, a hero.

* * *

"Today brought the first indication that spring may arrive on time in a week or so," noted the 535th's diarist on March 17. "Very warm, sunny, the air full of softness, larks and baseballs. It can't last."

Despite the fine weather, two planned missions to Augsburg and Frankfurt were scrubbed. The temperature also meant nothing to John Howland, who'd checked himself into the base hospital with a heavy cold. Still, his impending move to the Pathfinder Force was keeping his spirits up.

European weather conditions were set fair the next day when the crews attended a briefing for the group's 80th mission—an attack on Oberpfaffenhofen, some 13 miles southwest of Munich. It meant PFF B-17s weren't required. Even so, as navigator David McCarthy eyed the red ribbon stretching 550 miles across the European map, he was anxious.

"We couldn't spell it, we couldn't pronounce it, so how in the hell were we going to find it?"[9]

Harry Leber had hurriedly changed his briefing notes after the group's initial target—an aircraft components factory in Frankfurt—had been revised in favor of the airfield at Oberpfaffenhofen. Leber had then found his entry to the briefing room barred after he failed to give the correct password. When he eventually made it to the dais, he made sure his crews knew where they were heading.

"The colonel told us that only the [1st CBW] was assigned to the airfield," remembered David McCarthy. "But that there would be 700 bombers saturating the airspace over southern Germany."[10]

McCarthy was assigned to his usual B-17, *Our Mom*, which was piloted by his friend, Robert Miller, who'd been sweating out the mission for several days. Although Miller couldn't pronounce it, Oberpfaffenhofen represented his 25th and final destination.

The target for Miller's crew and 32 others was Oberpfaffenhofen's Dornier aircraft plant. Taking off from Ridgewell at 0800, the group joined almost 260 other bombers for the long trek in towards Germany. Reaching the IP with an escort of P-38s and no opposition, the 1st CBW then began maneuvering into its bombing formation.

"The lead group of the wing increased speed to create an opening for our group," noted McCarthy. "The high group was supposed to throttle back to make room for us, but for some reason they did not alter their speed or altitude."[11]

As *Our Mom* and the 381st ascended into position, the top turret gunner suddenly screamed at Robert Miller to turn. The high group was directly overhead, each of its B-17s with their bomb doors wide open. Miller immediately banked in order to avoid being demolished by bombs. It left *Our Mom* and those following out of position and having to make a 360-degree turn. By the time it was complete, the other groups had already released their loads and were banking away for England.

"There were [no guns, nor any planes] to oppose us," wrote David McCarthy. "Many of the buildings around the field were on fire and burning furiously."

Watching the 381st's bombs fall, McCarthy then spotted a German army truck racing around the perimeter track to the safety of a hangar. As soon as it entered, the 381st's bombs struck.

"That was the only time that I saw anyone killed as a direct result of our crews' efforts," McCarthy recalled. "He never had a chance."[12]

The 381st landed back at Ridgewell with no aborts, no damage and no wounded airmen. It was left to Robert Miller to buzz Ridgewell's control tower in celebration of his 25th mission. He'd successfully found, bombed and returned from a place he couldn't say.

* * *

After a day's break, during which time Ridgewell's airmen tended to their surroundings, carried out inspections and attended the monthly officers' dance ("a comedy of errors … uninvited guests, inebriates, broken glass … vomit," noted Ernest Gaillard),[13] the group returned to combat on March 20.

John Howland, who'd been released from hospital the previous day, was preparing to leave Ridgewell for his Pathfinder course at Chelveston. However, having met a nurse at the "swell dance" the evening before, he was cursing his luck.

"After more than two months in this place I finally met an interesting female companion, and now we are getting ready to ship out to PFF school," he wrote grudgingly.[14]

Veteran navigator David McCarthy was scheduled to take part in the group's next mission—a raid on Frankfurt's industrial areas. It was to be his 23rd and one that would see him fly with a new crew for the first time.

"My interest in the mission was purely one of getting there and getting home," he remembered. "I felt like an orphan, newly-accepted into a foster home. I missed *Our Mom* and her crew."[15]

Taking off just after 0730, the group's 30 B-17s left the English coast catapulted by a 100-knot tailwind. Even so, heavy contrails left by preceding wings hampered the 381st's trek to the target. By the time it arrived over Frankfurt, the contrails and clouds had become so bad that the formation ended up scattered. While most of the 1st BD's bombers abandoned the mission or became separated, the 381st overflew a flak area in the city of Mannheim. Dropping its bombs through the flak, the group then turned into headwinds.

Jaynee B was being flown by 14-mission veteran George McIntosh—former co-pilot of *Georgia Rebel*—who'd crash-landed in Sweden almost eight months earlier. Leading his squadron away from Mannheim, McIntosh's aircraft suffered flak damage to an engine, which he was unable to feather. Struggling to maintain a constant airspeed and making an "erratic" descent from his bombing altitude, McIntosh called for his deputy leader to take over. *Jaynee B* then slowly slipped back through the formation.

As the 381st flew "blindly" on, 535th BS navigator Ted Homdrom finally saw the ground down below but had no suitable charts to check his location. Grabbing a small European map that he'd been using to mark off areas of flak, he spotted a long river flowing "due west." He quickly deduced it was the Loire River and that the 381st was heading for the Bay of Biscay. Astonishingly, the group was almost 100 miles off course.

"I called the pilot, telling him that I had just discovered where we were and that we would have to fly almost due north … if we wanted to get back to England."

Homdrom's pilot decided his navigator was correct and made a solo, northerly turn. As he did so, the rest of the group followed.[16]

Like Homdrom's B-17, many in the formation were low on fuel after their nine-hour flight. Fortunately, most were able to continue on to Ridgewell, although several were forced to divert to airfields in Devon and Cornwall. Robert McIntosh's *Jaynee B*, however, was in trouble. Heavily-vibrating and with instruments being "shaken from their mounts,"[17] McIntosh flew low across northwestern France, only to attract German flak gunners who succeeded in damaging two more engines. He was finally left with no option but to ditch the bomber a mile from the French coast, near Quimper.

Jaynee B splashed down and floated for 20 minutes, allowing its crew to escape, eight of whom jumped into the only dinghy that would successfully inflate. McIntosh and his left waist gunner, Eugene S. Copp, were left clinging to its sides. Copp, a gunnery instructor on detached service from the US, had been flying the last of three missions before returning home. He and his nine crewmates were eventually picked up by a French boat carrying German soldiers. Once again, George McIntosh had arrived in captivity.

By the time elements of the 381st began arriving back over Essex, they were more than three hours late. Descending through clouds and fog so thick that some crews "couldn't see the wingtips," the B-17s landed at a rain-lashed Ridgewell. Among them was *Male Call*, being flown by 1st Lt. Bernard F. Beckman. He and most of his crew were ready to complete their tours as their B-17 touched down. However, three-quarters of the way along the runway, its undercarriage folded and the bomber slid to halt on its belly. Fortunately, the crew emerged unhurt, but shaken. It was left to the 381st's Catholic chaplain Martin J. Collett to "invoke benediction" on Beckman and his co-pilot, David H. Brophy, who were then photographed praying beneath their crashed bomber.

* * *

Having arrived at his new base at Chelveston, John Howland quickly learned that his new role would bring about much more responsibility.

"I will be either the lead or deputy lead navigator for a wing (54 ships)," he noted.[18]

Howland's was one of five crews ordered to "go to bed" on March 21, after they were scheduled to lead a mission the following day. When Howland asked his new commander when their training to become "a lead team" would begin, he was curtly informed he was a lead navigator "as of now" and to "get going." Howland was left dismayed.

"That was the shortest school and break in combat I ever saw or heard of," he wrote. "It's beginning to look like we might have been conned."[19]

Howland was not woken for a mission the next day, although 300 of his former 381st comrades were. The target for the group was a bomber assembly plant at Oranienburg, some 17 miles northwest of Berlin. The raid was to be led by former internee, Maj. Osce Jones flying in *Georgia Rebel II*, a bomber named in honor of his previous B-17F, *Georgia Rebel*, the first American aircraft to land in Sweden.

At "station time," a bombardier flying his third mission with another crew inadvertently knocked a propeller as he walked past his pre-flighted B-17. The engine suddenly burst into life, killing 2nd Lt. Clifford W. Collum instantly. Despite the horrific event, his crew—none of whom witnessed the tragedy—took off 90 minutes later.

Almost 700 heavy bombers left England bound for Oranienburg and the nearby town of Basdorf. They were led by nine PFF B-17s dispatched by the 482nd, which was due to be withdrawn from combat after the mission to serve as a radar development unit. Flying through "six major flak fields" and arriving over a completely cloud-covered Oranienburg, the 1st CBW formation diverted to its secondary—the city of Berlin. In addition to the release of over 50 tons of explosives, a sick bag with the regurgitated remains of the previous evening's meal was tossed out of *Return Ticket* by its queasy radio operator, Stephen M. Gasper. Scrawled on the bag were words to the effect that Adolf Hitler's Germany "didn't look so good from the air."[20]

* * *

The crews were sent back to Germany 24 hours later, when 33 of them took off at 0645 heading for an airfield at Werl, 10 miles southeast of Hamm. Leading the 1st CBW, the group was unable to pinpoint the airfield due to clouds. A target of opportunity was eventually bombed, which was believed to be a factory in the town of Ahlen. Having overflown "Happy Valley" and witnessed the "token appearance" of 12 *Luftwaffe* fighters, all 33 crews returned safely to Ridgewell.

"This was a milk run compared to Berlin," wrote tail gunner Wayne Pegg in his diary. "Thank God that's another in."[21]

Pegg had another eight missions to go when he was woken up at 0245 the following morning. He was one of over 200 airmen scheduled to fly the group's 84th mission. Like Pegg, Tommy LaMore had also flown the previous day and was left feeling lethargic after being woken.

"My clothes went on slow, I couldn't seem to wake up, and when we got outside, the weather was completely closed in," he wrote. "After we sat down in the briefing room, the curtain came back kind of slowly, almost sadly."[22]

It revealed a long, red line stretching towards a word that he and the other crews "knew and dreaded"—Schweinfurt.

Just after 0545, 22 B-17s began climbing into the overcast. Less than two minutes after lifting off, however, newly assigned 42-38102 was seen to veer "drunkenly" to the right, before suddenly diving into the ground.

"The plane pin-wheeled and exploded," recalled LaMore, who witnessed the accident from his tail gun position. "The explosion was a long, rippling, bright orange explosion that engulfed the trees and the brush. Then a flash of white light obliterated the whole area, throwing trees hundreds of feet into the air as the bomb load exploded."[23]

Once again, James Good Brown rushed to the scene of the crash, which was located on a farm near the village of Birdbrook, less than three miles from Ridgewell's main runway.

"I could not fathom how the parts of a plane could be sent so far," he later wrote. "We searched for the four engines, finally finding them. They had been sent hurling through space to unbelievable distances."[24]

The wreckage was spread over an area of some 700 yards. Twisted propellers, burning fuel and body parts littered the landscape. Fortunately, those on the ground had avoided the accident, but several farm buildings, 22 houses and the village school had been damaged.

Pilot 2nd Lt. Kenneth T. Haynes had been on his second mission. He'd been assigned to the 381st just eight days earlier. Some of his crew, including his stand-in co-pilot, 2nd Lt. Ralph Bemis Jr., were flying their first.

"The entire afternoon was spent picking up and identifying bodies," recalled Brown. "They were taken to the base hospital where they were placed in a row—six of them, lying there in the evening twilight."[25]

When the medical officers had finished the task of inspecting the remains, only seven men could be positively identified. The tragic event was captured by visiting war correspondent Lawrence Beall Smith, who'd arrived at Ridgewell four days earlier. Smith, an artist who'd previously designed posters for the war effort, had been sent to England to portray the USAAF's medical practices pictorially. According to senior officers, Ridgewell offered more "atmosphere" than other stations, so Smith had been attached to the 381st. When he had finished painting his account of the crash of Kenneth Haynes's bomber, it was entitled, *Death of a B-17*. Smith had vividly captured a scene of death and destruction in rural England.

* * *

As the 381st continued on towards Schweinfurt, its crews found the weather "lousy from the word go." Briefed to expect several cloud layers, they found a dense screen all the way to their assigned bombing altitude of 20,000 feet.

"The feeling of flying in clouds is like driving way too fast with no headlights," noted Tommy LaMore. "We flew like that for hours. My back began to ache from the anxiety … I looked out the left window trying to see where our wingman was when a B-17 tail section loomed up right underneath me."

LaMore had no time to react before there was a "grinding crunch" and a sharp dive, which "slammed" him into the ceiling. His unnamed B-17 had collided with another called, *Bar Fly*, chewing its cockpit with both starboard propellers. LaMore's aircraft had also lost its nose. Both aircraft became locked together and dropped from the formation.

"We were falling fast, dipping and rolling left and right. I was slammed around the fuselage. There was a loud pop, and we lurched left and up. Then we stopped. It was as if the plane had rolled up and parked. We were gliding."

LaMore found himself on the floor of the aircraft tangled up in his parachute, which had popped. As he struggled to make sense of his situation, he glanced out of the window to see *Bar Fly* banking sharply to the right before suddenly exploding. Only its tail gunner, Rivaldo Cavalieri survived the blast—blown free to become a prisoner of war. His pilot, 1st Lt. Thomas P. Thompson, and eight other crewmen were killed.

LaMore's B-17, meanwhile, turned back for England with wind blasting through the fuselage and two dead engines, one of which was on fire. When the flames were extinguished, the crew then set about jettisoning everything onboard, including the bombs and ball turret. Even so, for another hour, the aircraft continued "pitching and rolling" as LaMore's pilot, 2nd Lt. John A. Rickerson, fought to control it. Losing altitude and too low to bail out, he then ordered his crew to assume their crash positions in the radio room. The two remaining engines could go on no more.

"There was a lurch and a bump, then the earth grabbed the plane all at once with a vengeance," wrote LaMore.

Having dislocated his shoulder during the earlier collision, he felt it "grind and crunch" as his B-17 impacted the ground before shuddering to a halt near the French village of Camphin-en-Carembault, close to Lille. The crew, who all survived the crash-landing, immediately set about destroying the aircraft—LaMore helping to disable its Norden bombsight. They then made off from the burning bomber, each scattering in different directions. Although six would later be captured, four would ultimately escape, including LaMore. It was the start of an incredible journey for the Texan airman, one that would see him fight alongside the French Resistance and beyond.[26]

After the 381st reached Germany, worsening weather conditions forced its remaining B-17s to seek out the secondary target at Frankfurt. Despite heavy and accurate flak that wounded one of the 534th's bombardiers, the group's 19 bombers returned to Ridgewell, landing in haze and poor visibility at 1300. Still, another 30 men had been lost from the ranks of the 381st on its 18th consecutive mission into Germany. It had been a trying raid, as James Good Brown observed when the crews assembled for their interrogation.

> The lines in their faces showed more clearly. Eyes were strained. Their talk was rapid and serious. They looked as though they had lived in hell. They were disgusted. They were peeved at someone; they knew not whom. They thought someone higher up had not done his job; he had not read the weather properly. The fliers cannot conquer the cosmic forces.[27]

* * *

While the Anglo-American chiefs argued over how best to keep striking at the enemy after their planned European invasion (Eisenhower favored a "transportation plan," with attacks on marshaling yards and supply lines, while Spaatz wanted to persist with the "oil plan"), British Prime Minister Winston Churchill was keen to strike at the Germans' rocket sites in northern France. On March 26, the Eighth duly turned its attention back towards French "Noball" targets—but only after having changed objectives.

With the 482nd BG removed from regular PFF operations, John Howland and his crew had flown from Chelveston to Ridgewell the evening before, tasked with leading the 381st to Leipzig as a new PFF crew. However, when the briefing began at 0345, Howland and his crewmates were nowhere to be seen. Not being 381st regulars, no one had thought to wake them. Finally shaken awake at 0405 ("there was no time for breakfast"), they raced to the briefing hut, then to their bomber, only to find the mission scrubbed just prior to taxiing. They were duly sent back to Chelveston, while the 381st crews were briefed for a "milkrun raid" later that afternoon.[28]

Navigator David McCarthy had been one of those who'd attended the briefing for Leipzig. However, McCarthy's commander David Kunkel—aware that it would be his 26th and final raid—stood him down before the mission was scrubbed. Later that morning, McCarthy was ordered to report to the 381st headquarters.

"There were 23 officers in the room," he noted. "We were about to be briefed for a mission. And so we were."[29]

Unusually, the group was to attack targets in the Pas-de-Calais region by squadron. It meant the time-consuming procedure of forming into groups, wings and divisions wouldn't be necessary. As the 24 B-17s began moving out from their hardstands at 1300, one of them immediately ran off the perimeter track, blocking six others from taking off. Nevertheless, the squadrons eventually made their way individually, reaching 12,000 feet at the English coast before making an 11-minute crossing of the Channel to France.

"No mission was ever a sure thing," wrote David McCarthy. "This time I took extraordinary precautions. I acquired a sheet of armor plate to stand on, and two flak vests. I intended to wear them both."[30]

Aided by clear weather, each squadron made a 90-second bomb run through moderate flak, which remained "off-target." The site at Mimoyecques was roundly struck, although accurate observations were difficult due to the "indefinite nature" of the site. After 20 minutes over enemy-occupied territory, the B-17s then made their way back to Ridgewell—David McCarthy's *Colonel Bub* among them. He'd finished his tour and had survived 26 missions, but he harbored mixed feelings.

"As we approached the English coast, relaxed and for all intents and purposes finished with my combat tour, I felt no elation. My crew was gone. With whom would I celebrate?"

When he landed, David Kunkel was on hand to greet him. After driving McCarthy to the interrogation, Kunkel then arranged a pass for him to visit London later that evening. When McCarthy explained he had five days until he was paid, Kunkel offered to lend him £25. "Hell, you're not going to get killed now," he said. "You can pay me back on payday." McCarthy could only smile. His fear was no more.

"No more flak, no more Me 109s or Fw 190s, no more gut-wrenching wake-up calls in the early mornings, and no more fresh eggs."[31]

The same couldn't be said for 1st Lt. John Silvernale. Having safely delivered David McCarthy to Ridgewell 24 hours earlier, he was woken at 0245 again the next morning to prepare for his final mission—an 850-mile round trip on *Round Trip Jeannie* to bomb a *Luftwaffe* airfield at Saint-Jean-d'Angély in southwestern France.

After a three-hour delay caused by fog at Ridgewell, the group took off to lead the 1st CBW. Arriving over a crystal-clear target, its B-17s delivered their bombs in what was described by wing intelligence officers as "the best bombing ever." Having left a perfect circle "completely blanketed" and one hangar "split open like a flower," the 381st crews returned to Ridgewell, a happy John Silvernale among them. He and the crew of *Round Trip Jeannie* would later receive a certificate of commendation for destroying their target.

* * *

The next morning, and for a third consecutive day, the crews were briefed for yet another French target and another *Luftwaffe* airfield—Reims–Champagne, 85 miles northeast of Paris. Briefed at 0530, the crews again endured another delay to their planned 0830 departure time, eventually leaving Ridgewell two hours later. Led by *Rotherhithe's Revenge*, the group's 30 B-17s formed part of an armada of 182 heading for both Reims–Champagne and Dijon–Longvic airfield, some 150 miles further south.

As the 1st CBW's 59 bombers approached Reims–Champagne, German anti-aircraft gunners soon found their range, pounding the formation as it passed overhead. The 535th's *Superstitious Aloysius*, flown by James Liddle, was immediately hit in its number three engine. Unable to feather its propeller, Liddle quickly turned his bomber back to England, the bombs being salvoed in a nearby forest.

Just as it arrived over the target, another 381st B-17, *Whodat – The Dingbat!*, was also struck, although much more severely. A direct hit blasted a gaping hole in the side of the fuselage just behind the waist gunners' positions. It left three gunners dead and the bomber's tail visibly twisted and hanging by several braces. Vital control cables had also been destroyed, sending the bomber out of control. Fortunately, its quick-thinking engineer, TSgt. Sebastian Quaresma, spliced some wire to the severed cables, giving his pilot, 1st Lt. Daniel C. Henry, some directional control. By reducing and applying power to its engines, Henry then managed to control climb and descent. His would be a long and precarious flight home, which would only be aided by the appearance (and guidance) of a group of P-38s from the 20th FG.

The 381st, meanwhile, had let loose its 75 tons of bombs, which succeeded in hammering the airfield's hangars and aircraft. With several other damaged B-17s among its formation—including a flak-holed *Rotherhithe's Revenge*—the 381st headed back to England.

Nursing a violently windmilling propeller that was threatening to wrench itself free, *Superstitious Aloysius* was slowly nearing the English coast. John Burke, its ball turret gunner, then spotted engine flames. As the B-17 descended, so the fire worsened. Anxious the aircraft would soon explode, pilot James Liddle ordered his crew to jump.

"I was the second from the last to bail out," wrote Burke. "Liddle jumped last after heading the plane out to sea."

The pilot had steered his B-17 "in the direction of Germany" and switched on its AFCE, but *Superstitious Aloysius* fell far short, crashing in a field close to the Kent village of Hastingleigh. His crew, including John Burke, then descended on various locations around the village of Woodchurch.

Burke was immediately apprehended by a shear-wielding farmer, who quickly realized he wasn't German. The rest, including Native American and Purple Heart recipient, Emery Naha, landed together. They were put up in an Ashford hotel—navigator Joseph R. Scott even using his escape kit's French Francs as payment—while Burke made his way back to Ridgewell by train.

"I had my parachute and harness in a bundle that I carried; all the time wearing my sheepskin boots with heated slippers because I had no shoes."

When he arrived in London, Burke checked his parachute into a hotel.

"The women made a fuss over it because it was nylon," he recalled. "I did not know if I would get it back."[32]

* * *

As their crippled bomber approached Ridgewell, the surviving crewmen of *Whodat – The Dingbat!* were left wondering if they would get back. Although none had considered bailing out, it soon became apparent they would have to. As their bomber began circling Ridgewell, officers in the control tower could clearly see the extent of its damage.

Commanding officer Harry Leber radioed Daniel Henry, informing him that his aircraft wouldn't be able to land without there being a danger of its tail snapping off. The crew would have to bail out—some over the airfield, while the pilots would take the aircraft to the North Sea before bailing out themselves.

"The pilot was daring the impossible to bring the plane home in such a bad condition," wrote James Good Brown. "But it indicates how eager they are to get to Ridgewell Aerodrome. We wondered every second whether the plane would fall apart. It kept circling the base."[33]

As a sizeable crowd gathered to watch the spectacle, the first man jumped, landing safely on the airfield near the control tower. He was immediately surrounded by well-wishers before being whisked to the base hospital. Another three crewmen followed, each landing nearby. The crowd then gasped in unison as a fifth man free-fell several hundred feet before opening his parachute. It was navigator 1st Lt. Fred Beardsworth, who'd delayed the opening of his parachute in order to clear the aircraft. James Good Brown was driven across a ploughed wheat field to collect him. Fortunately, Beardsworth had landed unhurt. He then informed Brown of the deaths of the three gunners.

Shortly afterwards, pilot Daniel Henry and his co-pilot 2nd Lt. Robert W. Crisler left Ridgewell and flew towards the East Anglian coastline, where they bailed out 10 miles from the sea. *Whodat – The Dingbat!* and Staff Sergeants James F. Norcom, Frank J. Kurtz and Sgt. Richard Toler, were left destined for a watery grave.

* * *

That evening, the surviving crew members of *Whodat – The Dingbat!* were heavily sedated while plans were immediately drawn up to send them to a rest home. For other combat crews, however, there was no respite. Over 330 of them were woken at 0530 on March 29 for a return to Germany.

Some, like 535th navigator Ted Homdrom, had flown four consecutive missions in four days. He was "eager for a break."[34] John Howland, on the other hand, was set to fly his first as a qualified PFF navigator. With several changes to his crew prior to take-off—including the addition of Maj. George Shackley as co-pilot—Howland felt it wasn't "much of a PFF team." He also noted there would be seven officers and four enlisted men onboard ("lots of chiefs!"). Nevertheless, he couldn't help but marvel at his new PFF radar operator, David C. Flanagan, who insisted on wearing his formal dress for the mission.

"If we are to get shot up or shot down, he doesn't want to be caught dead or captured as a POW in anything but his Class A uniform," Howland wrote.[35]

Leading the 1st CBW, the 381st targeted an aircraft assembly and components factory sited on an airfield at Waggum, close to the city of Brunswick. However, on arrival, the group was unable to bomb the plant visually. David Flanagan soon zeroed in on the group's secondary target, the city of Brunswick, and instructed his bombardier to toggle the bombs. Amid moderate but accurate flak, the formation released a mix of high explosives and incendiaries before turning into a 100-knot headwind for the return to England.

The *Luftwaffe* then appeared "for the first time in weeks." Several passes were made by Me 109s, which resulted in three of the 533rd's B-17s being hit by cannon fire. *Honey*, carrying the 535th's commanding officer Maj. Charles Halsey as deputy group leader, suffered severe damage to its number three engine and radio room, although its crew remained unhurt. *Honey* soon slipped back through the formation, before coming under the protection of P-51s.

Sweet and Lovely was also struck—a direct hit in the waist wounding both gunners. Close by, *Princess Pat* was also hit, which hurled the engineer and top turret gunner, Favian R. Calderon, across his aircraft. Fortunately, like both waist gunners in *Sweet and Lovely*, Calderon's wounds from exploding shell fragments were minor.

Arriving back over England, the group's B-17s groped their way through clouds from 9,000 feet to 600 feet. Only 20 of them made it back to Ridgewell, landing in a swirling rainstorm. Thirteen more were forced to divert to six other airfields around East Anglia. While Favian Calderon was "really glad" *Princess Pat* made it back to Ridgewell, both he and his damaged bomber found themselves in hospital.[36]

* * *

As March came to a close with a scrubbed mission to Ludwigshafen and Oberpfaffenhofen, the 1st CBW congratulated itself for having "carried things off rather well during the biggest of all months to date." The 381st was singled out for its "outstanding performance," particularly for its non-abortive record, which attracted the attention of the 1st BD's commanding officer, Gen. Robert Williams, who wrote a glowing citation:

> During the period 6 March 1944, this unit was ordered to fly thirteen combat operations, four of which were to objectives in the Berlin area. In carrying out these attacks, eight missions were flown with no aircraft returning early. This includes twice flying three successive operations with no abortive aircraft. The record achieved by the 381st Bombardment Group (H) for this period indicates that 98.4% of the aircraft dispatched attacked targets in enemy territory. The exemplary conduct of the crewmen teamed with the untiring application to the task at hand by the administrative and maintenance personnel of this Group has made possible the carrying out of these successful missions.[37]

The recognition of the 448th Sub Depot, which was responsible for the repair and maintenance of the 381st's B-17s, was thoroughly merited. It had helped the

1st CBW achieve the lowest abortive rate of any of the 1st BD's wings. This was largely made possible by the fact the section had worked tirelessly on 172 aircraft during March alone—115 for routine maintenance, 28 for modifications and 29 for battle damage. A total of 58 engines had also been used by the 448th, one of which was fitted to *Stuff* after its number two engine had been shot out on the mission to Reims–Champagne.

The B-17F formerly known as *Miss Abortion* had flown 36 missions since being assigned. Seventy-two hours after entering one of Ridgewell's hangars, *Stuff* was ready for a test hop to check its engine. Technical Sergeant John W. Randall, who'd been responsible for painting out the aircraft's original name after it had previously been censored, was confident things were fixed. A photographer was on hand to capture the nose art as it was rolled out of the hangar. Randall then joined a skeleton crew of six for the flight, which comprised pilot 1st Lt. Wayne G. Schomburg and the 534th's engineering officer, Capt. Paul H. Stull, Jr.

"As a crew chief, I always flew on test hops," recalled Randall. "We taxied out for take-off, but near the end of the runway, I realized that I did not have my parachute."

While he went to collect his equipment, *Stuff* took off to perform a series of circuits before returning to collect him.

"I was watching *Stuff* circling for a landing and lining up for a final approach when all of a sudden … it turned to the left and nosed into the ground … crashed and burned."[38]

Although it was never proven, it was "generally assumed" that Paul Stull had been trying to land the aircraft when it stalled with a feathered propeller.

"His interest in flying has long been known to me," wrote surgeon, Ernest Gaillard. "I know he obtained as much unofficial stick time as possible."[39]

Stull's was one of two bodies identified by dog tags, the other being TSgt. Donald B. Carr, top turret gunner with John Silvernale's crew, who'd vowed never to fly with another pilot. He'd been persuaded to join the crew of *Stuff* for its 90-minute test flight. The bodies of pilot Wayne Schomburg; TSgts Charles L. Carter and Mervin F. Wilson; and Pfc Albert T. McClain were later identified by wallets, dental records, and "exclusion."

Once again, James Good Brown found himself at the death of another B-17 helping to recover more bodies. He then arranged their burials at Madingley.

"To all of us in the bomb group, it was a sad experience," he wrote in his diary. "Such accidents are not expected, but maybe they are part of an ugly war."[40]

CHAPTER 16

Do Much for Doolittle

April 1–19, 1944

By the end of March 1944, the 381st possessed a total of 55 B-17s. Nine of them were ageing B-17Fs, including *The Joker*—the group's only remaining "original" bomber. Pride and joy of its long-term crew chief, SSgt. Andrew "Whitey" Strednak, *The Joker* was without Tokyo tanks and thus deemed unsuitable for combat. Together with five other B-17Fs—including David McCarthy's much-loved *Our Mom*—it was set for transfer back to the US and training duties.

Despite the abundance of bombers at Ridgewell, the 381st was short of combat crews. By the beginning of April, only 31 were available. More replacement crews were needed. For over four months, the 381st, together with the 91st BG, had been supplying bombers and men to make up an entire wing. During April, news filtered through that the 398th BG would soon be arriving at Nuthampstead airfield, close to the border between Hertfordshire and Essex. The 398th, which had been serving as a replacement training unit in the US, was set to become the third bomb group assigned to the 1st CBW. Its arrival could not come soon enough.

As April began, so the pressures of combat were briefly lifted. A week-long period of stand downs allowed the hard-pressed 381st crews time to rest and refit. By April 7, another 12 B-17Gs had been received, although one was transferred out for special duties.

Avenger, which had been assigned to the group in September 1943 and had flown just six missions, was ferried to Knettishall airfield (AAF Station 136) in Suffolk. The plan was to tear its insides out, fill it with a highly explosive mix of nitrostarch and napalm, then equip it with radio-controlled equipment. *Avenger* had been earmarked for Operation *Aphrodite*, a new, top-secret program using remotely piloted bombers to attack "hardened" targets, such as U-boat pens and "Noball" sites.

The 381st's 89th mission on April 8 was to none of those targets, but a *Luftwaffe* airfield in the northwestern suburbs of the city of Oldenburg. Briefed at 0545, it was another five hours before the pilots began taxiing out from their hardstands. Fog and haze caused a lengthy delay, which kept the rest of the 1st BD's bombers grounded. Making up not just a complete bomb wing, the 91st's 30 B-17s and the 381st's 29 now formed an entire division.

Shortly after take-off, newly assigned B-17G *Carolina Queen* suffered a malfunction of its undercarriage, which failed to retract. One of the group's few B-17s left sporting its natural metal finish, its undercarriage had to be manually cranked into position. Under the command of 2nd Lt. Leslie A. Bond, who was flying his first mission, *Carolina Queen* flew on towards Germany.

Arriving over the target, the 381st was bracketed by heavy flak for almost 15 minutes.

"[It] was intense and we couldn't get out of it," wrote tail gunner Wayne Pegg. "Everywhere we turned was flak and more flak."[1]

Luckily, despite receiving a "few holes," his B-17G, *Spamcan*, was able to drop its bombs through the smoke of the 91st's preceding attack and safely head back to England. All 58 other B-17s also bombed successfully, including *Carolina Queen*. As it approached Ridgewell, however, Leslie Bond was faced with another mechanical problem.

> I tried to lower the gear electrically, but it would not lower. The engineer cranked the left gear down and tried to lower the right, but it would not lower. When we came over the field and the squadron peeled off to land, I flew out from the base and climbed to 4,000 feet … circled over the field and contacted the tower for instructions. I was asked if we had tools aboard with which to salvo the ball turret. We did not have any …[2]

Belly-landing a B-17 with a ball turret in place could destroy the fuselage. What should have been a 20-minute job for two men with two tools now involved much more. Conway Hall, who had been promoted as the group's deputy commander, wasted no time in flying to the rescue. Taking off in an A-20 Havoc (part of his famed, but unofficial "Hall's Air Force," which included an "off-paper" Flying Fortress, UC-78 Bobcat, P-47, P-38 and a J-3 Cub known as *Fearless Fosdick*), Hall flew above *Carolina Queen* with a "tool kit on a rope," which he attempted to lower into the B-17.

"The bag broke before we were able to get to it," noted Leslie Bond.[3]

Hall quickly decided to land and switch to his personal B-17, *Little Rock-ette*. Loading the stripped-back, faster B-17E with a longer rope and sandbag, he flew in formation "50 feet above and slightly ahead" of *Carolina Queen*, while one of his crew attempted to feed the bag of tools through its radio hatch.

"I instructed Lieutenant Bond to keep looking straight ahead during this maneuver and not to look at me," remembered Conway Hall.[4]

Eventually, after 20 minutes, the tools were delivered in what the *Stars and Stripes* newspaper later declared as, "the first successful tool-passing job in the ETO."

Leslie Bond steered *Carolina Queen* towards the North Sea, where its ball turret was successfully jettisoned. He then returned to Ridgewell "in a flawless belly landing" that resulted in several bent propellers and a "skinned undercarriage," but nothing worse. Four hours after its graceful, turretless landing, *Carolina Queen* was being worked on in one of Ridgewell's hangars.

"Afterwards, we made sure every aircraft in the squadron had those tools aboard," remembered Conway Hall,[5] whose exploits USAAF press officers likened to the "aerial refueling stunts of the old endurance fliers."

* * *

Endurance flying was necessary the next day when 29 crews were briefed for what was expected to be a 12-hour, round-trip flight to Gdynia on Poland's Baltic coast. For 2nd Lt. Harlan D. Soeder and his crew, however, their long-distance mission in *Shoo Shoo Baby* ended prematurely.

After two unsuccessful attempts at taking off, Soeder instructed his crew to move to the radio room to balance the aircraft. Carrying a payload of propaganda leaflets and reaching a speed of 160mph, Soeder's B-17F again failed to lift off. He was then unable to stop the bomber, which skidded into mud at the end of the runway and immediately nosed over. Despite a demolished nose compartment, Soeder and his crew clambered out uninjured.

The rest of the group's B-17s flew on to Poland, but two hours into the flight, while battling poor weather trying to stay in formation, the crews were recalled, and the mission scrubbed. However, two of the 381st's B-17s became lost and tacked onto other groups before bombing Marienburg and Posen. Their missions were credited, while others were not.

A much shorter mission was in store on April 10, when the group was ordered to fly a five-hour round trip to attack a *Luftwaffe* airfield at Melsbroek, northeast of the Belgian capital, Brussels. The mission also saw reduced crews assigned to some of the group's B-17s.

With the *Luftwaffe*'s noticeable attrition, it had been decided that one waist gun position could now be left vacant. For the first time, each of the 533rd's B-17s flew with just nine crew members.

Arriving over the target in two formations, the lead group circled the airfield twice, but was unable to sight through heavy clouds. Led by Arthur Briggs flying in *Sweet-Patootie*, 20 B-17s flew 35 miles northwest, making a 40-second bomb run over the Dutch airfield of Woensdrecht. The trailing formation—a composite group made up of 381st and 91st B-17s—succeeded in dropping their bombs on Melsbroek, after two bomb runs finally led to a break in the clouds. Both formations then arrived safely back at Ridgewell.

The joy of the successful short mission to Brussels was tempered the following day by the prospect of another long-range trek deep into Germany. Waking up on a crisp morning, the crews were again to be divided for two attacks—one on the city of Cottbus and another on the nearby town of Sorau. Both targets were aircraft factories.

Having recently been made the 535th's new squadron navigator, Ted Homdrom was now either leading the 381st or the 1st CBW. It also meant he was only flying every eighth mission. His tour, therefore, was taking much longer. On April 11, he was set to fly his 23rd mission, this time as the 1st CBW lead, with Maj. Osce Jones as the wing commander.

"We were told that our primary target was Cottbus, where Germany was producing the first jet fighters," wrote Homdrom. "It was a high priority target for our air war."[6]

At 0630, flares were fired from the control tower and the first group of B-17s, led by Homdrom's *Georgia Rebel II*, began taking off at 0715. They were followed 30 minutes later by the composite group. Leaving the Suffolk coast at Orford Ness, both formations then began a grueling 1,450-mile round trip that would eventually see them sweep north after bombing both targets, before returning to England over the Baltic Sea and Denmark.

Twenty minutes inside Germany, a mass of *Luftwaffe* fighters appeared. Although the 1st CBW was largely protected by a strong Allied fighter presence, trailing groups, including the 2nd BD's B-24s, came under heavy attack. As the 1st CBW approached Hanover, the city's flak gunners immediately opened up, quickly striking *Baboon McGoon* in the edge of its bomb bay doors, narrowly missing the bombload. Blast fragments also destroyed the radio operator's command set and table, but missed wounding Sgt. Phillip M. Smith, Jr. Nevertheless, the aircraft's rudder control cables had been severed and *Baboon McGoon* began to "slip-slide" from the formation. Using his AFCE, the pilot, 2nd Lt. Rolland O. Schindler eventually brought the aircraft under control after dropping some 2,000 feet. He was then covered by several P-51s that continued escorting.

During the commotion, the 534th's *Round Trip Jeannie* was also hit by flak, which damaged its number two engine. After feathering its propeller, 2nd Lt. Robert W. Hesse's aircraft slowly fell behind the formation. Jettisoning his bombs sometime later, he then attempted to catch up and move back into position but was singled out for attack by a German fighter, which succeeded in damaging another engine. That, too, had to be feathered. Shortly after, the same engine caught fire, the blaze spreading rapidly along the wing. Hesse ordered his crew to bail out, before their aircraft went into a dive. *Round Trip Jeannie* then plummeted into a forest near the village of Tzschelln, its wreckage being immediately descended on by local residents, eager for souvenirs.

Robert Hesse and his crew landed nearby, the majority quickly being caught. Hesse evaded capture for two days, as did bombardier 2nd Lt. Leo S. Bach, although both were eventually taken prisoner. Only the ball turret gunner, SSgt. Bernard J. Blanch, managed to evade for longer. After travelling almost 50 miles, he was picked up by a member of the German Home Guard 14 days later. Nevertheless, having accounted for only nine POWs, the crash of *Round Trip Jeannie* began to perplex the Germans. Unknown to them at the time, the crash of the B-17 was the 381st's first loss of a nine-man crew.

Baboon McGoon and its crew of nine, meanwhile, were struggling on—although under the close protection of several P-51s. The 381st's other bombers had also arrived over their targets, but Cottbus was found to be largely covered by cloud. Ted Homdrom's *Georgia Rebel II* made two 360-degree turns before the target was finally sighted. The 381st's formation of B-17s followed, becoming the only group to successfully bomb its primary. The 91st flew on to bomb a target of opportunity. The 1st BD formations, including the 381st bombers that had attacked Sorau, then began their long journey back to England.

By the time *Baboon McGoon* arrived back over Ridgewell, it had been escorted by a variety of P-51s, P-38s and P-47s. However, as the bomber made its final approach, it began gliding to the right. Two more attempts were made to line up with the runway, before its pilot, Rolland Schindler, and his co-pilot, 2nd Lt. Arthur J. Bailey, made a concerted effort to land using just their throttles, ailerons and elevators. *Baboon McGoon* touched down before coming to a halt just off the runway—its nine-man crew unscathed.

After "hooch" was served and the crews interrogated, the members of *Baboon McGoon* celebrated their homecoming with an evening at the *King's Head* pub in the village of Ridgewell. For many of the others, however, they could think of nothing but sleep. Co-pilot Troy Jones had flown his ninth mission. It had also been one of the 381st's longest so far.

> It was 11 hours and 20 minutes long—that's air time, mostly at altitude and on oxygen, which is more wearing and tiring than flying at lower altitudes. When you add to that 11:20 another three hours or so before the mission—getting up, eating, going to briefing; then at the end of the mission another hour or so for debriefing; you can see it was a pretty long day. Plus, with the tension of the mission itself, you can understand why no one needed to sing us to sleep that night.[7]

* * *

After receiving a stand down order overnight (rumored to be a "bouquet" for the 381st after its performance the day before), the men awoke to a thick fog enveloping the base. "Even the pigeons are walking," quipped the 535th's diarist. The weather then cleared sufficiently for the group's 92nd mission a day later. When the curtain was drawn back at the briefing, thick fog would have been much more preferable.

"The word 'Schweinfurt' is a bad word in the 381st Bomb Group," noted chaplain James Good Brown. "It brings too many unpleasant memories to our minds."

Brown sat through the briefing before being approached by 535th co-pilot 1st Lt. Thomas "Paxton" Sherwood, who asked Brown to accompany him outside.

"Together we walked out of the building and stood alone, looking up into the heavens," remembered Brown. "We stood there together a long time, not saying much—just thinking. There was a lot to think about. It was Sherwood's last mission."[8]

Paxton Sherwood, from Midway, Pennsylvania, had arrived in England in September 1942 as part of the 305th BG, then under the command of Curtis

LeMay. After helping to train LeMay's crews in blind landing techniques, Sherwood had then opted to transfer to the 381st as its chief instrument flight instructor. Re-entering combat, he'd soon been made the 535th Bomb Squadron's operations officer, replacing Capt. Elton Jukes in October 1943. However, just 11 days later, Sherwood had found himself replaced.

"Lieutenant Sherwood ... has been one of our problem children since he was assigned to this group," noted flight surgeon Ernest Gaillard. "He came to the ETO about 18–20 months ago and was grounded shortly thereafter for possible fear reaction."

Despite complaints "both real and imaginary," Gaillard felt Sherwood was "adjusting ... to his lot in life."[9]

Sherwood's *Our Desire* took off into hazy weather just after 1000, piloted by 2nd Lt. James F. Mullane. Their nine-man crew was leading the 535th on a three-hour flight in towards Schweinfurt. Leaving the English coast near Walton-on-the-Naze, *Our Desire* and the 381st slotted into a formation of 172 B-17s, all aiming for the city's ball bearing plants. Another 450 heavy bombers were heading for several other German targets.

Nearing the target, the 381st was skirted by a mass of Me 109s and Fw 190s that attacked other groups on both sides. Paxton Sherwood watched one Fw 190 zip across the formation, hotly pursued by P-51s. He resisted the urge to stand up and cheer the "aerial Seventh Cavalry" on, instead focusing on the flak *Our Desire* was fast-approaching.[10]

Passing through, the 381st was rocked by bursts, fragments of which struck *Our Desire* in its number three engine and disabled Sherwood's co-pilot controls. The propeller was quickly feathered by James Mullane, who then radioed his deputy leader to announce he was having problems with another engine and may have to feather that, too. *Our Desire* then dropped from the formation, losing 500 feet per minute while being followed by two P-47s.

The B-17 flew on, continually losing altitude while attracting more flak, which succeeded in destroying another engine. It soon became clear that Mullane and his crew should bail out. After crossing the Rhine River, all nine jumped, landing near the small town of Klosterkumbd, three miles north of Simmern. *Our Desire* then exploded in mid-air before crashing nearby. Sherwood and the rest of his crew were promptly rounded up by German troops.

When he was later questioned at the *Dulag Luft* interrogation center, Sherwood was told that another airman had been found in the wreckage. The interrogator suggested it would be better for the dead man's family if Sherwood named him. Fully aware that all nine crew members had landed safely, Sherwood refused to say. Once again, the Germans were left baffled. Where was the tenth crew member?

* * *

Thirty-two B-17s landed back at Ridgewell four hours later. A number of them were damaged, including *Shack Rabbit*, which had been hit in the wing by an errant 20mm cannon shell. Fortunately, there were no casualties.

The only loss was *Our Desire* and its crew, which included another of Ernest Gaillard's "problem children"—navigator 2nd Lt. Patrick D. O'Phelan. Like Paxton Sherwood, he'd also been nursed through numerous complaints. However, both men were now gone, imprisoned in *Stalag Luft I*.

"Despite the fact that it solves the problem for us, we would rather not have individuals disposed of in this way," noted a matter-of-fact Gaillard.[11]

Unknown to the crews, their futures were now firmly in the hands of Gen. Dwight Eisenhower, commander of SHAEF, who'd been given formal control of both the British and American strategic air forces. While it wasn't immediately apparent to the airmen, they were beginning to turn their attention towards pre-invasion targets. In the meantime, they were stood down from any operations, which allowed them to focus on preparing their base for Eisenhower's subordinates, who were expected to descend on Ridgewell a week later.

Two days after the Schweinfurt raid, the 535th's *Squat n' Droppit* rapidly descended into Ridgewell when its pilot, William E. Bartlett, encountered a problem. The B-17G had already suffered a minor mid-air collision on a training flight six weeks earlier. It had also sheared the tail off another B-17 while landing 45 days before that. Then, three days later, two trucks had driven into it. After landing on April 15, and while taxiing around the perimeter track, Bartlett was forced to shut down two engines that were overheating. Before he was able to cut the other two, they suddenly burst into flames. The blaze quickly spread along the port wing, burning the ill-fated *Squat n' Droppit* "flat to the ground." Luckily, William Bartlett and his crew were able to escape just in time.

* * *

On April 18, the 381st returned to combat when 33 crews were briefed for an attack on a Heinkel aircraft components plant at Oranienburg. Thought to be a key facility in the production of He 177 Greif bombers, the factory had avoided being bombed by the 381st on March 22. Cloud cover had saved it that day, but as the 381st's B-17s lifted off for the eight-hour round trip, the crews expected to find clear skies above their target.

After a lengthy dogleg over the middle of the North Sea, the 1st BD formation of some 280 B-17s turned southeast for a 75-minute flight in towards Oranienburg. Among them was the 535th's *Patches n' Prayers*, under the command of Harlan Soeder, whose crew had recovered from their unceremonious take-off on *Shoo Shoo Baby* nine days earlier.

Patches n' Prayers was flying in the relatively secure spot of the high squadron in the lead group. Out in front and approaching the bomb run, the leader, Capt. Douglas

L. Winter, was forced to descend by 500 feet to avoid a cloud bank. Nevertheless, he was still able to discern the target through flak bursts.

Second Lieutenant Lou W. Yank, a bombardier with the 533rd, was transfixed by the sight of a six-engine transport aircraft taking off from Oranienburg's airfield. The "big baby" was soon spotted by a P-51 pilot, who swooped down and attacked the transporter as it climbed to 500 feet.

"They smashed it flat," noted Yank. "I saw it crash less than 300 yards from the take-off field and it blew up with a great explosion when it hit the ground."[12]

By this time, *Patches n' Prayers* had been hit by flak in its number four engine. Feathering the propeller and dropping his bombs, Harlan Soeder began a slow turn off the target, but was left trailing the 381st. Unable to maintain altitude, and then losing another engine, Soeder called Douglas Winter to tell him he was going to bail out. Some 80 miles northwest of Oranienburg, the crew successfully jumped, all landing safely. *Patches n' Prayers* crashed near the town of Ludwigslust—the group's 89th bomber to be lost in 93 raids.

The rest of the 381st's B-17s began landing at Ridgewell after 1900, but the 535th's *Me and My Gal* was still lagging behind. Hit by flak over Oranienburg, its pilot, 1st Lt. John H. Hallecy, had struggled to control his B-17 after its horizontal stabilizer was damaged. When his co-pilot went back to investigate, he'd found a loose cable and tugged on it. Almost immediately, *Me and My Gal* went into a dive, which Hallecy fought to stop. Only when he was helped by his engineer heaving on the control column, was he able to arrest the dive. *Me and My Gal* eventually levelled out after losing 15,000 feet in altitude. Hallecy, who was flying his final mission, gingerly made his way back to Ridgewell for a safe landing.

* * *

John Howland and his crew had a narrow escape the following evening when they flew in from Chelveston to lead the 381st on a raid planned for the next morning.

"An air raid was in progress as we were flying to Ridgewell," he wrote. "We landed just prior to a red alert, and watched a helluva bomb attack on Chelmsford, about 30 miles south of us."[13]

The attack by German intruders was actually taking place on the 121st Station Hospital at Braintree, the nearest US Army hospital to Ridgewell. Nine wards were demolished and two completely flattened during the attack. Although the hospital was full of patients at the time, miraculously, no one was killed and only a handful of people were injured.

After safely landing at Ridgewell and climbing into bed at 0130, Howland's crew were woken just over an hour later. By 0315 they were in the briefing room planning for a raid on another Heinkel aircraft factory near Kassel in central Germany.

"It looked like an easy mission," noted Howland. "Really wanted to go on this raid …"[14]

Thirty minutes after his briefing, the rest of the crews assembled. Take-off was slated for 0645, with the target on an airfield at Eschwege. David McCarthy's usual waist gunner, SSgt. John L. Bristow, was one of those who'd been scheduled to fly.

"Bristow awakened me, asking for help," wrote McCarthy. "He was going on his last mission and had been assigned to another crew as their ball turret gunner. He was very upset with the assignment because he had never flown in the ball."

Bristow was anxious about the tight space in the turret, which would make it impossible for him to wear a parachute. McCarthy agreed to go with him to the operations office in order to have him stood down from the mission. However, the shortage of crews meant there were no gunners to fill the position—Bristow had to go.

After testing to see if he could squeeze into the ball turret with a parachute on (Bristow failed), McCarthy arranged with the crew chief of *Ol' Man Tucker* to have its gun sight removed, thus freeing more space.

"Borrowing tools from the crew chief, we managed to get the sight out of the ball, and Bristow, wearing his parachute, fitted comfortably within the tight confines of the turret," noted McCarthy.[15]

John Howland's PFF B-17 was also being furiously worked on by other mechanics who'd found a problem with one of its superchargers. By the time the 381st's other B-17s began taking off, Howland's was still grounded. When it was finally fixed, it was too late to intercept the formation halfway across the North Sea. A disappointed Howland gave his pilot a course for their return to Chelveston, their hoped-for milk run aborted.

Almost 800 heavy bombers escorted by 131 P-51s headed for seven aviation industry targets in Germany. Only the 1st CBW—flying in two contingents and led by Conway Hall—was aiming for Eschwege, 25 miles east of Kassel.

After flying past the target, both contingents then turned west for their bomb runs. The first, led by Hall, managed a 40-second bomb run, dropping through a "hole in the clouds," while the second formation's view was lost. They were forced to make a 360-degree over the target, which invited an estimated 50 *Luftwaffe* fighters to attack.

Having crash-landed his *Carolina Queen* at Ridgewell 11 days earlier, Leslie Bond's unnamed 42-3525 was struck by cannon fire, which saw it lurch away from the formation and into a dive. Only one parachute was seen to leave the aircraft before it exploded in mid-air. Several did manage to bail out, however, including Bond, who was later found dead on the ground. Only two of his crew survived—co-pilot 2nd Lt. Wilbur M. Mason and engineer SSgt. Neal V. Clyman, who'd manually cranked the undercarriage of *Carolina Queen* and caught the tools passed by Conway Hall on April 8. Both were taken prisoner.

The leading 534th BS was catching the worst of the fighter attacks, which succeeded in downing a second B-17G. It was *Ol' Man Tucker*, flown by 1st Lt. Robert W. Rayburn, but also carrying replacement ball turret gunner, John Bristow.

Ol' Man Tucker had a six-foot hole blasted in the side of its fuselage and instantly went spinning out of the formation, missing another B-17G, *Avengress*, by just 10 feet. Burning fiercely between its port engines, it went into a steep dive before blowing up. A single parachute was seen to leave the stricken bomber.

Luckily, John Bristow's insistence on wearing his parachute had paid off. He was one of six men to survive the explosion of *Ol' Man Tucker*. Three others were killed, including pilot Robert Rayburn and his co-pilot 2nd Lt. Maynard V. Craft (who'd been assigned to the squadron only nine days earlier and was flying his first mission). The crew's radio operator, SSgt. Donald C. Peterson, was also killed when the aircraft exploded before he could don his parachute.

After 10 frenzied minutes, the fighter attacks diminished as P-51s intervened. Yet, 2nd Lt. John A. Martyniak's B-17 had been mauled, his gunners bearing the brunt of the attacks. Staff Sergeant William P. Palmisano had been hit in the chest by 20mm shell fragments, which knocked him off his feet. He managed to crawl back to his machine gun and continued firing until the fighter attacks stopped. Palmisano would duly be awarded the Silver Star for his actions.

His fellow gunner, SSgt. Gerald A. Goodman, however, lay dead, with a bullet wound to the head. John Martyniak, who was also wounded in the left leg, continued flying the damaged bomber to England where it made an emergency landing at Framlingham airfield. Martyniak, Palmisano and three others were soon evacuated to the 65th General Hospital at Redgrave Park, Suffolk.

Despite seeing two of their fellow crews shot down in flames over Eschwege, the group's returning airmen were given another task as they approached Ridgewell.

"We finally had the inspection that the base has been preparing for the last two weeks at the expense of the war effort," wrote surgeon Ernest Gaillard.[16]

Gazing up at the 381st formation as it passed overhead was Eighth Air Force commander, Lt. Gen. Jimmy Doolittle. Stood beside him were Harry Leber, and the head of the 1st CBW, the now-promoted Brig. Gen. William Gross. They were flanked by a plethora of other officials, including Maj. Gen. Joseph T. McNarney, deputy chief of staff; Lt. Gen. John C. H. Lee, ETO deputy commander-in-chief; Maj. Gen. William E. Kepner, commander of the 2nd BD; Lt. Gen. Carl A. Spaatz, commander of USSTAF; Brig. Gen. Robert Williams, commander of the 1st BD; and Brig. Gen. Bartlett Beaman, chief of staff, 1st BD.

Outranking them all, despite being a civilian, was Assistant Secretary of War John J. McCloy, who had largely been responsible for establishing the draft, as well as overseeing the purchase of war materiel.

Watching the B-17s land, the party—which included commanders from many of the Eighth's other bomb groups—then toured the base, spending 45 minutes in its workshops and hangars, while also talking to the men of the 381st.

However, while he may have been an American military hero, Doolittle's recent decision to increase the combat crews' tours of duty still rankled as the airmen assembled in the interrogation room after yet another traumatic raid.

Intermission: Zero Hour

As soon as each bomb group headquarters received notification of a mission alert, the group operations staff immediately relayed the alert to those sections around the base to prepare the required number of aircraft and crews for the mission. The group's lead navigator and bombardier would be among the first to be notified. They would quickly report to the operations room for initial briefing by the S-3 (operations officer).

Once notified of the target, the S-2 (intelligence officer) would draw available photographs, maps, and intelligence information from the intelligence archive. This secret target information was then updated and augmented with the latest weather data—the result being a "target briefing pack" that could be disseminated to the now-waiting squadron operations rooms. In the case of a short-range milk run, this activity may well take place in the early evening. An afternoon warning usually indicated a larger, long-range raid into Germany, or even a "maximum effort."

While the air planners went about their business inside their heavily guarded bomb-proof operations blocks, the ground crews set about preparing their aircraft for battle. The entire bomb group was working towards a common target, the time designated for the first aircraft to take off—zero hour. All planning was worked backward and forward from this datum point in the mission timeline.

There were a significant number of stages to complete before a bomb group could be launched on a raid, all of which had to be factored into the structure of the mission. For example, most groups allowed a minimum of an hour to assemble over England before heading toward the hostile skies of Europe. This tricky, and often dangerous, process could take longer.

Even after fueling, arming, and loading bombs, there were other planning considerations. The lead crew officers needed more time to plan. Consequently, they were woken earlier—four-and-a-half hours before the mission briefing was not uncommon. Everyone scheduled to fly would be physically woken by the quartermaster sergeant responsible for their domestic site—the day beginning with the sergeant's voice calling out the names of those nominated to fly and the aircraft they were to crew. Once awake, the crews followed a well-established routine cocooned within the complex rhythm of the group's progress toward the all-important zero hour. Thirty minutes was allowed for a quick shave, essential to ensure that the oxygen mask fitted securely, breakfast for those that could face it, and a visit to the latrine.

The format of the pre-mission briefing cycle varied a little between different groups. In most cases, the gunners were briefed separately at a much shorter brief. This was the case at Ridgewell—the 381st chose to invest the time gained in checking and preparing guns and ammunition before zero hour. Once briefing was complete, the group moved through a graduated series of steps toward zero hour. Ten- to fifteen-minute gaps punctuated the transit of crews through the drawing of flight clothing and equipment, transit to aircraft on dispersal, crews to stations, the starting and warming of engines and, finally, taxiing into position for take-off.

RAF Ridgewell, later known as USAAF Station 167, under construction in the spring of 1942. This image was captured by the RAF's No. 1 Photographic Reconnaissance Unit. (Authors' collection)

Joseph J. Nazzaro (standing), the 381st's first commanding officer, with the crew of Edwin R. Manchester, Jr. (back to camera). Kneeling third from the left is Robert L. Weniger—responsible for "naming" their bomber, *T.S.* (Authors' collection)

The hulk of *Sweet Eloise* rests outside one of Ridgewell's two hangars. Despite reaching the ETO, the B-17F never had a chance to enter combat, becoming the 381st's first "hangar queen." (Fold 3)

Chaplain James Good Brown stands outside the door to Ridgewell's base chapel. For two years, he lived, worked and wrote his diary in this building. (Authors' collection)

Landon C. Hendricks (left), commander of the 533rd Bomb Squadron, shakes hands with his passenger, Frank O'Driscoll Hunter, commanding officer of VIII Fighter Command, beneath the nose of *Caroline*. This B-17 would be destroyed on its hardstand less than 24 hours later. (Fold 3)

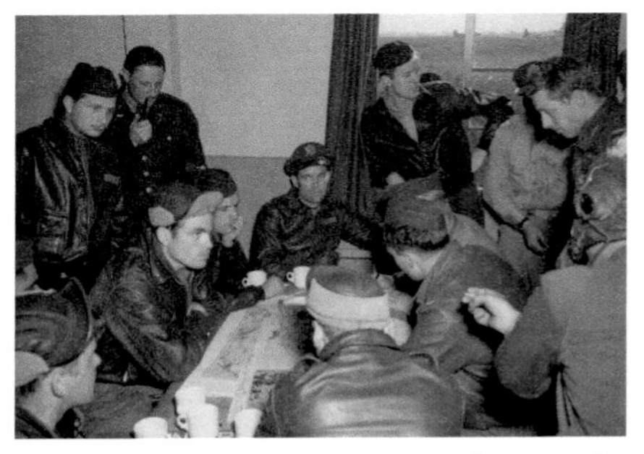

A pensive Joe Nazzaro (center) looks on as the combat crews are interrogated following the 381st's first mission—a raid on Antwerp—one that saw two of its crews lost. (Fold 3)

The wreckage of *Caroline* is strewn across its hardstand following an accidental explosion while being loaded for the 381st's second bombing mission on June 23, 1943. (Authors' collection)

Staff Sergeant Francis "Bud" E. Owens dons his flight clothing while training at Pyote, Texas. Hailed a hero after the *Caroline* explosion, Owens would also come to the aid of several others in the months that followed. (Geert Van Den Bogaert, Sean Claxton, Colleen Brennan)

Technical Sergeant John S. Comer enlisted in the USAAF at the age of 33. A former National Guard cavalryman from Texas, Comer joined the 381st as a replacement engineer/top turret gunner in July 1943. (Authors' collection)

Curious locals inspect *Georgia Rebel* shortly after it bellied into a boggy field just outside the Swedish hamlet of Vännacka. Osce V. Jones and his crew became the first Americans to be interned by the Swedish government. (Pär Henningsson)

The strain shows as Frank G. Chapman's crew is interrogated after the 381st's third mission on June 25, 1943. By now, the group had suffered 56 casualties. (Fold 3)

Navigator David A. McCarthy (back row, second right) and the crew of *Our Mom.* (Fold 3)

Captain Dexter Lishon (front row, second left) poses with his crew and their B-17F, *Bobby T*, just 24 hours before being shot down over Bremen on October 8, 1943. All 10 survived to be captured. (Fold 3)

Co-pilot Robert E. Nelson from Gresham, Oregon, is awarded the Silver Star by William J. Reed, 381st ground executive. Nelson and waist gunner Raymond A. Genz reputedly became the first American airmen to successfully evade capture and escape from Germany. (Fold 3)

Leonard L. Spivey experienced a rapid rise through the ranks of the 381st, becoming the 535th's squadron navigator and eventual stand-in group navigator. Spivey would lead his squadron on the infamous first Schweinfurt raid. (J. Ross Greene, Elizabeth Yee)

Co-pilot Thomas D. Sellers (far left) and the crew of the badly damaged *Tinker Toy* just days after their traumatic Bremen mission, which saw pilot William J. Minerich decapitated. (Fold 3)

Flight Surgeon Major Ernest Gaillard, Jr. and his English bride, Dorothy, leave the Savoy Chapel in London after being married on January 17, 1944. (Fold 3)

Captain Arthur Briggs, 535th operations officer, survived the weight of responsibility and his branding for "lack of moral fiber" to successfully return to his duties and higher status. (Authors' collection)

The wreckage of B-17G 42-31278 in a wood close to Ridgewell. The 381st's first major flying accident on January 4, 1944, claimed the lives of Cecil M. Clore and his crew, most of whom were close to finishing their tours. (Fold 3)

The 381st's second commanding officer, Harry P. Leber, Jr. (third from left), listens as the Mayor of Bermondsey, Albert Starr (holding a bottle of Bermondsey-made ale), names the 533rd's new B-17G, *Rotherhithe's Revenge.* (Fold 3)

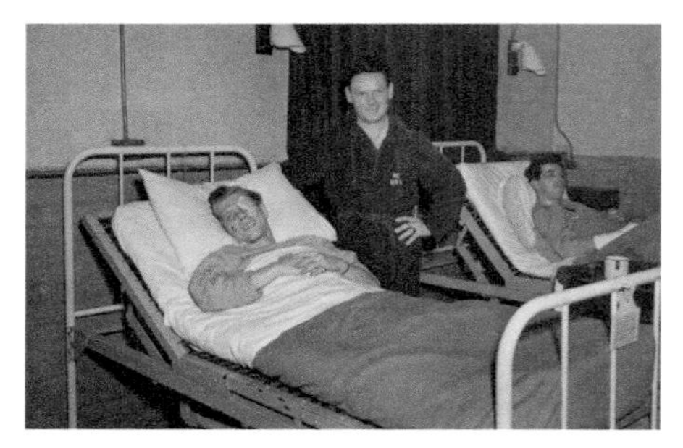

Technical Sergeant Lifford E. French stands next to the bed of Sergeant Herbert J. Burgasser, who lost his left eye during a mission to attack Avord airfield, France, on February 5, 1944. French would subsequently be awarded the 381st's second DSC. (Fold 3)

Pilot William D. Butler (left) is congratulated by James Good Brown after safely returning from his 25th and final mission. The picture appeared in the London newspaper, *The Sphere.* (Fold 3)

B-17G *Friday the 13th* (nearest the camera) piloted by Francis J. Flaherty, whose crew included Staff Sergeant Casimer "Casey" L. Bukowski, seen in flight sometime before February 1944. (Fold 3)

Navigator John Howland (front row, second left) poses in front of *Squat n' Droppit* after returning from a successful mission to Schweinfurt on February 24, 1944. The crew were handed donuts just before being photographed. (Fold 3)

A suitably equipped James Good Brown walks towards *Rotherhithe's Revenge* for his combat mission to Frankfurt on March 2, 1944. Despite it being prohibited for chaplains to take part in combat, Brown would eventually be awarded an Air Medal. (Bob Korkuc)

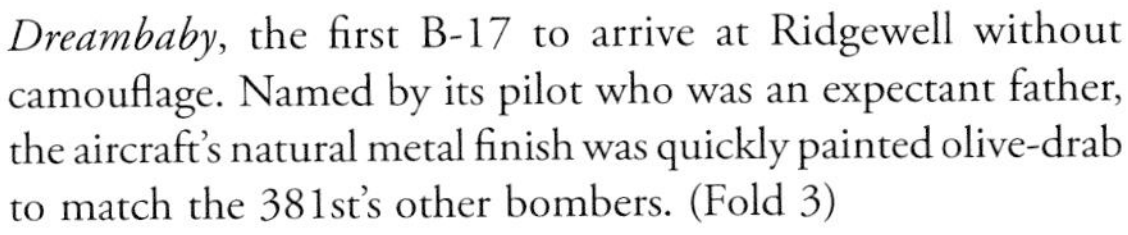

Dreambaby, the first B-17 to arrive at Ridgewell without camouflage. Named by its pilot who was an expectant father, the aircraft's natural metal finish was quickly painted olive-drab to match the 381st's other bombers. (Fold 3)

Troy H. Jones (back row, far left) and Charles E. Ackerman (back row, second left) pose with their crew in front of *Dee Marie*. Both men would volunteer for a second tour, but experience different outcomes towards the end of the war. (Fold 3)

The aftermath of the crash of Kenneth T. Haynes's unnamed B-17, which took place just eight days after the aircraft had been assigned to the 381st. The accident became the subject of a painting by war artist, Lawrence Beall Smith. (Fold 3)

Whodat–The Dingbat! overflies Reims-Champagne airfield just after receiving a direct flak hit to the waist. The blast left its tail visibly twisted and three gunners dead. The seven other crewmen were later forced to bail out, five over Ridgewell and two close to the North Sea coast. (Fold 3)

A 381st B-17 approaches Ridgewell across Suffolk's Stour Valley. It was standard practice for crews to fire flares, warning ambulance crews that a bomber was landing with wounded airmen. (Nathan Howland)

A photograph taken on the day *Stuff* (formerly known as *Miss Abortion*) took off to test a newly replaced engine. Hours later, its wreckage lay smoldering just yards from the end of one of Ridgewell's runways. (Fold 3)

James "Jimmy" H. Doolittle (far right) watches the 381st's B-17s return from a mission to Eschwege, Germany. Three weeks earlier, he had increased the combat crews' tours of duty to 30 missions. Stood alongside him are William M. Gross (center) and Harry P. Leber, Jr. (Fold 3)

Carolina Queen, under the command of Leslie A. Bond, makes a turretless belly landing after suffering mechanical problems during a mission to Oldenburg, Germany. Its safe return to Ridgewell was made possible by the aerial transfer of tools to jettison the ball turret. (Fold 3)

Subaltern Mary Churchill, daughter of the British prime minister, poses with a bottle of Coca Cola before twice attempting to smash it over the nose guns of the 381st's newest bomber, *Stage Door Canteen*. To her left are Alfred Lunt, Laurence Olivier and Vivien Leigh (far right). (Fold 3)

Ground crewmen pose with *Sunkist Special,* a Pathfinder Force (PFF) B-17G fitted with an *H2X* ground-scanning radar (the semi-retractable dome mounted in place of a ball turret). Assigned to the 381st in March 1944, it was lost almost exactly a year later in a landing accident. (Fold 3)

Wayne "Rusty" B. Pegg (back row, second from the right), tail gunner of the William A. Pluemer crew, flew 30 missions with the 381st before transferring to the Fifth Air Force in the Pacific. (Fold 3)

Superstitiously "unnamed" by its crew chief, but known by its crew as *Hit Parader*, the 532nd B-17G (nearest the camera) grapples with haze and contrails, as does the 533rd's *Martha the II*, whose bomb bay doors are open. Both aircraft would be lost in early 1944. (Fold 3)

June 6, 1944: D-Day. Pilots of the 381st are briefed in secret for the first of two missions to bomb gun emplacements overlooking the *Gold* invasion beach. By the end of the day, 46 sorties would be launched from Ridgewell. (Fold 3)

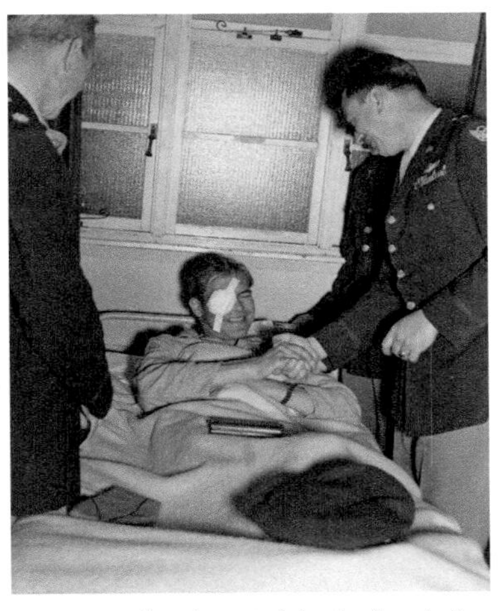

Laying in his hospital bed after being wounded on his 30th and final mission, a proud Theodore "Ted" Homdrom receives his DFC with Oak Leaf Cluster from the 1st CBW commander, William Gross. (Fold 3)

Checking a B-17's nose gun mount, Charles "Frenchy" A. Barbier waves to unicyclist George Grose as he rides past. Barbier was responsible for re-building the virtually destroyed B-17G *Big Mike*, which was subsequently renamed *Frenchy's Folly* in his honor. (Fold 3)

Damage sustained to the nose of the 535th's *Hell's Angel*, which was struck by a 100lb bomb dropped from another B-17. The accident killed bombardier, LeRoy Drummond. (Fold 3)

Movie star, Edward G. Robinson, is swamped by the 381st's airmen at Ridgewell after naming *Happy Bottom* in honour of his wife, Gladys—better known to him as "Glad-Ass." (Fold 3)

Eighteen-year-old Robert "Bob" B. Gilbert swapped his home in Long Beach, California, for a freezing B-17 ball turret over Europe in the autumn of 1944. He would survive 35 missions to return home in the spring of 1945. (Robert B. Gilbert)

The smoking remains of *Smashing Thru*, which slid into a railway cutting close to Ridgewell after suffering two engine failures shortly after take-off. Only the pilot, John M. Houston, and co-pilot, William M. Scruggs Jr., escaped the fully loaded bomber before it exploded, killing seven others on board. (Fold 3)

Bing Crosby arrived at a rainy Ridgewell on September 2, 1944. An estimated 4,000 people crammed into one of Ridgewell's hangars to hear him sing a number of his hits, including *White Christmas*. One of the 381st's audience members remembered that "even the rain drops seemed silent." (Fold 3)

Ground crewmen "sweat out" the 381st's bombers as they return from a mission. The waiting men sit around a signal square, which indicates the landing runway in use. Beyond is a smaller square displaying the letters "RD," identifying the airfield as Ridgewell. (Fold 3)

Ross "Bud" W. Perrin, Jr. pictured with his wife and former Miss America contestant, Thelma (née McGhee). Perrin was assigned to the 532nd Bomb Squadron at Ridgewell just four months before the birth of his daughter, Rosalind. (J. Ross Greene)

A member of the 534th's ground crews cleans the nose of *Schnozzle* using a baking powder solution. Tragically, despite their clear view, the crew of *Schnozzle* would not see *Egg Haid* as they returned from Aschaffenburg, Germany, on January 21, 1945. (Fold 3)

Conway S. Hall of Little Rock, Arkansas, joined the 381st as operations officer and rose through the ranks, eventually becoming its third and final commanding officer on February 6, 1945. (Authors' collection)

Robert "Bob" Armstrong (front row, far left) and his crew photographed in front of *The Joker*, the last B-17 they flew over Germany. Days later, Armstrong and several of his men left Ridgewell to join the USAAF's 5th Emergency Rescue Squadron. (Fold 3)

B-17 Flying Fortresses of the 381st Bomb Group taxi along the northeastern section of Ridgewell's perimeter track before turning onto its runway 24. The B-17 at the head of the queue is the 533rd's unnamed 42-97882. It would survive the war, having flown more than 80 missions. (Fold 3)

A 381st B-17 is photographed from another B-17 crossing a burning Berlin on February 3, 1945. The picture appeared in numerous British newspapers the following day. Ball turret gunner Bob Gilbert remained convinced he had captured the image from his position. (Getty Images)

Clarence B. Bankston, the crew chief responsible for maintaining the 381st's most famous B-17, *Stage Door Canteen*, is fed a huge slice of birthday cake by British actress, Anna Neagle. The event was held in recognition of the much-celebrated bomber's 105th mission. (Fold 3)

Charles "Hotrock" Carpenter and crew pose in front of their appropriately named *RAFAAF*, after mistakenly joining RAF Avro Lancasters over Cologne in March 1945. Both *RAFAAF* and the Carpenter crew would experience some extremely challenging moments before the war ended. (Fold 3)

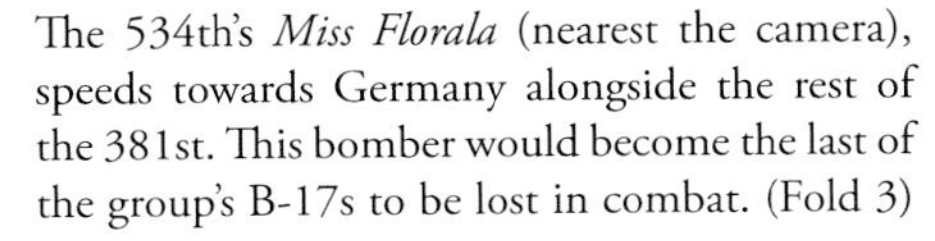

The 534th's *Miss Florala* (nearest the camera), speeds towards Germany alongside the rest of the 381st. This bomber would become the last of the group's B-17s to be lost in combat. (Fold 3)

The only recognizable part of what was a B-17 lies upright on the charred hillside of North Barrule, Isle of Man. Coming just two days before the 381st's final combat mission, the Isle of Man's worst aviation accident claimed the lives of 31 men, most of whom were ground crew members. (Authors' collection)

Andy Piter, Jr., an only son from Banning, Pennsylvania, was one of the 31 men killed in the Isle of Man tragedy. Piter had been at Ridgewell for almost exactly two years and was just two months away from being able to return home. (Donald J. Madar)

Some 24 hours before local civilians could officially celebrate the end of the war in Europe, the men of the 381st were already revelling at Ridgewell. Enlisted men sing and drink beer knowing they would soon be on their way home. (Fold 3)

On August 28, 1982, scores of American veterans and their wives returned to Ridgewell to dedicate a memorial to the 381st Bomb Group. They were led by their former chaplain, James Good Brown, dressed in his "pinks and greens." (Authors' collection)

Casimer "Casey" L. Bukowski of Buffalo, New York, stands on what remains of the threshold of Ridgewell's main runway. He had last taken off from here on February 22, 1944, to head to Oschersleben, Germany. Seventy-five years later, he finally returned. (Paul Bingley)

CHAPTER 17

The European Theater's Stage Door

April 20–May 8, 1944

A day after the 381st's high-ranking inspection, Adolf Hitler celebrated his 55th birthday. German propaganda minister Joseph Goebbels gave a congratulatory speech in which he extolled the virtues of "Our Hitler," claiming he was the only person who could deliver the German people their final victory. Goebbels also pondered how the history books would ultimately see the man "who stands above his times," claiming Hitler would become "the great historical figure." Goebbels then brought the air war into sharp focus.

"Few signs of the damage to Germany's cities caused by enemy air terror are likely to remain ten years after peace comes," he said. "What is likely to be recalled are the attitudes and behavior of those who withstood the terror."[1] Unknown to many, however, Hitler was already preparing his own form of terror, and the Allies were keenly aware.

At the request of the British government, Gen. Eisenhower was urged to give priority to attacks on "Noball" targets. Reconnaissance photographs showed that previous raids on the French "ski sites" had largely failed, with some being rebuilt while more had been constructed. There were also reports that rockets were being dispersed throughout northern France. On the day that Doolittle was touring Ridgewell, Eisenhower granted that Operation *Crossbow* be given priority over all other Allied air operations.[2]

"Briefing at 1400 hours and take-off at 1600 hours for the rocket gun installations—or whatever they are," wrote surgeon, Ernest Gaillard on April 20.[3]

After being delayed by poor weather conditions, 35 B-17s took off from Ridgewell bound for two "Noball" sites. Leonard E. Zapinski's B-17 soon suffered a technical fault while taxiing, which forced him and his crew to hurriedly switch to another aircraft. After missing the group's assembly, Zapinski then raced towards the coastal departure point to intercept his squadron.

"We never saw them," he wrote. "As we were about ready to come back home, someone on the crew noted a squadron formation, with only five planes, out over the sea."

After catching up with them, Zapinski found they were not sporting "Triangle L" on their tails.

"None of my crew recalled what markings they had, probably because it turned out to be a very traumatic mission."

Approaching the French coast at Calais, the small formation was buffeted by flak and severe turbulence. As they tried to locate their target, the B-17s made a series of circuits in order to avoid dropping bombs on French civilians.

"We made three 360s over the target all under heavy flak and each time around we could feel the airplane take hits," remembered Zapinski. "My co-pilot and radioman were both wounded."

Zapinksi's problems mounted when he lost two engines, one of which he was unable to feather. He then headed back to England with a vibrating engine, while his crew jettisoned everything, including their own flak suits.[4]

The 381st's other B-17s, meanwhile, found their targets covered by a solid undercast. Prohibited from releasing their bombs through clouds over occupied territory, they were forced to return with their loads intact. Even so, five of the 534th's bombers had been damaged by flak, while one of its co-pilots had been inexplicably struck in the leg by fragments of what was thought to be one of the group's own .50-caliber bullets.

As Leonard Zapinksi's B-17 neared the English coast, he soon spotted an RAF airfield. Radioing his predicament, he was invited to land. Before doing so, however, the windmilling propeller suddenly spun off and dropped away. Zapinski elected to press on towards Ridgewell, his crew firing flares on their approach to indicate they had wounded aboard.

"I stopped the plane on the runway and dropped out the front hatch, my legs too wobbly to hold me up," Zapinski wrote.

He was then approached by the 532nd's commanding officer, John E. Fitzgerald Jr., and operations officer Capt. Marvin Lord, who both berated the young officer for not locating his squadron, then going missing.

"My windshield had been all 'starred up' by a glancing flak piece at the last turn … I remember having to land looking out the side window … their questions were just a bit too much." Nevertheless, unlike the rest of his fellow airmen, Zapinski's mission was credited.[5]

* * *

"Londoners gaped in the streets last evening when wave upon wave of Fortress-Liberators flew high over the capital on their return from the Continent," read a *New York Times* article about the attacks on French "Noball" sites. Hitler's birthday had also been rounded off later that evening by RAF raids on French and German targets, in what was the highest number of bomber sorties flown (1,155) on a single night so far.[6]

Most of the 381st airmen could be excused for gaping when another group of celebrities arrived at Ridgewell the following morning.

"This particular occasion was quite outstanding," wrote chaplain, James Good Brown. "It was the first of its kind on the base and therefore attracted the attention of most of the men. Everyone was free, if at all possible, to assemble on the line to witness and take part in the christening."[7]

The subject of the christening was the brand-new B-17G-35-BO,[8] 42-31990, which had been assigned to the 535th exactly two weeks earlier. Its nose was freshly painted with a long, meandering nickname—*Stage Door Canteen*—which had drawn many an admiring glance.

"The noise of the men, a huge crowd, was unusual as they hovered underneath its wings, touching it, feeling its props and examining its guns," wrote Brown. "The crowd began to grow larger and larger until the plane seemed to be enveloped in a solid mass of men."[9]

Named in honor of a popular entertainment venue beneath the 44th Street Theater in New York, the new bomber was, in part, a tribute to the American Theatre Wing (ATW), which had been established in 1940 to raise funds for the British people.

The New York *Stage Door Canteen* had been opened by the ATW in March 1942 and was often staffed by entertainers volunteering their services to boost morale. Two of those were husband and wife movie stars, Alfred Lunt and Lynne Fontanne—also known as "The Lunts." Both had been seen "washing dishes and serving coffee" by "young, unknown hopeful," Lauren Bacall, who was also working in the venue as an usher.[10]

The Lunts's association with *Stage Door Canteen* had then led to both appearing in the 1943 Hollywood film of the same name. On April 21, 1944, Alfred Lunt's *Stage Door Canteen* connection finally took him to Ridgewell, where James Good Brown, for one, was delighted.

> The occasion was one long to be remembered in the 381st Bomb Group. The day was one of our highlights in our stay here in England. After all, our work is entirely directed toward destruction. Out of this comes no particular satisfaction or joy. No one is getting a kick out of loading bombs or dropping them, much less being shot at. Watching a prominent movie star christen a ship is much more fun.[11]

Alfred Lunt was not the star of the show, however. In addition to Winston Churchill's daughter, Mary, another famous married couple had also arrived to take part in the ceremony. *Wuthering Heights* actor Laurence Olivier and his wife, *Gone with the Wind* star Vivien Leigh, were also there to add their weight to the christening ceremony.

"Men were perched on top of jeeps, on the fenders of a command car, on top of airplane cranes, and on top of the wings and nose of the new ship—with all the hope of getting the best shot of Vivien Leigh and Laurence Olivier," wrote James Good Brown.

After a speech by her husband, Leigh then spoke to the crowd.

"I'd like to wish that the boys who fly in this plane will have the greatest good luck always," she said. "In fact, I hope that you all will, always."

It was then left to Winston Churchill's 20-year-old daughter, Mary, to christen the bomber. Dressed in her Auxiliary Territorial Service uniform, she declared, "I'm so very proud to have the privilege of christening this bomber. I name thee, *Stage Door Canteen*." She then tried to break a bottle of Coca-Cola over one of its nose guns, but failed. Swinging it a second time, she finally succeeded in smashing the bottle while showering its contents over several onlookers, including the 381st's commanding officer, Harry Leber. The Eighth Air Force's deputy head of operations, Maj. Gen. Frederick Anderson, stifled a laugh, while Churchill giggled, before quickly moving to wipe Leber's tunic with her handkerchief.

"After all alarms and excursions," she later wrote in her diary, "it was great fun."[12]

The christening party then moved on to Ridgewell's control tower, where they watched the 381st's B-17s take-off on a briefed mission to Merseburg, Germany. Owing to increasingly poor weather conditions, however, the mission was recalled 75 minutes later.

"We feel … that at times the people not directly in the center of the war are unaware of what war is," wrote James Good Brown. "Then when a ship is christened and the guests show some signs of awareness, it gives confidence to the men that perhaps they are not fighting this war in vain."[13]

* * *

After the party atmosphere of the day before, the men of the 381st went back to work on April 22, with an attack on the city of Hamm in western Germany. Taking off at 1615, 29 B-17s joined up with over 770 other heavy bombers—most heading for the city's marshaling yards, which served as a vital hub for the entire Ruhr Valley.

By the time the 381st arrived over the target, it was "buried under a pall of boiling black smoke" left by preceding bombers. The group's bombs then "went into the smoke," leaving hundreds of fires.

"I never saw so much smoke from a target," wrote tail gunner Wayne Pegg, who was flying his 25th mission. "Flak was meager and not too accurate, we got about four holes."[14]

All but one of the group's bombers returned to Ridgewell at the briefed time of 2200. They were aided by the base's high-intensity, low-visibility landing lights, but they also landed to the wail of air raid sirens.

Several German fighters infiltrated the bomber stream on the return, attacking a number of bombers as they landed at their bases. Fortunately, the 381st avoided any incidents, but one B-24 was forced to land at Ridgewell—its pilot having been warned away from his own base at Bungay.

The returning crews were then given just two hours' sleep before being woken again for another mission to Merseburg, which had been scrubbed two days earlier. Just after the briefing, the mission was scrubbed once again. The pace of combat was then stepped up a notch the next morning, when the group commenced a series of eight raids in as many days.

* * *

German airfields and aircraft production plants were the targets for all three divisions on April 24, as over 750 bombers were sent to attack seven different locations around Munich and Friedrichshafen in southern Germany. The 381st's target was Erding and its storage depot and *Luftwaffe* training base, 20 miles northeast of Munich—a 10-hour round trip.

John Howland, who hadn't flown a mission since March 29, was pleased to find perfect weather conditions crossing the English Channel from Beachy Head. Avoiding flak batteries over Europe, Howland's only discomfort came from sitting on an ammunition box for too long—the nose of his aircraft being crammed with radar equipment and two other crewmen. Passing Stuttgart, things "livened up" when German fighters made passes at other wings, but the 1st CBW continued on to Erding, where the group "smothered the target" before swinging south around Munich for the return to England.

"The beautiful Alps mountains and Switzerland were just 20 miles south of us," wrote Howland. "With their dazzling white cap of snow, the mountains were picturesque; too sparkling clean and pure to be associated with this ugly war."

Howland then watched battle-damaged B-17s "diving" towards the Swiss border. "I thought at the time, 'you lucky devils.'"[15]

* * *

John Howland and his fellow PFF crews were stood down the next day, when the 1st BD took off to attack several aviation targets in France. Leaving Ridgewell at 0615, 27 B-17s headed for the *Luftwaffe* airfield at Metz–Frescaty, 175 miles east of Paris, and just 20 miles from the German border.

Newly assigned navigator 19-year-old FO James "Hap" H. Chandler from Memphis, Tennessee, was flying his first mission along with the rest of his crew, led by 1st Lt. Samuel L. Peak. The Peak crew had been assigned to the 534th BS two weeks earlier and had been given a new B-17G the day before their first mission. Peak quickly named it *The-Betty-L*, in honor of his wife, who hailed from Louisiana, and his mother, Betty.

Hap Chandler, who had just become the youngest officer in the 381st, watched as the target approached. His B-17 then suddenly went out of control.

> We got caught in propwash that … threw us into a spin. When we pulled out of the spin, we were under the lead squadron, and they released their bombs on us. We were lucky not to get hit by the bombs, but a bomb shackle came through the wing. I think it is bad enough like it is, but when your own men try to bomb you out of the sky, that is too much.[16]

Two other 381st B-17s were also in trouble. *Return Ticket*, being flown by the 535th's 1st Lt. Emil L. Urban on his 30th and final mission, had lost power to its number three engine, while his number four was also giving trouble. Dropping behind the formation over the target, Urban issued an order to jettison all equipment, including the aircraft's ball turret. The B-17 immediately picked up speed and Urban was able to re-join the formation as it turned back for England. However, there were still over 300 miles to run.

Another 535th B-17—unnamed, because it had been transferred to Ridgewell two days earlier—was also having difficulty with its engines, caused mainly by flak damage. With one propeller feathered, another windmilling, and a third engine suffering a supercharger problem, 42-3511, under the command of 2nd Lt. Andrew G. Claytor, fell back from the formation, with its crew also jettisoning their equipment.

Most of the Claytor crew were flying their first mission. Only SSgt. Charles D. Middleton had any combat experience, with more than 20 missions to his name as Emil Urban's usual tail gunner. Falling seven miles behind the formation, the B-17 lost altitude as Claytor called for fighter support. After flying west for 170 miles, it became clear he couldn't keep up. He and his crew then bailed out at 11,000ft, before the B-17 came down near Précy-sur-Oise, 25 miles north of Paris. Claytor and six of his crew, including Charles Middleton, subsequently escaped and evaded capture, while two others were caught several hours later.

The 381st's remaining B-17s returned to Ridgewell after an eight-hour flight. Among them was *Return Ticket*, which had lived up to its name. Radio operator SSgt. Stephen M. Gasper couldn't be happier—it was his final mission.

"I was sweating out her ability to get home," he wrote. "But I guess I had nothing to worry about, for this is the third time she came home on three engines. She should be used to it by now."[17]

* * *

After two raids in two days (including an early wake-up call on the second mission), the men of the 381st had just got to sleep when they were woken again.

"One o'clock in the morning is a heck of a time to start a day's work," wrote John Howland.[18]

With their briefing set for 0215 and take-off three hours later, many of the men were already tired when they climbed into their B-17s. The 381st was soon leading the 1st CBW, which in turn was being led by group commander, Harry Leber. They were heading back to Brunswick airfield for a third visit in four months.

Pushed to the target by a "terrific tailwind," the 1st CBW found it covered by cloud. Dropping on the secondary in the city center using Howland's PFF B-17, the formation then returned to England, harried only by a few flak bursts along the way. Not one *Luftwaffe* fighter was seen and none of the 589 American bombers dispatched to Germany were lost.

Group bombardier Capt. William G. Fullick, who'd been flying with Leber (and who'd flown the group's first mission on June 22, 1943), was impressed with the "tremendous expansion" of the Eighth, which had occurred in a matter of just 10 months.

"It was tougher to go to France last summer than to go deep into Germany now," he remarked.[19]

John Howland was in total agreement. "Our escort was in complete control of the skies."

Howland, though, wasn't in control of his appetite when he arrived back at Chelveston.

"Don't know why it is," he wrote, "but after any long, tiring mission, I just can't seem to put any food down. Too nervous and exhausted I suppose."

Climbing into bed later that afternoon, he didn't wake up for the next 15 hours.

"I think I needed it."[20]

* * *

On April 27, new navigator Hap Chandler awoke to his 20th birthday. It was a day that would also see him help the 381st celebrate its own special milestone. After 10 months and five days in combat, the group was set for its 100th mission.

Briefed to attack another "Noball" site in northern France, 20 of its crews, including Hap Chandler's, left Ridgewell led by Osce Jones. They formed part of an armada of almost 600 heavy bombers heading for 25 separate sites in the Pas-de-Calais region.

"The early raids in France [were] characterized by small B-17 formations and intense hostile fighter attacks, and little, if any, fighter support," noted flight surgeon, Ernest Gaillard. "It certainly seems as though the Eighth Air Force has accomplished a tremendous amount now that it can raid almost any point ... with impunity."[21]

While *Luftwaffe* fighters were no longer such a threat, German flak gunners were.

"These Jerry gunners are the 'post graduates' in their line," noted the 535th's combat diarist. "They seemed to get plenty of unopposed practice."

Arriving over the target at La Glacerie on the Cherbourg Peninsula, some of the crews found the flak to be the worst they'd ever encountered. Although the weather was good, they were also unable to locate the target, which was camouflaged. After making one pass, during which time nine engines were damaged by flak, the group headed back to England—its bomb loads intact. Hap Chandler's B-17 was one of those whose engines were affected.

"Right after we passed over the target we noticed that number four engine was throwing oil, so we had to feather it," he wrote.

Another engine then malfunctioned across the English Channel. It, too, had to be feathered. Fortunately, Chandler made it back to Ridgewell in time for him to celebrate his birthday safely.

"... I still say that is heck of a way to spend your 20th birthday. I hope that my 21st birthday is spent in more pleasant surroundings."[22]

* * *

Hap Chandler found himself woken early again the next morning for an 0445 briefing involving another French destination—the *Luftwaffe* training base at Avord. The 381st had last visited the airfield 82 days earlier and caused significant damage. Since then, the *Luftwaffe* had converted it for "pathfinder" use. The group's B-17s were loaded with six 1,000lb bombs each, making it one of the heaviest loads yet carried. Twenty-eight crews were then assembled for the raid, which included the 535th's lead navigator, Ted Homdrom.

"I was told I was flying again with Major [Osce] Jones," Homdrom wrote.

Making his way to *Georgia Rebel II*, Homdrom was waiting for the rest of the crew when Maj. James E. Delano, the group's lead navigator arrived to tell him he was stood down (as lead navigator, Homdrom was needed for longer missions, "like Berlin").

"I must admit that I was pretty disgruntled ... having missed out on such a 'milk run'. I had also eagerly anticipated flying with Major Jones, whom I admired ..."[23]

Osce Jones, who'd been interned in Sweden the previous year, was leading the group for the second consecutive raid with 1st Lt. Harold F. Henslin as his pilot. Taking off at 0615, the group left Ridgewell at 9,000 feet, overflying London before leaving England at Selsey Bill on the Sussex coast. The B-17s then climbed to their bombing altitude of 14,000 feet, crossing south of Le Havre for a fairly straight run in towards the target.

Approaching Avord on the bomb run, light flak began tracking the formation. After bombing, the bombardier of *Georgia Rebel II* had just closed its doors when a direct flak hit blasted the number two engine, which was instantly wrenched away. The explosion also buffeted *Spamcan* flying behind. Osce Jones's left undercarriage then dropped from its nacelle and a long stream of flame trailed back. *Georgia Rebel II* banked sharply to the left and fell from the formation, tumbling through the low squadron.

"I saw it on its back and afraid no one had a chance," *Spamcan* tail gunner Wayne Pegg later wrote in his diary.[24]

Only three crew members survived the dive of *Georgia Rebel II*, which came down close to the village of Avord. Left waist gunner Sgt. William B. Blackmon, Jr.

parachuted inside the airfield's perimeter and dived into a bunker as the bombing raid continued. He was subsequently taken prisoner, as was the radio operator, TSgt. J. W. Padgett. The only other survivor was Maj. Osce Jones—original 381st crew member, 535th BS operations officer, and the first American pilot to be interned in Sweden. Jones would later join his former co-pilot and fellow internee, George McIntosh, in *Stalag Luft III*. Sadly, however, their navigator, 2nd Lt. Arthur L. Guertin—who'd been interned with them in Sweden and was also flying the Avord mission, having replaced Ted Homdrom—was KIA. It was particularly hard on Guertin's family, who had already received one telegram announcing he was missing after his forced landing in Sweden. It would be a further eight months before they learnt of his death in yet another telegram, this time received on New Year's Eve.

"There are no milk-runs," bemoaned the 535th's combat diarist. "Old timers among the combat men know that, and the newer ones learned it today in the loss of Maj. Jones and Lt. Henslin and crew in *Georgia Rebel II*."

It was one of two losses suffered by the 1st BD over Avord, the other being a 91st B-17, but it was the loss of Osce Jones that was "keenly felt."

The group's remaining B-17s landed at Ridgewell nursing some damage from flak and the few enemy fighters that had waited for the escorting P-47s and P-51s to briefly leave them before attacking. Nevertheless, their assault was deemed "ineffective," while the bombers left Avord's buildings "blazing" and its runways "pitted." Chaplain James Good Brown noted how the briefings for France were usually greeted with hope, yet they were proving not to be easy missions. The loss of *Georgia Rebel II* brought them back to reality.

"Daily we say: 'When will it ever end?'"[25]

* * *

Unfortunately, it was far from ending. Many of the combat crews were woken for their sixth consecutive mission on April 29—their target this time, the German capital, Berlin and its industrial areas. Twenty-seven B-17s were again loaded with 1,000lb bombs, while two PFF B-17s were sent from Chelveston. Navigator John Howland was stood down for the mission, but the 535th's lead navigator, Ted Homdrom, was selected to fly on one of the PFF B-17s, together with the 381st's operations officer, Lt. Col. David Kunkel. Both would lead the 1st CBW to Berlin.

Homdrom's past missions now stood him in good stead. After consulting with his unofficial flak map on the way to Berlin, he noticed the formation was due to overfly one of his previously experienced flak areas. Requesting Kunkel to adjust the formation's route to avoid the unbriefed flak, he was met with a testy reply. However, his assertion proved to be correct.

"When we were about five miles to the right and just out of range of the flak cloud, I gave the headings to get us back on track," remembered Homdrom, who was duly congratulated by Kunkel.[26]

Nearing the target, *Phyllis*, under the command of the 535th's 2nd Lt. Philip W. Gnatzig, lost a supercharger, rendering its number one engine unusable. Unable to feather the propeller, Gnatzig ordered the bombs to be jettisoned. He was then able to catch the formation as it approached Berlin.

Amid intense and accurate flak, another B-17G, *Big Mike*, was hit—the blast severing its hydraulic cables and damaging an engine. Its pilot, 2nd Lt. Ned W. Renick, slipped back through the 381st's formation before finding himself among another group. Renick still completed his bomb run and headed back for England.

Gnatzig's *Phyllis*, meanwhile, was slowed even further by the number three engine, which had also failed. With only two functioning engines and two windmilling propellers, he dropped back through successive formations before finally finding himself alone. Remaining undetected, *Phyllis* eventually landed at a "strange" English base, where the aircraft was found to have less than 25 gallons of fuel in each of its wing tanks.

The rest of the 381st's B-17s began landing at Ridgewell from 1600. One of the last to arrive was *Big Mike*, which touched down without brakes. Unable to stop, the B-17 careered off the end of the runway, crossed a field and smashed into a ditch.

"Luckily, no one was injured on that wild ride," remembered Maj. Raymond D. Jolicouer, commander of the 448th Sub Depot, the engineering unit responsible for the 381st's B-17s. "In the opinion of the inspectors … *Big Mike* had flown its last flight … the airplane was to be salvaged for parts."[27]

Even so, Jolicouer and his engineers—including crew chief, MSgt. Charles "Frenchy" A. Barbier—had other ideas. During slack periods, they would work to make the aircraft operational again.

* * *

April came to a close with a long-range mission to Lyon's Bron airfield in southeastern France. Only 12 crews were assigned for the raid, which saw them smother the target. Of 295 bombers sent by the Eighth, only one was lost, bringing its total losses for the month to 420, its highest of the war so far.

Despite this, the 1st CBW made several changes to its tactics. With the arrival of the 398th BG at Nuthampstead, the wing now formed five percent of the Eighth's bomber force. While the 1st CBW would still provide up to 60 bombers, some missions would be flown with 36—a dozen from each of its three groups. More importantly, the policy of removing one waist gunner would be formally adopted. The removal of one crewman and his ammunition would "correct" the B-17's tail heavy center of gravity, moving it forward by some five inches. It was hoped this would lead to less strain on engines, fewer aborts, and a decrease in fuel consumption.

A clear and cold May Day heralded the last of eight consecutive missions for the 381st. The crews were even allowed to sleep in longer. After an attack on Operation *Crossbow* targets carried out by other Eighth Air Force groups during the morning, a marshaling yard in central France came into the crosshairs of the 381st's crews later that day.

Briefed at 1145 and taking off at 1415, 25 B-17s attacked the French town of Troyes in what was considered by many to be a milk run. With no enemy opposition and only moderate flak on the way home, all 25 bombers landed safely, including 2nd Lt. Leonard Zapinski's newly named *So What?* Arriving with a violently windmilling propeller, Zapinski had already earned the nickname "Three Engine Zapinski," having lost one two days earlier, and another, nine days before that.

"I've come home on three so often that I can't remember them all," he joked. "That's partly why we're going to call the ship *So What?*"[28]

* * *

As the 381st returned from Troyes, so John Howland arrived at Bassingbourn. The Eighth's Pathfinder Force had been transferred from the 305th to the 91st's 324th BS, and Howland found his new base of operations "a real fine place."

"In fact, it is called the 'Country Club of the ETO'," he remarked.[29]

Howland was even closer to Cambridge, which was just 15 miles away. Like most 381st airman, he'd previously visited the town while taking advantage of the group's "Liberty Run"—a nightly truck service that delivered the crews to Cambridge, then returned them to Ridgewell six hours later. Since his departure from the 381st, however, its airmen had been restricted to just one trip per week. Together with a weekly 24-hour pass, it had become the extent of their freedom from the base.

John Howland returned to Ridgewell on the evening of May 3, after being briefed for a raid on Berlin the following day. Woken at 0200 the next morning, he then took off at 0615 in the lead B-17, *Sunkist Special*—an *H2X* bomber recently assigned to the 381st, but now loaned to Howland's 324th BS. With Conway Hall flying as co-pilot and "wing commander," the 381st climbed into overcast at 10,000 feet and groped its way to 22,000 feet to meet with the rest of the 91st. Reaching Lowestoft in "terrible visibility," the 381st's mission was scrubbed. Of 591 bombers sent on the raid, only 40 managed to reach the Netherlands, bombing a target of opportunity before returning to England.

* * *

With the pace of combat came maintenance pressures. During April, the 448th Sub Depot had built up 42 new engines, while 47 propellers had also been overhauled. With the group stood down from combat, a number of air tests could be carried out. One of the 532nd's new B-17Gs had undergone some work to its engines and the squadron's Capt. Douglas Winter was tasked with taking it up for an air test. In flight near Halstead, two engines caught fire and seized. Winter was forced to crash-land in a field eight miles from Ridgewell, where the month-old bomber was completely burnt out. Fortunately, Winter and his crew of three avoided any serious injury.

Although combat pressures had eased when the 381st embarked on its 105th mission on May 6, the target at La Glacerie had still seen the group sustain severe flak damage to a number of engines nine days earlier. Nevertheless, the group would no longer have to supply its B-17s to the 1st CBW's composite group. The 398th was now ready for its first mission as part of a new-look, three-group wing.

After another early wake-up call at Ridgewell, the crews were briefed to attack the "Noball" site at La Glacerie. While take-off went according to plan for the 381st, the 398th BG left Nuthampstead in a state of pandemonium.

During the lead-up to the mission, the 398th's kitchen staff hadn't been alerted to it. Consequently, when it came to the briefing (which was late and hurried), none of the crews had been fed. Some of the B-17s also hadn't been loaded with bombs, while the crews were left to wander around the airfield trying to locate their bombers when transportation trucks failed to arrive. By the time the new group began taking off, some of its B-17s only had partial bomb loads, while others had makeshift crews. Several more took off late and clung on to any bomb group they could find. Even so, the 398th flew on.[30]

Yet again, the 381st arrived over La Glacerie to find thick cloud cover and intense flak. Unable to release their bombs, the B-17s turned back for Ridgewell. Navigator Hap Chandler was happy to leave.

"Quite a number of holes in the plane, including one long gash just over my head, I was really scared," he wrote. "A number of other pieces of flak hit the wing, but by some miracle missed the gas tanks, thank God. I hope that I never go back there again, as even once was too much."[31]

As the ground crews sweated out the return of the group's B-17s at Ridgewell, a lone P-51 Mustang was seen to come out of the clouds in a slow roll and suddenly dive to the ground. The 381st's ambulances raced to the scene two miles away only to find the pilot, 2nd Lt. Ralph G. Boyce, dead. A new recruit on a training mission, Boyce had been assigned to the 4th FG at Debden airfield just four days earlier.

* * *

The following day, the 381st's attention was diverted away from France and back towards Germany. By now, the strategy of the Eighth was becoming clear to the 1st CBW's intelligence staff. When the weather over Germany was good, it was sent after "precision targets." When it was overcast, the groups would hit Berlin.

"We went over to the big 'B' again today," wrote Hap Chandler, who was flying his seventh mission. "But I can think of a lot better ways to spend Sunday than flying over Berlin."[32]

Six hundred B-17s were sent to the German capital, 29 of the 381st's among them. Led by Conway Hall in the group's new PFF B-17, *Dry Gulcher*, which had been assigned to the group the day before, the 381st steered the 1st CBW through intermittent and inaccurate flak.

"They were getting it up there, alright," noted Hall's pilot, 2nd Lt. Harold C. Blog. "But they appeared to be more interested in throwing it away than hitting us with it."[33]

Bombing through solid cloud cover, the group then returned to Ridgewell unopposed by the *Luftwaffe*, some of the men noting how "Big B" was "just another city now."

After an evening during which the 381st's officers enjoyed their monthly dance in the company of some 70 "show girls from London" ("the party progressed well with only a mild amount of trauma," noted Ernest Gaillard)[34], the crews were woken just a few hours later for a second consecutive raid on Berlin.

Taking off at 0545, the group—minus the 535th, which was assigned air–sea rescue patrols—formed part of over 800 heavy bombers heading for Germany. Again, the crews found a solid undercast, but this time, intense flak.

The only real cause for concern came when *Princess Pat* threw oil from its number one engine, forcing it to be feathered. An anxious few hours were spent alone, before the B-17 made it back to Ridgewell with only "5–6 holes."

Once again, the 381st's bombers had returned from Berlin largely unscathed and without any wounded airmen.

"Because of the influx of new crews, the missions do not seem to be causing any undue strain," noted surgeon Ernest Gaillard. "We have not had any psychiatric casualties that have required disposition for some time."[35]

As the happy 381st crews strode into the interrogation room at Ridgewell, Gen. Dwight Eisenhower had just made a momentous decision some 60 miles away at Bushy Park. In 28 days' time, the Allied ground invasion of Europe would begin.

CHAPTER 18

Brakes Off

May 9–30, 1944

Although rumors persisted, none of the 381st's airmen were aware a date for the European invasion had been decided. Even so, on May 9, all enlisted men were furnished with two clips of ammunition for their carbines (the thought being that when the invasion eventually took place, they would be suitably equipped to fend off any counterattack by German paratroopers), while some were attached to the base's military police to provide three-man perimeter defense platoons for "permanent base defense." Ridgewell was abuzz with gossip, weapons training and physical fitness tests.

When the field order came through overnight for an attack on an airfield at Saint-Dizier in France, the men were also unaware that it signaled the start of pre-invasion bombing. More than 800 heavy bombers were about to be dispatched to France, Belgium and Luxembourg in an attempt to destroy airfields and marshaling yards behind Hitler's Atlantic Wall.

The 381st sent 30 B-17s from Ridgewell to join 45 others from both the 398th and 91st. The now-full-strength 1st CBW made a 10-minute bomb run over the airfield, dropping 140 tons of incendiaries. Several major attacks on other targets were also visible to the returning crews, who reported "a mass of smoke" along the French coastline. Tail gunner Wayne Pegg of the 535th, who was flying in *Spamcan*, was overjoyed. He was on his way to surviving 30 missions.

"This was it and a beautiful one to finish on," he wrote. "No flak over the target and we really gave it 'hell'. Thank God."[1]

As Pegg prepared to leave Ridgewell (he would be transferred to the Fifth Air Force and the Pacific Theater), his fellow crews were woken the next morning for a return to Germany. Just minutes from the Dutch coast, however, the group was recalled due to bad weather. This was followed a day later by a scrubbed mission to Munich. The crews were then re-assembled for another briefing—this time for the French town of Sarreguemines and its boatyards, which lay at the confluence of the Saar and Blies rivers, close to the German border.

Thirty-one of the group's B-17s arrived over the target to find it obscured by cloud. Two runs were made through light flak, which damaged the lead B-17, *Dee Marie*, whose number three engine briefly caught fire. Nevertheless, the aircraft flew on, but surrendered its position. The weather then forced the group to seek out targets of opportunity. Two contingents bombed marshaling yards in the French town of Thionville, and Bettembourg, just across the Luxembourg border. The crews then caught sight of the *Luftwaffe* "for the first time in some time"—several Me 109s and Fw 190s making head-on passes at the low squadron. For the eighth consecutive mission, however, no bombers were lost and all returned safely.

* * *

Despite the focus on airfields and transportation facilities, the Eighth abruptly shifted its aim towards the German oil industry—in particular, those plants manufacturing both high grade aviation and motor fuel, as well as synthetic chemicals used in the production of explosives. On May 12, almost 900 heavy bombers and 735 fighters left England for the Eighth's preliminary attack on German oil production.

Leading the 1st CBW, the 381st's 19 B-17s were tasked with attacking Lützkendorf's oil facilities, 10 miles northwest of Halle. Several of its plants were known to be churning out some 300,000 tons of crude and synthetic oil each year.

Meanwhile, one of the Reich's biggest synthetic oil plants, Leuna, was being targeted by over 300 other 1st BD B-17s. Elsewhere, four other oil facilities were also being attacked by the 3rd BD's B-17s and 2nd BD's B-24s. Almost 1,700 tons of bombs were delivered for the loss of 46 bombers, including 14 from the 3rd BD's 452nd BG and 12 from its 96th.

The 1st CBW left "huge palls of smoke hanging" over Lützkendorf, which rose to some 15,000 feet. Although no enemy fighters were encountered, German anti-aircraft fire was accurate.

"The flak was extremely rough," noted navigator Hap Chandler. "But luckily we came home without a hole in the ship … knock on wood for me, because this squadron hasn't lost a ship since I went operational."[2]

Chandler was stood down the next day when the group went after another oil target, this time at Posen in western Poland. The group's 32 B-17s were divided into two contingents—one flying as part of the 1st CBW, while the other made up a composite group for the 40th CBW. After finding cloud and haze over both primary and secondary targets, the formations attacked separate targets of opportunity—the 1st CBW bombing the German Baltic city of Stralsund, while the 40th CBW dropped on the port of Stettin. All 32 returned to Ridgewell, with several crew members reaching the end of their tours.

Although no 381st airmen had been lost in combat during 10 missions, the group's surgeon, Ernest Gaillard, had noticed a distinct lack of "interest and drive" in both its officers and enlisted men, who, he claimed, had become "a bit stale."

> The war has lost its novelty for most of us and has taken on more drudgery than heretofore. Several officers have complained of being tired, fed up, irritable, and just plain sick of the

> routine, day-after-day work with no break. The answer will probably be one of two things: with awakened interest by the opening of the long awaited and delayed second front, or the number of passes and leaves will have to be increased if efficiency is to be maintained.[3]

Over the next few days, the men found themselves briefly freed from combat. A number of them were singled out for special praise during the group's first "review" and decorations parade, which took place on May 14. Stood to attention on Ridgewell's windswept main runway, they were inspected by Harry Leber, who presented an array of medals and "silver bracelets." The latter were mostly given to the ground crews for "meritorious achievement in performance of duty"—especially for servicing B-17s that went 25 consecutive missions without aborting. Leber was especially pleased the group as a whole had not seen a single abort in 10 consecutive raids.

The number of scrubbed raids frustrated the crews, however. Over a three-day period, two missions to Paris–Orly's *Luftwaffe* airfield and another to Rotenburg in Germany failed to get off the ground. Nevertheless, it gave the officers time to welcome new replacement crews to the 381st. It also allowed the squadrons to crew up their defense plans in case of an attack on the base. Finally, it was announced a different password would be issued by the 381st headquarters each evening. This would have to be used throughout the night by all personnel. Preparations for a "counter-invasion" took another step forward when a night-time guard was posted outside the 381st's headquarters building.

* * *

After five days without a mission, John Howland and his crew were briefed at Bassingbourn for one that would see them lead the 381st to Berlin the following morning. Flying their *Sunkist Special* to Ridgewell just after midnight on May 19, they managed two hours' sleep before being woken for breakfast and another briefing. Howland, who couldn't sleep, was even less keen on dining.

> Our reception at breakfast is becoming a depressing ritual. When we walk through the door of the mess hall, there is an audible groan as the men recognize the PFF team members and realize, for the first time, that the scheduled mission will be a Deep Penetration. Old friends and acquaintances that we lived with and flew alongside just two months ago now shun us like we have the plague. There is no compassion in their voices and no consideration of the fact that under a Plan "A" Deep Penetration, or a Plan "B" Milk Run to occupied territory, they get to go on the Milk Runs, but we don't. I try to tell myself that it is nothing personal; but it is hard to get a lift when the greeting is, "here come those poor forgotten … flyboys. Why don't you PFF guys stay home in Bassingbourn?"[4]

At the briefing, Howland learned that not only would he be leading the 381st, but he would also be out in front of the "whole damned Eighth Air Force." Three divisions of 888 B-17s and B-24s were set to attack both Berlin and Brunswick, escorted by 700 Allied fighters.

Thirty-nine B-17s, led by *Sunkist Special*, began taking off from Ridgewell at 0815 bound for Berlin's marshaling yards and industrial suburbs.

"This was the job for which we had been trained," wrote Howland. "Navigation is an art, and the hours and hours of practice coupled with the many mistakes made in the learning process, all combine to sharpen and polish our abilities to perform the task of being a lead navigator with the PFF team."[5]

Reaching the IP some five hours after take-off, the 1st BD formation turned east for a straight, 45-mile bomb run in towards Berlin. Nearing the target, Howland's bombardier found broken clouds, allowing him to make a visual bomb run. The *H2X* radar set was no longer needed, but the PFF's *Sunkist Special* flew straight and level towards "oily, black" clouds of flak.

"We could hear the bursts even over the roar of the engines and with our helmets and earphones pressed against our ears," remembered Howland.

A sudden explosion then rocked his B-17, and something struck him in the foot leaving it burning "like Hades." Howland later found only superficial damage to his boot and nothing to his foot.[6]

Just about the same time, the 532nd's recently assigned B-17, *Dry Gulcher*, was hit, its number three engine bursting into flames. Pilot 1st Lt. Harold Blog issued the bail-out order and all nine men jumped, seven of them being captured. Only Blog and his navigator, FO George W. Dennis, managed to evade the Germans, before being arrested by the Home Guard 48 hours later.

Another 381st B-17—the 533rd's unnamed 42-97454—was also hit just before dropping its bombs. Pilot 1st Lt. Earl Sharp immediately spotted flames beneath his wing. He was also unable to feather the propeller on his damaged number two engine. Sharp's bombardier, 2nd Lt. Francis W. Britenbaker, quickly dropped their bombs, while Sharp lowered the undercarriage to signal he was relinquishing the 533rd's lead position. Almost immediately, the B-17's entire electrical system failed, leaving him no option but to issue a bail-out order using only his hand signals. Partially anoxic after his oxygen hose had been cut, Sharp then managed to jump just before blacking out. Landing unconscious, the 17-mission pilot fractured his pelvis before being captured and hospitalized.

Britenbaker, meanwhile, had been helping the crew's replacement navigator, 2nd Lt. Wayne T. Hardwick, towards the forward escape hatch. Hardwick, who was flying his first mission, jumped ahead of Britenbaker, who was the last to leave the aircraft. It subsequently crashed 35 miles northeast of Berlin, the first 533rd BS B-17 to be lost in 34 consecutive missions.

"I saw a chute slipping as I was going down," Britenbaker later wrote.

It was Wayne Hardwick's, whose parachute had failed to open. He fell to his death. Britenbaker, who landed safely, was taken to view Hardwick's body after being captured by a German soldier.

"I was told … that he would receive a full military funeral with all honors due an officer of his rank," wrote Britenbaker.[7]

Veteran 533rd officer 2nd Lt. Frank R. O'Black was co-piloting *Lucky Me*, which turned away from Berlin after enduring five minutes of "extremely accurate" flak. Although he'd only been assigned to the squadron five days earlier, O'Black had already seen 18 months of combat in the Pacific. An enlisted member of the long-established 31st BS, O'Black had been undergoing gunnery training at Pearl Harbor's Hickam Field when it was bombed and strafed by the Japanese on December 7, 1941. O'Black had later flown on the first American bomber (a Douglas B-18 Bolo) to take-off from Hickam after the attack. Following service on Midway Island and the Solomons, O'Black had then returned to the US for cadet training. He'd "won his wings and commission" in August 1943 and was now escaping Berlin on his first mission in the ETO.

Two other airmen, both from the 535th, had narrow escapes over Berlin. Radio operator TSgt. Floyd C. Hanson and waist gunner Sgt. Nicholas M. Rotz were both hit by shrapnel. Unluckily, Hanson was struck in his side by a piece of flak, which found its way through the gap between the front and rear sections of his flak jacket. Despite a nasty wound, he survived. More fortunate was Nicholas Rotz, whose flak helmet and inner liner had stopped a large piece of metal from killing him.

At 1745, the remaining 37 B-17s returned to Ridgewell—John Howland's *Sunkist Special* continuing on to Bassingbourn, where it landed full of holes and its compass knocked out. Howland also discovered the explosion that had blown the hole in his shoe was caused by a ruptured oxygen bottle.

"I counted eight holes in the bottom of the plane, all within three feet of me," he wrote.[8]

Chaplain James Good Brown was saddened to learn the Blog and Sharp crews were missing. "These were now beginning to be the 'old timers' of the replacement crews," he noted. As their chaplain, Brown was also mindful he had a vital job to do.

> To write letters of condolence to the families of men who went down in combat is just as difficult as it was to write a letter for the very first man we lost over Antwerp, Belgium on June 22, 1943. I write fewer letters now, but I am nonetheless writing to a parent or a wife whose loss is just as heart-breaking.[9]

* * *

John Howland found himself back at Ridgewell later that evening. Woken at 0200 on May 20, he then trudged to breakfast.

"I was so tired, I felt numb," he wrote. "Even the groans and scorn the PFF team received as we walked into the mess hall didn't bother me."

Howland learned that his "Plan A" mission to Ludwigshafen had been scrubbed in favor of a "Plan B affair"—one that would take the 381st back to France and the *Luftwaffe* airfield at Villacoublay. Twelve B-17s soon took off from Ridgewell to form part of the 1st CBW's new 36-ship wing for the raid, which succeeded in scoring hits on Villacoublay's buildings, hangars and runways.

Despite a slight ground haze, the crews got a good look at Paris, even glimpsing the Eiffel Tower and Arc de Triomphe. They then arrived back over Ridgewell just as a disillusioned John Howland and his crew were landing back at Bassingbourn.

"I feel deceived, drained and desperately weary," wrote Howland.

Shortly after his arrival, however, he was handed a "silver bar" and promoted to first lieutenant. "It wasn't much of a lift."[10]

Former 535th navigator David McCarthy, on the other hand, found himself elevated to the higher echelons of the 1st CBW. He'd been made assistant wing navigator after successfully applying for a transfer.

"I spent a considerable amount of time trying to decide what to do," McCarthy wrote. "My wife wanted me to come home, but my understanding of the war in the Pacific convinced me there was no way the Army would permit all of the returned veterans to avoid a tour of duty against the Japanese."[11]

Hap Chandler, navigator with the 534th, was only a third of the way through his tour when he was woken for the group's 114th mission on May 22. The group's 26 B-17s dropped their incendiaries on Kiel's shipyards and naval base, led by the 534th's commanding officer, Arthur Briggs.

"I could see 250 Forts at one time, all in battle array," noted Briggs. "It really was an impressive sight."[12]

The eight-hour Kiel mission was followed 24 hours later by a return to France, and specifically an aircraft engine factory in the northern suburbs of the eastern city of Metz. Hap Chandler, flying his second consecutive mission, was glad to see it was being led by Harry Leber, who was also leading the 1st CBW. Although Leber was flying in one of the group's PFF B-17s, his radar operator was unable to distinguish the target beneath complete undercast. Going on to the secondary across the German border, the B-17s dropped on what the crews believed to be Saarbrücken's marshaling yards, although the group's intelligence officers later found it to be the town of Homburg. Nevertheless, all 25 B-17s returned from what Hap Chandler concluded was a milk run.

* * *

Second Lieutenant John J. Anderson, a co-pilot with the 533rd, knew not to expect a milk run the following day.

"At the early morning operational briefing we found out this mission was to Berlin," he wrote. "How about that? This would be my fourth mission to Berlin. This meant that I would have gone to Berlin on 25 percent of my missions so far."

Having bombed from 26,000 feet on each of his last three Berlin trips, Anderson was fearful when he saw the bombing altitude was to be the same on May 24.

"I thought to myself, that should make the Berlin flak batteries' jobs easier, knowing our altitude every time."[13]

Anderson was expecting to fly with his usual pilot, 2nd Lt. Arthur Bailey. Their usual B-17, *Baboon McGoon*, however, was out of commission. Instead, they were assigned the 535th's now famous *Stage Door Canteen*, before taking off with 38 others at 0600 for the near nine-hour round trip to Berlin's Friedrichstrasse district.

Led by the 534th, which in turn was leading the 1st CBW, the 381st's B-17s joined over 600 others making their way towards eastern Germany. Some 500 B-24s were also heading for several airfields in northern France. In total, over 1,000 heavy bombers and 800 fighters swept across Europe, most of them being hampered by dense clouds, persistent contrails and thick haze. Nevertheless, the 1st CBW reached its target just after 1100 and began its bomb run. A mix of general purpose and incendiary bombs were dropped through intense flak, before the formation began to bank away from the target, turning northwest towards Hamburg.

Troy Jones, flying as the lead pilot of the 534th, soon noticed about 60 enemy aircraft off to his right flying at the same altitude and in the same direction. They then half-circled to attack from head-on. Jones "reflexively" pushed his B-17's nose down to allow his top turret gunner a clear line of sight at the advancing fighters. Almost immediately, however, there was an explosion to his left. The 534th's *Avengress*, flown by 1st Lt. Carl A. Gardon, disappeared in a boiling inferno, followed in quick succession by *Carolina Queen*, piloted by 1st Lt. John A. Wardercki, and the 533rd's unnamed 42-31698, flown by 1st Lt. Clarence D. Wainwright, Jr. The 534th's *Joanne* was unable to avoid flying through the flaming debris, which immediately burnt through its rudder and horizontal stabilizers. The intense heat drove its desperate tail gunner, SSgt. Jack M. Ross, to bail out. He parachuted into captivity, while *Joanne* flew on.

The aggressive fighter attacks had also seen *Spamcan* lost from the formation. The B-17 was fired on by one Fw 190, before colliding with a second fighter as it followed up with another attack. *Spamcan*, flown by 2nd Lt. Walter K. Higgins, fell into a deep spin before exploding into several pieces.

Flying on the right, *Return Ticket*—its bomb bay doors still wedged open—was then riddled by 20mm cannon fire, which caused its left wing to break off. It then tumbled from the formation before exploding.

One of the 532nd's B-17s—the unnamed 42-38010, flown by 1st Lt. Clarence W. Ezzell—was also seen to drop from the group in a "slow let down" with its number one engine on fire. The bomber suddenly exploded at 20,000 feet. In a matter of seconds, six B-17s had been blown from the sky. Many others had also been badly mauled.

One of those was John Anderson's *Stage Door Canteen*, which had narrowly avoided the fiery collisions, but had been struck in its number three propeller hub by cannon fire. Blood-red hydraulic fluid had also spurted across the nose compartment's astrodome, with Anderson's pilot, Arthur Bailey, immediately fearing the worst. Fortunately, his navigator and bombardier were not wounded, although the aircraft's hydraulics were gone. He was also unable to feather the damaged propeller, which slowed the B-17 considerably.

"The vibrating propeller/engine was in turn shaking the aircraft's instrument panel so badly, we couldn't read the instruments," remembered Anderson. "Finally, the propeller seemed to break all connections with the rest of the engine and for a short period the vibration almost stopped."[14]

Despite this, *Stage Door Canteen* slipped from the formation and was soon flying alone.

Most B-17s were also being nursed back to Ridgewell, including *Me and My Gal*, which had suffered a fire in the nose that burnt both pilots. Elsewhere, 1st Lt. John W. Williams had managed to scrub the soot from his cockpit windows after steering *Joanne* through the burning wreckage of *Carolina Queen*. *Sweet-Patootie*, under the command of 1st Lt. Lawrence B. Wallerstein, was also wallowing along on only a single, fully functioning engine. Yet, it was *Stage Door Canteen* that was in most trouble.

With no radio compass, a failed oxygen system in the rear fuselage, and a number three propeller that kept working its way forward on the shaft, before shaking the "devil out of the plane," *Stage Door Canteen* then overflew Hamburg.

"We were getting intense flak," wrote Anderson. "The bursts were close enough we could see the individual explosions, even though we were in the clouds."[15]

Banking their lumbering bomber every 15 seconds, Anderson and Bailey wrestled with the controls for "what seemed like 20 minutes" before the flak diminished. Overflying Heligoland a short while later, they then encountered more, although its duration was shorter. The clouds then dissipated, enabling them to fix their position.

"Computations indicated there was perhaps enough fuel to get back to base," wrote Anderson.

Even so, they elected to jettison the ball turret to reduce the bomber's weight.

Arriving over Ridgewell hours after the rest the group, the crew hand-cranked the main gear one wheel at a time, while pushing and locking the tail wheel. They then discussed ways of stopping *Stage Door Canteen* without any brakes.

"I had read, in the *Stars and Stripes* paper, about a plane in Italy, which had lost its brakes and used parachutes after landing to stop their roll," remembered Anderson.

The crew duly fixed parachutes to the internal tail wheel assembly and close to the left waist gunner's window. On landing, the parachutes were deployed, slowing the aircraft as it reached three-quarters of the way down the runway. *Stage Door Canteen* then ground-looped and came to a halt, its windmilling propeller spinning off the shaft and rolling away from the aircraft. With some 200 flak holes and five 20mm gouges in the fuselage, *Stage Door Canteen* had made it.

"What a great plane to survive that punishment," wrote John Anderson. "Even more surprising, there was not a scratch on any of the crew."[16]

The same could not be said of many others, however. Fifty-six men were missing in action, 31 of whom were dead. Most never stood a chance of escaping their exploding bombers. Six of the men of *Spamcan*, including pilot Walter Higgins, had been killed. He and most of his crew had been assigned to the 381st just three weeks earlier, having already flown 30 missions from Italy with the Fifteenth Air Force.

By comparison, five of Carl Dasso's crew survived, although he didn't. Most were flying their first mission after being assigned two weeks before.

Not one of the crew of *Carolina Queen* survived. The B-17 that had crash-landed at Ridgewell in April after being helped by the tool-passing exploits of Conway Hall, now lay smoldering on the ground northeast of Berlin.

"BERLIN will be the last stand," wrote James Good Brown in his diary on May 24. "Therefore, when the line on the map points to Berlin, all our men know that there will be the last stand."[17]

* * *

Little known to the men, it would be their last visit to Berlin for some time. Instead, the following day they were France-bound, heading for Nancy–Essay's *Luftwaffe* airfield, a place the 381st had last visited in February. The group's 26 B-17s, led by Harry Leber in *Rotherhithe's Revenge*, were part of an armada of 400 bombers targeting 21 different airfields, marshaling yards and coastal batteries in France and Belgium. All 75 of the 1st CBW's B-17s dropped on Nancy–Essay, leaving "numerous explosions and columns of smoke" in an "eminently successful" mission.

It was the well-known *Stage Door Canteen* that continued to make the headlines, however. While the men were given a day's break from combat after the Nancy–Essay mission, they read about their celebrated new Fortress in a *Stars and Stripes* article about the aircraft's recent landing using parachutes as brakes. Badly damaged, *Stage Door Canteen* was still being repaired when the group prepared for its 118th mission on May 27.

German rail targets were the main objectives for the 1st BD, with the 381st forming part of the 94th CBW—its target being Ludwigshafen's marshaling yards. After taking off at 0745, the group's 19 B-17s crossed the English Channel from Beachy Head.

First Lieutenant Andrew H. Stuart of the 532nd, flying the unnamed 42-107023, soon called to say one engine was not giving enough power. As the group climbed to its bombing altitude over France, Stuart's B-17 was unable to. He then dropped behind the formation, before taking the decision to abort the mission.

Stuart's bombardier, 2nd Lt. Charles K. Eisen, salvoed the bombs and watched through the nose as Stuart "hit the deck" trying to make their escape across France. As the B-17 overflew the Montagne de Reims, however, his controls suddenly "gave" and the aircraft plunged into a forest before bouncing to a halt. The wrecked B-17 was soon discovered by a German patrol, who found Andrew Stuart and four of his crew, including Eisen, all alive. Only the navigator, 2nd Lt. Don H. Blyth, was dead. In the meantime, three others had managed to make their escape through the hills. It was the Stuart crew's first mission.

Ludwigshafen received a "bull's eye strike" by the rest of the group, which safely returned to Ridgewell. Less than 24 hours later, however, the crews were woken for another return to Germany, this time to attack an aircraft engine factory at Dessau.

Among the crews was that of 2nd Lt. Robert G. Beackley, who had been assigned to the 535th two weeks earlier. While Beackley had already flown one mission, his crew were flying their first.

Also flying the mission were John Howland and his "co-navigator," Ted Homdrom. Both were in the PFF B-17 flown by 1st CBW leader, Maj. Roy Halsey.

"We hit the enemy coast following our old highway … into Holland and on into Germany," wrote Howland. "There was a lot of haze over the target which, coupled with the smoke screen the Germans had put up to cover [the target], made it difficult for our bombardier to pinpoint the objective."

At the same time, several German fighters appeared, one of which hit Robert Beackley's *The Tomahawk Warrior*, disabling one of its engines. The aircraft then "dropped like a rock," its electrical system damaged. Nevertheless, it flew on.

Unable to sight the target in time, the formation flew past Dessau before finding a "large airport" at Polenz, 12 miles east of Leipzig.

"Really blew hell out of the hangar area," noted John Howland. "But the high group failed to see our bomb doors opening, and they didn't drop [with] us."[18]

The formation then turned back for England, eventually skirting the city of Frankfurt, where Halsey sent the high group in to bomb its marshaling yards. Intense flak then struck a number of the B-17s, wounding several crewmen and killing one. Sergeant George Samuelian, a tail gunner with the 532nd, was hit in the right leg and abdomen by flak and couldn't be saved. He was brought back to Ridgewell.

Another tail gunner, Sgt. William M. Cusick, flying in *Century Note*, had also been wounded in the thigh. Fortunately, through a combination of oxygen and artificial respiration, Cusick was revived by his crew and evacuated to hospital just after landing—a landing that almost saw bombardier 2nd Lt. Albert A. Saleeby killed. As *Century Note* slowed to a halt, a windmilling propeller spun off its shaft and slashed a three-foot hole in the fuselage just inches from him.

The Tomahawk Warrior, meanwhile, had slipped far behind the formation after suffering problems with a second engine. Flying at tree-top level, Robert Beackley ordered the crew to jettison everything they could. Bombs were manhandled out; the ball turret was salvoed; machine guns, clothing and anything else loose were also thrown. The crew then ducked as tracers "came up from time to time," while schoolchildren could be seen running out of their schools to wave. Eventually, *The*

Tomahawk Warrior landed back at Ridgewell with 217 holes and its tail gun position "blown away." Incredibly, none of the crew had been wounded.

* * *

After witnessing the fighter attacks over Dessau, John Howland had concluded the *Luftwaffe* wasn't "knocked out yet." Largely pegged back in Germany to protect the country's infrastructure, however, the opportunity to attack French and Belgian transportation targets could begin in earnest. Nevertheless, Eighth Air Force planners elected to press on with attacking German aircraft plants and major oil facilities. On May 29, almost 1,000 heavy bombers were dispatched to various targets in the east of the country. The 381st's objective lay in Posen, Poland, a target the group had failed to bomb 16 days earlier.

Taking off at 0800, 19 of the group's B-17s began a grueling 1,700-mile round trip, which navigator Hap Chandler noted was "the king of them all—an all-day hop." Despite a "very light fighter attack" and "meagre flak," most of the B-17s returned to Ridgewell, while several landed elsewhere after running short of fuel.

"I hope I never catch another one like that as long as I am ever here," wrote Chandler.

It wasn't to be, however. The next morning, he was woken early again. This time, Chandler was briefed for a round trip covering some 1,095 miles in six hours. But while he would be flying his 15th mission, newly assigned co-pilot 2nd Lt. William M. Scruggs, Jr., was flying his first. Even so, he and the rest of his crew were excited.

> Being young fellows, you know, ready to win this war, we were going to show them now that we could win it, and we were anxious for our first mission. We got up there, and we were flying, and we all had grins on our face. "Man, we made it! We're here! And you Krauts just watch out, because we're going to win the war now that they've got us over here." And we were absolutely just full of it, so eager and everything.[19]

Scruggs's *Via Panola Express* had arrived at Ridgewell two days earlier and was one of 30 B-17s lined up at Ridgewell ready for take-off. At the head of the line was *Spare Charlie*, a 534th B-17G being flown by a 533rd BS crew carrying the commander of the 1st CBW, William Gross. A few minutes earlier, he'd had his mission folder spread over the hood of his car while he briefed his crew. Now they were bound for Dessau, the target they'd tried to attack 48 hours earlier.

Spare Charlie was leading the entire 1st BD, which was heading for three separate targets in Germany. Leaving the English coast at Cromer by 0900, the 1st CBW formation neared its IP for Dessau two hours later. White contrails in the distance were an indication that some 50 German fighters were lining up and waiting. Just as the formation entered the bomb run, they attacked head-on—*Spare Charlie* one of the first to be hit. Cannon fire struck the B-17's batteries, which filled the cockpit and nose with smoke. Still, *Spare Charlie* flew on, its crew uninjured.

The 533rd's *Ol' Swayback*, which had been assigned just one week before, wasn't so lucky. It was hit by shells, causing a fire along its starboard wing. The aircraft slowly banked to the right and descended some 5,000 feet before exploding. The pilot, 1st Lt. Merrill O. Burton, who'd told his crew to "get the hell out," was unable to do so. He was killed when the aircraft crashed some 17 miles from the target. Three others were also killed, including top turret gunner John Eylens, who'd saved his burning bomber on March 16 after extinguishing a cockpit fire. Four others survived the explosion of *Ol' Swayback*. They included the navigator and bombardier, who were both blown clear and were able to deploy their parachutes. Most of Burton's crew were just five missions away from finishing their tours.

Another 533rd B-17G, *Connie*, was also badly damaged during the fighter attacks, which persisted throughout the bomb run. With its number two engine put out of action, *Connie* fell from the formation, two of its crew members killed by 20mm shells. Its pilot, 2nd Lt. John J. Monahan, then ordered the rest of his crew to bail out. Although he was seen to be preparing to jump, Monahan had inadvertently spilled his parachute. He was later found dead, along with three of his crew members.

Leonard Zapinski, flying his usual *So What?*, had been struggling with some "lousy formation flying" on the way to the target. Six Me 109s then attacked his B-17, causing damage to two engines and the ailerons. A long, thin stream of white smoke was also seen flowing from the right wing. With the aircraft starting to roll itself and on fire, Zapinski put the aircraft into a dive while his gunners fought off the attacks. It soon became clear, however, that *So What?* wouldn't be flying much longer. The long stream of "smoke" was fuel. Zapinski ordered his crew to bail out, all of them doing so. Seconds later, *So What?* exploded in mid-air.

As its radio operator TSgt. George J. Pastre descended, an Me 109 flashed past him, the rush of air almost collapsing his parachute. Just as he neared the ground, he was then shot at by civilians. Fortunately, he was picked up by German soldiers, as was Leonard Zapinski and the rest of his crew. "Three Engine Zapinski" wouldn't be making it back to Ridgewell this time.

Two more 381st crewman were also prevented from returning to base. The 535th's 2nd Lt. Robert E. Lutho and SSgt. James E. Dixon, who'd both been flying on *Me and My Gal* as co-pilot and top turret gunner respectively, had immediately bailed out after it was shot up during the first fighter attack. The shock had caused both of them to jump. Lutho found himself quickly captured by the Germans, while Dixon was later found to be dead. For *Me and My Gal*, however, its fight was far from over.

Pilot 2nd Lt. Howard R. Yates was aided by bombardier TSgt. Paul R. Van Derzee, who climbed into the empty co-pilot's seat. The two then fought to evade more fighter attacks, Yates, "diving, zooming, twisting and rolling" the B-17 for some 20 minutes. In the melee, they then lost another engine. With two engines out on the port side (one of which was windmilling), all six guns also out of action, and airspeed down to just 100mph, *Me and My Gal* was finally rescued by several P-38s, which fought off further attacks. When they felt sure the fight was over, the crew then threw out their flak suits and jettisoned the ball turret. Three hours later, they finally arrived back over Ridgewell—the hydraulic-less *Me and My Gal* landing without brakes.

"Lieutenant Yates and crew are excited and shaken, but in a good condition," noted surgeon Ernest Gaillard. "They are being admitted to the sick quarters for sedation this evening."[20]

Howard Yates and Paul Van Derzee were subsequently recommended for Silver Stars, although both later received DFCs.

Another three B-17s and 29 men were missing in action. William Scruggs and the crew of *Via Panola Express* were among the lucky ones to return to Ridgewell, albeit with a wounded gunner.

"All of a sudden, we all realized that this man's war was serious stuff," Scruggs later remembered. "That kind of calmed us down. And from then on, we weren't so eager and so revved up … we realized that this was serious business."

Intermission: Safety in Numbers

From the outset of operations, the defensive value of the massed firepower of mutually supporting bomber formations dominated the Eighth Air Force's thinking. The need to maintain the combat box remained prominent, even after the introduction of long-range fighter escorts that accompanied even the deepest missions into German airspace.

While achieving mission readiness dominated all thought and activity leading up to zero hour, every moment of the final hours on the ground was focused on ensuring that once launched, the group assembled as quickly and efficiently as possible.

Right from the instant they were woken, the crews were made aware of where in their squadron formation their individual aircraft was placed, and where in the group the squadron sat. Whether the squadron was nominated to fly as the high, lead, or low, had a direct influence on its position in the cab rank of bombers on the ground at zero hour.

The high squadron would take off first, the low squadron last, in the order of the three squadrons. The coordinating of the call forward, and subsequent sequencing of every single aircraft, therefore, required deliberate planning, regular practice, and choreography. All of this effort was designed to ensure that the aircraft arrived at the assembly point on time and in order.

The workload inside the cockpit matched the activity around the airfield. Maneuvering a B-17 on the ground required skill, judgement, and a degree of caution. The Flying Fortress was a huge tail dragger.[1] Its nose-up attitude prevented forward vision from the cockpit, and this blind spot increased the risk of ground collisions between taxiing B-17s. Braking to slow or halt a fully loaded B-17 on a wet or icy taxiway required anticipation, and the deft handling of brakes and throttles. With 50 or more other B-17s taxiing towards the main runway at one-minute intervals, there was little room for error.

Once in the air and clear of the airfield, each aircraft made its way to the altitude and location designated for assembly. Even in favorable weather with good visibility, assembling a group into a tight bombing formation could be challenging.

Different groups introduced their own methods to improve the speed of their assembly. Multi-colored assembly ships fitted with flashing lamps were employed by many. Chaser aircraft were another method of shepherding bombers into formation. The use of air-launched recognition flares, ground radio beacons, and signal lamps also became increasingly common.

Often described as a combat box, these formations were designed to maximize the collective defensive firepower of the heavily armed B-17s and B-24s. A close, uniform formation was also intended to improve bombing accuracy.

The term "box" came from the schematics showing the space occupied by each aircraft in the air; each aircraft shown as a brick that, when multiplied, collectively built a concentrated box. Bombing from a formation was a keystone of USAAF daylight bombing doctrine. The maintenance of a tight, well-ordered formation was considered critical to success.

CHAPTER 19

Triumphant We Fly

May 31–June 21, 1944

May had been a testing month for the 381st. Twelve aircraft had been lost, taking with them 108 men. A further three airmen had bailed out over enemy territory. Heavy damage to bombers that did return to Ridgewell also caused the 448th Sub Depot officers to cancel all passes and establish rolling 12-hour shifts for its engineers. The 24-hour coverage had seen 155 bombers worked on, 85 of which had required over a day's work. It was no wonder then, that by May 31, the group was among the highest achievers in the 1st BD, with an average of 25 B-17s dispatched per mission (versus 19 for the 1st BD) and only two aborts.

May closed with the 381st's 19th mission of the month—a briefed attack on a *Luftwaffe* airfield at Mulhouse, France. Heavy cloud cover forced the group's 25 B-17s to seek a target of opportunity, which was later discovered to be another airfield at Florennes, Belgium. The B-17s then returned to Ridgewell after a six-hour flight.

The next morning, the *New York Times* was categorical about the state of the Allied air offensive, proclaiming that, "at midnight the United States Army Air Forces and their allies in the European theaters had completed the greatest month of aerial warfare the world has ever seen."

John Howland and his crew had not flown a raid for three days. They'd been tasked with flying practice missions over The Wash instead—missions designed to hone the PFF's "through the cloud" bombing techniques. This involved the "camera bombing" of Skegness and its nearby coastline.

"Although we didn't know it at the time, we were practicing for the invasion," remembered Howland.

On June 1, his crew was alerted for a preliminary briefing involving an attack on gun batteries along the coast of France.

"At first, we thought the invasion was on," Howland wrote. "But the colonel assured us it wasn't. We were all a little disappointed."[1]

After flying to Ridgewell just before midnight, Howland "tossed and turned" before being roused at 0530 the next morning. After almost a year of operations, the 381st was set for its first "double header" mission.

The first of two objectives was a heavy gun emplacement in the Boulogne area. A total of 24 B-17s, each loaded with a dozen 500lb demolition bombs, set off at 0900 before splitting into two contingents. After overflying London and reaching Beachy Head, they turned east before reaching the IP at Dungeness, Kent.

"Our bomb bay doors were opened, damn near over England," noted John Howland.

Unimpeded by flak and fighters, the formations dropped through cloud cover using the PFF's smoke markers.

"It really was a milk run, and my first mission to France," Howland continued. "Sure was happy to get an easy one in for a change; but do hope we hit the coast, and the target through that thick layer of clouds. If we did, it might mean a few more easy ones to the coast for us."[2]

While Howland returned to Bassingbourn, 12 more 381st B-17s were readied for the group's second mission of the day. Taking off at 1730, they headed for a rail flyover at Massy-Palaiseau, on the southern outskirts of Paris. Set to bomb from 22,000 feet, the formation descended to 19,000 feet to drop through a partial overcast. All 12 B-17s then returned to Ridgewell at 2300.

The double header missions heralded the start of a seven-day period of consecutive attacks, all on various targets in northern France. The next day, June 3, the group's bombers returned to the Boulogne area to strike at more gun emplacements near Neufchâtel-Hardelot. Again, the group's B-17s remained unmolested, with Howland beginning to question the tactics of the Germans.

"I don't understand why they don't shoot at us," he wrote. "Perhaps they are saving their ammunition for more important targets."[3]

After what one crew member described as "the milk run of all milk runs," the group returned to Boulogne for a third consecutive day on June 4. Again, there was no flak, and the *Luftwaffe* remained absent.

This was followed a day later by another attack on French coastal defenses, this time at Tailleville, 10 miles north of Caen. After a short delay due to late loading, 39 B-17s were launched from Ridgewell. Crossing a cloud-covered English Channel, the crews eventually found clear weather over their target and made another unchecked bomb run, leaving "excellent results."

* * *

"Something is up," wrote chaplain James Good Brown. "We are smashing the coast of France. It feels to us in the briefing room that something is brewing. But we dare not say a word or give a hint."[4]

At 2200 on June 5, the lead pilots, navigators and bombardiers were called to the 381st headquarters building. Ted Homdrom was among them.

"As we had never before been called out in the evening, we sensed that something big was about to happen," he wrote. "As our Group CO, Col. Harry Leber pulled aside the curtain on the map in the briefing room, he pointed to the Normandy coast and said, 'Well, men, this is it.'"[5]

John Howland had heard similar words being uttered at his briefing at Bassingbourn. His was one of 17 PFF B-17s to take-off from Cambridgeshire and fan out across East Anglia to lead the Eighth's entire force of 40 heavy bomb groups. Ridgewell saw the arrival of Howland's and two other PFF aircraft. It was to be the start of a long day.

> We didn't get any sleep, and received our final briefing at 0130 hours. Security was extremely tight. Only pilots, navigators and bombardiers were allowed in the briefing room. All persons briefed were pledged to secrecy until the planes were in the air and the mission was underway. Only then could the location of the target be released to the crew.[6]

Ridgewell was alive with activity as men were "rushed to the line" armed with their carbines.

"The station defense was out in force and most of us were afraid of trigger-happy defense boys than we were of enemy action," wrote surgeon Ernest Gaillard.[7]

The combat crews had also been issued with their own .45 automatic pistols in case they were shot down over the Normandy beaches and had to join the battle. Overhead, "hundreds of glider-towing transports" could be heard heading towards northern France from bases in Lincolnshire.

"Today was D-Day! The day we have all been waiting for," wrote Gaillard.[8]

The 381st was tasked with carrying out two missions, the first of which was on a strongpoint northeast of Bayeux. The area overlooked the *Gold* invasion beach, which was to be stormed by British and Allied troops. The mission required a "lateral bombing pattern" by groups of 18 B-17s flying line abreast, directed by the PFF bomber in the center. John Howland, leading the first of two 381st groups, thought the "puny" bombload of 20 100lb demolition bombs scattered along a "one quarter mile stretch of beach" would never "wipe out a gun battery." He was then informed the bombs were intended to make foxholes for the troops.

After taking off, the formations assembled and left the English coast at Beachy Head, flying along a six-mile-wide corridor towards Normandy. A solid undercast blanketed the sea, the crews unable to witness the "history making events" below. Nevertheless, John Howland was made aware of it by his radar operator, who told him that his scope was "full of reflections" of hundreds of vessels on the water below.

"Until he said that, I didn't believe it was the real thing," wrote Howland. "I thought it was just a big practice mission."[9]

Howland and the 381st's first contingent arrived over the beach near Ver-sur-Mer and dropped their bombs at 0704, just 20 minutes before the troops began landing.

Meanwhile, the second group hit another target close to Courseulles-sur-Mer and *Juno* beach.

Once again, the B-17s were left alone by both flak and fighters, before banking west and then north, arriving back over the English coast at Weymouth, Dorset. Still, as the 381st's combat diarist pointed out: "The air crews, who had been sweating out D-Day, were completely browned off by the fact that the clouds deprived them of their box seats for the invasion."

While the two groups of 381st bombers were pounding Normandy's beaches, 12 more B-17s were loaded with 500lb demolition bombs for an attack on a road bridge leading to the city of Caen. Arriving over their target, the crews found solid cloud cover and were compelled to return their bombloads back to Ridgewell.

A third mission to another bridge at Villers-Bocage was also called, but the cloudy weather conditions saw the raid eventually cancelled. Rampant rumors then began to circulate that should the invasion falter, B-17s would be used to bomb and strafe from low altitude.

"The rumors really didn't bother us," wrote John Howland. "But the lack of sleep for more than 30 hours was wearing us down."

At the end of a long and tiring day, the men had been part of an aerial onslaught involving almost 2,600 heavy bombers and over 2,000 fighters. Their thoughts, however, were also with those on the beaches, as chaplain James Good Brown explained.

> The prevailing spirit of our fliers was their eagerness to help the invasion forces. They were aware of what the men on the beaches would face; therefore, they were glad to be of help from the air. To this extent, they felt a relation to our own ground forces which the original members of the 381st could never feel. Often they felt that they were fighting a lone battle.[10]

* * *

John Howland faced a battle on June 7 when he was suddenly alerted to fly to Ridgewell. Unbriefed and without a flight plan, Howland's crew arrived to find the 381st's 36 B-17s already lined up on the perimeter track waiting. With that, Harry Leber climbed aboard to act as wing commander for the mission to bomb a *Luftwaffe* airfield at Kerlin Bastard on the Brest Peninsula.

"What a name," Howland jibed, the lack of preparation annoying him. "That old saying about 5 minutes work on the ground being worth 30 minutes in the air is certainly true. Everything seemed screwed up."[11]

After a delayed assembly over Selsey Bill, broken clouds over the target then forced the B-17s to make a 360-degree turn, taking them over flak guns. *Our Captain*, flown by 1st Lt. John Martyniak, was hit, suffering damage to two of its engines. Slipping from the formation, his two other engines then began failing. Martyniak attempted to glide back to England, ordering his crew to jettison all loose items. The aircraft continued losing altitude, however, with Martyniak calling out his descent every 100 feet while the radio operator, SSgt. Paul E. Stewart, alerted RAF Air–Sea Rescue (ASR). Thirty miles southwest of Jersey, *Our Captain* struck the water tail-first and skimmed along on its belly. Seawater then swirled inside as the crew evacuated, all of them succeeding. Two minutes later, *Our Captain* sank beneath the waves.

By now, the 1st CBW had successfully bombed its objective, but the low group was missing. Harry Leber ordered his pilot to circle over Martyniak's dinghies, while waiting for the lost group to reappear. An already irked John Howland was angered by the decision.

"It was wasted time," he wrote. "The low group never showed up. They were long gone for home and we couldn't do a damned thing for that B-17 that was [ditched] below us."[12]

Fortunately, a "motor launch" was dropped to Martyniak and his crew by an RAF Vickers Warwick.[13] They were then towed back to England by an RAF ASR launch. "Marty" Martyniak, who had been wounded once and crash landed twice, had earned his reputation as the 381st's "original hard-luck kid."

For John Howland, who eventually landed back at Bassingbourn in darkness and cloud, "two stiff belts of bourbon" were needed before he could calm down. "I can't say that Col. Harry Leber is one of my favorite people," he wrote.[14]

The following day, almost 1,200 heavy bombers and over 1,300 fighters were again over France, attacking rail targets and airfields. The 381st sent 36 B-17s to bomb a bridge at Tours, some 145 miles from the Normandy beachheads. Flying his 18th mission, 534th navigator Hap Chandler was tired, but thrilled.

> I really am glad that I made this mission. As we hit the coast, I saw the landing barges pulled up on the beach, thousands of them. Then on the return trip we saw more boats than I have ever seen anywhere before in my life. They were all over the coastline and thousands more were coming over. It was really worth seeing. It is a wonderful show and I am glad that I have a front row seat, also that I am looking down at it all.[15]

The Tours mission marked the end of seven consecutive raids for the 381st. On June 9, the Eighth finally stood down its groups due to bad weather. Nevertheless, combat resumed the next day, with Allied aircraft operating from captured French airfields for the first time. The 381st was also tasked with returning to the gun emplacements near Neufchâtel-Hardelot—22 B-17s taking off at 0500. With no flak and fighters, each aircraft delivered its two 2,000lb demolition bombs before returning to Ridgewell four hours later.

Twenty-four hours later still, the group again left for France, heading to another *Luftwaffe* airfield at Beaumont-le-Roger, in what was another successful attack.

"Soon we'll be able to make no more sarcastic remarks about what the B-24 crews do for a living," quipped the 535th's combat diarist. "With the exception of flak, these missions are running quite uneventfully."

Despite some heavy heads the following morning after a party at the officers' club ("two officers had to be admitted to sick quarters and two had to be relieved from flying for non-operational reasons," noted Ernest Gaillard),[16] 36 B-17s took off at 0500 for Lille-Nord airfield, a target the group had previously attacked in September 1943. Once again, all B-17s returned undamaged.

Two scrubbed missions followed, before the group received a field order to attack another French airfield on June 14. The Eighth dispatched 1,525 B-17s and B-24s to bomb airfields, bridges and construction sites in France and the Low Countries. The 381st's target was Melun Villaroche, some 20 miles southeast of Paris, which it bombed successfully from 21,000 feet. Even so, the *Luftwaffe* made a brief appearance, hitting the 532nd's newly assigned *Flak Magnet*, killing its waist gunner, SSgt. Frederick A. Taylor. His body was later returned to Ridgewell.

Moderate flak over the French coast also struck the 533rd's *Second Year*, which had been assigned to the squadron only four days earlier. So named for the group's forthcoming anniversary in combat, its number two engine was left windmilling and the adjacent one failed shortly afterwards. Left without a radio, only one workable flap, and no instruments, *Second Year* almost piggy-backed another B-17 at Ridgewell, as it landed at high speed before ground-looping. Fortunately, the crew, led by 1st Lt. Milton F. Tarr, avoided injury; even despite the windmilling propeller falling from its mount and scything through the aircraft's wing, fuselage and horizontal stabilizer.

Tarr and his crew were back in the air the next day, only this time in another newly assigned B-17G, the unnamed 43-37561. It was one of 48 Fortresses split between two groups that would lead the 1st CBW to Bordeaux's Mérignac airfield.

Taking off at 0500, the formation flew west of London before leaving the English coast at Selsey Bill. Just after 0630, it reached the French coast west of Cherbourg and then began the long way down to Bordeaux. An hour later, flak began tracking the formation and struck an unnamed B-17 being flown by 2nd Lt. Charles H. Kelley. Its number four propeller was blown off, leaving the engine on fire. The two port engines were also badly damaged. At 12,500 feet, Kelley ordered his crew to bail out, all nine successfully reaching the ground. Having been assigned to the 534th BS just 12 days earlier, the entire Kelley crew would eventually escape and evade capture.

The group's 15th consecutive French mission had ended with its second combat loss in just over a fortnight. Nevertheless, with the Allies having linked up to create a single, 50-mile front across Normandy, the crews were glad to continue aiding the invasion with milk-run missions over France. All that was set to change, however.

* * *

Just before 0500 on June 16, the residents of the village of Bures, 10 miles southeast of Ridgewell, awoke to a strange "throbbing" noise.[17] The sound was then followed by complete silence before a loud explosion. While the "unknown explosive" had damaged several properties, there were no casualties. Nevertheless, the residents of the small village had avoided one of East Anglia's first flying bombs, a V-1 (*Vergeltungswaffen 1*)—"reprisal" weapons that would soon be commonly referred to as "buzz bombs" or "doodlebugs."

The men of the 381st were unaware of the sensation as they continued with their work. Another raid was planned for an oil refinery at Brüx in Czechoslovakia, but the mission was scrubbed. The men were allowed to continue with other duties, which included orientation talks for new crews and lectures on louse control. Nevertheless, the morning did provide some excitement for surgeon Ernest Gaillard.

An enlisted man being treated in Gaillard's sick quarters had shimmied up a wall and escaped out of a latrine window. The gunner, whose sanity had been called into question by Gaillard's medical officers (he'd been under observation for impersonating an officer, "malingering" and "pathological lying"), had claimed he'd made a suicide attempt the evening before. While under guard in the base hospital, he'd escaped.

"He took off across a pea patch and it looked for a while like he had made good his escape," wrote Gaillard. "[I] called out the station defense, home guard, civilian police, and as many men as the squadrons could supply … after about two hours, the prisoner was returned."[18]

It had been a busy 24-hour period for Gaillard, who'd also been smarting at the loss of one of the hospital's ambulances, which had been stolen the evening before and left "wrecked and abandoned."

Despite increasingly poor weather, John Howland and his PFF crew were alerted to a possible mission the next day. Landing at Ridgewell at 2100, the crew got three hours of fitful sleep before being woken just after midnight on June 18. Ernest Gaillard noted that the crews "look tired" as they assembled for their briefing.

"Four hours' sleep seems to be the least sleep than is beneficial to the individual," he wrote.[19]

The 381st was returning to Hamburg almost 11 months after its last visit. It was to be the Eighth's first major strategic strike since D-Day. Taking off at 0415, John Howland's *Sunkist Special* led 53 others to the Eurotank oil refinery at the city's port. Through broken clouds and extremely heavy flak, the formation dropped its array of 250lb bombs and turned back for England. On arrival, Howland's crew found numerous holes in *Sunkist Special*, including one that had been caused by a dud 88mm shell, which had sliced through one wing without exploding.

"People on the ground said our plane whistled like a banshee when we came in for landing," wrote Howland.[20]

Troy Jones had also returned from Hamburg onboard *Dee Marie*. Drinking in the officers' club with several other pilots later in the evening, they discussed their futures. Rumors were circulating about a new Eighth Air Force ruling increasing combat tours to 35 missions. Jones had just flown his 28th. Although there was no likelihood that his tour would be increased to 35, another edict stated that if an airman had more than 25 missions to his name and volunteered for another tour, he would be given an "immediate stand-down" and a "30-day leave" at home in the US.

"After a few more beers, the idea of volunteering for a second tour sounded better and better," Jones wrote.

He subsequently woke the 534th's commanding officer, Arthur Briggs, announcing his decision. Jones found himself immediately stood down.

"The next morning, we weren't sure the proposition sounded quite as attractive as it had the night before," he remembered. Nevertheless, he was soon packed and on his way home a few days later.[21]

* * *

More new crews continued to arrive at Ridgewell, even though the base's infrastructure was beginning to creak.

"We've got them living in tents, finishing their combat training with the group," noted the 535th's combat diarist, who rather acerbically added: "Crowding in as though the aerial war were only beginning instead of well past its climax—so far as innovations and technique are concerned."

The 381st was among 10 bomb groups tasked with attacking six French airfields the following day, when 51 of the group's B-17s traipsed back to Bordeaux to raid its Mérignac and Cazaux airfields.

Scheduled to bomb from 21,000 feet, thick clouds forced the group to climb to 26,000 feet. Turning due south at 0900 for the bomb run, heavy flak then bracketed the B-17s. The 532nd's unnamed 42-107088, flown by 2nd Lt. John B. Doyle, Jr. on his 13th mission, was struck in the starboard wing. His aircraft was seen to half-roll, with unshackled bombs loose in the bomb bay. Only those men at the extreme ends of the aircraft survived when it exploded in mid-air. Both the bombardier, 2nd Lt. Bernard S. Leavitt, and tail gunner Sgt. Robert T. Matthews parachuted down to be captured by the Germans. The other seven crew members, including Doyle, were killed.

A similar fate befell the crew of *Old Iron Gut* the next day when the 381st returned to bomb Hamburg's port area and oil refineries. It was one of 41 B-17s to lift off from Ridgewell at 0400. Approaching the target some four hours later, columns of smoke could be seen rising from the port, while the sky overhead was filled with flak. Making a long, straight bomb run, *Old Iron Gut* sustained three direct hits, which caused an instantaneous explosion. Bombardier 2nd Lt. Clifford Evans Jr. found himself "blown into mid-air" with only his back parachute remaining.

"While descending in my chute, large portions of the wing, a complete landing strut and wheel, thousands of fragments, a fully inflated dinghy … and an opened parachute with no one in it passed me up," wrote Evans, who was convinced his decision to wear a back parachute had saved his life. "The other members of the crew refused to wear this type of chute because they thought 'it was too awkward and too heavy.'"[22]

Only two other members of Evans's crew survived the explosion of *Old Iron Gut*. Waist gunner Sgt. Theodore E. Schmidt and tail gunner Sgt. Roger L. Beaman managed to escape the rear fuselage, which remained largely intact. When Evans and Beaman landed in a Hamburg railyard, they were immediately set upon by the rail workers, Beaman having his fingers "hammered" against the rails. When the surviving crew members were captured by German soldiers, Beaman was "almost unrecognizable." The six others, including pilot 2nd Lt. Mark R. Dunkel, were found dead at various points around the borough of Altona, along with the wreckage of *Old Iron Gut*, which had only arrived at Ridgewell two days earlier.

Several other 381st airmen were wounded by flak on the bomb run, including 1st Lt. Beverley W. Lessenger, pilot of *The Railroader*. He was hit in both knees by shrapnel, which caused him to collapse unconscious across the control column. The co-pilot, 2nd Lt. William R. Wetzel, managed to prise the pilot away with one hand, while steering the aircraft with the other. Lessenger was eventually removed from his seat and treated, while the top turret gunner, Sgt. Walter S. Gordon, assumed the role of co-pilot. *The Railroader* eventually landed back at Ridgewell with over 100 flak holes. Numerous other B-17s returned in similar condition.

* * *

"Our crew has been sweating out a trip home which we will make just three days from now, if we live that long," wrote John Howland on June 21.

His crew had been sent to Ridgewell after "someone screwed up" and assigned them for a raid, despite their tours supposedly being finished.

"I felt queer about the raid," Howland continued. "There was a deep, unexplainable feeling within that my number was up."[23]

Another early briefing saw Howland re-join Ted Homdrom for a mission to Berlin's Tiergarten district and its myriad of government buildings. As the briefing came to a close, Howland raised his hand to ask information about enemy fighter strength. His question was met with sniggers.

"We hadn't seen any appreciable enemy air activity in over a month, and many of the crews were newly arrived," Howland noted. "The response to my question was very upsetting and made me wonder, 'What the hell is wrong? Is it me, or is it them?'"[24]

Thirty-eight of the group's B-17s took off at 0430, led by Howland's *Dry Gulcher* (his usual PFF B-17, *Sunkist Special*, was still being repaired after being hit by flak over Hamburg three days earlier). Another protracted route over the North Sea took the formation across Denmark and on in towards Berlin. Having failed to rendezvous with its fighter escort, and just as the group was set to turn on its IP, some 60 enemy fighters were seen to be massing on the left of the formation. In a duel lasting 25 minutes, Me 210s, Me 410s and Ju 88s then swarmed around the 381st.

A rocket soon struck the 532nd's unnamed 42-31980, exploding in the radio room, while 20mm shells destroyed its oxygen tanks. Pilot 2nd Lt. Roger L. Dussault called for his crew to bail out, all of them acknowledging the order. Finding his parachute burnt, however, Dussault was forced to go back through the aircraft frantically searching for another. He then found the ball turret gunner, Sgt. Howard L. Corum, nursing a broken leg and trying to fasten his own parachute. Dussault helped him before searching for another. Corum, meanwhile, refused to jump without him. Both finally agreed to jump together with only one parachute.

As Dussault wrestled with the rear escape hatch, which had been damaged by the aircraft's slipstream, he suddenly found himself hanging beneath an open parachute. Although he could never be sure, Dussault believed he'd fallen unconscious at the door and Corum had hooked the parachute on him and attempted to hold onto his legs after pushing him out. Dussault was jolted by the shock of the parachute opening and felt a pulling on his legs. He then looked down to see something falling. It looked like Corum.

Together with Dussault's top turret gunner, SSgt. Elmer C. Meier, Howard Corum was later found dead by the Germans. Roger Dussault and six others survived, although they were soon captured. Having been assigned to the 381st on the same day as John Doyle and his crew, the Dussault crew had shared a similar fate two days apart.

The crew of *Baboon McGoon* weren't faring much better. A month after they'd slowed *Stage Door Canteen* using parachutes, they were now fighting off an assault that had left their number four engine on fire. Further attacks then put the aircraft into a dive, which pinned some of the crew to the ceiling.

Hearing a bail-out order, two of its officers jumped—bombardier 1st Lt. Erwin M. Brown and navigator 2nd Lt. Lloyd A. Peterson duly swapping their positions in the nose of *Baboon McGoon* for a wooden hut at *Stalag Luft III*. Their aircraft, under the command of 1st Lt. Arthur Bailey, flew on, however, eventually making a forced landing some 250 miles north of Berlin, near the Swedish village of Rinkaby. Bailey's crew had accounted for five Me 410s during their fight to escape. Now interned by the Swedish authorities, it would be another four months before they (and the repaired *Baboon McGoon*) returned to Ridgewell.

Navigator Hap Chandler, who was flying his 24th mission, was suddenly feeling pleased with himself. Like many of the 381st's crews, he was pouring fire into every passing German fighter, before finally hitting one.

"He came on and was so close that I could see him and the co-pilot," Chandler wrote. "[I] could see the bullets hitting the canopy and him, so I guess that I killed him, then he went into a spin and exploded. We really had a field day."[25]

The 381st's remaining B-17s were finally left alone as they approached the target, but they were then greeted by intense and accurate flak. Being the second wing over the target, the group's appearance invited the "toughest barrage" John Howland had ever flown through. His fellow navigator, Ted Homdrom, was flying his 30th and final mission. Homdrom had donned his steel helmet and flak vest and was stood looking over the shoulder of his bombardier when a piece of flak "the size of an egg" smashed through the plexiglass and narrowly missed them both.

"Seconds later a huge chunk of flak hit the bottom of the window about a foot from my head," Homdrom wrote. "The glass bits hit the back of my ... hand and neck and one piece bounced off my oxygen mask under my glasses, injuring my right eye."[26]

Nearby, *Marsha Sue* was also hit, badly wounding its bombardier, 2nd Lt. Peter Kowalski, his jaw lacerated. Barely conscious, Kowalski just managed to toggle his bombs and close the bomb bay doors before collapsing. As *Marsha Sue* turned off the bomb run, navigator 2nd Lt. Nelson F. Rekos tended to his wounded crewmate.

Leading the 534th was *Joanne*, the B-17 that had previously had its surfaces burnt during a collision between two others a month earlier. Ten minutes after leaving the target, flak hit its right wing, which immediately burst into flames. Pilot 1st Lt. Roy H. Pendergrist struggled to hold the aircraft as it dived some 5,000 feet before levelling off. Five men were able to bail out as *Joanne* turned 180 degrees. A further two parachutes were seen before the aircraft crashed into a forest 45 miles northwest of Berlin. While Roy Pendergrist and six of his crew survived, two were killed. Waist gunner Harold M. Lehman and tail gunner Byron E. King were later buried in a cemetery at Friesack by their crewmates.

The remaining 381st B-17s, most of them riddled with holes and several nursing feathered engines, flew back to Ridgewell. Three of them, including *Marsha Sue* landed without hydraulics. Copying the plight of *Stage Door Canteen*, its crew used three parachutes to slow the bomber, which turned off the runway and stopped neatly on the grass. Its wounded bombardier, Peter Kowalski, was immediately evacuated to the base hospital.

Button Nose also landed in the same manner, although its pilot, 1st Lt. Oscar E. Myerscough, was nursing burns after being covered by flaming hydraulic fluid during the fighter attacks. Fortunately, he was able to control his aircraft as it slewed to a halt aided by two parachutes. Meanwhile, the 535th's *Wild Bill* crashed into a fence near the bomb dump after its brakes failed while taxiing.

The largest daylight attack on Berlin to date had been a costly one—three of the group's bombers lost and 27 badly damaged. The day's toll was added to by 533rd crew chief, MSgt. Thomas F. Walsh, Jr., who accidentally shot himself in the right leg after finding a discarded .45 weapon in his B-17.

Ted Homdrom was also fortunate. Only the white of his eye had been cut by flak. Taken to the base hospital, he was convalescing when he was visited by

Brig. Gen. William Gross, Harry Leber, and surgeon Ernest Gaillard. Homdrom was awarded an Oak Leaf Cluster to his DFC for the mission to Berlin by the 381st's ground executive, William J. Reed.

"He then, for my completed tour of 30 missions, pinned the DFC on my pajamas!" wrote Homdrom. "It was one of the most thrilling moments of my life."[27]

John Howland was also greeted by William Gross, who congratulated him for completing his tour after leading the 1st CBW over Berlin's defenses.

"It was a helluva way to wrap up a tour of duty," Howland remembered. "However, it made no difference. We had successfully beaten the odds, and won our deadly game of tag. We were home free."[28]

CHAPTER 20

Marks in History

June 22–July 25, 1944

The 381st has "come of age"—we are one year old ... [but] the group is different from what it was in June, 1943 ... all the original members of the combat crews have either gone down in combat or have finished their 25 missions and returned to the States. Only about ten percent of the original members of the bomb group completed their 25 missions. This means that about 90 percent of our original bomb group flying personnel went down in combat.[1]

JAMES GOOD BROWN, JUNE 22, 1944

Both John Howland and Ted Homdrom were among the lucky ones not to have gone down in combat. While Homdrom had been wounded on his 30th and final mission, he'd survived. As he emptied his squadron navigator's desk, he discovered just how lucky he'd been.

"In doing statistics, I found that since my arrival in my squadron, we had had 27 navigators no longer on the roster to fly combat," he wrote. "Only four of us completed our tour. Of those four, three of us had received the Purple Heart."[2]

Flight surgeon Ernest Gaillard noticed the men were not coping well despite their recent run of short-range missions to France.

"The morale of the crews is lower than it has been for many months," he noted. "This is due to the decreased number of passes ... the frequent change in the definition of an operational tour ... the large number of missions flown in a comparatively short space of time, and the fact that many of the crewmembers are simply fatigued."

Gaillard concluded that unless the Eighth Air Force reviewed its "pass and leave policies," the crews' "anxiety reactions" and "failures" would only increase.[3]

On the group's first anniversary in combat, 36 crews were briefed to take part in a "1,000-bomber raid," targeting industrial areas and airfields in France. The 381st was split into three groups to attack power stations in the Pas-de-Calais region. Taking off at 1650, they overflew Dungeness after an hour, before turning on the IP at Le Tréport 20 minutes later.

Navigator Hap Chandler was flying in *Schnozzle* as part of 2nd Lt. Victor R. Romasco's crew. Romasco, Chandler's usual co-pilot, had been given command of his own B-17, while his and Chandler's regular crew (under the command of Samuel Peak) were flying in their usual *Spare Charlie*. Romasco's seat had been filled by 1st Lt. Robert F. Petroski, who'd volunteered to replace him. Petroski was flying his 30th and final mission.

Arriving over the target at Abbeville as the lead 534th B-17, *Spare Charlie* released its bombs, only to be struck by a direct flak hit in the bomb bay and its starboard wing. The aircraft immediately looped, before tumbling into a dive and disintegrating. No parachutes were seen, although waist gunner SSgt. Richard D. Oberlin survived the fall to be captured. Samuel Peak, Robert Petroski and the rest of his crew, including Hap Chandler's replacement, 2nd Lt. John K. Lundberg, were killed in action when the aircraft crashed into a marsh near the river Somme, two miles southeast of Abbeville. Lundberg's body would not be found for almost eight months, by which time his family had received his mail. "If you receive this letter I shall be unable to fill my desires," he'd written. "For I have requested that this letter be forwarded only in the event I do not return."[4]

Thirteen of the group's B-17s flew on to attack another power station at Tingry, 35 miles north, while others were unable to drop due to cloud cover. All 35 then returned to Ridgewell, including Hap Chandler's *Schnozzle*. What started out as a special day for the 381st, had become a sad one for him. His friends were lost.

"Maybe my luck will hold out," he wrote. "But you never can tell. All you can do is hope and pray. It has helped me so far. I have never been on a bomb run that I enter it [without] a prayer on the lips [and] I hope that they will continue to carry me on."[5]

* * *

While V-1s continued to rain down on London (some of Ernest Gaillard's colleagues had a close call when one landed next to their hotel, leaving them "sufficiently impressed"[6]), the group went back to France on June 23 in search of launch sites. An area at Bachimont was bombed through undercast using a PFF B-17, with all 18 returning to Ridgewell. It was the second of four consecutive visits to France for the men.

Hap Chandler was one of 360 woken the next morning for an attack on a railroad bridge over the Loire at La Riche, close to the city of Tours. Again, Chandler was flying with Victor Romasco, leading the 534th in *The-Betty-L*, the aircraft that had been named in honor of Samuel Peak's mother. In turn, it was leading the 1st CBW's high group.

Leaving the English coast at Selsey Bill, the formation made an almost direct run in towards Tours, before making a 360-degree turn just before reaching the target. At that point, the *The-Betty-L* received a direct flak hit in the waist, killing its radio operator, waist gunner and ball turret gunner. With severed control cables, the intercom out, and fire spreading along one wing, Victor Romasco clambered back through the aircraft to tell his crew to bail out. He then fell unconscious as he opened the nose escape hatch, before falling out—somehow opening his parachute as he went. Hap Chandler was the third to bail out.

"My chute opened after a bit of difficulty and [I fell] 22,000ft," he wrote. "Upon hitting the ground, I was quite shocked and also had a sprained ankle."

While he considered his options, two German soldiers wearing "skull and crossbones" immediately "took charge" of him. Flight Officer James "Hap" Chandler subsequently became POW 6525, *Stalag Luft III*, where he would spend the next 218 days, before ending his captivity at *Stalag VII-A*, Moosburg.[7]

* * *

Chandler was one of four men from *The-Betty-L* who'd been taken prisoner. Victor Romasco was another; so too, the top turret gunner and tail gunner. Romasco's bombardier, 1st Lt. Ray L. Stewart, who'd been part of the Martyniak crew that had ditched *Our Captain* in the English Channel 17 days earlier, made his escape courtesy of the French Resistance. He eventually linked up with American troops some two months later. Even so, the crew of *The-Betty-L* had become the seventh to be lost in seven missions.

The 381st returned to France the following day for an 11-hour trek to and from Toulouse Francazal airfield. Although several aircraft were hit by mobile flak guns, the group attacked and returned safely, some B-17s having to land elsewhere in England after running short of fuel. Then finally, after eight days in combat, the crews were given a brief break, which allowed the group time to take stock and re-evaluate.

"Men of high quality came feeding into the group day after day," remembered chaplain James Good Brown. "We had to become acquainted with them, and they had to learn quickly to adapt themselves to a new setting. They had to make new friends and had to acquire a loyalty to the 381st."[8]

Second Lieutenant James F. Grey was one of the new men assigned to the 535th. Raised in Wisconsin Rapids, Wisconsin, Grey had first served as an aviation cadet before graduating as a second lieutenant and navigator. On the day of the 381st's first anniversary in combat, he'd been assigned to the 535th, together with 2nd Lt. Floyd H. Metts's crew. After receiving ground training, and flying a two-hour practice mission on June 27, James Grey and the Metts crew prepared for their first combat mission.

Taking off in *Touch the Button Nell II* at 0415 on June 28, the Metts crew were commanded by the experienced 2nd Lt. Bob B. Bobrof. Flying alongside 35 other B-17s, *Touch the Button Nell II* headed for another French bridge, this time at Fismes, some 65 miles northeast of Paris. Arriving overhead, the group then dropped its load of 2,000lb bombs, all of them landing 200ft away. The bridge remained untouched, while the 381st wasn't. The 533rd's *Our Devotion* was struck in the tail by flak, which killed its gunner, Sgt. William F. Bursaw. The aircraft was able to return to England, as did *Touch the Button Nell II*, although it was forced to land at Great Ashfield, Suffolk, after weather closed in around Ridgewell. James Grey's aircraft then developed hydraulic problems just after landing. Fortunately, it was able to stop.

* * *

Poor weather conditions stopped the 381st from making any attacks for the next five days, although the group did attempt to reach Leipzig on June 29. After flying blindly for three hours over The Wash, the group's mission was scrubbed. Despite this, the 534th's *Carol Leigh* somehow managed to tack onto another CBW and flew on to the target. Pilot 2nd Lt. Robert L. Inscho and his crew returned from Leipzig to be rightly credited.

The 381st had flown a record 23 missions during June, losing nine B-17s in the process. Yet, the group was also singled out for praise by the 1st BD's commander, Robert Williams. The 381st had scheduled 716 aircraft for missions, only one of which returned early. But while the bombers of the Eighth remained grounded by bad weather, it didn't stop the Germans.

On July 2, James Good Brown was making his way to the nearby village of Clare to officially open its "Salute the Soldier Week." As he cycled the three miles from his chapel at Ridgewell, Brown instinctively looked up on hearing an aircraft passing overhead.

"It was the sound of the roar which struck me," he wrote. "The noise was not normal."

Thinking it was a Spitfire in trouble, Brown watched as it flew at low level, "spitting." Its engine then "shutdown" and the aircraft dived earthward, Brown imploring its pilot to bail out. The aircraft exploded with flames shooting high into the air.

"Too often on my base I had lifted the charred bodies of my men from a B-17," Brown wrote. "I knew the feeling of pain. Now I felt again the same pain for the RAF pilot trapped in his wrecked plane."

Anxiously pedaling to the local vicar's house to summon help, Brown arrived to be told that the "Spitfire" was in fact "just one of those buzz bombs."

"I shall not forget my consternation," remembered Brown. "I had utterly wasted all my sympathies on … a robot."[9]

Brown's men witnessed their second V-1 the following day when the base Tannoy broadcasted a red alert, closely followed by a distant explosion. Fortunately, no one was injured. Even so, the poor weather continued to keep the mood down, although it couldn't stop the 448th Sub Depot from rolling out an old bird under a new name.

After 3,037 man-hours and 65 days, the 533rd's *Big Mike* was fixed. Badly damaged during a crash-landing at Ridgewell on April 29, the B-17G had been fitted with a B-17F wing and four new engines, and had undergone countless modifications. Once declared "uneconomical" to repair, the reconstruction of *Big Mike* was a major boost for the group, thanks largely to its crew chief, MSgt. Charles Barbier. He'd overseen the work, which he had carried out, alongside a handful of others, during their spare time. It was fitting, then, that *Big Mike* should be renamed in his honor.

Hailing from Wallace, a rural community just outside New Orleans, Louisiana, Barbier's French parents had raised him to speak fluent French. It had given rise to his nickname, which had been stenciled on the B-17's nose. The renaissance of the freshly painted *Frenchy's Folly* may well have been fanciful when Charles Barbier set out to rebuild it but, through his tenacity, the 381st would come to rely on his B-17 until the end of the war.

* * *

While *Frenchy's Folly* was preparing for its new maiden flight on Independence Day, 36 of the group's other B-17s were lining up ready to take off on the 381st's 146th mission. Among them was James Grey's *The Tomahawk Warrior*, which had been named by a former pilot after his hometown of Tomahawk (in Grey's home state of Wisconsin). Grey's crew, including pilot Floyd Metts, were flying together for the first time. *Touch the Button Nell II*, which the crew had flown on five days earlier, was being crewed by Bob Bobrof and his men.

The group was being sent back to Tours for another attack on the railroad bridge at La Riche. After bright and clear weather at Ridgewell, the 381st formation found the continent shrouded by clouds. Approaching the IP, *Touch the Button Nell II* developed another mechanical problem, which saw Bob Bobrof feather one of its propellers. James Grey's tail gunner, Sgt. Leon S. Bucy, then watched the B-17 peel out of the formation.

"He was still losing altitude after salvoing his bombs," Bucy remembered. "Two P-38s turned back and the last I could see of them they were going into a cloud bank at about the same place we saw Lt. Bobrof."[10]

Bobrof's crew were desperately throwing out anything loose, but *Touch the Button Nell II* lost another engine, causing it to drop some 15,000 feet. It then developed a spin from which Bobrof was unable to recover. Two gunners—SSgt. Kenneth F. Hitchcock and TSgt. Clinton S. Word Jr.—both bailed out in time, while another's parachute became snagged on a propeller. Two others also bailed out too late for their parachutes to open. *Touch the Button Nell II* then struck the ground and exploded. Seven men, including Bob Bobrof, were killed. They were buried the next day by French civilians in the village of Persac—the mayor arranging for eight coffins to be interred (one being filled with rocks to confuse the Germans)[11]—while Hitchcock and Word were free to escape and evade capture thanks to the French Resistance.

Bobrof's loss hadn't been witnessed by the other 381st crews, who were forced to return their bomb loads back to Ridgewell after finding the target covered by cloud. All returned safely, but James Grey and his squadron were left wondering about the fate of the Bobrof crew.

"No one can imagine what happened to him," noted the 535th's diarist.

* * *

While James Grey waited to hear news of Bobrof and his men, James Good Brown was thrilled to listen to another who arrived at Ridgewell the next day.

"Of all the actors who came to the base, he showed the most human interest," wrote Brown of Hollywood movie star Edward G. Robinson. "He was never acting," Brown continued. "He just wanted to walk around the base talking to the men, and the men wanted to talk to him."[12]

A fortnight before his latest movie, *Mr. Winkle Goes to War* was released in the US, Robinson visited Ridgewell to christen a new bomber. Although the gleaming B-17G had arrived at Ridgewell six weeks earlier and had already flown several missions, it hadn't been named. Instead of christening it in honor of one of his characters, he swung a bottle of Coca-Cola declaring it to be, *Happy Bottom*. He then clarified that the term was, in fact, a tribute to his wife, Gladys, whose name he mispronounced as "Glad-ass."

James Good Brown, who'd jokingly sparred with Robinson in the officers' club earlier, was transfixed as the movie star then made a "remarkable" speech.

> He spoke decisively about the necessity for cooperation between the nations … And he strongly warned against groups and factions which would try … to separate the democratic nations … He literally captivated the crowd. The words flowed from his mouth, and the men were roaring. He stalked around in the middle of the ring, looking to one side and then to the other. He had them in the palm of his hand. The event was a roaring success, yet none of it was staged … Robinson got a wonderful hand from the men. He struck deeply into their hearts and minds and when he left the base, he left with several thousand men as his friends.[13]

* * *

The next day, the 381st returned to France for a successful attack on another V-1 launch site at Rely. A day later, the group took off for Leizpig's Erla aircraft and armaments factory, although not before two emergencies closer to home.

Earlier that morning, the 533rd's Robert L. Pospisil had installed his waist guns and was cycling back to the mess halls when he was hit by a truck on the perimeter track. Fortunately, he only suffered a broken leg, but soon found himself rushed to hospital. The 381st's hard-pushed medics then raced to the scene of a mid-air collision involving two B-17s of the 384th Bomb Group, which had been forming up over Withersfield, seven miles northwest of Ridgewell. They retrieved 16 dead bodies from the wreckage, while evacuating three lucky survivors.

Two further missions to France followed on July 8 and 9, during which time a total of 36 B-17s attempted to bomb a single Pas-de-Calais V-1 site. Bad weather largely foiled both attacks, although a road junction, and an airfield at Saint-Omer were bombed on both occasions—the last mission clocking up the group's 150th. After a day's break, the 381st then turned its attention back towards Germany, and the Nazi stronghold of Munich.

On the first of three consecutive missions, on July 11, the group attacked the Bavarian capital's marshaling yards. With the *Luftwaffe* absent, the group's B-17s—part of a force of almost 1,200 heavy bombers attacking the city—dropped "every imaginable size and type of bomb."

Twenty-four hours later, another 36 aircraft took off from Ridgewell to target the Bayerische Motoren Werke (BMW) plant in the northwest of the city. On both occasions, PFF B-17s were employed and the results unobserved. Even so, Conway Hall, leading the second mission, concluded the successful raids were like "running a big train on schedule."

All the while, a line of replacement crews filed into Ridgewell. Second Lieutenant Douglas E. Holt was a new co-pilot who'd been assigned to the 534th, having arrived from the US a week earlier. Holt, 19, hailed from Milwaukee, Wisconsin, and was part of 2nd Lt. Willis J. Black's crew. Still not slated for a mission, he was sleeping when the group took off for its third consecutive Munich mission on July 13.

After the 36 B-17s had gone and the roar subsided, Holt heard one of them return. It then immediately powered up to go around.

"It was only about seven a.m., but we crawled out of our sacks and went outside to see what was happening," he wrote. "The clouds were only about 200ft above the ground. We could hear the B-17, but could not see it."[14]

The B-17 Holt could hear was *Smashing Thru*, which belonged to his squadron. It was being flown by 2nd Lt. John M. Houston, who was having trouble returning to Ridgewell in poor visibility after losing one of his engines on take off. Having informed the tower that he would fly to the North Sea to jettison his bombs, Houston was told to return to Ridgewell to collect another B-17. After a second missed attempt, he asked for two high-intensity flares to be placed near the end of the runway so he could line up from further afield. The ground crews could only light one. It left Houston still unable to line up for a third approach. As he went around again, a second engine then failed. Fully loaded, *Smashing Thru* immediately lost altitude, narrowly missing Ridgewell's Hangar 1, before skimming over the base's domestic sites. It then dropped into a field less than a mile from the base's entrance. Houston's co-pilot, 2nd Lt. William Scruggs, held on as the B-17 bounced along on its belly.

> We slid across the wheatfield, and on the other side of the wheatfield was a railroad that was down in a cut. We slid across that railroad and hit the embankment on the other side, and the plane blew up … it caught fire. We still had the bombs on there and had all the live ammunition … it started going off and everything.
>
> Well, I crawled out through the fire over the wing, and crawled out, and when I came to, I was at a fence and I couldn't stand up … I was crawling … my hands were burning and my face was burning. I was hot and I was stinging … so I lifted my hands up, and the flesh was hanging off of my hands … my eyes were swelling, and my legs were hurting … so I just crawled the length … as far down the fence as I could go, and I was just about to give out when an English farmer came up, and he says, "let me help you."[15]

After they found some cover in a ditch, the aircraft exploded, bringing a tree down close by. Pilot John Houston had also managed to drag himself clear of the wreckage and was sheltering when another explosion took place. By this time, several airmen had run from the entrance of the base across two fields to reach the scene. They found Houston staggering towards them, badly burned.

James Good Brown, who'd been warned not to approach the area because of unexploded bombs, surreptitiously groped along some bushes next to the field when he came across Scruggs—"a quivering, moaning fellow." Brown remained with the "horribly burned" co-pilot while they waited for an ambulance to find its way to them. It took half an hour.

"What do you feel when your buddy lies there looking up into your eyes, calling your name, asking for help?" wrote Brown. "I knew him [and Houston] so well … They were now among the oldest friends I had among the fliers."

Houston and Scruggs, who were less than eight missions away from completing their tours, were evacuated to the 121st Station Hospital at Braintree. While Houston wasn't as badly injured, Scruggs didn't regain consciousness for five days. When he did, he found himself wrapped head-to-toe in a full body cast and with James Good Brown sat alongside him. Scruggs would spend the next three years in hospital, usually joking, but all the while hoping to fly again.

"Lieutenant Scruggs is strong in spirit," noted James Good Brown. "If anything will pull this fellow through, it will be his spirit. It cannot be put down."[16]

* * *

Seven of the crew of *Smashing Thru* were killed in the accident, only one of whom—Kenneth L. Spatz—could be positively identified. Their remains were subsequently interred at Madingley. The death of navigator 2nd Lt. Gerald J. Sullivan was particularly hard on one man in the group. Sullivan had been serving at Ridgewell alongside his brother, Padraig, a mechanic with the 448th Sub Depot.

"All of us are mindful of the sorrow which has befallen this one brother," noted James Good Brown.[17]

The loss of *Smashing Thru* was the only casualty of the day, the 381st's other B-17's returning from Munich. Two scrubbed missions to Merseburg were then followed by another visit to Munich on July 16. New co-pilot Douglas Holt, who'd already "had a feeling of war" after witnessing the demise of *Smashing Thru*, was woken to take part in his first mission.

"In the briefing they dwelt on the importance of not hitting the historic part of Munich," Holt remembered.

Yet, on his arrival over the cloud-covered city, and following the failure of the PFF's radars, he was surprised to find the 381st unleashing its bombs on smoke left by preceding groups.

"My thought was, 'this is precision bombing?'"[18]

The nine-hour round trip had taken its toll on the bombers' fuel, though. The 532nd's *Our Boarding House* just about made it back to English soil after losing two engines; while the newly named *Happy Bottom* wasn't so lucky. The squadron's new B-17G, which had been christened by Edward G. Robinson just 11 days earlier, lost three engines approximately 40 miles from the Essex coast, leaving its pilot, Lieutenant Jack M. McGregor, little choice but to ditch his aircraft. Fortunately, McGregor made a timed landing next to an ASR boat, allowing his crew to be rescued without even getting their feet wet. Nevertheless, 30 minutes later, *Happy Bottom* sank to the bottom of the North Sea.

* * *

As replacement B-17s continued to arrive at Ridgewell, new markings were soon being applied. After seeing some of the 2nd BD's bombers painted with distinctive colors, the 1st CBW's senior officers used the same idea, giving their B-17s a colorful identifier to help aid assembly in the increasingly crowded skies over England. As part of the 1st CBW, the 381st's B-17s' wingtips and horizontal stabilizers were duly painted bright red, while the center section of the tails were also painted the same color. John Comer's premonition that "red hot crews" needed "red hot ships" had now become official policy.

The new color experiment coincided with an attack on the Germans' experimental rocket facility at Peenemünde, a place the 381st had yet to visit. Thirty-eight B-17s took off at 0530 and approached the target over the Baltic Sea. On the bomb run, *Yardbird*, flown by Pearl Harbor veteran Frank O'Black, suffered engine problems. Feathering his number three, he dropped back through the formation. The 1st CBW was then forced to circle back over the target after finding it obscured by cloud. O'Black tried to keep up but was slipping further behind. Jettisoning his bombs, he then aimed his B-17 for neutral Sweden, landing at a small airfield in a suburb of Malmö an hour later. O'Black and his men became the third 381st crew to be interned by the Swedish authorities.

Three further attacks on Germany took place over the next three days, starting with an airfield at Lechfeld on July 19, and culminating with the group's fifth visit to Schweinfurt two days later. Although the 381st avoided losing any aircraft, its fellow 1st CBW group, the 91st, lost eight on the second of the three missions. A day earlier, the 381st almost lost one of its own men, and only a mile from the base.

At 0430 on July 19, *My Son Bob* took off for Lechfeld into darkness. It had been over three hours since its crew had been woken. As the Flying Fortress climbed away from Ridgewell, its bail-out bell suddenly rang. The alarm, which had been triggered accidentally, startled several crewmen, who immediately began donning their parachutes. One of the quickest was radio operator SSgt. Paul Stewart, who had been part of the Martyniak crew that had ditched in *Our Captain* six weeks earlier. Barging his way to the rear escape hatch, he immediately jumped out. *My Son Bob*, however, had only reached 400 feet. As the B-17 flew on, all pilot 1st Lt. Robert L. Inscho could do was call the control tower to explain that one of his crewmen had bailed.[19]

"The loudspeakers sounded on the base," wrote James Good Brown. "Where [we] would find him was not known. Since England is made up of patchwork-quilt fields surrounded by hedges, the task of finding a man is extremely difficult."

Stewart had delayed deploying his parachute and was hurled forward at 150mph. By the time it blossomed, he was at 30 feet. He hit the ground with a "terrific force," breaking his back and both ankles. Barely conscious and unable to move, he remained that way for the next eight hours, while jeeps and men scoured the wheatfields, a B-17 eventually being sent up to circle the area where it was thought Stewart had landed. Finally, his white parachute was spotted on the edge of a field. The crew also saw Stewart waving.

"The task then was to inform the drivers in the cars below as to where the fellow was," wrote Brown. "This was most difficult … Roads twist and turn and go nowhere in particular … The men in the plane overhead were at a complete loss to know how to tell the men in the jeeps … where to go …"[20]

Eight hours after bailing out, Paul Stewart was finally located in the corner of a field next to the base. He was in a critical condition, but still alive. Stewart was quickly evacuated to the 121st Station Hospital at Braintree, where doctors managed to "knead" his crushed bones together. He then sufficiently recovered to return home to Chicago, Illinois.

A day after Stewart's accident, Milwaukeean Douglas Holt was taking part in his second mission. He was co-piloting *Schnozzle*, so named because someone had thought the B-17's nose looked like comedian Jimmy Durante's. Even though Holt's introduction to war on the group's mission to Dessau was a long and fraught one, he had survived. "We did make it back to Ridgewell with everyone physically okay," he wrote. "But not so sure of everyone's mental state."[21]

Flight surgeon Ernest Gaillard was only too aware of the state of mind of some of the men. In a report to the Eighth's medical headquarters, Gaillard noted that a "large proportion" of ground crew personnel had become "fed-up, war-weary, stagnant, disinterested and indifferent to their work."

> There has been an increase in the number of Court Martials at this base. There were more in the month of June than in any previous three months ... Twenty percent [of personnel] stated that they were now drinking more than they had six months ago. Others stated that the only thing that keeps them from drinking more is the shortage of supply ... It is my considered opinion that we will see psychiatric problems and have a loss of technical efficiency of the group in the not too distant future unless some type of remedial action is instituted.[22]

* * *

On July 24, the Eighth was tasked with shifting its aim back towards tactical targets in support of US ground troops in northern France. Over 1,500 bombers were scheduled to attack German positions along a road linking the towns of Périers and Saint-Lô. It would herald the start of Operation *Cobra*, an offensive against German forces by the US First Army. Fifty-four B-17s were being readied at Ridgewell, the equivalent of a combat wing. It was the highest number of bombers supplied by all four squadrons so far.

Douglas Holt found himself flying his fifth mission—again in *Schnozzle*, and once more in thick overcast. Briefed to bomb from 10,000 feet on a "grid plan," low clouds soon forced the 381st down to 6,500 feet.

"Our specific target was to drop our fragmentation bombs in-train, starting south of the road running west out of St. Lô," he wrote. "The US Army troops had withdrawn several hundred yards north of the road and had lit colored smoke markers to prevent bombs landing on US troops."

Commander of American ground forces, Lt. Gen. Omar N. Bradley had agreed with air commanders that the safety zone for his troops would be 1,250 yards.

"With lowering clouds, and surface winds causing the smoke markers to blow around, and B-17s trying not to collide, the planned attack began to deteriorate," noted Holt. "When [our bombardier] released the bombs we were relieved to see [them] hit just south of the road."[23]

Others weren't so lucky, however. The 381st had been the last group to bomb, but just a few minutes after its B-17s had released their loads, the group's radio operators received a message to abort the attack and return to England. The crews were not sure if they'd bombed their own men or not, but it transpired the attacks had caused the deaths of a number of American troops.

Despite this, US ground forces finally broke out across the road the following day, although it required another concentrated attack by a huge force of almost 1,700 heavy bombers before they could.

"We did not get the job done yesterday, so we have to go to St. Lô again today," wrote Douglas Holt. "We got very strong instructions to do it right today."[24]

James Grey, 535th navigator, was flying his tenth mission and his second in two days. As his *Hell's Angel* overflew the target, visibility was better.

"This time we could see the ground and some of the heavy artillery fire," he wrote. "Really got shook around. Target was destroyed. Jerry radio called to try and get us to bomb over our target."[25]

While the 381st's 52 B-17s bombed as ordered, helping to saturate an area of less than five square miles, the raid left over a hundred American soldiers dead, including Lt. Gen. Lesley J. McNair, who was observing the fighting. He subsequently became the highest-ranking officer to be buried at Normandy's American cemetery. The 381st's surgeon, Ernest Gaillard, knew the group's 160th mission was a significant one when he closed his diary on July 25. "It is hoped that today will be another day marked in history."[26]

Intermission: The Sky Generals

Many of the men who built and commanded the Eighth Air Force traced their belief in the war-winning potential of air power back to a single point of origin—Col. William "Billy" L. Mitchell.

Billy Mitchell was a colorful World War I commander who fervently advocated the concept of strategic air power delivered by an independent air force. Outspoken in character, he developed his own air power doctrine, and passionately preached the gospel of the "strategic air offensive."

Mitchell died in 1936 and his passing was mourned by many air power disciples. Among them were the men who would, a few years later, put Mitchell's theories to the ultimate test over Europe. Today, the names of Arnold, Spaatz, Eaker, and Doolittle are synonymous with the American strategic, daylight bombing campaign of World War II, and each of them progressed to high command, heavily influenced by Mitchell.

Regarded by many as the father of American air power, Gen. Henry "Hap" H. Arnold was the head of the USAAC in 1940. In the summer of that year, President Franklin Roosevelt asked Congress for 50,000 aircraft a year. Hap Arnold oversaw that growth, as well as the formation of the USAAF in June 1941.

In May 1940, Arnold had sent the then Brig. Gen. Carl "Tooey" A. Spaatz—another product of the Mitchell era—over to England as an observer. Trusted by Arnold, Tooey Spaatz would later command the Eighth Air Force after acting as chief of the air staff of the USAAF in Europe.

However, if anyone deserves the accolade of being the architect of the Eighth Air Force, then perhaps it should be Brig. (later Lt.) Gen. Ira C. Eaker. Another accomplished aviator, he led the first group of USAAF officers to arrive in Britain in 1942.

Eaker was a polite and articulate Texan who understood the British mindset well. It was Eaker who forged close ties with RAF Bomber Command, working hard to maintain a good working relationship (and personal friendship) with its head, Air Chief Marshal Sir Arthur Harris. Eaker played a pivotal role in the expansion of the USAAF's own VIII BC. He nurtured the first bomb groups after their arrival in England; watching over the growth of the Eighth as it matured into the potent striking force it would ultimately become.

In December 1943, the US command structure in Europe underwent major reconstruction in preparation for Operation *Overlord*.[1] On January 1, 1944, Spaatz was brought in to command the newly established United States Strategic Air Forces in Europe (USSTAF) at Bushy Park. Amid some controversy, Eaker was moved out to the Mediterranean Theater. Impatient for a more aggressive bombing campaign, and a better, more effective use of fighters by the Eighth, Arnold replaced Eaker with Lt. Gen. James "Jimmy" H. Doolittle.

Hap Arnold was counting on the famous "Tokyo raider" to act as a catalyst. He and Spaatz soon pressured Doolittle into increasing the tempo of Eighth Air Force operations. Doolittle did not disappoint. One of his first major changes was to allow its fighter groups more freedom. A "freelance" directive was issued, allowing the fighters to range freely, hunting for *Luftwaffe* fighters wherever they found them—in the air, or on the ground. It was a hugely successful decision that many German commanders later described as a key turning point in the war.

CHAPTER 21

Buzz Bomb Alley to Happy Valley

July 26–September 2, 1944

On July 26, the 381st welcomed four South American diplomats, all of whom were given a red-carpet tour of Ridgewell and a ride in a B-17. However, the V-1s that continued to swoop over Ridgewell still garnered the most attention.

"The buzz bomb situation is becoming acute in that three or four have passed directly over this field," wrote surgeon Ernest Gaillard. "It is hoped 'Hans' continues to put enough petrol in them to get them over this field."[1]

Ridgewell received a welcome visitor the next day when Joe Nazzaro returned to inspect his former group. Nazzaro was in the throes of returning to the US to command a new bomb wing, one that would eventually be moved to the Pacific. For now, he was happy to see his 381st was largely in good shape, although its men were still facing the perils of "Piccadilly Flak." As he toured the base, a talk was being held in the station theatre on "venereal disease." It coincided with the unwelcome discovery of two cases of gonorrhea, which were promptly treated using the hospital's newly obtained supply of penicillin.

Across both days, two missions to Germany had been scrubbed, the second of which saw the B-17s briefly take off for Munich. On July 28 and 29, the group made it over Europe for two successive attacks on Merseburg's synthetic oil facilities. Bombed by PFF on both occasions, the group's aircraft returned safely, although seven had to land elsewhere on the latter after poor weather cloaked Ridgewell. Nevertheless, the group was met with the good news that it, together with all 1st BD groups, was being awarded a DUC for its part in the Oschersleben raid on January 11. All men, regardless of rank or position, were entitled to wear a "blue ribbon" on the right side of their uniforms.

July closed with the news that Hitler's own men had tried to kill him ("what will they think of next?" wrote Ernest Gaillard).[2] Even so, the group persisted with its attacks on Germany, returning to Munich on the last day of the month to strike at an engine factory in the northwest of the city. Taking off at 0830, the 381st's 36 B-17s skimmed "anvil-topped" clouds all the way to the target. Arriving over the suburb of Allach, the formation was then pounded by flak.

"They really threw up everything but their gun barrels at us," noted navigator James Grey, who was flying his 11th mission.[3]

As the formation turned off the target, the 533rd's *My Devotion* was damaged, its number one engine windmilling. Pilot Jack B. Pearson dropped from the formation until he was 3,000 feet below. He was then spotted "limping" towards Switzerland. Pearson's B-17G never made it, however. Less than 100 miles from Allach, *My Devotion* crash landed near the village of Staffiangen. Pearson and his men survived the belly landing, only to be captured—becoming the 27th 1st CBW crew to be lost that month.

On August 1, the group revisited France, and Melun Villaroche, an airfield it had previously bombed the week after D-Day. Arriving over the target, only part of the formation was able to attack through partial cloud cover. The low group failed to sight it and sought a target of opportunity instead. It found another airfield some 30 miles southwest at Étampes Mondésir and attacked. All 37 B-17s arrived back at base undamaged.

A new crew arrived at Ridgewell the following day. One of its members was co-pilot 2nd Lt. Robert "Bob" Armstrong from Scott City, Kansas. His crew had managed to engineer their assignment to the 381st while acclimatizing at Bovingdon.

Armstrong's pilot, 2nd Lt. Raymond L. P. LaPierre, had a brother, Roger, also a pilot, flying with the 533rd. Armstrong's "fraternity brother" Orlan D. Carmichael was also a bombardier with the 535th. After locating both at Ridgewell, Armstrong and the LaPierre crew then got "completely checked in." After escape pictures were taken, they were given lectures on POW procedures, then shown the base's layout. Armstrong also purchased a must-have used bicycle.

"By sunset, my billfold was twenty dollars lighter," he noted.[4]

On August 3, 37 of the group's B-17s took off to attack Mulhouse's marshaling yards, close to the French–Swiss border. Ball turret gunner Sgt. William Goudeket Jr., flying in the 533rd's *Minnie the Mermaid*, watched as the group's bombs fell.

"I remember watching the bombs go away when we dropped them, and I followed them all the way down to the ground and they hit the track—just bang, bang, bang—right down the track," he noted. "I don't know if the bombardier could see that from his location, but I got a bird's eye view of it."[5]

Mission planners had failed to see the flak batteries that tracked the formation as it overflew Antwerp on the return to England, however. "Real big and accurate," noted navigator James Grey.[6]

Fragments soon struck the 534th's *Yankee Rebel*, damaging its number four engine. Pilot 2nd Lt. John C. Wilcock called the 1st CBW leader to say his B-17 was in a "bad condition" and that his crew would have to bail out. Although it wasn't seen, *Yankee Rebel* was thought to have ditched somewhere in the North Sea, a fact confirmed 24 hours later when the body of John Wilcock was washed ashore near Felixstowe. The rest of his crew were never found.

* * *

On the day John Wilcock's body was recovered and returned to Ridgewell, Operation *Aphrodite*, the American plan to use radio-controlled B-17 drones, was put into effect with a mission attacking V-1 rocket sites in France. Meanwhile, the 1st BD was directed back to the Germans' experimental rocket facility at Peenemünde on the Baltic coast. Led by two PFF B-17s, *Sunkist Special* and *Dry Gulcher*, a new B-17G that had been assigned to the group a month earlier,[7] the 381st's formation of 37 aircraft were airborne at 0930.

While Bob Armstrong was still waiting to fly a mission, his new hut mate, 1st Lt. Russell J. Hadley, had been woken at 0430 to fly as the radar operator on *Dry Gulcher*. His aircraft, piloted by 1st Lt. Hanley G. Cupernall, and co-piloted by deputy mission lead, Capt. Irving J. Moore, was climbing up to 5,000 feet when there was a "sizzle" and a sudden rush of air. Moore immediately glanced round and saw a burst of flame behind him in the pilot's compartment. As smoke quickly filled the cockpit, Moore shouted for the crew to bail out and rang the alarm. Red and green magnesium flares then began "bouncing around" the cockpit. Captain Francis G. Hawkins, the 381st's photographer, who was flying on board *Dry Gulcher* as an observer, suddenly became aware of the disturbance.

"I had been up for a considerable time and had been working from at least four o'clock until flight time," he remembered. "I laid down on the floor and took a nap … sometime after that … I heard a lot of rustling around and I looked up."

Hawkins saw two of the gunners trying to prise open the escape hatch. When he asked what was happening, they told him the alarm had "gone off." Hawkins helped kick the escape hatch out, before both men jumped.

"I had not heard the bell and I was a little reluctant to leave the ship when it was still flying steady," remembered Hawkins. "So, as I put my chest chute on and turned around and looked, I saw the [aircraft's control] cables were sagging over the door."

Although Hawkins couldn't see any fire or smoke, he realized the situation was precarious.

"They [the cables] fell down low enough, about six inches or more, I lifted them out of the way and I left the ship."[8]

In the village of Shalford, eight miles south of Ridgewell, nine-year-old schoolboy Peter Morgan was playing outside in his garden when he heard a noise. "Like an aircraft in pain—engines screaming," he later remembered. As he looked up in the sky, Morgan's grandfather winked and said, "parachute practice." Morgan looked up and saw the crew of *Dry Gulcher* bailing out over his village.[9] Irving Moore, who'd kept the aircraft level while they jumped, was having difficulty breathing because of smoke in the cockpit. Opening his side window to breathe only fanned the flames. Unable to control the aircraft any longer, Moore tried squeezing out of the window, but couldn't. He then scrambled from the cockpit, falling as he did so, before grabbing his bombardier, 1st Lt. Charles W. Young. Both then jumped amid exploding .50-caliber shells and oxygen bottles.[10]

"My mother, who must have come out of the kitchen or somewhere, grabbed me by the scruff and hurled me through the kitchen door under a table," remembered Peter Morgan. "At which point there was this God-almighty explosion—a huge bang—and I was lying under this table, cowering there."[11]

Dry Gulcher had exploded in mid-air, showering the village with burning debris. Morgan's mother, Sybil, immediately dashed off in the direction of the crash, telling her son to "stay there." She then ran across a small bridge with local farmer Albert Tarbin and disappeared into the smoke.

"There was popping and banging going on all over the place," Morgan remembered. "And there was this almighty bang, something blew up, and I screamed and thought that's it, mother gone."

Morgan returned to his house to find it "raining inside." The concussion from the first explosion had ruptured the house's water tank. He also found a smoldering piece of generator, which had ploughed into the lawn nearby. "It was a very incredible thing to see when you're nine years-old," he remembered.[12]

Navigator James Grey also witnessed the crash as his B-17, *Hell's Angel*, circled overhead, before continuing on to Peenemünde. "Pretty disheartening to start a mission with," he noted. Grey had also counted nine parachutes dropping from *Dry Gulcher* just before it crashed. He was hopeful that all had landed.[13] Unknown to him, however, the doomed B-17 was carrying ten men. Peter Morgan's mother, along with Albert Tarbin and the local post mistress, Audrey Hayden, who'd all avoided the second explosion, found several of the airmen "standing around"—two of them nursing broken ankles. Irving Moore had also "spilled" his parachute to avoid power lines and landed heavily (he would be paralyzed from the waist down for several weeks). As Sybil Morgan comforted the crew, telling them no one had been killed in the accident, she was unaware that the body of tail gunner SSgt. Harold F. Norris lay in the wreckage. It was later thought that the severed control cables had prevented him from bailing out. Norris, whose baby son had been born after his arrival in England, was declared KIA.

* * *

Despite the loss of *Dry Gulcher*, the Peenemünde raid went ahead, with all 36 B-17s bombing successfully. A day later, the group was back in the air, heading for Germany and an oil storage depot at Nienburg, 35 miles southwest of Bremen.

Once again, a similar fate soon befell another PFF B-17, one that had been assigned shortly before *Dry Gulcher*.

The unnamed 42-97771 was being flown by 1st Lt. Salvatore J. Melomo, who'd been awarded a DFC for "excellent formation leadership" just nine days earlier. Unusually, his B-17 was carrying five officers and five enlisted men, including tail gunner SSgt. Louis F. Beneke, who was flying his final mission. Approaching the German coast at Cuxhaven, intense flak struck the B-17, which killed its navigator, 2nd Lt. Charles S. Freeman, and wounded the engineer, TSgt. Willard G. Gilbertson. Melomo immediately dropped the aircraft into the low group and jettisoned his bombs, before completing a 180-degree turn and heading back for England. With damage to both starboard engines, however, the B-17 caught fire some 70 miles out over the North Sea. Melomo rang the bail-out bell and all of the surviving crew jumped before the aircraft exploded.

Only five were able to survive in the water before they were finally located by a German patrol boat two hours later. Melomo was one of those who lost his life. Louis Beneke, the gunner drafted in on his last mission, survived to be captured.

Several other B-17s were damaged by flak—one seriously, although it continued on to Nienburg. Nevertheless, Harry Leber was furious when he returned to Ridgewell, informing the 1st CBW headquarters that his group could "use a stand down any time they cared to arrange it." Leber was tired of flying his "wagons on three engines."

The stand down wasn't to be, however. The group was given another field order on August 6 to attack an aircraft plant at Brandenburg, 35 miles west of Berlin. Yet again, another B-17 met a watery end, when *Underground Farmer* was disabled by flak just after bombs away. Unable to feather a badly damaged engine, and with three wounded crewmen, its pilot, 1st Lt. Allen W. Webb, began the long journey back to Ridgewell with a windmilling propeller. Approaching the city of Lübeck, however, Webb ordered his crew to bail out, most of them landing in its suburbs. *Underground Farmer* flew on before crashing into the Baltic. One crew member, tail gunner SSgt. Jack S. Patrick, was later found dead at a power plant in the city. He'd purportedly been killed by a civilian mob after landing.

* * *

Four of the *Underground Farmer* crew in German hands were hut mates of Bob Armstrong. Although he was still waiting on his first mission, their loss brought the total number of casualties in his hut to five.

"German air power is weakening and the 381st is suffering fewer losses," he wrote. "But that is hard to accept when it gets close to home."[14]

Although Armstrong was woken early the next morning, it wasn't to fly the group's 169th raid. While he and his crew set off on a training mission, 36 other B-17s took off to attack two fuel depots at Saint-Florentin and Bourron-Marlotte, both southeast of Paris. After four consecutive losses on each of the last four missions, all 36 returned.

It was a different story when the 381st returned to France as part of a formation of almost 700 B-17s a day later, however. The group was ordered to attack German gun emplacements at Cauvicourt, 10 miles southeast of Caen, and some 1,000 yards in front of dug-in Canadian troops. While the approach wasn't an easy one, the 381st led a formation of 231 B-17s to unleash more than 600 tons of ordnance on the German positions.

Flying "unusually low" across newly won territory, the 381st's bomb run took it over numerous flak gun positions. For a quarter of an hour, a hail of exploding 88mm shells bombarded the formation as it passed overhead.

"Every airplane was being hit," remembered Douglas Holt, co-pilot of *Passaic Warrior*. "My side window was hit and smashed. All pilots were having a problem holding close bombing formation."[15]

Also leading the 1st BD was the 535th's *Button Nose*, piloted by Capt. Thomas E. Barnicle. His aircraft received a direct hit in the bomb bay, which set it ablaze. Quickly jettisoning his bombs and banking away from the formation, Barnicle headed for the Allied lines with flames spreading along one wing. Unable to control the bomber, he then rang the bail-out bell and all nine men jumped from 10,000 feet, one of them landing in a tree. *Button Nose* then crashed into a school, which was fortunately unoccupied. Barnicle and his crew were aided by Canadian troops, who soon had them on their way back to Ridgewell.

Of the 37 B-17s sent by the 381st to Cauvicourt, 30 returned with battle damage—five of them classified as "major." The 532nd's *French Dressing* landed on the English south coast, although only after being slowed by two parachutes. After clambering out, the crew counted 110 flak holes and one wounded navigator. Thankfully, its lovingly painted Vargas girl nose art remained unblemished.[16]

"Certainly, we could use a stand down, for maintenance purposes," wrote the 535th's combat diarist. "The ships are flying flak patches. Today's is the sixth consecutive mission, most of them rough for flak."

Once again, no stand down came, however. Although only 24 serviceable B-17s could be scheduled, the crews were still briefed for another long-range trek to the BMW plants at Munich. Poor weather enroute subsequently forced a diversion to a target of opportunity—Saarbrücken's marshaling yards, which were duly attacked. All 24 aircraft then returned safely to base.

Ridgewell's hangars were swamped with all manner of repairs, however. After seven consecutive raids, the combat crews were finally stood down, allowing the sheet metal men to rivet patches on the group's many damaged B-17s. Still, the relentless pace of war only allowed for a brief period of respite before the group was back in the air 24 hours later.

Taking off at 1430 on August 11, 36 B-17s were sent to attack Brest's harbor fortifications, which were being stubbornly defended by German troops. Climbing to its bombing altitude over the English Channel, the 381st had to sharply level off to avoid colliding with scores of RAF Halifax bombers returning from attacking La Pallice. Arriving over its target, the group then bombed with "telling effect."

The first of four consecutive missions to France and Germany followed. On August 13, 36 B-17s left Ridgewell bound for a road junction in Rouen. Making a lengthy bomb run, the formation was tracked by accurate flak, which succeeding in striking *The Tomahawk Warrior*, whose navigator, 2nd Lt. William G. Haines Jr., suffered a "traumatic amputation" of his right leg. Despite attempts by his crew to stem the flow of blood, Haines died before his aircraft could reach Ridgewell.

The next day, the 381st left for Metz–Frescaty airfield, a target last visited in April. Among the group's 36 combat crews was that of Roger LaPierre, with Bob Armstrong flying alongside on his first mission as co-pilot. Without any opposition and only a few flak bursts at the coast, the 381st bombed successfully and returned.

"We were offered an ounce of whiskey [at the interrogation]," noted Armstrong. 'I felt this was the thing to do, so I gulped my shot down and I can assure you that was the first and last time I took the offered shot …"[17]

Armstrong was back in the air 24 hours later and on his way to Ostheim in the eastern suburbs of Cologne. The group's target was a *Luftwaffe* airfield, one of a number being targeted across Europe by both the USAAF and RAF. Led by Conway Hall, the 381st turned on its IP just west of Düsseldorf but was forced to climb along the bomb run to avoid intense flak being fired towards chaff[18] left by the formation in front. Even so, a number of 381st B-17s were struck, including Hall's *Whirlaway*, which sustained damage to its number three engine. Fortunately, Hall was able to continue the attack. Bombing results were deemed excellent and all 36 aircraft turned back for England.

"On the flight home, we passed over hundreds of British Lancaster bombers," remembered Bob Armstrong. "It was very unusual to see them out in daylight."[19]

The British attacks on Belgian and Dutch airfields were in preparation for a renewed night offensive against Germany.[20] That same day, the invasion of southern France had also begun.

Whether it was news of the Allied landings, or the passage of several more V-1s over the base (by now nicknamed "Buzz Bomb Alley"), something provoked high jinks at the headquarters site later that afternoon. Pistols and flares were being fired off, leading to all combat officers having to turn in their .45 pistols. On the orders of Harry Leber, every officer was then restricted to the base for the next five days.

Four days after celebrating his 20th birthday ("all I did was sleep in and eat three meals"), 534th co-pilot Douglas Holt was woken for his fourth consecutive mission and his 15th overall. Taking off in his regular B-17, *Lucky Dog*, Holt and the 381st were leading the 1st CBW towards an aircraft plant at Halle, 20 miles northwest of Leipzig. In clear weather, the 381st entered the bomb run, avoiding a sweep by enemy fighters, which struck at the groups behind, including the 91st. Six of its number were shot down. Only "accurate tracking flak" bothered Douglas Holt and his group. "My window broken again," he later noted in his diary. "Pretty mad!"[21] Yet, all 37 aircraft assigned for the mission landed back at Ridgewell—two with feathered engines and one with a wounded tail gunner. After six hours on oxygen, however, most of the men were left feeling "half-dead."

* * *

On the second anniversary of American heavy bomber operations from England, and exactly one year on from the catastrophic first Schweinfurt raid, deteriorating weather conditions forced a stand down on August 17. Three days on, and there was no let-up in the rain.

"Brother, we've had it," complained the 533rd's diarist. "The fins on our planes out on the line are really beginning to resemble fish now ..."

Moods worsened later that evening when the enlisted men's beer hall was forced to close because of a shortage of beer. Nevertheless, after an enforced absence lasting one week, the group returned to combat on August 24.

Led by the 533rd's new commanding officer, Maj. George K. Sandman, the 381st returned to Germany, and the city of Weimar, some 50 miles southwest of Leipzig. The target—an armaments factory believed to be producing components for rockets—was hit visually, with moderate flak along the way. The crews were surprised, however, by the sudden appearance of an Me 163 Komet, which tore past the formation at "startling" speed but didn't attack. All B-17s eventually returned to Ridgewell, logging a flying time in excess of nine hours.

"Wake up time for today's mission was at 0415," wrote Bob Armstrong on August 25. "For breakfast we had something unusual—two fried eggs, bacon, toast, dried fruit and oat meal." Although his breakfast was a pleasant surprise, Armstrong would soon learn that it was reserved for particularly demanding days.

Flying his third mission, Armstrong was heading for Neubrandenburg in the northeastern corner of Germany—a 1,100-mile round trip from Ridgewell. The target for his and 36 other 381st B-17s was an aircraft plant hidden in woods to the north of the city's airfield.

"I flew [*Our Boarding House*] over the target and since this is the most stressful time of the flight, I started to sweat," remembered Bob Armstrong. "This made my goggles fog over. I could barely make out the plane I was flying formation on, let alone see what else was going on."[22]

The target was also difficult to distinguish, with the hangars being completely missed by the lead squadron. However, all 37 B-17s released their bombs before heading back to England. With escort all the way, and no flak to contend with, all returned without damage and no wounded airmen—except one, who'd inadvertently "lodged an eraser" in his left ear.

More ears suffered a day later when the 381st took off for Gelsenkirchen, after a two-hour delay caused by fog. Crossing the English coast at 22,000 feet, the group then climbed to 29,000 feet—its highest bombing altitude so far. Despite intense and accurate flak, the B-17s "weathered it well" to bomb a synthetic oil refinery visually. Landing back at Ridgewell, some complained of "head colds and blocked ears," although none were wounded. Still, the group's "first trip back to 'Happy Valley' in some time" had proved successful.

On what was to be the group's 180th mission, the crews were briefed for "Big B" for the first time in two months.

"Talk about your moans and groans," wrote Bob Armstrong. "They were heard all over the briefing room."[23]

Taking off on August 27, the 37 B-17s soon encountered deteriorating weather to such an extent that the wing leader elected to turn back before reaching Berlin. Heading for Emden, the crews found its docks and marshaling yards, but also intense flak.

"Immediately after dropping our bombs, we had several flak bursts close to our plane," remembered Armstrong. "It had quite a devastating effect."

Fragments struck the cockpit of Armstrong's *Mizpah* and blew apart the bomber's radio, pieces of which struck Armstrong's pilot, Raymond LaPierre, in the neck.

> This temporarily paralyzed him. LaPierre was flying at the time and when he was hit he fell forward on the flight and engine controls. This put the plane in a sudden dive and changed the power settings of the engines. For a moment I felt I was viewing a movie where suddenly you see an injured soldier as he falls. I immediately grabbed the flight controls to pull the plane out of the dive with my right hand and using my left hand I reached over to pull LaPierre off the controls … there was pandemonium throughout the plane.

Armstrong had also been hit in the legs, but he continued flying *Mizpah* while LaPierre fell "in and out of consciousness." Roger LaPierre, flying ahead in the lead squadron, learnt about his brother's wounds over the radio. It was also clear many of the B-17s had been damaged and that one tail gunner, SSgt. Richard B. Ramsdell, had been killed. Fortunately, the bombers made it back to Ridgewell, including *Mizpah*, which landed without its rudder or brakes. Armstrong was able to let the bomber "roll off the runway" to a gentle stop. "That was only my second landing of a B-17," he recalled.

Raymond LaPierre was evacuated to the sick quarters, before being taken to the 121st Station Hospital at Braintree, where over 20 pieces of flak, glass and radio fragments were removed from his neck and hands. The wounds had paralyzed the right side of his body, but he was expected to recover.

"He looked bad," remembered Bob Armstrong. "He was told he would never fly combat again. Considering his condition, he was quite cheerful."[24]

None of the 381st's combat crews flew for the next two days due to "sluggish gray clouds." The playing of *Taps* over the base Tannoy both evenings also misled some into thinking a mission was planned for the next day. It wasn't until midday on August 30 that the group was called into action, though, despite being stood down earlier that morning.

Taking off for Kiel's harbor front, docks and warehouses, 36 B-17s embarked on the group's 16th mission of the month. Briefed for "unusual flak" from a nearby experimental facility, some crews witnessed "colored" explosions (thought to be helping the flak gunners find their range) and bursts with "sheets of burning material." Nevertheless, all B-17s returned safely, including *Fort Worth Gal*, whose throttle cables had been severed by flak. They had to be manipulated by the engineer, top turret gunner and "third pilot," SSgt. Nile E. Greathouse. It allowed *Fort Worth Gal* to "beat the formation back."

* * *

September began with the official opening of the London *Stage Door Canteen* at 201 Piccadilly. Among the stars lined up to perform was the American dancer, Fred Astaire. He was also joined onstage by actor and singer Bing Crosby, who'd already taken part in a live radio broadcast with Glenn Miller and his band. While Miller travelled to Thorpe Abbotts airfield to perform a show for the 100th BG later that evening, Crosby was driven to Lancashire, where he performed for American airmen at Warton and Burtonwood. The next morning, he travelled to Alconbury and Duxford, before arriving at a drizzly Ridgewell.

Crosby's arrival was preceded by the departure of the group's B-17s to Ludwigshafen. After reaching southwest of Paris in worsening weather, they were recalled, the crews not being credited for the mission despite flying over occupied territory for five hours. The group's return then coincided with the arrival of a new replacement crew led by FO Leo Belskis. He and his men, including bombardier 2nd Lt. Ross W. "Bud" Perrin from Knoxville, Tennessee, had arrived in England two weeks earlier. Their journey to Ridgewell could not have been better timed.

"He came with a troupe," wrote James Good Brown of Bing Crosby's arrival. "Not as the other movie stars who came to christen ships or just to meet the men. Bing Crosby came to stage a show."

Crosby was set to perform an outside concert at Ridgewell, but the persistent rain forced everyone inside the airfield's main Hangar 1. Crippled B-17s had to be dragged outside, while a makeshift stage was set up using two flatbed tractor trailers placed end-to-end.

"Nothing had been done like it here before on Ridgewell Aerodrome," noted Brown. "Nothing will be done like it again if we are to be here another two years."

The show, organized by the United Service Organizations, had been laid on to celebrate the American Red Cross Aeroclub's anniversary, as well as the last day of the Eighth Air Force's War Bond drive, which Jimmy Doolittle had launched after buying the first bond a month earlier. An estimated 4,000 people—including "42 truckloads" of wounded British and American troops "recently returned from battle fronts"—crammed inside the hangar. Many of the 381st men had to clamber up onto the building's girders to get a better view.

"The scene was electrifying, just to look through the great hangar and see this mass of humanity," wrote Brown. "The place looked like a monkey cage ..."

Crosby sauntered through his hits, playing to the crowd and jesting with a comedian. He was also accompanied by several musicians and two female singers.

"They were girls, and that is all that mattered," wrote Brown. "And they were here. They went over big with the boys, who always love to see and hear a girl." Yet, it was Bing Crosby himself who was the star attraction. "He was the limelight," Brown added.[25]

New bombardier Bud Perrin, whose wife, Thelma, had once enjoyed the limelight as a former Miss America contestant, hadn't written to her since he'd been preparing to leave Bovingdon for "some other place in England." His arrival at Ridgewell was a whirlwind, which culminated in the unexpected Bing Crosby concert. When he'd finally settled into his new surroundings and found his bearings, he began writing her a letter a day before their second anniversary.

"Bing Crosby was here on Saturday afternoon," he wrote. "I certainly enjoyed seeing him. Seems like a regular guy. He said it was sure good to be out on the road without Bob Hope."[26]

It had been 49 days since Bud Perrin had last seen his wife. She was now pregnant with their first child. His only hope was to survive 35 missions and get home.

CHAPTER 22

Friendly/Enemy Lines

September 3–October 17, 1944

After staying overnight at Ridgewell, Bing Crosby waved goodbye to the men of the 381st and continued his tour of USAAF bases with a visit to Raydon airfield in Suffolk. The group, meanwhile, continued with its day job, readying 37 B-17s for a visit to Ludwigshafen, Germany. Flying a long, circuitous route to the south of Paris, the bombers then turned northeast for the bomb run. It was the start of a 20-minute period of intense, accurate flak. Bob Armstrong, co-piloting *Little Guy* on his sixth mission, winced as he flew through it.

> To make myself as small a target as possible I moved my seat as far back and down as I could and still see to fly and check the engines on my side of the plane. For the first time I gave serious thought of keeping myself out of as much danger as possible. Flak was now making me quite nervous.[1]

Sweet-Patootie, flown by 2nd Lt. Omar P. Fulton, couldn't avoid the onslaught, however. It was hit in its number two engine and slid back through the formation. After jettisoning the bombs, Fulton then made for France and what he hoped would be Allied lines. Losing another engine along the way, he was then forced to crash land in a meadow near Damerey in the Burgundy region of France. Attempting to escape, Fulton and his crew were quickly rounded up and taken prisoner.

"Omar Fulton and I had gone all the way through aviation cadet flight training together," remembered Douglas Holt, who'd been stood down for the mission. "Fulton was a mature, tough guy from Brooklyn, New York. He was not going to accept the status of being a POW."

After being loaded into a box car, Fulton managed to prise open some floorboards, allowing his crew to escape. Eventually reaching Allied lines, they arrived back at Ridgewell three weeks later.[2]

* * *

By now, new crews were beginning to arrive in England without bombardiers. It was part of a new policy to use enlisted men as "toggliers."[3] Bud Perrin, who by now was "getting legs like a football player" riding his bicycle around Ridgewell, had become one of the last formally trained bombardiers to be assigned to the group. Nevertheless, he was also considering qualifying as a navigator in the hope it would speed up his mission count.[4]

Perrin was still waiting for his first mission when the 381st returned to Ludwigshafen on September 8. All 37 B-17s successfully attacked an oil refinery in the suburb of Oppau, although Douglas Holt's *Lucky Dog* received 18 holes on his 18th mission. Despite this, he was "over the hump at last."[5]

The 381st crossed to the opposite side of the Rhine the next day, when a larger force of 49 B-17s took off to bomb Ludwigshafen. Finding it covered in cloud, they flew on to bomb Mannheim's marshaling yards instead. Sixteen of them received battle damage, one of which, *Marsha Sue*, crash-landed at RAF Manston with a severely wounded togglier, SSgt. Robert J. Sharp. With the help of the 381st's surgeon, Ernest Gaillard, he survived a shattered pelvis.

As the 381st departed the next day for Gaggenau, 10 miles from the French border, James Good Brown and a group of others left Ridgewell for a 10-mile "unofficial hike" to the small Essex village of Hempstead—birthplace of the notorious highwayman Dick Turpin. Duly arriving, they then waited for a truck to return them to Ridgewell.

"We could just as easily have walked five miles, then returned the same five miles on foot," Brown joked.

A nervous child soon approached the men to ask if they were "German." When Brown replied they were "Yanks," the child responded with the words "an American will never forget. 'Have you any gum, chum?'" Brown laughed again.

"The Americans have left one blight on England," he wrote. "We have trained their children to chew gum."[6]

Over 400 miles way at Gaggenau, 24 of the 381st's B-17s began pummeling a motor factory thought to be manufacturing V-weapons. Moderate, but accurate flak struck *Fort Worth Gal*, damaging three of its engines. Pilot 2nd Lt. Ernest Germano turned away from the formation as if to head back to France. Ten minutes later—the aircraft fast-becoming uncontrollable—Germano ordered his crew to bail out. Eight of them, including Germano, were duly captured. The tail gunner, Sgt. Harry Siders, was found dead after apparently striking a tree on landing and breaking his neck.

By now, Allied troops from Normandy had linked up with those from southern France, while the British were entering the Netherlands. As Ernest Gaillard also noted in his diary, "the crews report that their feeling of security is much greater now they have so much friendly territory to fly over."[7]

On September 11, the Eighth made a concerted effort to destroy Germany's synthetic oil plants. The 381st was dispatched to Merseburg to attack its sprawling Leuna refinery, which was ringed by some 400 flak guns. While Bud Perrin and his crew set out on their first mission, Douglas Holt was enduring his 20th.

"Really rough!" he wrote. "A flak shell burst just in front of us and we flew right into the explosion of flak fragments."[8]

After losing its number one engine and hydraulics, Holt's *Patsy Ann* made it back to Ridgewell where it swung 180 degrees on landing, before skidding to a halt. Fortunately, no one was injured.

Another 381st B-17, *Egg Haid*, also lost two engines over the target and force landed at a recently liberated airfield in France—the crew eventually being billeted in a hotel that was previously a Nazi headquarters. Meanwhile, Bud Perrin found himself safely back in his hut at Ridgewell where he continued writing to Thelma. However, censors ensured he was unable to tell her anything of his first brush with the enemy.

* * *

An equally tough mission followed the next day when 37 B-17s took off for Brüx, Czechoslovakia. Again, the target was an oil plant, which was found to be partially obscured by cloud. Two squadrons bombed the area with "unobserved results," while the other two attacked a "target of last resort" in Plauen, Germany. In the process, *Honey*, of the 533rd suffered oxygen supply problems that resulted in the anoxic collapse of three of its gunners. Only two could be revived. The third—ball turret gunner Sgt. Lydell A. Hayes—was declared dead after *Honey* made an emergency landing at another liberated French airfield. Hayes's crewmates had vainly attempted artificial respiration for 90 minutes.

The 381st was stood down for the next four days, during which time the combat crews' discipline was called into question. An uncovered cache of German POW records revealed that "every one of the squadrons" (captured crew members) had volunteered details of formations, personnel and secret radio information to the Germans.[9] In a "special group meeting," the gunners were also criticized for being "lax" in their work, chiefly because the *Luftwaffe* was largely absent.

"At the time I did not agree," wrote Bob Armstrong. "But later, when I heard of a gunner making the following remark, I changed my mind. He said, 'He was so close (the enemy fighter), I would have shot him down if my guns had been loaded.'"[10]

On September 17, the 381st's armaments men loaded 42 of the group's bombers for a tactical raid on multiple targets near Eindhoven in the Netherlands. The targets, which were given in the form of map coordinates, indicated the locations of gun emplacements and tank concentrations. The mission was in direct support of ground and airborne troops set to take part in Operation *Market Garden*—an attempt to create an invasion route across the Rhine into northern Germany. The 381st's role had begun a day earlier, when *Passaic Warrior* was ferried to USAAF Station 467 at Aldermaston in Berkshire to collect one of the operation's key architects.

Lieutenant General Lewis H. Brereton, commander of the First Allied Airborne Army, was using the 534th's B-17G, flown by Frank L. Scurlock, to observe the assault. After watching the first glider elements take off on the morning of September 17, he climbed aboard *Passaic Warrior* to watch the "greatest airborne operation ever conceived." With him was journalist, W. B. Courtney, who wrote:

> Within the *Passaic Warrior*, there is a business-like tension. In the floor amidships, the rounded top of the underhung ball turret moves restlessly as its gunner scans the air and ground. Looking back through the narrowing fuselage, as through the big end of a telescope, you make out a little airman alert on his jockey seat at the tail guns. When you go forward to join the general in the nose, you have to sidle across a tiny, slippery catwalk in the bomb bay and then crawl between the legs of the top-turret gunner. Forts are for killing, not for comfort.[11]

Arriving over one of the drop zones, *Passaic Warrior* was targeted by flak, Brereton later noting the incident in his diary.

> We followed the southern course below the Thames estuary to Folkestone, then to a point north of Ostend, thence east over Ghent and past Antwerp to the I.P. at Gheel. Here we ran into flak. Remaining in this vicinity for approximately 20 minutes, we encountered light flak. Then we proceeded to the DZ at Eindhoven and watched our dive bombers take out the flak positions. Our B-17 was hit in several places by light flak.[12]

The 381st's other B-17s, meanwhile, took off to attack individually, which led to some interfering with each other's bomb runs and several near-misses.

"As we reformed into our group formation and headed back to England, we met what looked like an endless stream of C-47s towing gliders," wrote Douglas Holt. "I remember commenting that we could walk back to England on C-47s."[13]

Douglas Holt and his crew found themselves heading for one of the Eighth's rest homes the next day, while their fellow crews headed for Hamm's marshaling yards in the northeastern part of the Ruhr Valley. Accurate, tracking flak saw 10 of the 381st's 37 B-17s damaged, although all returned to England. This was followed a day later by a 24-hour break from combat, during which time Bob Armstrong was made "Officer of the Day." Although not much was necessary, events overhead took up most of his time.

"Buzz bombs started coming over, so I was on the phone helping plot their course," he wrote. "One came over our base at about 1,000 feet but it kept right on going."[14]

On September 21, 534th pilot Troy Jones made his way back across the Atlantic after his stateside leave. Jones was accompanied by his former pilot, Charles Ackerman—both men returning to Ridgewell for their second tours of duty. Their arrival coincided with the departure of the 381st's B-17s to Mainz, 20 miles southwest of Frankfurt. All but one of the group's aircraft returned to Ridgewell—the 532nd's *Carnival Queen* being forced to land in Brussels with two flak-damaged engines. Nevertheless, Arthur Bailey and his crew were safe.

After another successful mission to bomb Kassel's Henschel armaments factory a day later, the group was stood down again. The frequency of overflying buzz bombs hadn't abated, however. Bob Armstrong had just returned from visiting his former pilot, Raymond LaPierre, in hospital, when one landed uncomfortably close to his hut.

> We went outside to watch and for the first time we saw units trying to follow them with search lights. When the motor on the buzz bombs stopped the search lights would be turned off. When the bomb exploded we could see a large glow where it hit. One buzz bomb came over and it was being followed by a fighter. The fighter would fire every now and then but both were still going the last we saw or heard them.[15]

One had exploded near Great Yeldham, less than a mile from the base's domestic sites. Although there were no casualties, two houses were destroyed, 14 damaged, and overhead cables and telephone wires brought down.

"We had a little excitement a few minutes ago," Bud Perrin wrote in another letter to his wife, Thelma. "Fun in a way, but pretty close."[16]

Perrin was woken at 0400 and briefed for his fourth mission the following morning. His and 36 other crews were assembled for a strike on Frankfurt's marshaling yards. Bob Armstrong, set to fly his ninth mission, was among them.

"You can bet there were moans and groans when they pulled the curtain back and we could see the location of our target," he wrote. "The route in and out wasn't exactly like walking down a garden path."

Taking off after 0730, the group's B-17s climbed to 22,000 feet. Approaching the target, some of the radio operators then began throwing chaff to confuse the German flak gunners. It seemed to work. Their barrage from the IP onwards remained low and inaccurate. Even so, *Lucky Me!*, a 533rd B-17G under the command of 1st Lt. Oscar W. Gills, appeared to be hit, the ball turret gunner reporting that the aircraft was on fire.

Gills slipped out of the formation and ordered his crew to bail out. Tail gunner Sgt. Harold A. Mourning had already removed his flak vest, but inadvertently disconnected his intercom. Plugging it back in, he called Gills to seek confirmation of the bail-out but received no reply. He then found the aircraft empty. A former glider pilot, Mourning considered flying *Lucky Me!* towards Allied lines. Thinking it might explode, however, he chose to jump. Free-falling through two layers of clouds before pulling his cord, he then landed in a tree and hung five feet from the ground before being captured. In short order, the rest of Gills's crew were captured and taken 25 miles northeast to the *Dulag Luft* transit camp to begin their captivity.

* * *

Although the Eighth had been asked to focus its attacks on the German petroleum industry as first priority, the second priority targets—the country's rail networks—were bombed the next day. The 381st took off for Osnabrück to raid its marshaling yards, with the group's 37 B-17s bombing visually from 27,000 feet. Troy Jones, who was flying the first mission of his second tour after returning from Florida, was left unimpressed following two inopportune malfunctions.

> When I had left to go home on leave, the weather was warm and we were flying in our light flight gear, so unthinkingly on this mission, I carried no fleece-lined back-up gear, but instead wore my thin, electrically-heated flight suit. As luck would have it, not only did the bomb-bay doors stick open, but my flight suit failed to heat on the way home. So, there I sat for several hours—thin flight suit, bomb-bay doors open, and the outside air temperature registering -60 degrees Fahrenheit.[17]

While Jones was subsequently stood down with a blocked ear, Cologne came under attack on September 27, when 462 B-17s were dispatched by the 1st BD to bomb its marshaling yards. Through solid cloud cover and heavy contrails, the 381st's formation of 37 bombed, although the results remained unobserved. Again, one B-17 was forced down in Brussels with another anoxic ball turret gunner, although he was eventually revived.

For Bud Perrin, the Cologne mission marked a turning point. It was his first as a navigator—a position he was now officially training for.

"Being a navigator isn't so bad," he wrote to Thelma. "Keeps a fellow busy and makes time pass by much faster."

Perrin was woken the next morning for the group's fourth consecutive raid on Germany. He was scheduled to fly as navigator for the Harley L. Reed crew on *Little Guy*, which included Bob Armstrong as co-pilot. Their destination was a synthetic oil refinery at Magdeburg in central Germany.

"The anti-aircraft fire started as soon as we were over enemy territory," Armstrong wrote. "We were being shot at all the way to the target."[18]

Nevertheless, 35 of the group's B-17s dropped their bombs and returned after a nine-hour trip.

* * *

Two days earlier, another new crew had arrived at Ridgewell. Second Lieutenant Samuel Goldin's men were assigned to the 533rd BS and began settling into their new surroundings when a "deep-throated noise" startled them. The sight of a V-1 being chased by a fighter over Ridgewell was an eye-opener for Goldin's ball turret gunner, 18-year-old Californian, Sgt. Robert B. Gilbert.

"What we next witnessed was more exciting than any movie I had ever seen," he wrote. "The RAF pilot in his magnificent sweeping Spitfire finally scored a direct hit and the 'doodlebug' blew up in mid-air with a bright flash of light and a massive explosion."

The blast damaged 45 houses at Baythorne End, less than three miles from Gilbert's Nissen hut. "Wow, I thought, what an introduction to life in the ETO!"[19]

Experienced crews were becoming indifferent to the daily occurrence, however. "More buzz bombs came over during the morning hours," noted Bob Armstrong. "I didn't bother to get up to try and see them. They sure do interrupt my sleep."[20]

For others, though, the spectacle was made all the more exciting thanks to "blow-by-blow" accounts broadcast from the control tower over the Tannoy system. Even the crash landing of one of the 533rd's veteran B-17s (unnamed and returning from a training mission on October 1) couldn't upstage another V-1, which overflew later that evening, "an hour earlier than usual."

After flying 14 missions in September, the 381st recommenced combat operations on October 2 following a three-day break. The group returned to the Henschel works at Kassel, although not before two 533rd B-17s collided on the ground at Ridgewell just prior to take-off. Fortunately, the crews were uninjured, but both the unnamed 42-97882 and *The Railroader* were damaged—the latter's tail being "chewed" by one of the former's propellers.

On the mission itself, flak over the target struck Douglas Holt's *Avengress II*. Holt, who'd just returned from his seven days of rest and recuperation, found out what it was like when an aircraft loses control due to flak. Both he and his pilot, William Black were quickly called into action.

> Suddenly our nose went up. Both of us pushed forward on the control column but the response was slow and jerky. We shot up through the formation, barely missing other aircraft. We managed to get a level attitude before we stalled. We took up position at the back of the formation and asked our crew to report on damage. They reported that there was a large hole in the right tail at the hinge where the elevator attaches to the horizontal stabilizer. The damaged hinge and torn metal was interfering with the up and down movement of the elevator. While we were able to keep control for level flight we could not fly close formation.[21]

William Black was able to manipulate the aircraft's power settings to control its attitude, before eventually making a "beautiful landing" back at Ridgewell. His B-17 was followed by another 34 of the group's aircraft, all of which returned without any casualties.

Two days later, 35 B-17s began taking off from Ridgewell destined for Cologne. *The Railroader*, which had been fixed after its recent taxiing accident, was at the center of another incident immediately on take-off.

Reaching a speed of 90mph, its pilot, 2nd Lt. George E. Stevens, was unable to lift the aircraft, its tail "whipping." Slamming on the brakes, Stevens couldn't slow the bomber. *The Railroader* ran off the end of the runway before slamming into a ditch. Luckily, Stevens and his crew were largely uninjured, but the luckless B-17 had made its last attempt to fly.

Also failing to lift, another of the group's B-17s similarly struggled to take off. Losing control on the runway, it promptly ran off the end, crossed a field before finally getting airborne, only for the pilot to return to Ridgewell minutes later. The second consecutive mission featuring two aborts on take-off hadn't been well received at all.

"The group commander is very unhappy," noted surgeon, Ernest Gaillard. "And the pilots soon will be."[22]

While Ernest Gaillard packed his bags for an impending transfer to the 91st General Hospital at Cirencester, Gloucestershire, Harry Leber took it into his own hands to ensure his group faultlessly took off on its next mission. Leading the 381st to a synthetic oil plant at Pölitz in northern Germany on October 6, he discovered the primary and secondary targets were "closed in." Flying on to Stralsund, another 100 miles east, Leber's *Sunkist Special* then dropped on a power station before heading back to England. Douglas Holt, whose pilot, William Black, was suffering from a severe headache, flew the vast majority of the mission himself.

"Holding the control column in one hand and the other on the four throttles with constant adjustments to maintain close formation at 30,000ft, with a full load of bombs, and through flak barrages was a physical and emotional ordeal," he wrote. "At only 115 lbs. it took significant force for me to move the control column with just one hand."[23]

There was no rest for Douglas Holt, however. Less than 24 hours later, he was back in the air and heading for Brüx and its oil refinery, which the group had attacked a month earlier. Out in front was lead navigator James Grey, who was flying in the 532nd's PFF B-17, *Whirlaway*.

"My third wing lead and that turned out to be a division lead," he noted in his diary. "So, about 128 B-17s were to follow where I took them."[24]

On the way in, one of the B-17s following *Whirlaway* was struck by flak, which disabled one of its engines. The pilot of *Los Angeles City Limits*, 1st Lt. John J. O'Connor, found he was unable to keep up with the formation, so he jettisoned his bombs. He was then ordered to meet the formation on its return from bombing.

Arriving over the IP, David Kunkel, leading the mission in *Whirlaway*, learnt the target would be completely covered by cloud. He turned the formation back towards the secondary at Zwickau, which he'd spotted along the way as being "open." On arrival, however, it was found to be covered by "heavy haze." Kunkel took the formation on two "360s" overhead, but only the low group was able to sight the target, which it bombed. The lead and high groups continued on to Schneeberg, 10 miles southeast, and bombed its marshaling yards, while withholding their incendiaries. They were dropped on Nordhausen's airfield on the return.

The changes in the formation's route meant that *Los Angeles City Limits* was unable to meet it. Unfortunately for its crew, however, their B-17 met two Me 163 rocket-propelled fighters, which immediately began attacking. The attacks, which further damaged *Los Angeles City Limits*, caused it to drop to 4,000 feet, where it ran into flak. The severity, and the constant evasive action taken by John O'Connor, caused the tail gunner, SSgt. Marion O. Heilman, to bail out west of Hanover. He was promptly captured. After losing another engine in the fighter attacks, the rest of O'Connor's crew kept the Me 163s at bay before P-51s finally arrived to drive them off. Throwing everything moveable from the bomber, the crew allowed John O'Connor to hold *Los Angeles City Limits* at altitude, the aircraft limping back for a "soft landing" at Ridgewell. It was the bomber's 61st consecutive "non-abortive" mission.

The group's other B-17s also returned safely after over eight hours in the air. James Grey was happy to have made it, although later that evening, as he wrote his diary, another V-1 dropped and exploded just two miles away.

"Now it's evening and four buzz bombs just lit in our area," he wrote. "Cripes, flak all day. Buzz bombs at night, oh well."[25]

* * *

Following a scrubbed mission on October 8, the British radio comedian, Tommy Trinder arrived to entertain not only the men of the 381st, but also English civilians and wounded GIs.

"They say the buzz bomb [the previous evening] outdid Trinder," joked the 535th's diarist. "You've got to develop a taste for English music-hall humor."

The wake-up call for the group's next combat mission didn't come until 0600. Yet, by the time the crews assembled for the briefing, they'd have much rather listened to Tommy Trinder.

"Anytime the target of 'Schweinfurt' comes up I can assure you the moans and groans are long and loud," wrote Bob Armstrong, who was set to fly his 13th mission.[26] More significantly, however, the 381st's sixth visit to Schweinfurt would be its 200th mission.

Newly arrived ball turret gunner Bob Gilbert had been woken for his very first. After watching the other crews "casually eating and chatting" at breakfast, Gilbert was then taken to his B-17, *Princess Pat*, which he'd noticed the previous day was "covered in patches." He learnt from its crew chief that the bomber had "taken crews to Germany and delivered their bombs over 50 times."

Princess Pat was one of 37 B-17s to take off, joining over 300 others for the raid, which was carried out by PFF method amid flak that was "hardly up to Schweinfurt standard." Gilbert's *Princess Pat* and the others subsequently returned to Ridgewell after eight hours—Gilbert gleefully informing his hutmates that although his first mission had been to Schweinfurt, it was a "milk run."[27]

* * *

Despite the 381st's 200th mission-milestone, Harry Leber refused to sanction a party to celebrate.

"Apparently a couple of other bases went overboard with their celebrations, which included, according to reports, one suicide and a murder," noted the 535th's diarist.

For the next four days, the group flew no combat missions, while more V-1s passed overhead. Bob Armstrong, who'd spent the evening after the Schweinfurt raid reading and watching the buzz bombs, was in celebratory mood. He'd finally been checked out as a B-17 pilot, something he'd been aiming for since being assigned as a co-pilot in Dyersburg, Tennessee, six months earlier. Armstrong also learnt that his crew was now "on pass." It was "a most happy day."

A day after Armstrong's departure for London, the Mayor of San Antonio, Texas (and vice-president of the War Production Board), Maury Maverick arrived at Ridgewell to christen a newly assigned B-17. Driving home the idea that the US government would "provide funds for opening a small business" for returning servicemen, Maverick then swung a bottle at the bomber, which he named *The Alamo*.

It was another celebrity-christened B-17 that drew some of the 381st's airmen to London the next day, when they visited the real *Stage Door Canteen*. Harry Leber led the last crew to have flown *Stage Door Canteen*, together with its highly respected crew chief, MSgt. Clarence M. Bankston.

"Mary Churchill must have brought the bomber luck with the Coke she smashed on the nose," wrote the 535th's diarist. "For the aircraft has more than 70 consecutive missions to its credit."

The 381st returned to combat on October 14 with another attack on Cologne's marshaling yards. Bob Gilbert's crew was assigned the ageing *Rotherhithe's Revenge*.

"She was in a battered condition with holes and patches all over," Gilbert noted. "She was often assigned to newer crews because … of the higher incidence of calamitous events happening to them."[28]

Although *Rotherhithe's Revenge* avoided the worst of Cologne's "intense tracking and barrage" flak, it was still hit. But it was the 532nd's *Pella Tulip* that took the full force of one shell, which exploded directly in front of the bomber's cockpit as it flew along the bomb run.

Its pilot, 1st Lt. Charles W. Reseigh, was hit in the face, arms and legs; while his co-pilot, 1st Lt. David R. Rautio, was also incapacitated by the blast. With the aircraft in a dive, Rautio regained consciousness, before levelling out and jettisoning the bombs. The badly wounded Reseigh was then dragged from his seat, while engineer and top turret gunner TSgt. John M. Nushy took over co-pilot duties. With only two functioning port-side engines, jammed wing flaps, and its navigation equipment damaged, Rautio struggled to fly the aircraft for four hours, guided only by the navigator's magnetic compass. Finally arriving at Debach airfield in Suffolk, *Pella Tulip* landed with the aid of parachutes, before screeching to a halt just short of a parked B-17. Reseigh's crew had survived, but he would spend the next six weeks in hospital.

Bob Gilbert's *Rotherhithe Revenge* had survived Cologne, but his B-17 was also slightly damaged.

"As we walked around the trusty old bird that brought us home, we spotted 14 obviously new flak holes, but no major damage," noted Gilbert. "Some of us picked up small souvenir pieces of flak … in the future, we didn't bother to routinely look for and count holes; the novelty having worn off rather quickly."[29]

Bob Armstrong was dispatched to Debach the next day to collect the crew of *Pella Tulip*. "You could say the flak burst or bursts made the plane into an open cockpit job," he wrote. "I don't see how the pilot was able to get it back to England and get it landed."[30]

While he was at Debach, Armstrong's group took off from Ridgewell to revisit Cologne. Finding solid cloud cover and moderate flak, the group bombed and returned safely, although 17 B-17s were damaged, nine of them severely.

Thick fog allowed the ground crews time to patch up the damaged bombers in preparation for yet another raid on Cologne two days later. Led by the 535th's new commanding officer, Maj. Isaac N. Taylor, a former training squadron commander with more than 3,000 flying hours to his name, the group's 37 B-17s took off for the city's Gremburg marshaling yards on October 17. Onboard Taylor's *Stage Door Canteen* was lead navigator James Grey, flying his fourth wing lead.

Flying their first mission was 2nd Lt. John E. Rice, Jr. and his crew. As Rice flew *Green Hornet 2nd* to the 534th's squadron assembly area, he found himself too far south. Engine problems then left him trailing behind the rest of the group. By the time he reached the bomb run, Rice had already feathered one propeller. Another was then struck by flak. It caused the B-17 to drop some 8,000 feet before Rice arrested the descent. He then called Isaac Taylor to say he would be making an emergency landing at Brussels, while also requesting fighter support.

Rice's crew began jettisoning heavy equipment while *Green Hornet 2nd* was last seen losing altitude over the Belgian city of Ciney, before turning northwest towards Brussels. The flak-damaged engine finally gave out with the aircraft at just 1,800 feet. Issuing the bail-out order, Rice then prepared to jump, but his parachute spilled inside the cockpit. With five of his crew already gone, Rice returned to his seat and circled Kortrijk-Dutsel before spotting some flat land at Speelberg. He then glided the bomber in for a belly landing, which he and the remaining crew members walked away from.

Thinking he'd landed behind enemy lines, Rice was informed by local villagers that he was actually in friendly territory. The crew members who'd bailed out were also picked up by Canadian soldiers. They would soon be returned to Ridgewell, along with Rice, who would eventually complete his tour of duty. *Green Hornet 2nd*, which had flown 55 missions, was promptly stripped of its arms and ammunition, but remained in place for more than a year, where it was happily used by local children as their playground.

Intermission: Battle Stations—The Combat Crew

Conditions inside a B-17 were far from comfortable, even without the threat of enemy attack. From the moment a crew clambered on board in their bulky and uncomfortable flight clothing, they were working in a confined space. Once the engines were running, fumes penetrated every part of the fuselage. Communication also became difficult; often shouting was the only way to be heard. At high altitude, sub-zero temperatures and potential oxygen starvation became an omnipresent threat.

If a B-17 was to successfully complete its mission, every crew member had to remain constantly vigilant, looking out for themselves, and for their fellow crewmen. Up in the cockpit, the pilots sat in armored seats, the pilot sitting on the left. Often referred to as the "skipper," or the "old man," he was responsible for the aircraft and its crew. The average age of the "old man" was just 21. On his right, sharing the task of flying the B-17, sat the co-pilot. The two often took turns, hands on at the controls.

Forward and down into the nose of the B-17, is the bombardier's position. He sat on a small, armored seat, well forward in the plexiglass nose of the B-17 and right behind the Norden bombsight. Visibility was unrivalled, but it was also an incredibly exposed position. Once at the IP, the pilot would hand over control of the aircraft to the bombardier. The aircraft could then be flown from a panel on the left of his position.

Just behind the bombardier and in front of the pilots' feet was the navigator's table. From here, the navigator worked using ground references, dead reckoning, and radio aids. Later in the war, radar aids were added to his responsibilities. Like the bombardier, he was also required to man a gun.

The flight engineer was a busy man. As well as managing the aircraft's engines and systems in the air, he also manned the top turret behind the cockpit. During take-off, he would stand in the cockpit behind the two pilots monitoring the engines and assisting with the checks. With their all-round technical knowledge, flight engineers were often called upon to act as stand-in pilots in emergencies.

Moving rearwards to the center of the fuselage, beyond the bomb bay, is the radio operator's position. Probably the least glamorous role in the crew, the radio operator played a vital role. He could also be employed as a camera operator and as a gunner.

Behind and below the radio operator was the least popular position on the B-17, the ball turret. Protecting the underside of the B-17 and usually assigned to the smallest man on the crew, who was confined inside a claustrophobic, armored space hanging below the fuselage. Although perceived to be the most dangerous position, statistically ball turret gunners were less likely to be wounded than the other gunners.

Between the ball turret and the tail are the least protected stations on the B-17, the waist gunner positions. Silhouetted in the large open windows (of B-17s before the G) and with minimal protection, the waist gunners were vulnerable to shrapnel and enemy fire. More casualties were recorded in these positions than any other on the B-17.

Finally, in the rear most position of the B-17, lodged right beneath the tail, sat the vitally important tail gunner. In addition to head-on attacks, a stern attack was also favored by *Luftwaffe* fighter pilots. Consequently, tail gunners rarely returned home without firing their twin .50 caliber machine guns.

This brief insight into the composition of a B-17 crew illustrates how important every individual crew member was to the survival of his aircraft and his comrades.

CHAPTER 23

Leading the Way

October 18–December 11, 1944

Just as John Rice and his crew returned to Ridgewell to be sedated in its sick quarters, the other crews were briefed for a mission that was subsequently scrubbed. It did nothing for Bob Armstrong's nerves. He hadn't flown a mission since the group's 200th on October 9.

"This waiting for so many days between missions is giving me a case of the jitters," he wrote. "I will be glad when we can get going and get our missions out of the way."[1]

Bob Armstrong was stood down on October 19, while the 381st flew to Ludwigshafen in what turned out to be an uneventful mission. Again, the group crossed the Rhine to bomb Mannheim after finding the primary target closed in.

Bob Gilbert, flying in the group's first natural metal finish B-17G, *Dreambaby*, found some minor damage to his ball turret when he arrived back at Ridgewell. He didn't marvel for too long, however. Having flown every mission but one since Schweinfurt, he and his crew received their first 36-hour pass. "Old London Town" would prove to be much more interesting.

For the next five days, the group was not called for any missions, much to Bob Armstrong's consternation. "We went over to see how the gunners were doing. Think they are as restless as we are. We just don't understand why we are not scheduled for any missions."[2]

His only joy came when he attended a show at the officers' club in celebration of the group's 200th mission. "It seemed to me there were more and better looking girls than I had ever seen at the group parties," he wrote. "I asked around and learned our base always has its parties on Sundays so the show girls from London can come up."[3]

It wasn't until three days later that Armstrong finally climbed into *Little Guy* for his 14th combat mission—a raid on Hamburg's oil refineries. Despite the intensity of the city's flak, his B-17 and the 36 others safely returned to Ridgewell largely undamaged.

While Bob Armstrong took off the following day on a practice mission ("my first flight as first pilot"), the group was tasked with bombing Münster's marshaling yards. Poor weather and the malfunction of the PFF's radar equipment forced the group to find a target of opportunity in the form of Bielefeld. For ball turret gunner

Bob Gilbert, the mission marked a milestone—he was awarded his Air Medal on the eve of his 19th birthday.

Münster re-entered the 381st's sights on October 28, when 37 aircraft took off at 1050 led by James Grey's unnamed PFF B-17. Even so, another failure of the radar saw it relinquish the lead to Bud Perrin's *Sunkist Special*—Perrin finding himself leading the entire 1st BD as its lead bombardier.

The weather over the target was found to be "better than briefed" and the crews saw their bombs strike the city's marshaling yards. Very accurate flak then succeeded in damaging Kenyon W. Nashold's *Century Note*, but he was able to make an emergency landing in Brussels. Four crewmen from three squadrons were also wounded in action, although none seriously.

"My first squadron lead turned out to be a division lead—not a bad job," Perrin later wrote to his wife. "Remember, I ain't no hero. So keep it in the family."[4]

* * *

While Perrin was stood down on October 30, his fellow airmen were sent to bomb a synthetic oil plant at Gelsenkirchen. Not for the first time that month, they found solid cloud cover over their target. Continuing on for another 30 miles, they bombed Hamm's marshaling yards instead.

First Lieutenant John W. Berkley's unnamed 43-37791 had already lost power to its number two engine when he aborted the mission over the Netherlands. Feathering it proved unsuccessful and Berkley could only watch as the windmilling engine eventually ran away; so fast, that it burst into flames. As the fire spread along the port wing, the engine tilted up 45 degrees and suddenly tore away from the bomber. Berkley pushed the aircraft into a dive to extinguish the flames, before pulling up into a high-speed stall that saw it roll onto its back, which caused another engine to fail.

"We were still over the English Channel when that happened," remembered ball turret gunner William Goudeket. "[Berkley] thought it was inevitable that we were going to crash into the North Sea, so he gave the bail out signal and we all went to our assigned escape hatch."

Bombardier 2nd Lt. Harry L. Delaplane, Jr., raced past the navigator, 2nd Lt. Eugene L. Nelson, who noticed he wasn't wearing his parachute chest pack. Nelson handed him one and watched as Delaplane tucked it under his arm and immediately jumped out of the escape hatch. He was never seen again.[5]

In the rear, William Goudeket was also preparing to jump when the aircraft levelled out. He'd already seen the tail gunner, SSgt. Frank K. Gunderson, jump and wondered what to do himself.

"So, I got on the intercom and said to the pilot 'what's up?' and he said, 'stick with us'," remembered Goudeket. "But in the meantime, two guys had left the ship. And neither one of them were ever found. We even circled and dropped the life raft."[6]

Goudeket's aircraft eventually made it back to Ridgewell, despite losing another engine along the way. After turning off the runway, the remaining engine stopped. An inspection of the B-17 found the fuselage floor "littered with rivets," and its main wing spars "buckled"—so violent were Berkley's maneuvers to extinguish the fire. The crew's traumatic experience counted for nothing, however. Their mission was uncredited.

* * *

Despite good weather over Ridgewell, the 381st was stood down for the next four days, during which time it was announced that DFCs would no longer be automatically awarded to those completing their tours. The medal would only be given for special recognition.

"Missions, it's apparently figured, are getting easier," noted the 535th's diarist. "Jerry still has flak, but higher HQ seldom sees it."

Having already flown 30 missions to qualify, Douglas Holt, co-pilot with the 534th, was awarded his on November 2.

"All the members of our crew were also awarded the DFC," Holt wrote. "We were a good crew that always made it to the target … it was skill, plus a lot of luck."[7]

Holt's was one of 37 crews woken at 0430 on November 4 for a mission to Hamburg. Coming just three days after the Combined Chiefs of Staff had formally issued their directive listing the German petroleum industry as first priority, the Eighth dispatched over a thousand bombers to hit oil targets in the west of the country. The 381st, leading the 1st BD, dropped on a refinery in the borough of Harburg before returning to Ridgewell.

Twenty-four hours later, another 37 B-17s were loaded for the group's 210th mission, a raid on Frankfurt. Although the mission went according to plan, it almost started with a bang. The 535th's *Schnozzle* was in the process of warming its engines when the crew heard "something fall." They were shocked to discover an unshackled bomb had smashed through the bomb bay.

"We cut the engines, shut off the switches and everyone jumped out and started running," remembered co-pilot 2nd Lt. Boyd C. Fox, Jr. "When I went through the escape hatch, the props were still turning and a 1,000lb bomb was rolling towards the props. I hit the ground running."[8]

Fortunately, there was no explosion and Fox and the rest of his crew were able to switch to another B-17.

It was another early run for Boyd Fox the next day when he was woken at 0330 for his third raid on Hamburg. Assigned to fly *No Comment Needed* on his fifth mission, his was one of 37 B-17s to take off just before sunrise.

Entering the bomb run sometime later, the group was faced with thick clouds, a heavy smoke screen, and accurate, tracking flak. Just before reaching the target, the 535th's *Chug-a-Lug IV*, flown by 2nd Lt. Julius Levitoff, was struck, a burst of flak shattering its astrodome and disabling its number three engine. The aircraft then nosed up, but appeared to be under control, with Levitoff immediately jettisoning his bombs.

Trailing toggliers took this as the signal to release their bombs, which they did—dropping some two minutes short of their objective. With his aircraft on fire, however, Levitoff began ordering his crew to bail out. Seven, including Levitoff, were able to do so, all being captured after landing. Two others were found dead when the bomber crashed in Hamburg's Oschenwerder quarter. Navigator 2nd Lt. Joseph W. Byrnes was believed to have been killed in the initial flak strike; while co-pilot 2nd Lt. John F. Champion, Jr. was thought to have either been unable to escape through the burning bomb bay or killed during his fall. *Chug-a-Lug IV* had become the 535th's first total crew loss in 65 consecutive missions.

Turning off the bomb run, the formation eventually flew out of range of Hamburg's flak guns. Boyd Fox then noticed an engine oil leak coming from *No Comment Needed.* "I watched it and the instruments very close as everything seemed to be performing [alright]."

Approaching the Baltic coast, "puffs of smoke" were then reported passing by the tail gunner. Fox also spotted a flame "lick up" the left wingtip. Alerting his pilot, 2nd Lt. Dudley K. Brummett, the pair put *No Comment Needed* into a dive, reaching 320mph, which failed to extinguish the fire. Brummett then steered the bomber back inland, switched on the AFCE, and ordered his crew to bail out. Boyd Fox lowered himself feet first out of the escape hatch and clung on by his fingertips before letting go.

"The prop wash caught me and spun me around like a feather on a whirlpool," he wrote. "I was afraid I might blackout from the spinning so I pulled my ripcord and my parachute opened."[9]

Fox and the rest of the crew landed close to the small village of Plaggenburg, some 100 miles west of Hamburg. *No Comment Needed* then crashed near Wittmundhafen, five miles further on.

"I landed near a farmer's home in his rhubarb patch which was planted in rows," remembered Fox. "I had slipped out of my parachute and moved over a few rows, but there was no place for me to go."

Fox was then approached by the farmer and his wife, who immediately reached down to feel the silk of Fox's parachute. "I could tell that she would like to have the silk."

Quickly surrounded by other villagers, Fox found himself jostled into military custody. He fared much better than some members of his crew, however. Tail gunner Sgt. Frank N. Horsch managed to evade capture for 24 hours before finally being discovered. After being interrogated, he was then beaten, which left him needing a cane in later life. Engineer and top turret gunner Sgt. Thomas J. Lyons, who'd broken both his legs on landing, was immediately set upon by enraged civilians. By the time a German soldier intervened, Lyons had suffered broken ribs and nerve damage to his spine, which left him in hospital for six months.

"Hamburg, Germany, is still a tough target," noted James Good Brown in his diary on November 6. "There is as much dread to the fliers when they are briefed as when we flew our first raid to Hamburg on July 25, 1943. Today is one year and four months later. The loss of another 18 men is keenly felt."[10]

* * *

Two days after Franklin Roosevelt won a fourth term as US president, the 381st left Ridgewell bound for France—its first visit in almost three months. Using a new, British-developed *Gee-H* radar for the first time, the group flew a tactical mission to bomb gun emplacements and troop concentrations five miles southeast of Metz. The successful raid enabled Gen. George S. Patton's Third Army to bash through German defenses, advancing five miles and gaining 12 towns along the way.

The Metz raid was followed a day later by another attack on Cologne, which began with the death of a 533rd ground crewman. As he walked along the perimeter track, Corporal John J. Corley crossed the path of an approaching ordnance truck, which he was unable to hear above the noise of aircraft engines. Corley was struck, and immediately rushed to the base hospital, where he was pronounced dead just 10 minutes later.

The mission itself was also marred by tragedy. First Lieutenant Floyd Metts's *Hell's Angel* was smashed by several 100lb incendiary bombs, which had remained hung up in a B-17 flying above. Pulling off the bomb run, its crewmen unhooked three from the bomber—two of them taking the nose off of *Hell's Angel*, while one landed on Metts's bombardier, 1st Lt. LeRoy Drummond. The bomb failed to explode, but crushed the officer, fracturing his skull. His crew spent the next 45 minutes trying to dislodge the bomb from the aircraft, before landing back at Ridgewell where they were all hospitalized for shock.

"My letter to his father and mother … will not be pleasant to write," noted James Good Brown. "To say their son died 'in Service of his Country' is not sufficient to ease their suffering."[11]

With another 381st B-17, *Via Panola Express*, force landing in Brussels after its engineer bailed out, and Bob Gilbert's *Rotherhithe's Revenge* having landed at Ridgewell without brakes, the Cologne mission had been a testing one. It was partially tempered by the second of a two-night run of Noel Coward's stage play, *Blithe Spirit*, which was performed in one of Ridgewell's hangars by its London cast, including Peggy Wood.[12] Bud Perrin, who'd been stood down for the Cologne mission, had ended the night drinking with the actress.

"I told her all about my play-acting wife and that I was going to be a papa," he wrote to Thelma. "She was interesting to talk to. Said she would love to go on a mission with us, but we couldn't arrange it."

A few days later, Perrin found himself back in London—although this time, not as part of his crew.

"And can you imagine what I'm going to do?" he wrote excitedly in his next letter to Thelma. "I'm supposed to talk over the radio directly to WROL, Knoxville, Tenn. I thought they were kidding when they told me ... but I guess they weren't. Here I am, orders and all."[13]

The broadcast, recorded by the BBC, saw Perrin answer questions about his training and missions, before focusing on his thoughts about Thanksgiving.

"I'm thankful for my life mostly," he remarked. "But I'm thankful to have a strong ship to fly, and that the folks at home are working along with us, and backing us all the way. We couldn't have the faith we have if we weren't sure about that."[14]

* * *

Just as Perrin's group was gearing up for its next combat mission, a British Short Stirling bomber from nearby RAF Stradishall crash landed less than half a mile from one of Ridgewell's runways. It came to rest on its belly just yards from St Margaret's Church at Tilbury Juxta Clare, leaving a deep gouge across an adjacent field and two slightly injured crewmen. Bob Armstrong and several of his friends walked the short distance from their barracks to inspect the crashed bomber.

"Its construction is a steel frame that is covered with fabric," Armstrong noted. "We think our planes are quite austere but comparing ours with the English bombers, ours are 'fancy dandies'."[15]

Armstrong was stood down the following morning when 37 of the 381st's bombers were loaded with an array of 260lb fragmentation bombs, intended for enemy positions near the German city of Aachen, close to the Belgian and Dutch borders. The tactical mission on November 16 was in support of US ground troops pushing towards Germany.

"When we were briefed we were told ... we would see red crosses on the buildings," remembered 534th co-pilot Douglas Holt, who was flying his 34th mission. "They said that they had intelligence reports that this was actually an ammunition storage area that was camouflaged to look like a field hospital. While we accepted this information as true, there was an uneasy feeling as we dropped our bombs."[16]

Nevertheless, the huge explosions caused by the 381st's bombs confirmed the site was a munitions dump after all.

Several days of rain followed, pinning the combat crews to the ground. Only local training flights were carried out, including the check flight of one of the 534th's co-pilots.

Troy Jones, the squadron's assistant operations officer, took off in *My Son Bob* to qualify the officer as a first pilot. Landing back at Ridgewell, however, Jones's co-pilot "dropped" the B-17, causing its port landing gear to buckle. The aircraft then ground-looped.

"We came to a halt in the grass, while fire truck and ambulance came screaming out," wrote Jones. "Fortunately, nothing was damaged except the aircraft—and the pilots' public and self-images."[17]

The following morning, Douglas Holt flew as first pilot on his 35th and final mission, attacking the Leuna synthetic oil plant at Merseburg. Taking off in *Passaic Warrior*, he led the 381st's high group through heavy contrails and intense, accurate flak to reach the target.

Although his B-17 largely avoided any major damage, the 533rd's *Colonel Bub* didn't. It left the formation with several damaged engines and headed for Brussels, where it eventually "pancaked" after the crew abandoned it in flight. Co-pilot William G. Pettit, who'd struggled to open his flak-holed parachute, sprained his ankle on landing. He then watched as the locals "drained the gas" from his B-17's tanks.

Circling Ridgewell sometime later, Douglas Holt's *Passaic Warrior* was suddenly rocked by the propeller wash of another aircraft. Fighting to control his B-17, Holt banked wildly towards the control tower where he unintentionally did a "buzz job." Parking on the hardstand, he was then approached by an irate Harry Leber.

"He shouted that I was the last person on the earth that he would expect to pull a dumb stunt like that," remembered Holt. "He had previously issued orders that there was to be absolutely no more."

After Holt explained that he had prevented a disaster, Leber congratulated him for completing his tour, before asking what he wanted to do for his next assignment.

"[Col. Leber] said that for my size … I should be flying smaller aircraft and stated that he was changing my Pilot's rating from four engine back to two engine. He said that he would recommend me for Air Transport Command."[18]

* * *

For the next three days, the 381st's airmen undertook ground schools ("bail out over the North Sea … German interrogation … talk about a couple of downer subjects," wrote Bob Armstrong), but also enjoyed a Thanksgiving dinner of turkey, sweet potatoes and pumpkin pie. "Our food doesn't get any better than this," he later acknowledged.[19]

Bud Perrin, who so far had flown 13 missions, all of them over Germany, was packed off to Roke Manor in Hampshire for a seven-day furlough. While he was asleep, his voice echoed across the Atlantic as part of the WROL Knoxville radio broadcast. It was the first time his wife, Thelma, had heard him in over four months. In a letter to Perrin two days later, she excitedly told him about something his mother later heard on the radio.

"She happened to be walking in the kitchen and heard the announcer say that they had had so many requests for the special program carried last Thursday night that it would be repeated at this time—she ran in and called me, and we both got to hear it again, much to our delight."[20]

On November 25, Perrin's group was back in combat with a return to Merseburg. While Bob Armstrong found himself flying a newly assigned, nameless B-17G, 42-38780 ("nice and new and performed perfectly"), the almost uneventful mission saw another of the 381st's bombers make an emergency landing in Brussels. It returned the next day, just as the group was taking off for a new destination.

Over 1,100 heavy bombers left England bound for various marshaling yards, oil installations and bridges in western Germany. The 381st's target was a vital link in the German railroad network between the Ruhr and Kassel—a viaduct spanning the Beke valley, west of Altenbeken. Taking off into sunny skies, Harry Leber's *The Alamo* led 36 B-17s, all aiming for one of Germany's most important bridges.

Some 90 minutes after take-off, the 532nd's *Little Guy* developed an engine problem, which pilot 2nd Lt. Kyle S. Smith was forced to feather. As his B-17 dropped three miles behind the group, it was seen to come under attack by a German fighter—itself being shot down. Nevertheless, *Little Guy* was mortally damaged.

With only two functioning engines and two jammed bombs on board, Kyle Smith headed for Belgium. Reaching the IJssel River, a third engine failed, leaving him no choice but to issue the bail-out order. By the time his crew had jumped, *Little Guy* was too low for him to safely do so. The B-17 crashed on a small island in the middle of an Apeldoorn boating lake, killing Smith in the process.

Of the eight who bailed out of *Little Guy*, six were taken prisoner. Ball turret gunner Sgt. Gustavo E. Contreras was later found dead, while radio operator Sgt. Lester F. Colson died in hospital. Surviving crew members were led to believe that both men had been shot by German soldiers while descending beneath their parachutes.

The rest of the group's bombers attacked Altenbeken's viaduct though solid undercast aided by a *Gee-H* radar. "The only cloud in Germany hovered directly over our target," remarked Harry Leber on his return to Ridgewell, where a large crowd had assembled at the control tower to watch the bombers land.[21]

"Spirits were high—until the count showed one missing," wrote James Good Brown. "What was supposed to be a day of rejoicing and gaiety turned suddenly quiet and somber. No one felt like cheering."

* * *

Another 1,077 heavy bombers were dispatched from England on November 29 to attack more oil refineries and rail targets. The 1st BD's 445 B-17s were sent to an oil storage facility east of Hanover, near Dollbergen, with the 381st leading the way. Thick cloud cover forced a change of target to the secondary—an oil refinery at Misburg on the outskirts of Hanover. Flying between "two big flak barrages," the group turned off the target unscathed, although one B-17 had slipped behind the formation. *Minnie the Mermaid*, under the control of 2nd Lt. Joe D. Nelson, lost two engines due to mechanical problems. Lumbering on for another 180 miles, the B-17 force landed near the Dutch town of Meijel, 15 miles beyond the German border. Fortunately, Nelson and his uninjured crew were quickly evacuated by British troops.

They returned to Ridgewell the next day, just as the group was taking off for its final mission of November—an attack on another oil plant at Zeitz in eastern Germany. Ball turret gunner Bob Gilbert was flying his fourth raid in six days. The near eight-hour mission would once again leave him feeling drained and fatigued.

"An eight-hour mission actually took around 12 hours of more out of the day," he remembered. "So, when you have two such missions back-to-back it is like constantly being involved for 48 hours in preparing for and performing combat."[22]

On take-off, the 534th's *Ice Col' Katy* lost its number two engine while climbing out, forcing its pilot, 1st Lt. Robert W. Geise, to return to Ridgewell to collect another B-17. Making a hard landing, Geise's fully loaded bomber buckled its starboard landing gear and the aircraft collapsed.

"Several tons of gasoline, bombs and plane skidded halfway down the runway," noted the 535th's diarist. "The runway lost a couple of button lights and the 448th hangar boys got themselves a wreck to patch up, but there were no casualties."

There were also no casualties on the mission itself, despite Zeitz's heavy flak.

"Our togglier was knocked off his seat when a hunk of flak hit his flak vest," wrote Bob Gilbert. Fortunately, his crewmate wasn't wounded.

"We were able to bomb visually … it looked like all Germany was on fire, as other groups were also hitting their targets."[23] Gilbert's *Wild Bill* and the 381st's other bombers then returned to Ridgewell, landing in darkness.

* * *

December dawned with the arrival of a US war investigation committee, including Connecticut Republican, Clare Boothe Luce—renowned author, politician and wife of *Life* magazine publisher, Henry Luce. Although her party only remained at Ridgewell for an hour, the 381st's airmen were able to vent their frustrations—mainly about a cigarette shortage and its consequent hardships (sales had been reduced for combat crews and removed altogether for ground crews).

Luce, the "center of attraction," listened intently, before boarding a C-47 to head for France. A short while later, it was announced that sales of cigarettes would resume in the PX, with an allowance of seven packs per week for combat crews, and five for those on the ground.

That same day, non-smoker Bob Armstrong found himself agitated after discovering there was a DFC waiting for him at the 532nd's headquarters.

> We journeyed down and located the sergeant in charge ... he dug down in a drawer, pulled out some papers, looked them over and gave each of us a copy. Then he went to another drawer and took out two boxes. Each box contained the DFC medal, ribbon and lapel pin. We were not duly impressed with the awarding of our medals. My DFC was for flying the plane back to the base after we were shot up on August 27th. The orders show the effective date of the citation to be October 2nd. That was more than two months ago.[24]

Armstrong's mood was lifted when he picked up orders for his crew to travel to the Stanbridge Earls "flak house" at Romsey in Hampshire. Bud Perrin, meanwhile, journeyed in the opposite direction, having finished his rest and recuperation at the nearby Roke Manor. He duly swapped a soft bed for his lumpy cot.

Perrin was stood down for the group's 220th mission, a raid on Soest and its railroad storage sidings. Three divisions, comprising almost 1,200 heavy bombers, headed for a variety of marshaling yards in Germany, with the 381st attacking its target through solid cloud cover. An absence of flak and fighters saw all but one of the group's B-17s return to Ridgewell—the 533rd's unnamed 43-37560 landing safely in France after running short of fuel. "By all round agreement, this was a milk run," noted the 535th's combat diarist.

Despite being given a stand down from combat for the next four days, the crews were called for a long gunnery training mission over the North Sea on December 6. Many of the airmen were unhappy at having to fly for six hours shooting at tow targets over The Wash. There was one happy co-pilot, however. Douglas Holt finally received his orders to head home to the US and a furlough. He duly boarded the converted Caribbean cruise liner USS *Santa Rosa* for a stately voyage out of the ETO.

* * *

European combat resumed for the 381st on December 9, when 37 crews were briefed for an attack on Stuttgart's marshaling yards. Taking off at 0900, the group encountered bad weather at the German border that persisted all the way to the target. Moderate, but accurate flak then started bursting—a blast striking the 535th's *Boulder Buf*, knocking out two engines and badly wounding five crew members. With the oxygen system also out, the pilot, 1st Lt. William H. Clark, let down by some 12,000 feet while his uninjured crew members gave medical attention to those who needed it. Clark then battled through a storm of sleet and snow, before descending to 1,000 feet.

Narrowly avoiding a mountain, *Boulder Buf* was soon flying at 300 feet where it stayed for the next 90 minutes. With a flat tire and no hydraulics, Clark eventually landed at Nancy, France, bouncing to a halt in a "big mud puddle." Clark's five wounded crew members were immediately evacuated to hospital, including SSgt. Harold E. Hallstrom, who suffered a leg amputation.

Nine other B-17s had also been damaged by the flak, one of which, *Daisy Mae*, returned to Ridgewell with a severely wounded radio operator. TSgt. Rafael C. Larsen had been hit in the back. On arrival at Ridgewell, the ambulance crews attempted to administer plasma on the aircraft but were unable to because of Larsen's position. He was eventually given some at the sick quarters, before being transferred to the 121st Station Hospital at Braintree, with five blood donors in tow. Despite their best efforts, Rafael Larsen died two days later.

Chaplain James Good Brown was acutely aware of the "heartache and sorrow" the loss of an airman could bring. He saw it in the letters he'd received from those back home.

"All these letters must be answered, and the load is heavy," he wrote. "But heavier are the hearts of the loved ones back home who, most of all, suffer the loss of their son, husband or fiancé."

Rafael Larsen's fiancée later wrote to Brown seeking information on the cause of his death and the location of his body.

"Were I to publish all the letters I received from families of the men we lost, they would comprise a book."[25]

On December 10, Bud Perrin wrote another letter to his wife after being woken for a mission that was subsequently scrubbed.

"I had to get up real early again this morning, but got back to bed earlier than I usually get up, so I got plenty of sack time," he noted. "Didn't write yesterday because I was too tired after a rather tough day—it was long anyway."[26]

Perrin had endured the perils of the Stuttgart mission and found himself woken at 0400 on December 11 for another trip back to Germany. The 381st's task was to hit another railroad bridge linking Ludwigshafen and Mannheim. Its 37 B-17s would be joining the Eighth Air Force's largest force of bombers sent on a single operation so far. At 0630, a total of 1,586 began taking off from England, escorted by almost 860 P-51s and P-47s.

Bud Perrin's unnamed 43-38780 lifted off under the command of his usual pilot, Leo Belskis, before slotting into the low squadron of the 1st CBW formation. After crossing Belgium in fair weather, the formation climbed to avoid cumulus clouds half an hour from the target. Reaching Mannheim, intense and accurate flak then pounded the B-17s as they released their 2,000lb bombs through a solid undercast.

Almost as soon as he had released his bombs, Bud Perrin's B-17 was struck by a massive explosion, which caused it to lurch away from the formation with a blazing number two engine. As flames spread along the port wing, the engine then fell away and the B-17 dropped into a spin. Four men were seen to bail out at 21,000 feet, while two "objects" exited "possibly from the nose"—one of which was "on fire." The B-17 then crashed in a field close to Mannheim's Neckarau district, to the east of the Rhine.

Bud Perrin's body was found later that afternoon, together with those of six other crew members, including Leo Belskis. Two more—radio operator TSgt. Elvis A. McCoy and waist gunner SSgt. Durward V. Suggs—both survived to be taken prisoner. The only personal effects found by *Luftwaffe* officers from Mannheim's Sandhofen base were those of Bud Perrin. They included several "pictures," a wrist-watch, identification bracelet, and a wedding ring. It would be another three weeks before Perrin's wife learned he was "reported missing in action"—the telegram coming just two weeks before the birth of their daughter. Then, just as she was adapting to motherhood, Thelma received a knock at the door where she was presented with another telegram. It confirmed the death of her husband.

CHAPTER 24

Losing Friends, Burning Bridges

December 12, 1944–January 21, 1945

Returning from his rest and recuperation on December 12, Bob Armstrong soon learned of the loss of Leo Belskis and his crew.

"He and Lt. James V. Collett lived in our barracks and the other two officers … Glen C. Vaughn and Ross W. Perrin, lived in a different barracks located close by," wrote Armstrong. "One thing I did do was take the regular one-piece mattress off of Collett's bed and placed my three-biscuit mattress on his." It was, Armstrong admitted, a "rather natural step" when a crew was shot down.[1]

No one from the group was shot down that day, when the 381st sent 37 B-17s back to the Leuna oil facility at Merseburg. Two suffered a mid-air collision on the way to the target, however, one of which had only been assigned to the 533rd Bomb Squadron four days earlier. Fortunately, both were able to make emergency landings in Brussels, one with a "sheared" rudder.

Another of the 381st's B-17s was forced to land in Belgium two days later when the group flew to attack Kassel's marshaling yards. While none of the aircraft were damaged, they were confronted by stiff opposition in the form of heavy weather.

"The tops of the clouds were uneven, so we ended up flying in and out of the clouds as we flew along," wrote Bob Armstrong, who was flying his 22nd mission. "In addition to the clouds there were so many contrails being formed they added to our problem of reduced visibility. All things considered it was very hard flying formation."[2]

For ball turret gunner Bob Gilbert, the Kassel mission was a milk run that saw him "going over the hump." He was now halfway through his tour of 35 missions.

"We were superstitious about saying how many missions we had left to fly," Gilbert remembered. "We would never say we had so many missions to fly … but it was ok to say, 'I went over the hump today'."[3]

Nevertheless, the worsening weather was stymieing the crews' abilities to complete their tours. By the middle of December, the 381st had flown just five missions. On December 18, they were briefed for an attack on the Kalk marshaling yards in

Cologne. Climbing to 31,000 feet to overfly "stinking weather" along the route, the group was the only 1st CBW unit to successfully reach the target, despite not being able to see it. Still, the crews got a bird's-eye view of several large rockets streaking out of the clouds over the Netherlands.

Winston Churchill had previously announced that the Germans had been firing rockets "for the last few weeks." The new, long-range "V-2s" were capable of travelling at 3,000mph, taking just five minutes to reach England from launch sites thought to be in the Netherlands.

"The rumbling sound, like thunder, after the explosion, is the noise of the passage of the rocket through the air," stated an official Air Ministry report. "It is not heard until after the explosion as the rocket is travelling so much faster than sound."

On December 19, veteran 534th co-pilot, 1st Lt. Ashley Hamory and a group of enlisted men got a close-up look at one. Returning by train from London to catch the group's "Liberty Run" from Chelmsford, they were delayed by fog. Arriving in Essex, they found the 381st's trucks had already left for Ridgewell. Almost at the same time, a V-2 slammed into a factory less than half a mile from where they were standing. The resultant explosion devastated a large part of the Hoffmann's works, a plant responsible for manufacturing ball-bearings.

Rushing to the scene, Hamory and his men spent the rest of the night helping to search for survivors. They were joined by other US airmen from nearby Boreham airfield.

"Much gratitude is being expressed to the Americans," declared the *Essex Chronicle* newspaper three days later. "Two American soldiers were seen by a warden inside a burning house, part of which was in danger of collapsing. They had obtained a stirrup pump from somewhere, and were trying to put out the fire. They would not give up."

Despite their heroism, the Hoffmann's blast caused Chelmsford's greatest loss of life, leaving 39 dead and 138 injured. Many of them had been singing Christmas carols with a Salvation Army band before returning to their benches and machines when the rocket struck.

"Spirits had been high with the end to the war at last in sight and the festive season already begun," stated the *Essex Chronicle* article. "Many of the workers were young women who were still singing when without any warning the V-2 exploded yards away from them."

* * *

Three days later, James Good Brown found himself waiting to board a train at Clare station for a day trip to Colchester. He was accompanied by another 381st airman and two young English girls—Molly, 11, and Rowena, 8.

"One can shop even though it is the European [Theater] of Operations," Brown wrote in his diary. "And it can be fun, too. Well, I had that fun and it was one of the happiest days since coming to England."

Brown had been persuaded to help buy Christmas presents for "some English child," which the other airman usually did for his siblings—a "joy" he was missing out on. With the help of the vicar of the nearby village of Ashen, Brown was invited to take the two young girls to shop for clothes. Amid skeptical looks from a train conductor ("I mentioned that all was on the up and up and pointed to the cross on my uniform") and several others ("they looked at us as though we were kidnappers"), the two "army men—with two small girls" eventually found a store where they were also looked at quizzically by the shop assistants. Brown, however, instructed them to give the girls "the best the store has to offer, from shoes to hats and gloves…"

> The ladies were now convinced that we were not criminals, and soon there were five young lady clerks surrounding the girls, wanting to get in on the fun: Christmas shopping for two little English girls. They loved Molly and Rowena and showed them all kinds of garments, sometimes three or four kinds of clothes. I told the clerks that the girls were to make their own choices and that they could buy what they wished, regardless of price.

The happy party later arrived back in Ashen, where the two girls excitedly modelled the clothes for their parents.

"It was a great day," remembered Brown. "A great episode in the life of the 381st Bomb Group."

The episode continued when Brown cycled back to Ridgewell and arrived at the Red Cross Aeroclub. That afternoon, almost 400 local children descended on the base for its second Christmas party. Brown, who had not arranged the festivities, expected things to be "well-organized," just like the previous year. However, "chaos and general confusion" reigned in the "jammed" Nissen hut. With ripped and overflowing sweet bags, dripping ice cream and "two Santas"—one of whom "burnt out" after 90 minutes—the scene became increasingly frenzied.

"Only English children would have stood for it," Brown noted. "They have what Churchill describes as a 'grim, dogged determination to carry on'. If ever one saw it, he saw it at this Christmas party, which was like a London Blitz. I know now why the English are winning the war against Hitler."[4]

One of 50 airmen to help out at the party, Bob Gilbert was experiencing his second Christmas away from home. Yet, although he tried to enjoy himself, it "really wasn't Christmas." Two days later, Christmas Eve, he was woken for his 19th mission, the group's 226th, and the Eighth's 760th. For the first time in six days, the weather was clear over England, while a high-pressure system extended across much of central Europe. It allowed the Eighth to launch a maximum effort on communication targets just beyond the battle line.

* * *

For eight days, American troops had been fighting off a German attempt to open up a salient in the Ardennes Forest. The poor weather had prevented Allied bombers from providing air cover, while the *Luftwaffe* was able to support the German attack. The offensive, which later became known as the "Battle of the Bulge," was about to turn, however.

When Harry Leber marched to the front of the briefing room, the crews were "calmly elated" to hear they were finally being called upon to help their compatriots.

"We are going to give our ground forces, on the continent, a Christmas present they will never forget," announced Leber. "The Eighth Air Force is putting up 2,700 four-engined bombers to bomb in a 25-mile radius around Bastogne. There has never been that many bombers fly in a single day, much less bomb in such a small area."[5]

In fact, the true figure was 2,046 heavy bombers and 853 fighters—all dispatched to carry out what proved to be the largest air strike of the war.[6] The 381st sent 51—most of them forming "A" Combat Wing, which led the 1st BD. Its target was a *Luftwaffe* landing ground 100 miles beyond the lines at Ettinghausen. The group's other force of B-17s, meanwhile, joined the composite "C" Combat Wing, before flying to Kirch-Göns's *Luftwaffe* airfield, another 35 miles on. Both attacks proved successful, with the Ettinghausen force dropping its 100-pounders in a "big chrysanthemum pattern on the button."

The weather was not so clear over England on the return, however. Thick fog rolled across most of the 1st BD's airfields causing many bombers to divert. Ridgewell, the furthest east and mainly unaffected by fog, eventually saw the arrival of over 125 bombers, including most of the 398th's.

"Planes were parked on unused runways and some on muddy infields in order to keep one runway for landing planes," remembered 533rd co-pilot Edward C. Carr, who was returning from Kirch-Göns. "We landed ... before our field closed down."[7]

While the ground crews coped admirably with the huge influx of bombers, the adjutants and mess hall personnel struggled to accommodate almost 700 uninvited guests. The situation was further exacerbated when a planned mission called for the aircraft to be pre-flighted and loaded with bombs. A particularly heavy frost hindered the operation, which was then scrubbed. As Christmas Day dawned, the exhausted ground crews had to undo all their hard work.

* * *

> All of us had our appetites set for a big turkey dinner with all those good trimmings. We were ever shocked when we walked into the mess hall. They were serving Spam. Until we inquired, it hadn't dawned on us that they did not have enough "turkey dinner" and the trimmings to feed the men from our base plus the crew men from the other bases that had to spend the night with us. Rather than eating Spam many of the men returned to their barracks to check their Christmas packages and see what they could come up with.

Bob Armstrong, December 25, 1944[8]

Despite Bob Armstrong's grievances, the mess hall cooks were able to replenish and supply an evening Christmas meal, which he and his crew enjoyed later that evening. Free beer was also provided across the base, while Christmas carols rang out over the Tannoy. Senior sergeants were even allowed in the officers' club for the very first time. The mood at Ridgewell was merry.

Over the next 48 hours, the other bomb groups' crews departed for their own bases, while one of the 381st's B-17s was sent to Bury St. Edmunds to pick up a 533rd crew whose own B-17 had aborted the mission to Kirch-Göns.

"The plane did not have battle damage and there were no wounded," remembered Edward Carr, who was sent to collect its crew. "After [aborting] … the pilot would not get out of the plane. He just sat in the left seat on the flight deck staring straight ahead, not saying a word … [he] had to be carried from the plane because his legs were paralyzed."[9]

The same pilot had made an emergency landing after his aircraft had collided with another just two weeks earlier. The traumatized airman was later hospitalized.

One of those who had suffered a similar predicament 14 months earlier led the 381st on its next mission two days later. Arthur Briggs—now a lieutenant colonel and the group's operations officer—was tasked with commanding a formation of 37 B-17s for an attack on the Ludendorff Bridge, spanning the Rhine near the town of Remagen. The attack was successful.

"There was no flak, no enemy fighters, big escort, perfect weather at altitude and all clouds well below the formations," wrote the 535th's diarist, whose crewmen described it as "their easiest mission."

Another routine mission then took place on December 30, when, despite poor weather conditions, 37 B-17s bombed an ordnance depot at Mainz, 20 miles southwest of Frankfurt. Bob Armstrong—flying *Daisy Mae* under the watchful eye of 1st Lt. Everett E. Worrell—was hoping to be checked out as a section lead (a pilot in charge of a formation of six B-17s). On their return, Armstrong's radio operator tuned into a BBC radio frequency, which announced that "American heavy bombers were over Germany today."

"We knew they were right on that account," joked Armstrong. Landing in poor visibility, he was duly qualified as section lead.[10]

* * *

Just after Bob Armstrong took off on his first mission as section lead on New Year's Eve, another co-pilot was being checked out as first pilot by Capt. Troy Jones. Lifting off in *Dee Marie* with a skeleton crew of five, the B-17, under the control of 2nd Lt. Edmund E. Weynand, began the first of a series of "touch and go" landings[11] at Ridgewell.

"On final approach he set up a pretty nice rate of descent, and down we came," remembered Troy Jones. "At round-out, I thought he was still too high, and pushed the control column forward. Again, we landed hard and I could feel the left gear give way."

Learning from his previous collapsed landing gear landing six weeks earlier, Jones applied full power to both port engines to keep the B-17 on the runway. It failed to work. Worse still, the number one propeller touched the runway and a blade instantly snapped off, scything through the cockpit.

"I felt something strike my hand, but before I had time to realize what it was, Ed turned to me and calmly said, 'I lost my leg'. I glanced down. He was gripping his left leg above the knee, and I could see that he had, indeed, lost his leg."[12]

Dee Marie skidded to a halt several hundred feet from the runway, where an ambulance soon arrived. Within three minutes, the quick-thinking medics had applied a tourniquet and removed the unconscious Weynand from the aircraft. Some 1,600 units of plasma were then administered as the ambulance raced to Braintree hospital, 14 miles away.

"It was, indeed, a race with death," remembered James Good Brown, who had been called away from his Sunday morning worship to accompany Weynand. "One doctor was busy trying to keep the oxygen mask on Weynand's face. At times I held it in place while the doctor held down the arms so as not to interfere with the flow of the blood plasma."[13]

While Weynand was promptly wheeled into an operating room, Troy Jones was also being prepared for an operation to save his left hand, which was badly mangled.

"Before I was anaesthetized, I saw one person in gown and mask, sort of standing around," Jones wrote. "I thought he looked familiar, so called him over. From his eyes I recognized him as our base chaplain ..."

Jones immediately began laughing at James Good Brown, who was dressed in a white gown, having been given permission to watch the operation to save Jones's hand.

"I was put to sleep and when I awoke, found that the doctor had used a so-called 'banjo' splint," Jones remembered. "My arm, wrist, and about half the hand were covered with a cast." Thankfully, Jones's hand was saved, as was Edmund Weynand's life.

"During the several weeks we both were in the Braintree Hospital I never once heard him utter a single word of complaint or self-pity," wrote Jones of Weynand. "Now there was a hero."[14]

Both men subsequently returned to the US for further hospital treatment and remained in touch throughout their lives. Neither would ever fly in combat again.

* * *

Almost 300 miles from Ridgewell, the 381st's B-17s attacked a communications center at Prüm in support of American troops.

"There was no flak over the target [and] for the second time in a row, we weren't being shot at," noted Bob Armstrong. "Had the Germans fired at our aircraft their position would be given away and the American artillery would have blasted them. This is my kind of war, where you don't get shot at."[15]

Later that evening, the men of the 381st ushered in the New Year with dances at the officers' club and Red Cross Aeroclub. Brigadier General William Gross, who joined the officers, gave the crews an excuse to let their hair down by announcing a stand down for the next day.

"There were only a couple of unimportant fights in the beer parlor," noted the 535th's diarist. "Probably because everyone's worn out by what has been the longest single fight on record: the Allies against the weather man, who has consistently given the Jerry every break. 1945 couldn't be worse from that standpoint. So much for 1944."

* * *

During late-December, the 1st BD had been redesignated the 1st Air Division (1st AD), to which the 381st was formally assigned on New Year's Day. The move coincided with the group's first mission of the year, and a mass attack by hundreds of *Luftwaffe* aircraft on Allied airfields in Europe. It would turn out to be the last major German offensive of World War II.

Despite William Gross's promise of a stand down, 37 crews and hundreds of others were woken almost as soon as they had climbed into bed. Most were still drunk when they attended the briefing at 0415. All were then tasked with either visually attacking an oil plant at Magdeburg, or bombing Kassel by PFF, if conditions prevented it. The mission was expected to last 10 hours.

"Over half the men, including pilots and crewmen were still soused to the gills and were gulping huge amounts of coffee, trying to sober up," wrote 535th navigator 2nd Lt. George C. Kelley. "Some went to their planes and went on pure oxygen, which helped."[16]

Taking off at 0730, the group's 37 B-17s soon ran into difficulty, however. Two layers of clouds over the North Sea saw the formation climb through one to reach clearer air.

"You could see one minute and the next instant you could not see any of the surrounding planes," wrote Kelley, who was flying in *The Feathermerchant*. "It was 'panicsville' for everyone."[17]

Carrying out an emergency procedure to disperse the formation, the B-17s emerged out of the clouds, but were widely scattered. In the process of re-forming, the 381st then lost its position in the bomber stream. Arriving over Magdeburg at the tail end, the group made a visual run on the target, but found it cloud-covered. Interference from other groups then left the 381st's high and low squadrons both separated. They went to bomb the secondary target at Kassel, while the lead squadron, which included George Kelley's *The Feathermerchant*, made two further attempts on Magdeburg.

"As we went over the target for the third time, I did not see any flak, but it seemed as if the rest of the group accelerated and left us behind," remembered Kelley. "I looked out the window and could see that both number three and four engines were out."[18]

Kelley's pilot, 2nd Lt. Vincent J. Peters, found it increasingly difficult to control the B-17, which kept banking towards its dead wing. Peters's only counteraction was to repeatedly dive to pick up speed, then steer to the left. Even so, he was unable to maintain level flight for long. Jettisoning most of its heavy equipment, including the radios, *The Feathermerchant* flew a haphazard route towards France before George Kelley finally estimated they had reached Allied lines. However, they were also over hilly terrain.

"We decided the only way out—since I couldn't find a flat spot big enough to set a Piper Cub down let alone a B-17—we had to leave the ship," remembered Vincent Peters, who calmly announced to his crew: "Gentleman, it's time to leave."[19] He was the last to bail out—even having the coolness to destroy the Norden bombsight before jumping. Fortunately, all nine crew members landed in the lap of Patton's Third Army, near the town of Metz.

By then, and following the failure of the PFF B-17 to sight Magdeburg, the rest of Vincent Peters's squadron bombed Koblenz. Accurate flak at both Koblenz and Kassel severely damaged nine of the group's B-17s, however, with two forced down on the Continent, one carrying two seriously wounded crewmen.

Two consecutive missions to Germany followed when 74 sorties were flown against marshaling yards in both Gerolstein and Cologne. A 24-hour stand down was then followed by two further attacks on the German rail industry, which saw the group's bombers return safely from both Heimbach and, for the ninth time, Cologne. Even the sudden thump of a V-2 exploding eight miles away on January 6, and the crash-landing of *Ice Col' Katy* returning from a training mission 24 hours later, failed to prevent the 381st's combat operations from continuing. Nevertheless, snow, followed by frost on January 8, began to hinder operations as the group targeted a railroad bridge in the German town of Alzey.

A night of salting and sanding allowed the 37 B-17s to be loaded, before getting airborne just before 0700.

"It was still very dark," remembered Bob Armstrong. "Our heater didn't seem to be working and for the first time I used my electric gloves and jacket. There was a lot of flak in the target area. We had bursts all around us. Those close ones do help warm you up."[20]

Bombing through solid undercast using *Gee-H*, the results remained unobserved. The bombs, however, fell harmlessly on a hill next to the town—Alzey's inhabitants believing that its nearby *Wartbergturm* (Wartberg Tower) had been misinterpreted by the 381st crews as their aiming point. The tower duly became known as "Alzey's savior."

* * *

On January 10, the 303rd BG became the first to complete 300 combat missions. That same day, one of its *Gee-H*-equipped B-17s was supplied to the 381st to help the group attack Cologne's Ostheim airfield. Taking off into a snowstorm, Lt. Col. George Shackley led the group in another B-17, but engine failure forced him to leave the formation. In treacherous weather conditions, Shackley managed to make an emergency landing at Ghent, Belgium.

His position was taken over by the 303rd B-17, which successfully attacked the target. Banking away, heavy and accurate flak then struck the aircraft, severely damaging its tail and wounding the tail gunner SSgt. Arthur P. Hafner. His pilot, 1st Lt. Robert J. Roush, immediately fought to control the bomber, which he steered towards England. Unable to maintain altitude or speed, however, he soon diverted to Belgium. Making three passes at an airfield, Roush was unable to control the landing speed and overshot the runway, stopping in a turnip field. Surprisingly, it was the same airfield George Shackley and his crew had landed at two hours earlier. They raced towards Roush's bomber, which was tangled up in barbed wire, helping to evacuate the wounded tail gunner, Arthur Hafner, who had suffered the loss of his right leg.

While more snow blanketed Ridgewell ("makes it look almost habitable," quipped the 535th's diarist), the officers were lectured by a visiting fighter pilot, who gave them a useful insight into methods of fighter-bomber coordination. "This was a meeting where time was well spent," noted Bob Armstrong.[21]

At the same time, former World War I fighter pilot, co-designer of Supermarine seaplanes, and Member of Parliament for Birmingham Duddeston, Sir Oliver Simmonds toured the base to meet the 381st's ground crews. It was they who froze two days later while scraping ice from the runway for the group's next mission—another attack on another bridge—this time at Gemersheim.

Taking off into bad weather at 0930, the group crossed a largely cloud-free Europe to find the bridge completely blanketed. Using another 303rd *Gee-H* aircraft, the 381st dropped almost 98 tons of general-purpose 1,000-pounders. While the results were mostly unobserved, some gunners saw the impacts.

"As luck would have it, the clouds separated and I got to see our bombs hit smack on that railway bridge," wrote ball turret gunner Bob Gilbert. "All other considerations aside that was why we were here. It felt good!"[22]

Still, accurate tracking flak did strike some B-17s, including the 303rd BG's PFF bomber. It was forced to make a hydraulic-less, emergency landing in Belgium, stopping only by the use of two parachutes as brakes.

A day later, the group was handed another German bridge for its 238th target. An autobahn link, crossing the Rhine at Rodenkirchen in the southern suburbs of Cologne, was attacked by 37 of the group's B-17s. Nevertheless, an eight-minute bomb run—during which time the formation was bracketed by "continuous following fire"—did result in the loss of one of the group's aircraft.

A direct hit to *The Columbus Miss* and its number three engine saw the aircraft fall into a spin, its nine-man crew bailing out. While seven, including pilot 2nd Lt. Mead K. Robuck, were fortunate to land in Allied hands, two were less lucky. Ball turret gunner SSgt. Richard L. Shott and tail gunner Sgt. Fred Leiner were later found to have been killed, the causes unknown.

* * *

The Columbus Miss had been named by airmen who hailed from Columbus, Ohio—including Richard Shott. His surviving crew members made their way back to Ridgewell just as the base became the venue for another celebrity naming ceremony.

Christened in honor of another US city, the 533rd's new B-17G *Fort Lansing Emancipator* was to be flown by an "all-Lansing" crew, including pilot and squadron operations officer Capt. Ned Renick. Hollywood actress and USO entertainer Mary Brian, who had just returned from Europe having been caught in the fighting around Bastogne, safely arrived at Ridgewell with a Lansing radio commentator and BBC sound truck.

"I believe that she was the most popular of the actresses who appeared on Ridgewell Aerodrome," remembered chaplain, James Good Brown. "She was just plain nice, with no affectation whatsoever, and extremely friendly with the fellows … Mary Brian mingled freely with the enlisted men and this they liked."[23]

* * *

Over the next 48 hours, several missions were planned, but scrubbed. On January 16, two targets were selected and briefed.

"One was to bomb an oil refinery and fuel storage tanks near Merseburg. The other was to hit a power plant located in the western section of Berlin," wrote Bob Armstrong. "Those two places are about the hottest places in Germany for anti-aircraft fire. It was a bit hard on the nerves waiting for them to decide which target we would attack. Suddenly they scrubbed both plans."[24]

The 381st did get off the ground the next day, when 37 B-17s took off to attack some marshaling yards in Paderborn in western Germany. For once, the crews were unopposed—except for the weather, which closed in around the target. Despite this, all aircraft dropped their bombs, including SSgt. Robert Singleton's *Julie Linda*. The togglier, who was flying his sixth mission, excitedly wrote to his wife after returning from the mission.

"I really feel now, as if I gave him [Hitler] a sock in the belly ... When I say 'bombs away', then's when I thought of you. I was thinking to myself, 'there you are you dirty so and so, that comes from my dear wife, whom you're responsible for taking away from me'."[25]

After two days of bad weather, during which time high-tension power lines were brought down by 50mph gusts, leaving much of the base without electricity, the group returned to Germany to carry out its 240th mission. Again, the target was a rail and road bridge linking Mannheim with Ludwigshafen. The mission got off to an unusual start, however, when a 535th BS waist gunner decided he did not wish to fly in *Wild Bill.* Edward Carr watched events unfold from his trailing B-17:

> We were on the perimeter track ready to turn onto the runway behind another B-17 that was lining up for its take-off roll. Just as the plane started to move forward the waist hatch flew open. A gunner dressed in full flight gear jumped out of the plane. He ran as fast as he could across the field, across the perimeter and toward a nearby farm.[26]

The gunner, who had recently transferred from the 532nd to the 535th, subsequently turned himself in at the operations office, before he was swiftly processed through the base hospital, followed by the guardhouse.

"This is the first case of its kind in the squadron history," noted the 535th's diarist. "Only one other case of refusal to fly a combat mission as ordered is recorded in the entire group. This would have been [his] second mission."

With no losses on the Mannheim raid, the crews were woken again the next day for a mission to Aschaffenburg, 20 miles southeast of Frankfurt.

"They came through the barracks at 0400 and woke all but three men since this was to be a maximum effort," wrote Bob Armstrong, who was set to fly his 31st mission. The group's 38 B-17s would be led by Harry Leber's *Sunkist Special,* on what was to be his final combat mission.

"It was still dark at take-off and our instrument lights were flickering on and off," remembered Bob Armstrong. "That really made instrument flying difficult."

As the group formed up, the crews found the clouds were 10,000 feet higher than briefed. Continuing to climb, they eventually broke into clear skies.

"Upon reaching 25,000ft everyone seemed to be in a state of confusion," noted Armstrong. "There were a large number of planes that could not locate their groups. We ended up with several strangers in our group ..."[27]

Two of the group's B-17s then returned early, one of which made an emergency landing with engine problems.

Second Lieutenant Robert E. Coates's *Smashing Time!* suffered problems of its own over France. Unable to feather a malfunctioning engine, Coates flew on before another one failed. This was followed a short while later by the loss of a third. With a full bomb load and only one functioning engine, his B-17 slowly descended through the clouds, finally breaking clear at 1,000 feet. Still over France, Coates jettisoned his bombs, but was unable to maintain altitude. *Smashing Time!* then bellied into a potato field before sliding to a halt. As the uninjured crew clambered out, a group of civilians approached waving their arms and shouting. They were followed by a US Army truck. The crew's relief was short-lived, however. *Smashing Time!* had landed in a minefield. Nevertheless, Coates and his crew were carefully guided out to begin their journey back to Ridgewell.

The rest of the group's B-17s continued on to Aschaffenburg, once again dropping through a solid undercast unopposed by either flak or fighters. They then turned for home. The mission had taken just over eight hours when the formation approached Ridgewell in haze and high winds. Ball turret gunner Thomas R. Strong was busy closing the ball turret door when his B-17, *Sleepy Time Gal*, suddenly lurched up. Strong was sent crashing into the radio room bulkhead, severely bruising his arm. Bob Armstrong, flying *The Joker*, could see what had happened.

"As my section of six planes started to peel off [to land], the plane on my left wing, commanded by Flight Officer Nicholas F. Tauro, and the plane flying directly behind him commanded by Lieutenant James E. Smith had a mid-air collision."

Tauro's *Schnozzle* had sliced the tail off Smith's *Egg Haid*, sending both aircraft plunging 1,500 feet to the ground less than half a mile from the end of Ridgewell's main runway. The tail of *Egg Haid* came down a further half mile from both aircraft, its tail gunner, Sgt. Walter A. Streich, still inside, but barely alive. Shortly after being removed from the wrecked tail section, he died. Due to the intense flames engulfing both aircraft, the bodies of 17 others could not be retrieved until the following day.

"One of those killed was Lt. Charles F. Soper, a navigator," wrote Bob Armstrong. "His bunk was next to mine and we had breakfast together this morning. Since I was flying section lead I couldn't help but feel that I had lost one-third of my men. This has been a very sad day."[28]

James Good Brown greeted news of the accident with shock and sadness.

"During all our days in training in the States, through three phases of training, we did not have a single accident," he wrote. "Why could we not have been spared this sadness?" Brown's mood would not be lifted for several days.

> The weight was heavy on my heart when I stood over the graves of 18 men in the American Military Cemetery in Cambridge and conducted the funeral service. My heart was full of sorrow, and my soul was heavy with grief. These men were home, back to Ridgewell Aerodrome safely, so near and yet so far.
>
> What comfort can I give to the families back home? We can but say, "They died in combat," and "they gave their lives for their country."[29]

CHAPTER 25

Razing the Reich

January 22–March 15, 1945

The collision of *Schnozzle* and *Egg Haid* took place just over a year after the group's first major flying accident, when Cecil Clore's B-17 had crashed shortly after take-off from Ridgewell. Like then, the 381st's latest tragedy coincided with yet another change in leadership—this time, its third. Just as Harry Leber had taken over the group's reins in January 1944, so he prepared to relinquish them almost exactly 12 months later. On landing after leading the Aschaffenburg raid, he was awarded an immediate Silver Star by the 1st CBW commander, William Gross. He then readied himself for a move back to the US.

Four days later, Gross announced that Conway Hall, the group's deputy commander, had been chosen to replace Harry Leber. Rumors had been circulating that a new officer was being brought in. Gross's announcement, therefore, was greeted with "delight all over the base." James Good Brown was particularly thrilled.

"General Gross, our Wing Commander, told me personally that an exception to a binding rule was made in the one case of Colonel Hall," he wrote. "Due to the pressure of popular demand from the members of the 381st, they gave him to us rather than to another group to which he had been assigned."[1]

Following the announcement, and after a six-day break, the 381st resumed its combat operations with a briefed attack on Cologne's Hohenzollern Bridge. A combination of "unbriefed clouds" and *Gee-H* instrument failure caused the formation to overfly the target, before splitting up—several aircraft bombing another district of Cologne, while the majority flew on to attack Gütersloh. All 36 B-17s returned safely.

On January 29, the group then returned to Germany to hit the Niederlahnstein marshaling yards to the south of Koblenz. Although the target was covered by cloud, there was no failure of the *Gee-H* equipment this time, all 36 aircraft bombing successfully. However, Bob Armstrong, flying his 32nd mission, experienced a troubling moment.

While fumbling for his flak helmet on the bomb run, he found he had been issued the wrong size. Throwing it back over his shoulder in frustration, he inadvertently knocked the landing gear switch, which dropped the undercarriage, immediately slowing his bomber. In a state of confusion, Armstrong frantically tried applying power, only to be told by his ball turret gunner that the gear was down. He managed to swerve his lumbering B-17 from beneath another whose bomb bay doors were just opening, seconds before its twelve 500-pounders were released. "My luck was holding today," he later wrote.

After safely landing back at Ridgewell, Armstrong was then told to report to the group's operations officer, Arthur Briggs.

> [Briggs] advised me the [USAAF] was forming an Air Sea Rescue Squadron here in England. It would be composed of B-17s carrying airborne life boats. If I wanted the job, I would be in charge of the six B-17 crews. The tour of duty would run for six months and I would receive a promotion to captain. I would be given credit for a full combat tour and could take certain members of our present crew with me. The approved crew members would also be given credit for a full combat tour and would serve for six months before rotating back to the States. Man, we were a happy bunch. No more combat! All of us scheduled to go to the emergency rescue unit went to *The Fox* to drink beer and have one heck of a good time.[2]

Snow blanketed Ridgewell the next day, making the riding of bicycles treacherous. Frequent Tannoy announcements prohibited their use, while men stayed huddled in their huts or mess halls. Bob Armstrong calculated that he and his crew had been on the base exactly six months. He also noted that while eight of his hutmates had finished their tours, another eight had become casualties.

As January turned to February, Armstrong and his crew ventured out into the snow for an official photograph with *The Joker*—the B-17 they had flown over Niederlahnstein two days earlier. They then watched as 37 of the group's B-17s took off to attack Mannheim's marshaling yards.

Leading the Eighth's stream of 799 bombers to attack Germany's rail and industrial plants, the 381st was guided by a B-17 equipped with another new blind-bombing device—*Micro-H*.[3] The mission began calamitously for the group, however, when 2nd Lt. Curtis D. Kuhns's *Julie Linda* suffered engine failure and was forced to return early. Landing downwind, Kuhns was unable to stop his bomber, which careered off the runway and smashed through several huts, before ending in a crumpled heap near the 533rd's dispersals.

Although *Julie Linda* was damaged beyond repair, Kuhns and his crew escaped serious injury. Elsewhere, despite solid cloud-cover over the target, the rest of the group's B-17s successfully bombed Mannheim and returned safely.

* * *

Just as Winston Churchill, Franklin Roosevelt and the leader of the Soviet Union, Joseph Stalin, were meeting in Yalta on the Crimean Peninsula, the Americans were preparing to bomb Berlin in an effort to disrupt troop reinforcements to the Eastern

Front and "increase administrative confusion." Berlin's Tempelhof transportation district and government buildings became the 381st's next objective on February 3. Chaplain James Good Brown was present for the crews' briefing, as he had been for almost every one before. Yet, an "unpardonable slip of the tongue" soon left him feeling ashamed.

> We had just finished the briefing ... As always it was a long and dangerous mission. A flier expressed to me his apprehension about flying to Berlin. My reply was "Don't worry." No sooner had I spoken the words than I knew I had said the wrong thing ... The truth was, I was quite serious about what I said. I did not want him to worry. But, you see, the fellow did worry and had every right to worry ... No sooner had I said to him, "don't worry" than he replied, "I can see how you can say that!" I shall never forget this remark if I live to 100 years old. I hope I remember it to the end of time.[4]

Brown was set for his own "marvelous experience," however. Climbing into Conway Hall's *Little Rock-ette*, he took off to watch the Eighth Air Force assemble its largest formation of aircraft so far. Over 1,400 B-17s and B-24s, escorted by almost 1,000 P-51s and P-47s, formed up into a 300-mile bomber stream. Flying just above and behind the 381st, Brown found himself captivated by the sight.

"All knew where to rendezvous," he wrote. "There were no traffic signs, no crossroads, no hills and valleys as marking points, but the navigators knew where to meet."[5]

Despite a solid undercast all the way to the target, the clouds cleared by the time the 381st reached it, becoming the 12th group to do so. After its B-17s released almost 90 tons of bombs and incendiaries, tracking flak struck two of the group's aircraft. Second Lieutenant Paul C. Pucylouski's *Blind Date* made a sharp turn off the target and flew out of sight—the aircraft eventually crashing near Tutow, some 95 miles north of Berlin. Although eight of Pucylouski's crew managed to bail out to become POWs, his navigator, 2nd Lt. John E. Kelleher, was later found dead, the cause unknown.

The 532nd's *The Joker*, which had recently been flown by Bob Armstrong, was also hit in its number two engine. Flames licked around the wing for five minutes before its pilot, 2nd Lt. John B. Anderson, ordered his crew to bail out—eight of them doing so.

Unlike most ball turret gunners, SSgt. Michael J. Medzie had taken to wearing a parachute chest pack after his aircraft had been struck by flak on a previous mission. Hearing the bail-out order, Medzie immediately flipped open his turret door and fell out backwards. After landing in a tree and swinging some 50 feet above the ground, he managed to abseil down before being captured by two passing German soldiers. As they escorted him through the nearby town of Eberswalde, Medzie was set upon by angry civilians. Fortunately, he was locked up for his own good.

John Anderson, meanwhile, had held the B-17 long enough for his crew to escape. *The Joker* was then seen by other crews to go into a turning climb before exploding in mid-air. The wreckage landed in a forest 25 miles north of Berlin, where the body of John Anderson was also discovered. Together with three others in his crew, Anderson had been another hutmate of Bob Armstrong, who eventually learned they and *The Joker* were missing.

"The new score would be ten finished and twelve casualties," Armstrong noted later that evening.[6]

Ball turret gunner Bob Gilbert returned from Berlin having captured the post-strike photographs using a film camera mounted in his turret. He had also spotted a 381st B-17 flying across a burning Berlin below his. Thinking it was in trouble, Gilbert used the entire roll of film in case any of its crew bailed out. The B-17 then disappeared from view, leaving him unsure if it was one of those lost.

"The next day there were large headlines in the British papers," Gilbert wrote. "In one London tabloid, there was a half-page picture of a B-17 with the Triangle-L identifier … it dawned on me it was the same view as I had with my ball turret mounted camera."

Although he could never prove it, Gilbert was convinced the image—which became "one of the war's most famous"—came from his camera.[7]

* * *

Three days after the Berlin raid, Lt. Col. Conway S. Hall, 27, officially assumed command of the 381st Bomb Group. Having been a command pilot, operations officer and air executive, Hall's parents were informed of his new status by a delighted James Good Brown.

"This is an outstanding tribute to a man of whom you can rightly be proud," he wrote in a letter to them. "He is always a gentleman and so wonderful with the men in his command."[8]

One of Hall's early tasks as the 381st's commander was not to direct his men, though, but to placate the locals. He recalled the event vividly.

> This lady and her daughter came in and it seemed that one of our sergeants had borrowed their bicycle and he had been staying with them and he was missing … and she said that her husband would be coming home and "that bicycle had better be there."
>
> She said "now my daughter is pregnant by him and I'm also pregnant by him, but if that bicycle's not here my husband is going to really be mad." Well, this kind of stopped me for a minute and I'm thinking, and I said, "what you really want is your bicycle?" "Yes!"
>
> Well, when the men would go down [in combat], we'd pool the bicycles … I said to [one of the 381st's officers] "take her down and give her a bicycle and one for her daughter. And be sure they go out the front gate riding them." But that kind of shook me up. That husband's going to be real mad about that bicycle and couldn't care less about the rest. Oh boy.[9]

Hall's men flew to Lützkendorf on February 6 but found the target obscured by cloud. Unable to locate the secondary, the group then bombed a town "with a railroad running through it," which turned out to be Ohrdruf. Two bombers failed to drop, but continued on to bomb Steinbach, 15 miles further east.

The next day, the 381st took off to attack Osterfeld as part of a 1st AD force of 295 B-17s. However, a 30,000-foot cloud bank forced a recall, causing 294 of them to turn back. Only 2nd Lt. William H. Taylor's B-17 continued on. It had earlier suffered a supercharger problem and soon lost contact with the formation. Attempting to intercept it, Taylor cut across the briefed route, but was unable to locate any others. Unperturbed, he pressed on—his B-17 becoming the only heavy bomber over Germany.[10] Approaching Essen, he saw a target of opportunity, bombed it, then turned for home having been hit by flak. Landing back at Ridgewell with only three engines and major battle damage (and the threat of a possible court martial), Taylor was rightly awarded the DFC for his "extraordinary achievement."

* * *

After 192 days at Ridgewell, Bob Armstrong packed his DFC and Air Medal (with four Oak Leaf Clusters) to begin his new role with the 5th Emergency Rescue Squadron.

That day, February 9, the 381st flew to attack a viaduct at Arnsberg, bombing through solid undercast using *Gee-H*. It was followed by a four-day stand down, before the group received another field order in the early hours of February 14, to attack the city of Dresden, a target which had been heavily bombed overnight by almost 800 Avro Lancasters.

Part of Operation *Thunderclap*—a plan conceived the previous year to deliver a "sudden and devastating blow" in order to create transportation and urban confusion—the Eighth's 830th mission was intended to aid the Soviets' advance into eastern Germany.

Briefed at 0430, 37 of the 381st's crews took off from Ridgewell four hours later to attack the city's marshaling yards. With the 1st CBW leading the entire 1st AD, they were under strict instructions to maintain their place in the bomber stream. Any deviation could see their bombs falling on advancing Soviet troops. Unfortunately, the group ahead of the 381st led the formation through bad weather and contrails that left the entire division off course. Knowing the bomber stream had been interrupted, the 381st's lead pilot, Capt. James Tyson peeled his group off in search of a target of opportunity. Overflying Münster, heavy flak then struck a number of aircraft, including *The Fox*—a 535th B-17 named after the pub in Tilbury Juxta Clare. The damaged bomber, under the command of 2nd Lt. Dean L. Anderson, continued flying on.

Another 535th B-17, *Me and My Gal*, flown by 2nd Lt. Elmer B. Wulf, had also been hit. It was left with a damaged engine and out of formation. Heading back across Germany, it was struck by more flak near the Belgian border, which "lifted" the aircraft sideways. With fuel pouring out and two more engines lost, Wulf issued the bail-out order. Unable to locate his parachute, however, he remained with the aircraft while the rest of his crew jumped. He then crash-landed *Me and My Gal*, suffering minor injuries in the process, before being picked up by American troops.

Wulf's co-pilot, 2nd Lt. Hugh D. Robinson, was also found by GIs after successfully bailing out, although he was injured. Robinson's troubles were far from over, however. After being examined by a field medic, he was flown to a US Army hospital in Liège in a Stinson L-5 Sentinel aircraft. Flying into fog, the L-5's pilot lost his bearings and was unable to land. Calamitously, the aircraft then ran out of fuel forcing the hapless Robinson to bail out for a second time. Fortunately, he survived to return to Ridgewell—but not before the B-24 ferrying him to England suffered a collapsed landing gear while attempting to take off.

* * *

Near Dresden, James Tyson—John Howland's former pilot and now 535th operations officer—together with his bombardier, Capt. Frank Palenik, were still seeking a target of opportunity. Palenik eventually spotted a "vast industrial pile" free from cloud cover at Brüx, some 20 miles beyond the German–Czechoslovakian border. Making a 40-second bomb run, the lead and high squadrons let loose, while the low squadron failed to drop. Flying a further 50 miles south, it dropped on a target of opportunity at Pilsen. The 381st's bombers then made their escape back across Germany.

Dean Anderson's *The Fox* was trailing the group by some 200 miles. Having dropped his bombs at Brüx, flak had damaged another engine and jammed the bomb bay doors open. Further flak strikes on the flight across Germany then disabled a third engine, leaving the B-17 barely flyable. Anderson ordered his crew to bail out, four of them doing so from the rear. Those in the front were unable to prise open the forward escape hatch. They were forced to scramble their way back through the aircraft to the rear. Anderson was the last to bail out before *The Fox* crashed. He landed safely in a field but was soon approached by several farmers with pitchforks. The arrival of US troops moments later confirmed he and those in the front of *The Fox* had landed in friendly territory. The four in the back were less fortunate, however. Although they had bailed out safely, they'd landed on the wrong side of the lines.

Eighteen of the group's B-17s landed away from Ridgewell, most on the Continent due to a shortage of fuel. Returning from his 35th and final mission, Edward Carr was pleased to land *Fort Lansing Emancipator* at Ridgewell, despite a feathered propeller.

"On the ground and taxiing to our hardstand the thought came to my mind that I would not have to fly from Ridgewell again," he wrote. "I cut the engines, the props stopped, and then silence. It didn't sink in. This was the last time I would be at the controls of a B-17."[11]

Although there was great relief among the returning combat crews, Conway Hall and the intelligence officers were in a dither trying to establish if the group had dropped its bombs on Soviet-held territory. Poring over strike photos taken by the B-17s, it was found that 25 had "absolutely clobbered" Brüx's Sudetenländische Treibstoff Werke—an "A-Plus Priority" synthetic oil and gas plant, which the Allies had previously tried knocking out. The other 12 B-17s that bombed Pilsen were also found to have struck the Škoda armaments plant.

"We turned what might have been a miserable and costly failure into one of our outstanding combat performances," boasted the 381st's combat diarist.

* * *

Despite the loss of two B-17s on the group's last mission, James Good Brown was positive about the direction of the air war.

"The 381st [has] now moved into a more cheerful atmosphere with respect to our combat flying," he wrote. "It is evident that Germany is fast losing the war. Their defenses are weakening as ground forces are steadily moving toward Berlin. And the Air Force is winning the war in the air."[12]

All but two of the Eighth's bomb groups were sent back to eastern Germany a day later, when two oil refineries were selected as the primary targets. The 381st headed for Ruhland, 30 miles north of Dresden. A weather scout flying ahead of the formation found the target cloud-covered, however. The 381st was diverted south, dropping by PFF method on the city of Dresden, which was still smoldering after heavy Allied raids across the previous two days.

Of the 24 B-17s sent from Ridgewell, 21 bombed what were thought to be the city's marshaling yards, while two others struck targets of opportunity on the Ems–Weser canal and at Lingen. Nevertheless, the bulk of the Dresden bombs had missed their aiming point.

"Not a single detached building remains intact or capable of reconstruction," a Nazi official later declared on German radio. "The town area [of Dresden] is devoid of human life. A great city has been wiped from the map of Europe."[13]

Central Germany came back into the group's sights on February 16, when 37 B-17s lifted off to bomb another oil refinery near Dortmund. Once again, clouds extending to 27,000 feet impeded the 381st's attack. It was forced to shift its aim to the secondary target—Langendreer's marshaling yards. The majority of the group's B-17s successfully struck the site, while 13 looked for other targets of opportunity—which fortuitously included an ammunition dump—a "tremendous flash" and a "huge column of smoke" confirming the nature of the site.

Although a number of B-17s were damaged by seven minutes of accurate, tracking flak, the 381st returned to Ridgewell intact. Only the unnamed 43-38771 suffered any serious damage—due to "friendly fire" when two bombs released from an overflying

B-17 punched through its starboard wing. Fortunately, the crew remained unhurt, and the rattling bomber landed back at Ridgewell.

* * *

A day after the 381st had flown its 250th mission, German radio reported that the head of USSTAF, Lt. Gen. Carl Spaatz was being awarded a "special decoration"—the "Order of the White Feather." The announcer declared it was for "exceptional cowardice in laying a carpet of bombs across a city crowded with hundreds of thousands of refugees." The seven-minute broadcast largely referred to the raid on Berlin, which had taken place on February 3, but it was clear the incessant attacks under Operation *Thunderclap* were having a shocking effect. Even the *Associated Press* news agency was beginning to accuse the "Allied Air Chiefs" of adopting the "deliberate terror bombing of German population centers as a ruthless expedient to hastening Hitler's doom."

At Ridgewell, the first larks could be heard as the 381st welcomed an unusual visitor a day later. Avro Lancaster R5868 PO-S ("S for Sugar")[14] of 467 Squadron, Royal Australian Air Force, visited Station 167 as part of a six-week "goodwill tour" of Eighth Air Force bases. Adorned with eight full rows of operations symbols and the words, "No enemy plane will fly over the Reich territory" (attributed to *Luftwaffe* general Hermann Göring), the 128-operation bomber was keenly inspected by the 381st's airmen.

Unlike the group's B-17s, "S for Sugar" had visited the German city of Dortmund once before. On February 19, the 381st made its first visit, heading for the Hoesch benzine oil refinery, successfully dropping almost 100 tons of general-purpose bombs. All 37 B-17s safely returned to Ridgewell, closely followed by 13 of the 398th BG's bombers, which were unable to find Nuthampstead airfield in a heavy ground haze.

A day later, the 381st made the first of two consecutive strikes on the southeastern German city of Nürnberg. Bombing its marshaling yards by PFF method on both occasions, the results remained unobserved.

Ball turret gunner Bob Gilbert, who was flying his 32nd mission on the second of the two raids, was "lost in personal thoughts" as his B-17 droned back to Ridgewell. His day had started badly when he had been woken, only to fall asleep before reawakening to find the Nissen hut's lights switched on and his crew gone. Missing breakfast and frantically stumbling across a ploughed field in near-darkness, he had finally reached his B-17 just prior to take-off. "This screw-up by me didn't help any of my feelings of impending doom," he later wrote.[15]

Gilbert didn't have too long to wait for his 33rd mission. Waking up at the first time of asking on February 22, his B-17 was one of 37 to take off from Ridgewell to attack the German road and rail infrastructure as part of Operation *Clarion*. The Eighth had scheduled almost 1,300 heavy bombers and approximately 700 fighters for low level attacks on numerous "undefended" and "unbombed" targets. They were to be joined by elements of the Ninth and Fifteenth Air Forces, as well as RAF Bomber Command, attacking railroads, bridges and roads from bases in England, France, the Netherlands, Belgium and Italy.

The 381st's target was a road and rail junction at Gardelegen, some 85 miles west of Berlin. However, the sheer number of Allied aircraft in the skies over Germany forced the 381st out of position on its approach to the target. Instead, the group's leader, James Tyson, decided to seek a target of opportunity. Finding another overpass 15 miles from Gardelegen, at Köbbelitz, the 381st's lead and low squadrons successfully bombed from an "unusually low" 12,000 feet, while the high squadron missed the opportunity altogether. It flew five miles further on to bomb another station at Klötze. Bob Gilbert's B-17 was among them.

"My viewing position today was exceptional," he wrote. "Everything was very clear as I witnessed the bombs smacking into the rail yard with large explosions … Bomb strike photos are fine, but watching the real thing in real time is exhilarating."[16]

Gilbert got another opportunity to watch his bombs fall 24 hours later, when the group took part in a second consecutive day of *Clarion* operations. Although the target this time was the Bavarian town of Hof, a solid undercast all the way saw the 381st seek another target of opportunity 65 miles west at Meiningen. Once again, Gilbert's 533rd BS misjudged its bomb run, having to make a 360-degree turn over Meiningen, before attacking Adelsberg 50 miles away. The search for the targets had left many of the 381st's bombers short of fuel, however. After an almost 10-hour round-trip, 11 were forced to land away from Ridgewell, including Gilbert's unnamed B-17, which diverted to Rivenhall.

Following an evening of drinking and singing with their British and Commonwealth counterparts, Gilbert's crew returned to Ridgewell the next morning. By the time they arrived, the group had already left for its next raid on a more familiar target, the Blohm & Voss shipyards at Hamburg. Yet, the day had also begun with a tragedy. Long-serving 534th BS assistant crew chief Sgt. Thomas S. Downey was killed as he attempted to fight a fire that had enveloped an engine on the B-17 he was servicing. With its propeller still spinning, Downey inadvertently stumbled into it. He was pronounced dead at the scene.

* * *

Senior crew chief MSgt. Clarence Bankston was congratulated the next day as he shared the stage with several English actresses, including Anna Neagle. The star of the show, however, was Bankston's *Stage Door Canteen*, the veteran 105-mission bomber, which had been christened by Mary Churchill 10 months earlier.

"To keep a ship any length of time is heartening and no one should envy us the joy and delight of seeing a ship remain with us," noted James Good Brown. "To keep a ship a long time is the coveted wish of every base."[17]

Neagle, who had recently had a B-17 christened *Lady Anna* in her honor by the men of the 379th BG at Kimbolton, swung another bottle of Coca Cola at *Stage Door Canteen*. Delivering a speech, she then cut through a huge birthday cake containing almost enough candles to represent its mission-count. "They managed to dig up 99 little white ones," noted the 535th's diarist, "which isn't bad." Clarence Bankston, who had been "charged" with only one mechanical abort during its mission tally, was then fed a "monster mouthful" as the newspaper cameras flashed.

Earlier that morning, the 381st had dispatched another 37 B-17s to attack Munich's central station and marshaling yards. With the ground visible all the way to the target, the Germans tried (and failed) to cover the area using smokepots, the wind blowing their smoke across the city's flak gunners, who were unable to sight the group as it turned off the target. The 381st's bombs then "walked right across the tracks."

Bob Gilbert had seen the Alps while on approach to Munich, "bright white with sharp canyons of pink and blue." After turning away from the city, he then looked down from his ball turret.

"From five miles up, I gazed silently at the map-like arrangements of towns, villages and farms connected by roads and rivers," he later wrote. "It was hard to realize what was happening down there in that beautiful tapestry of greens and browns ..."

The mission marked Gilbert's 35th and final one. Not wishing to jinx it, none of his crew had mentioned it to him. Not until his B-17 had parked on its hardstand at Ridgewell was he confident of celebrating.

"I slowly climbed out of the waist door and just said, 'thank you', as I patted the horizontal stabilizer."

Gilbert, who was two missions ahead of the rest of the crew, was then asked by his pilot, 2nd Lt. Samuel Goldin, if he would fly two more missions so the crew could "finish together." Gilbert "respectfully declined."[18]

* * *

Goldin's crew flew the next day as the 381st targeted Berlin for the 11th time. On this occasion the group attacked the city's Schlesisches rail station, dropping almost 90 tons of high explosives and incendiaries through a solid undercast. Despite a moderate flak barrage in the target area, several of the B-17s were equipped with new "spot jammers," radar devices designed to jam those used by the German flak gun crews. Operated by newly trained waist gunners, the equipment worked "beautifully"—one 381st crewman stopping "32 separate leaks" over Berlin.

The spot jamming technique was just one of several new measures adopted by the Eighth Air Force. It had been decided that with the reduction in fighter attacks, the remaining waist gunner could be removed altogether, with some retraining as spot jammers. The Eighth's B-17s would largely be crewed by eight men. Additionally, the

1st CBW was also planning to remove the ball turrets from some of the 381st's B-17s, and the chin turrets from a number of the 398th's bombers. Their removal would lessen drag and increase speed, although this was of no benefit when flying in formation.

On February 27, over 1,100 heavy bombers took off from England to carry out attacks on seven rail targets in Germany. The 381st struck Leipzig's marshaling yards by PFF method, with all 36 B-17s returning safely to Ridgewell. Among them was Samuel Goldin's. He and his crew had finally completed their 35 missions having flown on six of the previous seven days.

"In our outfit when one finished his tour of duty, he was given a 'Happy Warrior' pass of 72 hours," wrote Goldin's former ball turret gunner Bob Gilbert.

As they prepared to travel to London, Gilbert and the rest of the Goldin crew toasted each other while swigging a "very foul tasting" mix of scotch and champagne, which they named "The Happy Warrior Cocktail."

"We all drank way too much, but we were young … and no one begrudged us our release of emotions," remembered Gilbert.

After a brief 24-hour stand down, Gilbert's group was back in the air on March 1. Mission 260 saw the 381st heading for Neckarsulm's marshaling yards, 30 miles north of Stuttgart. Largely unimpeded, the B-17s dropped their 500-pounders, which burst across the marshaling yards, although slightly off target.

As the group made its return to Ridgewell, the 532nd's *Flak Magnet* experienced engine problems. A long stream of fuel was seen trailing behind its number four engine. Its pilot, 1st Lt. Edgar H. Price, Jr., attempted to feather the propeller, but the engine immediately burst into flames. Price instructed his crew to prepare to bail out, prompting his engineer and top turret gunner, Sergeant Donald R. Hawkins, to immediately do so. Jumping through the bomb bay at 14,000 feet, Hawkins was seen to be in a "good fall" before disappearing into clouds. Fortunately, he was over Arras, France and landed in friendly territory.

Edgar Price was also fortunate to see the flames extinguished on his burning engine. He was able to return *Flak Magnet* to Ridgewell with the rest of his crew still on board. Their good fortune was highlighted by crew chief, Whitey Strednak, who believed that another 30 seconds of fire would have seen the B-17's firewall breached and its fuel ignited.

Another engine problem the next day led to an unusual incident for the 533rd's 2nd Lt. Charles H. Carpenter. As deputy group lead, Carpenter had been briefed to bomb a synthetic oil plant at Böhlen, 10 miles south of Leipzig. On take-off, his B-17 quickly suffered a technical fault. Landing back at Ridgewell, his crew raced to another bomber, before taking off some 20 minutes later. Carpenter "poured on the coal" to catch the 381st, which he presumed was a "great blob of ships" in the distance. By the time he caught up, he discovered they were RAF Lancasters.

Determined to "give the English a hand," Carpenter remained with the Lancasters, joining them as they attacked Cologne in what turned out to be the last RAF raid on the city.[19] Landing back at Ridgewell having "frolicked" with the British bombers on the way back, Carpenter, who was known by the nickname "Hotrock," was stunned to learn his B-17's nickname was *RAFAAF*—an amalgam of the British and American air force abbreviations.

* * *

Although the 381st had found Böhlen cloud-covered, the group did manage to attack the secondary target at Chemnitz, some 35 miles southeast. More importantly, it was its 13th consecutive raid on Germany without loss.

While the 381st was stood down on March 3, over 1,100 American B-17s and B-24s attacked a variety of German targets. Later that evening, almost 350 RAF bombers attacked Kamen and an aqueduct crossing the Dortmund–Ems canal. However, on their return, an estimated 200 German night fighters concealed themselves in the bomber stream. For the next five hours, the *Luftwaffe*'s Operation *Gisela*—an aerial intruder operation—was carried out in an effort to support the German air defense system by making an all-out attack against the Allies and their airfields. Although no raids were made on Ridgewell, a red alert Tannoy announcement was made and a total blackout enforced. Nevertheless, 24 RAF aircraft were lost in what proved to be the *Luftwaffe*'s last major night fighter intrusion of the war.

Three hours after the red alert, the combat crews were woken for the group's next mission, an attack on a tank factory near Ulm in southern Germany. The mission passed without incident. "It was 37 up, 37 over and 37 back," noted the 381st's combat diarist.

The next day, another 37 B-17s took off bound for Ruhland in eastern Germany. Its oil refinery was due to be attacked visually but was found to be covered by cloud. Instead, the group flew on to the secondary at Chemnitz—two of the squadrons bombing through clouds, while the high squadron selected a target of opportunity 40 miles southwest at Plauen. This time, however, only 35 returned to Ridgewell, two force landing on the Continent, including Edgar Price's *Carnival Queen*. Luckily, both crews were safe.

A two-day stand down followed, during which time several of the group's officers visited London. They included new commanding officer, Conway Hall, who was invited by the Conservative Member of Parliament for Buckingham, Lionel Berry, to hear a debate. Hall and his men were then taken to the Savoy Hotel by renowned aviation author, Clarence Winchester, who had been present at the recent *Stage Door Canteen* celebrations. They were also joined by the commander of the RAF's PFF training unit at RAF Warboys, Group Captain Thomas "Hamish" Mahaddie. Elsewhere in London, Charles "Hotrock" Carpenter and one of his crew members participated in a radio broadcast to tell of their exploits with the RAF over Cologne a few days earlier.

The 381st's next mission was an assault on the Auguste Victoria benzol plant at Hüls, 35 miles northwest of Cologne. With no opposition except meager and inaccurate flak, the group's 37 B-17s dropped by PFF on the MPI of previous attacks, leaving a column of smoke some 15,000 feet high. It could still be seen 75 miles away.

The only downside to the day was the loss of one of the 381st's PFF B-17s, *Sunkist Special*, which crash landed at Glatton in Huntingdonshire. Although veteran pilot James Tyson and his crew were uninjured, the 63-mission bomber was written off with significant damage.

By March 9, Conway Hall had returned to Ridgewell, where he climbed aboard one of the 381st's other PFF B-17s to lead his group to Kassel's marshaling yards in central Germany. Finding the target clear, the group's 37 B-17s prepared to bomb visually. However, intense, accurate flak struck the 532nd's fatefully named *Miss Fortune*. A direct hit between the number three engine and bomb bay left the "whole right side" on fire and its nose blown off. Two parachutes were seen to exit 2nd Lt. Paul J. Scherrman's B-17, which glided from the formation, seemingly under control. At 10,000 feet it was then seen to explode. Only one crew member survived the explosion of *Miss Fortune*—its radio operator, Sgt. George M. Gasparovich. The Scherrman crew had been assigned to the 532nd just 25 days earlier, two days before the group's previous combat loss.

* * *

Three consecutive raids followed, with the 381st bombing marshaling yards at Sinsen; submarine pens at Bremen; and a railroad center at Dillenburg in the Ruhr Valley. All B-17s returned safely from all three missions, the last of which saw a message of congratulations received from General of the Army, Henry "Hap" Arnold. He praised the group (and the rest of the 1st AD) for its contributions over the previous five weeks.

More congratulations were in order the next day, when the group, led by Conway Hall, flew to attack a single-track rail bridge across the Weser River at Vlotho in northwestern Germany. The 381st made a visual run leaving the bridge "covered with bomb blasts." On his return, Hall then received a telephone call from the 1st CBW commander, William Gross, congratulating him on having "one of the best formations ever seen." Events later that evening put a dampener on any further celebrations, however.

One of the group's B-17s, flying a practice mission, crash landed close to Ridgewell's north–south runway, half a mile from the village of Little Yeldham. Fortunately, the crew of five all survived, although two of its officers were badly injured. Bob Gilbert's former co-pilot, 2nd Lt. Alfred J. Reynolds, had been flying the B-17 when it came down. The former "trained fighter pilot" had previously been transferred to bombers due to a shortage of pilots, but he was never that happy flying a "big lumbering bird."

* * *

The 381st carried out its 270th mission a day later, when 37 B-17s lifted off at 1000 to bomb Oranienburg's marshaling yards—a site of considerable movement to the Eastern Front. Flying "Tail end Charlie" at the rear of the entire Eighth Air Force, the 381st was being led by 22-year-old, Hotrock Carpenter.

His aircraft was first over a target that was already covered by smoke from attacks made by 575 other bombers. Although the *Luftwaffe* made an appearance, the 381st avoided any attacks and swung south for the return to England. Thirty minutes later, however, accurate flak over Wittenberg saw Carpenter's B-17 rocked by a direct hit in the waist. The blast killed the waist gunner, SSgt. Walter J. Ahl, and incapacitated several others. It also left a 15-foot gash in the right side of the fuselage ("big enough to push a piano through"), while severing all control cables to the rudder and stabilizers. Carpenter was only able to fly using his ailerons and throttles for control. Worse still, four of the crew's parachutes had either been sucked out of the aircraft or destroyed by flak.

For almost five hours, Carpenter and his co-pilot, FO Albert R. Gembler, nursed their "flying wing" across Germany and France. Arriving back over England in darkness, Carpenter crossed RAF Woodbridge's blacked-out emergency landing ground before ordering his engineer to fire flares to attract attention. With the runway lights promptly illuminated, Carpenter made a wide, flat turn before using full throttles to avoid stalling. His aircraft crossed the threshold at 200 miles per hour before thumping into the ground, where its landing gear immediately buckled. The bomber then broke in two, its tail section "snapping off," while flames engulfed two engines.

The forward section of the bomber finally came to a grating stop, allowing its dazed crew to clamber out. Carpenter then climbed onto the cockpit before coolly taking a roll call. Sadly, one of his crew was dead, while another was evacuated to hospital. Carpenter and the others were then served a meal of fresh eggs and "whisky-laden tea" by their hosts.

Back at Ridgewell, James Good Brown was pleased to see 36 of the B-17s return, but his "joy was dimmed" when he learnt of the death of Walter Ahl.

"We are ever mindful of the grief which strikes the hearts of his wife and family when the telegraph arrives at the door of their home," he wrote. "The end of the war cannot come too soon for us."[20]

Intermission: "Keep 'em Flying"—The Ground Crew

Each B-17 had its own ground crew, commanded by a crew chief—a master sergeant—who supervised the servicing and maintenance of his allocated aircraft. The crew chief was responsible for every aspect of preparing his B-17 for its next mission. Every piece of work carried out on the aircraft was recorded in a Form 1A, which the pilot used to identify any faults and snags. This told the crew chief the items that needed attention.

The ground crew, under the crew chief, worked long, unforgiving hours on the aircraft hardstands, to repair, prepare, or modify their aircraft to fly. Many worked on the same B-17 for months. They also rarely worked under cover and were constantly exposed to the changing extremes of the British weather. Protective clothing was generally good, and the USAAF was well supplied with portable generators and inspection lights. All these things were needed to cope with the severe winter weather of 1944–45.

Although casualties from enemy action were light among ground crews, *Luftwaffe* raiders occasionally attacked USAAF airfields. Those on the ground were keenly aware of the threat, and many vividly recall air raids and V-1 flying bombs passing overhead.

Daily routine was tough. In some cases, the farthest hardstands could be two miles from the mess halls, where the ground crews were expected to eat, and the huts in which they slept. Vehicles were not always available to make the journey to and from hardstands. Making the transit on foot or by bicycle was sometimes impractical in the dark—especially due to workload, or during bad weather. Consequently, many groundcrews built rudimentary shacks near the flight line and lived, slept, and ate on the hardstand with their aircraft.

Crew chiefs often flew in the right-hand co-pilot's seat during the air testing of newly changed engines, or after major servicing. Many of them were also experienced enough to taxi their B-17 off the hardstand, to its allocated position in the squadron order of the march along the taxiway.

The crew chief would supervise the fueling and loading of his aircraft. Once complete, he would then walk the pilot around the aircraft noting any observations made on the Form 1A. Once the pilot had accepted his aircraft and signed with the crew chief, it was his responsibility.

Notification of an imminent mission was usually received in the early hours of the morning. The ground crew were immediately involved in pre-flighting the aircraft, warming up engines, and finishing any outstanding maintenance tasks. Even after the aircraft had taken off, the ground crew remained at the hardstand in case the B-17 aborted the mission and had to be fixed quickly. Any reason for a mission abort was closely investigated.

While a mission was in progress, the ground crew routinely "sweated it out," waiting for the return of their B-17 and its crew. After a mission, an undamaged Fortress could be turned around and prepared for flight in a matter of hours. However, damaged aircraft were an entirely different proposition, often requiring ground crews to work through the night, or for several days to get their B-17 back online.

Almost every wartime memoir from the Eighth Air Force recalls the dedication of the ground crews and their monumental efforts to repair and maintain the aircraft that flew on every mission mounted. But they could not have done it without those who backed them—the mechanics, the sheet metal men, the armorers, the electricians, and even the cooks.

CHAPTER 26

Hitting the Home Run

March 16–April 23, 1945

Unknown to James Good Brown and the men of the 381st, a peace offer had reportedly been made by Adolf Hitler through British and American circles in Sweden. The Stockholm newspaper, *Svenska Dagbladet*, ran an unconfirmed story claiming Hitler had been persuaded to make a peace overture to the Allies by his foreign minister, Joachim von Ribbentrop. Dispatching a high-ranking government official to Stockholm to deliver Hitler's message, Ribbentrop's envoy duly returned to Berlin empty handed. The Allies were convinced that "one big hit" would end any last real German resistance.[1]

After a scrubbed mission to Böhlen on March 16, the 381st finally struck its oil plant a day later. Of the 37 B-17s sent from Ridgewell, only 12 bombed the refinery—the 25 others being forced to attack the secondary—the Carl Zeiss optical factory at Jena, 40 miles distant. Despite a combination of 15,000 feet of solid cloud cover, PFF instrument failure, and persistent contrails, the group returned to Ridgewell without mishap.

The weather improved the next day, enabling the Eighth to dispatch over 1,300 heavy bombers to Berlin for what was described as "the biggest daylight raid ever made" on the city. Thirty-seven of the 381st's B-17s were tasked with returning to its Schlesisches rail station, a target the group had last visited three weeks earlier. Although the run across Germany was clear, an undercast soon built up some 50 miles from Berlin. Then, just as the group was about to unleash its 105 tons of bombs and incendiaries, another squadron of bombers emerged from the clouds beneath. The 381st's leader, Maj. Joseph Krieger, Jr., deviated to avoid hitting them and continued his attack, with only the lead and low squadrons succeeding in dropping on the target. The high squadron—its lead aircraft's AFCE malfunctioning—flew on to bomb the secondary at Zehdenick, 30 miles north of Berlin. The group's formation then escaped back to Ridgewell, avoiding the sudden appearance of Me 262s in the target area, while nursing 20 flak-damaged B-17s—three of them "major."

* * *

After attacking a variety of industrial targets, the 381st's aim was then switched to those of a military nature. Taking off into a gray, windy morning on March 19, the group's B-17s flew at the front of the entire Eighth Air Force to destroy flak batteries surrounding Böhlen's synthetic oil plant. Clouds intervened, however, forcing the group to divert to Plauen's industrial areas instead. The 381st's 14th mission of the month ended with all 37 B-17s bombing and returning to Ridgewell.

Two days later, the Eighth commenced a series of raids on German airfields in preparation for a crossing of the lower Rhine River by Allied ground troops. The target for the 381st's 37 B-17s was a supposed Me 262 base at Rheine in northwestern Germany. Despite three aborts due to mechanical problems, the group's other bombers blasted the airfield, leaving an excellent pattern, which, surprisingly, failed to elicit a response from the *Luftwaffe*.

Twenty-four hours later, the 381st embarked on its 275th mission. Thirty-seven of its B-17s were loaded with enough ordnance to bring the total tally dropped by the group on enemy targets to over 18,000 tons. James Good Brown was convinced the war would be finished within a month.

"An optimism has grown up which we thought would not be broken as we come to the end of our combat missions," he wrote.[2]

Over 1,330 of the Eighth's heavy bombers were scheduled to attack military encampments, barracks, and airfields in western Germany. The 381st's objectives were hut installations at Dorsten and Feldhausen, 10 miles north of Essen.

Taking off at 0730, the group was led by the 533rd's unnamed PFF B-17G, 44-8175, which was flying its 23rd mission. Piloted by 2nd Lt. Robert D. Fawcett, it was carrying the group's mission leader, Robert J. Gotthardt, who had been promoted to captain four days earlier. Unusually, the aircraft consisted of a 10-man crew made up of seven officers and three enlisted men. Among the officers was navigator Capt. George J. Stone, who was due to complete his second tour and 50th mission—the first man in the 381st to do so.

As the formation entered the bomb run, a swirling mix of ground haze, smoke screen, and smoke from previous raids caused difficulty in distinguishing the targets. Accurate flak then gradually increased from moderate to intense as the group released its bombs.

Almost immediately, 44-8175 received a direct hit between its number three engine and fuselage, leaving a gaping hole "right through the cockpit." The aircraft was seen to burst into flames—its fuel tanks igniting—before entering a "slow spin" and rapidly disintegrating. Watching crews counted six parachutes before the aircraft crashed south of Essen. However, it would be another five months before they eventually discovered that all 10 of their senior comrades had been killed.

"The 381st Bomb Group has had many shocks since we flew our first mission on June 22, 1943," wrote James Good Brown. "We endured about every blow that a Bomb Group could take ... But today ... the blow struck like a hammer on an anvil."

Robert Gotthardt and his crew were all highly regarded and their loss sent shock waves through the group.

"All of these men were top men in their field," Brown continued. "They had proven themselves. And being with us so long they had won the hearts and affections of everyone. They are more than names to us. They are our friends."[3]

Brown was particularly saddened by the loss of his close friend George Stone, with whom he had often "chewed the rag" in the officers' lounge. Stone had even helped Brown locate his nephew, who was flying C-47s elsewhere in England. The result of a "casual meeting" while visiting a USAAF troop transport base, Stone had delivered Brown's nephew to Ridgewell for a surprise meeting. "Our visit was very pleasant," Brown acknowledged, "and Captain Stone was a part of it."[4]

"It is no secret that the enemy wants to get the lead ship," Brown noted in his diary on the evening of Stone's loss. "Get the leader. Get the man out front. Get the colonel. Get the general. By doing so, the unity and spirit of the whole group may be adversely affected. On this, our 275th mission, the enemy got our BEST."[5]

* * *

The 381st's recent attacks had helped pave the way for Operation *Plunder*, the planned Allied crossing of the Rhine. Just before it was launched, the group was called back into action to attack Coesfeld's marshaling yards 35 miles northeast of the intended crossing point. Flying through beautiful weather, over light ground haze, and with no enemy opposition, the group made an excellent bombing run. The day's events were rounded off by the safe return of all 37 B-17s, including Capt. Gottfried H. Klinksiek's. He had managed to survive his second tour of duty and 50th combat mission, 24 hours after the loss of the 49-mission veteran George Stone.

On March 24, the 381st's crews were set for their first "double header" since D-Day. In the early hours of the morning, 37 crews were woken and briefed for an attack on a *Luftwaffe* landing ground at Fürstenau, 75 miles northwest of the Rhine crossing point. An improvised airfield that had been in existence for a year, Fürstenau's infrastructure was rudimentary, mainly comprising a hangar, several barracks and numerous dispersals hidden beneath trees. Nevertheless, it housed Fw 190s flown by elements of the *Luftwaffe*'s JG 26.

James Good Brown had cycled to Ridgewell's crowded briefing room to find its atmosphere "all astir." As well as the Fürstenau raid, he was told a second mission would take place later that day—with 12 of the group's B-17s being sent to attack another airfield at Twente, near Enschede, just across the Dutch border. Brown was confounded by the number of aircraft being readied on the ground at Ridgewell. He was also surprised by what was taking place overhead.

> I stood in the tower waiting for my planes to take off. It was yet dark. At the break of dawn, I looked out and through the dim light of the rising dawn and saw something phenomenal: gliders were trailing behind troop transport ships. They were directly over the tower only a few hundred feet above us. We spotted them by the lights on their wings. As I scanned the dark skies, I saw one light after another. The troop transport planes, with their gliders, were coming in a steady stream over our field … I stood for an hour at the window watching these airborne troops headed for ground combat in Europe … This was THE BIG PUSH. This was a second D-Day.[6]

Operation *Varsity*, a massive airborne operation supporting *Plunder*, was now under way. The first of the group's B-17s then began taking off at 0615 into a cloudless sky. Second Lieutenant Robert E. Jankowiak, a 533rd pilot flying his 11th mission, was maneuvering his unnamed B-17G along the perimeter track for take-off.

"The tranquility of taxiing through a rural farm area was in sharp contrast to what was to come," Jankowiak noted. "Here it seemed like you were in the most peaceful part of the world."

Despite the vast number of Allied aircraft in the skies over western Europe, the flight to the IP was also calm, with clear weather extending for miles. As the group neared its target, flak was then seen in the distance.

"It wasn't heavy, but somehow appeared to be at a dangerous level," wrote Jankowiak. "The right altitude and in the heading we were taking."

As the 381st began its bomb run, a violent jolt shook Jankowiak's B-17 shortly after the bomb bay doors were opened.

"Easily I could see that our entire No. 4 engine, prop and cowling dissipated into a cloud of black dust. A direct hit."

Jankowiak immediately jettisoned his bombs and briefly considered turning back towards the Rhine, but with the aircraft on fire and its starboard wingtip "folding up," he ordered his crew to bail out.

"By now the control cables … were damaged and my control column began to slam forward and backward," Jankowiak remembered. "By what force I could muster, I pushed the column forward and was able to reach the parachute chest pack from under the seat."

As his B-17 entered a spin, Jankowiak struggled to reach the escape hatch. The centrifugal force then flung him out, where he was smashed against the side of the fuselage—his hand involuntarily pulling the ripcord, which popped the chute. In an instant, his parachute draped itself around the aircraft's horizontal stabilizer. Jankowiak then found himself being buffeted beneath the tail.

"Looking out over the fluttering canopy, directly into a blue sky and a bright sun, my thought was 'why this way?'"

Resorting to prayer, Jankowiak then watched as the wing folded completely before a tremendous blast broke the aircraft in two. He was thrown free, falling rapidly beneath a torn parachute.

"The silence during the descent was short lived," he wrote. "As objects on the ground started to become more clear, tracer bullets from small arms fire came my way and severed some of the shroud lines. It was like the sound of violin strings breaking."

Jankowiak landed quite hard in a bomb crater on what appeared to be another *Luftwaffe* airfield. As he briefly considered escaping to a nearby pine forest, he noticed his left leg was "pointing at 9 o'clock" while he was "facing 12 o'clock." Moments later, a German soldier appeared, forcing Jankowiak to hop into captivity using his rifle "like a baseball bat." Although he wouldn't know the fate of most of his crew until much later (four had been KIA), it would be less than four months before he was repatriated home as a RAMP (Recovered American Military Personnel).[7]

* * *

While the rest of the 381st's B-17s hit Fürstenau "dead on the target," several others were also damaged by flak. The "Anglo-American" bomber, *RAFAAF* had its number three and four engines silenced; one propeller twisting off and falling away after its bombs were released. Another 535th BS bomber, *Buckeye*, also lost two engines—although like *RAFAAF*, it was able to return on its remaining two.

"Red flares were seen spurting from the planes," wrote James Good Brown, as he watched the B-17s land. "Could we not go through this one day without wounded?"[8]

The answer was no. Two wounded men were removed from *RAFAAF*, including its pilot, 2nd Lt. Turner G. Brashear. Worse still, the 535th's *Tinker Toy-Too* was brought back to Ridgewell with a dead waist gunner. Staff Sergeant Robert B. Bolin had previously bailed out over friendly territory on New Year's Day, when *The Feathermerchant* had crashed after being hit by flak over Magdeburg.

"I hear *Taps* for Staff Sergeant Robert B. Bolin …" wrote Brown. "A hero. He died for his country. One of THE MIGHTY MEN OF THE 381st."[9]

The group's second mission of the day went ahead, nonetheless. Twelve more B-17s took off at 1415 to join another 140 from the 1st AD to bomb Twente's airfield. Despite a heavy ground haze, almost 350 tons of explosives were dropped on the base—the 381st leaving its 140 500-pounders on the main cross runway. Three hours and 15 minutes after taking off, the 12 B-17s landed back at Ridgewell, one of the 381st's shortest flying times on record.

Chaplain Brown cycled back to Ridgewell's main runway to find all 12 crews safely back home. He was also happy to find them in great spirits. But his thoughts were also with those who were now fighting on the ground in Europe.

"Do they have a well-cooked supper as we had?" he wrote. "Did they have plenty to eat? Do they have a movie to go to—a warm room in which to sit and talk? Or—are they alive? And what of Lieutenant Robert Jankowiak's crew?"[10]

* * *

Another short combat flying mission took place the next day, when the group took off to attack Zeitz, only to be turned back an hour later due to bad weather. To compound the combat crews' frustrations, they were then forced to fly a further four hours' practice, which culminated in the loss of *Princess Pat.*

Chaplain Brown was typing in his chapel when he heard a distant explosion. After being told that one of the ships was "burning up," he raced outside.

"To my amazement, I saw flames shooting high into the air," he wrote. "It was raining. I seized my raincoat and hopped on my bicycle."

Brown rode to the runway where he found its crew had managed to escape the burning bomber. With ammunition popping off, however, he was fearful for the men who were fighting the fire.

"The fire trucks were pouring gallons of water on the burning ship which had already crumbled to the ground, a mass of ruins ... the metal burned like paper, and there was nothing left but the heavy engines."[11]

Ironically, the veteran bomber had been nicknamed *Princess Pat* after a "campfire song" made famous during World War I.

Another B-17 was named by US Army nurses the following day, when a bottle of Coca-Cola was broken over the guns of the 535th's newly assigned *The South Boston Shillelagh*. Bad weather failed to dampen the occasion, which then saw other B-17s take off for Zeitz's synthetic oil plant—the target the group had been prevented from bombing a day earlier.

Although the mission did get off the ground, it became a "mixed-up deal" from the start. Filthy weather on the way in, coupled with cloud banks over Zeitz, saw the group make two "360s" over the target. The low squadron bombed, but missed, while the lead and high squadrons flew on to Plauen, 40 miles south; making another "360," which invited yet more flak. By the time the group's 279th mission had ended, one of the 533rd's B-17s had crash landed at Vitry in France with two wounded crewmen, while five others were forced to divert elsewhere after running short of fuel.

* * *

Just as Winston Churchill was writing a pointed letter to his chief of the air staff, Sir Charles Portal, questioning the bombing of German cities "for the sake of increasing terror," the 381st was sent back to Berlin to bomb its armaments and tank factories. Togglier Robert Singleton was among 330 airmen flying the group's 280th mission.

"Only had 45 minutes from briefing until take-off," he wrote. "Weather worst yet!"[12]

Singleton's *PFC's Ltd* was one of 446 B-17s groping their way towards Berlin. On arrival over the target, the 381st found solid cloud cover, no *Luftwaffe*, and only meager and inaccurate flak. Bombing by *H2X*, the group then headed back to England, although one was forced to land on the Continent short of fuel. Its crew would initially be listed as MIA, causing some upset when they returned to Ridgewell the following day. One of the enlisted men found his bunk had been stripped and most of his belongings gone.

Robert Singleton's *PFC's Ltd* managed to land back at Ridgewell after the Berlin mission, although not without difficulty.

"We flew home alone, from France to base, due to bad weather," he wrote. "Flew at 500' most of time. What fun!"[13] However, he had survived his 20th mission.

The group's 280th mission was followed two days later by another visit to Germany—this time, Bremen and its submarine pens. More than 1,400 heavy bombers were dispatched to hit several targets connected with U-boat construction and operation. Led by group commander, Conway Hall, the 381st sent 37 B-17s, including the 535th's *In Like Errol*, flying its 91st raid.

Piloted by 2nd Lt. Robert A. Bennett, its crew consisted of 10 men, including spot jammer SSgt. Charles L. Majors. The Bennett crew had recently suffered the loss of their waist gunner, Robert Bolin, while several of them had also been forced to bail out of *The Feathermerchant* on New Year's Day—an experience their co-pilot, 2nd Lt. Alexander D. Nelson, Jr. said he would never repeat.

Arriving over Bremen at 26,000 feet, *In Like Errol* suffered a direct flak hit to its number one engine. Bennett succeeded in feathering its propeller, but the aircraft rolled out of the formation and was unable to keep up. Just then, four P-51s flew across the front of *In Like Errol*, while one peeled away, flying underneath the bomber. Ball turret gunner SSgt. Calvin J. Hockley thought the P-51 had begun firing at him when shells began striking the B-17.

"I was tracking him with the turret, but being a P-51 and so close in, I never got a chance to fire back, because I wasn't expecting that, of all things," he later wrote.[14]

The attack had actually been made by an Me 262, which Hockley had not seen. The German fighter had raked the left side of *In Like Errol*, destroying its number two engine and setting fire to the aircraft. Robert Bennett briefly considered flying towards friendly territory, but with a damaged horizontal stabilizer and the oxygen system out, he issued the bail-out order instead—only to find his interphone cut. Bennett's co-pilot, Nelson, then went back through the aircraft to ensure the gunners were bailing out. As he did so, *In Like Errol* dropped into a dive, which pinned several of them to the ceiling. Fortunately, Bennett—both feet firmly planted on the instrument panel—managed to wrench the aircraft level, after losing some 20,000 feet in altitude. Nevertheless, he was unable to prevent the B-17 from going down.

Only seven of the crew survived the crash of *In Like Errol*. They bailed out and were taken prisoner by members of the German *Kriegsmarine*. Some of them were then shown Alexander Nelson's personal effects, including his dog tags, cap, and a picture of his wife. The Germans claimed Nelson's badly mutilated body had been found in the wreckage of *In Like Errol*. Some of his crew failed to believe it, however. Nelson's belongings were in good condition despite the aircraft ending in a mass of flames.

Tail gunner SSgt. Charles F. Knaus was also killed in action, possibly as the result of an unopened parachute. Once again, some of Knaus's crewmates were skeptical about the Germans' claims that he had been killed in a failed jump, several believing he may have been murdered by German civilians.

The fate of engineer TSgt. Chester M. Slomzcenski also remained a mystery. Although he had been seen to land in a small patch of woods, his whereabouts were unknown. Some of the crew thought the 20-year-old from Detroit, Michigan, had evaded capture thanks to his fluency in several languages, including German. However, three months later, Slomzcenski's family received a telegram stating he had been KIA. It was the conclusion of some of his crew that he had also been killed by German civilians.

Charles Majors was fortunate to avoid a similar fate, having been captured by German soldiers.

"Four of us … were quickly rounded up together and were being marched in a single file," he wrote. "One yelling, red-faced civilian attempted to charge me but was tackled by one of our guards. They both hit the ground."[15]

After being held in a small farm shack overnight, Majors was eventually transported to *Stalag Luft I*.

The rest of the 381st's crews safely returned to Ridgewell unaware of the fate of *In Like Errol* and its men. Nevertheless, they would continue with their missions, the group flying its 23rd raid of the month the following day. A long-distance trek to Halle in eastern Germany on March 31 ended with just over 100 tons of bombs and incendiaries being deposited on the city's marshaling yards.

March ended with the Eighth Air Force having carried out 31,169 heavy bomber sorties, the highest monthly number launched so far. Although four crews had been lost from the 381st, and 90 of its B-17s battle-damaged, the general mood was positive.

"For us it had been an exciting and elating month," wrote the group's public relations officer, Saul Schwartz. "Victory talk became more and more outspoken and frequent bets were made on the date that hostilities would cease."[16]

* * *

The first three days of April saw the 381st take off on the 2nd for a mission to the Danish town of Skrydstrup and its nearby *Luftwaffe* airfield. Halfway across the North Sea, however, the group was recalled due to bad weather. Another *Luftwaffe* landing ground at Hoya in Germany was subsequently attacked by the 381st on April 4, resulting in one airman being severely wounded by flak over the target.

Flight Officer Ralph A. Thomas from Fayette, Iowa, had become firm friends with James Good Brown, who found Thomas's disposition "positively radiant." A former semi-professional baseball player, Thomas had been eager to join the 381st's baseball team, having arrived at Ridgewell two months earlier. With the new season about to commence, he had been busy practising.

"How happy he was!" noted Brown. "If he had a care on his mind, one would never have known it."

Brown had sat with Thomas at the briefing for the group's mission to Hoya. "While the others filed out of the room past us, he [Thomas] laughingly said to them, 'Got any troubles? Bring them to the chaplain.'" Yet, it was Brown who was troubled after the group's return from Hoya. In the nose of *Century Note*, Ralph Thomas lay dead. He had died from his wounds on the way back. Brown found himself burying his friend at Madingley two days later.

"He lighted up the surroundings, no matter how dark they were," Brown remembered. "In truth, I never saw dark surroundings when he was around."[17]

After two successful missions on April 5 and April 7 (an ordnance depot at Grafenwöhr in southeastern Germany and a jet fighter base at Kohlenbissen in northern Germany respectively), the group was tasked with attacking an underground oil storage facility at Derben, 60 miles west of Berlin on April 8.

Take-off for the group's 37 bombers was at 0920. Three hours later they arrived over the target to find it cloud-covered. Flying a further 15 miles north, they unloaded on the secondary target—a railroad workshop at Stendal. Nevertheless, tracking flak bracketed the group for 90 seconds, damaging several of the group's B-17s and knocking one from the formation.

Miss Florala had been assigned to the 534th the previous June and was named by its original pilot, co-pilot and engineer after their home states of Mississippi, Florida and Alabama. Over Stendal and under the command of 2nd Lt. Harvey E. Adelmeyer, *Miss Florala* had just released its bombs when flak struck its starboard wing and set the number three engine on fire. Adelmeyer dived 10,000 feet in an attempt to extinguish the flames, but it failed to work. As the gunners in the rear of the aircraft discussed bailing out, the aircraft suddenly exploded. Two were blown clear and quickly managed to open their parachutes.

Radio operator TSgt. James H. Hayden and tail gunner Sgt. Edward P. Houser floated down to find themselves being shot at from below. Both evaded the bullets, with Houser eventually landing in a tree. After extricating himself, he then met up with Houser, the two making their escape. Three days later, they came across a US Army patrol, whose troops arranged for their return to Ridgewell. Hayden and Houser were the only two survivors of the loss of *Miss Florala*, which would subsequently become the group's last B-17 to be lost in combat.

"The loss of six men on this 286th mission was as sad as the loss of the men on our first mission," wrote James Good Brown. "We had hoped that, as we came to the end of our combat flying, we would lose no more men. But war is not like that. War did not lend us favors, not from the first mission to the last. War was cruel to the very end."[18]

* * *

Although another 381st B-17 was lost in a crash landing at RAF Lympne the following day (*Our Boarding House* had been damaged by flak over Oberpfaffenhofen), the group's missions had remained largely *Luftwaffe*-free. However, the German air force did make an appearance 24 hours later.

The 381st was dispatched to attack a munitions depot at Oranienburg, 17 miles northwest of Berlin. The group's 37 B-17s were part of a force of 1,315 heavy bombers also sent to bomb airfields known to be used by the *Luftwaffe*'s jet fighters. Flying in cloudless skies, the 381st arrived over its target where the crews "dropped their eggs," leaving excellent results. Even so, pulling off the bomb run, around 40 Me 109s and several Me 262s suddenly appeared, although the focus of their attacks was on other groups.

One Me 262 came barreling through the 381st, giving a brief moment of concern, but it was moving too fast for any of the gunners to hit it. The day ended with 19 of the Eighth's bombers being shot down, mostly by the German jets. Fortunately, all 381st B-17s returned safely to Ridgewell.

One aircraft that was lucky to return to Ridgewell a day later was the much-vaunted *RAFAAF*. One of 37 B-17s sent to attack another underground oil storage depot at Freiham in the western suburbs of Munich, *RAFAAF* had successfully bombed and was returning in formation over Ludwigshafen. Another of the 535th's B-17s—the unnamed 44-8826, flying on the right of *RAFAAF* and under the command of 2nd Lt. Arthur T. Greenspan—suddenly lurched down. Sergeant Jack W. Prillaman, the tail gunner on *RAFAAF*, shouted to his pilot, 2nd Lt. Turner Brashear, to "drop it," but it was too late. Greenspan's left wing slammed down on Brashear's right stabilizer, snapping it off completely. *RAFAAF* instantly dropped into a flat spin sending its crew into the aircraft's ceiling, Turner Brashear having to pull himself down using the control column as a lever. After falling some 7,000 feet, Brashear and his co-pilot, 2nd Lt. Robert P. Horn, finally arrested the descent, both having to place their feet on the instrument panel to do so. However, once in level flight and with the throttles cut back, *RAFAAF* began adopting a nose up attitude, threatening to stall.

Brashear's quick thinking, and the mechanical expertise of his engineer, Sgt. James Edwards, saw two dials immediately removed from the instrument panel. A length of recovered control cable was then fed through and wrapped around the control column, while an axe handle was spliced to the wire. This crude turnbuckle enabled Brashear to manipulate his remaining elevator by slackening or tightening the control cable.

Although Brashear and his crew had twice discussed the possibility of bailing out, it was rejected both times. Some four hours after the collision (Arthur Greenspan's 44-8826, although damaged itself, had safely landed back at base), *RAFAAF* approached Ridgewell's landing circuit, where Conway Hall was informed of Brashear's predicament. Hall advised the pilot to let his crew bail out over the field, before taking the aircraft out over the North Sea where he would have to bail out. Again, Brashear discussed the idea with his crew, who all refused. Brashear then advised Hall he would attempt a landing at Ridgewell.

With the aircraft prone to stalling at less than 140mph, Brashear banked to make a long approach at speed. As Robert Horn adjusted the throttles and Brashear worked the turnbuckle, the crew assembled in the radio room. *RAFAAF* then shot across Ridgewell's threshold before Brashear used every inch of runway to stop while burning out the brakes. Astonishingly, *RAFAAF* came to a halt on the tarmac.

"One of the best landings ever seen here," glowed the 535th's combat diarist.

* * *

That evening, while Turner Brashear and his crew celebrated their remarkable survival, they and the rest of the 381st learnt of the sudden death of Franklin D. Roosevelt.

"At London's Rainbow Corner, hundreds of soldiers stood for several minutes in stunned silence when they heard the news," noted a *Stars and Stripes* correspondent. "Some paled and others made no effort to hide wet eyes. Military police along Shaftesbury Avenue and around Piccadilly Circus reported the gloom swept over British and American alike … Two British bobbies couldn't recall such midnight gloom, even during the Blitz."

Former 381st ball turret gunner, now armorer–gunner, Bob Gilbert was on a 36-hour pass and found himself among the crowds gathered at Rainbow Corner.

"A reporter from the International News Service interviewed me to get an American soldier's reactions," Gilbert wrote. "I expressed how sad I thought it was that after he had given so much, for so many years, he didn't get to live to see the end of this noble effort in Europe."[19]

At Ridgewell, a "30-day period of mourning" began with the American flag being flown at half-mast. All social activities were also cancelled for the month. Nevertheless, the war had to go on. At 0710, on Friday, April 13, 37 B-17s took off in perfect weather bound for Neumünster's marshaling yards in northern Germany. The group's bombs duly "smacked right on the target."

Following a 24-hour stand down, the 381st then returned to France for the first time in five months, with the tactical bombing of German gun emplacements at Soulac-sur-Mer, 55 miles northwest of Bordeaux, on the Gironde estuary. One of the last remaining pockets of German resistance, the area was blasted by 100 tons of the group's ordnance, leaving a "terrific smoke." The aerial attack was then followed by a terrific bombardment from French warships just as the bombers turned off the target.

"With American and Russian armies only 100 miles apart in the Dresden area, and British and American troops in northern Germany, cutting across country towards Berlin almost without opposition, London daily [newspapers] are carrying wide-open 'Any minute now' headlines," noted the 535th's combat diarist. "Everyone feels the end of organized German resistant is imminent."

Just as the 381st's B-17s returned from France, Ridgewell underwent something of a reorganization itself, when most of the 381st's subordinate commands, including the 448th Sub Depot, were absorbed into the newly formed 432nd Air Service Group. Its crews had recently completed the modification of a brand-new B-17G, 44-6975, which was planned to be used as a "command scout" by the 1st CBW's commanding officer, William Gross. With its ball and chin turrets removed, the streamlined, lightweight bomber was capable of a true air speed of almost 300mph. Gross had flown his new "luxury liner" for the first time over the Gironde estuary. The aircraft would soon be christened by his English secretary, Ella Prentice, who was also known as "Bridget." Assigned to the 91st BG at Bassingbourn, it would eventually carry her image and the name *Our Bridget* in her honor.

* * *

On April 16, Eighth Air Force commander, Jimmy Doolittle received a directive from Carl Spaatz, who had just been promoted to general.

"The advances of the Ground Forces have brought to a close the Strategic Air War ..." Spaatz wrote. "It has been won with a decisiveness becoming increasingly evident as our armies overrun Germany. From now on, our Strategic Air Forces must operate with our Tactical Air Forces in close cooperation with our armies."

That same day, the 381st dispatched 37 B-17s to attack a railroad bridge spanning the Danube at Regensburg, in the southeast of Germany. Despite clear weather conditions, no enemy aircraft, and moderate flak, the group's bombs fell short. Just before the bomb run, though, the 534th's unnamed 43-38907, flown by 2nd Lt. Fred J. Fink, had suffered a problem with its number four engine, which ran away. Feathering the propeller and dropping from the formation, Fink then salvoed his bombs in a field before suffering another engine failure, this time to its number two. Fink was finally forced to land on a "newly-steel-matted runway" on the outskirts of Mannheim, which had recently become the new home of a P-47 group. In addition to having to carry out an engine change, Fink's engineer, Sgt. William Szigetti (who had yet to fire a single shot during his 24 missions) was also tasked with accompanying a group of US Military Police (MPs) on a hunt to capture a former Waffen-SS and Nazi Party official. A fluent German speaker, Szigetti helped the MPs discover the man hiding in a house "stashed with food, money and a huge store of clothing for his wife."[20]

While the group's other bombers returned to Ridgewell, a familiar aircraft was seen pirouetting in the skies over the airfield. Former 533rd pilot 1st Lt. Joseph D. Nelson, who had been assigned to the 381st in July 1944, and had since been re-assigned to the 364th FG having completed his tour of duty, buzzed Ridgewell's control tower in his weather reconnaissance P-51.

Frequently seen "knocking leaves from the trees" around his former base, Nelson attempted to dive into a slow roll, but his engine cut out and the P-51 nose-dived into a field close to the village of Little Yeldham. By the time emergency crews reached the blazing wreckage, Nelson's body was so badly burned that it took some time before he could be formally identified.

* * *

On April 17, the Eighth sent over 1,000 heavy bombers to hit rail targets across the southeast of Germany and Czechoslovakia. At the head of the entire formation was the 381st, which was aiming for Dresden's marshaling yards. Accompanying the group was 1st CBW commander William Gross in *Our Bridget*. Gross had decided to fly alongside the first box on the bomb run, before circling back to accompany the second, then third. Escorting the 381st, which bombed visually (although the results were "not too good"), Gross then circled back, only to be confronted by an Me 262, which succeeded in hitting his B-17's empty bomb bay and bulkhead with cannon fire. Fortunately, *Our Bridget* flew on, its crew, including William Gross, unharmed. Nevertheless, Gross headed for the nearest formation and remained with it until landing back at Bassingbourn.

While the men enjoyed a brief stand down and some early summery weather a day later, one of their number left Ridgewell for a new assignment. Lieutenant Colonel Arthur Briggs, who had suffered crash landings, the terror of the first Schweinfurt raid, and had been diagnosed with pyscho-neurosis and severe operational fatigue, left his role as the 381st's operations officer to become the new commanding officer of its 1st CBW sister unit, the 398th BG at Nuthampstead. Briggs's remarkable fortitude and strength of character had been officially recognized.

By April 19, Leipzig had been captured by US troops. Meanwhile, the 381st was tasked with attacking another rail target at Elsterwerda, some 50 miles east of the city. Deemed an important link in the east–west German supply lines, the lead bombardier struggled to synchronize his bombsight over the town due to a stiff crosswind. Three circuits were made, before the 533rd and 535th finally unloaded their bombs—the lead squadron flying on to attack Falkenberg's marshaling yards, 15 miles northwest. The mission, according to the 535th's combat diarist, was "one of those things best forgotten."

More railroad facilities came in for attack the following day, when the 381st took off to bomb Brandenburg's marshaling yards. However, after the fiasco of the day before, almost "every ranking flying man on the base" was scheduled to fly, Conway Hall among them. He piloted his unarmed *Little Rock-ette*.

No fewer than 40 B-17s took off from Ridgewell at 0625, before arriving over Brandenburg to drop a good concentration of general-purpose bombs across the target. Except for some meager flak—a burst of which caused a brief fire in the lead B-17—all aircraft returned to Ridgewell.

A day later, just as Soviet troops reached the outer suburbs of Berlin, the 381st arrived over Munich for the seventh time. The city's marshaling yards were being targeted by 113 B-17s, although bad weather across Germany prevented visual bombing—*H2X* being used by the 1st AD.

While the mission was described as "completely uneventful" by the group's diarist, one 532nd B-17 suffered a series of technical problems—including the loss of its radio, a smoking chin turret, and three hung up bombs. Despite growing concerns that British anti-aircraft gunners might fire on the B-17, its pilot, 2nd Lt. Wesley E. Huff, Jr., managed to return to Ridgewell.

The group's 296th mission had seen Conway Hall ask William Gross to consider giving his 381st the lead in the 1st CBW formation for its 300th raid, a request Gross accepted. Nevertheless, the group was stood down on April 22, allowing its men some rest and relaxation, while also enjoying the London stage play, *Love in Idleness*, starring husband and wife stars, Alfred Lunt and Lynn Fontaine. The play, which was performed at Ridgewell without scenery or costumes (and with props scrounged from the base), was declared "the best show ever given." "The Lunts" then toasted the 534th's *Passaic Warrior*, a B-17 that had joined the growing list of those that had reached 100 missions.

* * *

One of the 381st's pilots nearing his 50th combat mission was Capt. Charles Ackerman of San Bernardino, California. A close friend of Troy Jones, Ackerman had returned to Ridgewell the previous September after completing his first tour. On April 23, just two missions short of completing his second, the 22-year-old was given a special task to add to his 455 hours of flying experience.

With the group's combat missions almost over, Conway Hall granted his men more freedom by allowing some of them to see something of the country.

"They have been confined to the base except for brief passes," wrote James Good Brown. "A trip to Ireland! Gosh! What a pleasure! Who would not like to take it?"[21]

Captain Robert W. Marelius had originally been tasked with flying the men, but he declined after being told he wouldn't be getting off in Ireland, not even for a coffee. Charles Ackerman had subsequently been selected to fly the group of 381st "holidaymakers" to Belfast's RAF Nutts Corner for their 72-hour pass.

Although Brown hoped to go on the Irish excursion, he was unable to because of a chaplains' meeting. Instead, 26 others—those thought to be most deserving—were selected. Among them was Technician Fourth Grade Sgt. Andy Piter, Jr. from Banning, Pennsylvania.

The former mine worker had arrived at Ridgewell a day after the *Caroline* explosion to begin his work as a motor transport mechanic. Piter's US Army pay from his two years at Ridgewell had since allowed him to buy a new home for his parents. He was also no stranger to Ireland, having visited Londonderry just a month earlier.

William L. Palmer, a member of the 381st's operations staff was also eager to go and asked Conway Hall's permission.

"I said 'we're finished for the war, practically, and I would just like to be able to take the time off' and he said 'no, I need you here. You stay here.'"[22]

Others were luckier—some winning the trip on the toss of a coin. Gunnery officer 1st Lt. Wayne W. Hart was given the surprise opportunity to take the place of his boss, the 535th's executive officer, Capt. Richard L. Tansey, who had been offered a seat, but had to cancel his plans at the last minute. Just before 0800, shortly after Charles Ackerman had started the B-17's engines, Hart was seen sprinting towards the aircraft. Its waist door was opened and he jumped aboard, the bomber taxiing a few moments later.

Reputedly nicknamed *Dottie Jeanne*,[23] the B-17G had been assigned to the 534th the previous October. Designed to carry a crew of 10 and a maximum bomb payload of less than eight tons, *Dottie Jeanne* lifted off from Ridgewell at 0800 with 31 people and a dog on board. Among the occupants were five crew members, including Charles Ackerman; his co-pilot, FO Edwin A. Hutcheson, plus a navigator, engineer and radio operator. They soon set course for Belfast, routing north of the Isle of Man.

Just over two hours after *Dottie Jeanne* had taken off from Ridgewell, the aircraft neared the Isle of Man. Farm worker Harold Ennett spotted the "four-engined, silver-colored" aircraft flying in from the coast at "no more than 500ft." It was so low, Ennett could clearly see the USAAF insignia under its wing as it passed overhead. He then watched as it disappeared into the mist that covered the island's second highest peak, North Barrule. Moments later, a "terrific explosion" told Ennett all he needed to know.

* * *

Dottie Jeanne had impacted North Barrule's southern slope just 200 feet from its summit—scattering flaming wreckage, bodies, playing cards and dollar bills across the scorched hillside. Despite the elevation, members of the RAF from nearby Andreas soon scaled its 1,850-foot slope to begin the task of recovering the bodies of the 31 men, all of whom had been killed instantly. They were brought down on stretchers to a waiting vehicle, which then transported them to Andreas.

News didn't reach Ridgewell until later in the evening, shocking everyone across the base. Every section had lost at least one of its men. Most of them had been at Ridgewell for two years. Returning from his chaplains' meeting, James Good Brown was told as soon as he arrived back at Ridgewell.

"It was then that I received the shock," Brown wrote. "One of the worst shocks of my stay in England."

Brown was informed of the deaths of all 31 men, including his chapel organist and assistant SSgt. Ralph L. Gibbs.

"To say that a dark cloud has been cast over the base is not even to begin to express our feelings."[24]

The next day, Conway Hall and a team of orderlies, including a dentist and flight surgeon, flew to Andreas in *Little Rock-ette* to assist in the task of identifying the bodies. Hall and his deputy, George Shackley, then climbed North Barrule to survey the crash site. RAF officers informed them that they would have to proceed through diplomatic channels to repatriate the bodies to Ridgewell. Not wanting to prolong the already unpleasant task, Hall ignored the instruction and promptly loaded all 31 bodies on *Little Rock-ette* before flying back to Ridgewell.

"My actions resulted in some diplomatic flak, but since the bodies were back in England, nothing came of it," Hall later recalled.[25]

On landing, he instructed James Good Brown to write to the mothers, telling them that "not one body was burned, not one dismembered" and to "take comfort in the thought they knew no mental anguish before death, for they never sensed danger."[26] Brown, however, was in a daze.

> Even though we have been here two years, and even though we have gone through hard months of fighting and have seen death all around us, with the attending heartaches ... when this accident occurred, it left the men completely stunned. They are as severely shocked as they were on June 23, 1943.[27]

CHAPTER 27

An Understandable Corner of the World

April 24–August 28, 1945

Not only were the men of the 381st left reeling from events on the Isle of Man, so too were the local civilians, many of whom who had lost friends in the tragedy. James Good Brown's organist, Ralph Gibbs, for example, was married to an English girl from Cambridge, Brown having attended their wedding.

"These were not newcomers to the base," he noted, "they were the backbone of the 381st Bomb Group."[1]

Brown soon began planning yet another major funeral ceremony at Madingley, one that would become the largest ever seen.[2]

Although an investigation took place into the crash of *Dottie Jeanne*, no specific cause could be established. Surprisingly, another B-17 had crashed on the island just 10 days earlier, when the 306th BG's *Combined Operations* hit the southern tip, killing all 11 men onboard. More remarkable was the crash of a 27th Air Transport Group B-24 *Flassie*, which occurred nine months before the loss of *Dottie Jeanne*. It had also smashed into North Barrule killing its five crew members.

In a strange twist of fate, however, *Flassie* had been flown by 1st Lt. Ronald B. Dorrington, a former 381st pilot who had accompanied Charles Ackerman on 10 missions. Dorrington had completed his tour of duty with the 381st the previous May. It was conceivable that Ackerman was attempting to look for the spot where his friend had come to grief. Whatever the cause, the crash of *Dottie Jeanne* eventually became the Isle of Man's deadliest aviation accident.[3]

While the bodies of the 31 men were being prepared for burial, the 381st received a field order to take part in the Eighth's 968th mission and the group's 297th. Thirty-seven B-17s took off from Ridgewell to join 270 others for a raid on Pilsen, Czechoslovakia, a city last visited on February 14, when elements of the 381st attacked its Škoda armaments factory. On April 25, the 1st AD returned to bomb both the Škoda plant and a nearby airfield—the 381st heading for the latter.

The Pilsen raid had been requested by Allied ground forces to stem the flow of guns and tanks to German forces still fighting in the east. The 2nd AD, meanwhile, was dispatched to Salzburg to attack its marshaling yards, which were teeming with enemy troops and supplies.

"As a bombing expedition it was a washout," wrote the 381st's diarist. Of the group's B-17s, only two dropped their bombs on smoke markers left by a previous group. Because of solid cloud cover and the possibility of their bombs falling on friendly forces, the others returned to Ridgewell with their loads still onboard. Nevertheless, intense and accurate flak caused the loss of six B-17s from other groups, while the 381st escaped the worst of it, despite having to make several "360s" over the target.

"I'll brain the next guy who tells me the war is over," barked mission leader Maj. Charles W. Bordner on landing at Ridgewell. Yet, unknown to him and the men of the entire Eighth Air Force, it would turn out to be the last heavy bomber mission of the European war.[4]

* * *

The 381st and other bomb groups were stood down just as American and Soviet troops met at the Elbe River, leaving less of Nazi Germany for the Eighth to attack. Instead, the group focused on domestic duties, flying a practice mission.

A day after the Pilsen raid, the 97-mission B-17G, *The Tomahawk Warrior* was flying under the command of 2nd Lt. Albert J. Cotea and was loaded with a 5,000lb payload of bombs "just in case" the 381st was called for a combat mission. As Cotea approached Ridgewell, a fire broke out along the starboard wing. Luckily, he was able to land *The Tomahawk Warrior* before turning off the runway. Then, noticing the flames were spreading rapidly, Cotea ordered his crew to abandon the aircraft. They watched from a safe distance as the fully loaded bomber blazed for 15 minutes before its bomb load erupted spectacularly. *The Tomahawk Warrior* was torn to shreds, leaving behind an 800 square-foot, 18-inch-deep crater in the perimeter track. Nevertheless, four hours later, the station utility men had the taxiway patched up.

They were among 700 mourners to leave a drizzly Ridgewell the next day to travel 30 miles to Cambridge's American military cemetery. All work stopped on the base as 17 trucks and numerous cars and jeeps made their way to Madingley for the burials of those killed on the Isle of Man. London newspapers estimated that a crowd of 2,000 people attended the service, which was presided over by James Good Brown.

"I only wish I could give these fine boys back to you mothers," he said. "But they are with God … They are martyrs to a holy cause, for they gave their lives in a war to exterminate evil."

As the final casket was lowered into its grave, it brought the total number of men buried by the chaplain in England to 188.[5]

While other groups were tasked with dropping food supplies to beleaguered Dutch civilians still being held in the Nazi grip, the 381st wasn't called upon to take part in Operation *Chowhound*. As the men waited for the next field order, they welcomed New Jersey Congressman, Gordon Canfield, who travelled to England after visiting the recently liberated concentration camp at Buchenwald. Canfield arrived at Ridgewell to toast the group's 71-mission bomber, *Passaic Warrior*, in one of the lighter moments of his European tour.

The day after his visit, British newspapers carried the German announcement that Adolf Hitler was dead. However, the men waited—the only briefed mission to take place, a single photographic reconnaissance flight over Oschersleben, scene of the 381st's second worst day for combat losses on January 11, 1944.

Finally, at 0200 on May 7, the teletype machine in the 381st headquarters building spewed out an announcement stating that the German High Command had surrendered. The men were left asleep for several hours, while plans were put in place for the rest of the day—a day that would include 24 hours of free beer. Ridgewell's *Daily Bulletin* declared:

> All department heads will free as many men as possible in order to participate in the activities for the day. Officers' mess bar, NCO club bar, station beer parlor and Aero Club open 1000 to midnight today, no special activities are planned. No regular meals will be served (morning or evening). Snacks available 1100 to 2400 today. All personnel restricted to limits of station except those on official business until 0700 08/05/45. From 0700 08/05 until 0700 09/05 personnel restricted to a travel radius of 20 miles. Station theater shows 7 times today. All personnel to remember they're in a foreign country and must conduct ourselves in an exemplary and agreeable manner.

It almost wasn't to be, however. The crews were woken at 0600 and told to assemble at the control tower. Group commander Conway Hall then climbed onto its roof where he informed them of the German surrender. He then listed a summary of the 381st Bomb Group's activities.

Most men were aware of the grim coincidence between the group's first mission (the deaths of 24 men in the explosion of *Caroline* 24 hours after) and its last (the loss of 31 others on the Isle of Man 48 hours before), but many were unaware that the group had lost (in raids and non-operational accidents) "165 aircraft and approximately 1,290 men." Hall also stated that 223 enemy aircraft had been destroyed by the group's gunners (along with 40 probables and 167 damaged)—their biggest day being January 11, 1944, when 28 had been shot down over Oschersleben. Yet, Schweinfurt represented the group's heaviest single loss in a day—11 aircraft and 10 crews missing. Hall then confirmed the group had dropped 22,159.5 tons of bombs and 24 tons of leaflets. Furthermore, in addition to two DUCs, its airmen had also been awarded two DSCs, 21 Silver Stars and countless DFCs.

* * *

Twenty-four hours earlier, James Good Brown had been called away to Paris by the head of the Eighth Air Force's chaplains. Knowing the Germans might surrender while he was away, Brown had the foresight to plan the base's victory ceremony.

He also drafted his own message, which was read to the men by personnel officer Maj. LeRoy C. Wilcox, who had been with the group since its days at Pyote.

"The war has not been won," Brown wrote. "So far we have done only the ugly work. We have dug up the weeds, and I'm glad to say, have burned them. It now remains to plant the soil … Let us be happy. Let us be joyful. Let us sing. Let us be merry in ways that we ought."[6]

The men took this as their cue to celebrate—bolstered by gallons of free beer—one crewman estimating that "80%" were quickly inebriated.

"The boys got out an assortment of flares and incendiaries," wrote 533rd pilot Wilbur Larson, who had completed 22 missions. "They had a 'small war' going on for a while. It really wasn't safe to be outside."

A "newsman" was also present capturing Technicolor film footage of the "biggest celebration" Larson had ever seen—one that was set to get even bigger.

"They are supposed to blow the bomb dump up at 11pm," he noted. "It should be quite a noise … all trucks and cars are locked up and no one is allowed off the base. The enlisted men are getting tighter, and I have had a few myself."[7]

East Anglia had been full of rumors, but no official word came through. Those on Ridgewell's doorstep, however, were only too aware of the excitement thanks to frequent fireworks—a local teacher even calling the base to ask if "the holiday" was official. Conway Hall then found his telephone ringing.

> A group commander from another base called and said, "what are you people doing?" There's no secret, I told him. Well, it wasn't long until General [William] Gross called me … and said "what in the world are you doing?" This was about 11–12 o'clock. I said, "well, we're celebrating over here. The war's over." He said, "there's been no announcement" and "you know, every group in my outfit and half of the Eighth Air Force is celebrating … what you started." He said "if we have a mission, and everybody's too drunk to go, you're going to lead it." He was unhappy.

Hall was also called by an anxious officer from his own base who claimed the crews were "about to burn the place down." Hurrying to the scene with his deputy George Shackley, Hall calmed the men down.

"We lined them up and threatened them with everything—but going home," he recalled. "Celebrate all you want to," Hall told them. "But damage nothing."[8]

Even so, he was glad to be proven right 24 hours later (for celebrating a day early), when Winston Churchill officially proclaimed "Victory in Europe Day."

That day, commander of the Eighth, Jimmy Doolittle authorized aerial tours of Germany, allowing some of the 381st's Bronze Star holders to leave the base to "rubberneck." Others found their movements limited. Most were only allowed short passes of less than six hours within the local area. All were told to keep their contact with civilians to a minimum and for their conduct to remain absolutely above reproach.

* * *

While James Good Brown was in Paris, he had bumped into ("among millions of Parisians walking the streets celebrating the end of the war") Guerdon Humason, the 532nd pilot who had been shot down in July 1943 during the so-called "Blitz Week." Their surprise meeting followed Humason's two years in captivity (he had made his own way to Paris after his "prison gates were opened"). However, there were still many more waiting for their turn to be set free.

On May 10, 30 B-17s left Ridgewell led by Conway Hall to bring hundreds of downed airmen out of Germany. Wilbur Larson's B-17 was among them. Flying first to Lübeck, then to Rheine; Larson collected 25 POWs before delivering them to Roissy, near Paris. "They were so happy to leave," he wrote.[9]

Two days later, Operation *Revival*—the evacuation of American POWs from *Stalag Luft I*—formally began. First Combat Bombardment Wing commander William Gross—flying *Our Bridget*, and in command of the operation—set out for the nearby airfield of Barth to equip it with an improvised radio tower in the form of another B-17. The 1st AD would then send 200 aircraft to collect as many of the almost 9,000 POWs as they could.

On May 13, 40 modified B-17s left Ridgewell bound for Barth. Leading them was *Frenchy's Folly*, flown by Wilbur Larson and carrying Conway Hall. With its bomb bay gutted and fitted with a table and "portable mess hall," *Frenchy's Folly* crossed Europe at 4,000 feet along a fixed corridor (to avoid possible ground fire). The route over Wilhelmshaven and Hamburg allowed those on board a perfect view of towns and cities they had previously only seen from five miles high. Once on the ground at Barth, *Frenchy's Folly* then parked to allow Conway Hall to oversee the operation, while scores of other B-17s taxied in single file—their two starboard engines throttled back at a loading point to allow up to 30 POWs to be ushered onboard.

"I could see B-17s coming into the airfield at Barth," remembered 533rd pilot, Robert Jankowiak, who had been shot down on the group's mission to Fürstenau 50 days earlier.

"What a sight. Unbelievably, I could see some 'Triangle L' markings of the 381st."

Within 15 minutes of landing, each loaded B-17 took off from Barth—those of the 381st flying to Laon's Couvron airfield, France, where the POWs (now known as RAMPs) were offloaded and transferred to Paris before heading to Camp *Lucky Strike* in Saint-Valery—the largest of 10 staging camps and chief assembly point for newly-liberated POWs.

The following day, the 381st's crews flew the same route and altitude, collecting another batch of RAMPs. The 533rd's Gilbert C. Schrank, co-pilot of *LON BOY*, was able to note down the effects of war on Europe (and the effects of flying on his passengers) as he took them to Laon.

> Flew over Osnabruck, Munster, Happy Valley, Cologne, Aachen. Saw cathedral in Cologne, damage very severe. Places where large cement blocks had been blasted out of the ground, probably Siegfried Line positions. Aachen had very much damage, most factories inoperative.

> Most buildings only the walls standing with no windows. Some small towns wiped out completely. Saw some trenches at different places, usually accompanied by spots caused by artillery fire. Had 30 passengers, some of which got sick while flying. Air a little rough.[10]

The very last B-17 to leave Barth on May 14 was *Our Bridget*. It was carrying not just William Gross, but also Col. Hubert "Hub" Zemke, former commander of the 56th and 479th FGs, and the senior Allied officer in *Stalag Luft I*. As they left behind an empty prison camp and headed for Paris, Gross acknowledged that his 1st CBW had flown its final mission. "The Wing is dead," he declared. "Long live the Wing."[11]

* * *

Among the group's B-17s that had survived the war was *Rotherhithe's Revenge*. Having flown 102 missions since being purchased by the residents of Bermondsey 15 months earlier, a crowd of Londoners returned to Ridgewell to take part in a ceremony of farewell and appreciation for the bomber. *Rotherhithe's Revenge* was one of 72 earmarked to return to the US when orders came through to the 381st headquarters on May 16.

Earlier, Conway Hall and his squadron commanders had been summoned for a special meeting at the 1st AD's headquarters at Brampton Grange, Huntingdonshire. There, they learned that the group's two years of life in rural England were about to end almost as suddenly as they had begun.

Robert Singleton, a togglier with the 535th, was notified that he was to leave with a group of B-17s on June 1. Thanks to his strong standing, owing to his length of service, overseas time, combat credits and number of dependents, he had earned a seat on one of the first B-17s scheduled to leave Ridgewell. Two days later, he wrote to his wife, Norma.

"I told you I had some news to tell you, so brace yourself, as here it is: I'm coming home!"[12]

Of the 1,875 personnel at Ridgewell, a select band of 220 climbed aboard 11 B-17s on May 20 ready for their return to the US—destination Bradley Field, Windsor Locks, Connecticut. Loading their 55-pound luggage allowance, the men left English soil for the last time, many not having the time or opportunity to say goodbye to their friends and acquaintances in the surrounding villages. For others, including Robert Singleton, however, it would be the start of an interminable wait.

Poor weather conditions over the North Atlantic, combined with large numbers of American aircraft now staging through airfields en route (RAF Valley in Wales and Meeks Field in Iceland being particularly congested) meant that the next group of bombers, including Singleton's, were delayed. It gave the men the chance to continue packing crates and to transfer some of its bombers to the 306th Bomb Group, which had been selected for duty with the occupational air forces in

Germany. *The South Boston Shillelagh* and *The Alamo* were among six to be ferried to Thurleigh on May 23.

The men listed to fly back to the US were also assigned their aircraft—532nd crew chief, Whitey Strednak being slated to return on *Flak Magnet*, the B-17G he had faithfully maintained for over a year. Known by him as "Nan" thanks to its assigned aircraft letter (N), *Flak Magnet* had briefly been called *Patches* due to the number of times flak holes had to be fixed by him and his crew. It would soon join the rebuilt *Frenchy's Folly* and the group's much-celebrated veteran B-17, *Stage Door Canteen*, for the exodus to the US. (*Flak Magnet* appears on the cover of the book.)

Second Lieutenant Eugene R. Ilten, who had been assigned to the 535th three months earlier, was waiting to navigate *Buckeye*. In between watching shows at the station theater and packing his bags, Ilten was becoming frustrated, especially when June 1 came and went.

"Getting stir crazy," he wrote. "Rumor has it that we have the 5th. That will be Tuesday. Hope it will not be any later than that. Got two blankets—it's cold. We sleep all morning and stay up to 1 or 2am. Makes the day seem shorter ... Would just as soon work as do this."[13]

The men's growing frustrations were not helped by the American Red Cross Aeroclub, which had been stripped down to a bare snack bar and games room. Except for the "jammed" theater, which remained open for nine hours, there was almost nothing for the men to do, except eat, sleep and loaf. Most had been stuck on the base for almost a month, leading to some personal issues.

"Last night some guy got drunk and started shooting at guys," Eugene Ilten wrote. "We had a couple slugs whistle through our walls. He's in the clink today. Hope they throw the book at him."

Having packed, then unpacked, before being briefed for the North Atlantic crossing (which was then scrubbed), Ilten's mood was not lifted by worsening weather.

"Place is getting me down," he wrote on June 6. "Our diversions are cards, soft ball, volleyball. Cards mainly because it is raining most of the time. Nuts."[14]

The skies cleared a day later, however, allowing 61 bombers to be loaded with 20 men, their belongings and equipment. The B-17s then lined up ready for departure. Conway Hall had been planning to fly his *Little Rock-ette* to Bradley, but just prior to departure he had received a telephone call from Gen. William Gross.

"I'm coming over and taking over Hall's Air Force [Conway Hall's off-paper fleet of aircraft, including *Little Rock-ette*]," Gross had told him, "You will be flying my stripped airplane back [*Our Bridget*]. It's on-paper."[15]

Our Bridget duly became the last 381st Bomb Group B-17 to take off from Ridgewell on June 7—almost two years to the day since Joe Nazzaro's *Nobody's Baby* had first landed.

* * *

As the fleet of bombers began their journey, they left behind some 700 men under the command of a new ground executive, LeRoy Wilcox. Among them were 65 officers and enlisted men who had been tasked with staying at Ridgewell to provide care and maintenance while a decision was made on its future. For the ground crews, the bombers' departures heralded the start of two weeks of intense packing and loading.

Of the 61 B-17s that left for the US, only one encountered any difficulty en route. *Ice Col' Katy* developed engine problems over Canada and was forced to land at Mingan, Quebec, for an engine change. Others began arriving at Bradley Field in the afternoon of June 9. However, due to overcrowding, most of the 381st's B-17s were diverted to Grenier, New Hampshire. Still, they were home. The base's newly opened telephone exchange soon became "a seething, sweating mass of eager soldiers" calling back to their families.

Back in England, the majority of the 381st ground crews began moving out of Ridgewell on June 23 (the remaining 65 would not leave until July 17). Travelling in a convoy of trucks to Great Yeldham station, they drove along roads that were lined with waving villagers. Arriving at a jammed station, they were able to say their goodbyes as men who had "arrived as strangers and were leaving as friends." In many cases, there were some who were leaving as husbands and sweethearts.

As several trains pulled out of Great Yeldham station for the journey to Scotland, it marked the end of a cycle that had started two years earlier. Moored at Gourock was RMS *Queen Elizabeth*, the liner that had originally brought the ground echelon to England in 1943. Two days later, the men of the 381st were finally on their way home.

"The ship slipped down the Clyde past villages and dwellings where men and women, waving sheets, flags and anything else sufficiently large and bright, added their send-off to this first great homecoming boatload of the Eighth Air Force men and women who had been America's spearhead into the Reich," noted the group's diarist.

After a six-day crossing of the Atlantic, *Queen Elizabeth* docked at Pier 90, New York. The men of the 381st then returned to Camp Kilmer, where they were soon separated into regional groups for transfer to separation centers across the US. They were also given 30 days of rest and recuperation, before being told to report to Sioux Falls Army Air Field, where they were to be screened and processed for possible overseas service.

As the men of the 381st waited and wondered if they would be sent to the Pacific, they subsequently learned that their group was to be deactivated. The majority would find themselves transferred to the Second Air Force, which was tasked with training new B-29 Superfortress groups and replacement crews for units still fighting in the Pacific. It wasn't until the dust had settled in Hiroshima and Nagasaki that it became clear most of them would be discharged from the USAAF. Finally, on August 28, 1945, the 381st was officially deactivated.

"And that," wrote the group's diarist, "under the decorations and citations, the foolishness and fun, the frustration and bitterness, the camaraderie and the novelty of life in a strange but essentially understandable corner of the world, was quite what the war proved to be for the 381st Bombardment Group."

Epilogue

> One by one I recalled the faces of my crew—a group of young men from diverse locales and backgrounds, thrown together by chance and placed under intense pressure. We were such ordinary men from whom the extraordinary was demanded.[1]
>
> JOHN COMER, *COMBAT CREW*, 1988

A month after the 381st left Ridgewell, a BBC radio correspondent travelled to the village of Great Yeldham to record a broadcast entitled, "The Deserted Village." Drawing on interviews with local residents, the program examined how Great Yeldham was faring in the wake of "the most dramatic incident in its long history"—the two-year period when "American flying men" had "crossed through."

"Can any good friend in America write and tell us a use for discarded chewing gum?" asked one resident, who kept finding it stuck "snugly in all odd cracks and crevices."

Others were more specific. "I shall always remember the party and celebration we had when Otto … of Michigan Avenue, Bay City, Michigan, and friends got back after escaping from Germany."[2]

Most prevalent, though, was the wistful sense that Great Yeldham had been left "lonely." "What do the people of an English village feel about the thousands of American fliers who have come and are now gone?" asked the BBC correspondent. "They hope they'll come back again."

John Comer was among the first to return three decades later. Having survived 25 missions, he'd left Ridgewell at the start of 1944 to transfer to Gulfport, Mississippi, where he was tasked with training the USAAF's new bomber crews. Discovering that flying in combat was safer than working with raw recruits, Comer soon volunteered to return to Europe. He flew a further 50 missions with the Fifteenth Air Force from bases in Italy, before returning home. Ridgewell, however, was burned deeply into his memory. "To me this was ground as hallowed as Lincoln's Gettysburg," he wrote.[3]

Comer returned to Ridgewell in 1972 following a distinguished career as a sales manager for America's largest coatings manufacturer, Sherwin-Williams. By 1975, he had retired to become both a business mentor and volunteer guide at the *Frontiers of*

Flight Museum. In 1988, his wartime memoir, *Combat Crew*, was published. Based on his hand-written journals, it has been acknowledged as one of the finest personal accounts of the European air war, vividly describing "the most intensely lived year" of his life, a life that ended in 2005 when he was 95.

A decade after John Comer's visit to England, a party of his compatriots returned to dedicate a memorial to the 381st Bomb Group. The ceremony took place on August 28, 1982—37 years to the day of the group's deactivation. Constructed of South African granite and weighing twice the payload of a B-17, the monument was funded by the group's former members. It was erected just yards from the Nissen huts that made up Ridgewell's sick quarters, the former home of flight surgeon Ernest Gaillard, Jr., MD.

Gaillard had transferred to a US Army hospital in Gloucestershire 10 months after marrying his English fiancée, Dorothy. Six months later, just as Buchenwald's concentration camp was liberated, his medical skills were "conscripted" so he could tend to its victims. He was subsequently transferred to Berlin to treat wounded civilians there. Both became experiences that Gaillard would never speak about. In April 2004, after retiring to San Diego, California, with 32 more years' surgical experience, Ernest Gaillard passed away aged 90.

The 381st memorial ceremony at Ridgewell was led by former chaplain, James Good Brown, who caused something of a stir arriving at London's Heathrow Airport dressed in his "pinks and greens." Hoisting the same flag that had flown over Ridgewell during the war (Brown had retrieved and kept it), he introduced the service. "We stand on hallowed ground, made sacred by the deeds of noble and brave men," he said. Brown then went on to describe how the wounds could not be healed without returning to dedicate the memorial to those "lost and loved." "When they died," he said, "they took some of our life with them."[4]

James Good Brown lived a long life—107 years in all. He was the only chaplain to remain with the same bomb group throughout World War II.[5] In 1945, Brown returned home to Connecticut to complete 50 years of service as a minister. He could never forget the men of the 381st, however. Using the diaries he had written across 970 days between 1943 and 1945, Brown published his book, *The Mighty Men of the 381st: Heroes All*. First printed two years after Ridgewell's ceremony, Brown never thought of it as a book, more a memorial. "It's a testament to both the living and the dead," he said. James Good Brown passed away in Haverhill, New Hampshire on Christmas Day, 2008.

Brown outlived all but one of his commanding officers. His friend, and the group's final commander, Conway Hall, became its last surviving senior officer. Hall retired from the United States Air Force (USAF) as a "full-bird" colonel in 1970 and moved back to his native Arkansas to be with his wife and two daughters. When asked about the confidence he inspired in his men towards the end of the war, the ever-popular, but stern Conway Hall replied, "It's something to be in it, and live in it, and when you have a good chance of surviving it—that's what made the morale go so high."[6] Conway Hall passed away in 2012 at the age of 94.

On February 5, 1990, the group's first commanding officer, Joseph Nazzaro, died in Tucson, Arizona, the same city he had left on New Year's Day 1943 to establish the 381st Bomb Group. A career officer who rose to the rank of four-star general, Nazzaro served in Okinawa, Japan, before being appointed commander-in-chief of the US Strategic Air Command. He then commanded the Pacific Air Forces—a role which saw him oversee Operation *Rolling Thunder*, the aerial bombing campaign carried out against the North Vietnamese during the Vietnam War.

The 381st's second commanding officer, Harry Leber, returned to the US to take up a role as director of operations with the Fifteenth Air Force at Colorado Springs. After attending command school in Alabama, he then returned to England in 1948 as the USAF liaison officer at the RAF's Staff College. Shortly after his return to Alabama two years later, however, Leber contracted polio and was hospitalized for three years. He retired from the USAF in 1951 and moved to Deerfield Beach, Florida, with his wife, Ester. In 1966, Harry Leber passed away at the young age of 54. He is buried in Arlington National Cemetery.

A 381st officer who had a strained relationship with higher authority was Pathfinder navigator John Howland. His ability to read the landscape was put to further use after the war. Finishing his military career with the 91st Bomb Group at Bassingbourn, Howland returned to his home in Colorado Springs, where he completed a Bachelor of Science degree in Geology. He then worked for several mining companies, including Gulf Oil. In 2014, John Howland was awarded the French Légion d'Honneur for his wartime service. He passed away a year later at the age of 95.

Ironically, Howland's fellow navigator David McCarthy ended up spending 15 years working in oil pollution control after starting his own business. McCarthy had left the USAAF in November 1945, having transferred to the 1CBW as Combat Wing Navigator after completing his 25 missions with the 381st. Returning to the US, he had then studied electrical engineering before finding employment in industrial sales. McCarthy wrote his memoir, *Fear No More*, in 1991. He passed away four years later in Pittsburgh, Pennsylvania, aged 74.

Another navigator, Ted Homdrom, wrote his book a decade after David McCarthy. *Mission Memories* was published in 2001, although its title could equally describe Homdrom's post-war years. "Reverend Ted" and his wife Betty, together with their two young children, left Minnesota to spend 35 years as missionaries in South Africa, a country beset by the struggles of apartheid. "I had already demonstrated my willingness to serve in extreme danger overseas," he later admitted.[7] The family returned to the US in 1985, where Homdrom began work as a green card coordinator. In 2019, Reverend Theodore Homdrom (DFC) passed away in Saint Paul, Minnesota, aged 100.

Post-war, the 381st's navigators were seemingly able to weave their words as well as their B-17s. In 2011, the 535th's James Grey published *Vanishing Contrails*, a set of memoirs detailing the "vanishing of an entire way of life." He remained in the military for 22 years, before retiring at the rank of lieutenant colonel. Grey and his family then moved to Sacramento, California, where he entered the world of commercial banking, a career that would not end until he was 85. Just before retiring, Grey's house was burgled, the thieves taking almost everything of value, including his car. Particularly painful was the loss of his wartime memorabilia, uniforms and A-2 jacket, which had been hand-painted with the name of his B-17, *Hell's Angels*. "To me, they were priceless treasures that held immeasurable personal value," he said.[8] Three weeks after turning 96, James Grey passed away.

Edward Carr was another 381st man who rose to become a lieutenant colonel, before retiring from the USAF Reserve in 1970. A former National Guard officer from Tacoma, Washington, Carr found himself transferred to Honolulu just after the Pearl Harbor attack. Realizing he might be drafted into the infantry to fight at Guadalcanal, Carr eventually managed to maneuver himself into the USAAF for pilot training. "I had never before been in an airplane, had no burning desire to fly, but knew that the Air Force would be better than the Infantry," he said.[9] After flying 35 missions with the 533rd Bomb Squadron, Carr returned to the US in February 1945. He gained a degree in economics and enjoyed a career in insurance. In 1983, a year after the 381st memorial was dedicated at Ridgewell, he returned to his former base. Some 20 years later, he wrote his first book, *On Final Approach*, about his wartime experiences in England. In October 2020, Edward Carr passed away at the age of 98.

In a way, enlisted man, Wayne "Rusty" Pegg went back to his roots on being assigned to the 381st in England. His paternal grandfather was a coal miner from Bolton, Lancashire. Pegg never published a book, but he did write a secret combat diary, which opened with the group's second deadliest mission (Oschersleben, January 11, 1944). "Rough, very rough for the first one!" he had written. After surviving another 29 missions, Pegg was transferred to the Fifth Air Force in the Pacific. He then returned to Pennsylvania to work as an engineer with Bell Telephone Company. Pegg, who was eventually married with three sons, passed away in 1993 at the age of 69.

Douglas Holt also kept his own diary, although he used his as the basis for his 2007 book, *Lucky Dog*. Having completed 35 missions in November 1944, Holt left England a month later to return to his home in Milwaukee, Wisconsin. Subsequently awarded a degree in electrical engineering, he enjoyed a near 40-year career as an engineer. His interest in aviation never left him, however, and he continued flying his yellow Piper PA-17 Vagabond after he retired. Douglas Holt passed away in October 2015 aged 91.

Another 381st pilot who continued flying long after his 32nd and final mission was Bob Armstrong. On returning to Kansas, he immediately co-founded a flying service in Scott City, but was called back to active duty two years later. He became a B-29 Superfortress co-pilot, finding himself back in England for three months during the Berlin Blockade. Released from duty a year later, Armstrong re-entered the commercial aviation world and became a Federal Aviation Administration pilot examiner. By January 1969, he had written his name into the history books after carrying out the "longest period of daily flying on record," taking off every day for three years, seven months and 15 days. The achievement saw him entered into the 1984 edition of the *Guinness Book of Aircraft Facts and Feats*. Despite his aerial prowess, however, Armstrong never returned to Ridgewell. He passed away on October 14, 2013, at the age of 92.

Former ball turret gunner Bob Gilbert was another crewman who never managed to return to Ridgewell. Arriving back home in Long Beach just as the 381st was preparing to leave England, Gilbert returned to his studies under the GI Bill, a financial aid program to help World War II veterans. In 1949, he left to begin work as a template maker for Douglas Aircraft in Long Beach, before marrying and raising two daughters. His career in the aerospace industry then saw him become a senior quality control manager at McDonnell Douglas, a role which involved working on the Apollo, Concorde and Space Shuttle programs. Gilbert retired in 1991, before publishing his memoir, *The View from the Bottom Up* in 2012. He passed away a year later, aged 87.

* * *

Of the total casualties suffered by the 381st during World War II, it is thought that some 619 were KIA. By 1957, 298 of them were buried in cemeteries across Europe, 97 at Madingley alone.

In 1946, the US War Department had issued a notice on the "Disposition of World War II Armed Forces Dead," allowing the next-of-kin an opportunity to have their relatives' remains returned home. The family of Andy Piter, killed in the Isle of Man tragedy, chose to have his body exhumed and returned for reinterment at the Olive Branch Cemetery, Pennsylvania, five miles from his parents' home at Banning. Piter's burial took place on July 15, 1948.

The family of bombardier, Bud Perrin, killed over Mannheim on December 11, 1944, also elected to have his body returned to Knoxville, Tennessee; the reinterment taking place at the city's Lynnhurst Cemetery in May 1949. Perrin's four-year-old daughter, who had been named Rosalind in his honor, was held back from the ceremony. Sixty years after her father's burial, she discovered over 1,000 letters written between her parents during the war. Passing them to her cousin, J. Ross Greene, he subsequently wrote *A Fortress and a Legacy*, a fact-based novel using the letters as his guide. The book was "a gift" to the daughter Perrin never knew.

Similarly, the family of Andy Piter were also able to learn and appreciate the role he played in England thanks to the efforts of his great-nephew, Donald J. Madar. His *An Only Son of the 381st* is a fine tribute to just one of the 381st's ground crews—those individuals who, all too often, have been overlooked in the wider context of the Eighth Air Force.

Thanks to modern technology and aviation, the second and third generations of those who served with the 381st at Ridgewell are also beginning to trace their relatives' footsteps. In 2015, members of Bud Owens's family followed his route through France to the Pyrenees (Owens was shot down on July 4, 1943, and perished near Andorra). Their epic journey was captured in a moving documentary, *In the Footsteps of Bud Owens*, which also told the story of his heroics and ultimate sacrifice.

Unfortunately, the ability to visit most 381st wartime locations is limited to crash sites (if they can be found) and former POW camps. Much of the group's story took place some five miles above the earth. Sadly, there are no battle markers in the sky. Only the group's base shows any signs of its war, although much of it has been erased.

Ridgewell's time as an operational military airfield ended soon after Conway Hall's *Our Bridget* took off to return to the US. However, it did become Essex's only long-term, wartime heavy bomber base. After the 381st left Ridgewell, the airfield was transferred back to the RAF, whose 94 and 95 Maintenance Units stored thousands of tons of unused wartime ordnance along its runways. In 1957, the Air Ministry dispensed with the site. The farmers who had been ejected some 15 years before were allowed to return, while the base's infrastructure was torn down. With most of the runways and all of the hardstands broken up, only sections of its perimeter track were retained. By 1978, much of the airfield's former taxiways were converted into public roads, more than any other British Eighth Air Force base.[10]

In the late 1980s, only two buildings still stood on the airfield. Both maintenance hangars were commandeered by the USAF for use as supplementary storage facilities for its units based at nearby RAF Wethersfield. When the Americans finally relinquished control of Wethersfield in 1990, Ridgewell's hangars were dismantled, taking with them some of the last vestiges of its wartime past.

By the turn of the millennium, the airfield's past was being faithfully restored by a group of enthusiasts at the Ridgewell Airfield Commemorative Museum. Located in one of the former hospital Nissen huts, its exhibits and stories were perfectly positioned next to the memorial that was dedicated by James Good Brown and the 381st veterans two decades earlier.

It is here that Casey Bukowski of Buffalo, New York, returned in September 2019. He remembered his crew: First Lieutenant Francis J. Flaherty; Second Lieutenant John I. Hoffer; Technical Sergeant Notra J. Bright; Staff Sergeant Burling Larson; Staff Sergeant Henry R. Krzyak; Staff Sergeant Arthur N. Butler. Six of so many who failed to return to Ridgewell. Staff Sergeant Casimer L. Bukowski finally could; 75 years, six months and 29 days later. He's one of a dwindling number of American airmen who flew from scores of British airfields during World War II. One of the "Mighty Men of the 381st"—"the hottest outfit to reach the ETO"—he may ultimately be one of the last to make it back.

Glossary

AFCE – Automatic Flight Control Equipment
ASR – Air–Sea Rescue
BD – Bombardment Division
BG – Bombardment Group
BMW – Bayerische Motoren Werke
BS – Bombardment Squadron
BW – Bombardment Wing
CBO – Combined Bomber Offensive
CBW – Combat Bombardment Wing
DFC – Distinguished Flying Cross
DSC – Distinguished Service Cross
DUC – Distinguished Unit Citation
ETO – European Theater of Operations
FG – Fighter Group
IFF – Identification Friend or Foe antenna
IP – Initial Point
JG 26 – *Jagdgeschwader* 26
KIA – killed in action
MIA – missing in action
MPI – Mean Point of Impact
PCBW – Provisional Combat Bombardment Wing
PFF – Pathfinder Force
POW – prisoner of war
RAF – Royal Air Force
RAMP – Recovered American Military Personnel
SHAEF – Supreme Headquarters Allied Expeditionary Force
USAAC – United States Army Air Corps
USAAF – United States Army Air Forces
USSTAF – United States Strategic Air Forces in Europe
VIII BC – VIII Bomber Command
VIII FC – VIII Fighter Command
WIA – wounded in action

APPENDIX I

Internal Mission Numbers Used by the 381st Bomb Group between June 1943 and April 1945

No.	Date	Location	Target Type	B-17s Lost
1	22/06/43	Antwerp	Industrial	2
2	23/06/43	Bernay-Saint-Martin	Airfield	0
3	25/06/43	Hamburg	Aircraft factory	1
4	26/06/43	Vélizy-Villacoublay	Airfield	0
5	28/06/43	Saint-Nazaire	U-Boat pens	0
6	29/06/43	Triqueville	Airfield	0
7	04/07/43	Le Mans	Aircraft factory	1
8	10/07/43	Vélizy-Villacoublay	Airfield	0
9	14/07/43	Amiens–Glisy	Airfield	2
10	17/07/43	Hanover	Synthetic rubber factory	0
11	24/07/43	Herøya	Aluminum plant	1
12	25/07/43	Hamburg	Port	3
13	26/07/43	Hamburg	Aircraft factory	0
14	28/07/43	Kassel	Industrial	0
15	29/07/43	Kiel	U-Boat yard	0
16	30/07/43	Kassel	Aircraft factory	1
17	12/08/43	Gelsenkirchen	Oil facility	3
18	15/08/43	Brussels	Airfield	0
19	16/08/43	Le Bourget	Airfield	0
20	17/08/43	Schweinfurt	Ball-bearing factories	11
21	19/08/43	Gilze-Rijen	Airfield	1
22	24/08/43	Vélizy-Villacoublay	Airfield	0
23	27/08/43	Watten	V-weapon site	0

No.	Date	Location	Target Type	B-17s Lost
24	31/08/43	Amiens–Glisy	Airfield	0
25	03/09/43	Romilly-sur-Seine	Airfield	1
26	06/09/43	Stuttgart	Aircraft factory	0
27	07/09/43	Brussels	Industrial	0
28	09/09/43	Lille-Nord	Airfield	0
29	15/09/43	Romilly-sur-Seine	Airfield	0
30	16/09/43	Nantes	Airfield	0
31	23/09/43	Nantes	Port	0
32	26/09/43	Meulan-les-Mureaux	Aircraft factory	0
33	27/09/43	Emden	Port	0
34	02/10/43	Emden	Port	0
35	04/10/43	Frankfurt	Industrial	0
36	08/10/43	Bremen	Industrial	7
37	09/10/43	Anklam	Aircraft factory	3
38	10/10/43	Münster	Rail and waterworks	0
39	14/10/43	Schweinfurt	Ball-bearing factories	1
40	20/10/43	Düren	Industrial	0
41	03/11/43	Wilhelmshaven	Port	0
42	05/11/43	Gelsenkirchen	Industrial	1
43	07/11/43	Wesel	Industrial	0
44	16/11/43	Knaben	Molybdenum mine	0
45	26/11/43	Bremen	Port	0
46	01/12/43	Leverkusen	Industrial	4
47	05/12/43	Ivry-sur-Seine	Ball-bearing factory	0
48	11/12/43	Emden	Industrial	0
49	13/12/43	Bremen	Port	0
50	16/12/43	Bremen	Port	0
51	20/12/43	Bremen	Port	4
52	22/12/43	Osnabrück	Marshaling yards	0
53	24/12/43	Cocove	V-weapon site	0
54	30/12/43	Ludwigshafen	Industrial	0
55	31/12/43	Cognac-Châteaubernard	Airfield	1

No.	Date	Location	Target Type	B-17s Lost
56	04/01/44	Kiel	U-Boat yards	2
57	05/01/44	Tours	Airfield	1
58	07/01/44	Ludwigshafen	Synthetic rubber factory	1
59	11/01/44	Oschersleben	Aircraft factory	8
60	21/01/44	Belleville-en-Caux/ Saint-Adrien	V-weapon sites	0
61	29/01/44	Frankfurt	Industrial	2
62	30/01/44	Brunswick	Aircraft factory	3
63	03/02/44	Wilhelmshaven	Port	0
64	04/02/44	Frankfurt	Marshaling yards	0
65	05/02/44	Avord	Airfield	0
66	06/02/44	Nancy-Essey	Airfield	0
67	11/02/44	Ludwigshafen	Target of opportunity	1
68	20/02/44	Leipzig/Oschersleben	Airfields	1
69	21/02/44	Achmer	Airfield	0
70	22/02/44	Bünde	Airfield	6
71	24/12/44	Schweinfurt	Ball-bearing factories	0
72	25/12/44	Augsburg	Aircraft factory	1
73	02/03/44	Frankfurt	Industrial	1
74	03/03/44	Wilhelmshaven	Target of opportunity	1
75	04/03/44	Düsseldorf	Target of opportunity	1
76	06/03/44	Berlin	Industrial	3
77	08/03/44	Erkner	Ball-bearing factory	1
78	09/03/44	Berlin	Industrial	0
79	16/03/44	Gessertshausen	Marshaling yards	0
80	18/03/44	Oberpfaffenhofen	Aircraft factory and airfield	0
81	20/03/44	Mannheim	Industrial	1
82	22/03/44	Berlin	Aircraft factory	0
83	23/03/44	Ahlen	Airfield	0
84	24/03/44	Frankfurt	Marshaling yards	3
85	26/03/44	Marquise-Mimoyecques	V-weapon site	0
86	27/03/44	Saint-Jean-d'Angély	Airfield	0

No.	Date	Location	Target Type	B-17s Lost
87	28/03/44	Reims-Champagne	Airfield and aircraft factory	1
88	29/03/44	Brunswick	Aircraft factory	0
89	08/04/44	Oldenburg	Airfield	0
90	10/04/44	Brussels/Woensdrecht	Airfield/aircraft factory	0
91	11/04/44	Cottbus/Sorau	Aircraft factories	1
92	13/04/44	Schweinfurt	Ball-bearing factories	1
93	18/04/44	Oranienburg	Aircraft factory	1
94	19/04/44	Eschwege	Airfield	2
95	20/04/44	Le Plouy Ferme	V-weapon site	0
96	22/04/44	Hamm	Marshaling yards	0
97	24/04/44	Erding	Air equipment depot	0
98	25/04/44	Metz-Frescaty	Airfield	1
99	26/04/44	Brunswick	Industrial	0
100	27/04/44	La Glacerie	V-weapon site	0
101	28/04/44	Avord	Airfield	1
102	29/04/44	Berlin	Marshaling yards	0
103	30/04/44	Lyon-Bron	Airfield	0
104	01/05/44	Troyes	Marshaling yards	0
105	06/05/44	La Glacerie	V-weapon site	0
106	07/05/44	Berlin	Industrial	0
107	08/05/44	Berlin	Industrial	0
108	09/05/44	Saint-Dizier	Airfield	0
109	11/05/44	Bettembourg/Thionville	Targets of opportunity	0
110	12/05/44	Lützkendorf	Oil facility	0
111	13/05/44	Stralsund/Stettin	Targets of opportunity	0
112	19/05/44	Berlin	Marshaling yards	2
113	20/05/44	Vélizy-Villacoublay	Airfield	0
114	22/05/44	Kiel	Port	0
115	23/05/44	Homburg	Target of opportunity	0
116	24/05/44	Berlin	Marshaling yards	6
117	25/05/44	Nancy-Essey	Airfield	0
118	27/05/44	Ludwigshafen	Marshaling yards	1

No.	Date	Location	Target Type	B-17s Lost
119	28/05/44	Brandis-Polenz Wüsten-Sachsen/Frankfurt	Airfields/Industrial	0
120	29/05/44	Posen	Marshaling yards	0
121	30/05/44	Dessau	Aircraft factory	3
122	31/05/44	Florennes	Target of opportunity	0
123	02/06/44	Boulogne	Gun installations	0
124	02/06/44	Massy-Palaiseau	Railroad station	0
125	03/06/44	Boulogne	Gun installations	0
126	04/06/44	Boulogne	V-weapon sites	0
127	05/06/44	Tailleville	Gun installations	0
128	06/06/44	Ver-sur-Mer/ Courseulles-sur-Mer	Gun installations	0
129	06/06/44	Caen	Gun installations	0
130	07/06/44	Kerlin-Bastard	Airfield	1
131	08/06/44	Tours (La Frillière)	Railroad bridge	0
132	10/06/44	Neufchâtel-Hardelot	Gun installations	0
133	11/06/44	Beaumont-le-Roger	Airfield	0
134	12/06/44	Lille-Nord	Airfield	0
135	14/06/44	Melun Villaroche	Airfield	0
136	15/06/44	Bordeaux-Mérignac	Airfield	1
137	18/06/44	Hamburg	Port	0
138	19/06/44	Bordeaux-Mérignac	Airfield	1
139	20/06/44	Hamburg	Oil facility and docks	1
140	21/06/44	Berlin	Industrial	2
141	22/06/44	Tingry/Abbeville	Power station	1
142	23/06/44	Bachimont	V-weapon site	0
143	24/06/44	Tours-La Riche	Railroad bridge	1
144	25/06/44	Toulouse-Francazal	Airfield	0
145	28/06/44	Fismes	Railroad bridge	0
146	04/07/44	Tours-La Riche	Railroad bridge	1
147	06/07/44	Rely	V-weapon site	0
148	07/07/44	Leipzig-Mockau	Armaments factory	0

No.	Date	Location	Target Type	B-17s Lost
149	08/07/44	Andres/Coubronne/Rely	Targets of opportunity	0
150	09/07/44	Saint-Omer	Airfield	0
151	11/07/44	Munich	Marshaling yards	0
152	12/07/44	Munich	Industrial	0
153	13/07/44	Munich	Target of opportunity	0
154	16/07/44	Munich/Augsburg	Aircraft factories	1
155	18/07/44	Peenemünde	Rocket establishment	1
156	19/07/44	Lechfeld	Airfield	0
157	20/07/44	Dessau	Aircraft factory	0
158	21/07/44	Schweinfurt	Ball-bearing factories	0
159	24/07/44	Saint-Lô	Gun installations	0
160	25/07/44	Saint-Lô	Gun installations	0
161	28/07/44	Merseburg	Oil facility	0
162	29/07/44	Merseburg	Oil facility	0
163	31/07/44	Munich	Aircraft factory	1
164	01/08/44	Melun Villaroche/ Étampes Mondésir	Airfields	0
165	03/08/44	Mulhouse	Marshaling yards	1
166	04/08/44	Peenemünde	Rocket establishment	1
167	05/08/44	Nienburg	Oil facility	1
168	06/08/44	Brandenburg	Armaments factory	1
169	07/08/44	Saint-Florentin/ Bourron-Marlotte	Oil storage facilities	0
170	08/08/44	Cauvicourt	Gun installations	1
171	09/08/44	Saarbrücken	Target of opportunity	0
172	11/08/44	Brest	Coastal battery	0
173	13/08/44	Rouen	Road junction	0
174	14/08/44	Metz-Frescaty	Airfield	0
175	15/08/44	Ostheim	Airfield	0
176	16/08/44	Halle	Aircraft factory	0
177	24/08/44	Weimar	Armaments factory	0
178	25/08/44	Neubrandenburg	Airfield and aircraft factory	0

No.	Date	Location	Target Type	B-17s Lost
179	26/08/44	Gelsenkirchen	Oil facility	0
180	27/08/44	Emden	Target of opportunity	0
181	30/08/44	Kiel	Port	0
182	03/09/44	Ludwigshafen	Oil facility	1
183	08/09/44	Ludwigshafen	Oil facility	0
184	09/09/44	Mannheim	Marshaling yards	0
185	10/09/44	Gaggenau	Engine factory	1
186	11/09/44	Merseburg	Oil facility	0
187	12/09/44	Brüx/Plauen	Oil facilities	1
188	17/09/44	Eindhoven	Ground defenses	0
189	19/09/44	Hamm	Marshaling yards	0
190	21/09/44	Mainz	Marshaling yards	0
191	22/09/44	Kassel	Armaments factories	0
192	25/09/44	Frankfurt	Marshaling yards	1
193	26/09/44	Osnabrück	Marshaling yards	0
194	27/09/44	Cologne	Marshaling yards	0
195	28/09/44	Magdeburg	Oil facility	0
196	02/10/44	Kassel	Armaments factory	0
197	05/10/44	Cologne	Target of opportunity	0
198	06/10/44	Stralsund	Target of opportunity	0
199	07/10/44	Schneeburg/Zwickau	Marshaling yards	0
200	09/10/44	Schweinfurt	Ball-bearing factories	0
201	14/10/44	Cologne	Marshaling yards	0
202	15/10/44	Cologne	Marshaling yards	0
203	17/10/44	Cologne	Marshaling yards	0
204	19/10/44	Mannheim	Industrial	0
205	25/10/44	Hamburg	Oil facility	0
206	26/10/44	Bielefeld	Oil facility	0
207	28/10/44	Münster	Marshaling yards	0
208	30/10/44	Hamm	Marshaling yards	0
209	04/11/44	Hamburg	Oil facility	0
210	05/11/44	Frankfurt	Marshaling yards	0

No.	Date	Location	Target Type	B-17s Lost
211	06/11/44	Hamburg	Oil facility	2
212	09/11/44	Metz	Gun installations	0
213	10/11/44	Cologne	Airfield	0
214	16/11/44	Eschweiler	Gun installations	0
215	21/11/44	Merseburg	Oil facility	0
216	25/11/44	Merseburg	Oil facility	0
217	26/11/44	Altenbeken	Railroad viaduct	1
218	29/11/44	Misburg	Oil facility	0
219	30/11/44	Zeitz	Oil facility	0
220	04/12/44	Soest	Marshaling yards	0
221	09/12/44	Stuttgart	Marshaling yards	1
222	11/12/44	Mannheim	Bridge	1
223	12/12/44	Merseburg	Oil facility	0
224	15/12/44	Kassel	Marshaling yards	0
225	18/12/44	Cologne	Marshaling yards	0
226	24/12/44	Ettinghausen/Kirch-Göns	Airfield	0
227	28/12/44	Remagen	Bridge	0
228	30/12/44	Mainz	Armaments	0
229	31/12/44	Prüm	Military communications	0
230	01/01/45	Koblenz/Kassel	Marshaling yards	1
231	02/01/45	Gerolstein	Marshaling yards	0
232	03/01/45	Cologne	Marshaling yards	0
233	05/01/45	Heimbach	Railroad	0
234	06/01/45	Cologne	Bridge	0
235	08/01/45	Alzey	Bridge	0
236	10/01/45	Ostheim	Airfield	0
237	13/01/45	Germersheim	Bridge	0
238	14/01/45	Rodenkirchen	Bridge	1
239	17/01/45	Paderborn	Marshaling yards	0
240	20/01/45	Mannheim	Bridge	0
241	21/01/45	Aschaffenburg	Armaments	2
242	28/01/45	Gütersloh	Marshaling yards	0

No.	Date	Location	Target Type	B-17s Lost
243	29/01/45	Niederlahnstein	Marshaling yards	0
244	01/02/45	Mannheim	Marshaling yards	0
245	03/02/45	Berlin	Marshaling yards	2
246	06/02/45	Ohrdruf	Target of opportunity	0
247	09/02/45	Arnsberg	Viaduct	0
248	14/02/45	Brüx/Pilsen	Target of opportunity	2
249	15/02/45	Dresden	Target of opportunity	0
250	16/02/45	Langendreer	Target of opportunity	0
251	19/02/45	Dortmund	Oil facility	0
252	20/02/45	Nürnberg	Marshaling yards	0
253	21/02/45	Nürnberg	Marshaling yards	0
254	22/02/45	Köbbelitz/Klötze	Target of opportunity	0
255	23/02/45	Meiningen/Adelsberg	Target of opportunity	0
256	24/02/45	Hamburg	Port	0
257	25/02/45	Munich	Marshaling yards	0
258	26/02/45	Berlin	Marshaling yards	0
259	27/02/45	Leipzig	Military Communications	2
260	01/03/45	Neckarsulm	Marshaling yards	0
261	02/03/45	Chemnitz	Marshaling yards	0
262	04/03/45	Ulm	Armaments	0
263	05/03/45	Chemnitz/Plauen	Marshaling yards	0
264	08/03/45	Hüls	Oil facility	0
265	09/03/45	Kassel	Marshaling yards	1
266	10/03/45	Marl-Sinsen	Railroad supplies center	0
267	11/03/45	Bremen	Marshaling yards	0
268	12/03/45	Dillenburg	Marshaling yards	0
269	14/03/45	Vlotho	Railroad bridge	0
270	15/03/45	Oranienburg	Marshaling yards	0
271	17/03/45	Böhlen/Jena	Oil facility/armaments	0
272	18/03/45	Berlin/Zehdenick	Railroad station	0
273	19/03/45	Plauen	Gun installations	0
274	21/03/45	Rheine	Airfield	0

No.	Date	Location	Target Type	B-17s Lost
275	22/03/45	Dorsten/Feldhausen	Military camps	1
276	23/03/45	Coesfeld	Marshaling yards	0
277	24/03/45	Fürstenau/Vechtel	Airfields	1
278	24/03/45	Twente Enschede	Airfield	0
279	26/03/45	Zeitz/Plauen	Oil facility	0
280	28/03/45	Berlin	Industrial	0
281	30/03/45	Bremen	U-Boat yards	1
282	31/03/45	Halle	Marshaling yards	0
283	04/04/45	Hoya	Airfield	0
284	05/04/45	Grafenwöhr	Armaments	0
285	07/04/45	Kohlenbissen	Airfield	0
286	08/04/45	Stendal	Railroad workshops	1
287	09/04/45	Oberpfaffenhofen	Airfield	1
288	10/04/45	Oranienburg	Armaments	0
289	11/04/45	Freiham	Oil facility	0
290	13/04/45	Neumünster	Marshaling yards	0
291	15/04/45	Soulac-sur-Mer	Gun installations	0
292	16/04/45	Regensburg	Railroad bridge	0
293	17/04/45	Dresden	Railroad depot	0
294	19/04/45	Elsterwerda/ Falkenburg	Railroad bridge/ Marshaling yards	0
295	20/04/45	Brandenburg	Marshaling yards	0
296	21/04/45	Munich	Marshaling yards	0
297	25/04/45	Pilsen	Airfield	0

APPENDIX 2

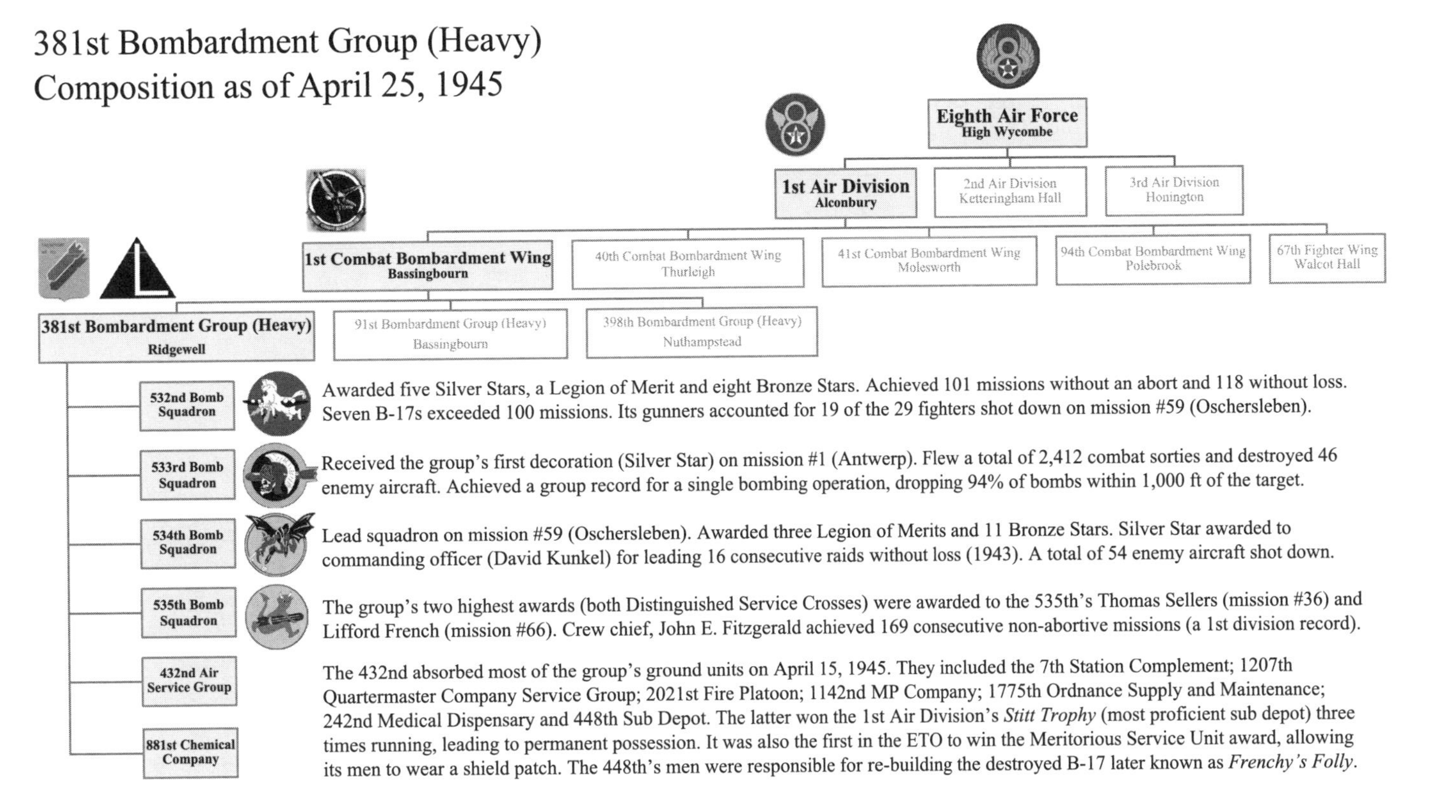

381st Bombardment Group (Heavy)
Composition as of April 25, 1945
Eighth Air Force
High Wycombe
1st Air Division
Alconbury
2nd Air Division
Ketteringham Hall
3rd Air Division
Honington
1st Combat Bombardment Wing
Bassingbourn
40th Combat Bombardment Wing
Thurleigh
41st Combat Bombardment Wing
Molesworth
94th Combat Bombardment Wing
Polebrook
67th Fighter Wing
Walcot Hall
381st Bombardment Group (Heavy)
Ridgewell
91st Bombardment Group (Heavy)
Bassingbourn
398th Bombardment Group (Heavy)
Nuthampstead
532nd Bomb Squadron
Awarded five Silver Stars, a Legion of Merit and eight Bronze Stars. Achieved 101 missions without an abort and 118 without loss. Seven B-17s exceeded 100 missions. Its gunners accounted for 19 of the 29 fighters shot down on mission #59 (Oschersleben).
533rd Bomb Squadron
Received the group's first decoration (Silver Star) on mission #1 (Antwerp). Flew a total of 2,412 combat sorties and destroyed 46 enemy aircraft. Achieved a group record for a single bombing operation, dropping 94% of bombs within 1,000 ft of the target.
534th Bomb Squadron
Lead squadron on mission #59 (Oschersleben). Awarded three Legion of Merits and 11 Bronze Stars. Silver Star awarded to commanding officer (David Kunkel) for leading 16 consecutive raids without loss (1943). A total of 54 enemy aircraft shot down.
535th Bomb Squadron
The group's two highest awards (both Distinguished Service Crosses) were awarded to the 535th's Thomas Sellers (mission #36) and Lifford French (mission #66). Crew chief, John E. Fitzgerald achieved 169 consecutive non-abortive missions (a 1st division record).
432nd Air Service Group
The 432nd absorbed most of the group's ground units on April 15, 1945. They included the 7th Station Complement; 1207th Quartermaster Company Service Group; 2021st Fire Platoon; 1142nd MP Company; 1775th Ordnance Supply and Maintenance; 242nd Medical Dispensary and 448th Sub Depot. The latter won the 1st Air Division's Stitt Trophy (most proficient sub depot) three times running, leading to permanent possession. It was also the first in the ETO to win the Meritorious Service Unit award, allowing its men to wear a shield patch. The 448th's men were responsible for re-building the destroyed B-17 later known as Frenchy's Folly.
881st Chemical Company

APPENDIX 3

Casualty Statistics

By the end of World War II, the Eighth Air Force had flown some 600,000 sorties. At its peak, approximately 250,000 men and women were wearing the Eighth's winged badge. However, of those engaged in combat, around 47,000 did not return, with an estimated 26,000 KIA.

It is believed that the 381st experienced 1,407 casualties—619 of those were KIA. A further 686 became POWs, while 61 evaded capture. Those interned in Sweden numbered 41.

In early 1944, the Eighth Air Force published a report of casualty figures recorded over an 18-month period.[1] It found that between June 1942 and December 1943, 335,450 combat crew members had been dispatched on operational missions. Of that number, 13,868 became casualties (MIA, KIA and WIA—wounded in action):

MIA: 9,921
KIA: 411
WIA: 3,536

Eighty percent of those WIA were either hit by flak or 20mm cannon fire. Another 20 percent were injured by machine gun fire or "plane parts." Those WIA were in the following positions:

Navigator:	12%
Tail Gunner:	12%
Bombardier:	11%
Radio Operator:	10%
Waist Gunner (1):	10%
Waist Gunner (2):	10%
Top Turret Gunner:	8%
Pilot:	7%
Ball Turret Gunner:	6%
Co-Pilot:	6%

The report also looked at the rate of loss (KIA and MIA) across five bomb groups—the 91st, 94th, 305th, 384th and 381st. It found that of 2,085 crewmen studied, 5.4 percent were lost in the first five missions of their 25-mission tours, most of them on mission number five. Over half were either KIA or MIA, while 17 percent were lost due to physical disability, death in non-operational aircraft accidents, or "lack of moral fiber." It concluded that just 25 percent completed their tour.

Endnotes

Prologue

1 European Theater of Operations.

Chapter 1

1 Gordon W. Prange, *At Dawn We Slept* (New York: McGraw-Hill Book Company, 1991), 467.
2 Ibid., 500–501.
3 Daniel Allen Butler, *Pearl, December 7, 1941* (Havertown: Casemate Publishers, 2020), 158.
4 Ibid., 196.
5 This is the aircraft's serial number. The 40 refers to the year the construction contract was issued.
6 Butler, *Pearl*, 196.
7 Edward Jablonski, *Flying Fortress* (London: Sidgwick and Jackson Ltd, 1974), 46.
8 Ernest L. Reid Collection (AFC/2001/001/00756), Veterans History Project, American Folklife Center, Library of Congress.
9 Jablonski, *Flying Fortress*, 47.

Chapter 2

1 Thomas E. Alexander, *The One and Only Rattlesnake Bomber Base* (Abilene: State House Press, 2005), 87.
2 James Good Brown, *The Mighty Men of the 381st: Heroes All* (Salt Lake City: Publishers Press, 1986), 4.
3 "Retired chaplain's life shining example of duty, faith," Air Force Print News, November 23, 2006. Available at: https://www.af.mil/News/Article-Display/article/128962/retired-chaplains-life-shining-example-of-duty-faith/.
4 Conway S. Hall, *From Pyote to Fortress Europe*. Interview by Vernon L. Williams. Old Segundo Productions, 2013.
5 Ibid.
6 Brown, *The Mighty Men of the 381st: Heroes All*, 1–2.
7 Charles D. Butts, *From Pyote to Fortress Europe*. Interview by Vernon L. Williams. Old Segundo Productions, 2013.
8 Brown, *The Mighty Men of the 381st: Heroes All*, 3.
9 The turret protecting the belly of the aircraft from attacks from below.
10 Ken Stone, *Triumphant We Fly* (Paducah: Turner Publishing Company, 1994), 27.
11 Brown, *The Mighty Men of the 381st: Heroes All*, 15.
12 The classic leather bomber jacket, its designation was "Jacket, Pilot's (Summer)," but it was worn by most aircrew and even servicemen who weren't flyers.
13 Brown, *The Mighty Men of the 381st: Heroes All*, 8.
14 Ibid., 19.
15 Ibid., 22–23.
16 Winston Churchill speech, May 19, 1943. Joint Session of Congress, Washington, D.C.
17 Effectively changing radio channels.
18 The name for flying control in Prestwick, Scotland.
19 Brown, *The Mighty Men of the 381st: Heroes All*, 17–18.

20 Ibid., 19.
21 Ibid., 19.
22 To rotate the blades until they are edgewise to the flight direction and airflow, thereby reducing drag.
23 James Good Brown, *A Cup of Tea* (Unpublished), 2.
24 Brown, *The Mighty Men of the 381st: Heroes All*, 25.
25 In the case of the *Queen Elizabeth*, and similar liners like the RMS *Queen Mary*, the ship used her high, sustained speed to elude U-boats. This was too fast for the Allied convoys plodding across the Atlantic.
26 Brown, *The Mighty Men of the 381st: Heroes All*, 25.
27 Ibid., 27.
28 Ibid., 27.
29 Ibid., 2.
30 Ibid., 27.

Chapter 3

1 Paul Francis, Richard Flagg and Graham Crisp, "Nine Thousand Miles of Concrete: A Review of Second World War Temporary Airfields in England." (Historic England, January 2016), 7.
2 Paul Bingley, "Taking the Fortress to War," *FlyPast Magazine*, May 2016: 18–21.
3 Brown, *A Cup of Tea*, 38.
4 Olive Foulds, "Wartime Services Canteen in Ridgewell." Interview by BBC Essex, 1990. Essex Record Office.
5 Brown, *The Mighty Men of the 381st: Heroes All*, 30.
6 Ibid., 30–31.
7 Arthur Travers Harris and Sebastian Cox, *Despatch on War Operations: 23 February 1942, to 8 May 1945* (Routledge: 1995), 196.
8 Cliff T. Bishop, *Fortresses of the Big Triangle First* (Bishop Stortford: East Anglia Books: 1986), 60.
9 Brown, *The Mighty Men of the 381st: Heroes All*, 39.
10 Ibid., 42.
11 The point where the "bomb run" towards the target commenced.
12 An acronym for the German word *Flugabwehrkanone*, meaning "air defence cannon" (anti-aircraft fire).
13 The USAAF numbered its aircraft engines left to right (1–4) as viewed from the pilot's seat.
14 An abbreviation for *Stammlager Luft III*, meaning 'Main Camp, Air, III'—a *Luftwaffe*-run POW camp near Sagan, Germany (now Żagań, Poland).
15 Essentially an autopilot, but also used also used to transfer flight control to the bombardier and the Norden bombsight during the bomb run.
16 Brown, *The Mighty Men of the 381st: Heroes All*, 45.
17 Conway S. Hall, *From Pyote to Fortress Europe*. Interview by Vernon L. Williams. Old Segundo Productions, 2013.
18 Brown, *The Mighty Men of the 381st: Heroes All*, 46.
19 Joe H. Willis, *From Pyote to Fortress Europe*. Interview by Vernon L. Williams. Old Segundo Productions, 2013.
20 Ibid.
21 Brown, *The Mighty Men of the 381st: Heroes All*, 51.
22 Lt. Col. Ernest Gaillard, Jr., *Flight Surgeon* (Bloomington: 1stBooks, 2005), 6.
23 Brown, *The Mighty Men of the 381st: Heroes All*, 52.
24 Ibid., 52.
25 Derek Wyndham Mayes, *The Airmen of Ridgewell: A History of Ridgewell Airfield* (Self-published: 2007), 94–98.
26 Roger A. Freeman, *Mighty Eighth War Diary* (London: Jane's Publishing Company Limited, 1981), 70.
27 Brown, *The Mighty Men of the 381st: Heroes All*, 53.
28 Joe H. Willis, *From Pyote to Fortress Europe*. Interview by Vernon L. Williams. Old Segundo Productions, 2013.
29 Brown, *The Mighty Men of the 381st: Heroes All*, 55.
30 381st Bombardment Group (Heavy). "535th Bomb Squadron War Diary." [Accessed 2015]. Available at: http://www.381st.org/Unit-History/War-Diaries/535th-BS-War-Diary.

31 Colloquial name given to an "administrative aircraft" used for a variety of non-combat roles.
32 Headquarters, 1st Bombardment Wing, AOP 634, B-A/G-3, 452.1, dated 7 June 1943, Subject: 'Naming of Aircraft," Signed by Bartlett Beaman, 1st Air Division Headquarters Heritage Society Archives.
33 John M. Carah, Lt. Col. USAF (Ret.), *Achtung! Achtung! Die Flugfestungen Kommen!* (Brighton: Elbow Lane Books, 2006), 14. John Carah would go on to become Assistant Air Attaché with the US Legation in Bern, while working closely with the head of the country's Office of Strategic Services, Allen Dulles.
34 Ibid., 12.
35 Brown, *The Mighty Men of the 381st: Heroes All*, 58–60.
36 Ibid., 66.
37 Ron Mackay, *Ridgewell's Flying Fortresses: The 381st Bombardment Group (H) in World War II* (Atglen: Schiffer Publishing, 2000), 30.
38 Ibid., 31.
39 The Wall of Valor Project. "Charles Pershing London." [Accessed 2015]. Available at: https://valor.militarytimes.com/hero/31832.
40 Mackay, *Ridgewell's Flying Fortresses*, 32.
41 Brown, *The Mighty Men of the 381st: Heroes All*, 64.

Chapter 4

1 Brown, *The Mighty Men of the 381st: Heroes All*, 62.
2 A portion of the Casablanca Directive detailing (among others) the German aircraft industry and the country's transportation system as primary targets.
3 Roger W. Burwell, *My War* (Self-published: 1990), 7.
4 Ibid., 8.
5 John Comer, *Combat Crew* (Great Britain: Leo Cooper, 1988), 1.
6 Ibid., xiv.
7 Ibid., 4.
8 Donald L. Miller, *Masters of the Air: America's Bomber Boys Who Fought the Air War Against Nazi Germany* (New York: Simon & Schuster, 2007), 7.
9 Martin Middlebrook and Chris Everitt, *The Bomber Command War Diaries* (Great Britain: Midland, 2011), 410.
10 A gyroscope-stabilized bombsight developed by Dutch engineer Carl L. Norden in the 1930s.
11 Pär Henningsson, "The Story of Georgia Rebel." *Sweden After the Flak*, December 1999: 3–4.
12 Stone, *Triumphant We Fly*, 34.
13 Ibid., 34.
14 Ibid., 34.
15 Ibid., 36.
16 Brown, *The Mighty Men of the 381st: Heroes All*, 86.
17 Ibid., 87.
18 Middlebrook and Everitt, *The Bomber Command War Diaries*, 413–414.
19 Comer, *Combat Crew*, 11.
20 Ibid., 13.
21 Brown, *The Mighty Men of the 381st: Heroes All*, 91.
22 Ibid., 94.
23 Ibid., 93.

Intermission: The Bomb Group

1 Robin Neillands, *The Bomber War: Arthur Harris and the Allied Bomber Offensive 1939–1945* (London: John Murray, 2001), 166.

Chapter 5

1 Bishop, *Fortresses of the Big Triangle First*, 65.
2 Gaillard Jr., *Flight Surgeon*, 19.

3 Ibid., 24–28
4 Spivey, Leonard, Oral History, National World War II Museum. [Accessed 2015]. Available at: https://www.ww2online.org/view/leonard-spivey#segment-4.
5 Ibid.
6 Brown, *The Mighty Men of the 381st: Heroes All*, 99.
7 Everett F. Malone, unpublished combat diary.
8 Stone, *Triumphant We Fly*, 40.
9 381st Bombardment Group (Heavy). "534th Bomb Squadron War Diary." [Accessed 2015]. Available at: http://www.381st.org/Unit-History/War-Diaries/534th-BS-War-Diary.
10 Brown, *The Mighty Men of the 381st: Heroes All*, 103.
11 Comer, *Combat Crew*, 24.
12 Ibid., 25.
13 Ibid., 29.
14 Ibid., 31.
15 Ibid., 33.
16 Brown, *The Mighty Men of the 381st: Heroes All*, 109.
17 Martin Middlebrook, *The Schweinfurt–Regensburg Mission* (Barnsley: Pen & Sword, 1983), 71.
18 Stone, *Triumphant We Fly*, 41.
19 Middlebrook, *The Schweinfurt–Regensburg Mission*, 192.
20 Ibid., 209–210.
21 An acronym for *vier motoriges* or "four engines."
22 Middlebrook, *The Schweinfurt–Regensburg Mission*, 242.
23 Stone, *Triumphant We Fly*, 47.
24 Middlebrook, *The Schweinfurt–Regensburg Mission*, 228.
25 Stone, *Triumphant We Fly*, 41.
26 Ibid., 45.
27 Spivey, Leonard, Oral History, National World War II Museum. [Accessed 2015]. Available at: https://www.ww2online.org/view/leonard-spivey#segment-5.
28 Stone, *Triumphant We Fly*, 44.
29 Ibid., 44.
30 Brown, *The Mighty Men of the 381st: Heroes All*, 114.
31 Stone, *Triumphant We Fly*, 41–42.
32 Conway S. Hall, *From Pyote to Fortress Europe*. Interview by Vernon L. Williams. Old Segundo Productions, 2013.
33 Burwell, *My War*, 11.
34 Mackay, *Ridgewell's Flying Fortresses*, 45.

Chapter 6

1 Brown, *The Mighty Men of the 381st: Heroes All*, 117–118.
2 Ibid., 118–119.
3 Comer, *Combat Crew*, 45.
4 Spivey, Leonard, Oral History, National World War II Museum. [Accessed 2015]. Available at: https://www.ww2online.org/view/leonard-spivey#segment-6.
5 Gaillard Jr., *Flight Surgeon*, 28–29.
6 Comer, *Combat Crew*, 51.
7 Gaillard Jr., *Flight Surgeon*, 29.
8 Comer, *Combat Crew*, 57.
9 Ibid., 60.
10 Norman Longmate, *Hitler's Rockets* (Barnsley: Frontline Books, 2009), 69.
11 Gaillard Jr., *Flight Surgeon*, 31.
12 National Archives Catalog, Nelson, Robert E (1st Lt.), 5554811, E and E 170.
13 Ibid.
14 Freeman, *Mighty Eighth War Diary*, 102.
15 Gaillard Jr., *Flight Surgeon*, 31.

16 Comer, *Combat Crew*, 71.
17 Missing Air Crew Report 473, Charles F. Bang, Letter, March 1, 1946.
18 Missing Air Crew Report 473, Statement Concerning Missing Aircraft, Elton D. Jukes.
19 Comer, *Combat Crew*, 79.
20 Ibid., 80.
21 Ibid., 92.
22 Middlebrook and Everitt, *The Bomber Command War Diaries*, 430.
23 Comer, *Combat Crew*, 97.
24 Ibid., 99.
25 Ibid., 102.

Intermission: Evolution of the B-17

1 Jablonski, *Flying Fortress*, 6.

Chapter 7

1 Gaillard Jr., *Flight Surgeon*, 33.
2 351st Bomb Group "Mission 39 – 15 Sep. 1943." [Accessed 2015]. Available at: http://www.351st.org/351st-Missions/Mission039/Mission39.html.
3 Comer, *Combat Crew*, 105–106.
4 Gaillard Jr., *Flight Surgeon*, 35.
5 Comer, *Combat Crew*, 107–108.
6 Gaillard Jr., *Flight Surgeon*, 35.
7 Ibid., 35.
8 Ibid., 35–36.
9 Comer, *Combat Crew*, 112–113.
10 BBC, *WW2 People's War* "A Teenage Boy's Memories." [Accessed 2015]. Available at: https://www.bbc.co.uk/history/ww2peopleswar/stories/08/a9900008.shtml.
11 Middlebrook and Everitt, *The Bomber Command War Diaries*, 432.
12 Brown, *The Mighty Men of the 381st: Heroes All*, 157.
13 BBC, *WW2 People's War* "A Teenage Boy's Memories." [Accessed 2015]. Available at: https://www.bbc.co.uk/history/ww2peopleswar/stories/08/a9900008.shtml.
14 Gaillard Jr., *Flight Surgeon*, 37.
15 Brown, *The Mighty Men of the 381st: Heroes All*, 157.
16 381st Bombardment Group (Heavy). "1st Combat Bombardment Wing (H)." [Accessed 2015]. Available at: http://www.381st.org/Unit-Histories/War-Diaries/1st-CBW-War-Diary.
17 381st Bombardment Group (Heavy). "Two War Time Articles Featuring Melvin Hecker." [Accessed 2015]. Available at: http://www.381st.org/Unit-History/Stories/Authors-E-H/Articles.
18 Comer, *Combat Crew*, 115–116.
19 John C. Leverette, unpublished combat diary.
20 Marshall J. Thixton, George E. Moffat and John J. O'Neil, *Bombs Away* (Connecticut: FNP Military Division, 1998), 65.
21 Lightweight and designed to be expendable as the fighters would drop them once empty or before engaging the enemy.
22 Brown, *The Mighty Men of the 381st: Heroes All*, 155.
23 Everett F. Malone, unpublished combat diary.
24 Stone, *Triumphant We Fly*, 54.
25 Ibid., 54–55.
26 Ibid., 55.
27 Ibid., 55.
28 Comer, *Combat Crew*, 116.
29 Burwell, *My War*, 14.
30 Ibid., 14.
31 Ibid., 15.

32 David A. McCarthy, *Fear No More: A B-17 Navigator's Journey* (Pittsburgh: Cottage Wordsmiths, 1991), 19.
33 Ibid., 19.
34 Ibid., 16–17.
35 Ibid., 23.
36 Stone, *Triumphant We Fly*, 61.
37 351st Bomb Group "Mission 46 – 8 Oct. 1943." [Accessed 2015]. Available at: www.351st.org/351stMissions/Mission046/Mission46.html.
38 McCarthy, *Fear No More*, 24.
39 Comer, *Combat Crew*, 125.
40 Burwell, *My War*, 15.
41 Stone, *Triumphant We Fly*, 62.
42 Ibid., 62.
43 Burwell, *My War*, 17.
44 Stone, *Triumphant We Fly*, 62.
45 Ibid., 58.
46 Ibid., 60.
47 Missing Air Crew Report 885, Edwin D. Frost, Individual Casualty Questionnaire.
48 Missing Air Crew Report 885, William F. Cormany, Jr., Individual Casualty Questionnaire.
49 Stone, *Triumphant We Fly*, 57.
50 Comer, *Combat Crew*, 127.
51 Ibid., 128.
52 Ibid., 128.
53 Brown, *The Mighty Men of the 381st: Heroes All*, 166.
54 McCarthy, *Fear No More*, 29.
55 Ibid., 27.
56 Ibid., 28.
57 Brown, *The Mighty Men of the 381st: Heroes All*, 188–189.
58 Freeman, *Mighty Eighth War Diary*, 123.
59 The Wall of Valor Project. "Thomas Duncan Sellers." [Accessed 2015]. Available at: https://valor.militarytimes.com/hero/32753.
60 Brown, *The Mighty Men of the 381st: Heroes All*, 170–183.

Chapter 8

1 Brown, *The Mighty Men of the 381st: Heroes All*, 169.
2 Ibid., 192.
3 Gaillard Jr., *Flight Surgeon*, 43.
4 Comer, *Combat Crew*, 135.
5 McCarthy, *Fear No More*, 44.
6 Comer, *Combat Crew*, 139.
7 Brown, *The Mighty Men of the 381st: Heroes All*, 207.
8 Ibid., 191.
9 McCarthy, *Fear No More*, 54.
10 The Library of Congress. "Churchill and the Great Republic." Winston Churchill letter to Jacob Devers, October 11, 1943. [Accessed 2021]. Available at: https://www.loc.gov/exhibits/churchill/interactive/_html/wc0205.html.
11 Freeman, *Mighty Eighth War Diary*, 125.
12 McCarthy, *Fear No More*, 55.
13 Gaillard Jr., *Flight Surgeon*, 54.
14 Comer, *Combat Crew*, 164.
15 Used by crews to describe a mission where minimal resistance from the enemy was expected.
16 Comer, *Combat Crew*, 166.
17 McCarthy, *Fear No More*, 70.
18 Comer, *Combat Crew*, 168–169.

19 A ground loop occurs when the aircraft inadvertently spins around on one wheel, sometimes digging a wingtip into the ground in the more severe cases, or even cartwheeling. It can be caused by a sudden crosswind, a burst tire or stuck brake, or loss of power on one side for multi-engine aircraft and can even happen at low speeds when there is little to no "authority" from the control surfaces (not enough airflow for them to effectively counter the pending loss of control). A ground loop can also be deliberately performed by the pilot if unable to stop in time due to brake loss or limited space.
20 Miller, *Masters of the Air*, 210.
21 Comer, *Combat Crew*, 171.
22 McCarthy, *Fear No More*, 71.
23 Gaillard Jr., *Flight Surgeon*, 48.
24 Brown, *The Mighty Men of the 381st: Heroes All*, 214.
25 McCarthy, *Fear No More*, 72.
26 Brown, *The Mighty Men of the 381st: Heroes All*, 215.
27 Olof M. Ballinger eventually returned to England on December 3, after crossing the Pyrenees himself, guided only by the sun and stars.

Chapter 9

1 381st Bombardment Group (Heavy). "1st Combat Bombardment Wing (H)." [Accessed 2015]. Available at: http://www.381st.org/Unit-Histories/War-Diaries/1st-CBW-War-Diary.
2 Comer, *Combat Crew*, 178.
3 McCarthy, *Fear No More*, 80.
4 Comer, *Combat Crew*, 179.
5 Gaillard Jr., *Flight Surgeon*, 56.
6 Comer, *Combat Crew*, 180–181.
7 Paid for by funds raised by US civilians, in this case the residents of Franklin County, Missouri.
8 Stone, *Triumphant We Fly*, 75.
9 The wreckage of *Blowin' Bessie* was eventually discovered during Dutch dredging operations in 1969.
10 Comer, *Combat Crew*, 184.
11 Ibid., 185.
12 Brown, *The Mighty Men of the 381st: Heroes All*, 217.
13 McCarthy, *Fear No More*, 88.
14 Gaillard Jr., *Flight Surgeon*, 58.
15 McCarthy, *Fear No More*, 88.
16 Gaillard Jr., *Flight Surgeon*, 59.
17 381st Bombardment Group (Heavy). "535th Bomb Squadron War Diary." [Accessed 2015]. Available at: http://www.381st.org/Unit-History/War-Diaries/535th-BS-War-Diary.
18 381st Bombardment Group (Heavy). "532nd Bomb Squadron War Diary." [Accessed 2015]. Available at: http://www.381st.org/Unit-Histories/532nd-Bomb-Squadron-War-Diary.
19 Stone, *Triumphant We Fly*, 75.
20 351st Bomb Group "Mission 54 – 16 Nov. 1943." [Accessed 2015]. Available at: www.351st.org/351stMissions/Mission054/Mission54.html.
21 Gaillard Jr., *Flight Surgeon*, 59.
22 Brown, *The Mighty Men of the 381st: Heroes All*, 222.
23 Bob Korkuc, *Finding a Fallen Hero* (Norman: University of Oklahoma Press, 2008), 144.
24 McCarthy, *Fear No More*, 91–92.
25 Robert L. Singleton Jr., *To Great Yoho and Back* (West Stockbridge: Bearcliff Publishing, 2002), 129.
26 McCarthy, *Fear No More*, 89.
27 Brown, *The Mighty Men of the 381st: Heroes All*, 226–227.
28 381st Bombardment Group (Heavy). "1st Combat Bombardment Wing (H)." [Accessed 2015]. Available at: http://www.381st.org/Unit-Histories/War-Diaries/1st-CBW-War-Diary.
29 Brown, *The Mighty Men of the 381st: Heroes All*, 222.
30 Ibid., 227.
31 McCarthy, *Fear No More*, 97.

32 Bill M. Yancy, *December 1, 1943: We Knew We Were in for a Long Day* (Self-published, 2013), 22–23.
33 Ibid., 23.
34 Ibid., 23.
35 Ibid., 32.
36 McCarthy, *Fear No More*, 101.
37 Brown, *The Mighty Men of the 381st: Heroes All*, 225.

Chapter 10

1 Stone, *Triumphant We Fly*, 53.
2 Brown, *The Mighty Men of the 381st: Heroes All*, 230.
3 Gaillard Jr., *Flight Surgeon*, 63.
4 American slang term for sexually transmitted diseases.
5 Gaillard Jr., *Flight Surgeon*, 63.
6 Comer, *Combat Crew*, 210.
7 Ibid., 212.
8 Brown, *The Mighty Men of the 381st: Heroes All*, 238.
9 Gaillard Jr., *Flight Surgeon*, 66.
10 Comer, *Combat Crew*, 214.
11 McCarthy, *Fear No More*, 104.
12 Comer, *Combat Crew*, 220.
13 Ibid., 223.
14 Brown, *The Mighty Men of the 381st: Heroes All*, 250.
15 Ibid., 250.
16 Gaillard Jr., *Flight Surgeon*, 66.
17 The Tortoise stove was a patented solid fuel heating appliance first built in 1830 by Charles Portway, an ironmonger of Halstead, Essex (just eight miles from Ridgewell). The success of Portway's Tortoise stove saw 17,000 sold worldwide.
18 Ibid., 66.
19 Ibid., 67.
20 Stone, *Triumphant We Fly*, 77.
21 John C. Leverette, unpublished combat diary.
22 Comer, *Combat Crew*, 226.
23 Ibid., 229.
24 Ibid., 230.
25 Ibid., 230.
26 B-17 Flying Fortress. "B-17 42-3563 / Great Profile." [Accessed 2016]. Available at: https://b17flyingfortress.de/en/b17/42-3563-great-profile/. B-17G-5-DL, Serial Number 42-3563.
27 Missing Air Crew Report 1724, Richard J. Niederriter, Missing Crew Statement.
28 Gaillard Jr., *Flight Surgeon*, 69.
29 Comer, *Combat Crew*, 232.
30 A device fitted externally to the aircraft that measures flow velocity, i.e., airspeed.
31 Gaillard Jr., *Flight Surgeon*, 70.
32 Comer, *Combat Crew*, 241.
33 McCarthy, *Fear No More*, 127.
34 Brown, *The Mighty Men of the 381st: Heroes All*, 259.
35 Comer, *Combat Crew*, 247–248.
36 Ibid., 248.
37 Brown, *The Mighty Men of the 381st: Heroes All*, 279.

Intermission: Manning the Forts

1 Miller, *Masters of the Air*, 164.

Chapter 11

1 Gaillard Jr., *Flight Surgeon*, 185–193.
2 McCarthy, *Fear No More*, 145.
3 Ibid., 146.
4 Brown, *The Mighty Men of the 381st: Heroes All*, 285.
5 McCarthy, *Fear No More*, 147.
6 Self-sealing fuel cells installed in the wings of newer B-17s to extend their range.
7 McCarthy, *Fear No More*, 148.
8 Ibid., 149.
9 Brown, *The Mighty Men of the 381st: Heroes All*, 291–292.
10 Comer, *Combat Crew*, 251.
11 Freeman, *Mighty Eighth War Diary*, 163.
12 Comer, *Combat Crew*, 255.
13 Ibid., 256.
14 Missing Air Crew Report 1962, Otis A. Montgomery.
15 Missing Air Crew Report 1962, Frank R. Bisagna.
16 Comer, *Combat Crew*, 258.
17 Brown, *The Mighty Men of the 381st: Heroes All*, 288.
18 Ibid., 337.
19 Theodore Homdrom, *Mission Memories* (Self-published, 2002), 16.
20 Ibid., 36.
21 Missing Air Crew Report 1873, Harry H. Ullom, Individual Casualty Questionnaire.
22 Stone, *Triumphant We Fly*, 81.
23 Comer, *Combat Crew*, 258.
24 John W. Howland, Capt. USAF (Ret.), *Diary of a Pathfinder Navigator* (private papers, 1994), 15.
25 Brown, *The Mighty Men of the 381st: Heroes All*, 298.
26 Gaillard Jr., *Flight Surgeon*, 79.
27 Comer, *Combat Crew*, 263.
28 Howland, *Diary of a Pathfinder Navigator*, 15.
29 *Hellcat* was eventually recovered during Dutch dredging operations in June 1966.
30 Missing Air Crew Report 1876, Bernard M. Keene and L. T. Patterson, Individual Casualty Questionnaires.
31 McCarthy, *Fear No More*, 152.
32 Brown, *The Mighty Men of the 381st: Heroes All*, 299–301.

Chapter 12

1 Howland, *Diary of a Pathfinder Navigator*, 16.
2 Gaillard Jr., *Flight Surgeon*, 80.
3 American slang for a London prostitute. Howland, *Diary of a Pathfinder Navigator*, 17.
4 Aircraft take off and land into wind to generate as much lift as possible at low speeds.
5 Howland, *Diary of a Pathfinder Navigator*, 18.
6 Homdrom, *Mission Memories*, 43.
7 Howland, *Diary of a Pathfinder Navigator*, 18.
8 Middlebrook and Everitt, *The Bomber Command War Diaries*, 466.
9 Howland, *Diary of a Pathfinder Navigator*, 18.
10 Ibid., 19.
11 Brown, *The Mighty Men of the 381st: Heroes All*, 302.
12 Gaillard Jr., *Flight Surgeon*, 81.
13 Howland, *Diary of a Pathfinder Navigator*, 20.
14 381st Bombardment Group (Heavy). "533rd Bomb Squadron War Diary." [Accessed 2015]. Available at: http://www.381st.org/Unit-Histories/War-Diaries/533rd-Bomb-Squadron-War-Diary.
15 Gaillard Jr., *Flight Surgeon*, 82.

16 Brown, *The Mighty Men of the 381st: Heroes All*, 306.
17 Ibid., 310.
18 Missing Air Crew Report 2495, Bill Ridley, Statement.
19 Brown, *The Mighty Men of the 381st: Heroes All*, 311.
20 Howland, *Diary of a Pathfinder Navigator*, 21.
21 Ibid., 21.
22 Brown, *The Mighty Men of the 381st: Heroes All*, 316.
23 Howland, *Diary of a Pathfinder Navigator*, 24–25.
24 Ibid., 26.
25 David R. Osborne, *They Came from Over the Pond* (Madison: 381st Bomb Group Memorial Association, 1999), 65.
26 The News-Courier. "WWII hero's life vest discovered in France." [Accessed 2015]. Available at: http://www.cnhinewsservice.com/national/index.php?mode=view&id=6624.
27 Ibid.
28 Howland, *Diary of a Pathfinder Navigator*, 29.
29 Ibid., 31.
30 Fold3. "WWII US Air Force Photos." [Accessed 2016]. Available at: https://www.fold3.com/image/32018524.
31 Howland, *Diary of a Pathfinder Navigator*, 32.
32 James Holland, *Big Week* (London: Penguin Books Ltd, 2018), 249.

Chapter 13

1 Middlebrook and Everitt, *The Bomber Command War Diaries*, 473–474.
2 McCarthy, *Fear No More*, 180.
3 Ibid., 180.
4 Mackay, *Ridgewell's Flying Fortresses*, 92.
5 Matthew Walsh, PhD. "Lost Flyboys: The story of World War II airmen, Marvin Dille and William Meehan." *Iowa History Journal*, May/June 2019. http://iowahistoryjournal.com/lost-flyboys.
6 Howland, *Diary of a Pathfinder Navigator*, 33.
7 Brown, *The Mighty Men of the 381st: Heroes All*, 323–324.
8 Gaillard Jr., *Flight Surgeon*, 90.
9 Howland, *Diary of a Pathfinder Navigator*, 33.
10 Ibid., 34.
11 381st Bombardment Group (Heavy). "533rd Bomb Squadron War Diary." [Accessed 2015]. Available at: http://www.381st.org/Unit-Histories/War-Diaries/533rd-Bomb-Squadron-War-Diary.
12 Howland, *Diary of a Pathfinder Navigator*, 34.
13 Tommy LaMore and Dan A. Baker, *One Man's War* (Lanham: Taylor Trade Publishing, 2002), 68.
14 Casey Bukowski. Interview by Paul Bingley. September 5, 2020. Audio, 26:10.
15 Howland, *Diary of a Pathfinder Navigator*, 34.
16 Ibid., 34.
17 LaMore and Baker, *One Man's War*, 69.
18 Missing Air Crew Report 2936, AAA Group – Muenster, AAA Sub-Group – Bielefeld, Combat Report, translation.
19 A sideslip is where the longitudinal axis of the aircraft is at an angle to the flightpath but the aircraft continues on the same heading. It is aerodynamically inefficient so can be used deliberately to lose height quickly (for example, in a short-field landing).
20 LaMore and Baker, *One Man's War*, 72–73.
21 Brown, *The Mighty Men of the 381st: Heroes All*, 331.
22 Ibid., 330.
23 Howland, *Diary of a Pathfinder Navigator*, 35.
24 McCarthy, *Fear No More*, 186.
25 Howland, *Diary of a Pathfinder Navigator*, 36.
26 *Star-Spangled Banner*, an air-dropped newspaper written in German.

27 Korkuc, *Finding a Fallen Hero*, 124.
28 Howland, *Diary of a Pathfinder Navigator*, 37.
29 Korkuc, *Finding a Fallen Hero*, 229.
30 381st Bombardment Group (Heavy). "533rd Bomb Squadron War Diary." [Accessed 2015]. Available at: http://www.381st.org/Unit-Histories/War-Diaries/533rd-Bomb-Squadron-War-Diary.
31 381st Bombardment Group (Heavy). "1st Combat Bombardment Wing (H)." [Accessed 2015]. Available at: http://www.381st.org/Unit-Histories/War-Diaries/1st-CBW-War-Diary.
32 Miller, *Masters of the Air*, 264.
33 Holland, *Big Week*, 355.
34 Howland, *Diary of a Pathfinder Navigator*, 38.

Chapter 14

1 The Army Air Forces Aid Society, *The Official Guide to the Army Air Forces AAF* (New York: Pocket Books Inc., 1944), 128.
2 Edward C. Carr, *On Final Approach* (Coupeville: Self-published, 2002), 135.
3 Benjamin W. Bishop, *Jimmy Doolittle: The Commander Behind the Legend* (Montgomery: Air University Press, 2015), 88.
4 McCarthy, *Fear No More*, 196.
5 Brown, *The Mighty Men of the 381st: Heroes All*, 337–338.
6 Ibid., 336–356.
7 Howland, *Diary of a Pathfinder Navigator*, 41.
8 Ibid., 41.
9 Gaillard Jr., *Flight Surgeon*, 96.
10 McCarthy, *Fear No More*, 192.
11 Mackay, *Ridgewell's Flying Fortresses*, 103.
12 Howland, *Diary of a Pathfinder Navigator*, 42.
13 Ibid., 42.
14 McCarthy, *Fear No More*, 193.
15 Homdrom, *Mission Memories*, 69.
16 Howland, *Diary of a Pathfinder Navigator*, 43.
17 Mackay, *Ridgewell's Flying Fortresses*, 104.
18 McCarthy, *Fear No More*, 195.
19 Howland, *Diary of a Pathfinder Navigator*, 44.
20 Gaillard Jr., *Flight Surgeon*, 96.
21 Howland, *Diary of a Pathfinder Navigator*, 45.
22 Ibid., 45.
23 Ibid., 46.
24 Gaillard Jr., *Flight Surgeon*, 98–99.
25 Howland, *Diary of a Pathfinder Navigator*, 46.
26 McCarthy, *Fear No More*, 199.
27 Howland, *Diary of a Pathfinder Navigator*, 46.
28 Ibid., 47.
29 McCarthy, *Fear No More*, 200–201.
30 Howland, *Diary of a Pathfinder Navigator*, 48–49.

Chapter 15

1 LaMore and Baker, *One Man's War*, 84.
2 381st Bombardment Group (Heavy). "535th Bomb Squadron War Diary." [Accessed 2015]. Available at: http://www.381st.org/Unit-History/War-Diaries/535th-BS-War-Diary.
3 Howland, *Diary of a Pathfinder Navigator*, 50.
4 Nankivell, Barbara. "The Deserted Village." Transcript of an interview by John Irwin. BBC, July 27, 1945.
5 Howland, *Diary of a Pathfinder Navigator*, 50.
6 Troy H. Jones, Jr., *Some Recollections of a Florida Cracker* (Unpublished memoir: 1992), 58.

7 An Air Medal was awarded for the first five sorties or to an individual airman who shot down an enemy aircraft. Oak Leaf Clusters (ribbon devices) were added for each additional accomplishment.
8 Gaillard Jr., *Flight Surgeon*, 99.
9 McCarthy, *Fear No More*, 203.
10 Ibid., 203.
11 Ibid., 204.
12 Ibid., 205.
13 Gaillard Jr., *Flight Surgeon*, 100.
14 Howland, *Diary of a Pathfinder Navigator*, 51.
15 McCarthy, *Fear No More*, 208.
16 Homdrom, *Mission Memories*, 76.
17 Mackay, *Ridgewell's Flying Fortresses*, 108.
18 Howland, *Diary of a Pathfinder Navigator*, 52.
19 Ibid., 52.
20 Mackay, *Ridgewell's Flying Fortresses*, 107.
21 Wayne B. Pegg, unpublished combat diary.
22 LaMore and Baker, *One Man's War*, 85.
23 Ibid., 86.
24 Brown, *The Mighty Men of the 381st: Heroes All*, 376.
25 Ibid., 377.
26 LaMore and Baker, *One Man's War*, 87–90.
27 Brown, *The Mighty Men of the 381st: Heroes All*, 378.
28 Howland, *Diary of a Pathfinder Navigator*, 53.
29 McCarthy, *Fear No More*, 210.
30 Ibid., 211.
31 Ibid., 212–213.
32 Stone, *Triumphant We Fly*, 95–96.
33 Brown, *The Mighty Men of the 381st: Heroes All*, 383.
34 Homdrom, *Mission Memories*, 87.
35 Howland, *Diary of a Pathfinder Navigator*, 54.
36 Favian R. Calderon, unpublished combat diary.
37 381st Bombardment Group (Heavy). "1st Combat Bombardment Wing (H)." [Accessed 2015]. Available at: http://www.381st.org/Unit-Histories/War-Diaries/1st-CBW-War-Diary.
38 Stone, *Triumphant We Fly*, 96.
39 Gaillard Jr., *Flight Surgeon*, 106.
40 Brown, *The Mighty Men of the 381st: Heroes All*, 389.

Chapter 16

1 Wayne B. Pegg, unpublished combat diary.
2 Accident Report No. 44-4-8-520. Leslie A. Bond, Statement.
3 Ibid.
4 Ibid., Conway S. Hall, Statement.
5 Ibid.
6 Homdrom, *Mission Memories*, 91.
7 Jones, *Some Recollections of a Florida Cracker*, 75.
8 Brown, *The Mighty Men of the 381st: Heroes All*, 393.
9 Gaillard Jr., *Flight Surgeon*, 108.
10 Mackay, *Ridgewell's Flying Fortresses*, 121.
11 Gaillard Jr., *Flight Surgeon*, 108.
12 381st Bombardment Group (Heavy). "533rd Bomb Squadron War Diary." [Accessed 2015]. Available at: http://www.381st.org/Unit-Histories/War-Diaries/533rd-Bomb-Squadron-War-Diary.
13 Howland, *Diary of a Pathfinder Navigator*, 58.
14 Ibid., 58.
15 McCarthy, *Fear No More*, 215–216.

16 Gaillard Jr., *Flight Surgeon*, 112.

Chapter 17

1 Calvin University. "Our Hitler," Goebbels's 1944 Speech on Hitler's 55th Birthday. Available at: https://research.calvin.edu/german-propaganda-archive/unser44.htm.
2 Adam L. Gruen, *Preemptive Defense, Allied Air Power Versus Hitler's V-Weapons, 1943–1945*, (Air Force History and Museums Program, 1998), 4.
3 Gaillard Jr., *Flight Surgeon*, 112.
4 Osborne, *They Came from Over the Pond*, 87–88.
5 Ibid., 88.
6 Middlebrook and Everitt, *The Bomber Command War Diaries*, 497.
7 Brown, *The Mighty Men of the 381st: Heroes All*, 549–550.
8 Three aircraft manufacturers built the B-17: Boeing (BO), Douglas (DL) and Vega (VE).
9 Brown, *The Mighty Men of the 381st: Heroes All*, 551.
10 Emily Yellin, *Our Mothers' War* (New York: Free Press, 2005), 83.
11 Brown, *The Mighty Men of the 381st: Heroes All*, 550.
12 Emma Soames, *Mary Churchill's War* (Two Roads, Unabridged Audiobook, 2021), 16:55–17:13.
13 Brown, *The Mighty Men of the 381st: Heroes All*, 552.
14 Wayne B. Pegg, unpublished combat diary.
15 Howland, *Diary of a Pathfinder Navigator*, 60.
16 James H. Chandler, unpublished combat diary.
17 Osborne, *They Came from Over the Pond*, 91.
18 Howland, *Diary of a Pathfinder Navigator*, 62.
19 Osborne, *They Came from Over the Pond*, 91.
20 Howland, *Diary of a Pathfinder Navigator*, 62.
21 Gaillard Jr., *Flight Surgeon*, 115.
22 James H. Chandler, unpublished combat diary.
23 Homdrom, *Mission Memories*, 94–95.
24 Wayne B. Pegg, unpublished combat diary.
25 Brown, *The Mighty Men of the 381st: Heroes All*, 396.
26 Homdrom, *Mission Memories*, 99.
27 Stone, *Triumphant We Fly*, 100.
28 Osborne, *They Came from Over the Pond*, 94.
29 Howland, *Diary of a Pathfinder Navigator*, 63.
30 Freeman, *Mighty Eighth War Diary*, 237.
31 James H. Chandler, unpublished combat diary.
32 Ibid.
33 Osborne, *They Came from Over the Pond*, 95.
34 Gaillard Jr., *Flight Surgeon*, 118.
35 Ibid., 118.

Chapter 18

1 Wayne B. Pegg, unpublished combat diary.
2 James H. Chandler, unpublished combat diary.
3 Gaillard Jr., *Flight Surgeon*, 119.
4 Howland, *Diary of a Pathfinder Navigator*, 64.
5 Ibid., 65.
6 Ibid., 66.
7 Missing Air Crew Report 2495, Francis W. Britenbaker, Statement.
8 Howland, *Diary of a Pathfinder Navigator*, 67.
9 Brown, *The Mighty Men of the 381st: Heroes All*, 398.

10 Howland, *Diary of a Pathfinder Navigator*, 67–68.
11 McCarthy, *Fear No More*, 218–219.
12 Osborne, *They Came from Over the Pond*, 99.
13 Stone, *Triumphant We Fly*, 102.
14 Ibid., 102.
15 Ibid., 103.
16 Ibid., 104.
17 Brown, *The Mighty Men of the 381st: Heroes All*, 404.
18 Howland, *Diary of a Pathfinder Navigator*, 70.
19 William Scruggs. Interview by David Gregory. May 8–17, 2000.
20 Gaillard Jr., *Flight Surgeon*, 134.

Intermission: Safety in Numbers

1 A colloquial term for an aircraft with a tailwheel, as opposed to those with tricycle landing gear, i.e., with a nosewheel.

Chapter 19

1 Howland, *Diary of a Pathfinder Navigator*, 72.
2 Ibid., 72.
3 Ibid., 73.
4 Brown, *The Mighty Men of the 381st: Heroes All*, 411.
5 Homdrom, *Mission Memories*, 111.
6 Howland, *Diary of a Pathfinder Navigator*, 76.
7 Gaillard Jr., *Flight Surgeon*, 135.
8 Ibid., 135.
9 Howland, *Diary of a Pathfinder Navigator*, 76.
10 Brown, *The Mighty Men of the 381st: Heroes All*, 415.
11 Howland, *Diary of a Pathfinder Navigator*, 78.
12 Ibid., 79.
13 The Warwick, supposed to be a successor for the venerable Vickers Wellington medium bomber, became best known for its ASR duties. Carrying an "airborne lifeboat" that could be dropped to downed airmen in the sea, Warwick crews often flew along known return routes to hopefully assist downed aircrew as quickly as possible.
14 Howland, *Diary of a Pathfinder Navigator*, 80.
15 James H. Chandler, unpublished combat diary.
16 Gaillard Jr., *Flight Surgeon*, 138.
17 R. Douglas Brown, *East Anglia 1944* (Lavenham: Terence Dalton Ltd, 1992), 95.
18 Gaillard Jr., *Flight Surgeon*, 139.
19 Ibid., 140.
20 Howland, *Diary of a Pathfinder Navigator*, 81.
21 Jones, *Some Recollections of a Florida Cracker*, 77.
22 Missing Air Crew Report 5991, Clifford Evans Jr., Statement.
23 Howland, *Diary of a Pathfinder Navigator*, 81.
24 Ibid., 82.
25 James H. Chandler, unpublished combat diary.
26 Homdrom, *Mission Memories*, 118–119.
27 Ibid., 121.
28 Howland, *Diary of a Pathfinder Navigator*, 84.

Chapter 20

1 Brown, *The Mighty Men of the 381st: Heroes All*, 421.

2 Homdrom, *Mission Memories*, 121.
3 Gaillard Jr., *Flight Surgeon*, 143.
4 Brown, *The Mighty Men of the 381st: Heroes All*, 410.
5 James H. Chandler, unpublished combat diary.
6 Gaillard Jr., *Flight Surgeon*, 144.
7 James H. Chandler, unpublished combat diary.
8 Brown, *The Mighty Men of the 381st: Heroes All*, 423–424.
9 Ibid., 572–575.
10 Missing Air Crew Report 6779, Leon S. Bucy, Statement.
11 Stone, *Triumphant We Fly*, 119.
12 Brown, *The Mighty Men of the 381st: Heroes All*, 559.
13 Ibid., 561–562.
14 Douglas E. Holt, *Lucky Dog* (Self-published, 2007), 60–61.
15 William Scruggs. Interview by David Gregory. May 8–17, 2000.
16 Brown, *The Mighty Men of the 381st: Heroes All*, 453.
17 Ibid., 451.
18 Holt, *Lucky Dog*, 63.
19 Brown, *The Mighty Men of the 381st: Heroes All*, 454.
20 Ibid., 455–456.
21 Holt, *Lucky Dog*, 67.
22 Gaillard Jr., *Flight Surgeon*, 210–211.
23 Holt, *Lucky Dog*, 70.
24 Ibid., 71.
25 James F. Grey, *Vanishing Contrails* (Bloomington: Worldclay, 2011), 371.
26 Gaillard Jr., *Flight Surgeon*, 152.

Intermission: The Sky Generals

1 The battle of Normandy following the landings on June 6, 1944.

Chapter 21

1 Gaillard Jr., *Flight Surgeon*, 152.
2 Ibid., 154.
3 Grey, *Vanishing Contrails*, 371.
4 Robert "Bob" Armstrong, *Friendly and Enemy Skies* (Hutchinson: Self-published, 2003), 44.
5 William Goudeket Jr., *From Pyote to Fortress Europe*. Interview by Vernon L. Williams. Old Segundo Productions, 2013.
6 Grey, *Vanishing Contrails*, 371.
7 The PFF *Dry Gulcher* (42-97594) was given the same name as the 532nd's 42-32088, which had been lost on mission #112 on May 19, 1944.
8 Francis G. Hawkins, *Dry Gulcher Down*. Interview by Vernon L. Williams. Old Segundo Productions.
9 Peter Morgan, *Dry Gulcher Down*. Interview by Vernon L. Williams. Old Segundo Productions.
10 For his actions in holding the burning *Dry Gulcher* for his crew to escape, Irving Moore was awarded a second DFC. He would subsequently go on to become a prominent television director, most notably of the 1980s series' *Dynasty* and *Dallas*, including the famed "Who Shot J.R.?" episode.
11 Peter Morgan, *Dry Gulcher Down*. Interview by Vernon L. Williams. Old Segundo Productions.
12 Ibid.
13 Grey, *Vanishing Contrails*, 372.
14 Armstrong, *Friendly and Enemy Skies*, 46.
15 Holt, *Lucky Dog*, 78.
16 The "Vargas girl" depicted on *French Dressing* was one of a number of "pin-ups" drawn by Peruvian-American artist, Alberto Vargas for *Esquire* magazine.

17 Armstrong, *Friendly and Enemy Skies*, 58.
18 Foil-backed strips of paper dumped from an aircraft to confuse ground-based anti-aircraft radars.
19 Armstrong, *Friendly and Enemy Skies*, 61.
20 Middlebrook and Everitt, *The Bomber Command War Diaries*, 563.
21 Holt, *Lucky Dog*, 84.
22 Armstrong, *Friendly and Enemy Skies*, 68.
23 Ibid., 72.
24 Ibid., 73–78.
25 Brown, *The Mighty Men of the 381st: Heroes All*, 562–564.
26 J. Ross Greene, *A Fortress and a Legacy* (CreateSpace Independent Publishing Platform: Self-published, 2015), 200.

Chapter 22

1 Armstrong, *Friendly and Enemy Skies*, 81.
2 Holt, *Lucky Dog*, 92.
3 A gunner who "toggled" a push-button to release an aircraft's bombs on the signal of a lead bombardier.
4 Greene, *A Fortress and a Legacy*, 190.
5 Holt, *Lucky Dog*, 93.
6 Brown, *The Mighty Men of the 381st: Heroes All*, 471.
7 Gaillard Jr., *Flight Surgeon*, 163.
8 Holt, *Lucky Dog*, 95.
9 Gaillard Jr., *Flight Surgeon*, 169.
10 Armstrong, *Friendly and Enemy Skies*, 90.
11 W. B. Courtney, "Army in the Sky," *Collier's Weekly*, November 11, 1944.
12 Lewis H. Brereton, *The Brereton Diaries* (New York: William Morrow and Company, 1946), 344.
13 Holt, *Lucky Dog*, 101–102.
14 Armstrong, *Friendly and Enemy Skies*, 92.
15 Ibid., 94.
16 Greene, *A Fortress and a Legacy*, 252.
17 Jones, *Some Recollections of a Florida Cracker*, 79.
18 Armstrong, *Friendly and Enemy Skies*, 97.
19 Robert Gilbert, *The View from the Bottom Up* (Bennington: Merriam Press, 2012), 66–67.
20 Armstrong, *Friendly and Enemy Skies*, 98.
21 Holt, *Lucky Dog*, 104.
22 Gaillard Jr., *Flight Surgeon*, 172.
23 Holt, *Lucky Dog*, 106.
24 Grey, *Vanishing Contrails*, 376.
25 Ibid., 376.
26 Armstrong, *Friendly and Enemy Skies*, 104.
27 Gilbert, *The View from the Bottom Up*, 79.
28 Ibid., 80.
29 Ibid., 81–82.
30 Armstrong, *Friendly and Enemy Skies*, 108.

Chapter 23

1 Armstrong, *Friendly and Enemy Skies*, 109.
2 Ibid., 110.
3 Ibid., 110.
4 Greene, *A Fortress and a Legacy*, 296.
5 Carr, *On Final Approach*, 120.
6 William Goudeket Jr., *From Pyote to Fortress Europe*. Interview by Vernon L. Williams. Old Segundo Productions, 2013.

7 Holt, *Lucky Dog*, 116.
8 Armstrong, *Friendly and Enemy Skies*, 129.
9 Ibid., 130.
10 Brown, *The Mighty Men of the 381st: Heroes All*, 486–487.
11 Ibid., 487
12 American actress whose final screen appearance was as Mother Abbess in *The Sound of Music* (1965).
13 Greene, *A Fortress and a Legacy*, 317.
14 Ibid., 328.
15 Armstrong might be remembering the structure of the Vickers Wellington in this case, the fuselage and wings of which were a metal geodetic frame covered with doped fabric. The Stirling, besides its fabric-covered control surfaces, was of all-metal construction.
16 Holt, *Lucky Dog*, 119.
17 Jones, *Some Recollections of a Florida Cracker*, 80.
18 Holt, *Lucky Dog*, 124.
19 Armstrong, *Friendly and Enemy Skies*, 149.
20 Greene, *A Fortress and a Legacy*, 331.
21 381st Bombardment Group (Heavy). "535th Bomb Squadron War Diary." [Accessed 2015]. Available at: http://www.381st.org/Unit-History/War-Diaries/535th-BS-War-Diary.
22 Gilbert, *The View from the Bottom Up*, 136.
23 Ibid., 135.
24 Armstrong, *Friendly and Enemy Skies*, 154–155.
25 Brown, *The Mighty Men of the 381st: Heroes All*, 491.
26 Greene, *A Fortress and a Legacy*, 5.

Chapter 24

1 Armstrong, *Friendly and Enemy Skies*, 160.
2 Ibid., 161.
3 Gilbert, *The View from the Bottom Up*, 140.
4 Brown, *The Mighty Men of the 381st: Heroes All*, 508.
5 Mackay, *Ridgewell's Flying Fortresses*, 172.
6 Freeman, *Mighty Eighth War Diary*, 400.
7 Carr, *On Final Approach*, 112.
8 Armstrong, *Friendly and Enemy Skies*, 168.
9 Carr, *On Final Approach*, 108.
10 Armstrong, *Friendly and Enemy Skies*, 170.
11 Also known as "circuits and bumps," this is a series of short flights where the aircraft takes off, but immediately joins the circuit around the airfield to land. This process built pilot proficiency.
12 Jones, *Some Recollections of a Florida Cracker*, 82.
13 Brown, *The Mighty Men of the 381st: Heroes All*, 513.
14 Jones, *Some Recollections of a Florida Cracker*, 83.
15 Armstrong, *Friendly and Enemy Skies*, 171.
16 Stone, *Triumphant We Fly*, 130.
17 Ibid., 130.
18 Ibid., 130.
19 Ibid., 133.
20 Armstrong, *Friendly and Enemy Skies*, 175–176.
21 Ibid., 178.
22 Gilbert, *The View from the Bottom Up*, 153.
23 Brown, *The Mighty Men of the 381st: Heroes All*, 554.
24 Armstrong, *Friendly and Enemy Skies*, 181.
25 Singleton, *To Great Yoho and Back*, 179.
26 Carr, *On Final Approach*, 108.

27 Armstrong, *Friendly and Enemy Skies*, 184.
28 Ibid., 185.
29 Brown, *The Mighty Men of the 381st: Heroes All*, 526.

Chapter 25

1 Brown, *The Mighty Men of the 381st: Heroes All*, 519.
2 Armstrong, *Friendly and Enemy Skies*, 189–190.
3 A "twin-beacon" beam radar combined with *H2X*.
4 Brown, *The Mighty Men of the 381st: Heroes All*, 529.
5 Ibid., 532.
6 Armstrong, *Friendly and Enemy Skies*, 192.
7 Gilbert, *The View from the Bottom Up*, 168.
8 Brown, *The Mighty Men of the 381st: Heroes All*, 522.
9 Conway S. Hall, *From Pyote to Fortress Europe*. Interview by Vernon L. Williams. Old Segundo Productions, 2013.
10 Freeman, *Mighty Eighth War Diary*, 435.
11 Carr, *On Final Approach*, 128.
12 Brown, *The Mighty Men of the 381st: Heroes All*, 533.
13 Miller, *Masters of the Air*, 433.
14 Now on display at the Royal Air Force Museum, London.
15 Gilbert, *The View from the Bottom Up*, 182.
16 Ibid., 184.
17 Brown, *The Mighty Men of the 381st: Heroes All*, 556–557.
18 Gilbert, *The View from the Bottom Up*, 189–190.
19 Middlebrook and Everitt, *The Bomber Command War Diaries*, 673.
20 Brown, *The Mighty Men of the 381st: Heroes All*, 540.

Chapter 26

1 *Medera Tribune* article, "Hitler Made Peace Offer but Refused," 15 March 1945, 1.
2 Brown, *The Mighty Men of the 381st: Heroes All*, 541.
3 Ibid., 542.
4 Ibid., 544.
5 Ibid., 545.
6 Ibid., 577–578.
7 Stone, *Triumphant We Fly*, 146–148.
8 Brown, *The Mighty Men of the 381st: Heroes All*, 580.
9 Ibid., 580.
10 Ibid., 583.
11 Ibid., 539.
12 Singleton, *To Great Yoho and Back*, 197.
13 Ibid.
14 Missing Air Crew Report 13542, Calvin J. Hockley, Individual Statement.
15 Stone, *Triumphant We Fly*, 154.
16 381st Bombardment Group (Heavy). "381st Bomb Group." [Accessed 2015]. Available at: http://www.381st.org/Unit-Histories/War-Diaries/381st-Bomb-Group-War-Diary.
17 Brown, *The Mighty Men of the 381st: Heroes All*, 584.
18 Ibid., 587–588.
19 Gilbert, *The View from the Bottom Up*, 200.
20 Stone, *Triumphant We Fly*, 149.
21 Brown, *The Mighty Men of the 381st: Heroes All*, 604.
22 William L. Palmer, *From Pyote to Fortress Europe*. Interview by Vernon L. Williams. Old Segundo Productions, 2013.

23 Donald J. Madar, *An Only Son of the 381st* (CreateSpace Independent Publishing Platform: Self-published, 2017), 48–49.
24 Brown, *The Mighty Men of the 381st: Heroes All*, 603.
25 Conway S. Hall, *From Pyote to Fortress Europe*. Interview by Vernon L. Williams. Old Segundo Productions, 2013.
26 Ibid.
27 Brown, *The Mighty Men of the 381st: Heroes All*, 607.

Chapter 27

1 Brown, *The Mighty Men of the 381st: Heroes All*, 607.
2 381st Bombardment Group (Heavy). "381st Bomb Group." [Accessed 2015]. Available at: http://www.381st.org/Unit-Histories/War-Diaries/381st-Bomb-Group-War-Diary.
3 *Isle of Man Examiner*, Isle of Man Newspapers Ltd (Johnston Press Publishing, 2015), 20.
4 Freeman, *Mighty Eighth War Diary*, 497.
5 Brown, *The Mighty Men of the 381st: Heroes All*, 652.
6 Ibid., 611.
7 Stone, *Triumphant We Fly*, 152.
8 Conway S. Hall, *From Pyote to Fortress Europe*. Interview by Vernon L. Williams. Old Segundo Productions, 2013.
9 Stone, *Triumphant We Fly*, 152.
10 Gilbert C. Schrank, unpublished combat diary.
11 381st Bombardment Group (Heavy). "1st Combat Bombardment Wing (H)." [Accessed 2015]. Available at: http://www.381st.org/Unit-Histories/War-Diaries/1st-CBW-War-Diary.
12 Singleton, *To Great Yoho and Back*, 203.
13 Eugene R. Ilten, unpublished combat diary.
14 Ibid.
15 Conway S. Hall, *From Pyote to Fortress Europe*. Interview by Vernon L. Williams. Old Segundo Productions, 2013.

Epilogue

1 Comer, *Combat Crew*, xi.
2 Otto F. Bruzewski was one of four crewman who escaped and evaded capture after *Chug-A-Lug Lulu* was shot down over Belgium on the first Schweinfurt raid, August 17, 1943.
3 Comer, *Combat Crew*, xii.
4 Brown, *The Mighty Men of the 381st: Heroes All*, 683.
5 Retired chaplain's life shining example of duty, faith," Air Force Print News, November 23, 2006. Available at: https://www.af.mil/News/Article-Display/article/128962/retired-chaplains-life-shining-example-of-duty-faith/.
6 Conway S. Hall, *VE Day Plus 50 Years: WWII Remembered*. Interview by CH 11 Little Rock, April 27, 1995.
7 Homdrom, *Mission Memories*, 154.
8 Grey, *Vanishing Contrails*, 299.
9 Carr, *On Final Approach*, 37.
10 Roger Freeman, *Airfields of the Eighth Then and Now* (London: Battle of Britain Prints International Limited, 1978), 199.

Appendix: Casualty Statistics

1 Gaillard Jr., *Flight Surgeon*, 185–193.

Bibliography

Articles

Bingley, Paul. "Taking the Fortress to War." *FlyPast Magazine*, May 2016.
Courtney, W. B. "Army in the Sky." *Collier's Weekly*, November 11, 1944.
Francis, Paul, Richard Flagg and Graham Crisp. "Nine Thousand Miles of Concrete: A Review of Second World War Temporary Airfields in England." Historic England, January 2016.
Henningsson, Pär. "The Story of Georgia Rebel." *Sweden After the Flak*, Volume 1, Issue 4, December 1999.
Walsh, PhD, Matthew. "Lost Flyboys: The story of World War II airmen, Marvin Dille and William Meehan." *Iowa History Journal*, May/June 2019. Available at: http://iowahistoryjournal.com/lost-flyboys.

Books

Alexander, Thomas E. *The One and Only Rattlesnake Bomber Base*. Abilene: State House Press, 2005.
Alling, Charles. *A Mighty Fortress*. Havertown: Casemate Publishers, 2006.
Armstrong, Robert "Bob." *Friendly and Enemy Skies*. Hutchinson: Self-published, 2003.
Bishop, Benjamin W. *Jimmy Doolittle: The Commander Behind the Legend*. Montgomery: Air University Press, 2015.
Bishop, Cliff T. *Fortresses of the Big Triangle First*. Bishop Stortford: East Anglia Books, 1986.
Bowman, Martin. *1st Air Division, 8th Air Force, USAAF 1942–45*. Barnsley: Pen & Sword, 2007.
Bowman, Martin. *Clash of Eagles*. Barnsley: Pen & Sword, 2006.
Bowman, Martin. *Echoes of England*. Stroud: Tempus Publishing Ltd, 2006.
Bowman, Martin. *The Mighty Eighth at War*. Barnsley: Pen & Sword, 2010.
Bowyer, Michael. *Action Stations Revisited*. Manchester: Crecy Publishing, 2010.
Brereton, Lewis H. *The Brereton Diaries*. New York: William Morrow and Company, 1946.
Brown, James Good. *The Mighty Men of the 381st: Heroes All*. Salt Lake City: Publishers Press, 1986.
Brown, James Good. *A Cup of Tea*. Unpublished.
Brown, R. Douglas. *East Anglia 1944*. Lavenham: Terence Dalton Ltd, 1992.
Bruning, John. *Bombs Away!* Minneapolis: Zenith Press, 2011.
Burwell, Roger W. *My War*. Self-published, 1990.
Butler, Daniel Allen. *Pearl, December 7, 1941*. Havertown: Casemate Publishers, 2020.
Caidin, Martin. *Black Thursday: The Story of the Schweinfurt Raid*. Brecksville: Rocket Press, 1960.
Caldwell, Donald and Muller, Richard. *The Luftwaffe Over Germany*. London: Frontline Books, 2014.
Caldwell, Donald. *Day Fighters in Defence of the Reich 1942–45*. London: Frontline Books, 2011.
Caldwell, Donald. *JG26 Top Guns of the Luftwaffe*. London: Frontline Books, 2013.

Carah, John M. Lt. Col. USAF (Ret.). *Achtung! Achtung! Die Flugfestungen Kommen!* Brighton: Elbow Lane Books, 2006.
Carr, Edward C. *On Final Approach.* Coupeville: Self-published, 2002.
Carty, Pat. *Secret Squadrons of the Eighth.* Minnesota: Speciality Press, 1990.
Coffey, Thomas. *Decision Over Schweinfurt.* Thetford: Robert Hale Ltd, 1977.
Comer, John. *Combat Crew.* London: Leo Cooper, 1988.
Cooper, Glynis. *Cambridgeshire at War.* Barnsley: Pen & Sword, 2020.
Crosby, Harry H. *A Wing and a Prayer.* New York: Harper Collins Publishers Inc, 1993.
Darlow, Stephen. *D-Day Bombers: The Veterans' Story.* London: Grub Street Publishing, 2004.
Delve, Ken. *How The RAF & USAAF Beat The Luftwaffe.* Barnsley: Greenhill Books, 2021.
Delve, Ken. *The Military Airfields of Great Britain, Northern Home Counties.* Ramsbury: Crowood, 2006.
Doolittle, Gen. James H., *I Could Never Be So Lucky Again.* New York: Bantam Books, 1991.
Ethell, Jeffrey and Fry, Gary. *Escort To Berlin.* New York, Airco Publishing Inc, 1980.
Ethell, Jeffrey and Price, Alfred. *Target Berlin.* Pennsylvania: Greenhill Books, 1981.
Freeman, Roger A. *Mighty Eighth War Diary.* London: Jane's Publishing Company Limited, 1981.
Freeman, Roger A. *The Mighty Eighth War Manual.* London: Cassell, 2001.
Freeman, Roger, *Airfields of the Eighth, Then and Now.* London: Battle of Britain Prints International Limited, 1978.
Freeman, Roger. *B-17 Fortress at War.* London: Ian Allan Ltd, 1977.
Freeman, Roger. *The Mighty Eighth.* London: Macdonald and Janes Publishing, 1970.
Gaillard Jr., Ernest, Lt. Col. MD USAAF-MC (Ret.). *Flight Surgeon.* Bloomington: 1stBooks, 2005.
Gilbert, Robert. *The View from the Bottom Up.* Bennington: Merriam Press, 2012.
Greene, J. Ross. *A Fortress and a Legacy.* CreateSpace Independent Publishing Platform: Self-published, 2015.
Grey, James F. *Vanishing Contrails.* Bloomington: Worldclay, 2011.
Gruen, Adam L. *Preemptive Defense, Allied Air Power Versus Hitler's V-Weapons, 1943–1945.* Washington, D.C.: Air Force History and Museums Program, 1998.
Harris, Arthur Travers and Sebastian Cox. *Despatch on War Operations: 23 February 1942, to 8 May 1945.* Routledge: 1995.
Holland, James. *Big Week.* London: Penguin Books Ltd, 2018.
Holt, Douglas E. *Lucky Dog.* Self-published, 2007.
Homdrom, Theodore. *Mission Memories.* Self-published, 2002.
Howland, John W, Capt. USAF (Ret.). *Diary of a Pathfinder Navigator.* Private papers, 1994.
Jablonski, Edward. *Flying Fortress.* London: Sidgwick & Jackson Ltd, 1974.
Jackson, Robert. *B-17 Flying Fortress.* London: Amber Books, 2018.
Jones, Jr., Troy H. *Some Recollections of a Florida Cracker.* Unpublished memoir, 1992.
Kaplan, Philip. *With Wings as Eagles.* New York: Sky Horse Publishing, 2020.
Korkuc, Bob. *Finding a Fallen Hero.* Norman: University of Oklahoma Press, 2008.
LaMore, Tommy and Dan A. Baker. *One Man's War.* Lanham: Taylor Trade Publishing, 2002.
Lande, David. *From Somewhere in England.* Airlife Publishing, 1991.
Longmate, Norman. *Hitler's Rockets.* Barnsley: Frontline Books, 2009.
Mackay, Ron. *Ridgewell's Flying Fortresses: The 381st Bombardment Group (H) in World War II.* Atglen: Schiffer Military History, 2000.
Madar, Donald J. *An Only Son of the 381st.* CreateSpace Independent Publishing Platform: Self-published, 2017.
McCarthy, David A. *Fear No More: A B-17 Navigator's Journey.* Pittsburgh: Cottage Wordsmiths, 1991.
McLachlan, Ian and Zorn, Russell. *Eighth Air Force Bomber Stories.* Yeovil: Patrick Stephens Ltd, 1991.
McLachlan, Ian. *Night of the Intruders.* Barnsley: Pen & Sword, 1994.

Michel, Marshall. *Schweinfurt-Regensburg*. Oxford: Osprey Publishing, 2020.
Middlebrook, Martin and Chris Everitt. *The Bomber Command War Diaries*. Hersham: Midland Publishing, 2011.
Middlebrook, Martin. *Firestorm Hamburg*. Barnsley: Pen & Sword, 2020.
Middlebrook, Martin. *The Schweinfurt–Regensburg Mission*. Barnsley: Pen & Sword, 1983.
Miller, Donald. *Eighth Air Force, The American Bomber Crews in Britain*. London: Aurum Press, 2007.
Miller, Donald. *Masters of the Air: America's Bomber Boys Who Fought the Air War Against Nazi Germany*. New York: Simon & Schuster, 2007.
Morgan, Col. Robert. *The Man Who Flew the Memphis Belle*. London: Penguin Books Ltd, 2001.
Neillands, Robin. *The Bomber War: Arthur Harris and the Allied Bomber Offensive 1939–1945*. London: John Murray Ltd, 2001.
Osborne, David R. *They Came from Over the Pond*. Madison: 381st Bomb Group Memorial Association, 1999.
Overy, Richard. *The Bombing War, Europe 1939–1945*. London: Penguin Books Ltd, 2013.
Prange, Gordon W. *At Dawn We Slept*. New York: McGraw-Hill Book Company, 1991.
Richardson, Charles J. *35 Missions To Hell and Back*. Conneaut Lake: Page Publishing, 2019.
Simons, Graham and Friedman, Harry. *Boeing B-17, The Fifteen Ton Flying Fortress*. Barnsley: Pen & Sword, 2020.
Singleton, Robert L. Jr. *To Great Yoho and Back*. West Stockbridge: Bearcliff Publishing, 2002.
Sion, Edward M. *Through Blue Skies to Hell*. Havertown: Casemate Publishers, 2008.
Smith, Graham. *The Mighty Eighth in the Second World War*. Newbury: Countryside Books, 2001.
Soames, Emma. *Mary Churchill's War* (Two Roads, Unabridged Audiobook, 2021).
Stanaway, John. *479th Fighter Group, Riddle's Raiders*. Oxford: Osprey Publishing Ltd, 2009.
Stone, Ken. *Triumphant We Fly*. Paducah: Turner Publishing Company, 1994.
Tarashuk, Pat. *Andrew "Whitey" Strednak and the Mighty Eighth Air Force of the United States of America*. Self-published, 2014.
The Army Air Forces Aid Society. *The Official Guide to the Army Air Forces AAF*. New York: Pocket Books Inc., 1944.
Thixton, Marshall J., George E. Moffat and John J. O'Neil, *Bombs Away* (Connecticut: FNP Military Division, 1998), 65.
Watkins, Robert. *Battle Colors, Insignia & Aircraft Markings of the Eighth Air Force*. Volume 1, Atglen: Schiffer Military History, 2004.
Wyndham Mayes, Derek. *The Airmen of Ridgewell: A History of Ridgewell Airfield*. Self-published, 2007.
Yancy, Bill M. *December 1, 1943: We Knew We Were in for a Long Day*. Self-published: 2013.
Yellin, Emily. *Our Mothers' War*. New York: Free Press, 2005.

First-hand Accounts

Accident Report No. 44-4-8-520. Leslie A. Bond, Statement.
Charles D. Butts, *From Pyote to Fortress Europe*. Interview by Vernon L. Williams. Old Segundo Productions, 2013.
Conway S. Hall, *From Pyote to Fortress Europe*. Interview by Vernon L. Williams. Old Segundo Productions, 2013.
Conway S. Hall, *VE Day Plus 50 Years: WWII Remembered*. Interview by CH 11 Little Rock, April 27, 1995.
Ernest L. Reid Collection (AFC/2001/001/00756), Veterans History Project, American Folklife Center, Library of Congress.

Francis G. Hawkins, *Dry Gulcher Down*. Interview by Vernon L. Williams. Old Segundo Productions, 2014.

Isle of Man Examiner, Isle of Man Newspapers Ltd (Johnston Press Publishing, 2015), 20.

Joe H. Willis, *From Pyote to Fortress Europe*. Interview by Vernon L. Williams. Old Segundo Productions, 2013.

Missing Air Crew Reports can be found at www.archives.gov/research/military/ww2/missing-air-crew-reports.

Nankivell, Barbara. "The Deserted Village." Transcript of an interview by John Irwin. BBC, July 27, 1945.

National Archives Catalog, Nelson, Robert E (1st Lt.), 5554811, E and E 170.

Olive Foulds, "Wartime Services Canteen in Ridgewell." Interview by BBC Essex, 1990. Essex Record Office.

Peter Morgan, *Dry Gulcher Down*. Interview by Vernon L. Williams. Old Segundo Productions, 2014.

William Goudeket Jr., *From Pyote to Fortress Europe*. Interview by Vernon L. Williams. Old Segundo Productions, 2013.

William L. Palmer, *From Pyote to Fortress Europe*. Interview by Vernon L. Williams. Old Segundo Productions, 2013.

William Scruggs. Interview by David Gregory. May 8–17, 2000.

Unpublished combat diaries of Favian R. Calderon, James H. Chandler, Eugene R. Ilten, John C. Leverette, Everett F. Malone, Wayne B. Pegg and Gilbert C. Schrank can be found at Ridgewell Airfield Commemorative Museum, Essex, England.

Websites

www.351st.org
www.381st.org
www.381st.com
www.398th.org
www.8thafhs.org
www.91stbombgroup.com
www.rafcamuseum.co.uk
www.fold3.com
www.americanairmuseum.com
www.mightyeighth.org
www.ww2online.org/view/leonard-spivey

Index